Eng'd by H.B. Hall's Sons, New York.

McCLELLAN'S OWN STORY

THE WAR FOR THE UNION

THE SOLDIERS WHO FOUGHT IT

THE CIVILIANS WHO DIRECTED IT

AND

HIS RELATIONS TO IT AND TO THEM

BY

GEORGE B. McCLELLAN

LATE MAJOR-GENERAL COMMANDING THE ARMIES

NEW YORK
CHARLES L. WEBSTER & COMPANY
1887

ISBN 1-58218-007-5

Digital Scanning, Inc.
344 Gannett Road
Scituate, MA 02066
© 1998 All Rights Reserved.

CONTENTS.

CONTENTS.

CONTENTS.

CONTENTS.

CONTENTS.

ILLUSTRATIONS.

NOTE. - Mr. A. R. Waud accompanied the Army of the Potomac while under McClellan's command, and the illustrations drawn by him are from his original sketches made on the spot in 1862.

STATUETTE BY J. A. BAILLY.

BIOGRAPHICAL SKETCH

OF

GEORGE B. McCLELLAN

BY

W. C. PRIME, LL.D.

xiii-xiv

THE

LIFE, SERVICES, AND CHARACTER

OF

GEORGE B. McCLELLAN.

GEORGE BRINTON McCLELLAN, son of George McClellan, M.D., and Elizabeth Brinton McClellan, was born in Philadelphia, Penn., Dec. 3, 1826. His school education was in that city; in 1841 and 1842 in the preparatory school attached to the University of Pennsylvania. He entered the Military Academy at West Point in 1842, graduating in 1846, when he was assigned to the Corps of Engineers as second lieutenant. In Sept. of the same year he went with the army to Mexico, where he served with distinction during the war. He was breveted first lieutenant for gallantry at Contreras and Churubusco, captain for Chapultepec.

At the close of the Mexican war he commanded the engineer company and brought it to West Point, where he served with it, acting also as assistant instructor of practical engineering until 1851. In that year he superintended the construction of Fort Delaware. In 1852 he accompanied Capt. R. B. Marcy on the Red river exploring expedition. In 1853 and 1854 he was on duty in Washington Territory and Oregon, as an engineer officer, exploring a proposed route for the Pacific Railroad.

In the spring of 1855 the government sent a commission of army officers to Europe, instructed to obtain and report information on military service in general, and the practical working of changes then recently made in military systems.

The commission was specially instructed to give attention to the organization of armies, transports for men and horses, embarking and disembarking them, hospitals and ambulances, clothing and camp equipage, arms and ammunition, fortifications and sea-coast defences, engineering operations of a siege in all its branches, siege-trains, bridge-trains, boats, wagons - in short, to study and report on the whole art of war in Europe. As the Crimean war was then in progress, and the British and French forces were besieging Sebastopol, this was an important point for the objects of the commission, which consisted of three officers - Maj. R.

Delafield, Maj. A. Mordecai, and Capt. G. B. McClellan. They proceeded to Europe in the spring of 1855, amply accredited to American representatives and the several governments on whose courtesy they would have to depend for opportunities of study and observation.

The British government extended to them every possible courtesy. From the French and the Russian they could obtain no facilities. They were received in the Crimea with soldierly kindness by Gen. Simpson, who had succeeded Lord Raglan in command of the British forces. Here they had ample opportunity for the study of military operations on a grand scale. Leaving the Crimea in Nov., they pursued their duties in various European states, The list of military posts and fortresses which they examined is very long, abounding in names illustrious in the history of wars. McClellan's Report on the arms, equipments, and organization of "the three arms" was, says a distinguished soldier, "a model of conciseness and accurate information, and added to his already brilliant reputation." It may be noted as an interesting fact that the Secretary of War who issued the elaborate instructions to this commission, and selected its members for their special ability and fitness, was Jefferson Davis. Five years later, when he was at the head of a political and military rebellion, one of the commissioners utilized his experience and information in organizing and leading the armies of the Union for its suppression.

In Jan., 1857 McClellan, then captain in the 1st Cavalry, resigned his commission and accepted employment, first as chief-engineer, afterward as vice-president, of the Illinois Central Railroad Company. Later he became president of the Eastern Division of the Ohio and Mississippi Railroad Company.

On the 22d May, 1860, he married Ellen Mary Marcy, daughter of Capt. (afterward Gen.) Randolph B. Marcy, and established his residence at Cincinnati, O., where he was occupied in his business when the civil war began, and he offered his services to his country.

No volunteer in the army made greater personal sacrifices. He was in the enjoyment of a large income; his prospects in life were brilliant. Like all soldiers of the old army, he had led a wandering life, with no one place to call a home. He had now for the first time made for himself a place of rest with his young wife, in which they were gathering those personal belongings which go so far to make life happy and rest delightful. The sacrifices of the soldier's wife are as great, often greater, than those of the husband. McClellan's wife was a soldier's daughter. The spirit of obedience to the call of duty ruled them both alike. No words can fitly express the perfectness of that love which was the light of both their lives. It was expressed in a few lines of his letters which I have suffered to appear in this volume, in a thousand passages and words which are omitted.

His life from April, 1861, to Nov., 1862, forms the subject of this narrative, which I have entitled "McClellan's Own Story."

He was commissioned major-general of volunteers in Ohio on the 23d April, 1861.

On the 14th May he was made major-general in the United States army and placed in command of the Department of the Ohio.

On the 26th May he issued a proclamation to the Union men of Western Virginia, and an address to his soldiers whom he led to what has been known as the Western Virginia campaign. On the 22d July, having freed Western Virginia from secessionists and preserved its people to the Union, he was summoned to Washington, and, arriving there on the 26th, was assigned to command the Division of the Potomac.

He found Washington in a perilous condition. The defeat at Bull Run had demoralized the administration and the army. No one had formed any, the most vague, idea of what was to be done or how to do anything. Up to this time the administration had shared with the people of the North and an unconsidering press the opinion that the rebellion was but a mob, to be scattered in one or two free fights by impetuous onsets of patriotic men. Now the shout, "On to Richmond," had been suddenly and appallingly hushed. Paralysis had followed. Not even Scott or McDowell, or any military adviser of the administration and people, had thought of making ordinary military provision for the defence of Washington against an enemy whose shell might at any moment shatter the dome of the Capitol. The military condition of the whole country, Western Virginia alone excepted, was chaotic.

Probably there were other men in America as well fitted by natural ability and education for the great work in hand, but they did not appear. No other one has been indicated as the proper man for the occasion. That occasion demanded a calm foresight of the vast needs of the country in the coming, the then present, peril, the ability to provide for every one of them, and the expression is homely but precise - the staying power to make the provision perfectly, calmly, completely, unmoved by the cries, however honest and anxious, of an alarmed people, equally unmoved. by the criticisms of the envious and the clamors of the unprincipled.

If the wisdom which sought the ablest military advice in that moment of alarm had been displayed throughout the war by entrusting to military knowledge and ability the conduct of campaigns and the direction and execution of the work of war, the expense of treasure and blood would have been vastly less, and the end would have been much more speedy. Instead of this, after McClellan had assured the safety of the capital, and the alarm of the civilians had subsided, they assumed the direction, interfered with and delayed military preparations, and undertook the specific management of campaigns and armies, while they took care that the delays and defeats which they caused should be charged on soldiers in the field.

We who were then living can with the utmost difficulty carry our minds back to the conditions under which McClellan was called to save the capital and country. It is impossible for the present generation to realize the blindness of the people or appreciate the prevision of the young general. We now look back to all that which he foresaw, foretold, and provided for. So intense had been popular, feeling that it was regarded:

as treason to think or say that secession was in great strength, that the
South would not be easily conquered,

He was alone in the clear atmosphere, above the scene of physical and
political warfare, and saw what others could not or would not see. Mr.
Lincoln probably came nearer to accepting his views than any one else.
From this time on the President reposed confidence in him; and there is
small reason for doubt that, but for the interference of politicians, Lincoln
and McClellan would have brought the war to an end in the summer of
1862. But Mr. Lincoln soon had two wars on his hands.   He was at the
head of the Union and at the head of a political party.   Both were threatened with division.   He desired to save both, probably believing that the
unity of his party was essential to the saving of the country.   In this view
can be explained much which is otherwise inexplicable in his dealings
with the general, to whom up to the very last he gave the most frank and
full private assurances of his confidence.

The "staying" powers of McClellan were the salvation of the Union.
Alone in his outlook, he was alone in the execution of his great work.
The fortification of Washington accomplished, and a sufficient force
organized and disciplined for its defence, he directed his labors to the
next great need - an army. The people, the sovereigns, had not the remot-
est conception of the meaning of the word "army." Very few soldiers in this country had grasped the idea. No one but McClellan had
observed that the able and educated soldiers of the South had long been
organizing that vast machine which, once created, moves with irresistible
force over all obstacles until met by another machine of like construction
and greater power, or which is handled with greater skill.   The Army of
the Potomac grew like a vast engine constructed by a master-mind.   Its
history is the reward of the constructor, ample, and the only reward he
ever received.

There was one characteristic of McClellan's mind which some would
regard as a defect, and which certainly placed him at a disadvantage in
his relations with the men in Washington.   He was slow to suspect evil
of any man. This trait was exhibited in his private life, and he never
wholly lost it.   The philosophic reader will find interest in the indications
afforded in his letters of his gradual awakening to the controlling presence
in Washington of a class of men known as politicians.   Soldiers, accustomed to honest service for definite purposes, imbued with high principles
of honor, can with difficulty recognize the existence of men in public life
who are willing to manage public interests for private or party gain.

He knew the past history of his country by heart.   He remembered
the illustrious names and records of men whose high ambition had been
to serve the people as statesmen, whom no one had ever thought to charge
with personal or party motive in any of their acts as trustees and representatives of the people.   Was the day of such American senators and representatives gone by?   Was legislation henceforth to be for the perpetuation
of hold on office, for the success of party, with the mere pretence of good
to country? Now that the general trust of governmental powers had

become a specific trust of blood to be poured out and treasure to be expended for the salvation of the Union, it did not occur to him that any of the trustees could dream of using that treasure and blood for personal advantage. When men professed honest patriotism he believed them.

Nor do the people themselves, in times of excitement, yield readily to the belief that among their leaders are some who are not honest and patriotic. But in calm retrospect they are generally more wise. It would not be difficult already to make a Catalogue of names of men who were prominent in Washington and elsewhere during the war, who secured for the time the reputation of patriotic leaders of opinion and directors of events, whose memories have been allowed, as they deserved, to rot.

All our history demonstrates how such men abound, and secure influence and power at every seat of government, municipal and general, wherever patronage is to be distributed and money to be expended. They are very ignorant indeed who imagine that, in the greatest opportunity for such men ever afforded in America, there were none of them at the front. They were legion.

The history of the war is inextricably involved in the history of party politics. No one can understand the former without knowledge of the latter. Nor can the great services of McClellan be in any way estimated, his marvelous steadfastness in duty, his herculean work in Washington, and his brilliant career at the head of the Army of the Potomac, without giving full value to the fact that from a short time after his arrival in Washington politicians formed an enemy in his rear often more formidable to him and his army than the enemy in their front toward whom alone the eyes of the people were then directed.

The Republican party which re-elected Mr. Lincoln in 1864 was not the same party, either in principles or in voters, which had elected him in 1860. The Democratic party of later years is not in any aspect the party of Mr. Buchanan's time. Old issues were dead, annihilated by the fire on Fort Sumter. The Republican party-machinery existed, the machine politicians held it in hand, and ardent partisans throughout the country kept up a semblance of party distinction by denouncing all opponents as sympathizers with secession and traitors. But in the early summer of 1861 there was but one party in the North, the party of the Union and Constitution. Here and there was a Southern sympathizer whose utterances furnished material for newspapers and orators to grow wild about, but the number of these was insignificant. The entire body of the Northern people were united in one sentiment. And this enthusiastic unanimity was the more wonderful because there had been a very widespread sympathy in the North with the doctrine of secession, on which the leaders of the South had based much expectation. This sympathy was not in one political party alone. Startling as the statement may be to some, the fact is easily demonstrated that there had been as many if not more secessionists among Northern Republicans than Democrats. There is no more trustworthy indication of a man's political opinions than the doctrines taught by the newspaper he takes regularly and reads religiously. One powerful Northern journal taught that the right of secession was as clear as the rights asserted in the Declaration of Independence, that a Union pinned together by bayonets was not worth having, that the erring sisters ought to be let go. This journal claimed and had 200,000 subscribers, which implies at least a half million regular readers, a large part of whom accepted the doctrine of secession. There was a body of men in the North, of considerable numbers, known as the Abolitionists, who had steadily advocated disunion, their motto being, "The Constitution of the United States is a league with death and a covenant with hell." Many of them were voters with the Republican party. It is therefore unquestionable that a considerable portion of the Republican party had been indoctrinated into a belief not only of the right but of the desirableness of the secession of the Southern States. That a considerable portion of the Democrats had held the same views no one doubts. But the challenge to arms was accepted by Republicans and Democrats with one voice and act. All sympathy with secession vanished, and it would be absurd now to deny that there were as many Democrats as Republicans among the volunteer soldiery of the war.

The people and the army thought of one subject only-the suppression of the rebellion, while politicians, Democrats as well as Republicans, looked to the spoils of present power and the means of confirming that power in future elections.

Congress, at the moment of McClellan's arrival in Washington, as if to instruct him in his duty, expressed the unanimous sentiment of the North in a resolution which declared "that the present deplorable civil war has been forced upon the country by the disunionists of the Southern States, now in revolt against the constitutional government, and in arms around the capital; that in this national emergency Congress, banishing all feeling of mere passion or resentment, will recollect only its duty to its country; that this war is not waged, on our part, in any spirit of oppression, nor for any purpose of conquest or subjugation, nor purpose of overthrowing or interfering with the rights or established institutions of those States, but to defend and maintain the supremacy of the Constitution and to preserve the Union, with all the dignity, equality, and rights of the several States unimpaired; and as soon as these objects are accomplished the war ought to cease."

McClellan accepted this instruction. It expressed his own views and those of every lover of his country in the North.

But if this purpose were achieved in this way the Southern States, kept in the Union by a strong hand, would reappear in future elections as a solid South against the machine politicians who had gained power in 1860. If the white vote could be suppressed and the slaves be freed with the immediate right of suffrage, their vote might be controlled and a solid South secured for those who had given them the right of voting. But how could the people be led to favor this policy?

Various schemes were devised to accomplish the desired end. For a time efforts were made to induce the North to adopt a policy which

Mr. Chase formulated in an interview with Mr. Wade of the Senate and Mr. Ashley of the House, Dec. 11, 1861.

Mr. Chase said (Warden, p. 390) that a State attempting to secede, the State government being placed in hostility to the Federal government, "the State organization was forfeited, and it lapsed into the condition of a Territory"; that "we could organize territorial courts, and, as soon as it became necessary, a territorial government"; that "those States could not properly he considered as States in the Union, but must be readmitted from time to time as Congress should provide." Mr. Wade and Mr. Ashley were understood to concur in this doctrine; and, as matter of fact, it was given out as sound doctrine and was widely advocated in newspapers and at war-meetings engineered by politicians in various parts of the North.

Mr. Chase was too good a lawyer not to recognize the absurdity of the doctrine as American law. It was pure secession doctrine at bottom, and subversive of the whole system of government in all the States. The firmness of conservative Republicans, and the adherence of Mr. Lincoln to the doctrine of the Congressional resolution, kept a large portion of the people from accepting it. Perhaps the greatest service which Mr. Lincoln rendered his country was in the sagacious manner in which he prevented this revolutionary doctrine from becoming the avowed policy of a party. Its success would have been more fatal to the Constitution than the acknowledgment of the Southern Confederacy.

The abolition of slavery as "a war measure" was proposed and advocated at the same time. This was more popular. But neither Mr. Lincoln nor any military authority could perceive its practical use as a weapon of war, and, although a tremendous pressure was brought to bear on the President, he steadily refused to issue "a bull against a comet." The political position was therefore complicated. The process of coalition, by which politicians who had been Democrats as well as Republicans came together and formed the radical wing of the Republican party, is worthy the study of every one interested in the history of popular government. A powerful combination was formed. It had no leader, for too many of its members were "every man for himself," while each was seeking one or another personal benefit. Its common purpose was to manage the war in such way as to secure control of the country in the elections in 1864 and afterwards.

There was a body of noble, conservative, and patriotic men in the old Republican party strong enough to interpose many obstacles in the way of the radicals. The latter adopted the customary tactics of unscrupulous partisans in this country, and visited on all who opposed them storms of foul epithets and charges of sympathy with the rebellion. Mr. Lincoln was alternately praised and vilified. But no one of the radical coalition was his friend or desired his continuance at the head of the party. Some old Democratic politicians, recognizing good prospects of its success, joined the radical party. Congress in time yielded to its control. A committee called The Committee on the Conduct of the War was created, to be the machine of partisan politics, in control of the most unscrupulous leaders of the combination, who used it to good effect in the deception of the confiding people of the country.

It is profoundly interesting, and there is something grotesque in it also, to observe how the shrewd and far-seeing Lincoln kept the headship of both elements, conservative and radical, prevented their often-threatened division into two parties, defeated each of the rival candidates for his office, and finally compelled his own renomination and their support in his re-election.

To secure for their purposes the leader of the armies had been one of the first and most important objects of the radicals. If a victor he was morally certain to become the idol of the people. "What can we make out of McClellan?" was the question of all; "What can I make out of McClellan?" was the question of each. Thus in that marvelous apocalypse, his private diary, Mr. Chase writes (Warden, p. 500) that a friend said to him, "Col. Key often expressed his regret that McClellan had not conferred with me and *acted in concert with me.* I replied that I thought if he had that the rebellion would be ended now." "I . . . was quite willing he should repeat to McClellan what I had said." Undoubtedly had McClellan attached himself to Mr. Chase, or any other Presidential candidate, in the manner suggested, he would have been supported by a powerful political combination. But the bargains of politics were foreign to his work and nature. He was creating an army and using it for the people, not for himself; certainly not for Mr. Chase or any other aspirant to position.

The success of McClellan in 1862 would have been doubly fatal to the politicians. The old Union would have been restored and the general would command the political situation. Therefore McClellan must not be successful. His popularity must be destroyed. Whatever of falsehood could be invented must be published concerning him. His successes must be decried. Above all, he must not be allowed to win a decisive victory. Neither a quick ending of the war nor a victorious campaign by McClellan would ensure to party success.

The argument of personal rivalry and party requirement was pressed on Mr. Lincoln without success. However loyal McClellan was to his country, the Secretary of the Treasury said he urged his removal because "he was not loyal to the administration."

As it began to be evident that Mr. Lincoln would not adopt the radical policy, nor discharge McClellan and appoint some general suited to radical purposes, nor manage war matters with special regard to future partisan considerations, it became important to gain the War Department, and place in it a secretary who would do what the President would not. Thus the course of the war could be controlled, generals could be driven with reins, the President himself could be deceived, misled, to some extent managed.

Mr. Edwin M. Stanton was selected, and Mr. Chase, with great adroitness, described by himself, induced Mr. Lincoln to appoint him as successor to Mr. Cameron. The religious emotion with which Mr. Chase recorded the success of this scheme indicates the view he had of its vital importance to the radical cause.

Mr. Stanton was a lawyer of moderate abilities, a man of peculiar mental constitution. Without moral principle or sense of personal honor, he was equally ready to change front in public politics and to betray private friendship, and was therefore eminently suited to the purposes for which he was selected by the men with whom he had formed a secret alliance. But he was as untrustworthy in that as in other associations, and at the very moment when Mr. Chase, confiding in him, was intriguing to bring him into the cabinet, he betrayed Mr. Chase's confidences and defeated his plans, for his own purposes. Those who knew him well were in the habit of describing him as one of those who "always kick down the ladder by which they have climbed." His ambition was unbounded and his self-reliance absolute. He did not depend, as do ordinary politicians, on a larger or smaller body of followers and political dependants. No one shared his aspirations, and none were to claim gratitude or reward in his successes.

All times of great popular excitement and national peril bring into view remarkable characters. None more remarkable than his appears in the history of the civil war; none will be a more interesting subject to the student of human nature. With opportunity to achieve greatness and win a people's gratitude such as few others had, he used it in such way that in the calm retrospect of a quarter of a century his countrymen look at him with sorrowful shame, and few name him with respect, except here and there a survivor of the alliance whose purposes he served. He was supposed to be energetic, but he was only spasmodic, and in his spasms of impulsive judgment and action committed errors costly beyond all measurement in the money of the treasury and the lives of soldiers. Himself honest in money matters, a host of plunderers fattened without check on the money provided by the people and scattered in his improvident and reckless management of the department. With the men and means lavishly placed at his disposal by the people, a War Secretary of sound sense, cool discretion, honest purpose, and the good judgment to accept military advice and instruction for military operations, would have conducted the war at an expense of hundreds where it was thousands of millions. But Mr. Stanton's errors of self-reliance were aggravated by the fact that he not only had no military knowledge, but by his peculiar disposition was incapacitated to receive military instruction. A very foolish letter which he published revealed his ignorance of the simplest principles on which success in war depends. His suspension of all recruiting at the moment of opening active operations in the field was a blunder unparalleled in military history, as well as a crime. His inability to receive military instruction has singular illustration in a letter, recently made public,*

*Letter to Rev. H. Dyer, dated May 18, 1862, read in the House of Representatives June 8. 1886.

which he wrote to a friend a few weeks after the siege of Yorktown. When McClellan entered on the Peninsular campaign his entire plan of campaign rested on his purpose to throw the 1st corps in rear of Yorktown, turn that fortified position, and clear the way for a rapid advance to Richmond. The withdrawal of the 1st corps from his army at the very instant it was to have been thus utilized defeated the plan of campaign, rendered necessary the siege of Yorktown and the adoption of a new plan with a reduced army. Innumerable letters and despatches besides those given in McClellan's narrative made these facts clear to all, excepting the War Department. Mr. Stanton wrote in this private letter to a confidential friend: "The force retained from his [McClellan's] expedition was not needed, and could not have been employed by him"!

One of his co-secretaries says that his hostility to McClellan began when he entered the cabinet. He was, indeed, but one of the organized enemy in the rear of the Army of the Potomac and their commander, but he was the executive of their plots as well as of his own. Professing always devoted personal attachment to and admiration of the general, he opened his private correspondence with his wife; circulated with vindictive malice falsehoods and slanders, petty and great, to his injury; misrepresented him to, and sought to embroil him with, the President; and deliberately planned and executed the defeat of the Peninsular campaign. The accusation is most grave and terrible; but it was made to him in person by the general of the army, and his reception of it was a confession of its awful truth. For at midnight, June 27-28, when McClellan found his army in the toils into which Mr. Stanton had led them and there abandoned them, the general, anticipating his own possible death with thousands of the men he loved, sent a despatch to the secretary the like of which was never sent by commander in the field to superior at home. Every line was weighty, every word solemn. It was the free outpouring of a great soul conscious of the approach of death. There are no erasures in the original draft which lies before me. It concluded with this denunciation: "If I save this army now, I tell you plainly that I owe no thanks to you or to any other persons in Washington. *You have done your best to sacrifice this army.*"

The secretary received the accusation in silence which was the confession of its truth. If it were not true, McClellan deserved, and would have received, quick punishment for the gross insubordination, and the country would have justified any imposed penalty. If Mr. Stanton had dared dispute its truth and appeal on the facts to the honest judgment of a court-martial or the country, he would, of course, have done so. Not only did he fail to resent it, but he kept the despatch secret; and when, some time later, it was laid before the Committee on the Conduct of the War, the concluding sentences above quoted were suppressed! It appears thus mutilated in that mass of worthless because falsified and untrustworthy rubbish which forms a large part of the printed report of that committee. The secretary's personal reply to the general was the affectionate letter of July 3 professing his devotion. His practical reply was to go with Mr. Chase to the President and urge the sending of Gen. Pope to supersede McClellan.

The soldiers of the Union went into the field everywhere with a mind of this sort to use them as it would. If conscience ever asserted itself in that strange mind, always alternating in passionate emotions of anger and fear, the set faces of a half-million dead soldiers must have haunted it waking and sleeping.

While politicians were plotting McClellan was working. It is impossible to over-estimate the laborious character of the general's life. His whole soul was in his work; his every energy and thought was given to it. He was always, while in Washington and while in the field, in the habit of seeing personally, as far as possible, to the execution of important orders. Out of countless illustrations of this which might be given, let one suffice. The lieutenant-colonel of that superb regiment, the 1st Conn. Artillery, wrote to me from the works before Yorktown that, a little after midnight the previous rainy night, while the men were at work in the trenches, McClellan rode up, attended by a single orderly, sprang from his horse, inspected the work, gave some directions, remounted, and rode away. About three A.M. he reappeared as before, approved the work, gave further directions, and vanished. My correspondent met him at his headquarters before seven A.M., and also met there a friend, whose regiment was stationed some miles away, who told him that the general had surprised them by a visit and inspection at about two A.M. The soldiers soon learned not to be surprised at his appearance among them anywhere, at any hour of day or night.

He made Washington secure, he created the Army of the Potomac, he gathered the vast material for a war. Called to the chief command, he brought order out of chaos in all the armies; he organized the first and only plan for the war in all the country; he sent successful expeditions, with detailed orders, to North Carolina, New Orleans, and elsewhere, in pursuance of his comprehensive scheme, in which concerted action everywhere was to be in direct relation to the chief act - the taking of Richmond. On this plan the war went on after his retirement. When he was ready to wield the vast power he had created, he left Washington at the head of the Army of the Potomac to strike the decisive blow at Richmond. Instantly the operations of the enemy in the rear began. He was removed from the command-in-chief, and no successor appointed. All his comprehensive plan was shattered. The War Secretary, succeeding practically to the command, neglected even to carry out his orders for the completion of the defences of Washington. The subsequent defeat of Pope was directly chargeable to this neglect, and other like neglects led to other disasters.

When he reached the Peninsula and met the enemy his army was suddenly reduced by the withdrawal of one-third of its force. He had planned to turn Yorktown; he now went over it. The country rang with the preconcerted outcry which the politicians raised. The siege of Yorktown was denounced as slow. It occupied less than twenty days, and has no parallel for swiftness in the history of the war.

The plan of campaign having been overturned by the reduction of the army, the general formed a new plan and advanced rapidly on it. Again the War Department interfered and defeated it, ordering him to stretch his right to the north of Richmond to effect the junction of McDowell's corps, now promised, but to come overland. Again and again McDowell was coming, but never came. His advance was within sound of McClellan's cannon when he was finally withdrawn. Assuredly if the Secretary had deliberately planned the destruction of the army he would have given precisely the orders he did, and would have handled the 1st corps exactly as he did handle it. No trap could have been better set by an enemy. Only the consummate generalship of McClellan and the heroism of the Army of the Potomac in the successful battles of the Seven Days saved it from the fate to which it had been consigned.

The Army of the Potomac was recalled to Washington instead of being reinforced on the banks of the James. All the lives and all the agonies of the country which were expended in regaining that same position two years afterwards were wasted for the only purpose of getting rid of McClellan.

There are many open questions in regard to the treatment which McClellan received from the power behind the throne in Washington, which will be answered only when more such records as Mr. Chase's private diary shall be discovered and published. Why was Gen. Halleck authorized to assure McClellan that he was recalled to Washington to take command of the combined forces, his own army and Gen. Pope's? Was there then, and continuously afterward, in the minds of Mr. Stanton and his associates, a fear of McClellan and the army? The charge was not infrequently made that he intended to seize the government. The devotion of the army to him, with their indignation at his and their treatment by the War Department, might arouse apprehension in minds not noted for personal courage. It is no secret that this fear prevailed in the War Department after Sept. 2, and especially when the final order was sent relieving McClellan. Possibly such apprehension had something to do with the holding out to the general the idea that he was to command the combined forces, and with the adoption of the plan of withdrawing the army from his command instead of relieving him. That the President had no part in this ultimate purpose can hardly be doubted. He honestly desired to see an army always between Washington and the enemy, nor did he or Mr. Stanton learn till years afterward, when Grant was south of Richmond, the military truth which McClellan reiterated, that the true defence of Washington was on the bank of the James river.

It is hardly worth while now to say that if any such fears prevailed among the men in Washington it was because they could not realize the possible existence of such an upright, pure, and unselfish servant of his country as McClellan. He entertained no thought of anything to be done by him except duty. Absolutely obedient to orders, he accepted as his work whatever his superiors set before him. It was not till the fate of the country depended on his assuming power and exercising it without orders that, staking his life for the people, he led the army to South Mountain and Antietam.

There is no passage in the history of any man who has ever lived more startling in the contrasts it presents than the story of McClellan's recall and return to Washington. The commander who had for months been the victim of political intrigues, baffled in every effort to serve his country, ordered against his judgment and protest hither and thither by ignorant and inimical superiors, the general loving and loved by a great army now removed from his command, sat, or paced to and fro, with a little group of staff officers and a few wounded veterans around him in his tent, listening in anxiety beyond words to the sound of distant cannon firing on his old troops, and was even compelled to ask the password for the night from the military governor of the small city in whose outskirts his tent was pitched. His personal enemies had triumphed. The war was now to be very long and very bloody. They had effected his disgrace. But a few hours changed the scene. The defeated army of the Union was rushing homeward in broken masses. An exultant enemy was marching on the capital. The War Secretary and the nominal general-in-chief, the trustees of the Union and the military heads of the squad of politicians who had brought about the disaster, had ordered the arsenal to be emptied and abandoned - it was said also, to be burned. Frightened at the awful catastrophe they had caused, the politicians disappeared from sight and were not seen or heard by the people again until, with recovered breath, in assured safety, they reopened their attack on the general toward whom, for the time, all eyes in the land were directed as the only possible saviour of his country.

The people, in the person of their President, who alone in Washington preserved sound judgment and a serene mind, went to the lately insulted and displaced general, and, with tears not unfitting the occasion (for his tears were the emotion of a betrayed and outraged nation), asked him to forget his wrongs and save the country. The falsehood was afterward circulated that he hesitated and sought to make conditions. He accepted the new responsibility instantly, for every second was of priceless value. He saved the arsenal which cowardice would have destroyed. The wild scene of joy with which the army received him can never be the subject of the artist's pencil, for it was in the darkness of night, among the Virginia forests, when the good horse of the general, accompanied by one faithful aide, the gallant Colburn, brought him at that tremendous pace the soldiers knew, to meet them retreating, gloomy as the black night that lay on the hills around them. But the wild shout of welcome that rolled from company to company and corps to corps was prophetic of South Mountain and Antietam

Who shall say that the soldiers of the Army of the Potomac did not know that man, and that he did not merit their admiring love?

He gathered them in his hand. He made a new army of the defeated, disorganized, and decimated regiments of his own army and the Army of Virginia, reorganized it and supplied its pressing needs as it marched, followed and overtook the exultant enemy, flushed with success, in Maryland, and in fifteen days after that night of disastrous retreat led his heroic troops to the victorious fields of South Mountain and Antietam.

It is one of the settled truths of history that constant reiteration of a statement, however untrue, will impress many minds with its truthfulness. The impatience of the people afforded to the enemies of McClellan the opportunity to represent him as constitutionally slow. There are not a few who believe it. There was no foundation for the slur; and any one who studies dates and informs himself of the actual time occupied by him in any of his work will be surprised at the currency which such a criticism obtained. He was calm and cool in judgment, never impulsive, but always as rapid in action as the circumstances required. If campaigns are to be compared, it is well to note that in the West Virginia and the Maryland campaigns he was his own master and director, while the Peninsular campaign was actually three several campaigns, so made by the interference of the War Department, and all three subject to that constant interference.

The order of Aug. 30 had removed McClellan from the command of the Army of the Potomac. The order of Sept. 2 had only placed him in command of the fortifications of Washington. The history of this order is sufficiently discussed in a note on page 538, etc. He had, for the safety of the country and the preservation of the Union, assumed command and fought the battles of South Mountain and Antietam with "a halter around his neck." No change was made in his command after the battle of Antietam. The entire confidence with which he had received the orders of the President on the morning of Sept. 2 was characteristic. When asked afterward why he did not on that occasion ask written orders, he replied, with a smile, "It was no time for writing, and in fact I never thought of it."

The President fully approved of his determination not to lead the army on an offensive campaign into Virginia without shoes, clothing, and supplies, and without horses for cavalry and transportation. The table which will be found on pages 632, 633 of this volume demonstrates beyond cavil both the necessities of the troops and the dates at which they were supplied. Without supplies, cavalry, or transportation, no general would have moved an hour sooner than he did. When ready he moved with his accustomed rapidity and skill. The movement accomplished his purpose. He had placed the enemy at a fatal disadvantage. If he were brought to battle there was no reasonable doubt that McClellan had so divided him that he would be beaten in detail. If he declined battle the Army of the Potomac had the inside track in a race to Richmond. In either event McClellan was about to win another and a decisive victory.

Some one reported to the politicians in Washington the imminent danger of a great Union victory by the army under McClellan. Perhaps when time reveals correspondence it will be known who sent the intelligence. McClellan's despatches had communicated facts, not expectations. There was no visible reason for interfering with him at this moment. But the final pressure now brought to bear on the President was successful. He issued a discretionary order to Gen. Halleck, who made haste to exercise the discretion at once, and Nov. 5, 1862, McClellan was ordered to turn over the command to Burnside and go to Trenton, N. J. He lies there now on a hill overlooking the Delaware. But he never received there, or elsewhere, order, thanks, or any recognition from the government of his country.

Nor did he ever expect or desire it. To him, as to all pure minds, the ample compensation for labor and self-sacrifice was in the consciousness of duty done. He held himself in readiness to serve the cause should his services be needed, but they were not sought.

In 1864 the political elements were still in a chaotic condition. Two parties had been evolved from the exciting conditions caused by the war and the ambitions of politicians. The great body of conservative men were practically unattached to either. The Democratic party nominated him for the Presidency. His reluctant acceptance of the nomination was a new - service, not his smallest, to the Republic, concentrating the conservative element in the country on a platform which he made for himself in his letter of acceptance, placing his supporters firmly on the principle of supporting the war and prosecuting it vigorously till the Union and Constitution should be established in safety. How many votes he received will never be known, for the "count " was in the hands of those who had not scrupled to defeat him in battles with the enemies of the Union. The soldiers' votes were effectually disposed of by the Secretary of War.

He had not expected to be elected, and the result was a great relief to him. His earnest desire had always been to regain the enjoyments of home life, of which he had had so brief an experience.

He resigned his commission as major-general in the army on the day of the Presidential election, Nov. 8, 1864, and immediately sought work as a civilian for the support of his family.

But the bitterness of political enmity followed him into private life. His eminent abilities made his services desirable to many great corporations, and he was offered one and another position of honorable employment, such as he desired. In each case he ascertained that the offer was made by a majority over a minority who had strong prejudices against him and opposed his appointment. Acceptance was impossible to him under such circumstances. In Jan., 1865, he went to Europe with his family. His reasons were sad enough, expressed to me in a sentence I well remember: "I cannot find a place to earn my living here, and I am going to stay abroad till I am forgotten, then come back and find work, which I may get when these animosities have cooled down."

But the people would not forget him. In 1868, when it was rumored that he was coming home, soldiers and citizens proposed to receive him with honors. He wrote emphatically protesting against any such demonstration, and after his return insisted on declining it. The demand of his old comrades and friends became so pressing that he at last consented to receive a procession on a designated evening a few days in advance, provided it should be spontaneous, without previous advertisement in newspapers. He expected a few hundred old soldiers and friends, and an affair of a few minutes. Instead he received the most impressive ovation which has ever been given to a private citizen of this country, perhaps not excepting those in times of the highest political excitement. The vast and broad procession of men who honored him passed hour after hour in front of the balcony on which he stood, while fifty or a hundred thousand crowded the street and square to witness and share in the demonstration. At midnight that night he said to me: "Well, it is over now, and I hope I can be quiet hereafter." But an American with such a hold on the hearts of people cannot be quiet.

There was no man in America, up to the day of his death, to whom so many of his fellow-citizens were attached by ties of affection and respect. There was what men call a magnetism about him which won all hearts. To politicians such a man, honest and unapproachable, is always a subject of apprehension. Party politicians, Democrats as well as Republicans, feared him as a possible rival or opponent. He received no favors from either, and to his death owed no gratitude to either party or any of their leaders. He was as carefully neglected by one as by the other, except when his great personal influence was wanted in a political campaign.

He established his residence, known as Maywood, on Orange Mountain, in New Jersey, where he built a house, and brought around him treasures of literature and art, memorials of faithful friends, of far travel, of scenes in his life which were pleasant to remember. Conspicuous in his own room was a shining mass of the long black hair of the horse Dan Webster, faithful among the faithful on a score of battle-fields.

In 1877 he was elected Governor of New Jersey. Had it been possible for Democratic party politicians to control the nomination he would not have been selected. His administration was eminently successful, rich in benefit to the educational, industrial, and judicial systems of the. State, and wholly free from partisanship. And here it may be added that his experience had taught him to recognize the party politician whenever he came in contact with one, and to estimate him at his precise worth. He had accepted the governorship, urged on him as an opportunity of doing good service to his State; but he was glad when the end of his term of office came. He had resolved to pass the remainder of his life as a private citizen. During its later pears he went abroad several times, to Europe, Egypt, and the Holy Land, enjoying travel and study and the pleasure of warm social intercourse with many of the most distinguished soldiers, statesmen, and scholars of various countries, who were his correspondents and friends. His ample knowledge of modern languages made him at home in all countries, and enabled him to accumulate stores of information. He was thoroughly familiar with the progress of political as well as military thought and events in Europe and at home.

In the autumn of 1885 he had several severe attacks of pain in the region of the heart. After one of these he yielded to the advice of his excellent physician and remained at home, resting for some days. On the afternoon of Oct. 28 he drove out with his daughter, and passed the evening in pleasant conversation with his family. Towards eleven o'clock, after the evening prayers which were the family custom, he went to his working-room, wrote for a brief time, and then went to bed, taking, as he generally did, a book, which he read for a while. A sharp attack of the same acute pain suddenly seized him. The physician summoned to his side administered remedies, but the agony continued. He left his bed for a large chair in which he sat. No expression of suffering escaped him. On the contrary, he spoke only cheerfully and pleasantly to the servants whom he was sorry to call up, and to his wife and daughter, to whom he once in a while addressed a bright word of affection. About three o'clock in the morning he looked towards Mrs. McClellan and said in a low voice to the physician, "Tell her I am better now." The next moment his head rested on the chair-back and the good soldier was gone. The rewards which are withheld here, whether by reason of the malice of enemies or the neglect of friends, are of no account there.

His funeral was, in accordance with his own wishes often expressed, that of a private citizen. His body was brought to New York to my house, in which he had always been at home. While thousands of citizens filled the neighboring streets, he lay life-like, and around him stood a group of great men. The commanders of the opposing armies which had met at Yorktown and in the Peninsular campaign were both there - one living, the other dead. Strong men, generals, old soldiers of many battle-fields, his comrades and his foes, looked at his calm face. I have never seen, never expect to see again, such a scene, so many stout men in tears. Such eyes shed tears only for the great and good.

Then followed the simple services in the Madison Square Presbyterian Church, of which he had been a member until he became a ruling elder in the church at Orange. From the church he was carried to Trenton. Great throngs awaited the arrival of the train at the station and crowded the streets through which the procession passed for two miles. Thousands of silent mourners were assembled in the cemetery. His grave was in his private plot, on a hill overlooking the flow of the Delaware. A clergyman, one who loved him, said the last words of faith and hope as he was laid in the grave. So we buried him.

Most public men live two lives - the one that which the people see, the other that which none see unless it be a few intimate friends and companions of hours of freedom. McClellan, the soldier and patriot, is well known to the people, has been diversely judged by them according to the amount of correct information they have received, and according to those prejudices of political and other associations which affect all our opinions of public men of our own time.

Whatever be their judgment of the soldier and statesman, few if any outside of the circle of his intimate friends have had any idea of the real man. Public men are too often measured by the familiar standards of public life. He was a man such as we seldom know. His experiences in life were varied. Educated as a soldier, he had devoted his life to his profession, and was one of the most accomplished military scholars of the world. His military library was large, in various languages, always increasing, every book thoroughly studied. He continued these studies faithfully to his death. Military operations in every part of the world commanded his close observation. He supplied himself with maps and all information in current literature, followed movements of armies, kept himself familiar with every phase of campaigns, whether in Europe, in Afghanistan, in Egypt, or in South Africa.

While this was his professional study, he occupied himself with almost equally thorough study of subjects very - remote from military matters. He was a general student of the literature of the world. He read freely most of the languages of Europe, and kept up with the progress of thought and discussion in history, philosophy, and art. He was especially interested in archæology, and, having all his life retained and used his knowledge of ancient languages, found abundant delight in reading archæologic publications and in following the work of explorers. In all departments of scholarly reading, he was constant and unwearying, and he never forgot what he had once learned. Fitted by his attainments for the society of the learned, he had the marked characteristic of the true scholar - the desire to know more, and therefore the habit of seeking instead of offering information. Few suspected his mastery of subjects on which he only asked questions when thrown in contact with recognized masters. In general conversation he more frequently sought information than gave it; but when drawn out to give it his expression was concise, vigorous, clear. His extended knowledge of ancient and modern languages made him master of his own. His public papers are models of pure style. His habit of writing was swift, and he never hesitated for the precise word to express the exact shade of meaning he intended. His despatch-books, containing the autograph originals of his despatches during the war, are marvels, since, with whatever haste he wrote, he wrote without erasure or alteration on subjects where each word was of vital importance.

That his life was one of constant occupation may be judged from what has been said. He had no idle hours - for those cannot be called idle which were given to social duties and the enjoyments of that home life whose beauty and happiness were perfect. His wife and children were his companions, and a perpetual sunshine was in the household. He was full of cheer, life, vigor, always ready for whatever would make any one of them happy.

And this leads me to say that of all men I have ever known McClellan was the most unselfish. Neither in his public life nor in his private life did he ever seek anything for himself. He was constantly doing something for some one else; always seeking to do good, confer pleasure, relieve sorrow, gratify a whim, do something for another. He had his own amusements, but in those he sought the good of others. He had devoted a great deal of attention to ceramic art, and had collected many fine examples. He was an excellent judge of genuineness of specimens. But his love of "old china" was not for mere pleasure - it was for historical and industrial considerations; and New Jersey owes him a vastly larger debt than she knows for the great advance made in her pottery productions through his special personal efforts while and after he was governor of that State. In his elegant home, with ample table furniture of old historic porcelains, gathered with admirable judgment and taste in his European trips, he was especially proud of, and fond of using and showing, beautiful services made at Trenton in potteries which he often visited, and to whose advancement he had, while governor and afterward, directed earnest attention.

The personal affection which existed between McClellan and the soldiers of the Army of the Potomac is historical. It grew with years on both sides. On his it was a marked trait of his character. He would make great sacrifices of his own pleasure and comfort to render a service to any one of them. They were a vast family, and not a few of them came to him for aid in distress. None came in vain.

His charity was abundant. He sympathized with every one who was in trouble or sorrow; and his sympathy was practical and useful, for his person and his purse were devoted to its uses. An Irish servant in a New York house saw her brother's name in the list of killed at Antietam, and started off forthwith to find his grave. When she came back she told her story to the family. She found her way to the battle-field, and after a while to the graves where some one told her the men of her brother's regiment were buried. It was a lonesome place above ground then, for the army had moved away. She was searching among the graves for a familiar name on the stakes. when she saw, riding down the road which passed at some distance from the burial place, what she called a lot of soldiers on horseback. When they came abreast of her the leader, who was a little in advance, called a halt, sprang to the ground, and walked across the open field to her. "What are you looking for, my good woman?' he said. She told him. "What was your brother's regiment ?" She answered. "You are only one of thousands who want to know to-day where their dead are lying here," he said. "I hope you will find your brother's grave. Don't mourn too much for him. He died a soldier's death." Then, turning, he called, "Orderly!" A soldier came. "Stay with this woman and help her find her brother's grave. Report to me this evening." And he went back, remounted. and the company rode on at a gallop. After a while the orderly found the grave, and she knelt there and prayed. Then she asked the soldier: "Who was that gentleman that told you to help me?" "That?" said the orderly. "Why, didn't you know him? That was 'Little Mac.' "God bless him! I said," was the end of her story. Innumerable like prayers of grateful souls of men and women, with those words, "God bless him!" have "battered the gates of heaven."

It is surely unnecessary to say that he was a gentleman in every sense of the word.   In social life he was perfectly simple in his manner, wholly unaffected, always genial, having rare conversational powers with all classes of persons, devoutly respectful to ladies. This deference to the female sex was a marked characteristic.   I note an illustration of it which I find in many of his private letters, some in this volume.   When at the head of the army, and occupying a position only second to the President, he received thousands of visitors who came from mere curiosity, introduced by senators or others, to see the young general. In mentioning such visits he invariabry says that he "was presented to the ladies"- never uses what would have been a perfectly correct expression under the circumstances: "the ladies were presented to me."

In person McClellan was five feet nine inches tall, with great breadth of shoulders and solid, not superfluous, muscle.   He measured forty-five inches around the chest.   His physical strength in his younger life was very great. He seldom exerted it in later years.   He contracted disease in the Mexican war which never wholly left him, and which doubtless somewhat impaired his strength.   But in 1863 I have seen him bend a quarter-dollar over the end of his thumb by pressure between the first and second finger of his hand.   That same evening we were sitting together, three, one of whom was a distinguished officer who weighed over two hundred and fifty. "They tell me, general," said I, "that McClellan can throw you over his head." "So they say," was the somewhat uncertain response. McClellan sprang from his chair and crossed the room rapidly with hands stretched out to seize the giant. "Let me alone, general!" he exclaimed -"let me alone! He can do it - he has done it. He can toss me in his arms like a baby." To the very last day of his life his step was quick, firm, elastic, the expression of that uniform cheerfulness, bouyancy, and enjoyment of life which he possessed and which he always communicated to those around him.   I think I shall be understood in saying that his physical bearing was such that of all men he was the very last with whom those who knew him could connect any thought of death.

I have left to the last to speak of the controlling feature of McClelI-Ian's character and life.   His religion was deep, earnest, practical; not vague or ill-defined to himself or others, not obtrusive, but outspoken when occasion required, and, when outspoken, frank and hearty. For it was part and parcel of his soul.   I must use brief words, and I seek to make them distinct, in defining his creed, which was clear as crystal, more steadfast than the hills - the faith once delivered to the saints in its pure simplicity.   With his intellectual powers, which were of the highest. and with his heart, which was supremely gentle, as trustful all his life as any child's, he was servant and follower of Jesus Christ, in whom he believed as God, of God.

In all his life, public and private, every purpose was formed, every act done in the light of that faith.   It was this which not only produced in him that stainless purity of walk and conversation which all who knew him recognized, but also gave him strength for all the great works of a great life. It was this which created that magnetic power so often spoken of, won to him that marvellous devotion of his soldiers, made all who knew him regard him with affection, those who knew him best love him most.

Out of the private correspondence which has come into my hands I have selected, and venture to make public here, two letters. These, better than anything I can say, will serve to open, for those who only knew him as a public man, a view of that inner life - his real life - which he lived among his familiar friends:

" NEW YORK, Aug. 18, 1879.

"MY DEAR GENERAL: Passing through South Street I saw a magnificent yacht-like ship, apparently new, called the *Gen. McClellan.* You have probably seen her. If not, she deserves a visit. I am sure you are tired of being governor or anything else, for, no matter what the title be, the result is always the same - work, work unceasingly. Now, suppose we gather our household gods and sail away in this good ship, until we come to 'the land where it is always afternoon'? This would be better than Orange Mountain or the salt sea of Long Island.

"With kind regards to Mrs. McClellan, believe me, yours,

"S. L. M. BARLOW.

"Gen. McCLELLAN."

ORANGE, Sept. 3, 1879.

MY DEAR SAM: Your welcome note of the 18th Aug. reached me when on the point of starting off for a trip from home. I was very glad to see those "leaning-back" characters once more.

Some few years ago I saw - near Mr. Alsop's office - a ship named for me, probably the same you saw the other day. I fancy Sam, that we will never reach that "land where it is always afternoon" in any ship built by mortal hands. Our fate is to work, and still to work, as long as there is any work left in us; and I do not doubt that it is best. For I can't help thinking that, when me reach that other and far better land, we shall still have work to do throughout the long ages, only we will then see, as we go on, that it is all done for the Master and under His own eye; and we will like it, and never grow weary of it, as we often do here when we don't clearly see to what end me are working, and our work brings us in contact with all sorts of men and things not pleasant to rub against. I suppose that the more we work here the better we shall be trained for that other work, which, after all, is the great end towards which we move, or ought to be moving.

Well, I did not start out to sermonize, but somehow or other your letter started my thoughts in that direction. I *would* like to take the "belongings" and sail for that quiet land; but we will have to wait some little time yet, and I suppose each one will reach it alone, and the first arrived wait for the others.

I hear that Elsie is to leave you in October. Is it possible that time can fly so rapidly? Before many years May will perhaps leave us; and just now me are getting ready to send Max to boarding-school - an awful business, as you can tell from your own experience in sending Pete to Dr. Coit's. I think this scattering of children is the worst wrench we get down here; but there is nothing to be done but do the best for them as we understand it, and to thank God that they don't and can't feel it as we do.

What changes since we first crossed the Atlantic together - how many years ago? What a mess in politics! I am trying to take the least possible interest in such matters, as the only way to keep one's temper. Mrs. McClellan unites with me in love to Mrs. Barlow, Elsie, and yourself And I am always your friend,

                                                    GEO. B. MCCLELLAN.
S. L. M. B.

In editing this volume for the press I have tried to do that which my friend would approve. The discretion which he gave me was ample. I have exercised it by omissions, not by changes. Of course his work was unfinished when he left it. Living prepared for the call whenever it might come, serving God as he had served his country, always ready for whatever command he might receive, it is nevertheless certain that, when the order came to go to duty in another life, he was not expecting it.

In writing his memoirs he had made no haste to complete them. Probably had he lived to extreme old age there would still have been much to be written. For years after the civil war he declined to write anything about it. He had no anxieties for himself and his own reputation. An abiding faith in time and the calm judgment of his country kept him from any care about the misstatements, misrepresentations, and falsehoods of which he, more perhaps than any American who had lived before him, excepting Washington, had been made the subject. Besides, he always gave less thought to himself and his own reputation than any man I ever knew or heard of. He was a man of very deep feeling, with the passions of all ardent souls; but so absolute had become his habitual self-control and subjection of all passionate resentment, so complete the self-abnegation which characterized him, I can affirm with certainty that he always felt more sorrow for the man who maligned him than for himself. Once when I showed him a slander, a pure fabrication, which had been published on the authority of Gen. Burnside, he read it, laid down the magazine with a quiet laugh, said, "Poor Burn! he didn't know what he was saying," and, after a few kindly words about his old friend, dropped the subject. In vain was he urged to publish the demonstrations he possessed of the falsehood of this and similar attacks.

His happiness in life consisted in what he was always doing for others, without thought of self. As he had never sought position, command, or promotion, so he never asked his countrymen to give him honor or thanks.

It was only when I urged on him that his children had a right to possess his own story that he took the subject into consideration. Afterward, while in Europe, he began to write out personal reminiscences, which from time to time he continued after his return to America. A fire destroyed all his manuscript. In 1881 he resumed the work. He did not labor at it continuously, with intent to produce a book, but wrote as the humor seized him.

His Report, made in 1863, but held back by the War Department for some months, had been full, accurate, and exhaustive. It was published in 1864. No statement in it has ever been controverted. This Report did not include any accounts of his personal relations to the civilians who directed the course of political events and misdirected military operations during the first two years of the war. These accounts he wrote, accompanying them with letters, despatches, documents - whatever might throw light on history. He rewrote and extended a large part of the military history - which his Report had given in brief, and from time to time inserted pages of manuscript here and there in those parts of it which he had not rewritten. Thus as years passed he was extending and annotating a history, at all times complete in itself as a narrative; and, however long he had lived, would probably have enriched it from year to year with more and more of interesting material. His sudden death interrupted the progress of his work. When I came to examine the collected and arranged papers which he entrusted to me, verbally while living, and by his last will, I found not only the narrative which I have styled MCCLELLAN'S OWN STORY, but sufficient illustrative and explanatory documents, letters, and despatches to form several volumes.

He had not written with reference to publication. It was expressly for his children that he was preparing his memoirs, and there was a great deal in them which was intended solely for their eyes. A century hence every word, perhaps, might be interesting to those who enjoy personal memoirs, but, as a matter of course, it has been my duty to withhold such portions as I think he would not have published now. I have exercised my discretion in reserving for future publication much of the material he had arranged, which would now be valuable, and doubtless acceptable, but would have extended this volume to a series of two or three. All the foot-notes in the volume are mine.

Another class of material came into my hands. McClellan had been married only a few months before the outbreak of the war. Not the least sacrifice which he made in entering the service was the breaking up of the home - his first home - in which he had found the first happiness of a laborious life. Sometimes during his public service Mrs. McClellan was able to be with him, especially while he was in Washington. When they were separated he found his only rest and refreshment in writing to her. To no other person in the world did he open his whole soul. The perfection of their love, the absolute confidence which he reposed, and wisely reposed, in her, made his letters not only graphic accounts of daily events, great and small, but an exposure of his inmost feelings I found among his papers some extracts from these letters, which he had made to aid him in writing his memoirs; but the letters were supposed to have vanished in the fire. When they were discovered, carefully sealed for the one only person to whom they belonged, I asked for fuller extracts. I confess that I hesitated very much about giving any part of these letters, written in the most sacred confidence of life, to the public eye. Others advised that, as he belonged to his country, and innumerable citizens and soldiers loved him with devout affection, they could well be allowed, had indeed a right, to read portions of these letters which reveal McClellan the man, as his narrative shows McClellan the soldier.

By far the larger portion of the letters, and of every letter, belongs to that confidence which not even death affects. In determining what parts may and what may not be published I have been influenced by the wish to present to his fellow-citizens who honored him, and his soldiers who loved him, some of that view of his character which those nearest to him always had; and I have done this with the guiding trust that he will approve what I have done when I again meet him.

W. C. PRIME.

AUGUST 10, 1886.

McCLELLAN'S OWN STORY

November 8, 1881.

The labor of years in the preparation of my memoirs having been destroyed by fire, it remains to recommence the tedious work and replace the loss as best I may. Fortunately my original papers are preserved. I have no present intention of publishing anything during my lifetime, but desire to leave, for the use of my children, my own account of the great events in which it was my fortune to take part. Therefore, should I live to complete my work, it will probably be found too voluminous for publication, and I anticipate the necessity of a judicious pruning to fit it for the public use.

I have thus far abstained from any public reply to the various criticisms and misrepresentations of which I have been the subject, and shall probably preserve the same attitude during the remainder of my life. Certainly, up to within a brief period, party feeling has run so high that the pathway for the truth has been well-nigh closed, and too many have preferred to accept blindly whatever was most agreeable to their prejudices, rather than to examine facts.

Moreover, during the civil war I never sought rank nor command. Whenever of that nature came to me came by force of circumstances and with no effort of my own. In the performance of the duties thus thrown upon me, I can with a clear conscience say that I never thought of myself or of my own interests, but that I steadily pursued the course which commended itself to me as best serving the true interests of my country, and of the gallant troops whom I had the honor to command.

I have, therefore, been able to maintain a calm front under abuse, and - while far from claiming immunity from error - have remained satisfied with the conviction that, after my death at least, my countrymen will recognize the fact that I loyally served my country in its darkest hour; and that others, who during their lifetimes have been more favored than myself, would probably have done no better, under the circumstances which surrounded me, when, twice at least, I saved the capital, once created and once reorganized a great army.

McCLELLAN'S OWN STORY.

CHAPTER I.

Causes of the war - Principles of the Union - State-rights and secession - Slavery - Immediate and gradual emancipation - Douglas and Lincoln - War imminent - The South responsible - A slander refuted - McClellan always for the Union - Enters the service - Made major-general of volunteers in Ohio.

WHEN the occurrences at Fort Sumter in April, 1861, aroused the nation to some appreciation of the gravity of the situation, I was engaged in civil life as president of the Eastern Division of the Ohio and Mississippi Railroad, having resigned my commission as a captain of cavalry in January, 1857. My residence was then in Cincinnati, and the fact that I had been in the army threw me in contact with the leading men of the State. My old army associations had placed me in intimate relations with many Southern men, and I had travelled much in the South, so that I was, perhaps, better prepared to weigh the situation than the majority of Northern men. So strongly was I convinced that war would ensue that when, in the autumn of 1860, I leased a house in Cincinnati for the term of three years, I insisted upon a clause in the lease releasing me from the obligation in the event of war.

The general current of events during the winter, and many special instances of outrage or insult offered to unoffending Northern travellers in the Southwest (coming to my knowledge as a railway official), reduced this impression to a certainty in my mind, even before the firing upon Sumter.

After all that has been said and written upon the subject, I suppose none now doubt that slavery was the real knot of the question and the underlying cause of the war. It is now easy to perceive how the war might have been avoided if for two or

29

three generations back all the men of both sections had been eminently wise, calm, unselfish, and patriotic. But with men as they are, it would be difficult indeed to indicate how a permanent pacific solution could have been reached. It is no doubt true that events were precipitated, perhaps rendered inevitable, by the violent course of a comparatively small number of men, on both sides of the line, during the thirty years preceding the war.

But it is the distinct lesson of history that this is always so; that the great crises in the world's history are induced by the words and actions of a few earnest or violent men, who stir up the masses and induce them blindly to follow their lead, whether for good or evil. As a rule the masses of civilized men, if left to themselves, are not prone to disturb the existing order of things or to resort to violent measures, unless suffering under intense evils which come home to each man individually and affect either his personal safety or personal possessions and prosperity; and even in such cases spontaneous uprisings of the masses are rare.

In our own case the people of the two sections did not understand each other before the war, and probably neither section regarded the other as seriously in earnest. The wide difference existing in social organization and habits had much to do with this.

In the South the habit of carrying, and using on slight provocation, deadly weapons, the sparse settlement of the country, the idle and reckless habits of the majority of the illiterate whites, the self-assertion natural to the dominant race in a slave-holding country, all conspired to impress them with an ill-founded assumption of superior worth and courage over the industrious, peaceful, law-abiding Northerners. On the other hand, the men of the North had become somewhat habituated to the boastful assertions too common among the Southerners, and had learned to believe that no real purpose of using force lay concealed beneath their violent language. Both were mistaken. The Southerner, with all his gasconading, was earnest in his intention to fight to the last for slavery and the right of secession. The peaceful Northerner, unaccustomed to personal warfare and prone to submit his disputes to the regular ordeal of law, was ready to lay down his life for the cause of the Union.

More gallant foes never met on the field of battle than these men of the same race, who had so long lived under the ample folds of the same flag; more desperate battles were never fought than those now about to occur. The military virtues of patriotism, patience, endurance, self-abnegation, and heroism were about to receive their most striking illustrations.

In judging the motives of men at this great crisis it must be remembered that the vast majority of Southern men had been educated in the doctrine of secession and of extreme State-rights -which is, that allegiance was due first to the State, next to the general government, and that the State when it entered the Union retained the right to withdraw at will; while in the North the doctrine was generally held that allegiance to the general government was paramount and the Union indissoluble. The masses on each side were honest in their belief as to the justice of their cause. Their honesty and sincerity were proved by the sacrifices they made, by the earnestness with which so many devout Christians on both sides confidently relied upon the aid of God in their hour of trial, and by the readiness with which so many brave men laid down their lives on the field of battle.

When the generation which took part in this contest shall have passed away, and the question can be regarded in the cold light of dispassionate historical and philosophical inquiry, it will be clearly seen that in this case also history has repeated itself, and that the truth lay midway between the extreme positions assumed by the controlling spirits at the time. The right of secession would virtually have carried us back to the old Confederacy, which proved so weak from lack of cohesion between its parts and of the necessary force in the executive. The tendency of Northern Republicans was towards a centralized power, under which the autocracy of the States would disappear.

It is impossible for any government to recognize the right of secession unless its assertion is supported by such overwhelming force as to render opposition entirely hopeless, and thus practically convert rebellion into successful revolution. There can be no stability, no protection of person and property, no good government, no power to put down disorder at home or to resist oppression from without, under any other principle.

On the other hand, in a country so vast as ours, with such

great differences of topography and of climate, with a population so numerous and derived from such a variety of sources, and, in consequence of all this, such diversities of habits, local laws, and material interests, it is impossible for a centralized government to legislate satisfactorily for all the domestic concerns of the various parts of the Union.

The only safe policy is that the general government be strictly confined to the general powers and duties vested in it by the old Constitution, while the individual States preserve all the sovereign rights and powers retained by them when the constitutional compact was formed.

As a corollary from this I am convinced that no State can be deprived of any of these retained rights, powers, and duties without its own consent; and that the power of amending the Constitution was intended to apply only to amendments affecting the manner of carrying into effect the original provisions of the Constitution, but not to enable the general government to seize new power at the expense of any unwilling State.

A strict adherence in practice to this theory presents, in my opinion, the only possibility of the permanent maintenance of our Union throughout the long years of the future.

The old Southern doctrine of extreme State-rights, including that of secession, would reduce the Union to a mere rope of sand, and would completely paralyze the general government, rendering it an object of just contempt at home and abroad.

The doctrine of centralization, if carried to its legitimate conclusions, in substituting the legislation of the general government for that of the States in regard to the local and domestic affairs of the people, would soon cause so much discontent and suffering as to result in a resort to secession as the only practical remedy. And in this case the Union could only be maintained by the superior force of a strong military central government, thus rendering the Union valueless for its great object of securing the liberties of the people.

In the course of my narrative the fact will appear - a fact well known to all who intelligently followed the events of the time- that, at the beginning of the great civil war, the general government was powerless, both in the East and West, to maintain its rights and vindicate its authority, and that the means to accomplish these vital ends were furnished by the individual States, acting in their capacity as sovereigns. The history of that period is the best possible vindication of the Northern doctrine of State-rights.

And no impartial observer of the events of the war can fail to see that all the subsequent violations of the Constitution and of the rights of the loyal States, by the general government, were not only wholly unnecessary but positively pernicious at the time. The safety of the republic at no time during the war required or justified any departure from the provisions of the Constitution. That great instrument was broad enough to cover even the necessities of that most eventful period. The loyalty of the great masses of the Northern people was so marked and so strong that they could be trusted far more than most of the selfish servants whom a minority had placed in power. The happiest condition of affairs for us would no doubt be found in a return to the situation before the war, when the action of the general government, being strictly confined to its legitimate purposes, was so little felt by individual citizens that they almost forgot its existence, and were almost unaware that there was any other government in the land than those of the States and municipalities,

Soon after my arrival in Washington in 1861 I had several interviews with prominent abolitionists - of whom Senator Sumner was one - on the subject of slavery. I invariably took the ground that I was thoroughly opposed to slavery, regarding it as a great evil, especially to the whites of the South, but that in my opinion no sweeping measure of emancipation should be carried out, unless accompanied by arrangements providing for the new relations between employers and employed, carefully guarding the rights and interests of both; and that were such a measure framed to my satisfaction I would cordially support it. Mr. Sumner replied - others also agreed with him - that such points did not concern us, and that all that must be left to take care of itself. My reply was that no real statesman could ever contemplate so sweeping and serious a measure as sudden and general emancipation without looking to the future and providing for its consequences; that four and a half millions of uneducated slaves should not suddenly be manumitted without due precautions taken both to protect them and to guard against them; that just there was the point where we differed radically and probably irreconcilably.

My own view was that emancipation should be accomplished gradually, and that the negroes should be fitted for it by certain preparatory steps in the way of education, recognition of the rights of family and marriage, prohibition against selling them without their own consent, the freedom of those born after a certain date, etc.   I was always prepared to make it one of the essential conditions of peace that slavery should be abolished within a fixed and reasonable period.   Had the arrangements of the terms of peace been in my hands I should certainly have insisted on this.

During the autumn of 1861, after arriving in Washington, I discontinued the practice of returning fugitive slaves to their owners.

In Western Virginia, after Pegram's surrender, when I had been directed to parole the prisoners, I collected the large number of negro slaves captured with their masters, and gave them their choice as *to* returning with the latter, remaining in camp under pay as laborers, or going North.   With one or two exceptions they decided to return with their masters.   From that time forward I never returned a negro slave to his master, although many such requisitions were made on me.   I followed the principle that there could be no slave in my camp.

On the Peninsula I not only received all negroes who came to the camps, but (especially when on the James river) frequently sent out parties to bring in negroes, because I required them for certain work around the camps and depots too severe for white men in that climate.   They were employed upon police work, loading and unloading transports, etc., and sometimes upon entrenchments.   They were fed and received some small wages. As a rule much strictness was necessary to make them work; they supposed that in leaving their masters they left all labor behind them, and that they would be clothed, fed, and allowed to live in idleness in the North.   That was their only idea of liberty.   It was very clear that they were entirely unfit for sudden emancipation and the reception of the electoral franchise, and should have been gradually prepared for it.

While on this subject I must say that, although I was a strong Democrat of the Stephen A. Douglas school, I had no personal political ambition.   I knew nothing about "practical politics," had never even voted except for Douglas, and during the whole period of my command I never did or wrote anything, or abstained from doing or writing anything, in view of its political effect upon myself. My ambition was fully gratified by the possession of the command of the army, and, so long as I held that, nothing would have induced me to give it up for the Presidency. Whenever I wrote anything of a political nature it was only with the hope of doing something towards the maintenance of those political principles which I honestly thought should control the conduct of the war. In fact, I sacrificed my own interests rather than acquiesce in what I thought wrong or impolitic. The President and his advisers made a great mistake in supposing that I desired political advancement.

Many of the Democratic leaders did me great harm by using my name for party purposes without my knowledge or consent; and, without intending it, probably did more than my armed enemies in the way of ruining my military career by giving the administration some reason to suppose that in the event of military success I might prove a dangerous political rival.

Regarding, as I did, the restoration of the Union and preservation of the national life to be the great object of the war, I would, no doubt, have acquiesced in any honorable measure absolutely necessary to bring about the desired result, even to the forcible and general abolition of slavery, if found to be a military necessity. I recognized the fact that as the Confederate States had chosen to resort to the arbitrament of arms, they must abide by the logical consequences of the stern laws of war. But, as I always believed that we should fight to bring them back into the Union, and should treat them as members of the Union when so brought back, I held that it was a matter of sound policy to do nothing likely to render ultimate reconciliation and harmony impossible, unless such a course were imperative to secure military success. Nor do I now believe that my ideas were quixotic or impracticable.

Since the war I have met many of my late antagonists, and have found none who entertained any personal enmity against me. While acknowledging, with Lee and other of their generals, that they feared me more than any of the Northern generals, and that I had struck them harder blows when in the full prime of their strength, they have all said that I fought them like a gen-

5

tleman and in an honorable way, and that they felt nothing but respect for me.

I remember very well, when riding over the field of South Mountain, that, passing by a severely wounded Confederate officer, I dismounted and spoke with him, asking whether I could do anything to relieve him. He was a lieutenant-colonel of a South Carolina regiment, and asked me if I was Gen. McClellan; and when I said that I was Gen. McClellan, he grasped my hand and told me that he was perfectly willing to be wounded and a prisoner for the sake of taking by the hand one whom all the Confederates so honored and admired. Such things happened to me not unfrequently, and I confess that it gave me no little pleasure to find that my antagonists shared the feelings of my own men for me.

To revert to politics for a moment: Then residing in Chicago I knew Mr. Stephen A. Douglas quite well. During his campaign for the senatorship against Mr. Lincoln they were on one occasion to hold a joint discussion at Bloomington, and, as my business called me in that direction, I invited Mr. Douglas to accompany me in my private car. We started late in the evening, and Mr. Douglas brought with him a number of his political henchmen, with whom he was up all night. We reached Bloomington early in the afternoon of the nest day, and about half an hour before arriving I warned Mr. Douglas, who had continued his amusements up to that time, not having slept at all. I dreaded a failure in the discussion about to take place, for the Little Giant certainly had had no opportunity of thinking of the subject of the debate, and did not seem to be in fit condition to carry it on. Not that he was intoxicated, but looking unkempt and sleepy. He, however, retired to my private cabin, and soon emerged perfectly fresh and ready for the work before him; so much so that I thought his speech of that day his best during the campaign.

Mr. Lincoln entertained a very high respect for Mr. Douglas's powers, and no doubt had the latter survived he would have exercised a great and most favorable influence upon Mr. Lincoln, as well as upon the Democratic party of the North. His death was a severe blow to the country. He would, in all probability, have been able to control the more flighty leaders of the Northwestern Democracy, and have kept the party in the eyes of the world, as its masses really were, united in a hearty support of the war.

While giving due weight to all said or done by the ultra abolitionists of the North, I hold the South directly accountable for the war. If the election of Mr. Lincoln meant a more determined attack upon slavery, they of the South were responsible for the result, in consequence of their desertion of Mr. Douglas and the resulting rupture of the Democratic party. Even after that, if they had chosen to draw near the Northern Democrats again, seeking their remedy and protection within the Union, the Constitution, and the laws, they would have retained the right on their side. If left to their own cool judgment it is probable that the majority of the Southern whites would have realized that slavery could not exist much longer, and that their wisest course was to recognize that fact, consent that it should not be extended beyond its existing limits, and provide for its gradual extinction. But, for various reasons, more reckless counsels prevailed. The Southern States rallied to the support of their peculiar institution, declared it to be a holy ordinance, demanded that it might be extended over the Territories, and bitterly opposed the idea that general manumission should be provided for in any form. Thus a state of feeling arose, more particularly in the South, which could only be quieted by the drastic methods of war.

In the early part of 1861, as has already been stated, it became almost impossible for any Northern man to travel in the Southwest without being subjected to gross insults or to personal maltreated; this conduct soon produced a counter irritation, and, as for myself, I confess that ere long I came to the conclusion that there was but one way to put an end to such proceedings, and that the sooner we entered upon that way the better it would be. When Sumter was fired upon there was no longer room for discussion, and the question was narrowed to the issue of the life of the Union and the honor of the flag. For men who thought as I did there was but one course open.

It was clear that, even if a peaceable separation were arranged, we would soon come to blows on some secondary issue, such as boundaries, the division of public property, the slavery question on the borders, the free navigation of the Mississippi, the territorial domain, etc., etc., and in that view it was better to throw everything else to one side and fight upon the main underlying issue - the preservation of the Union and the observance of the laws of the general government.

It is perhaps hardly worth while to notice here any of those unfounded slanders which some papers uttered concerning me-that is, the statement that at the outbreak of the war I entertained offers to enter the Southern service. I need only say that there was not the shadow of a foundation for this. The leading men on the Southern side knew perfectly well that of all men I would be the last to waver in my allegiance to the general government and its flag.

At no period, either before or after the war broke out, did any one suggest to me, either directly or indirectly, the idea of my taking part with the South. No one ever made me any offer to join the rebel service; no one ever suggested the possibility of my dreaming of espousing that side. I never, in any manner, intimated to any one that it would be possible for me to take any other side than that of the general government and the Union, nor did such a thought ever pass through my mind. I always stated distinctly that, should the apprehended crisis arrive, I should stand by the Union and the general government. I make this record because there have been people so foolish as to believe the statements made by radical newspapers to the effect that I had offered my services to the secessionists. Those papers must have known their statements to be entirely false and void of foundation, when they made them for the sole purpose of serving party political ends.

The secession of South Carolina, Dec. 20, 1860, was closely followed by that of six other States, and on the 8th of Feb., 1861, the Southern Confederacy was formally proclaimed and its president elected. But, without even awaiting the organization of the new Confederate government, the seceding States seized all the unprotected United States arsenals and fortifications within their limits, together with all the arms, stores, and munitions of war they contained. Forts Moultrie and Sumter in Charleston harbor, Fort Pickens at Pensacola, and the fortresses at Key West and Tortugas in Florida were about the only forts within the seceded States which remained in the possession of the general government.

How soon the work of organizing and instructing troops began in the South will appear from the fact that as early as the 9th of Jan., 1861, an expedition for the relief of Fort Sumter was turned back by the fire of the Southern batteries near the entrance of Charleston harbor. About the same time the navy-yard at Pensacola was occupied by an armed force under Bragg, and the works at the mouth of the Mississippi garrisoned.

In brief, at least from the beginning of Jan., 1861, and probably in many cases yet earlier, the work of organizing, arming, and instructing troops began throughout the seceded States, and not improbably in such of the slaveholding States also as had not yet formally joined the movement of secession. As early as Feb. 18, Gen. Twiggs surrendered the forces under his command in Texas.

Meanwhile neither the general government nor the Northern States were doing anything to counteract this movement and meet the impending storm. Not only were there no additional troops raised, no steps taken to organize and arm the militia and volunteers, but, so far as the general government was concerned, the authorities seemed to dread even the semblance of a movement to reinforce the few forts still in their possession. The little regular army, scattered over the vast area of the West, was left without orders, and not even concentrated for self-defence, much less brought in where its services might be available against the active forces of the secessionists, as common prudence would have suggested, as early as the passage of the South Carolina ordinance of secession.

Such was the condition of affairs when Fort Sumter surrendered on the 14th of April, 1861. The general government and the Northern States were utterly unprepared for war; not a man enlisted, not a musket procured, not a cartridge made, not a piece of clothing or equipment provided, beyond those maintained during a state of profound and apparently permanent peace. The Southern States for nearly four months had been actively preparing for the eventuality they intended to force on, and had made no little headway in the collection of material, the organization and instruction of troops.

Moreover, on the breaking-out of hostilities they possessed another and very considerable advantage over the Northerners: that is to say, one of the results of the peculiar institution of the South was that the class of slaveholders, the highly educated whites, had always composed an aristocracy, which furnished the social and political leaders to whom the poor whites were, as a rule, accustomed to defer, so that when the time arrived to raise troops the aristocratic class furnished officers always accustomed to control, and the poor whites furnished the mass of the private soldiers, always habituated to that deference to their leaders which under the new circumstances rapidly passed into obedience.   Discipline was thus very easily established among them.

Among the Northern men there was little difficulty in establishing discipline when the officers were intelligent gentlemen; but, in the early part of the war particuiarly, it occurred that the officers were sometimes inferior in intelligence and education to the soldiers, and in these cases the establishment of discipline presented far greater difficulties.

Here let me say that, given good officers, there are no men in the world who admit of a more thorough and effective discipline than the native-born Americans of the North.   Their intelligence soon shows them the absolute necessity of discipline in an army, and its advantages to all concerned; but the kind of discipline best adapted to them differs materially from that required by other races. Their fighting qualities are second to none in the world.

When the catastrophe occurred - the firing upon Fort Sumter - the excitement in Cincinnati and along the Ohio river was naturally intense.   The formation of regiments began at once, and all who had military knowledge or experience were eagerly sought for, myself among others.   I did what I could in the way of giving advice to those who sought it, and in allaying the excitement in Cincinnati. About this time I received telegrams from friends in New York informing me that the governor of that State desired to avail himself of my services; another from Gen. Robert Patterson, offering me the position of chief-engineer of the command of militia then organizing under his orders; and one from Gov. Curtin, of Pennsylvania, offering me the command of the Pennsylvania Reserves, afterwards given to McCall.   I promptly arranged my business affairs so as to admit of a short absence, and started for Pennsylvania to see what was best to be done.   At the request of several gentlemen of Cincinnati I stopped at Columbus to give Gov. Dennison some information about the conditions of affairs in Cincinnati, intending to remain only a few hours and then proceed to Harrisburg.

According to the then existing laws of Ohio the command of the militia and volunteers called out must be given to general officers of the existing militia establishment. The legislature being in session, the governor caused to be presented a bill permitting him to appoint as major-general commanding, any resident of the State. This was intended for my benefit, was passed by both houses in a few hours, and the appointment offered to me the same day, the 23d of April, 1861. I at once accepted and without an hour's delay entered upon the performance of my duties, abandoning my intended trip to the East.

CHAPTER II.

Beginning of the war in the West - Apathy at Washington - Value of
State governments - Incidents in organizing Western army - Kentucky - campaign in Western Virginia - McClellan called to Washington.

AT the time of my appointment in Ohio we were cut off from
direct communication with Washington in consequence of the
unfortunate occurrences in Baltimore, and the attention of the
national authorities was confined exclusively to the task of relieving the capital from danger and of securing its communications with the loyal States. We in the West were therefore left
for a long time without orders, advice, money, or supplies of any
kind, and it was clear that the different States must take care of
themselves and provide their own means of defence.

At this critical juncture the value and vitality of the State
governments was fully tested. Fortunately they proved equal to
the emergency and saved the country. Any one who coolly and
dispassionately reviews the occurrences of that exciting period
must arrive at the conclusion that, in a country so large as ours,
the safety of the nation imperatively demands the entire preservation of the rights and autonomy of the several States as
secured by the original Constitution; of course with the proviso
that the vexed question of the right of secession has been for
ever settled in the negative by the result of the civil war. The
Eastern States were to a certain extent provided with arms, the
material of war, and some tolerably organized and instructed
militia regiments. Their prompt action saved the capital.

The Western States were almost entirely without the means
of defence, but the governors (cordially supported by the legis-
latures) at once took steps to obtain by purchase and by contract, at home and abroad, the requisite arms, ammunition,
clothing, camp equipage, etc. The supplies thus provided were
often inferior in quality and insufficient in quantity, but they
answered the purpose until better arrangements could be made.

In addition to the Ohio volunteers called for by the general government, the governor placed under my command twelve or thirteen regiments of State troops; and for several weeks I remained at Columbus, without a staff, working night and day at the organization of the entire Ohio contingent.

The condition of affairs in the West was not satisfactory or reassuring. We were entirely unprepared for war. It was already clear that Missouri was likely to be the scene of a serious struggle, and the attitude of Kentucky was very doubtful. The secessionists were gathering forces in Tennessee and upon the Mississippi river, as well as in Western Virginia, and many well-informed persons felt great anxiety in respect to the loyalty of large numbers of the inhabitants of southern Illinois, Indiana, and Ohio. In brief, our situation was difficult. We were surrounded by possible, or even probable, dangers; were without organization, arms, supplies, money, officers We had no idea of the policy which the general government intended to pursue; we had no "head" to direct affairs. It fell to me, perhaps more than to any one person, to supply these pressing wants, and at this distance I may say that the task was not unsatisfactorily performed.

My civil career ended at this time, for from the evening when I received the appointment as major-general of the Ohio Volunteers all my thoughts and efforts were directed to my military duties. I never again went to the office of the Ohio and Mississippi Railroad, unless it may have been for a few minutes when my advice was needed on matters of importance. The owners of the road refused to accept my resignation for many months, until it .was certain that I was inextricably involved in military affairs; but I drew no pay from them after I ceased to do the duty. The salary I gave up to re-enter the military service was ten thousand dollars per annum.

On the night of my appointment as major-general in Ohio I wrote a letter to Gen. Scott (probably directed to the adjutant-general) informing him of the fact, reporting for orders, giving all the details I possessed in regard to my command, the arms, etc., at my disposal, and asking for staff officers to assist me. This was sent by a special messenger, there being then no mail communication with Washington. Within a few days I sent by similar means another letter to the general, suggesting that

the Western States between the Alleghanies and the Mississippi
be placed under one head; stating that I intended bringing all
the Ohio troops into one camp of instruction (Camp Dennison);
asking for arms, funds, etc.; urging the necessity of artillery and
cavalry; renewing the request for staff officers; suggesting a
plan, or rather plans, of Western campaigns. It is possible that
some of the ideas here mentioned as being in the second letter
may have been in the first, or in another letter written soon
after; for about this time I wrote several letters to the headquarters at Washington. One movement that I suggested was
in connection with the operations of the Eastern army then
being assembled around Washington; a movement up the valley of the Great Kanawha, and across the mountains upon Richmond or upon Staunton, as circumstances might render advisable.
Another was a movement upon Nashville, and thence, in combination with the Eastern army, upon Chattanooga, Atlanta, Montgomery, Savannah, etc., etc. The importance of Eastern Tennessee, and of the railroad from Memphis through Chattanooga
and Knoxville, was very early impressed upon my mind, and at
a very early date brought before the Washington authorities.
Fortunately, or unfortunately, they were too busy to think of
the West, and these letters received little or no attention, so that
we were allowed to go on pretty much as we pleased, with such
means as the States could get possession of.

On the 13th of May, 1861, I received the order, dated May
3, forming the Department of the Ohio - consisting of the States
of Ohio, Indiana, and Illinois - and giving the command to me.
A short time afterwards were added to the department a small
portion of Western Pennsylvania and that part of Western Virginia north of the Great Kanawha and west of the Greenbriar
rivers. I was still left without a single instructed staff officer

Capt. (afterwards Maj.-Gen.) Gordon Granger, U. S. Mounted Rifles, was sent to Ohio to muster in volunteers. I appointed him division inspector, and repeatedly applied for him as
a member of my staff; but these requests were constantly
refused, and he was not permitted to retain the post of inspector. During the short time he was with me he rendered remarkable services. Capt. Lawrence Williams, 10th U. S. Infantry,
was soon after ordered to Ohio as a mustering officer, and my
application for him as an aide-de-camp was granted. He con-

tinued with me during the Western Virginia campaign and until a short period after my arrival in Washington, when with great difficulty I procured for him the appointment of major in the 6th U. S. Cavalry. This much-abused officer always served me faithfully, and exhibited great gallantry in action. I was and am fully satisfied that he always behaved with thorough loyalty.

Soon after this Gen. Harney and Col. McKinstry lent me Capt. Dickerson, A. A. Q. M. After much difficulty I succeeded in retaining him, and he proved to be a most valuable officer. Capt. Burns, A. C. S., happened to pass through Cincinnati unemployed, so that I detained him, and at last kept him permanently. Both this officer and Capt. Dickerson were more than once ordered away from me to less important functions, and it was with the utmost difficulty that I finally retained them. At a subsequent period, but before the Western Virginia campaign, Maj. Seth Williams was assigned to duty as adjutant-general of the department, Maj. R. B. Marcy as paymaster (subsequently assigned by me as chief of staff and inspector-general), Capt. Kingsbury as chief of ordnance.

During the first organization of the department my great difficulty was encountered from the unwillingness of the Washington authorities to give me any staff officers. I do not think they had an idea beyond their own safety, and consequently that of Washington; except the Blairs, who were naturally much interested in the State of Missouri, and Mr. Chase. As will be seen hereafter, Kentucky and West Virginia received a very small share of the attention of the functionaries in Washington.

In the course of May and June I made several tours of inspection through my command. Cairo was visited at an early day, and after a thorough inspection I gave the necessary orders for its defence, as well as that of Bird's Point, which I also visited. Cairo was then under the immediate command of Brig.-Gen. Prentiss, and, considering all the circumstances, the troops were in a remarkably satisfactory condition. The artillery, especially, had made very good progress under the instruction of Col. Wagner, a Hungarian officer, whom I had sent there for that object. I inspected also at Springfield (Ill.), Chicago, several points on the Illinois Central Railroad, several times at Indianapolis, Cleveland, and Columbus. Maj. Marcy also inspected the points left unexamined by me. In connection with Gov. Dennison I had several meetings with the governors of the Northwestern States for the purpose of urging on military preparations.

During the period that elapsed from my assignment to the command in Ohio until I commenced sending troops to West Virginia, my time was fully occupied in expediting the organizstion and instruction of the troops, and in endeavoring to provide for their food, armament, and equipment. The difficulties arising from the apathy and contracted views of the authorities at Washington were very great, and could never have been overcome but for the zeal and intelligence of the governors of the Western States, foremost among whom was Gov. Dennison, of Ohio. It seemed that the Washington people had quite for gotten the existence of the West; certain it is that for a long time we were left entirely to our own resources, and it frequently became necessary to assume responsibilities not at all in accordance with the ordinary proprieties of a well-regulated service.

Gen. Scott and the other military authorities all this time refused to allow the organization of cavalry and artillery for my command, being clear that neither of these arms of service would be needed! With the exception of the "Michigan Battery" (Capt. Loomis), which was authorized by Gen. Wool during the time when communication with Washington was cut off, there was no battery in the United States service at my disposal for a long time. Upon my recommendation the governors of the States organized State batteries on their own responsibility. Finally three companies of the 4th U. S. Artillery, serving as infantry, arrived at Cincinnati *en route* to the East from Fort Randall. I at length received permission to retain them, and sent Capt. (afterwards Maj.-Gen.) George Getty, the commander of one of them, to Washington, with a letter for the general commanding, in which I repeated my wants in regard to artillery, and urged that the three companies should at once be mounted. The result was a tardy and reluctant consent that one of them, Capt. (afterwards Gen.) A. P. Howe's, should be mounted. But Gen. Scott expressed to Capt. Getty no little indignation that I should presume to make such a request, and, among other things, said: "I know more about artillery than Gen. McClellan does, and it is not for him to teach me." So tedious were the movements of the Ordnance Bureau that Capt. Howe's battery was not mounted until after I left for West Virginia, and joined me there in a perfectly raw condition. Cavalry was absolutely refused, but the governors of the States complied with my request and organized a few companies, which were finally mustered into the United States service and proved very useful.

Soon after Gen. Patterson commenced his operations in the vicinity of Williamsport (when on the cars returning from Indianapolis, where I went to inspect some regiments of Indiana troops) I received from him a telegraphic despatch stating that he had largely superior forces in front of him, that he was in a critical condition and wanted assistance. I at once telegraphed and wrote to Gen. Scott what Gen. Patterson stated, and suggesting that I should move out, with all my disposable force, by the Baltimore and Ohio Railroad to Piedmont and beyond, and thus, in connection with Gen. Patterson, clear out the Shenandoah Valley. The reply to this was in substance, and as nearly as I remember in these very words: that "the region beyond Piedmont is not within Gen. McClellan's command. When his opinion is desired about matters there it will be asked for." After this encouraging reply I very carefully abstained from unnecessary communication with Washington. It may be remarked that my suggestion was not uncalled for, but directly induced by Gen. Patterson's official despatch to me; and, further, that if my suggestion had been adopted the result would have been that no "Bull Run No. 1" would have been fought.

I think it was during my absence on this very trip (to Indianapolis) that Grant came to Cincinnati to ask me, as an old acquaintance, to give him employment, or a place on my staff. Marcy or Seth Williams saw him and told him that if he would await my return, doubtless I would do something for him; but before I got back he was telegraphed that he could have a regiment in Illinois, and at once returned thither, so that I did not see him. This was his good luck; for had I been there I would no doubt have given him a place on my staff, and he would probably have remained with me and shared my fate.

Shortly before West Virginia was placed under my command (May 24) I received two identical despatches from Gen. Scott and the Secretary of War (Mr. Cameron) stating that it was understood that the rebels were collecting troops in that region, and asking me whether I could do anything to protect the Union men against them. I immediately replied that, if they desired it, I would clear West Virginia of the rebels. I received no reply whatever to this despatch, nor did I afterwards receive any other despatch or order from Washington that could be construed into an order or permission to operate in West Virginia. The movements that were subsequently made were initiated and conducted entirely on my own responsibility and of my own volition.

A few weeks before I took the field in West Virginia, and while my headquarters were in Cincinnati, I received one morning a telegram from Samuel Gill, an old graduate of West Point, and at that time superintendent of the Louisville and Lexington Railroad, stating that S. B. Buckner (afterwards the rebel general) wished to see me, and asking when I would be at home. I replied that I would see him that night. Accordingly the two (Buckner and Gill) reached my house about ten o'clock that evening. I received them alone, and we spent the night in conversation about the condition of affairs in Kentucky. Buckner was at that time the commandant of the "State Guards," a militia organization in Kentucky, but neither numerous nor efficient. It was, however, the only organization existing there, and Buckner was in close relations with Gov. McGoffin - was, in fact, his military adviser. Buckner brought me no letter or other credentials from the governor, nor did he assume to be authorized to make any arrangement in his name. The object of the interview was simply that we, as old friends, should compare views and see if we could do any good; thus I understood it. Buckner's main purpose seemed to be to ascertain what I should do in the event that Kentucky should be invaded by the secession forces then collecting under Gen. Pillow at various points in Tennessee near the Kentucky line. Buckner was very anxious that the Ohio and other Federal forces should respect the neutrality of Kentucky, and stated that he would do his best to preserve it, and drive Pillow out should he cross the boundary-line. I could assent to this only to the extent that I should be satisfied if the Kentuckians would immediately drive out any rebel force that might invade Kentucky, and continued, almost in these very words: "You had better be very quick about it, Simon, for if I learn that the rebels are in Kentucky I will, with or without orders, drive them out without delay."

I expressly told Buckner that I had no power to guarantee the neutrality of Kentucky, and that, although my command did not extend over it, I would not tolerate the presence of rebel troops in that State. Not many days afterwards I accidentally met Buckner again at Cairo, and had a conversation with him in the presence of John M. Douglass, of Chicago. Buckner had then just returned from a visit to Pillow, and he clearly showed by his conversation that he understood my determination at the first interview just as I have related it above. Among other things he said that he found Pillow (with whom he had had serious personal quarrels before) sitting on a log; and, referring to his (Pillow's) purpose of entering Kentucky, said to him that "if he did McClellan would be after him"; to which, he said, Pillow replied, "He is the very person I want to meet." It may be remarked that Gen. Pillow had reason to be inimical to me. Buckner's letter to Gov. McGoffin, subsequently published, stating that in our first interview I had agreed to respect the neutrality of Kentucky, gave an incorrect account of the case, which was as I have stated it.

Before the necessity arose for action in West Virginia my views were turned towards Tennessee; for from the beginning I saw the great importance of aiding the loyal men in the mountainous portion of that State, of holding the railways there, and of occupying in force the great projecting bastion formed by that district. I was satisfied that a firm hold there in force, and with secure communications to the Ohio river, would soon render the occupation of Richmond and Eastern Virginia impossible to the secessionists. Unhappily the state of affairs brought about by the first Bull Run rendered it impossible to act upon this theory when the direction of military movements came into my hands, nor did any of my subordinates in the West seize the importance of the idea, frequently as I presented it to them. Had not the general direction of the war been taken from my hands at the time I was about inaugurating the Peninsular campaign, I should then have carried out the movement upon East Tennessee and Atlanta.

The plan of operations which Gen. Scott soon imparted to me confidentially was to occupy the summer and early fall in the equipment, discipline, and instruction of the three-years troops, who were to be collected in numerous small camps of instruction, and to form in the fall "an iron band of sixty thousand troops" to be placed under my command, who were to move down the valley of the Mississippi by roads parallel with that stream, their supplies following in boats on the river. I think that subsequent events proved that the occupation of the central mountain region at an early period of the war would have produced more rapid and decisive results than any movement down the Mississippi.

While engaged in pushing forward the preparations of the troops, and doing all in my power to preserve the peace in Kentucky, events occurred which made it necessary for me to direct my attention more particularly to West Virginia.

It may be repeated here that my movements in West Virginia were, from first to last, undertaken upon my own authority and of my own volition, and without any advice, orders, or instructions from Washington or elsewhere.

The proclamations I addressed to the inhabitants of West Virginia and to my troops were also entirely of my own volition. I had received no intimation of the policy intended to be pursued by the general government, and had no time to seek for instructions. When, on the afternoon of May 26, I received at Camp Dennison confirmation of the movement of the secessionists to destroy the Baltimore and Ohio Railroad, and at once ordered by telegraph Kelly's and other regiments to remove from Wheeling and Parkersburg along the two branches of that railway, I wrote the proclamation and address of May 26 to the inhabitants of West Virginia and my troops, in my dining-room at Cincinnati, in the utmost haste, with the ladies of my family conversing in the room, and without consulting any one. They were at once despatched by telegraph to Wheeling and Parkersburg, there to be printed.

PROCLAMATION.

HEADQUARTERS, DEPARTMENT OF THE OHIO,
May 26, 1861.

To the Union Men of Western Virginia:

VIRGINIANS: The general government has long enough endured the machinations of a few factious rebels in your midst. Armed traitors have in vain endeavored to deter you from expressing your loyalty at the polls. Having failed in this infamous attempt to deprive you of the exercise of your dearest rights, they now seek to inaugurate a reign of terror, and thus force you to yield to their schemes and submit to the yoke of the traitorous conspiracy dignified by the name of the Southern Confederacy. They are destroying the property of citizens of your State and ruining your magnificent railways. The general government has heretofore carefully abstained from sending troops across the Ohio, or even from posting them along its banks, although frequently urged to do so by many of your prominent citizens. It determined to await the result of the late election, desirous that no one might be able to say that the slightest effort had been made from this side to influence the free expression of your opinions, although the many agencies brought to bear upon you by the rebels were well known. You have now shown, under the most adverse circumstances, that the great mass of the people of Western Virginia are true and loyal to that beneficent government under which we and our fathers have lived so long. As soon as the result of the election was known the traitors commenced their work of destruction, The general government cannot close its ears to the demand you have made for assistance. I have ordered troops to cross the Ohio river. They come as your friends and brothers; as enemies, only to the armed rebels who are preying upon you. Your homes, your families, and your property are safe under our protection. All your rights shall be religiously respected, notwithstanding all that has been said by the traitors to induce you to believe that our advent among you will be signalized by interference with your slaves. Understand one thing clearly: not only will we abstain from all such interference, but we will, on the contrary, with an iron hand crush any attempt at insurrection on their part. Now that we are in your midst, I call upon you to fly to arms and support the general government. Sever the connection that binds you to traitors; proclaim to the world that the faith and loyalty so long boasted by the Old Dominion are still preserved in Western Virginia, and that you remain true to the stars and stripes.

GEO. B. McCLELLAN,
Maj.-Gen. U. S. A., commanading Dept.

ADDRESS.

HEADQUARTERS, DEPARTMENT OF THE OHIO,
CINCINNATI, May 26, 1861.

SOLDIERS: You are ordered to cross the frontier and enter upon the soil of Virginia.

Your mission is to restore peace and confidence, to protect the majesty of the law, and to rescue our brethren from the grasp
6

of armed traitors. You are to act in concert with Virginia troops and to support their advance. I place under the safeguard of your honor the persons and property of the Virginians. I know that you will respect their feelings and all their rights.

Preserve the strictest discipline; remember that each one of you holds in his keeping the honor of Ohio and the Union. If you are called upon to overcome armed opposition I know that your courage is equal to the task; but remember that your only foes are the armed traitors, and shorn mercy even to them when they are in your power, for many of them are misguided. When under your protection, the loyal men of Western Virginia have been enabled to organize and arm, they can protect themselves, and you can then return to your homes with the proud satisfaction of having saved a gallant people from destruction.

GEO. B. McCLELLAN,
Maj.-Gen. U. S. A., Commanding.

I, of course, sent copies to the President, with a letter explaining the necessity of my prompt action without waiting to consult with him. To this letter I never received any reply or acknowledgment; nor did the President, or any of his civil or military advisers, ever inform me whether they approved or disapproved the course I had taken. I must give to the Washington functionaries at least this much credit - viz., that although they gave me no assistance or orders towards initiating the campaign, they never interfered with me after its commencement. And when they saw me in a fair way toward success they were much more ready to listen to my requisitions for supplies. But I must claim the credit, if credit there be, of having begun and carried on and finished this short campaign on my own resources and against every possible disadvantage.

During my whole career in West Virginia, as well as before I went there, I was kept in complete ignorance of the intentions of the Washington people in regard to movements in the East.

As I write this (Nov., 1883) I propose omitting for the present the story of the West Virginia campaign, but intend supplying it when my history of the Army of the Potomac is completed.

By the middle of July I had obtained complete possession of the country west of the mountains and north of the Kanawha, holding also the lower portion of the last-named valley, where

Gen. J. D. Cox had been checked in his advance. I held the Baltimore and Ohio Railroad as far as Cumberland, and covered all the roads leading into West Virginia from the Potomac as far south as those uniting about eighteen miles south of Beverly, and held the country north of the Kanawha by garrisons and moving columns.

The time of the three-months regiments was now rapidly expiring, and my movements were stopped for a time by the necessity of reorganizing them and getting up the three-years regiments.

My advance into West Virginia had been without orders and entirely of my own volition, to meet the necessities of the case, and all I knew about the movements in front of Washington was derived from the newspapers and private sources; I received no official information of McDowell's intended movements, and had no communication from headquarters on the subject until Gen. McDowell was actually in contact with the enemy. Consequently the projects I formed for operations, as soon as my command should be reorganized, were utterly independent of the state of affairs at Washington and based entirely upon my views of the condition of affairs in the West.

I pushed the reorganization with the utmost energy, and prepared a light column of five Ohio regiments and the incomplete 1st Virginia, with which I intended to march on the 22d or 23d of July, via Suttonsville, Somersville, and the Dogwood Ridge, to strike the Kanawha near Fayetteville Court-House, and there cut off the troops under Gens. Floyd and Wise, who were then in front of Cox, at and below Charleston.

Having entirely cleared the Kanawha valley of Confederates, I intended to secure my left flank by the line of the Upper Kanawha and New river, and to move upon Wytheville, in order to cut the line of railroad from Memphis to Lynchburg and to hold the country from New river to Abingdon. The objects I had in view were to cut the great east and west line of railroad, so as to deprive the Confederates of its use, and thence to employ the very circuitous route by Atlanta; and to rally the Union men of the mountain region, to arm and embody them, and at least hold my own in that mountain region until prepared to advance in whatever direction might prove best for the general good. In a letter to Gen. Scott from Buckhannon, dated July 6, I stated my desire to move on Wytheville after clearing the country north of the Kanawha.

Had my designs been carried out Gen. Lee's attempt to recover West Virginia would have been made (if at all attempted) under very different auspices, and with much more decisive results in our favor. I am confident that I should have been in possession of Wytheville and the mountain region south of it in a very few weeks.

In this brief campaign the telegraph was for the first time, I think, constructed as the army advanced, and proved of very great use to us; it caused a very great saving of time and horseflesh.

On the evening of July 21, 1861, I first received intelligence of the advance of Gen, McDowell and the battle of Bull Run. I had received no intimation whatever in regard to the projected operations in the East, although I might have aided them very materially had I been asked to do so. The first telegram I received from Gen. Scott, early in the evening of the 21st, was to the effect that McDowell was gaining a grand victory, had taken four redoubts on the enemy's left, and would soon defeat them utterly. Then came a despatch not quite so favorable ; finally a telegram stating that McDowell was utterly defeated, his army routed and, as a mere mob, streaming towards Washington. The despatch closed with a question as to whether I could do anything across the mountains to relieve McDowell and Washington.

I did not then know that Gen. Joe Johnston had left Winchester and joined Beauregard, supposing that Gen. Patterson had retained him in the Shenandoah Valley. Therefore, after a half-hour's consideration, I proposed that I should move *via* Romney, unite with Patterson, and operate against Johnston in the Shenandoah Valley. I offered, however, to move on Staunton, if they preferred that movement in Washington, provided the three-months men (of whom my army was mainly composed) would consent to remain a few weeks longer. No reply ever came to these propositions; and it may here be stated that none of the three-months men would consent to remain beyond the termination of their enlistments, to move either towards the Gauley or eastward. For the Gauley movement I had, however, enough three-years men disposable.

On the next day, the 22d of July, I received a despatch from the adjutant-general stating that the condition of public affairs rendered my immediate presence in Washington necessary, and directing me to turn over my command to the next in rank, who happened to be Gen. Rosecrans.

I started next morning at daylight, rode on horseback sixty miles to the nearest railway station, and took the cars to Wheeling, where I found my wife awaiting me, and then proceeded to Washington, which I reached on the 26th of July, 1861.

Immediately after the affair of Rich Mountain I was instructed by Gen. Scott to release upon parole all the prisoners I had taken, with the exception of such as had left the United States service with the evident intention of joining that of the secessionists.

Col. John Pegram and a surgeon (Dr. Campbell) were the only ones who came under the latter category; and the order was promptly carried out in regard to the others. From the moment the prisoners came into my hands they were treated with the utmost kindness. The private baggage of the officers was restored to them whenever it could be found. The men, most of whom were starving when they surrendered, were at once fed; the same care was extended to their wounded as to our own. All of them were unanimous in their gratitude for the treatment they received. The slaves taken in attendance upon officers were allowed their choice whether to go North, remain with us, or return to their masters. Nearly all chose the latter alternative. Among the prisoners was an entire company composed of students of the William and Mary University, commanded by the president. Many of these were mere boys, among whom some were severely wounded. These last I sent home to their parents, without awaiting orders from Washington. It was a singular fact that the wounded preferred the attendance of our surgeons to that of their own, saying that the former were more kind and attentive to them. I mention thus particularly my treatment of these prisoners for the reason that they were the first in considerable numbers taken during the war, and that the course I pursued ought to have been reciprocated by the secessionists. Their treatment of our officers and men captured so soon afterwards at Bull Run is, therefore, without excuse. Whatever hardships prisoners afterwards suffered on either side, the blame of the initiation of ill-treatment must fall on the rebels and not on us.

The successor of Gen. Garnett, Gen. Jackson (formerly U. S. Minister at Vienna), sent a flag of truce to thank me for the kindness I had extended to their wounded and unwounded officers and men. On subsequent occasions I received proofs of their appreciation of my course. Application was also made to me, under a flag, for the body of Gen. Garnett, which I agreed to deliver up; but before my orders in the case could reach Grafton the corpse had been taken East by the father of his late wife.

The successes just achieved in West Virginia by the troops under my command created great excitement through the loyal States. They were the only ones of importance achieved up to that time by the Union arms, and, since public attention had not been especially directed to that quarter, the people were all the more dazzled by the rapidity and brilliancy of the results. Although the telegram ordering me to the East contained no mention of the purpose in view, it was easy, under the circumstances, to divine it. I fully realized the importance and difficulty of the task to be imposed upon me, and naturally felt gratified by the proof of confidence the order afforded. Yet I felt great regret at leaving the West, for I should have been very glad to carry out the Kanawha and Wytheville movement, and thereby quiet affairs in that region before giving up the command.

It would probably have been better for me personally had my promotion been delayed a year or more. Yet I do not know who could have organized the Army of the Potomac as I did; and I have the consolation of knowing that, during the war, I never sought any commission or duty, but simply did my best in whatever position my superiors chose to place me.

CHAPTER III.

[*June 21 to July 21, 1861.*]

Marietta, June 21, 1861. - I must snatch a few moments to write you. We got off at 11.30 yesterday morning, and had a continual ovation all along the road. At every station where we stopped crowds had assembled to see the "young general" gray-headed old men and women, mothers holding up their children to take my hand, girls, boys, all sorts, cheering and crying, God bless you! I never went through such a scene in my life, and never expect to go through such another one. You would have been surprised at the excitement. At Chillicothe the ladies had prepared a dinner, and I had to be trotted through. They gave me about twenty beautiful bouquets and almost killed me with kindness. The trouble will be to fill their expectations, they seem to be so high. I could hear them say, "He is our own general"; "Look at him, how young he is"; "He will thrash them"; "He'll do," etc., etc. *ad infinitum.* . . .

We reached here about three in the morning, and at once went on board the boat, where I got about three hours' sleep until we reached Parkersburg. I have been hard at work all day, for I found everything in great confusion. Came up here in a boat about an hour ago, and shall go back to Parkersburg in two or three hours. . . We start from Parkersburg at six in the morning. With me go McCook's regiment (9th Ohio), Mack's company (4th U. S. Artillery), the Sturgess Rifle Co., a battery of six guns (Loomis's), and one company of cavalry (Barker's Illinois). Two Indiana regiments leave in the morning just after us. I shall have five additional regiments at Grafton to-morrow afternoon. I shall have some eighteen regiments two batteries, two companies of cavalry at my disposal - enough to thrash anything I find. I think the danger has been greatly exaggerated, and anticipate little or no chance of winning laurels.

. . . A terrible storm is passing over us now; thunder and lightning terrible in the extreme. . . .

Grafton, Sunday, June 23, 1861.- . . . We did not reach here until about two in the morning, and I was tired out. . . . Everything here needs the hand of the master and is getting it fast.   I shall hardly be able to move from here for a couple of days. . . . The weather is delightful here: we are well up in the hills and have the mountain air. . . .

Grafton, June 26, 1861.- . . . I am detained here by want of supplies now on the way, and which I hope to receive soon. . . . It is very difficult to learn anything definite about our friends in front of us. Sometimes I am half-inclined to doubt whether there are many of them; then again it looks as if there were a good many. We shall soon see, however. I am pretty well tired out and shall be very glad to get on the march.

What a row the papers have raised about the Buckner letter! B. has represented a personal interview as an official treaty. . . .

Captain Howe is at Clarksburg-Guentler with him. Mack is here with us. . . . I don't know exactly when I shall be able to leave here; certainly not before to-morrow, and perhaps not until next day. . . .

Grafton, June 27.- . . . I shall be after the gentlemen pretty shortly.   You must be under no apprehensions as to me or the result.   I never worked so hard in my life before; even take my meals in my own room. . , .

Grafton, June 29.- . . . I am bothered half to death by delays in getting up supplies. Unless where I am in person, everything seems to go wrong. . . . I expect in the course of an hour or two to get to Clarksburg - will probably march twelve miles thence to-day - with Howe's battery, Mack's and the Chicago companies, and one company of cavalry.   I shall have a telegraph line built to follow us up. Look on the maps and find Buckhannon and Beverly; that is the direction of my march. I hope to thrash the infamous scamps before a week is over. All I fear is that I won't catch them. . . . What a strange performance that of Buckner's was!   Fortunately I have secured the testimony of Gill and Douglass (present at the Cairo interview) that

Buckner has entirely misrepresented me. It has annoyed me much, but I hope to do such work here as will set criticism at defiance. . . .

Clarksburg, June 30. - . . . Again great delays here; will certainly get off by four A.M. to-morrow, and make a long march, probably twenty-eight miles. After the next march I shall have a large tent, borrowed from the Chicago Rifles; your father and I will take that, make it reception-room, sleeping-apartment, mess-room, etc. . . . One thing takes up a great deal of time, yet I cannot avoid it: crowds of the country-people who have heard of me and read my proclamations come in from all directions to thank me, shake me by the hand, and look at their "liberator," "the general"! Of course I have to see them and talk to them. Well, it is a proud and glorious thing to see a whole people here, simple and unsophisticated, looking up to me as their deliverer from tyranny.

Camp 14 miles south of Clarksburg, July 2. - . . . We start in a few moments to Buckhannon. I have with me two regiments, a battery, two cavalry companies, three detached companies. Had several heavy rains yesterday. Rosecrans is at Buckhannon. I doubt whether the rebels will fight; it is possible they may, but I begin to think that my successes will be due to manœuvres, and that I shall have no brilliant victories to record. I would be glad to clear them out of West Virginia and liberate the country without bloodshed, if possible. The people are rejoiced to see us.

Buckhannon, July 3. - . . . We had a pleasant march of sixteen miles yesterday through a beautiful mountain region: magnificent timber, lovely valleys running up from the main valley; the people all out, waving their handkerchiefs and giving me plenty of bouquets and kind words. . . .

We nearly froze to death last night. I retired, as I thought, at about midnight, intending to have a good night's sleep. About half an hour after I shut up my tent a colonel in command of a detachment some fifteen miles distant came to report, so I received him in bed, and fell asleep about six times during the three hours I was talking with him. Finally,

however, he left, and I alternately slept and froze until seven
o'clock. This morning I sent Bates on an expedition and raked
up a couple of horse-blankets, by the aid of which I hope hereafter to be reasonably comfortable.

I hope to get the trains up to-morrow and make a final start
during the day. We have a good many to deal with. I ordered
the Guthrie Grays to Philippi this P.M. to resist a stampede attack that Gen. Morris feared.

Buckhannon, July 5, 1861. - . . . Yesterday was a very busy
day with me, reviewing troops all the morning and giving orders
all day and pretty much all night. . . . I realize now the dreadful responsibility on me - the lives of my men, the reputation of
the country, and the success of our cause. The enemy are in
front, and I shall probably move forward to-morrow, but not
come in contact with them until about the next day. I shall
feel my way and be very cautious, for I recognize the fact that
everything requires success in first operations. You need not be
at all alarmed as to the result; God is on our side. This is a
beautiful country in which we now are - a lovely valley surrounded by mountains, well cultivated. The people hail our parties
as deliverers wherever they go, and we meet with perfect ova-
tions. Yesterday was very hot, and my head almost roasted as I
stood bareheaded while the troops passed by in review. We
have a nice little camp of our own here: Mack's and Steele's
companies, Howe's battery next, two companies of cavalry, and
two well-behaved Virginia companies. When we next go into
camp we shall have the German regiment (9th Ohio) with us in
camp. I intend having a picked brigade with me all the time.
—'s regiment is on the march up from Clarksburg; they signalized their entrance into the country by breaking into and rob-
bing a grocery-store at Webster! The Guthrie Grays are at Philippi; they leave there to-day, and will be here to-morrow night,
following us up in reserve, or perhaps overtaking us before we
meet the enemy. . . .

Buckhannon, July 7, 1861. - I have been obliged to inflict
some severe punishments, and I presume the papers of the
Western Reserve will be hard down on me for disgracing some
of their friends guilty of the small crime of burglary. I believe

the army is beginning to comprehend that they have a master over them who is stern in punishing and means what he says. I fear I shall have to have some of them shot or hung; that may convince some of the particular individuals concerned that they are not in the right track exactly. . . I have not told you about our camp at this place. It is in a large grass-field on a hill a little out of town, a beautiful grove near by. Your father and I share the same tent, a very large round one, pitched under a tree. Seth has one near by–an office; Lawrence Williams another as office and mess-tent. Marcy, the two Williamses, Judge Key, and Lander mess with me. Poe and the rest of the youngsters are in tents near by. . . . I had a very complimentary despatch from Gen. Scott last night. He said he was "charmed with my energy, movements, and success." Pretty well for the old man. I hope to deserve more of him in the future.

Move at six to-morrow morning to overtake advanced guard, which consists of three regiments, a battery, and one company of cavalry. I take up headquarters escort and four regiments infantry; three more follow next day. The large supply-train up and ready to move. Brig.-Gen. Garnett in command of enemy.

July 10, *Roaring Creek.* - We have occupied the important position on this line without loss. The enemy are in sight, and I am about sending out a strong armed reconnoissance to feel him and see what he is. I have been looking at their camps with my glass; they are strongly entrenched, but I think I can come the Cerro Gordo over them.

Telegram - *Rich Mountain, July* 12, 1861. - Have met with complete success; captured the enemy's entire camp, guns, tents, wagons, etc. Many prisoners, among whom several officers. Enemy's loss severe, ours very small. No officers lost on our side. I turned the position. All well.

July 12, *Beverly.* - Have gained a decided victory at small cost, and move on to Huttonsville to-morrow in hope of seizing the mountain-pass near that point before it is occupied in force by the enemy. If that can be done I can soon clear up the rest of the business to be done out here, and return to see you for a time at least. . . .

I had an affecting interview to-day with a poor woman whom we liberated from prison, where she had been confined for three weeks by these scoundrels merely because she was a Union woman. I enclose a flower from a bouquet the poor thing gave me.

Telegram - *July* 13, 1861. - Success complete. Enemy routed. Lost everything he had - guns, tents, wagons, etc. Pegram was in command. We lost but 10 killed and 35 wounded. Garnett has abandoned his camp between this and Philippi, and is in full retreat into Eastern Virginia. I hope still to cut him off. All well.

July 13, *Huttonsville.* - Since you last heard from me I received from Pegram a proposition to surrender, which I granted. L. Williams went out with an escort of cavalry and received him. He surrendered, with another colonel, some 25 officers, and 560 men. . . . I do not think the enemy in front of us in the Cheat Mountain pass, but that they have fallen back in hot haste. If they have, I will drive them out to-morrow and occupy the pass. . . . It now appears we killed nearly 200; took almost 900. . . .

The valley in which we are is one of the most beautiful I ever saw, and I am more than ever inclined to make my headquarters at Beverly and have you with me. Beverly is a quiet, old-fashioned town, in a lovely valley; a beautiful stream running by it - a perfectly pastoral scene, such as the old painters dreamed of but never realized. . . . I find that the prisoners are beyond measure astonished at my humanity towards them. The bearer of the flag from Pegram reached me about five this morning. He had been two days without food. I at once gave him some breakfast, and shortly after gave him a drink of whiskey; as he drank it he said: "I thank you, general I drink that I may never again be in rebellion against the general government."

July 14, 1861. - I have released the doctor this morning of whom I told you. Also sent a lieutenant to carry back the body of his captain. Also those poor young boys of good family who had lost their limbs. I have tried to temper justice with mercy. I think these men will do me no harm, but that some mothers and sisters and wives will bless the name of your husband. . . .

Started this morning with a strong advanced guard, supported by two regiments, to test the question as to whether the rebels were really fortified in the Cheat Mountain pass. I went prepared for another fight, but found that they had scampered. We picked up some of their plunder, but they have undoubtedly gone at least to Staunton. The pass was strong, and they might have given us an immense deal of trouble. I went with a few men to Cheat river, the other side of the mountain. . . . I have made a very clear sweep of it. Never was more complete success gained with smaller sacrifice of life. Our prisoners will exceed one thousand.

On my return I found a telegram from Gen. Scott, sent before he had received information as to the full results of my victory. It was:

"The general-in-chief, and what is more the cabinet, including the President, are charmed with your activity, valor, and consequent success. We do not doubt that you will in due time sweep the rebels from West Virginia, but do not mean to precipitate you, as you are fast enough.
"WINFIELD SCOTT."

. . . Our ride to-day was magnificent; some of the most splendid mountain views I ever beheld. The mountain we crossed is fully three thousand feet above its base, and the lovely little valleys, the cleared farms, the long ranges of mountains in the distance, all made a varied scene that I cannot describe to you. At the mountain-top was a pretty little farm, neat as neat could be. A very old couple lived there, the old lady as rosy and cheerful as a cricket. It is sad that war should visit even such sequestered spots as that.

Monday evening. - After closing my letter last night a courier arrived with the news that the troops I had sent in pursuit of Garnett had caught him, routed his army, captured his baggage, one gun, taken several prisoners, and that Garnett himself lay dead on the field of battle! Such is the fate of traitors: one of their leaders a prisoner, the other killed; their armies annihilated, their cause crushed in this region. . . . You ask what my plans are. Why, don't you know that my movements depend much on those of Monsieur l'Ennemi? I expect to hear in a few hours of the final extermination of the remnants of Garnett's army. Then I am almost hourly awaiting news of Cox's success in the Kanawha. Should Cox not be prompt enough I will go down there myself and bring the matter to a close.

West Virginia being cleared of the enemy, I have then to reorganize and consolidate the army. The time of the three-months men is about expiring, and they form so large portion of my force that some delay will ensue. . . .

Telegram - *July* 15, *Hutonsville.* - Garnett and whole concern have retreated. None nearer than Staunton. Crossed Cheat Mountain to-day and returned.

July 18, *Beverly.* - I am awaiting news from the Kanawha which will determine my movements. I do not see now but that I can leave here in a couple of days; but do not count upon it, as there are so many chances in war.

July 19, 1861. - I enclose Bulletin No. 5, printed with our portable press. You see we have carried civilization with us in the shape of the printing-press and the telegraph-institutions decidedly neglected in this part of the world heretofore, and, I fear, not likely to be paying institutions in this vicinity after we go. The good people here read but little and have but few ideas. Gen. Scott is decidedly flattering to me. I received from him yesterday a despatch beginning, "Your suggestion in respect to Staunton would be admirable, like your other conceptions and acts." I value that old man's praise very highly, and wrote him a short note last night telling him so. I enclose some scraps clipped off a dirty rebel flag captured at Rich Mountain. . . .

Am engaged now in arranging to march home the three-months men to be reorganized, and in clearing up matters generally. . . . I suppose McDowell drove the enemy from Manassas Junction yesterday; if so the way will be pretty well cleared for the present. If any decided movement is made towards Richmond I shall feel sure that they cannot intend to trouble my people here.

July 21, Beverly. - . . . Were you satisfied with the result?

Nine guns taken, twelve colors, lots of prisoners, and all this done with so little loss on our side! We found yesterday some more guns abandoned by Garnett, bringing the number taken up to nine. . . Gen. Cox has been badly checked in the Kanawha; one wounded colonel (Newton) taken prisoner, two others and a lieutenant-colonel (Neff) captured while amusing themselves by an insane expedition in advance of the pickets - served them right!   Cox lost more men in getting a detachment thrashed than I did in routing two armies.   The consequence is, I shall move down with a heavy column to take Mr. Wise in rear, and hope either to drive him out without a battle or to catch him with his whole force.   It is absolutely necessary for me to go in person; I have no one to whom I can entrust the operation.   More than that, I don't feel sure that the men will fight very well under any one but myself; they have confidence in me and will do anything that I put them at.   I lose about fourteen regiments now whose term of service is about expiring, and am sorry to say that I have as yet found but few whose patriotism is sufficient to induce them to remain beyond their time.   I expect to get away from here by day after to-morrow at latest. The march to the Kanawha will require about seven days.   I hope to be able to start for Cincinnati in about two weeks from to-morrow.   I expect the Guthrie Grays here to-day, and will take them with me to the Kanawha.

CHAPTER IV.

Arrival at Washington - Reception by Gen. Scott and the President - Condition of the capital - Takes command of the Division of the Potomac - State of the army - Numbers, increase, and position of troops.

I REACHED Washington late in the afternoon of Friday, July 26. I called on Gen. Scott that evening, and next morning reported to the adjutant-general, who instructed me to call upon the President, by whom I was received cordially and informed that he had placed me in command of Washington and all the troops in its vicinity. He directed me to return to the White House at one o'clock to be present at a cabinet meeting. I called again on Gen. Scott, then commanding the army of the United States, and, after conversing with him for some time on the state of affairs, casually remarked that I must take my leave, as the President had desired me to attend a cabinet meeting at one o'clock. Upon this the general became quite indignant and said that it was highly improper that I should receive such an invitation to his exclusion, and insisted upon keeping me until too late to attend the meeting. He then instructed me to ride around the city immediately and send stragglers back to their regiments. The general appeared to know and think very little about the defensive condition of the city and its approaches, and was more concerned about the disorganized condition of the stragglers in the city itself. I explained to the President later in the day the cause of my apparent lack of courtesy, at which he seemed more amused than otherwise.

After leaving the general I rode around the outskirts of the city on the Maryland side towards Tennallytown, Seventh Street, etc., and examined some of the camps, but did not devote myself individually to the police work of picking up drunken stragglers. I found no preparations whatever for defence, not even to the extent of putting the troops in military positions. Not a regiment was properly encamped, not a single avenue of approach guarded, All was chaos, and the streets, hotels, and bar-rooms were filled with drunken officers and men absent from their regiments without leave - a perfect pandemonium. Many had even gone to their homes, their flight from Bull Run often terminating in New York, or even in New Hampshire and Maine. There was really nothing to prevent a small cavalry force from riding into the city. A determined attack would doubtless have carried Arlington Heights and placed the city at the mercy of a battery of rifled guns. If the secessionists attached any value to the possession of Washington, they committed their greatest error in not following up the victory of Bull Run.*

On the 25th had been issued the order constituting the Division of the Potomac and assigning me to its command. The division consisted of the Department of Northeast Virginia, under McDowell, which comprised all the troops in front of Washington on the Pennsylvania bank of the river, and the Department of Washington, under Mansfield, which comprised all the troops in Washington and its vicinity on the Maryland side. Neither of these officers seemed pleased with the new arrangement, more particularly Mansfield.

On the 27th I assumed command and lost no time in acquainting myself with the situation and applying the proper remedies. On the next day, Sunday, I rode along the lines on

*The defenceless condition of Washington on this very day was described by Mr. Edwin M. Stanton, afterwards Secretary of War in Mr. Lincoln's cabinet, in a private letter, historic and prophetic, to ex-President Buchanan, as follows:

"WASHINGTON, July 26, 1861.

" DEAR SIR: . . The dreadful disaster of Sunday can scarcely be mentioned. The imbecility of this administration culminated in that catastrophe; an irretrievable misfortune and national disgrace never to be forgotten are to be added to the ruin of all peaceful pursuits and national bankruptcy as the result of Lincoln's 'running the machine' for five months. . It is not unlikely that some change in the War and Navy Departments may take place, but none beyond those two departments until Jeff Davis turns out the whole concern. The capture of Washington seems now to be inevitable; during the whole of Monday and Tuesday it might have been taken without any resistance. The rout, overthrow, and demoralization of the whole army is complete. Even now I doubt whether any serious opposition to the entrance of the Confederate forces could be offered. While Lincoln, Scott, and the cabinet are disputing who is to blame, the city is unguarded and the enemy at hand. Gen. McClellan reached here last evening. But if he had the ability of Cæsar, Alexander, or Napoleon, what can he accomplish? Will not Scott's jealousy, cabinet intrigues, and Republican interference thwart him at every step? . . .
"Yours truly, EDWIN M. STANTON."

the Virginia side, beginning at Gen. W. T. Sherman's position opposite Georgetown. I found Sherman somewhat nervous. He attempted to dissuade me from passing outside of his pickets, believing the enemy to be close at hand. As that was precisely what I wanted to know, however, I did ride some distance beyond the pickets and found no enemy.

The condition of things on the Virginia side was not much better than on the other. The troops were on the river-banks or on the high ground immediately overlooking them. Few were in condition to fight, and but little had been done in the way of entrenching the approaches.

Fort Ellsworth, near Alexandria; Forts Runyon and Allan, at the end of the Long Bridge; Fort Corcoran, at the head of Aqueduct Bridge, with one or two small adjacent batteries, comprised all the works completed on the south side. A small battery at the Maryland end of the Chain Bridge was the only one on the Washington side of the river. Two or three small entrenchments had just been commenced on Arlington Heights. These detached works simply covered some of the principal direct approaches from the Virginia side, but in no sense formed part of any general defensive line.

The condition of affairs which thus presented itself to me upon assuming command was one of extreme difficulty and fraught with great danger. The defeated army of McDowell could not property be called an army - it was only a collection of undisciplined, ill-officered, and uninstructed men, who were, as a rule, much demoralized by defeat and ready to run at the first shot. Positions from which the city could be commanded by the enemy's guns were open for their occupation. The troops were as insufficient in number as in quality. The period of service of many regiments had expired, or would do so in a few days. There was so little discipline that officers and men left their camps at their own will, and, as I have already stated, the city was full of drunken men in uniform. The executive was demoralized; an attack by the enemy was expected from hour to hour; material of war did not exist in anything like sufficient quantities; and, lastly, I was not supreme and unhampered, but often thwarted by the lieutenant-general.

I may be permitted to say that my arrival was hailed with delight by all, except, perhaps, the two generals whom I superseded; and that the executive and the country soon passed from a state of abject despair to confidence, as will appear from the newspapers of the time.

The first and most pressing demand upon me was the immediate safety of the capital and the government. This was provided for by at once exacting the most rigid discipline and order; by arresting all ignorant officers and men, and sending them back to their regiments; by instituting and enforcing strict rules in regard to permission for leaving the camps; by prohibiting civilians and others not on duty from crossing the river or visiting the camps without permits from headquarters; by organizing permanent brigades under regular officers, and by placing the troops in good defensive positions. I threw them further out from the city, so as to have space in rear for manœuvring, and selected positions which commanded the various avenues of approach to the city and enabled the different brigades to afford reciprocal support.

I lost no time in acquiring an accurate knowledge of the ground in all directions, and by frequent visits to the troops made them personally acquainted with me, while I learned all about them, their condition and their needs, and thus soon succeeded in inspiring full confidence and a good *morale* in place of the lamentable state of affairs which existed on my arrival.

Thus I passed long days in the saddle and my nights in the office-a very fatiguing life, but one which made my power felt everywhere and by every one. There were about one thousand regular infantry with McDowell at Arlington. These, with a regular battery and a squadron of regular cavalry, I at once brought to the city and employed as a provost-guard, with the most satisfactory results. It was through their discipline, steadiness, and devotion that order was so promptly established. The following order explains itself :

General Order No. 2.

HEADQUARTERS, DIVISION OF THE POTOMAC,
WASHINGTON, July 30, 1861.

The general commanding the division has with much regret observed that large numbers of officers and men stationed in the vicinity of Washington are in the habit of frequenting the streets

and hotels of the city.   This practice is eminently prejudicial to good order and military discipline, and must at once be discontinued. The time and services of all persons connected with this division should be devoted to their appropriate duties with their respective commands. It is therefore directed that hereafter no officer or soldier be allowed to absent himself from his camp and visit Washington except for the performance of some public duty or for the transaction of important private business, for which purpose written permits will be given by the commanders of brigades. The permit will state the object of the visit. Brigade commanders will be held responsible for the strict execution of this order. Col. Andrew Porter, of the 16th U. S. Infantry, is detached for temporary duty as provost-marshal in Washington, and will be obeyed and respected accordingly.   Col. Porter will report in person at these headquarters for instructions.
> By command of Maj.-Gen. McClellan.
> (Signed)   S. WILLIAMS,
> *Asst. Adjt.-Gen.*

The effect of all this was that on the 4th of August I was able to write to one of my family: "I have Washington perfectly quiet now; you would not know that there was a regiment here. I have restored order very completely already."

In re-arranging the posts and organization of the troops I brought over to the Washington side of the river those regiments which had been most shaken and demoralized by the defeat of Bull Run, and retained them there, with the newly arriving regiments, until in fit condition to be trusted on the side towards the enemy.   My report (made in 1863) gives in sufficient detail the measures taken to expedite the instruction, discipline, and equipment of the new regiments on the Washington side before assigning them to brigades in front of the enemy.   I also proceeded at once to reorganize the various staff departments on a footing commensurate with the actual and future condition of affairs, and used every effort to hasten the arrival of new regiments, as well as the manufacture and purchase of war material of all kinds.

Fortunately I had some excellent officers at my disposal and at once made use of them.

At this period I committed one of my greatest errors - that was in retaining Gen. McDowell on duty with the troops under my command.   I knew that he had been a close student of military affairs, and thought that he possessed sufficient ability to be useful in a subordinate capacity.   Moreover, I pitied him extremely, and thought that circumstances had as much to do with his failure at Bull Run as any want of ability and energy on his part. I knew that if I sent him away he would be ruined for life, and desired to give him an opportunity to retrieve his military reputation. I therefore left him in the nominal command on the Virginia side of the river until the order forming the Army of the Potomac was issued; he doing some little bureau work and retaining a large staff, while I performed the real military labor demanded by the occasion. I was sadly deceived. He never appreciated my motives, and felt no gratitude for my forbearance and kindness. Subsequent events proved that, although in some respects a very good bureau officer and a fair disciplinarian and drill-officer for a school of instruction, he lacked the qualities necessary for a commander in the field. After Pope's campaign it was not safe for McDowell to visit the camps of his troops; the men declared that they would kill him. I have long been convinced that he intrigued against me to the utmost of his power. His conduct towards Fitz-John Porter on the second Bull Run campaign, his testimony in the latter's trial, and subsequent rehearing in 1880, show what manner of man he was. In all human probability I should have been spared an infinite amount of trouble had I relieved him upon reaching Washington: and allowed him to sink at once into obscurity.

When I resumed command it was clear that a prompt advance was wholly impracticable; for, as I have already stated, the mass of the troops placed under me were utterly demoralized and destitute of organization, instruction, discipline, artillery, cavalry, transportation. I repeat that it was not worthy to be called an army. The request to bring with me, or cause to follow, a few of the victorious regiments from West Virginia was denied. As it was, nothing remained but to create an army and material as rapidly as possible from the very foundation.

The result of the first Bull Run had changed the conditions of the problem and complicated them exceedingly. In West Virginia I had raw troops against raw troops; my opponents had all the advantages of knowledge of the ground, strong positions, and a country peculiarly adapted to the defensive. Yet I did not hesitate to attack, and gained complete success. I felt that against troops who had never been under fire and were not particularly well commanded the offensive offered great advan-

tages, and also felt entire confidence in my ability to handle my
men, many of whom had attained a certain rough kind of discipline at Camp Dennison. But at Washington everything was
different. The enemy not only had all the advantages of position, of entrenchments, of the *morale* resulting from success,
but his discipline and drill were far better than our own. It
would have been madness to renew the attempt until a complete change was made, for all the advantages of a sudden
movement had been lost. The problem now was to attack victorious and finely drilled troops in entrenchment. I knew that
this could be done only by well-organized and well-drilled troops,
well supplied with artillery and other arms of service; the future
of the war proved the correctness of this view. I had, therefore,
no choice but to create a real army and its material out of
nothing. The contest had already assumed such a phase that
large masses were necessary to decide it. To use such masses
they must be organized and instructed. Perhaps even then a
few thousand regulars would have decided the war. But we
had them not!

Let those who criticise me for the delay in creating an army
and its material point out an instance when so much has been
done with the same means in so short a time.

Not only was it necessary to organize, discipline, and drill
the troops, but the immense labor of constructing the fortifications required to secure the city in the absence of the army was
also to be performed by the troops. Not only did this consume
much time and greatly retard the preparation of the army for the
field, but it tied down the troops to the line of the defences, and
rendered it impossible to take up a more advanced position until
the works were finished.

Before my arrival no one had contemplated the complete fortification of the city. I at once conceived the idea and carried it
into effect; for I saw immediately that the safety of the capital
would always be a great clog on the movements of the army, unless its security were amply guaranteed by strong entrenchments.
I cannot speak in too high terms of the cheerfulness, zeal, and
activity with which these raw troops performed this arduous and
disagreeable labor. They gave thus early an earnest of what
might be expected from them under more trying circumstances.

The system adopted was that of detached earthworks. The

most important points were occupied by large bastioned forts closed at the gorge, with magazines, platforms, etc.; the scarps and counterscarps often reveted with timber, the parapets usually sodded. The intermediate points were occupied by lunettes, redoubts, batteries, etc., and in a few cases these were united by infantry parapets. The entire circumference of the city was thus protected. Towards Manassas the very important advanced points of Upton's and Munson's Hills were held by strong works, with some small batteries near by. This was the key to the approach in that direction.

In weighing the magnitude of the task of organizing the Army of the Potomac it must be borne in mind that the deficiency of instructed officers was almost as great as that of well-instructed non-commissioned officers and soldiers.

It is important to emphasize the condition of affairs at this juncture. If the enemy advanced in fair condition and reasonable force direct upon Washington, there were no means of preventing his occupation of Arlington Heights and the bombardment of the city. If he availed himself of the low water in the Potomac and crossed at or above the Great Falls, at the same time making a feint on the direct approaches, he could enter the city unopposed. For when I arrived there were neither entrenchments nor troops in position on the Maryland side, and Banks's command, near Harper's Ferry, was so distant, so unorganized, demoralized, and unfit to march or fight, that it could exercise no influence on the result.

Soon after my arrival I called upon Gen. McDowell, then in command of all the troops on the Virginia side, for a report as to the condition of his command. On the 30th of July he reported as follows:

"An inspection commenced yesterday by all the regular officers who were available, and is still going on, of all the regiments in this department. When the reports are made I shall be able to give something more than a mere opinion as to their condition to take the field. In the absence of any precise information I should say that but few regiments, if any, are in such condition at this time. Those who were in the last movement are not yet recovered, and the others are raw. Such as they are, about twenty regiments could be set in motion in two or three days. But few would have any organization with which they would be at all acquainted, and would have but little confidence in them-

selves or each other. But one battery of artillery ready; the
others are refitting. The three companies of cavalry are a good
deal run down.   One New York regiment (Quimby's) is in a
state of utter demoralization and asking to be discharged. In
another (Bruin's) all the field officers tendered their resignation.
An inspection of Quimby's, made by Major Wadsworth, seems to
show that we have but one ultimatum - to dissolve it as worthless.
I shall be at your headquarters this P.M."

On the 2d of August I received from Col. F. J. Porter, who
had been on duty with Gen. Patterson, and continued with his
successor, Gen. Banks, a letter from Sandy Hook, under date of
the 1st of Aug., from which I give the following extract:

"That the government should not suffer by my withdrawal
from this command, on the arrival of Gen. Banks I consented to
remain, and had myself assigned to the position of acting inspector-general, in order to accomplish what no one else here can
- a reorganization of this demoralized force.   I think within a
week I shall have placed it in excellent order for brigade commanders to perfect. My occupation will then be gone, unless
this force is to take the initiative and enter on an active campaign. If to be active, with confidence reposed in me, I can be
of much use and render the country essential services.   But can
I do so in other positions and more satisfactory to myself?
Should the campaign turn out as the last, the odium which has
been thrown unjustly upon Patterson will be reflected upon me
and his other advisers. Time and orders from high authority
will show he was right, and the country should be thankful. But
I cannot bear another such, and see my companions, my juniors,
rising to distinction and position, while I must plod away in a
beaten and sandy track. . . ."

Every one in Washington realized the imminent danger of its
capture, and none dreamed of a renewal of the attack upon
Manassas under the circumstances and with the means at hand.
They were but too well satisfied with the assurance that the measures I took would secure order and preserve the capital from
insult or capture. A new advance made soon after the first
would, if unsuccessful, have been certainly followed by the
prompt occupation of Washington by the enemy. Until the
new army was in such condition as to make success certain, it
would have been unpardonable folly to advance without leaving
Washington so well entrenched and garrisoned as to afford a safe
retreat to the entire army if repulsed. This was impracticable

when I assumed command, and the Confederates, while receiving large accessions of force, lost no time in constructing strong entrenchments at Centreville, Manassas, etc.

There was so much misunderstanding and there were so many misrepresentations during the war as to the effective strength of the Army of the Potomac that it is necessary to explain briefly the manner in which the returns were made up.

They showed -

1st. The number of officers and men "present for duty."

2d. The number of officers and men "present sick."

3d. The number of officers and men "present in arrest."

4th. The total present, this being the sum of the three preceding items.

5th. The number absent.

6th. The total present and absent, made up by taking the sum of items 4th and 5th.

It is, of course, clear that the first item comprises all the officers and men who are effective for the immediate work of the army, yet-either through ignorance, or to injure me by exaggerating the force at my disposal - often the "total present," often the "aggregate present and absent," was given, by those occupying official positions, as the effective strength of the Army of the Potomac. In the latter case this sometimes involved an exaggeration of over sixty per cent; as, for example, on July 10, 1862, the total present for duty was 89,549, while the aggregate present and absent was 144,886.

Nor, as our returns were made during the first two years of the war, were the numbers given as "present for duty" by any means a true measure of the effective force, because one of the instructions for making out the returns was that "all officers and enlisted men present on extra or daily duty will be borne in the column of 'present for duty.'" Therefore there were included among the "present for duty" all camp, train, and special guards, all men detailed for duty as teamsters, laborers, and otherwise, in the headquarters, commissary, engineer, medical, and ordnance departments; all orderlies, cooks, officers' servants-in short, those who form no part of the fighting strength of an army, and who in every European and other service, except our own, are borne in a separate column as present on special extra or daily duty, so that the column of "present for duty" then gives the actual available fighting force. After careful study, and with ample means to reach accurate results, Gen. A. A. Humphreys estimates the number of extra-duty officers and men, not including camp-guards, orderlies, cooks, etc., etc., who were not in the ranks of the Army of the Potomac at all on the 20th of June, 1862, to be from 17,000 to 18,000 out of 105,000, or about one-sixth. This is, doubtless, very near the truth, and not above it; so that, as the Confederates reported only the officers and men in ranks as present for duty, there must always be deducted from the "present for duty" strength of the Army of the Potomac during the first two years of the war about one-sixth to make a fair comparison with the enemy. But, allowing for camp-guards and officers' servants, etc., a deduction of one-fifth at least should be made.

On the 1st of Aug., 1861, I had, according to the returns, less than 50,000 infantry, 1,000 cavalry, 650 artillerists with 30 guns, present. Bearing in mind what has just been stated, and making the proper deduction for the sick, in arrest, and on extra duty, it appears that there were certainly not more than 37,000 infantry in the ranks. The term of service of many of these regiments was about expiring, and they were gradually replaced by perfectly raw new regiments. On the 19th of Aug. I had less than 42,000 effective of all arms, such as they were; and the most necessary defences still required about a week to enable them to resist assaults with tolerable certainty. On the 20th of Aug. I had 80 guns and less than 1,200 cavalry. On the 25th of Aug. I had about 50,000 effective of all arms and perhaps 100 guns. The return for Aug. 31, 1861, shows that, excluding Gen. Dix's command, there was an "aggregate present" of 76,415 of all arms. This comprised Banks's command near Harper's Ferry and above, and Stone's corps of observation at Poolesville. It included the sick, those under arrest, and all extra-duty men. Making the proper deduction on these accounts, the effective force, including Banks's and Stone's, is reduced to 58,680 officers and men of all arms; many of these being still unfit for service through lack of discipline and instruction, unserviceable arms, etc. This is just about the number of effectives reported by the Confederates as composing Johnston's command.

After providing, even very insufficiently, for watching the Potomac and guarding the communication with Baltimore, there would not have been left more than 45,000 effectives for the garrison of Washington and active operation. Certainly not 10,000 of these troops were in any condition to make an offensive movement, nor were they sufficient in numbers to furnish an active column which would give the slightest hope of success after making even a small provision for the safety of the capital.

On the 15th of Oct., 1861, the troops under my command "present for duty" numbered . .		133,200
Of these there were unarmed and unequipped .		12,000
		121,200
Deduct one-sixth for extra - duty men, etc.,		20,200
		101,000
Total effectives, without regard to instruction, Gen. Dix was charged with the defence of Baltimore, occupation of the east shore, garrison of Fort Delaware, the communications to Philadelphia, and the immediate approaches to Baltimore, including Annapolis. In view of the strong secessionist feeling in his district it would have been dangerous to leave him with less than	10,000	
The upper Potomac, from Washington to Cumberland, a distance of more than one hundred and sixty miles by the river, could not safely be watched and guarded by less than	15,000	
The lower Potomac, the south part of Maryland, and communication with Baltimore required at least	5,000	
For the garrison of Washington and its defences, and securing the flanks and communication of the main army during its advance on Manassas, a very moderate estimate would have been	30,000	60,000
Leaving for the active column		41,000

In estimating the force of the above detachments it must be remembered that I was obliged to regard the apprehensions of the administration and the state of feeling in Maryland, as well as the purely military considerations. I was not then in com-

mand of all the armies of the United States, far less free to disregard the administration. Had I been chief of the state the
conditions of the problem would have been very different. In
that case, with the discipline, instruction, and armament sufficiently advanced-which was not the fact - I would not have
hesitated to throw Banks on Winchester with 15,000 men, to act
on the left flank of the enemy at Manassas, and, reducing the
garrison of Washington to 10,000 men, advance on Manassas
with 60,000 men; that would have been the best that could have
been done, and in that event 10,000 must have watched the line
of the Occoquan, leaving 50,000 available for the attack on Manassas.

On the 27th of Oct. the "present for duty" were . . 147,695
Deduct unarmed and unequipped, ... 13,410

134,285
Deduct one-sixth for extra duty, etc., ... 22,360

111,925
Deduct garrisons and corps of deserters, . . . 60,000

Leaving available for active operations, ... 51,925

On the 4th of Nov. the "present for duty" were . . 152,748
Deduct unarmed and unequipped, . . . 8,706

144,042
Deduct one-sixth for extra-duty men, etc., . . . 24,007

120,035
Garrisons, etc., ... 60,000

For active operations, officers and men of all arms, . 60,035

Up to the beginning of November, and still later, many of
the infantry were insufficiently drilled and disciplined, and they
were to a considerable extent armed with unserviceable weapons.
Few of the cavalry were completely armed, and most of the volunteer cavalry were still very inefficient. The artillery numbered
228 guns, but many of the batteries were still entirely unfit to
take the field. Transportation was still lacking for any extended
movements.

On the 1st of Dec. there were "present for duty". . .169,452
Of these there were unequipped and unarmed, at least   5,000

                                                     164,452
Deduct   extra-duty   men,   etc., ... 27,600

                                                     136,852
Deduct   garrisons,   etc.,   as   before, ... 60,000

For   active   operations, ... 76,852

    On the 27th of Aug., when I assumed command of the Division of the Potomac, Gen. Banks had just been relieved by Gen. Dix in the command of the Department of Maryland, and in his turn relieved Gen. Patterson - whose term of service expired on that day - in the command of the Department of the Shenandoah. On the 1st of Aug. Gen. Banks's headquarters were at Sandy Hook, in the immediate vicinity of Harper's Ferry. In consequence of the expiration of service of the three-months regiments this command was in a state of disorganization for the moment.

    As the geographical Division of the Potomac extended along that river somewhat beyond the Monocacy, and it fell within my province to guard that part of the river, within two or three days after assuming command I organized a brigade of four regiments, under Gen. C. P. Stone, and ordered him to the vicinity of Poolesville to observe and guard the Potomac between the Great Falls and the limits of Gen. Banks's command. On the 2d of Aug. the seven regiments of the Pennsylvania Reserve Corps, then arrived, were organized as a brigade under Gen. G. A. McCall, and ordered to Tennallytown to guard the important roads meeting at that point, and to observe the river as far as the Great Falls. At this place the brigade was in position to support Stone and the troops at the Chain Bridge, and, in case of necessity, would rapidly move by the Aqueduct Bridge to support the troops at Fort Corcoran and Arlington Heights. On the 1st the two regiments at the Chain Bridge were placed under the command of Col. W. F. Smith, and within three days his command was increased to four regiments of infantry, one battery, and one company of cavalry. At the same time Couch's brigade was posted at the Toll-Gate on the Seventh Street road, where the Milkhouse Ford and Blagden's Mill

roads intersect it. Hooker's brigade was posted on the Bla-
densburg road, near the position afterwards entrenched. Gen.
W. T. Sherman's brigade, reinforced by three regiments of infantry, with one battery and one company of regular cavalry,
occupied Fort Corcoran, at the head of the Georgetown Aqueduct Bridge. Gens. Hunter's and Keyes's brigades held the
Arlington Heights. Col. Richardson's brigade was posted in
advance of the Long Bridge, with one regiment in Fort Runyon. Near this were a couple of light batteries under Col. H.
J. Hunt, ready to move whenever required. Col. Blenker's brigade was in advance of Roach's Mills, in the valley of Four-
Mile Run. Gens. Franklin's and Heintzelman's brigades were
in front of Alexandria, in the vicinity of the Seminary. Kearny's brigade was at Cloud's Mills, on the Annandale turnpike.
One regiment was stationed at Fort Ellsworth, immediately in
front of Alexandria.

I had thus provided against all eventualities as well as the
means in my possession permitted. If the enemy confined himself to a direct advance the probable points of attack were held
by eight brigades, so posted that they could render mutual assistance, if all were not simultaneously assailed in force, while
the brigades of McCall, Couch, and Hooker could move by
good roads to support them; Hooker having about five miles
to march to the Long Bridge, Couch about six to the Long
Bridge, the Aqueduct, or to the Chain Bridge, and McCall having a little over three miles to the Chain Bridge or the Aqueduct, or about six miles to the Long Bridge.

If the enemy crossed the Potomac for the purpose of attacking on the Maryland side, Stone was in position to fall back on
McCall or Couch after retarding their passage of the river; so
that there would have been four brigades, with good communication to either flank, in readiness to oppose them, while troops
could have been brought from the Virginia side to their support.

In the city were the few regulars acting as a provost-guard,
and ready to be thrown wherever their services might be required.

On the 5th of Aug. the first three regiments of the Excelsior Brigade and the 79th New York were formed into a
provisional brigade and posted in the suburbs of Washington;
they were soon moved south of the Anacostia to the vicinity of

Uniontown. On the 7th McCall received a battery of regular artillery; and on the 9th Kearny and Sherman each received another company of volunteer cavalry, and on the same day King's brigade of three regiments was formed, and posted on Meridian Hill. Three days afterwards it was increased by two regiments.   On the 10th a battery was sent to Stone, and a second one to McCall, who received another regiment on the 12th.

The formation of divisions was thus:

Aug. 24, 1861: McDowell's division, consisting of Keyes's and Wadsworth's brigades.   King's brigade was added on Oct. 5.

About the same date - *i.e.,* within two or three days after the formation of the Army of the Potomac - the troops under Gen. Banks were organized as a division.

Aug. 28, 1861: Franklin's division, consisting of Kearny's and Franklin's old brigade. A third brigade added Sept. 4.

Aug. 30, 1861: F. J. Porter's division, consisting of two brigades. A third brigade added Sept. 27.

Sept. 12, 1861: Stone's division, consisting of two brigades, Lander's and Peck's.   Baker's brigade was added towards the end of the month or early in October.

Sept. 14, 1861: Buell's division, consisting of Couch's and Graham's brigades. A third brigade added early in October.

Sept. 16, 1861: McCall's division; on the 25th of that month he received the last two regiments of the Pennsylvania Reserves, so that his division consisted of thirteen regiments in three brigades, under Meade, J. F. Reynolds, and Ord.

Sept. 28, 1861: W. F. Smith's division, consisting of the Vermont brigade (afterwards Brooks's), J. J. Stevens's and Hancock's brigades.

Oct. 5, 1861: Heintzelman's division, consisting of Richardson's, Sedgwick's, and Jameson's brigades.

Oct. 11, 1861: Hooker's division, consisting of his own (afterwards Naglee's) brigade and Sickles's brigade.   In November a third brigade (Starr's New Jersey) was added.

Oct. 12, 1861: Blenker's division, consisting of Stahl's and Steinwehr's brigades. A third brigade added during the winter.

Nov. 25, 1861: Sumner's division, consisting of Howard's, Meagher's, and French's brigades.

Dec. 6, 1861: Casey's division, consisting of three brigades.

CHAPTER V.

PRIVATE LETTERS.

[*July* 27 to *Sept.* 30, 1861.]

July 27, 1861, *Washington,* D. C. - I have been assigned to the command of a division composed of the departments of northeastern Virginia (that under McDowell) and that of Washington (now under Mansfield). Neither of them like it much, especially Mansfield; but I think they must ere long become accustomed to it, as there is no help for it. . . . I find myself in a new and strange position here: President, cabinet, Gen. Scott, and all deferring to me. By some strange operation of magic I seem to have become the power of the land.

I see already the main causes of our recent failure; I am sure that I can remedy these, and am confident that I can lead these armies of men to victory once more. I start to-morrow very early on a tour through the lines on the other side of the river. It will occupy me all day long, and a rather fatiguing ride it will be, but I will be able to make up my mind as to the state of things. Refused invitations to dine to-day from Gen. Scott and four secretaries; had too many things to attend to. . . .

I will endeavor to enclose with this the "thanks of Congress," which please preserve. I feel very proud of it. Gen. Scott objected to it on the ground that it ought to be accompanied by a gold medal. I cheerfully acquiesce in the thanks by themselves, hoping to win the medal by some other action, and the sword by some other fait *d'éclat.*

July 30, *Washington* - . . Had to work until nearly three this morning. . . . I am getting my ideas pretty well arranged in regard to the strength of my army; it will be a very large one. I have been employed in trying to get the right kind of general officers. . . . Have been working this morning at a bill allowing me to appoint as many aides as I please from civil life and from the army. . . .

I went to the Senate to get it through, and was quite overwhelmed by the congratulations I received and the respect with which I was treated. I suppose half a dozen of the oldest made the remark I am becoming so much used to: "Why, how young you look, and yet an old soldier!" It seems to strike everybody that I am very young. They give me my way in everything, full swing and unbounded confidence. All tell me that I am held responsible for the fate of the nation, and that all its resources shall be placed at my disposal. It is an immense task that I have on my hands, but I believe I can accomplish it. . . . When I was in the Senate chamber to-day and found those old men flocking around me; when I afterwards stood in the library, looking over the Capitol of our great nation, and saw the crowd gathering around to stare at me, I began to feel how great the task committed to me. Oh! how sincerely I pray to God that I may be endowed with the wisdom and courage necessary to accomplish the work. Who would have thought, when we were married, that I should so soon be called upon to save my country?

Aug. 2. - Rode over the river, looked at some of the works, and inspected three or four regiments; worked at organizing brigades - just got through with that. I handed to the President to-night a carefully considered plan for conducting the war on a large scale. . . . I shall carry this thing on en grand and crush the rebels in one campaign. I flatter myself that Beauregard has gained his last victory. We need success and must have it. I will leave nothing undone to gain it. Gen. Scott has been trying to work a traverse to have - made inspector-general of *my* army and of *the* army. I respectfully declined the favor. . . .

I have on the staff Seth Williams as adjutant-general; Barnard as chief-engineer; Van Vliet, chief-quartermaster; H. F. Clarke, chief-commissary; Barry, chief of artillery; Meade will be senior topographer; Dr. Tripler, medical director. I have applied for Kingsbury as chief of ordnance, and for Armstrong and Sweitzer as aides-de-camp. I dine with the President to-morrow, where I presume I shall meet Prince Napoleon. . . . You would laugh if you could see the scores of queer letters I receive in these days. I am sorry to say I do not answer any of them; I do no writing myself, except to you. . . . I was in the saddle
8

nearly twelve hours yesterday. I broke down your father and sent Seth home half an hour since, neither of them having been out all to-day.

Aug, 4. - I dined at the President's yesterday. I suppose some forty were present - Prince Napoleon and his staff, French minister, English ditto, cabinet, some senators, Gen. Scott, and myself. The dinner was not especially interesting; rather long, and rather tedious, as such things generally are. I was placed between Col. Pisani, one of the prince's aides, who spoke no English, and a member of the - legation who labored under the delusion that he spoke our native tongue with fluency. I had some long talks with the prince, who speaks English very much as the Frenchmen do in the old English comedies. He is an intelligent man. . . . It made me feel a little strangely when I went in to the President's last evening with the old general leaning on me; I could see that many marked the contrast. . . . I have Washington perfectly quiet now. You would not know that there was a regiment here. I have restored order very completely already.

Aug. 8. - . . . Rose early to-day (having retired at three A.M.), and was pestered to death with senators, etc., and a row with Gen. Scott until about four o'clock; then crossed the river and rode beyond and along the line of pickets for some distance. Came back and had a long interview with Seward about my "pronunciamiento" against Gen. Scott's policy. . . . I have scarcely slept one moment for the last three nights, knowing well that the enemy intend some movement and fully recognizing our own weakness. If Beauregard does not attack to-night I shall look upon it as a dispensation of Providence. He ought to do it. Every day strengthens me. I am leaving nothing undone to increase our force; but the old general always comes in the way. He understands nothing, appreciates nothing.

Aug. —. - On Sunday, instead of going to church, was sent for by the President immediately after breakfast, and kept busy until midnight, when I returned from a long ride too tired to talk even. Yesterday in the saddle from ten to five, and then persecuted until after midnight. To-day the President sent for me before I was up; have been at work ever since, and soon start out to receive a brigade and some batteries.

Aug, 9, 1861, A.M. - I have had a busy day: started from here at seven in the morning, and was in the saddle until about nine this evening; rode over the advanced position on the other side of the river, was soundly drenched in a hard rain, and have been busy ever since my return. Things are improving daily. I received three new regiments to-day; fitted out one new battery yesterday, another to-day, two to-morrow, about five day after. Within four days I hope to have at least 21 batteries - say 124 field-guns - 18 companies of cavalry, and some 70 regiments of infantry. Gen. Scott is the great obstacle. He will not comprehend the danger. I have to fight my way against him. To-morrow the question will probably be decided by giving me absolute control independently of him. I suppose it will result in enmity on his part against me; but I have no choice. The people call upon me to save the country. I must save it, and cannot respect anything that is in the way.

I receive letter after letter, have conversation after conversation; calling on me to save the nation, alluding to the presidency, dictatorship, etc. As I hope one day to be united with you for ever in heaven, I have no such aspiration. I would cheerfully take the dictatorship and agree to lay down my life when the country is saved. I am not spoiled by my unexpected new position. I feel sure that God will give me the strength and wisdom to preserve this great nation; but I tell you, who share all my thoughts, that I have no selfish feeling in this matter. I feel that God has placed a great work in my hands. I have not sought it. I know how weak I am, but I know that I mean to do right, and I believe that God will help me and give me the wisdom I do not possess. Pray for me, that I may be able to accomplish my task, the greatest, perhaps, that any poor, weak mortal ever had to do. . . . God grant that I may bring this war to an end and be permitted to spend the rest of my days quietly with you!

I met the prince (Napoleon) at Alexandria to-day and came up with him. He says that Beauregard's head is turned; that Joe Johnston is quiet and sad, and that he spoke to him in very kind terms of me.

Aug. 12. - . . . Every day shows some progress.   If Beauregard will give me another week or ten days I will feel quite comfortable again. I have been anxious, especially as the old man and I do not get along very well together.

Aug. 13. - I am living in Com. Wilkes's house, the northwest corner of Jackson Square, close by where you used to visit Secretary Marcy's family. It is a very nice house. I occupy the three front rooms on the second story; Van Vliet the room in rear of mine; Judge Key behind him; Colburn the story above. I receive the staff every morning until ten and every evening at nine. Quite a levee it makes, and a rather fine-looking set they are. Kingsbury arrived last night. Did I tell you that Hudson is one of my regular aides?

Aug. 14. - Rode to McCall's camp, out to the line of pickets, and followed that to the Aqueduct Bridge, thence home by W. F. Smith's camp; got home at ten P.M.

Midnight, 15th. - . . . I am almost tired out; I cannot get one minute's rest during the day, and sleep with one eye open at night, looking out sharply for Beauregard, who, I think, has some notion of making a dash in this direction.   Gen. Scott is the most dangerous antagonist I have. Our ideas are so widely different that it is impossible for us to work together much longer - *tant pour cela.* My day has been spent much as usual. . . . Rose at 6.30; did any reasonable amount of business, among which may be classed quelling a couple of mutinies among the volunteers; started on my usual ride at 4.30, came home at nine; have been hard at work ever since. As to my mutinous friends, I have ordered sixty-three of the 2d Maine regiment to be sent as prisoners to the Dry Tortugas, there to serve out the rest of the war as prisoners at hard labor.   I reduced the others (79th N. Y.) by sending out a battalion, battery, and squadron of regulars to take care of them.   The gentlemen at once laid down their arms, and I have the ringleaders in irons. They will be tried and probably shot to-morrow.   An example is necessary to bring these people up to the mark; and if they will not fight and do their duty from honorable motives, I intend to coerce them and let them see what they have to expect if they pretend to rebel. I deprived the 79th of their colors, and have them down-stairs, not to be returned to them until they have earned them again by good behavior. The great trouble is the want of officers of regiments. We have good material, but no officers.

Aug. 14, 1861. - I was so occupied yesterday that I could not write. Profs. Mahan and Bache at breakfast. Then came the usual levee. Then Burnside turned up, and I had to listen to his explanation of some slanders against him; then some naval officers; then I don't know how many others before dinner. After dinner I rode out until about nine, when I found the President had been to see me and wanted me at the White House. After I got through there I went to see Montgomery Blair on business. Then, on my return, found some more of the cabinet, McDowell, etc., so that it was after midnight when I got to my room, completely fatigued. So my days and nights pass, a steady course of conversations and orders all day. Except when I get out for a ride, no relief for mind or body.

Washington, 16th. - . . . I am here in a terrible place: the enemy have from three to four times my force; the President, the old general, cannot or will not see the true state of affairs. Most of my troops are demoralized by the defeat at Bull Run; some regiments even mutinous. I have probably stopped that; but you see my position is not pleasant. . . . I have, I believe made the best possible disposition of the few men under my command; will quietly await events, and, if the enemy attacks, will try to make my movements as rapid and desperate as may be. If my men will only fight I think I can thrash him, notwithstanding the disparity of numbers. As it is, I trust to God to give success to our arms, though He is not wont to aid those who refuse to aid themselves. I am weary of all this. I have no ambition in the present affairs; only wish to save my country, and find the incapables around me will not permit it. They sit on the verge of the precipice, and cannot realize what they see. Their reply to everything is, "Impossible! Impossible!" They think nothing possible which is against their wishes.

Aug. 16, 6 P.M. - . . Gen. Scott is at last opening his eyes to the fact that I am right and that we are in imminent danger.

Providence is aiding me by heavy rains, which are swelling the Potomac, which may be impassable for a week; if so we are saved. If Beauregard comes down upon us soon I have everything ready to make a manœuvre which will be decisive. Give me two weeks and I will defy Beauregard; in a week the chances will be at least even.

Aug. 18. - My command is at last extended, so that I take in Banks in the Shenandoah and Dix at Baltimore. . . . The true reason why I did not bring you here was that I did not deem it safe. We may have to fight a battle under the defences of Washington within a week, and I did not care to have you exposed to the chances. If Beauregard does not attack within two days he has lost every chance of success. If by the time you receive this letter you have not heard of a battle through the telegraph you may be easy and contented.

Aug. 19. - . . . If this week passes without a battle, and reinforcements come in, I shall feel sure that the dangerous point is turned.

6 P.M. - I have been inspecting the defences over the river and find them quite strong. We are becoming stronger in our position every day, and I hope for large reinforcements this week.

Aug. 20. - . . . If Beauregard does not attack this week he is foolish. He has given me infinite advantages, and you may be sure I have not neglected the opportunity. Every day adds to the strength of my defences, to the perfection of the organization, and some little to our forces. I have now about 80 field-guns (there were but 49 at Bull Run), and by Saturday will have 112. There were only some 400 cavalry at Bull Run; I now have about 1,200, and by the close of the week will have some 3,000. I am gaining rapidly in every way. I can now defend Washington with almost perfect certainty. When I came here it could have been taken with the utmost ease. In a week I ought to be perfectly safe and be prepared to defend all Maryland; in another week to advance our position.

. . . The men were very enthusiastic and looked well. My old State will come out handsomely. I have been much vexed to-night by sundry troublesome things; the only comfort has been

your father's arrival, which is a great relief to me.   I like to see
that cool, steady head near me.

Aug. 23. - . . . Yesterday I rode to Alexandria and reviewed four brigades - that is, seventeen regiments. . . Beauregard has missed his chance, and I have gained what I most
needed-time! . . .

I do not *live* at all; merely exist, worked and worried half to
death. I have no privacy, no leisure, no relaxation, except in
reading your letters and writing to you.   We take our meals at
Wormley's: a colored gentleman who keeps a restaurant just
around the corner in I Street.   I take breakfast there pretty
regularly; sometimes have it sent over here.   As to dinner, it
takes its chances, and generally gets no chance at all, as it is often
ten o'clock when I get back from my ride, and I have nothing to
eat all day. . . .

Aug. 25. - Yesterday started at nine A.M., rode over Long
Bridge and reviewed Richardson's brigade, then went three miles
further and at twelve reviewed Blenker's brigade at Roach's
Mills, then rode some ten miles looking for a position in which
to fight a battle to cover Alexandria should it be attacked. I
found one which satisfies me entirely.   I then returned to Fort
Runyon, near the head of Long Bridge, and reviewed the 21st
New York, after which reviewed four batteries of light artillery.
. . . This morning telegram from other side announcing enemy
advancing in force.   Started off aides and put the wires at work;
when fairly started alarm proved false. . . Friend Beauregard
has allowed the chance to escape him.   I have now some 65,000
effective men; will have 75,000 by end of week.   Last week he
certainly had double our force.   I feel sure that the dangerous
moment has passed.

26th - . . . Reviewed Sherman's command (seven regiments)
near Fort Corcoran; then McDowell's (eight regiments) at the
race-course; then rode to the ground in front of Alexandria-
twelve hours in saddle,

Aug. 31. - Drove out yesterday as far as McCall's camp, and
to-day down over the river for several hours.   Have not yet ven-

tured on horseback again; may try it to-morrow. . . . Our defences are becoming very strong now, and the army is increasing in efficiency and numbers quite rapidly. I think Beauregard has abandoned the idea of crossing the river above us, and I learned to-day again that my movements had entirely disconcerted their plans and that they did not know what to do. They are suffering much from sickness, and I fancy are not in the best possible condition. If they venture to attack us here they will have an awful time of it. I do not think they will dare to attack. We are now ready for them. The news from every quarter to-night is favorable. All goes well.

Sept. 4, 1861. - I took an early dinner, and then mounted the bay, Sturgis's horse, and rode to McCall's camp at Tennallytown. Sweitzer and Colburn went with me, as usual when hard riding is expected ; also the ordinary escort of a sergeant and ten dragoons. . . . Learned that the firing at Great Falls amounted to little, and that the orders I had before given to send another regiment and another battery were sufficient. Then rode to Little Falls (Chain Bridge) and went along the whole picket-line.

Sept. — . - . . . Had my dinner just after writing the above, and then rode to review a brigade and 32 guns away over beyond the Capitol. Just as I got through Seth rode up with a message to the effect that the enemy were in force near Smith (W. F.) I rode rapidly home, changed my horse, and rode out to Smith's camp. I determined at once to throw Smith across the river, and went over with his brigade myself till I saw him in position, and then came back at 1.30 pretty well tired out.

Sept. 6. - Rode along pickets from Corcoran to Chain Bridge. Found everything in good condition and ready for a battle. If B. attacks now he will inevitably be defeated with terrible loss. . . . I feel now perfectly secure against an attack; the next thing will be to attack him.

Sept. 8. - What a shame that any one should spread such a wicked rumor in regard to my being killed! I beg to assure you that I have not been killed a single time since I reached Washington. So don't believe any such absurd rumors. How lucky that you did not hear the report until after you received the telegram! I had another bouquet this morning, one from the "Lady President." Mr. Lincoln came this morning to ask me to pardon a man that I had ordered to be shot, suggesting that I could give as a reason in the order that it was by request of the "Lady President."

Sept. — . - Inspected works from Corcoran to Albany; reviewed McDowell's division and another brigade; condition of troops excellent. Received proceedings of court-martial sentencing a dozen men to death; too severe and unjust.

Sept. 27. - . . . He (the President) sent a carriage for me to meet him and the cabinet at Gen. Scott's office. Before we got through the general "raised a row with me." I k e p t c o o l. In the course of the conversation he very strongly intimated that we were no longer friends. I said nothing, merely looked at him and bowed. He tried to avoid me when we left, but I walked square up to him, looked him fully in the eye, extended my hand, and said, "Good-morning, Gen. Scott." He had to take my hand, and so we parted. As he threw down the glove and I took it up, I presume war is declared. So be it. I have one strong point-that I do not care one iota for my present position.

Sept. — . - I started early in the day to be present at the presentation of colors to McCall's division by Gov. Curtin. It was long and fatiguing. I then rode over the Chain Bridge and back by Fort Corcoran. When I returned I had a great deal of tedious work to do and fell asleep in the midst of it. This morning I have had a siege with the Sanitary Committee, and don't think I will ride out to-day. How did you learn that Buckner and Smith have joined the rebel army? I can hardly believe it. You have no idea how the men brighten up now when I go among them. I can see every eye glisten. Yesterday they nearly pulled me to pieces in one regiment. You never heard such yelling. Did I tell you that Lawrence Williams has been promoted and leaves my staff? I do not in the least doubt his loyalty. I enclose a card just received from "A. Lincoln"; it shows too much deference to be seen outside.

No date. - The enemy were stampeded this morning, and while they were in terror I rapidly occupied all their positions and had the satisfaction of going out with our advance and seeing the last of their cavalry.

No date (Sept. 30?) - A most unhappy thing occurred last night among some of W. F. Smith's raw regiments. They three times mistook each other for the enemy and fired into each other. At least six were killed and several wounded, besides two horses were killed. It is dangerous to make night - marches on that account; but Smith's march was delayed by causes I could not foresee, and it was necessary to advance at all hazards. The manœuvring in advance by our flanks alarmed the enemy, whose centre at Munson's and Upton's was much advanced. As soon as our pickets informed me that he had fallen back I rushed forward and seized those very important points. We now hold them in strength and have at once proceeded to fortify them. The moral effect of this advance will be great, and it will have a bad influence on the troops of the enemy. They can no longer say that they are flaunting their dirty little flag in my face, and I hope they have taken their last look at Washington. . . .

CHAPTER VI.

The defence of Washington - Growth of an army - Foresight of the magnitude of the war - Memorandum to the President - Letter to Secretary Cameron.

REFERENCE to any good man will show that Washington is situated on the point of confluence of the main Potomac with the Anacostia, or eastern branch thereof. The ground occupied by the city is low, though by no means flat, and is commanded from all directions by heights within the easy range of even modern field-artillery.

Moral and political considerations alike rendered it necessary to retain the seat of government in Washington, although its situation was the most unfavorable that could be conceived under the circumstances of the case. So far as military operations were concerned, it would have been well could the capital have been removed to New York; but this was impossible. The defence of the capital, containing, as it did, the executive and legislative, the archives of the government, the public buildings, the honor and prestige of the nation, and, as time moved on, vast amounts of military supplies, was a matter of vital importance, and it was necessary to protect it not only from capture, but also against insult. To accomplish this without fortifications would have required an army of great strength, so large as to detract fatally from the efficiency of the active armies. It was, therefore, absolutely necessary to resort to fortifications, and circumstances required that they should be of a temporary nature.

As I have already stated, I found the capital entirely defenceless, and at once determined upon the system to be pursued.

During the months of August and September the work of organization and fortification proceeded as rapidly as circumstances permitted. Naturally there were frequent reports as to the movements of the enemy in advance; sometimes of intended

93

crossings below Alexandria, sometimes above the city. In the
early part of August, when we were so entirely open to attack,
these reports gave me no little uneasiness. And even after we
had reached a point of comparative security, so far as the safety
of Washington was concerned, the probable effects of an inroad
in any form into Maryland rendered it necessary to be constantly on the alert and take every precaution to prevent a crossing
of the river. As soon as Gen. Banks came under my command,
Aug. 20, 1861, I directed him to cross to the eastern bank of
the Monocacy, leaving one regiment to observe the Potomac
above Harper's Ferry, and another to watch it from the latter
place to the mouth of the Monocacy, and to put his main body
not far from Hyattstown; thus placing him in position to oppose
any attempt at crossing the river above Harper's Ferry, while his
junction with the force at Washington would be secure of the enemy's crossing below the Monocacy. In his former position, at
Sandy Hook, he was too far from Washington. He was ordered
to move his surplus and heavy stores from Frederick to Baltimore or Washington, and his surplus transportation to the latter
place; to oppose any passage of the Potomac by the enemy, provided it would not involve his separation from the main army;
also to support Stone when necessary, and, if forced back by
superior numbers, to retreat on Rockville. He was also instructed to protect the railroad as well as practicable without
making too heavy detachments.

Up to this period, and until about the beginning of September, there was reason to apprehend some attack of the enemy;
at all events, reports to that effect frequently arrived, and we
were not for some time in condition to offer successful resistance.

It must never be forgotten that at this period the spirit of
secession was active and bitter in many parts of Maryland.
Baltimore had given too full proof of the feeling of a large
part of its inhabitants of all classes; in the northern and western counties there were many secessionists, though the Union
party was also strong; but in the southern and southeastern
counties the Union people were very few. In this condition
of affairs, with our communications and lines of supply all passing through Maryland, it was too dangerous to even allow small
portions of the enemy to cross the river, and it was therefore

necessary to employ much larger numbers of troops on the frontier, on the line of communication, and in observation through the State than would have been the case if Pennsylvania, for example, had been the frontier State.

Before the middle of August Gen. Smith's pickets were thrown across the river at the Chain Bridge. On the 3d of Sept., while reviewing troops east of the Capitol, I received despatches to the effect that the enemy had appeared in force opposite the Chain Bridge and towards Great Falls; also that they were probably on the point of advancing along their whole line. After giving the necessary orders at other points I rode to Gen. Smith's headquarters at the Chain Bridge, and determined to move his brigade across the river during the night and to entrench a position on the Virginia side as the surest method of saving the bridge. I ordered up King's brigade and a battery to support him, and directed the cavalry and reserve artillery and other troops in the city to be held in readiness to move up if necessary. McCall was also ordered to send an additional regiment and two more guns to Great Falls, and to hold the rest of his command in readiness to move either towards Great Falls or the Chain Bridge, as circumstances might require. Early during the night Smith crossed and at once commenced the construction of Forts Maury and Ethan Allen - positions which I had already examined.

On the 28th of Sept. Smith's division marched out to Falls Church, which movement, in connection with an advance of a part of Franklin's division on the Leesburg pike, of McDowell's on Ball's cross-roads and Upton's Hill, and of Porter's on Hall's Hill, determined the evacuation of Munson's, Upton's, and Taylor's hills by the enemy's outposts, who had now seen the last of Washington until Early's raid in 1864.

Taylor's, Perkins's, Upton's, and Munson's hills were occupied by a brigade of McDowell's division, who at once commenced work upon the necessary fortifications. The occupation of this point was of great importance, as it gave ample room in rear for moving the troops in any direction, and, in the event of my deciding to attack Centreville, would enable me to reach that place in one march from the outposts. Immediately after the occupation of this new position the camp of Porter's division was moved forward to Hall's and Munson's hills, in easy supporting distance; a few days later Smith's division was moved to Marshall's Hill. To support this movement McCall's division was, on the 9th of Oct., brought to the Virginia side to Langley's, and a few days later to Prospect Hill. He was replaced at Tennallytown by a brigade of Buell's division.

On the 5th of Oct. Heintzelman's division was formed, and posted at Fort Lyon, south of Alexandria, forming the left of our line on the Virginia side. During the months of September and October Sickles's brigade, posted on the south side of the eastern branch, sent frequent reconnoissances into lower Maryland.

Early in November Hooker's division was organized and moved to the vicinity of Budd's Ferry to observe the enemy, who were active in that direction, and to prevent, as far as possible, the crossing of the river by emissaries of the enemy. So that early in November the positions of the command were as follows:

On the right McCall's division at Prospect Hill; Smith's division at Mackall's Hill, holding Lewinsville by an advanced guard; Porter's division at Minor's and Hall's hills; McDowell at Arlington, with one brigade at Munson's Hill, etc.; Blenker's division at Hunter's Chapel; Franklin at the Theological Seminary; Heintzelman at Fort Lyon. There were thus on the Virginia side seven divisions, so posted as to cover every avenue of approach, and able to afford assistance to every point that could be attacked, and, moreover, in position to advance on Centreville if necessary. On the north of Washington, Buell's division held Tennallytown and the other important points (supported by Casey's provisional brigades), the reserve artillery and the cavalry depots; while Stone's division at Poolesville, and Banks's division at Darnestown, observed the upper river and were in position to retire upon Washington if attacked by superior forces. Hooker was in the vicinity of Budd's Ferry. By the 30th of Sept. several of the principal works were pretty well advanced, but a great deal still remained to be done to complete the system.

I shall refer elsewhere to the inconveniences resulting from the position of Washington and the nature of the frontier formed by the Potomac; in this place it will suffice to say that as the Potomac is often fordable, and many of the inhabitants on the

Maryland side were favorable to the enemy, it was a very necessary and difficult task to guard it properly.

In view of its exposed position and immense political importance it was impossible to allow Washington to be endangered; so that a garrison was always necessary, and all that could be done was to make the fortifications so strong that a comparatively small garrison would suffice. After the experience of the first Bull Run the executive would never consent to leave Washington without a large garrison.

At this juncture it would have been wise to adopt a definite policy with regard to the regular army - viz., either virtually break it up, as a temporary measure, and distribute its members among the staff and regiments of the volunteer organization, thus giving the volunteers all possible benefit from the discipline and instruction of the regulars, or to fill the regular regiments to their full capacity and employ them as a reserve at critical junctures. I could not secure the adoption of either plan, and a middle course was followed which resulted less favorably than either of the plans indicated; but it must be said that, even as things were, the regulars were in every way of immense benefit to the service. As a general rule the officers (and, of course, the non-commissioned officers) of the volunteer regiments were entirely ignorant of their duties, and many were unfitted, from their education, moral character, or mental deficiences, for ever acquiring the requisite efficiency.

These latter were weeded out by courts-martial and boards of examination, while the others were instructed *pari passu* as they instructed their men. The small number of regular officers available rendered it impossible to furnish all the staff officers from among them; so that a regiment was very fortunate if its colonel was a regular officer, and a brigade was lucky to have a regular as its commander. The generals were usually, and colonels always, obliged to appoint their staff officers from civil life, and instruct them as best they could. It speaks wonders for the intelligence and military aptitude of our people that so much was well done in this way on both sides. Many of these raw civilians, who were men of pride, intelligence, and education, soon became excellent officers; though these very men most keenly regretted their lack of a good military education in early life.

The frequent reviews I held at Washington were not at all for the benefit of the public, nor yet for the purpose of examining the individual condition of the men, although I did much of that even on these occasions - for a general with a quick eye can see things when riding at a gallop which would seem impossible to a civilian. But they were to accustom the regiments to move together and see each other, to give the troops an idea of their own strength, to infuse *esprit de corps* and mutual emulation, and to acquaint myself with the capacity of the general officers. These reviews also had a good effect in accustoming the troops to see me, although they saw so much of me in their camps and on the picket-lines that this was of minor importance. With new troops frequent reviews are of the greatest utility and produce the most excellent effect. Those I held did much towards making the Army of the Potomac what it became.

Some persons, who ought to have known better, have supposed that in organizing the Army of the Potomac I set too high a model before me and consumed unnecessary time in striving to form an army of regulars. This was an unjustifiable error on their part. I should, of course, have been glad to bring that army to the condition of regulars, but no one knew better than myself that, with the means at my command, that would have been impossible within any reasonable or permissible time.

What I strove for and accomplished was to bring about such a condition of discipline and instruction that the army could be handled on the march and on the field of battle, and that orders could be reasonably well carried out. No one cognizant of the circumstances and possessed of any knowledge of military affairs can honestly believe that I bestowed unnecessary time and labor upon the organization and instruction of that army whose courage, discipline, and efficiency finally brought the war to a close.

In spite of all the clamor to the contrary, the time spent in the camps of instruction in front of Washington was well bestowed, and produced the most important and valuable results. Not a day of it was wasted. The fortifications then erected, both directly and indirectly, saved the capital more than once in the course of the war, and enabled the army to manœuvre freely and independently. The organization and discipline then acquired, and so much improved during the campaign of the Peninsula which converted the men into veterans, enabled the army to pass gloriously through the many sanguinary conflicts and harassing campaigns that proved necessary to terminate the war. They learned to gain victories and to withstand defeat. No other army we possessed could have met and defeated the Confederate Army of Northern Virginia. And, with all the courage, energy, and intelligence of the Army of the Potomac, it probably would not have been equal to that most difficult task without the advantage it enjoyed during its sojourn in the camps around Washington.

Early in August more or less trouble and discontent appeared among some of the regiments in relation to their term of service. In fact, many of those who enlisted during the first excitement had no expectation of engaging for a long war, and, when they found the three-months regiments returning home in large numbers, became much dissatisfied. In two cases this culminated in open mutiny on the part of large numbers of the officers and men. In the case of one regiment I brought them to order by directing the transportation of sixty-three of the number as prisoners to the Dry Tortugas, to labor there during the remainder of the war. In the case of the other the following order was issued:

Special Order No. 27.

HEADQUARTERS, DIVISION OF THE POTOMAC,
WASHINGTON, Aug. 14, 1861.

The general commanding this division learns with the utmost pain that decided insubordination, if not open mutiny, has been displayed by a large portion of the 79th regiment of N. Y. Volunteers. The general commanding does not desire, at this time, to enter into any statement of the alleged grievances of this regiment, further than to say that he has examined into them and finds that they are frivolous and unfounded. This conduct is disgraceful in the extreme, both as soldiers and citizens, to all concerned in it. Those who have participated in this shameful affair have utterly disgraced themselves; they are unworthy of the sympathy of their fellow-soldiers, and in acting such a part at a time when the services of every true man are required by the nation they have rendered themselves liable to the suspicion that motives of the basest cowardice have controlled their conduct. This regiment has chosen to make the issue, and the commanding general is prepared to meet it. The regiment is ordered to return at once to its duty. All members of the regiment, whether officers or privates, who do not forthwith, on this order being read to them, return to duty will be required to lay down their arms and will be placed in arrest, and, refusing to do so, they

9

will be fired upon. Of those who obey the order and return to their duty the mutinous ringleaders will alone be punished.

The regiment will be deprived of its colors, which will not be returned until its members have shown by their conduct in camp that they have learned the first duty of soldiers-obedience - and have proved on the field of battle that they are not wanting in courage. A copy of this order, with the names of the officers and men implicated, will be sent to the governor of New York, to be filed among the State archives.

(Signed)   GEO. B. McCLELLAN
             Maj.-Gen. Commanding.

The execution of this order was entrusted to Col. A. Porter, who took with him a battalion, a squadron, and a battery of regulars. They were drawn up in front of the mutineers, who promptly submitted. The ringleaders were placed in irons and the rest marched over to the Virginia side. In the course of a couple of months I was able to return their colors to this regiment as a reward for good conduct in camp and in several skirmishes. The regiment afterwards accompanied Sherman's expedition to Carolina and did good service. I think the trouble arose rather from poor officers than from the men.

As an additional means of preserving discipline, and to guard the camps from the presence of spies, the following order was issued:

General Order No. 4.

HEADQUARTERS DIVISION OF THE POTOMAC,
WASHINGTON, Aug. 16, 1861.

All passes, safe-conducts, and permits heretofore given to enter or go beyond the lines of the United States army on the Virginia side of the Potomac are to be deemed revoked, and all such passes will emanate only from the War Department, the headquarters of the United States army or of this division, or from the provost-marshal at Washington. Similar passes will be required to cross the river by bridge or boat into Virginia. A strict military surveillance will be exercised within the lines of the army on the northern side of the Potomac, and upon all the avenues of every kind, by land and water, leading to and from the city of Washington, as well over persons holding passes as all others. Passes will not be required at or within the lines of the army north of the Potomac, but disloyal or suspected persons will be liable to arrest and detention until discharged by competent authority; and contraband articles will be seized.

Officers and soldiers of the army will obtain passes as heretofore ordered. All complaints of improper seizures or searches made, or purporting to be made, under military authority will be received by the proper brigade commanders or provost-marshals, who will at once investigate the same, and in each instance make report to these headquarters.

By command of Maj.-Gen. McClellan.

(Signed)   S. WILLIAMS,

Asst. Adjt.-Gen.

In describing the steps taken toward the creation of the Army of the Potomac it will be well to begin with the Memorandum of Aug. 2, 1861, submitted to the President at his request. In my Report the date is erroneously given as of the 4th. This paper was necessarily prepared in great haste, as my time was fully occupied both by day and night with the incessant labors incident to my assumption of the command and the dangerous condition of affairs.

MEMORANDUM.

The object of the present war differs from those in which nations are usually engaged, mainly in this: that the purpose of ordinary war is to conquer a peace and make a treaty on advantageous terms; in this contest it has become necessary to crush a population sufficiently numerous, intelligent, and warlike to constitute a nation. We have not only to defeat their armed and organized forces in the field, but to display such an overwhelming strength as will convince all our antagonists, especially those of the governing, aristocratic class, of the utter impossibility of resistance. Our late reverses make this course imperative. Had we been successful in the recent battle (Mansssas) it is possible that we might have been spared the labor and expense of a great effort; now me have no alternative. Their success will enable the political leaders of the rebels to convince the mass of their people that we are inferior to them in force and courage, and to command ail their resources. The contest began with a class, now it is with a people; our military success can alone restore the former issue.

By thoroughly defeating their armies, taking their strong places, and pursuing a rigidly protective policy as to private property and unarmed persons, and a lenient course as to private soldiers, we may well hope for a permanent restoration of a peaceful Union. But in the first instance the authority of the government must be supported by overwhelming physical force.

Our foreign relations and financial credit also imperatively demand that the military action of the government should be prompt and irresistible.

The rebels have chosen Virginia as their battle-field, and it seems proper for us to make the first great struggle there. But while thus directing our main efforts, it is necessary to diminish the resistance there offered us by movements on other points both by land and water.

Without entering at present into details, I would advise that a strong movement be made on the Mississippi, and that the rebels be driven out of Missouri.

As soon as it becomes perfectly clear that Kentucky is cordially united with us, I would advise a movement through that State into Eastern Tennessee for the purpose of assisting the Union men of that region and of seizing the railroads leading from Memphis to the East.

The possession of those roads by us, in connection with the movement on the Mississippi, would go far towards determining the evacuation of Virginia by the rebels. In the meantime all the passes into Western Virginia from the East should be securely guarded, but I would advise no movement from that quarter towards Richmond, unless the political condition of Kentucky renders it impossible or inexpedient for us to make the movement upon Eastern Tennessee through that State. Every effort should, however, be made to organize, equip, and arm as many troops as possible in Western Virginia, in order to render the Ohio and Indiana regiments available for other operations.

At as early a day as practicable it would be well to protect and reopen the Baltimore and Ohio Railroad. Baltimore and Fort Monroe should be occupied by garrisons sufficient to retain them in our possession.

The importance of Harper's Ferry and the line of the Potomac in the direction of Leesburg will be very materially diminished so soon as our force in this vicinity becomes organized, strong, and efficient, because no capable general will cross the river north of this city when we have a strong army here ready to cut off his retreat.

To revert to the West, it is probable that no very large additions to the troops now in Missouri will be necessary to secure that State.

I presume that the force required for the movement down the Mississippi will be determined by its commander and the President. If Kentucky assumes the right position not more than 20,000 will be needed, together with those that can be raised in that State and Eastern Tennessee to secure the latter region and its railroads, as well as ultimately to occupy Nashville.

The Western Virginia troops, with not more than five to ten thousand from Ohio and Indiana, should, under proper management, suffice for its protection.

When we have reorganized our main army here 10,000 men ought to be enough to protect the Baltimore and Ohio Railroad and the Potomac; 5,000 will garrison Baltimore, 3,000 Fort Monroe, and not more than 20,000 will be necessary at the utmost for the defence of Washington.

For the main army of operations I urge the following composition:

250	regiments of infantry, say, ...	225,000 men.
100	field-batteries, 600 guns, ...	15,000 "
28	regiments of cavalry, ...	25,500 "
5	regiments engineer troops, ...	7,500 "
	Total, ...	273,000 "

The force must be supplied with the necessary engineer and pontoon trains, and with transportation for everything save tents. Its general line of operations should be so directed that water-transportation can be availed of from point to point by means of the ocean and the rivers emptying into it. An essential feature of the plan of operations will be the employment of a strong naval force to protect the movement of a fleet of transports intended to convey a considerable body of troops from point to point of the enemy's sea-coast, thus either creating diversions and rendering it necessary for them to detach largely from their main body in order to protect such of their cities as may be threatened, or else landing and forming establishments on their coast at any favorable places that opportunity might offer. This naval force should also co-operate with the main army in its efforts to seize the important seaboard towns of the rebels.

It cannot be ignored that the construction of railroads has introduced a new and very important element into war, by the great facilities thus given for concentrating at particular positions large masses of troops from remote sections, and by creating new strategic points and lines of operations.

It is intended to overcome this difficulty by the partial operations suggested, and such other as the particular case may require. We must endeavor to seize places on the railways in the rear of the enemy's points of concentration, and me must threaten their seaboard cities, in order that each State may be forced, by the necessity of its own defence, to diminish its contingent to the Confederate army.

The proposed movement down the Mississippi will produce important results in this connection. That advance and the progress of the main army at the East will materially assist each other by diminishing the resistance to be encountered by each.

The tendency of the Mississippi movement upon all questions connected with cotton is too well understood by the President and cabinet to need any illustration from me.

There is another independent movement that has often been

suggested and which has always recommended itself to my judgment. I refer to a movement from Kansas and Nebraska through the Indian Territory upon Red river and Western Texas for the purpose of protecting, and developing the latent Union and free-State sentiment well known to predominate in Western Texas, and which, like a similar sentiment in Western Virginia, will, if protected, ultimately organize that section into a free State. How far it will be possible to support this movement by an advance through New Mexico from California is a matter which I have not sufficiently examined to be able to express a decided opinion. If at all practicable, it is eminently desirable, as bringing into play the resources and warlike qualities of the Pacific States, as well as identifying them with our cause and connecting the bond of union between them and the general government.

If it is not departing too far from my province, I will venture to suggest the policy of an ultimate alliance and cordial understanding with Mexico; their sympathies and interests are with us, their antipathies exclusively against our enemies and their institutions. I think it would not be difficult to obtain from the Mexican government the right to use, at least during the present contest, the road from Guaymas to New Mexico; this concession would very materially reduce the obstacles of the column moving from the Pacific. A similar permission to use their territory for the passage of troops between the Panuco and the Rio Grande would enable us to throw a column of troops by a good road from Tampico, or some of the small harbors north of it, upon and across the Rio Grande, without risk and scarcely firing a shot.

To what extent, if any, it would be desirable to take into service and employ Mexican soldiers is a question entirely political, on which I do not venture to offer an opinion.

The force I have recommended is large; the expense is great. It is possible that a smaller force might accomplish the object in view, but I understand it to be the purpose of this great nation to re-establish the power of its government and restore peace to its citizens in the shortest possible time.

The question to be decided is simply this: Shall we crush the rebellion at one blow, terminate the war in one campaign, or shall we leave it as a legacy for our descendants?

When the extent of the possible line of operations is considered, the force asked for for the main army under my command cannot be regarded as unduly large; every mile we advance carries us further from our base of operations and renders detachments necessary to cover our communications, while the enemy will be constantly concentrating as he falls back. I propose, with the force which I have requested, not only to drive the enemy out of Virginia and occupy Richmond, but to occupy Charleston, Savannah, Montgomery, Pensacola,

Mobile, and New Orleans; in other words to move into the heart of the enemy's country and crush the rebellion in its very heart.

By seizing and repairing the railroads as we advance the difficulties of transportation will be materially diminished. It is perhaps unnecessary to state that, in addition to the forces named in this memorandum, strong reserves should be formed, ready to supply any losses that may occur.

In conclusion, I would submit that the exigencies of the treasury may be lessened by making only partial payments to our troops when in the enemy's country, and by giving the obligations of the United States for such supplies as may there be obtained.

GEO. B. McCLELLAN,
Maj.-Gen.

In the light of the experience of the twenty-two years which have elapsed since this Memorandum was so hastily prepared, and after full consideration of all the events of the long and bloody war which followed it, I still hold to the soundness of the views it expressed. Had the measures recommended been carried into effect the war would have been closed in less than one-half the time and with infinite saving of blood and treasure. So far as I know, it was the first general plan of operations proposed upon a scale adequate to the case. It recognized the importance of railways as a new element in strategy; it emphasized the vital importance of the railway system leading from Memphis to the East; it marked out the advantages to be derived from coast expeditions; it stated the part to be played upon the Mississippi; it foreshadowed the marches upon Atlanta and the sea-coast; it called for a force which the future proved to be fully within our means, and which would have crushed the rebellion in one or two campaigns.

In this connection I would refer to the letters written by me to Gen. Scott from Columbus in April and May of 1861.

The following was received Sept. 7 and answered Sept. 8:

" GENERAL : It is evident that we are on the eve of a great battle-one that may decide the fate of the country. Its success must depend on you and the means that may be placed at your disposal. Impressed with this belief, and anxious to aid you with all the power of my department, I will be glad if you will inform me how I can do so. Very truly yours,

"7th Sept., 1861.   SIMON CAMERON.

"MAJ.-GEN. McCLELLAN."

HEADQUARTERS, ARMY OF THE POTOMAC,
WASHINGTON, Sept. 8, 1861.

Hon. Simon Cameron, Secretary of War:

SIR: Your note of to-day is received. I concur in your views as to the exigency of the present occasion. I appreciate and cordially thank you for your offers of support, and will avail myself of them to the fullest extent demanded by the interests of the country. The force of all arms within the immediate vicinity of Washington is nearly 85,000 men. The effective portion of this force is more than sufficient to resist with certain success any attacks on our works upon the other side of the river. By calling in the commands of Gens. Banks and Stone it will probably be sufficient to defend the city of Washington from whatever direction it may be assailed. It is well understood that, although the ultimate design of the enemy is to possess himself of the city of Washington, his first efforts will be directed towards Baltimore, with the intention of cutting our line of communication and supplies, as well as to arouse an insurrection in Maryland. To accomplish this he will no doubt show a certain portion of his force in front of our positions on the other side of the Potomac, in order to engage our attention there and induce us to leave a large portion of our force for the defence of those positions. He will probably also make demonstrations in the vicinity of Acquia Creek, Mathias Point, and the Occoquan, in order still further to induce us to disseminate our forces. His main and real movement will doubtless be to cross the Potomac between Washington and Point of Rocks, probably not far from Seneca Mills, and most likely at more points than one. His hope will be so to engage our attention by the diversions already named as to enable him to move with a large force direct and unopposed on Baltimore. I see no reason to doubt the possibility of his attempting this with a column of at least 100,000 effective troops. If he has only 130,000 under arms, he can make all the diversions I have mentioned with his raw and badly organized troops, leaving 100,000 effective men for his real movement. As I am now situated I can by no possibility bring to bear against this column more than 70,000, and probably not over 60,000, effective troops.

In regard to the composition of our active army, it must be borne in mind that the very important arms of cavalry and artillery had been almost entirely neglected until I assumed command of this army, and that consequently the troops of these arms, although greatly increased in numbers, are comparatively raw and inexperienced, most of the cavalry not being yet armed or equipped. In making the foregoing estimate of numbers I have reduced the enemy's force below what is regarded by the War Department and other official circles as its real strength, and have taken the reverse course as to our own. Our situation, then, is simply this: if the commander-in-chief of the enemy follows the simplest dictates of the military art we must meet him with greatly inferior forces. To render success possible the divisions of our army must be more ably led and commanded than those of the enemy. The fate of the nation and the success of the cause in which we are engaged must be mainly decided by the issue of the next battle to be fought by the army now under my command. I therefore feel that the interests of the nation demand that the ablest soldiers in the service should be on duty with the Army of the Potomac, and that, contenting ourselves with remaining on the defensive for the present at all other points, this army should at once be reinforced by all the effective troops that the East and West and North can furnish. In view of these facts I respectfully urge that all the available troops in Ohio, Indiana, Michigan, Wisconsin, and at least ten thousand Illinois troops (there being fifteen thousand there unarmed), and all those of the Eastern and Northern States, be at once directed to report to me for duty. I beg leave to repeat the opinion I have heretofore expressed: that the Army of the Potomac should number not less than three hundred thousand men in order to insure complete success and an early termination of the war. I also request that Brig.-Gens. Don Carlos Buell and J. F. Reynolds-both appointed upon my recommendation and for the purpose of serving with me-be at once assigned to duty with this army; also that no general officer appointed upon my recommendation shall be assigned away from this army without my consent; that I shall have full control of all officers and troops within this department; and that no one, whatever his rank may be, shall give any orders respecting my command without my being first consulted. Otherwise it is evident that I cannot be responsible for the success of our arms.

Very respectfully, your obedient servant,

GEO. B. MCCLELLAN,
Maj.-Gen. U. S. A.

CHAPTER VII.

Organization of the army - What an army is - Infantry, artillery, cavalry, engineer Troops - The staff and its departments - Details of the creation of the Army of the Potomac.

THE organized armies of modern times consist of two well-defined parts: the fighting force, or "line," and "the staff," which directs, inspects, and supplies the former. The line is made up of infantry, artillery, cavalry, and engineer troops.

As INFANTRY can move wherever a man can set his foot, can fight on all kinds of ground, gives the most destructive fire of all the arms, and is the least expensive and most easily instructed, it constitutes the great bulk of all large armies, and is decidedly the most important.

With equally good generals, that army which has the best infantry is pretty sure to win, for no reasonable superiority in the other arms of service can compensate for marked inferiority in the infantry.

The essential qualities of good infantry are: the ability to make long marches, with their full equipment, without straggling; accuracy of fire; confidence in their ability to use the bayonet - for this will prevent their breaking upon the very near approach of a hostile line - coolness, intelligence, determination, and mutual confidence in attacking or receiving an attack; the ability to reform rapidly after a successful attack, and to rally when driven back, either after a repulsed attack or when obliged to retreat from a defensive position; the power of enduring fatigue, exposure, and hunger.

Next in importance is the ARTILLERY, whose work it is to open the way for, and cover the movements of, the other arms by destroying the enemy's defences at long range, silencing his artillery, and demoralizing his infantry; or, at short ranges, to crush them by a rapid fire of case and shrapnel. It is also a part of its duty to cover the retreat of beaten infantry, and to assist in the operations of detached bodies of cavalry.

There is thus heavy artillery, whose business it is to handle siege-guns and those used in permanent defences, and field-artillery, who accompany an army in the field. Field-artillery is made up of three kinds - viz., the mounted batteries, whose cannoneers usually march on foot, but during rapid movements ride upon the carriages and caissons, and which serve with the regiment, division, and army corps; the horse-batteries, whose cannoneers are provided with saddle-horses, and which are especially intended for service with the cavalry; and the batteries of position, consisting of the heaviest field-guns, intended especially for action against the enemy's material defences.

The field-guns, at the period of which I write, were generally provided in the ratio of at least two and a half guns to each thousand infantry, and three or four guns to each thousand cavalry, the exact proportion depending somewhat on the nature of the field of war and the quality of the troops. With raw troops a somewhat larger proportion is necessary than with veterans.

The technical information necessary for the artillery officers and men renders it difficult to improvise thoroughly efficient artillery.

The CAVALRY is an indispensable part of every army. It not only takes part, as occasion demands, in general battles, but, with a due proportion of horse-artillery, is capable of independent action, even at long distances from the main body of the army. Upon it devolves to a great extent the duty of observing and discovering the positions, movements, and strength of the enemy, as well as masking those of its own army. It is capable of making extensive inroads into the enemy's country, and is usually employed to threaten and attack his communications, supply-trains, etc. The modern improvements in firearms have certainly affected the employment of cavalry on the field of battle against infantry and artillery, but have not lessened the importance of its other duties. Nor is it probable that the number of these arms will in the future be materially diminished. The employment of breech-loading small arms has added very much to the strength of cavalry, and it is certain that in future wars large bodies of cavalry will be employed as mounted infantry. That is, they will use their horses to move rapidly to the point of action, and fight on foot. Under ordinary circumstances it has usually been re-

garded as advisable to furnish cavalry to the extent of one-sixth
to one-eighth of the infantry force.

To render cavalry efficient it is necessary that the officers and
men should be of a superior order of intelligence, and that they
should fully understand the care of their horses, which should
be active and enduring. Officers and men should be excellent
horsemen, skilful in the use of their weapons, and thoroughly
instructed in the work of reconnoissance. It is really much
more difficult to form reliable cavalry at short notice than to
instruct artillery and infantry.

It is the duty of ENGINEER TROOPS to conduct siege operations; to supervise and construct temporary defences and the
works for their attack; to construct, repair, and destroy bridges
of all kinds, fords, roads, etc. The repair and destruction of railways should also be under their direction. The performance of
these duties requires a superior order of men, skilled in some
mechanical trade, and needs careful instruction. In ordinary
cases the engineer troops should number about one-fortieth of
the infantry.

To direct the movements and supply the wants of the com-
batants is the business of THE STAFF which in modern armies is
a complicated and extensive organization. It includes:

1st. The Adjutant-General's Department.

This department issues, in the name of the commander, all
orders relating to the discipline, instruction, movements, and
supply of the troops, whether directly to the fighting organization or to the other staff corps; and through it pass to the
commander all written reports on such subjects. It has direct
charge of all returns relating to the force and condition of the
command, and to it all such returns are directed.

2d. The Inspector-General's Department.

To this department is committed the work of ascertaining by
rigid and careful inspection the exact condition of the various
elements comprising the command; verifying returns and reports; ascertaining the exact state of discipline, instruction,
morale, and general efficiency; the number present for duty;
the observation of sanitary rules; the quantity and condition
of transportation, arms, ammunition, equipment, clothing, food,

medical stores, etc. As so much depends upon the faithful and intelligent discharge of these very important duties, it is absolutely necessary that the officers of this corps should be thoroughly instructed soldiers of long experience, the highest integrity, the greatest intelligence, with great industry and method in the performance of these duties.

3d. Aides-de-Camp.

These constitute the personal staff of the general to whom they are attached. They carry his orders and watch over their execution. They should be thorough soldiers, of great activity, intelligence, and devotion.

4th. The Engineers.

In our service the conduct of reconnoissances falls chiefly upon them; the selection of positions, especially for defence; the conduct of all siege operations, and the construction of all field-works, temporary defences, bridges, roads, etc.

On the part of these officers the most thorough knowledge of the highest branches of the profession, accurate judgment of ground, and great intelligence are required. They cannot successfully be improvised.

5th. The Quartermaster's Department.

Upon this department devolves the purchase of horses for all military purposes, the providing of all means of transportation, ambulances, litters, the supply of clothing, camp equipage, cooking utensils, the forage for animals, the conduct of supply-trains, and, in fact, providing all material that is not especially assigned to some other department.

6th. The Commissary Department.

It is the duty of this department to provide and have ready for issue at the proper time and place all articles of food required by the army. The task of this department is often very difficult and of the greatest possible importance, for upon its proper performance the success of the army depends.

7th. The Medical Department.

Upon this department devolves the general charge of the

sanitary condition of troops in camps and on the march; the care of the sick and wounded; the use of ambulances and litters; the providing of medical stores and comforts; the installation and direction of all military hospitals.

8th. The Ordnance Corps.

This corps furnishes all arms, ammunition, artillery carriages and harness, cavalry equipment, and makes in the field all repairs which cannot be executed by the armorers and mechanics of the regiments of the line.

9th. The Pay Department.

Its duty is to pay the troops at proper times.

10th. The Department of Military Justice.

It has the supervision of all proceedings by court-martial, military commission, etc.

11th. The Signal Corps.

It is in charge of the various systems of communicating intelligence by signals, telegraph, balloons, etc.

In large armies, with numerous staff corps charged with such manifold and important duties, it has been found necessary to establish the position of CHIEF OF STAFF, who might supervise and co-ordinate the various branches, and thus relieve the commanding general from a multiplicity of detail. This office, found in all European armies, had never been established in our own. I soon found it necessary for the Army of the Potomac. The officer holding such a confidential relation with his commander should always be a man possessing the latter's entire confidence. I therefore selected for this place Col. R. B. Marcy, inspector-general of the army, whose rank was also superior to that of all the staff officers on duty with the Army of the Potomac.

My orders for the movements and fighting of the troops were generally issued through the chief of staff.

One of my earliest measures was the formation of permanent BRIGADES of infantry. The new levies of infantry, upon their arrival in Washington, were formed into provisional brigades and placed in camps in the suburbs on the Maryland side of the river, for equipment, instruction, and discipline. As soon as regiments were in fit condition for transfer to the forces across the Potomac they were assigned to the brigades serving there. Brig.-Gen. F. J. Porter was at first assigned to the charge of the provisional brigades. Brig.-Gen. A. E. Burnside was the next officer assigned this duty, from which, however, he was soon relieved by Brig.-Gen. Casey, who continued in charge of the newly arriving regiments until the Army of the Potomac departed for the Peninsula, in March, 1862. The newly arriving artillery troops reported to Brig.-Gen. William F. Barry, the chief of artillery, and the cavalry to Brig.-Gen. George Stoneman, the chief of cavalry, and were also retained on the Maryland side until their equipment and armament were essentially completed and some rudimentary instruction obtained.

A few days after reaching Washington Gen. Scott asked me what I intended to do in the way of organization. I replied that I wished the force under my command to be organized as and denominated an army instead of a geographical division; that I should first form brigades, then divisions, and, when in the field, army corps. My reason for postponing the formation of the latter was that with untried general officers it would be too dangerous an experiment to appoint any to such high and important commands without first proving them in actual campaign and in battle.

He objected to all I proposed, save the brigade formation, saying that under our system and regulations it would be impossible to administer the affairs of an "army," and that the retention of the system and nomenclature of geographical divisions and departments was an absolute necessity; he also objected to the formation of divisions as unnecessary, for the reason that in Mexico he had only brigades.

I called to his attention the fact that, all the world over, fighting forces were organized as armies; that I had done so in West Virginia ; and that his force in Mexico was a very small affair in comparison with that soon to be collected in front of Washington. He did not change his views. So I quietly went to work in my own way. The result was that on the 20th of Aug. the order constituting the ARMY OF THE POTOMAC was issued; and in addition to the two departments originally under my command, the troops in the Shenandoah, Maryland, and Delaware were also included in the Army of the Potomac, the old departments being broken up and merged in the newly created army. Thus I had command of all the troops on the line of the Potomac and as far to the rear as Baltimore and Fort Delaware.

During the first days of August I procured the passage of an act authorizing the appointment of additional aides-de-camp to general officers; these might be taken from civil life or from the army, and were to be of no higher grade than that of colonel. I used this lam not only to furnish the requisite number of actual aides-de-camp, but also to give additional pay and rank in the regular army to officers whose duty made such a step necessary. For instance, I gave to Maj. Barry, chief of artillery, and to Maj. H. J. Hunt, commanding the reserve artillery, the grade of colonel; to Van Vliet and Clarke the same. When the organization of the brigades was well established, and the troops somewhat disciplined and instructed, divisions of three brigades each were gradually formed.

I intended to compose each division of three infantry brigades of four regiments each, four batteries, and one regiment of cavalry, which would have given a nominal strength of 12,000 infantry, 1,000 cavalry, and 24 guns, or an effective of about 10,000 infantry, 700 cavalry, and 24 guns. It was determined to collect whatever regular infantry could be obtained to form the nucleus of a reserve. The measures taken for recruiting these regiments were so insufficient and the results so meagre that as late as the 30th of April, 1862, there were only 4,600 men in the 71 companies, regular infantry, on duty with the Army of the Potomac. These, together with the 5th and 10th N. Y. Volunteers, finally formed part of the 5th corps as a division under Brig.-Gen. Sykes, 3d U. S. Infantry.

The creation of an adequate ARTILLERY establishment for an army of so large proportions was a formidable undertaking; and had it not been that the country possessed in the regular service a body of accomplished and energetic artillery officers, the task would have been almost hopeless.

The charge of organizing this most important arm was confided to Maj. (afterwards Brig.-Gen.) William F. Barry, chief of artillery, whose industry and zeal achieved the best results The following principles were adopted as the basis of organization:

1. That the proportion of artillery should be in the proportion of at least two and one-half pieces to 1,000 men, to be expanded, if possible, to three pieces to 1,000 men.

2. That the proportion of rifled guns should be restricted to the system of the United States ordnance department; and of Parrott and the "smooth-bores" (with the exception of a few howitzers for special service) to be exclusively the 12-pounder gun, of the model of 1857, variously called the "gun-howitzer," the "light twelve-pounder," or the "Napoleon."

3. That each field-battery should, if practicable, be composed of six guns, and none to be less than four guns, and in all cases the guns of each battery should be of uniform calibre.

4. That the field-batteries were to be assigned to divisions, and not to brigades, and in the proportion of four to each division, of which one was to be a battery of regulars, the remainder of volunteers, the captain of the regular battery to be the commandant of artillery of the division. In the event of several divisions constituting an army corps, at least one-half of the divisional artillery was to constitute the reserve artillery of the corps.

5. That the artillery reserve of the whole army should consist of 100 guns, and should comprise, besides a sufficient number of light "mounted batteries," all the guns of position, and, until the cavalry were massed, all the horse-artillery.

6. That the amount of ammunition to accompany field-batteries was not to be less than 400 rounds per gun.

7. A siege-train of 50 pieces. This was subsequently expanded, for special service at the siege of Yorktown, to very nearly 100 pieces, and comprised the unusual calibres and enormously heavy weight of metal of two 200-pounders, five 100-pounders, and ten 13-inch sea-coast mortars.

As has been before stated, the whole of the field-artillery of the Army of the Potomac, July 28, 1861, was comprised of 9 imperfectly equipped batteries of 30 guns, 650 men, and 400 horses. In March, 1862, when the whole army took the field, it consisted of 92 batteries of 520 guns, 12,500 men, and 11,000 horses, fully equipped and in readiness for active field service; of the whole force 30 batteries were regulars and 62 batteries volunteers. During the short period of seven months all of this immense amount of material was manufactured or purchased, and issued by the ordnance department and placed in the hands of the artil-

10

lery troops after their arrival in Washington. About one-fourth of all the volunteer batteries brought with them from their respective States a few guns and carriages, but they were nearly all of such peculiar calibre as to lack uniformity with the more modern and more serviceable ordnance with which the other batteries were armed, and they therefore had to be withdrawn and replaced by more suitable material. While about one-sixth came supplied with horses and harness, less than one-tenth were apparently fully equipped for service when they reported; and every one even of these required the supply of many deficiencies of material, and very extensive instruction in the theory and practice of their special arm.

The operations on the Peninsula by the Army of the Potomac commenced with a full field-artillery force of 49 batteries of 274 guns. To this must be added the field-artillery of Franklin's division of McDowell's corps, which joined a few days before the capture of Yorktown, but was not disembarked from its transports for service until after the battle of Williamsburg, and the field-artillery of McCall's division of McDowell's corps (4 batteries, 22 guns), which joined in June, a few days before the battle of Mechanicsville (June 26, 1862), making a grand total of field-artillery at any time with the army of the peninsula of 57 batteries of 318 guns.

When there were so many newly organized volunteer field-batteries, many of whom received their first and only instruction in the entrenched camps covering Washington during the three or four inclement months of the winter of 1861-62, there was, of course, much to be improved. Many of the volunteer batteries, however, evinced such zeal and intelligence, and availed themselves so industriously of the instructions of the regular officers, their commanders, and the example of the regular batteries, their associates, that they made rapid progress and attained a degree of proficiency highly creditable.

Gen. Barry served as chief of artillery with the Army of the Potomac until the close of the Peninsular campaign; he performed his duties with great zeal, patience, and ability. The artillery reserve was originally commanded by Col. H. J. Hunt, who gave up the command only when appointed chief of artillery in place of Gen. Barry. The artillery reserve was then commanded by Col. George W. Getty, an excellent officer.

Gen. Hunt retained the position of chief of artillery until the close of the war. I regarded him as the best living commander of field-artillery. He was a man of the utmost coolness in danger, thoroughly versed in his profession, an admirable organizer, a soldier of a very high order. As I write this (July, 1882) Hunt is likely to be retired as a colonel - a man whose services in any other army would have been rewarded by titles, high rank, and ample pension. He is one of the most marked instances within my knowledge of the highest merit and services passed over unacknowledged and unrewarded.

Hunt's merits consisted not only in organizing his command to the best advantage, but in using it on the field of battle with the utmost skill and power. The services of this most distinguished officer in reorganizing and refitting the batteries prior to and after Antietam, his gallant and skilful conduct on that field, at Malvern, and in fact during the whole Peninsular campaign, merit the highest encomiums in my power to bestow.

The country in which operations were to be conducted was so obstructed by forests as to present few favorable opportunities for the employment of long-range artillery. I therefore desired to compose the artillery two-thirds of the Napoleon gun - a light 12-pounder-and one-third of rifled guns. But the facilities for the construction of army guns were so limited, while those for iron guns were comparatively so great, that in the first armament it was impossible to observe these proportions, so that when the army took the field less than one-third were Napoleon guns, and it was only during the reorganization for the Antietam campaign that it was possible to approach the proportions originally fixed upon. Our experience in battle proved the correctness of these views. The shrapnel and canister from the Napoleons was always most destructive to the hostile infantry at close range. We seldom saw the enemy at long range in large bodies.

On the 20th of Aug., 1861, I had 80 guns. The returns of Oct. 15 show that there were 27 batteries of divisional artillery. Of these 17 were regulars and 10 volunteers, and, as several had only 4 guns, there were not more than 140 guns in all, and of these the rifled guns composed a good deal more than two-thirds.

Including Banks and Dix, there were 33 batteries, of which 19 regulars and 14 volunteers, making not over 168 guns in all, to a force of 143,647 present on Oct. 15, and out of these guns must be provided those required for the garrisons of Washington and Baltimore, and the defences of the line of the Potomac.

In regard to the 140 guns, they belonged to a force of about 120,000 men, and out of the number would come those required for the garrison of Washington and the defences of the Potomac.

It was not until after this date that artillery material and equipment flowed in with any considerable rapidity, so that, even disregarding the question of instruction, it was not until after the season for active operations had passed that a sufficient number of equipped batteries were disposable to finish the requisite reserve and divisional artillery. The mass of the artillery was not in condition to move until the following April, and even then several of the volunteer batteries were deficient in instruction.

The difficulties attending the organization of a suitable CAVALRY FORCE were very great, and it cannot be said that they were ever satisfactorily overcome.

The newly arriving regiments reported to Gen. Stoneman, the chief of cavalry, and, as with the artillery and infantry, were, as far as circumstances would permit, retained for a certain time on the north bank of the Potomac. There was at first a total lack of equipment for the cavalry, and it was very long before this difficulty was removed. So great was the lack of cavalry arms that I was obliged to organize Rush's regiment (6th Penn.) as lancers, it being impossible to provide other weapons.

Many of the officers and men were quite ignorant of the management of horses, and could not even ride well. Moreover, there was too little appreciation on the part of the government of the necessity and advantages of that arm of service. With the cavalry, as with the other arms of service, every effort was made to weed out inefficient and incompetent officers by means of courts-martial and boards of examination.

As rapidly as possible every cavalry soldier was armed with a sabre and revolver, and at least two squadrons in each regiment with the carbine.*

It was intended to assign at least one regiment of cavalry to each infantry division so long as the division organization was the highest, and, when army corps should be formed, to attach

*On the margin of his manuscript Gen. McClellan has written, "Here note experience in West Virginia."

a strong brigade of cavalry to its headquarters, leaving with the division only enough for the necessary duty; also to form a general cavalry reserve. On the 15th of Oct. there were serving with the Army of the Potomac, including General Banks's command, one regiment and two companies of regular cavalry, and eleven regiments of volunteer cavalry. When the army took the field there were on its rolls four regiments and two companies of regular cavalry, eighteen regiments and five companies of volunteer cavalry, besides four regiments yet unprovided with horses.

Of these there went to the Peninsula the regulars and four regiments and five companies of volunteers, making eight regiments and seven companies; and there remained with Gen. Banks and at Washington twenty-one regiments, besides the four unprovided with horses. Circumstances beyond my control rendered it impossible for me to carry out my views as to the cavalry, and it was entirely against my wishes and judgment that I was left in the field with so small a force of this arm. Of the field force one regiment of regulars were necessarily employed on provost duty, and two companies of regulars and one of volunteers at headquarters, leaving only three regiments of regulars and four regiments and four companies of volunteers, certainly not over four thousand men at most, to do all the cavalry and mounted orderly duty for the army of eleven divisions - a force so ridiculously insufficient, less than one-fourth of what it should have been, as to render it strange that the enemy contented themselves with riding around our lines only once on the Peninsula.

As there were but three weak companies of ENGINEER TROOPS available, I did the best in my power to supply the deficiency by detailing as volunteer engineer troops the 15th and 50th N. Y. Volunteers, which comprised an unusual number of sailors and mechanics in their ranks. These were formed into an engineer brigade, and placed under the command, first of Col. E. S. Alexander, U. S. Corps of Engineers, and finally under that of Col. D. V. Woodbury, of the same corps. These regiments rendered good service as engineer troops, and at length became admirable pontoniers, as their services under fire more than once testified.

We had no bridge trains whatever, for the remains of the India-rubber pontoon trains constructed for the Mexican war were of no possible use. Therefore I gave directions for the construction of trains on the model of the latest French bridge.

Capt. Duane, commanding the battalion of regular engineer troops, was charged with this duty, as well as the preparation of the other engineer trains. Capt. Duane performed this duty, as he did all that was assigned to him, in the most satisfactory manner. He on all occasions proved himself an admirable soldier and most excellent engineer.

As already stated, I found it necessary to create the office of CHIEF OF STAFF, and selected Col. R. B. Marcy for the place.

One of the greatest defects in our military system is the lack of a thoroughly instructed STAFF CORPS, from which should be furnished chief of staff of armies, army corps and divisions, adjutant-general, and aides-de-camp and recruiting officers. Perhaps the greatest difficulty that I encountered in the work of creating the Army of the Potomac arose from the scarcity of thoroughly instructed staff officers, and I must frankly state that every day I myself felt the disadvantages under which I personally labored from the want of that thorough theoretical and practical education received by the officers of the German general staff.

Under our system of government, and in the circumstances which surround us, it is perhaps impossible, certainly very improbable, that this most vital point can ever be satisfactorily covered. Political and personal considerations now control so completely the appointment to places in the various branches of the staff that the chances are against their being filled by the most competent men. In fact, judging from the experience of the past few years, it is almost a certainty that incompetent men will be selected for these most important positions. Inefficiency and waste must surely result from our present system, even in times of peace; but in the event of our being thrown into collision with a well-organized European army, the results will be disastrous. Should we ever have a Secretary of War who understands his business and possesses the full support of the administration and of Congress, the work may be done. But even if commenced in the right way, the danger would be that in the course of time presidents would appoint to the corps political or personal favorites, unless the law so hedged in the corps that appointments could only be made upon the recommendation of the chief of the corps and a board of its officers after a proper test of their qualifications. I am very sure that every general officer who served in the late war will agree with me that his

labors would have been immensely lightened and the efficiency
of his command very much increased if he could have had a
competent staff at his disposal.

In comparison with the difficulties of the work that fell to
my lot the task of a general officer of the German army seems
mere child's play. None of the officers at my disposal had ever
seen large armies or the operations of war on a grand scale.
Those who came from West Point had a good education, so far
as the theory of war was concerned. That was a great advantage, but by no means all that was required. Those whom I
selected were usually comparatively young men, and, under my
direction, soon grasped the situation; but one very great obstacle arose from the incompetence of many of the permanent heads
of departments, who found it very difficult to get out of the ruts
in which they had been accustomed to move. To pass suddenly
from the small scale on which the affairs of an army of 10,000
men in time of peace had been conducted, to that required for
an army of half a million in the midst of a desperate war, was no
easy task.

I have dwelt somewhat at length on this subject in order to
accentuate the difficulties of the position, and to show that the
time consumed in organizing the Army of the Potomac was far
from unreasonable.

During the war many improvements were made in the details
of the administration of the staff corps; but unfortunately no
change whatever has been made in the organization of the various departments, and their only gain by the war is in the
personal experience of the officers who served therein. When
they have passed away there will be little or no trace left of the
experience of the war.

Our own experience, and that of other armies, agree in
determining the necessity for an efficient and able staff. To
obtain this our staff establishment should be based on correct
principles, and extended to be adequate to the necessities of the
service, and should include a system of staff and line education.

Moreover, the officers of the staff should be required occasionally to serve with troops as officers of the line, and when the
turn of each comes for promotion it should be determined not
only whether he is fit for promotion, but whether he is fit to
remain in the corps.

[The following memorandum by Gen. McClellan was found lying among his manuscript at this point:]

General Staff Corps. - Abolish the adjutant-general and inspector-general's departments, and merge their functions in those of the general staff corps. Make the chief of the general staff a major-general, and let the corps be composed somewhat as follows, viz :

1. The major-general.

2. {
One brigadier-general, to perform the present duties of adjutant-general.
One brigadier-general, to perform the present duties of inspector-general, etc.
}

8. {
One colonel, assistant to the chief.
One colonel, in charge of the department of military inspection (maps), statistics, etc.
Two colonels, inspection duty.
Two colonels, assistant adjutant-generals.
Two colonels, aides-de-camp.
}

11. {
One lieutenant-colonel, assistant to chief.
One lieutenant-colonel, military statistics.
Two lieutenant-colonels, inspection duty.
Four lieutenant-colonels, assistant adjutant-generals.
Three lieutenant-colonels, aides-de-camp.
}

19. {
Four majors, inspection duty.
Eight majors, assistant adjutant-generals.
One major, statistics.
Six majors, aides-de-camp.
}

30. {
Four captains, assistant to chief.
Four captains, military statistics.
Eight captains, military inspection.
Eight captains, assistant adjutant-generals.
Six aides, general duty.
}

The affairs of the ADJUTANT-GENERAL'S DEPARTMENT, while I commanded the Army of the Potomac, were conducted by Brig.-Gen. S. Williams, assisted by Lieut.-Col. James A. Hardie, aide-de-camp. Their management of the department during the organization of the army in the fall and winter of 1861 and during its subsequent operations in the field was excellent.

They were, during the entire period, assisted by Capt. Richard B. Irwin, aide-de-camp, and during the organization of the army by the following-named officers: Capts. Joseph Kirkland, Arthur McClellan, M. T. McMahon, William P. Mason, and William F. Biddle, aides-de-camp.

My PERSONAL STAFF, when we embarked for the Peninsula, consisted of Col. Thomas M. Key, additional aide-de-camp; Col. E. H. Wright, additional aide-de-camp and major 6th U. S. Cavalry; Col. T. T. Gantt, additional aide-de-camp; Col. J. J. Astor, Jr., volunteer aide-de-camp; Lieut.-Col. A. V. Colburn, additional aide-de-camp and captain adjutant-general's department; Lieut.-Col. N. B. Sweitzer, additional aide-de-camp and captain 1st U. S. Cavalry; Lieut.-Col. Edward McK. Hudson, additional aide-de-camp and captain 14th U. S. Infantry; Lieut.-Col. Paul Von Radowitz, additional aide-de-camp; Maj. H. Von Hammerstein, additional aide-de-camp; Maj. W. W. Russell, U. S. Marine Corps; Maj. F. Le Compte, of the Swiss army, volunteer aide-de-camp; Capts. Joseph Kirkland, Arthur McClellan, L. P. d'Orleans, R. d'Orleans, M. T. McMahon, William P. Mason, Jr., William F. Biddle, and E. A. Raymond, additional aides-de-camp.

Of these officers, Col. Gantt performed the duty of judge-advocate-general; Maj. Le Compte was a spectator; Capts. Kirkland, McClellan, McMahon, Mason, and Biddle were on duty in the adjutant-general's office; Capt. Raymond with the chief of staff; Capt. McMahon was assigned to the personal staff of Brig.-Gen. Franklin, and Capts. Kirkland and Mason to that of Brig.-Gen. F. J. Porter, during the siege of Yorktown. They remained subsequently with those general officers. Maj. Le Compte left the army during the siege of Yorktown; Cols. Gantt and Astor, Maj. Russell, Capts. L. P. d'Orleans, R. d'Orleans, and Raymond at the close of the Peninsular campaign.

To this number I am tempted to add the Prince de Joinville, who constantly accompanied me through the trying campaign of the Peninsula, and frequently rendered important services.

Soon after we reached the Chickahominy I took as one of my aides Lieut. G. A. Custer, 5th U. S. Cavalry, as a reward for an act of daring gallantry. This was the beginning of the distinguished career of one of the most gallant soldiers of the army and an admirable cavalry leader. Before the termination of the Peninsular campaign Capts. W. S. Abert and Charles R. Lowell, of the 6th U. S. Cavalry, joined my staff as aides-de-camp, and remained with me until I was relieved from the command of the Army of the Potomac. All of these officers served me with great gallantry and devotion; they were ever ready to execute any service, no matter how dangerous, difficult, or fatiguing.

The duties of the INSPECTOR-GENERAL'S DEPARTMENT, during the whole period of my command of the Army of the Potomac, were performed by Col. D. B. Sackett, assisted by Majs. N. H. Davis and Roger Jones, of the inspector-general's corps. The value of the services rendered by these officers merits all the commendation that I can bestow. No duty was ever slighted by them and no labor too great for them. Their reports were always full, satisfactory, and thoroughly to be relied upon. Nor did they confine themselves to the mere routine work of their duties, but on the field of battle rendered most valuable services as aides-de-camp under heavy fire.

When I assumed command of the Division of the Potomac I found Maj. J. G. Barnard, U. S. Engineers - subsequently brigadier-general of volunteers-occupying the position of chief-engineer of McDowell's command. I continued him in the same office, and at once gave the necessary instructions for the completion of the defences of the capital and for the entire reorganization of the department.

Under his direction the entire system of defences was carried into execution. This was completed before the army departed for Fort Monroe, and is a sufficient evidence of the skill of the engineers and the diligent labor of the troops.

The ENGINEER DEPARTMENT presented the following organization when the army moved for the Peninsula:

Brig.-Gen. J. G. Barnard, chief-engineer; First Lieut. H. C. Abbott, topographical engineers, aide-de-camp. Brigade volunteer engineers, Brig.-Gen. Woodbury commanding: 15th N. Y. Volunteers, Col. McLeod Murphy; 50th N. Y. Volunteers, Col. C. B. Stewart. Battalion, three companies U. S. Engineers, Capt. J. C. Duane commanding; companies respectively commanded by First Lieuts. C. B. Reese, C. E. Cross, and O. E. Babcock, U. S. Engineers. The chief-engineer was ably assisted in his duties by Lieut-Col. B. S. Alexander and First Lieuts. C. R. Comstock, M. D. McAlester, and Merrill, U. S. Engineers. Capt. C. S. Stuart and Second Lieut. F. U. Farquhar, U. S. Engineers, joined after the army arrived at Fort Monroe.

The necessary bridge equipage for the operations of a large army had been collected, consisting of bateaux, with the anchors and flooring material (French model), trestles, and engineers' tools, with the necessary wagons for their transportation.

The small number of officers of this corps available rendered it impracticable to detail engineers permanently at the headquarters of corps and divisions. The companies of regular engineers never had their proper number of officers, and it was necessary, as a rule, to follow the principle of detailing engineer officers temporarily whenever their services were required. Constantly during the construction of the defences of Washington, and during the subsequent campaigns, we suffered great inconvenience and delay from the want of a sufficient number of officers of engineers.

To the corps of TOPOGRAPHICAL ENGINEERS was entrusted the collection of topographical information and the preparation of campaign maps. Until a short time previous to the departure of the army for Fort Monroe, Lieut-Col. John W. Macomb was in charge of this department and prepared a large amount of valuable material. He was succeeded by Brig.-Gen. A. A. Humphreys, who retained the position throughout the Peninsular campaign. These officers were assisted by Lieuts. O. G. Wagner, N. Bowen, John M. Wilson, and James H. Wilson, topographical engineers. This number, although the greatest available, was so small that much of the duty of the department devolved upon parties furnished by Prof. Bache, Superintendent of the Coast Survey, and other gentlemen from civil life.

Owing to the entire absence of reliable topographical maps, the labors of this corps were difficult and arduous in the extreme. Notwithstanding the energy and ability displayed by Gen. Humphreys, Lieut.-Col. Macomb, and their subordinates, who frequently obtained the necessary information under fire, the movements of the army were sometimes unavoidably delayed by the difficulty of obtaining knowledge of the country in advance. The result of their labors was the preparation of an excellent series of maps, which were invaluable to the armies afterwards traversing the same ground.

During the campaign it was impossible to draw a distinct line of demarcation between the duties of the two corps of engineers, so that the labors of reconnoissances of roads, of lines of entrenchments, of fields for battle, and of the position of the enemy, as well as the construction of siege and defensive works, were habitually performed by details from either corps, as the convenience of the service demanded.

I desire to express my high appreciation of the skill, gallantry, and devotion displayed by the officers of both corps of engineers under the most trying circumstances.

During the Maryland campaign I united the two corps under Capt. J. C. Duane, U. S. Engineers, and found great advantages from the arrangement. The permanent union of the two corps, since made, was no doubt a wise measure.

Surgeon Charles S. Tripler and Surgeon Jonathan Letterman in turn performed the duties of medical director of the Army of the Potomac, the former from Aug. 12, 1861, until July 1, 1862, and the latter after that date. The difficulties to be overcome in organizing and making effective the MEDICAL DEPARTMENT were very great, arising principally from the inexperience of the regimental medical officers, many of whom were physicians taken suddenly from civil life, who, according to Surgeon Tripler, "had to be instructed in their duties from the very alphabet," and from the ignorance of the line officers as to their relations with the medical officers, which gave rise to confusion and conflict of authority. Boards of examination were instituted, by which many ignorant officers were removed; and by the successive exertions of Surgeons Tripler and Letterman the medical corps was brought to a very high degree of efficiency. With regard to the sanitary condition of the army while on the Potomac, Dr. Tripler said that the records showed a constantly increasing immunity from disease. "In Oct. and Nov., 1861, with an army averaging 130,000 men, we had 7,932 cases of fever of all sorts; of these about 1,000 were reported as cases of typhoid fever. I know that errors of diagnosis were frequently committed, and therefore this must be considered as the limit of typhoid cases. If any army in the world can show such a record as this I do not know when or where it was assembled." From Sept., 1861, to Feb., 1862, while the army was increasing, the number of sick decreased from 7 per cent. to 6.18 per cent. Of these the men sick in the regimental and general hospitals were less than one-half; the remainder were slight cases, under treatment in quarters. "During this time, so far as rumor was concerned, the army was being decimated by disease every month." Of the sanitary condition of the army during the Peninsular campaign, up to its arrival at Harrison's Landing, Dr. Tripler says: "During this campaign the army was favored with excellent health. No epidemic disease appeared. Those scourges of modern armies, dysentery, typhus, cholera, were almost unknown. We had some typhoid fever and more malarial fevers, but even these never prevailed to such an extent as to create any alarm. The sick-reports were sometimes larger than we cared to have them; but the great majority of the cases reported were such as did not threaten life or permanent disability. I regret that I have not before me the retained copies of the monthly reports, so that I might give accurate statistics. I have endeavored to recover them, but have been unsuccessful. My recollection is that the whole sick-report never exceeded eight per cent. of the force, and this including all sorts of cases, the trivial as well as the severe. The Army of the Potomac must be conceded to have been the most healthy army in the service of the United States."

The service, labors, and privations of the troops during the Seven Days' Battles had, of course, a great effect on the health of the army after it reached Harrison's Landing, increasing the number of sick to about twenty per cent. of the whole force.

The nature of the military operations had also unavoidably placed the medical department in a very unsatisfactory condition. Supplies had been almost entirely exhausted or necessarily abandoned; hospital tents abandoned or destroyed; and the medical officers were deficient in numbers and broken down by fatigue.

All the remarkable energy and ability of Surgeon Letterman were required to restore the efficiency of his department; but before we left Harrison's Landing he had succeeded in fitting it out thoroughly with the supplies it required, and the health of the army was vastly improved by the sanitary measures which were enforced at his suggestion.

The great haste with which the army was removed from the Peninsula made it necessary to leave at Fort Monroe, to be forwarded afterwards, nearly all the baggage and transportation, including medical stores and ambulances, all the vessels being required to transport the troops themselves and their ammunition. When the Army of the Potomac returned to Washington after Gen. Pope's campaign, and the medical department came once more under Surgeon Letterman's control, he found it in a deplorable condition. The officers were worn out by the labors they had performed, and the few supplies that had been brought from the Peninsula had been exhausted or abandoned, so that the work of reorganization and resupplying had to be again performed, and this while the army was moving rapidly and almost in the face of the enemy. That it was successfully accomplished is shown by the care and attention which the wounded received after the battles of South Mountain and Antietam.

Among the improvements introduced into his department by Surgeon Letterman, the principal are the organization of an ambulance corps, the system of field-hospitals, and the method of supplying by brigades, all of which were instituted during the Maryland campaign, and found so efficient that they remained unchanged until the close of the war, and were to a great extent adopted by the other armies of the United States.

On assuming command of the troops in and around Washington I appointed Capt. S. Van Vliet, assistant quartermaster (afterwards brigadier-general), CHIEF QUARTERMASTER to my command, and gave him the necessary instructions for organizing his department and collecting the supplies requisite for the large army then called for.

The disaster at Manassas had but recently occurred, and the army was quite destitute of quartermaster's stores. Gen. Van Vliet, with great energy and zeal, set himself about the task of furnishing the supplies immediately necessary, and preparing to obtain the still larger amounts which would be required by the new troops which were moving in large numbers towards the capital. The principal depot for supplies in the city of Washington was under charge of Col. D. H. Rucker, assistant quartermaster, who ably performed his duties. Lieut.-Col. R. Ingalls, assistant quartermaster, was placed in charge of the department on the south side of the Potomac. I directed a large depot for transportation to be established at Perryville, on the left bank of the Susquehanna, a point equally accessible by rail and water. Capt. C. G. Sawtelle, assistant quartermaster, was detailed to organize the camp, and performed his duties to my entire satisfaction. Capt. J. J. Dana, assistant quartermaster, had immediate charge of the transportation in and about Washington, as well as of the large number of horses purchased for the use of the artillery and cavalry. The principal difficulties which Gen. Van Vliet had to encounter arose from the inexperience of the majority of the officers of his department in the new regiments and brigades.

The necessity of attending personally to minor details rendered his duties arduous and harassing in the extreme. All obstacles, however, were surmounted by the untiring industry of the chief quartermaster and his immediate subordinates, and when the army was prepared to move the organization of the department was found to be admirable.

When it was determined to move the army to the Peninsula the duties of providing water transportation were devolved by the Secretary of War upon his assistant, the Hon. John Tucker. The vessels were ordered to Alexandria, and Lieut-Col. Ingalls was placed in immediate charge of the embarkation of the troops, transportation, and material of every description. Operations of this nature, on so extensive a scale, had no parallel in the history of our country.

The arrangements of Lieut-Col. Ingalls were perfected with remarkable skill and energy, and the army and its material were embarked and transported to Fortress Monroe in a very short space of time and entirely without loss.

During the operations on the Peninsula, until the arrival of troops at Harrison's Landing, Gen. Van Vliet retained the position of chief quartermaster, and maintained the thorough organization and efficiency of his department. The principal depots of supplies were under the immediate charge of Lieut.-Cols. Ingalls and Sawtelle.

On the 10th of July, 1862, Gen. Van Vliet having requested to be relieved from duty with the Army of the Potomac, I appointed Lieut.-Col. Ingalls chief quartermaster, and he continued to discharge the duties of that office during the remainder of the Peninsular and the Maryland campaigns in a manner which fully sustained the high reputation he had previously acquired.

The immense amount of labor accomplished often under the most difficult circumstances, the admirable system under which the duties of the department were performed, and the entire success which attended the efforts to supply so large an army, reflect the highest credit upon the officers upon whom these onerous duties devolved.

On the 1st of Aug., 1861, Col. H. F. Clarke, commissary of subsistence, joined my staff, and at once entered upon his duties as CHIEF COMMISSARY of the Army of the Potomac. In order to realize the responsibilities pertaining, to this office, as well as to form a proper estimate of the vast amount of labor which must necessarily devolve upon its occupant, it is only necessary to consider the unprepared state of the country to engage in a war of such magnitude, and the lack of practical knowledge on the part of the officers with reference to supplying and subsisting a large, and at that time unorganized, army. Yet, notwithstanding the existence of these great obstacles, the manner in which the duties of the commissary department were discharged was such as to merit and call forth the commendation of the entire army.

During the stay of the Army of the Potomac in the vicinity of Washington, prior to the Peninsular campaign, its subsistence was drawn chiefly from the depots which had been established by the commissary department at Washington, Alexandria, Forts Corcoran and Runyon. In the important task of designating and establishing depots of supplies Col. Clarke was ably seconded by his assistants, Col. Amos Beckwith, C. S., U. S. A.; Lieut.-Col. George Bell, C. S., U. S. A.; Lieut-Col. A. P. Porter, C. S., U. S. A.; Capt. Thomas Wilson, C. S., U. S. A.; Capt. Brownell Granger, C. S., U. S. Volunteers; Capt. W. H. Bell, C. S., U. S. A.; Capt. J. H. Woodward, C. S., U. S. Volunteers; and Capt. W. R. Murphy, C. S., U. S. Volunteers.

A full knowledge of the highly creditable manner in which each and all of the above-mentioned officers discharged their duties was given in the detailed report of Col. Clarke. The remarks and suggestions contained in his report afford valuable rules for the future guidance of the subsistence department in supplying armies in the field. The success of the subsistence department of the Army of the Potomac was in a great measure attributable to the fact that the subsistence department at Washington made ample provision for sending supplies to the Peninsula, and that it always exercised the most intelligent foresight. It moreover gave its advice and countenance to the officers charged with its duties and reputation in the field, and those officers, I am happy to say, worked with it and together in per-

fect harmony for the public good. During the entire period that
I was in command of the Army of the Potomac there was no
instance within my knowledge where the troops were without their rations from any fault of the officers of this department.

I am quite within bounds when I say that no one could have
performed his vitally important duties more satisfactorily than
did Gen. Clarke. He never caused me the slightest anxiety, and
I soon learned that he would always carry out my wishes, were
it in the power of man to do so. A stranger to all petty intrigue,
a brave and able officer, a modest man intent only upon the
proper performance of his duty, he has never received the reward
and appreciation his invaluable services merited. He held the
post of chief-commissary of the Army of the Potomac until the
close of the war, discharging his duty to the entire satisfaction
of its successive commanders. Yet he was overslaughed in favor
of an inferior who had never held a post of great importance, and
whose only claim was the personal friendship of the President
who committed the injustice. As I write (Sept., 1882) he has
just received the grade of colonel in the ordinary course of promotion, and will ere long be retired with that grade, his only
reward having been the empty brevet of major-general.

The ORDANCE DEPARTMENT, that very important branch
of the service, was placed under the charge of Capt. C. P. Kingsbury, ordnance corps, colonel and aide-de-camp. Great difficulty existed in the proper organization of the department for the
want of a sufficient number of suitable officers to perform the
duties at the various headquarters and depots of supply. But
far greater obstacles had to be surmounted, from the fact that
the supply of small arms was totally inadequate to the demands
of a large army, and a vast proportion of those furnished were
of such inferior quality as to be unsatisfactory to the troops and
condemned by their officers. The supply of artillery was more
abundant, but of great variety. Rifled ordnance was just coming
into use for the first time in this country, and the description
of gun and kind of projectile which would prove most effective,
and should, therefore, be adopted, was a mere matter of theory.
To obviate these difficulties large quantities of small arms of foreign manufacture were contracted for; private enterprise in the
construction of arms and ammunition was encouraged; and by

11

the time the army was ordered to move to the Peninsula the amount of ordnance and ordnance stores was ample.

But it was not until the close of 1861, too late for active operations, that the infantry were reasonably well provided with serviceable arms; and even after that the calibres were too numerous, and many arms really unfit for service. The artillery material, likewise, arrived in insufficient quantities until the early part of 1862. I mention these facts, not as in any way reflecting upon the ordnance department, which accomplished all that was in the power of men to do, but as showing the actual difficulties of the situation. Much also had been done to bring the quality, both of arms and ammunition, up to the proper standard. Boards of officers were in session continually during the autumn and winter of 1861 to test the relative merits of new arms and projectiles.

The reports of these boards, confirmed by subsequent experience in the field, have done much to establish the respective claims of different inventors and manufacturers. During the campaigns of the Peninsula and Maryland the officers connected with the department were zealous and energetic, and kept the troops well supplied, notwithstanding the perplexing and arduous nature of their duties. One great source of perplexity was the fact that it had been necessary to issue arms of all varieties and calibres, giving an equal diversity in the kinds of ammunition required. Untiring watchfulness was therefore incumbent upon the officers in charge to prevent confusion and improper distribution of cartridges. Col. Kingsbury discharged the duties of his office with great efficiency until July, 1862, when his health required that he should be relieved. First Lieut. Thomas G. Baylor, ordnance corps, succeeded him, and performed his duty during the remainder of the Peninsular and Maryland campaigns with marked ability and success.

Immediately after I was placed in command of the Division of the Potomac I appointed Col. Andrew Porter, 16th Regiment Infantry, PROVOST-MARSHALL of Washington. All the available regular infantry, a battery, and a squadron of cavalry were placed under his command, and by his energetic action he soon corrected the serious evils which existed, and restored order in the city.

When the army was about to take the field Gen. Porter was appointed provost-marshal-general of the Army of the Potomac, and held that most important position until the end of the Peninsular campaign, when sickness, contracted in the untiring discharge of his duties, compelled him to ask to be relieved from the position he had so ably and energetically filled.

The provost marshal-general's department had the charge of a class of duties which had not before, in our service, been defined and grouped under the management of a special department. The following subjects indicate the sphere of this department:

Suppression of marauding and depredations, and of all brawls and disturbances, preservation of good order, and suppression of disturbances beyond the limits of the camps.

Prevention of straggling on the march.

Suppression of gambling-houses, drinking-houses or bar-rooms, and brothels.

Regulation of hotels, taverns, markets, and places of public amusement.

Searches, seizures, and arrests. Execution of sentences of general courts-martial involving imprisonment or capital punishment. Enforcement of orders prohibiting the sale of intoxicating liquors whether by tradesmen or sutlers, and of orders respecting passes.

Deserters from the enemy.

Prisoners of war taken from the enemy.

Countersigning safeguards.

Passes to citizens within the lines and for purposes of trade.

Complaints of citizens as to the conduct of the soldiers.

Gen. Porter was assisted by the following named officers: Maj. W. H. Wood, 17th U. S. Infantry; Capt. James McMillan, acting assistant adjutant-general, 2d U. S. Infantry; Capt. W. T. Gentry, 17th U. S. Infantry; Capt. J. W. Forsyth, 18th U. S. Infantry; Lieut. J. W. Jones, 12th U. S. Infantry; Lieut. C. F. Trowbridge, 16th U. S. Infantry; and Lieut. C. D. Mehaffey, 1st U. S. Infantry.

The provost-guard was composed of the 2d U. S. Cavalry, Maj. Pleasonton, and a battalion of the 8th and 17th U. S. Infantry, Maj. Willard. After Gen. Porter was relieved Maj. Wood was in charge of this department until after the battle of Antietam, when Brig.-Gen. Patrick was appointed provost-marshal-general.

When the army took the field, for the purpose of securing

order and regularity in the camp of headquarters, and facilitating its movements the office of COMMANDANT OF GENERAL HEAD- QUARTERS was created, and assigned to Maj. G. O. Haller, 7th U. S. Infantry.   Six companies of infantry were placed under his orders for guard and police duty.

From Aug., 1861, the position of JUDGE-ADVOCATE was held by Col. Thomas T. Gantt, aide-de-camp, until compelled by ill- health to retire, at Harrison's Landing, in Aug., 1862. His reviews of the decisions of courts-martial during this period were of great utility in correcting the practice in military courts, diffusing true notions of discipline and subordination, and set- ting before the army a high standard of soldierly honor.   Upon the retirement of Col. Gantt the duties of judge-advocate were ably performed by Col. Thomas M. Key, aide-de-camp.

The method of conveying intelligence and orders invented and introduced into the service by Maj. Albert J. Myer, signal officer U. S. Army, was first practically tested in large operations during the organization of the Army of the Potomac.   Under the direction of Maj. Myer a SIGNAL CORPS was formed by detailing officers and men from the different regiments of volun- teers, and instructing them in the use of the flags by day and torches by night.

The chief signal officer was indefatigable in his exertions to render his corps effective, and it soon became available for service in every division of the army.   In addition to the flags and torches Maj. Myer introduced a portable insulated telegraph- wire, which could be readily laid from point to point, and which could be used under the same general system.   In front of Wash- ington and on the lower Potomac, at any point within our lines not reached by the military telegraph, the great usefulness of this system of signals was made manifest.   But it was not until after the arrival of the army upon the Peninsula, and during the siege and battles of that and the Maryland campaigns, that the great benefits to be derived from it on the field and under fire were fully appreciated.

There was scarcely any action or skirmish in which the signal corps did not render important services.   Often under heavy fire of artillery, and not unfrequently while exposed to musketry, the officers and men of this corps gave information of the move- ments of the enemy, and transmitted directions for the evolutions of our own troops. The weak point in the signal corps as then constituted was that its officers were not trained soldiers, and therefore their judgment could not always be relied upon.

The TELEGRAPHIC OPERATIONS of the Army of the Potomac were superintended by Maj. Thomas J. Eckert, and under the immediate direction of Mr. Caldwell, who was, with a corps of operators, attached to my headquarters during the entire campaigns upon the Peninsula and in Maryland.

The services of this corps were arduous and efficient. Under the admirable arrangements of Maj. Eckert they were constantly provided with all the material for constructing new lines, which were rapidly established whenever the army changed position, and it was not unfrequently the case that the operatives worked under fire from the enemy's guns; yet they invariably performed all the duties required of them with great alacrity and cheerfulness, and it was seldom that I was without the means of direct telegraphic communication with the War Department and with the corps commanders.

From the organization of the Army of the Potomac up to Nov. 1, 1862, including the Peninsular and Maryland campaigns, upwards of twelve hundred (1,200) miles of military telegraph line had been constructed in connection with the operations of the army, and the number of operatives and builders employed was about two hundred (200).

To Prof. Lowe, the intelligent and enterprising aeronaut, who had the management of the BALLOONS, I was indebted for information obtained during his ascensions. In a clear atmosphere, and in a country not too much obstructed by woods, balloon reconnoissances made by intelligent officers are often of considerable value.

I more than once took occasion to recommend the members of my staff, both general and personal, for promotion and reward. I once more record their names in the history of the Army of the Potomac as gallant soldiers, to whom their country owes a debt of gratitude, still unpaid, for the courage, ability, and untiring zeal they displayed during the eventful campaigns in which they bore so prominent a part.

CHAPTER VIII.

Various generals - Scott, Halleck, Hunter, Sumner, Franklin, Porter,
Sedgwick, and others - Blenker's brigade - Scenes in his command -
The Hungarian Klapka - The French prisoners - Events in Maryland.

It is a great mistake to suppose that I had the cordial support
of Gen. Scott; the contrary was too much the case.   While in the
West I failed to obtain from him the assistance needed, and when
I reached Washington I soon found that he was unnecessarily
jealous of me.   On the very day of my arrival he interfered, as
already described, to prevent my keeping an appointment with
the President, because he was not invited to be present. He
directed me to ride around the streets of Washington and see
that the drunken men were picked up, which I naturally did not
do! He opposed the bill for increasing the number of aides, on
the ground that he had only two in Mexico.   Soon after assuming the command I saw the absolute necessity of giving a name
to the mass of troops under my command, in order to inspire
them with *esprit de corps;* I therefore proposed to call my
command "The Army of the Potomac." Gen. Scott objected
most strenuously to this step, saying,   that the routine of service
could be carried on only under the "department" system, etc.
I persisted, and finally had my own way in the matter in spite
of the opposition. I also told him that I proposed to organize
brigades at first; then, when that organization was fairly established, to form divisions; and finally, after everything was well
arranged and I could be sure of selecting the right commanders-
probably after having been in the field for a time - to form army
corps.

The general objected to this also, insisting that no higher
organization than that of brigade was necessary; that it was
impossible to organize the troops under my command as an
army! Consequently, when the proper time arrived, I organized
the divisions without further discussion of the matter.

Gen. Scott was no longer himself when the war broke out.
The weight of years and great bodily suffering pressed heavily
upon him, and really rendered him incapable of performing the

duties of his station. For some time before he retired he was simply an obstacle, and a very serious one, in the way of active work. He did not wish me to succeed him as general-in-chief, but desired that place for Halleck, and long withheld his retirement that Halleck might arrive East and fall heir to his place.

Speaking of Halleck, a day or two before he arrived in Washington Stanton came to caution me against trusting Halleck, who was, he said, probably the greatest scoundrel and most barefaced villain in America; he said that he was totally destitute of principle, and that in the Almaden Quicksilver case he had convicted Halleck of perjury in open court. When Halleck arrived he came to caution me against Stanton, repeating almost precisely the same words that Stanton had employed.

I made a note of this fact soon after its occurrence, and lately, Dec. 4, 1883, I saw for the first time, on page 833, vol. viii., series 1, "Official Records of the War of the Rebellion," Gen. E. A. Hitchcock's letter to Halleck, in which the former transmits a message from Stanton on the very same subject. This is eminently characteristic of Stanton, who would say one thing to a man's face and just the reverse behind his back."

Of all men whom I have encountered in high position Halleck was the most hopelessly stupid. It was more difficult to get an idea through his head than can be conceived by any one who never made the attempt. I do not think he ever had a correct military idea from beginning to end.

I left Gen. Hunter in nominal command of his brigade, because he bore an excellent reputation in the old army and had been wounded; I have never met him personally. He did not assume command of the brigade, for as soon as he recovered from his wound the President appointed him major-general of volunteers, that he might go to Illinois and, in the words of Mr. Lincoln, "be a sort of father to them out there."

*The following is an extract from the letter of Gen E. A. Hitchcock to Gen. H. W. Halleck, dated Washington, March 22, 1862:

"I then bid the secretary (Stanton) good-evening and left him, but he called me back, and added that if I was going to write to you he wished to convey his respects, and his future confidence in your ability and patriotism, explaining that he had been employed against you in the mine case in California. and that his partner had some difficulty or controversy with you of a somewhat personal nature, but that, for his part, he had taken no interest in it, and had never had any other than the highest respect for you, and he hoped you would not imagine that he ever had."

Heintzelman also received a brigade; he, too, had been wounded at Bull Run, and bore a good reputation in the old army. He was a very brave man and an excellent officer.

W. T. Sherman was almost immediately taken from me to accompany Robert Anderson to Kentucky. I had a high opinion of him and parted from him with regret.

Philip Kearny received a brigade; but, though he stood high as a remarkably daring man and good cavalry captain in the Mexican war, I had not sufficient confidence in his brains to give him one of the first divisions. I have since sometimes thought that I would have done well had I given him command of the cavalry.

Sumner was in California when I assumed command; he returned not long before we took the field, and at once received a division. He was an old and tried officer; perfectly honest; as brave as a man could be; conscientious and laborious. In many respects he was a model soldier. He was a man for whom I had a very high regard, and for his memory I have the greatest respect. He was a very valuable man, and his soldierly example was of the highest value in a new army. A nation is fortunate that possesses many such soldiers as was Edwin V. Sumner.

Franklin was one of the best officers I had; very powerful. He was a man not only of excellent judgment, but of a remarkably high order of intellectual ability. He was often badly treated, and seldom received the credit he deserved. His moral character was of the highest, and he was in all respects an admirable corps commander; more than that, he would have commanded an army well. The only reason why I did not send him to relieve Sherman, instead of Buell, was that I could not spare such a man from the Army of the Potomac.

Blenker I found, and retained, in command of the Germans. Born in Bavaria, it was said he had served in Greece as a non-commissioned officer, and subsequently as a colonel or general officer in the revolutionary army of Baden in 1848. He was in many respects an excellent soldier; had his command in excellent drill, was very fond of display, but did not, or could not, always restrain his men from plundering. Had he remained with me I think that he and his division would have done good service, and that they would have been kept under good discipline. It would be difficult to find a more soldierly-looking set of men than he had under his command. Of his subordinate officers the best was Gen. Stahl, a Hungarian, who had served with distinction under Georgei. His real name, I believe, was Count Serbiani.

Richardson was in command of a regiment of Michigan volunteers when I went to Washington; I at once gave him a brigade. He was an officer of the old army, "bull-headed," brave, a good disciplinarian. He received his mortal wound at Antietam.

To Stone I gave a detached brigade on the upper Potomac-ground with which he was familiar. He was a most charming and amiable gentleman; honest, brave, a good soldier, though occasionally carried away by his chivalrous ideas. He was very unfortunate, and was as far as possible from meriting the sad fate and cruel treatment he met with.

I found Couch in command of a regiment, and soon gave him a brigade. He was an honest, faithful, and laborious man, a brave, modest, and valuable officer.

Fitz-John Porter was on duty with Gen. Patterson, as adjutant-general, when I assumed command. As soon as possible I had him made a brigadier-general and gave him the command vacated by W. T. Sherman. Take him for all in all, he was probably the best general officer I had under me. He had excellent ability, sound judgment, and all the instincts of a soldier. He was perfectly familiar with all the details of his duty, an excellent organizer and administrative officer, and one of the most conscientious and laborious men I ever knew. I never found it necessary to do more than give him general instructions, for it was certain that all details would be cared for and nothing neglected. I always knew that an order given to him would be fully carried out, were it morally and physically possible. He was one of the coolest and most imperturbable men in danger whom I ever knew - like all his race. I shall have occasion to revert to him hereafter, and will now only add that he was treated with the grossest injustice - chiefly, I fear, because of his devotion to me.

Buell was in California, a lieutenant-colonel of the adjutant-general's department. I had him appointed a brigadier-general and sent for him at once. He possessed a very high reputation in the Mexican war, and I found him to be an admirable soldier in every regard.

To Sedgwick I gave a brigade. Not knowing him well, I did not at first appreciate his high qualities, but soon discovered them and gave him the first vacant division - that originally commanded by Stone. He was one of the best and most modest soldiers we had. Possessing excellent ability and judgment, the highest bravery, great skill in handling troops, wonderful powers in instructing and disciplining men, as well as in gaining their love, respect, and confidence, he was withal so modest and unobtrusive that it was necessary to be thrown closely in contact with him to appreciate him. He was thoroughly unselfish, honest, and true as steel. His conduct during the battle of Chancellorsville in storming the works on Marie's Heights, and afterwards holding his own against tremendous odds, was a remarkable and most brilliant feat of arms.

Hancock received a brigade early in the formation of the Army of the Potomac. He was a man of the most chivalrous courage, and of a superb presence, especially in action; he had a wonderfully quick and correct eye for ground and for handling troops; his judgment was good, and it would be difficult to find a better corps commander.

John Reynolds was commandant of the corps of cadets when the war broke out. He gained a high reputation in the Mexican war as an officer of light artillery, and was among the first whom I caused to be appointed brigadier-general. He was a splendid soldier and performed admirably every duty assigned to him. Constantly improving, he was, when killed at Gettysburg, with Meade and Sedgwick, the best officer then with the Army of the Potomac. He was remarkably brave and intelligent, an honest, true gentleman.

Meade was also one of my early appointments as brigadier-general. He was an excellent officer; cool, brave, and intelligent; he always did his duty admirably, and was an honest man. As commander of an army he was far superior to either Hooker or Burnside.

Col. Ingalls was, in my experience, unequalled as a chief-quartermaster in the field.

When first assigned to the command in the Department of the Ohio, I applied for Fitz-John Porter as my adjutant-general, but he was already on duty with Gen. Patterson in the same capacity, and could not be spared. Soon afterwards I obtained Maj. Seth Williams, who had been on duty with Gen. Harney at St. Louis, and he remained with me as my adjutant-general until I was finally relieved from the command of the Army of the Potomac. I never met with a better bureau officer, perhaps never with so good a one. He thoroughly understood the working of the adjutant-general's department, was indefatigable in the performance of his duty, made many and valuable suggestions as to the system of returns, reports, etc., and thus exerted a great influence in bringing about the excellent organization of the Army of the Potomac. He was thoroughly honest and a gentleman; he was, if anything, too modest, for he would probably have accomplished more had he possessed more self-reliance. He won universal regard by his kind and considerate manner towards those with whom he was officially brought in contact. I never knew a more laborious and conscientious man.

During the autumn of 1861, as already stated, I spent my days chiefly in the saddle, rarely returning from my rides until late at night. Most of the night and the morning hours were given up to office-work.

Of course I rode everywhere and saw everything. Not an entrenchment was commenced unless I had at least approved its site; many I located myself. Not a camp that I did not examine, not a picket-line that I did not visit and cross, so that almost every man in the army saw me at one time or another, and most of them became familiar with my face. And there was no part of the ground near Washington that I did not know thoroughly.

The most entertaining of my duties were those which sometimes led me to Blenker's camp, whither Franklin was always glad to accompany me to see the "circus," or "opera," as he usually called the performance. As soon as we were sighted Blenker would have the "officer's call" blown to assemble his polyglot collection, with their uniform as varied and brilliant as the colors of the rainbow. Wrapped in his scarlet-lined cloak, his group of officers ranged around him, he would receive us with the most formal and polished courtesy. Being a very handsome and soldierly-looking man himself, and there being many equally so among his surroundings, the tableau was always very effective, and presented a striking contrast to the matter-of-fact way in which things were managed in the other divisions.

In a few minutes he would shout, *"Ordinanz numero eins!"* whereupon champagne would be brought in great profusion, the bands would play, sometimes songs be sung. It was said, I know not how truly, that Blenker had been a non-commissioned officer in the German contingent serving under King Otho of Greece.

His division was very peculiar. So far as "the pride, pomp, and circumstance of glorious war" were concerned, it certainly outshone all the others. Their drill and bearing were also excellent; for all the officers, and probably all the men, had served in Europe. I have always regretted that the division was finally taken from me and sent to Fremont. The officers and men were all strongly attached to me; I could control them as no one else could, and they would have done good service had they remained in Sumner's corps. The regiments were all foreign and mostly of Germans; but the most remarkable of all was the Garibaldi regiment. Its colonel, D'Utassy, was a Hungarian, and was said to have been a rider in Franconi's Circus, and terminated his public American career in the Albany Penitentiary. His men were from all known and unknown lands, from all possible and impossible armies: Zouaves from Algiers, men of the "Foreign Legion," Zephyrs, Cossacks, Garibaldians of the deepest dye, English deserters, Sepoys, Turcos, Croats, Swiss, beer drinkers from Bavaria, stout men from North Germany, and no doubt Chinese, Esquimaux, and detachments from the army of the Grand Duchess of Gerolstein.

Such a mixture was probably never before seen under any flag, unless, perhaps, in such bands as Holk's Jagers of the Thirty Years' War or the free lances of the middle ages.

I well remember that in returning one night from beyond the picket-lines I encountered an outpost of the Garibaldians. In reply to their challenge I tried English, French, Spanish, Italian, German, Indian, a little Russian and Turkish;* all in

* It is proper to say that this is doubtless a simple statement of fact.

vain, for nothing at my disposal made the slightest impression upon them, and I inferred that they were perhaps gipsies or Esquimaux or Chinese.

Mr. Seward's policy of making ours "a people's war," as he expressed it, by drumming up officers from all parts of the world, sometimes produced strange results and brought us rare specimens of the class vulgarly known as "hard cases." Most of the officers thus obtained had left their own armies for the armies' good, although there were admirable and honorable exceptions, such as Stahl, Willich, Rosencranz, Cesnola, and some others. Few were of the slightest use to us, and I think the reason why the German regiments so seldom turned out well was that their officers were so often men without character.

Soon after Gen. Scott retired I received a letter from the Hungarian Klapka informing me that he had been approached by some of Mr. Seward's agents to get him into our army, and saying that he thought it best to come to a direct understanding with myself as to terms, etc. He said that he would require a bonus of $100,000 in cash and a salary of $25,000 per annum; that on his first arrival he would consent to serve as my chief of staff for a short time until he acquired the language, and that he would then take my place of general commanding-in-chief. He failed to state what provision he would make for me, that probably to depend upon the impression I made upon him.

I immediately took the letter to Mr. Lincoln, who was made very angry by it, and, taking possession of the letter, said that he would see that I should not be troubled in that way again.

Cluseret - afterwards Minister of War under the Commune- brought me a letter of introduction from Garibaldi, recommending him in the highest terms as a soldier, man of honor, etc. I did not like his appearance and declined his services; but without my knowledge or consent Stanton appointed him a colonel on my staff. I still declined to have anything to do with him, and he was sent to the Mountain Department, as chief of staff, I think.

On the recommendation of the Prussian minister I took upon

Gen. McClellan was able to converse freely in most of the languages named, including two dialects of North American Indian, and had sufficient practical knowledge of all of them (as well as others) to make him independent of an interpreter.   W. C. P.

my staff, as aides-de-camp, two German officers whose subsequent histories were peculiar and suggestive. One was a member of a very noble family, whose father had held high official rank in his native land, the son having been a lieutenant in the Guard Cavalry. He was one of the handsomest young fellows I have ever seen, polished to the last degree, and a splendid soldier. He remained with me during my command, and always performed difficult and dangerous duties in the best possible manner. He remained with the army on staff-duty after I was relieved.

Being in Germany when the Austro-Prussian war broke out, I determined to call upon the War Minister and advise him to recall the officer in question, as an admirable soldier whose experience in our war would be valuable; for I had been led to believe that his original separation from his own army had been caused by some trivial breach of discipline. Within a few days I learned that he had been dismissed from our service. The last I heard of this poor fellow - for one cannot help feeling sorry for the waste of such excellent gifts - was that he made his living as croupier in a gambling-den.

The other was of an old military family; his father had been a general, and I had met his brothers and cousins as officers in the Austrian army. He also was an admirable and most useful aide in difficult times. After I left the field he became lieutenant-colonel, and probably colonel, of a regiment, and did good service. At the close of the war, failing to be retained, he enlisted in a regular cavalry regiment, hoping to be examined and promoted to a commission; but his habits were against him. At last, in carrying the mail during the winter between the posts on the plains, his feet were frozen and, I think, amputated. Finally his family sent for him, and he returned home to die.

Of a different order were the French princes who formed part of my military family from Sept. 20, 1861, to the close of the Seven Days. They served as captains, declining any higher rank, though they had fully earned promotion before the close of their connection with the army. They served precisely as the other aides, taking their full share of all duty, whether agreeable or disagreeable, dangerous or the reverse. They were fine young fellows and good soldiers, and deserved high credit in every way.

Their uncle, the Prince de Joinville, who accompanied them

as a Mentor, held no official position, but our relations were always confidential and most agreeable. The Duc de Chartres had received a military education at the military school at Turin; the Comte de Paris had only received instruction in military matters from his tutors. They had their separate establishment, being accompanied by a physician and a captain of chasseurs-à-pied. The latter was an immense man, who could never, under any circumstances, be persuaded to mount a horse: he always made the march on foot.

Their little establishment was usually the jolliest in camp, and it was often a great relief to me, when burdened with care, to listen to the laughter and gayety that resounded from their tents. They managed their affairs so well that they were respected and liked by all with whom they came in contact. The Prince de Joinville sketched admirably and possessed a most keen sense of the ridiculous, so that his sketch-book was an inexhaustible source of amusement, because everything ludicrous that struck his fancy on the march was sure to find a place there. He was a man of far more than ordinary ability and of excellent judgment. His deafness was, of course, a disadvantage to him, but his admirable qualities were so marked that I became warmly attached to him, as, in fact, I did to all the three, and I have good reason to know that the feeling was mutual.

Whatever may have been the peculiarities of Louis Philippe during his later life, it is very certain that in his youth, as the Duc de Chartres, he was a brave, dashing, and excellent soldier. His sons, especially the Ducs d'Orléans, d'Aumale, Montpensier, and the Prince de Joinville, showed the same characteristics in Algiers and elsewhere; and I may be permitted to say that my personal experience with the three members of the family who served with me was such that there could be no doubt as to their courage, energy, and military spirit. The course pursued by the Prince de Joinville and the Duc de Chartres during the fatal invasion of France by the Germans was in perfect harmony with this. Both sought service, under assumed names, in the darkest and most dangerous hours of their country's trial. The duke served for some months as Capt. Robert le Fort, and under that name, his identity being known to few if any beyond his closest personal friends, gained promotion and distinction by his gallantry and intelligence.

Should the Comte de Paris ever reach the throne of France - as is more than probable - I am sure that he will prove to be a wise, honest, and firm constitutional king, and that the honor and prosperity of France will be safer in his hands and those of his soldierly family than for many years past.

Information from various sources received in Aug. and Sept., 1861, convinced the government that there was serious danger of the secession of Maryland.

The secessionists possessed about two-thirds of each branch of the State legislature, and the general government had what it regarded as good reasons for believing that a secret, extra, and illegal session of the legislature was about to be convened at Frederick on the 17th of Sept. in order to pass an ordinance of secession. It was understood that this action was to be supported by an advance of the Southern army across the Potomac - an advance which the Army of the Potomac was not yet in a condition to desire. Even an abortive attempt to carry out this design would have involved great civil confusion and military inconvenience. It was impossible to permit the secession of Maryland, intervening, as it did, between the capital and the loyal States, and commanding all our lines of supply and rein-forcement. I do not know how the government obtained the information on which they reached their conclusions. I do not know how reliable it was. I only know that at the time it seemed more than probable, and that ordinary prudence required that it should be regarded as certain. So that when I received the orders for the arrest of the most active members of the legislature, for the purpose of preventing the intended meeting and the passage of the act of secession, I gave that order a most full and hearty support as a measure of undoubted military necessity.

On the 10th of Sept. Hon. Simon Cameron, Secretary of War, instructed Gen. Banks to prevent the passage of any act of secession by the Maryland legislature, directing him to arrest all or any number of the members, if necessary, but in any event to do the work effectively.

On the same day the Secretary of War instructed Gen. Dix to arrest six conspicuous and active secessionists of Baltimore, three of whom were members of the legislature. They were to be sent to Fort Monroe, their papers seized and examined. A special agent was sent to take immediate charge of the arrests.

On the 10th of Sept. Gen. Dix sent to Secretary Seward and myself marked lists of the legislature. In his letters he strongly approved of the intended arrests, and advised that those arrested should be sent to New York harbor by a special steamer.

The total number of arrests made was about sixteen, and the result was the thorough upsetting of whatever plans the secessionists of Maryland may have entertained. It is needless to say that the arrested parties were ultimately released, and were kindly treated while imprisoned. Their arrest was a military necessity, and they had no cause of complaint. In fact, they might with justice have received much more severe treatment than they did.

On the 28th of Oct. I received from the chief of the Secret Service a report in reference to the elections to be held in Maryland, on the 6th of Nov., for governor, members of the State legislature, etc. In this report he states that he had information of a general apprehension among the Union citizens of the southern part of the State of a serious interference with their rights of suffrage by the disunion citizens of that district on the occasion of the election; that it was said that several hundred persons, who had left that part of Maryland with the avowed purpose of aiding the secessionist cause by taking up arms or otherwise, had recently returned to their homes, as was supposed, for the purpose of controlling the State election; also, that it had been reported to him that a large quantity of arms were concealed in a designated locality for use in endeavoring to control the election by the disunionists.

I laid this report immediately before the President, who caused the following endorsement (also issued separately in the form of an order) to be made upon it:

" DEPARTMENT OF STATE,
" WASHINGTON Oct. 28, 1861.
" *Maj.-Gen. George B. McClellan, etc., etc., etc.:*
"The President desires that Gen. McClellan will direct such disposition of the military force as will guard effectually against invasion of the peace and order of Maryland during the election,. and for this purpose he is authorized to suspend the habeas corpus and make arrests of traitors and their confederates in his discretion.
"(Signed) WILLIAM H. SEWARD."

To carry out these instructions the necessary orders were
12

issued to Gens. Banks, Stone, and Hooker. I give a copy of the order issued to Gen. Banks; the others were the same, *mutatis mutandis:*

HEADQUARTERS, ARMY OF THE POTOMAC,
Oct. 29, 1861.

To Maj.-Gen. N. P. Banks, Commanding Division at Muddy Branch, Md.:

GENERAL: There is an apprehension among Union citizens in many parts of Maryland of an attempt at interference with the rights of suffrage by disunion citizens on the occasion of the election to take place on the 6th of Nov. next. In order to prevent this the major-general commanding directs that you send detachments of a sufficient number of men to the different points in your vicinity where the elections are to be held, to protect the Union voters and see that no disunionists are allowed to intimidate them or in any way interfere with their rights. He also desires you to arrest and hold in confinement till after the election all disunionists who are known to have returned from Virginia recently and who show themselves at the polls, and to guard effectually against any invasion of the peace and order of the election.

For the purpose of carrying out these instructions you are authorized to suspend the *habeas corpus.* Gen. Stone has received similar instructions to these. You will please confer with him as to the particular points that each shall take control of.

I am, very respectfully, your obedient servant,

R. B. MARCY, *Chief of Staff*

CHAPTER IX

Conspiracy of the politicians - Edwin M. Stanton - Interview at the President's office - Salmon P. Chase - Relations with Mr. Lincoln - Anecdotes - President's military orders - Reduction of army.

I HAVE already stated in a general way what occurred between myself and some of the radical leaders shortly after I reached Washington. They then saw clearly that it would not be possible to make a party tool of me, and soon concluded that it was their policy to ruin me if possible.

It had been clearly stated by Congress and the general government that the sole object of the war was the preservation of the Union and the prevention of the secession of the Southern States." We fought to keep them in the Union, and the practically unanimous sentiment of the army, as well as of the mass of the people, was at that time strongly in favor of confining the war to that object. Although the Free-Soil element was strong in the North, the Abolitionists proper were weak, and a declaration of their true purposes would have seriously interfered with the progress of the war. A clear indication of the correctness of this statement lies in the fact that the executive never disowned my proclamation to the West Virginians nor the policy I pursued in reference to Kentucky.

The real object of the radical leaders was not the restoration of the Union, but the permanent ascendency of their party, and to this they were ready to sacrifice the Union, if necessary.

* A few days before the arrival of McClellan in Washington Congress had stated the purposes of the war in a resolution:

"That the present deplorable civil war has been forced upon the country by the disunionists of the Southern States, now in revolt against the constitutional government, and in arms around the capital; that in this national emergency Congress, banishing all feeling of mere passion or resentment, will recollect only its duty to its country; that this war is not waged, on our part, in any spirit of oppression, nor for any purpose of conquest or subjugation, nor purpose of overthrowing or interfering with the rights or established institutions of those States, but to defend and maintain the supremacy of the Constitution and to preserve the Union, with all the dignity, equality, and rights of the several States unimpaired; and as soon as these objects are accomplished the war ought to cease."

They committed a grave error in supposing me to be politically ambitious and in thinking that I looked forward to military success as a means of reaching the presidential chair. At the same time they knew that if I achieved marked success my influence would necessarily be very great throughout the country - an influence which I should certainly have used for the good of the whole country, and not for that of any party at the nation's expense.

They therefore determined to ruin me in any event and by any means: first by endeavoring to force me into premature movements, knowing that a failure would probably end my military career; afterwards by withholding the means necessary to achieve success.

That they were not honest is proved by the fact that, having failed to force me to advance at a time when an advance would have been madness, they withheld the means of success when I was in contact with the enemy, and finally relieved me from command when the game was in my hands. They determined that I should not succeed, and carried out their determinations only too well and at a fearful sacrifice of blood, time, and treasure. In the East alone it is quite safe to say that we unnecessarily lost more than a quarter of a million in killed, wounded, and prisoners in consequence of my being withdrawn from the Peninsula and not properly supported. Taking both East and West, and counting the losses also by disease, I do not doubt that more than half a million of men were sacrificed unnecessarily for the sake of insuring the success of a political party.

I do not base my assertions as to the motives of the radical leaders upon mere surmises, but upon facts that have frequently come to my knowledge during the war and since. For instance, Maj. Charles Davies, once professor of mathematics at West Point, told me, and at a different time told Gen. Jos. E. Johnston, the following story:

He said that during the very early part of the Peninsular campaign he was one of a commission sent from New York to urge more vigorous action in supporting me. They called upon the President, and found Mr. Stanton with him. In reply to their statement of the purpose of their visit Mr. Stanton stated that the great end and aim of the war was to abolish slavery.

To end the war before the nation was ready for that would be a failure. The war must be prolonged, and conducted so as to achieve that. That the people of the North were not yet ready to accept that view, and that it would not answer to permit me to succeed until the people had been worked up to the proper pitch on that question. That the war would not be finished until that result was reached, and that, therefore, it was not their policy to strengthen Gen. McClellan so as to insure his success.

I have heard, from the best authority, many instances in which the same views were expressed by other prominent radical leaders. Under date of April 7, 1862, Gen. Franklin, in a letter informing me of the circumstances attending the withholding of McDowell's corps, of which his division formed part, writes: "McDowell told me that it was intended as a blow at you. That Stanton had said that you intended to work by strategy and not by fighting; that all of the opponents of the policy of the administration centred around you - in other words, that you had political aspirations. There was no friend of yours present to contradict these statements, of course."

As a further proof that the administration did not intend the Peninsular campaign to be successful may be cited the fact that on the 3d of April, 1862, ten days after left Washington to assume command in the field, there was issued General Order No. 33, closing all the recruiting depots for the volunteers and stopping all recruiting. It is hardly credible that the members of the administration were ignorant of the fact that an army in the field must meet with some losses under the most favorable circumstances, and that to stop all supplies of men at such a juncture is the most unpardonable of follies.

From the light that has since been thrown on Stanton's character I am satisfied that from an early date he was in this treasonable conspiracy, and that his course in ingratiating himself with me, and pretending to be my friend before he was in office, was only a part of his long system of treachery.

Judge Black's papers in the *Galaxy* showed the character of the man; and it is somewhat singular that the judge began the papers for the purpose of vindicating Stanton, but that as he proceeded he became enlightened as to what the man really was.

I had never seen Mr. Stanton, and probably had not even

heard of him, before reaching Washington in 1861. Not many weeks after arriving I was introduced to him as a safe adviser on legal points. From that moment he did his best to ingratiate himself with me, and professed the warmest friendship and devotion. I had no reason to suspect his sincerity, and therefore believed him to be what he professed. The most disagreeable thing about him was the extreme virulence with which he abused the President, the administration, and the Republican party. He carried this to such an extent that I was often shocked by it.

He never spoke of the President in any other way than as the "original gorilla," and often said that Du Chaillu was a fool to wander all the way to Africa in search of what he could so easily have found at Springfield, Illinois. Nothing could be more bitter than his words and manner always were when speaking of the administration and the Republican party. He never gave them credit for honesty or patriotism, and very seldom for any ability.

At some time during the autumn of 1861 Secretary Cameron made quite an abolition speech to some newly arrived regiment. Next day Stanton urged me to arrest him for inciting to insubordination. He often advocated the propriety of my seizing the government and taking affairs into my own hands.

As he always expressed himself in favor of putting down the rebellion at any cost, I always regarded these extreme views as the ebullitions of an intense and patriotic nature, and sometimes wasted more or less time in endeavoring to bring him to more moderate views, never dreaming that all the while this man was in close communication with the very men whom he so violently abused. His purpose was to endeavor to climb upon my shoulders and then throw me down.

Several weeks before Mr. Cameron was finally removed from the War Department it came to my knowledge that a committee of New York bankers were urging upon Secretary Chase the removal of Mr. Cameron. I interfered, and by my action with the President no doubt saved him. The fact is that, so far as purely military matters were concerned, Mr. Cameron had not at all interfered with me, but gave me full support. He, so far as I knew, occupied himself solely with contracts and political affairs. The only difficulty I ever had with him - and I do not think that this point had arisen before the time in question, at all events to a very considerable degree - was that I could not always dispose of arms and supplies as I thought the good of the service demanded. For instance, it often happened, especially toward the close of his administration, that when a shipment of unusually good arms arrived from Europe, and I wished them for the Army of the Potomac, I found that they had been promised to some political friend who might be engaged in raising a prospective regiment in some remote State, and I could not get them. So with regard to other articles of equipment, and to batteries and regiments which I desired for the Army of the Potomac. As I had no idea who might be selected in Mr. Cameron's place, and as he supported me in purely military matters, I objected to his removal and saved him. He was made aware of this at the time.

Finally, one day when I returned to my house from my day's work and was dressing for dinner, a lady of my family told me that Col. Key, one of my aides, had just been there to inform me that Mr. Cameron had resigned and that Mr. Stanton was appointed in his place. This was the first intimation that I had of the matter. Before I had finished my toilet Mr. Stanton's card came up, and as soon as possible I went down to see him. He told me that he had been appointed Secretary of War, and that his name had been sent to the Senate for confirmation, and that he had called to confer with me as to his acceptance. He said that acceptance would involve very great personal sacrifices on his part, and that the only possible inducement would be that he might have it in his power to aid me in the work of putting down the rebellion; that he was willing to devote all his time, intellect, and energy to my assistance, and that together we could soon bring the war to an end. If I wished him to accept he would do so, but only on my account; that he had come to know my wishes and determine accordingly. I told him that I hoped he would accept the position.

Soon after Mr. Stanton became Secretary of War it became clear that, without any reason known to me, our relations had completely changed. Instead of using his new position to assist me he threw every obstacle in my way, and did all in his power to create difficulty and distrust between the President and myself. I soon found it impossible to gain access to him. Before he was in office he constantly ran after me and professed the most ardent friendship; as soon as he became Secretary of War his whole manner changed, and I could no longer find the opportunity to transact even the ordinary current business of the office with him. It is now very clear to me that, far from being, as he had always represented himself to me, in direct and violent opposition to the radicals, he was really in secret alliance with them, and that he and they were alike unwilling that I should be successful. No other theory can possibly account for his and their course, and on that theory everything becomes clear and easily explained.

Had I been successful in my first campaign the rebellion would perhaps have been terminated without the immediate abolition of slavery. To gain their ends with the President they played upon his apprehensions for the safety of Washington-growing out of his complete ignorance of war - as well as upon his personal aspirations. I believe that the leaders of the radical branch of the Republican party preferred political control in one section of a divided country to being in the minority in a restored Union.

Not only did these people desire the abolition of slavery, but its abolition in such a manner and under such circumstances that the slaves would at once be endowed with the electoral franchise, while the intelligent white man of the South should be deprived of it, and permanent control thus be secured through the votes of the ignorant slaves, composing so large a portion of the population of the seceded States.

Influenced by these motives, they succeeded but too well in sowing the seeds of distrust in Mr. Lincoln's mind, so that, even before I actually commenced the Peninsular campaign, I had lost that cordial support of the executive which was necessary to attain success. It may be said that under these circumstances it was my duty to resign my command. But I had become warmly attached to the soldiers, who already had learned to love me well; all my pride was wrapped up in the army that I had created, and I knew of no commander at all likely to be assigned to it in my place who would be competent to conduct its operations.

Nor did I at that time fully realize the length to which these men were prepared to go in carrying out their schemes. For instance, I did not suspect, until the orders reached me, that

Fort Monroe and the 1st corps would be withdrawn from my control; and when those orders arrived they found me too far committed to permit me to withdraw with honor. With the troops under fire it did not become me to offer my resignation.

The difficulties of my position in Washington commenced when I was first confined to my bed with typhoid fever in December and January (1861 and 1862) for some three weeks, and culminated soon after Mr. Stanton became Secretary of War. Up to this time there had been no serious difficulty; there were slight murmurs of impatience at the delay in moving, but all sensible and well-informed men saw the impossibility of entering upon a campaign at that season, and no party was as yet openly formed against me.

My malady was supposed to be more serious than it really was; for, although very weak and ill, my strong constitution enabled me to retain a clear intellect during the most trying part of the illness, so that I daily transacted business and gave the necessary orders, never for a moment abandoning the direction of affairs. As is often the case with such diseases, I sometimes passed days and nights without sleeping, and it more than once happened that the President called while I was asleep after such intervals of wakefulness, and, being denied admittance, his anxiety induced him to think that my disease was very acute and would terminate fatally. The radical leaders skilfully availed themselves of the state of affairs to drive in an entering wedge. They represented to the President that as I kept my own counsels and was not in the habit of consulting or advising with others, but acted entirely on my own judgment, no one but myself knew the exact condition of the army, its state of preparation, or the designs I had in view; that, should my malady terminate suddenly and fatally, great confusion would ensue, and that it was necessary to provide against such an emergency by causing a secret examination to be made immediately. My first inkling of this came through Mr. Stanton, not yet Secretary of War, who said to me: "They are counting on your death, and are already dividing among themselves your military goods and chattels."

The fact was that, although I was in the habit of acting solely on my own judgment, and never told more of my intentions than was absolutely necessary, I always consulted freely with the chiefs of the staff departments, each of whom knew the exact condition of affairs in his own department and could give to any properly authorized person all necessary explanations. So that a secret examination was not only unnecessary, but could not produce as good results as the honest, direct way of coming to me and directing me to instruct my staff to explain the state of affairs to the President or Secretary of War. Gens. McDowell, Franklin, and, I think, Meigs were entrusted by the President with this business.

McDowell, who was probably at the bottom of the affair, undertook it *con amore,* hoping to succeed me in command. Franklin was unwilling to touch it, and simply acted under orders. This information reached me when the crisis of my malady was over, and learning - also through Mr. Stanton - that a grand conclave was to assemble without my knowledge, I mustered strength enough on Sunday morning (Jan. 12, 1862) to be driven to the White House, where my unexpected appearance caused very much the effect of a shell in a powder-magazine. It was very clear from the manner of those I met there that there was something of which they were ashamed.

I made no allusion to what I knew, nor was anything said to me on the subject. But I took advantage of the occasion to explain to the President in a general and casual way what my intentions were; and before I left he told me that there was to be a meeting at the White House next day, and invited me to attend, but made no reference to the object of the meeting. At the designated hour I went to the President's office and there met a party consisting of the President, Secretaries Seward, Chase, and Blair, Gens. McDowell, Franklin, and Meigs. I do not think that the Secretary of War (Mr. Cameron) was present. I sat by Secretary Blair and Gen. Meigs, and entered into conversation with them upon topics of general interest having no possible bearing upon any subject that could be brought before the meeting. Meanwhile there was a good deal of whispering among the others, in which I do not think Franklin took any special part. Finally McDowell said he wished to explain to me the part he had in the examination, which had commenced, into the state of the army.

Exactly what he said has escaped my memory, except that he

disclaimed any purpose hostile to me, and based what had been done on the ground of the supposed critical nature of my illness. I stopped the explanation by saying that as I was now again restored to health the case had changed, and that, as the examination must now cease, further explanations were unnecessary. Franklin then said a few words clearing himself of any improper motives, which was needless, as I could not suspect him of anything wrong. I then quietly resumed my conversation with Blair and Meigs, awaiting further developments.

The whispering then recommenced, especially between the President and Secretary Chase; when at length the latter (Chase) spoke aloud, for the benefit of all assembled, in a very excited tone and manner, saying that he understood the purpose of the meeting to be that Gen. McClellan should then and there explain his military plans in detail, that they might be submitted to the approval or disapproval of the gentlemen present. The uncalled-for violence of his manner surprised me, but I determined to avail myself of it by keeping perfectly cool myself, and contented myself with remarking-what was entirely true - that the purpose he expressed was entirely new to me; that I did not recognize the Secretary of the Treasury as in any manner my official superior, and that I denied his right to question me upon the military affairs committed to my charge; that in the President and Secretary of War alone did I recognize the right to interrogate me. I then quietly resumed my conversation with Blair and Meigs, taking no further notice of Mr. Chase.

I must again state that this meeting had been arranged when I was supposed to be too ill to attend, and that the original and real purpose was not as Mr. Chase stated it, but "to dispose of the military goods and chattels" of the sick man so inopportunely restored to life. Mr. Chase's disappointment at this sudden frustration of his schemes accounts, I suppose, for his anger. In another connection I have already stated that some weeks before the date of this meeting I had given Mr. Chase a sketch of the proposed Urbana movement, and that he was much pleased with it. Here I need only say in addition that I did this entirely of my own volition, for the purpose indicated, and that Mr. Swinton is entirely mistaken in stating that it was by direction of the President. Mr. Chase knew at the time that the President had no knowledge of my intention of talking to him about my plans. At this previous interview Mr. Chase seemed very grateful for the confidence I reposed in him and for my thoughtfulness in thus seeking to relieve his mind in his troubles. I presume the after-thought, and the object of the intrigues, cut short by my recovery, was to take advantage of this plan by having it carried into effect by McDowell. In no other way can I account for the uncalled-for irritation displayed. This impression is strengthened by other circumstances which will appear as I proceed with my story.

To return to the meeting. After I had thus disposed of the Secretary of the Treasury he resumed his whispering with the President, who, after the lapse of some minutes, said: "Well, Gen. McClellan, I think you had better tell us what your plans are" - or words to that effect.

To this I replied, in substance, that if the President had confidence in me it was not right or necessary to entrust my designs to the judgment of others, but that if his confidence was so slight as to require my opinions to be fortified by those of other persons it would be wiser to replace me by some one fully possessing his confidence; that no general commanding an army would willingly submit his plans to the judgment of such an assembly, in which some were incompetent to form a valuable opinion, and others incapable of keeping a secret, so that anything made known to them would soon spread over Washington and become known to the enemy. I also reminded the President that he and the Secretary of the Treasury knew in general terms what my designs were. Finally, I declined giving any further information to the meeting, unless the President gave me the order in writing and assumed the responsibility of the results.

This was probably an unexpected *dénouement*. The President was not willing to assume the responsibility; and, after a little more whispering between him and Mr. Chase, Mr. Seward arose, buttoned his coat, and laughingly said, "Well, Mr. President, I think the meeting had better break up. I don't see that we are likely to make much out of Gen. McClellan." With that the meeting adjourned. I do not think that Mr. Seward took any special part in the affair, and believe that he was on my side. Mr. Chase still continued his whispered conversation with the President. I waited until that had ceased, then walked up to the President, begged him not to allow himself to be acted upon by improper influences, but still to trust me, and said that if he would leave military affairs to me I would be responsible that I would bring matters to a successful issue and free him from all his troubles.

The radicals never again lost their influence with the President, and henceforth directed all their efforts to prevent my achieving success. After this time Secretary Chase worked with them and became my enemy.

One of their next steps was to secure the removal of Mr. Cameron, in order to replace him by Mr. Stanton, who, while pretending to be my friend, was secretly allied with them, and no doubt made use of his pretended friendship for me to secure his appointment; for I have no reason to doubt the sincerity of the President's assertion that he had appointed him because he thought it would be agreeable to me.*

* Note by the *Editor.* - The question will naturally be asked, How came it about that Mr Edwin M. Stanton, then a pronounced and violent opponent of the President and the administration, knew of this secret proceeding, which was concealed from all but a few confidential friends of the President and three soldiers under orders of secrecy? Also, how came it that a few days after this Mr. Stanton was brought into Mr. Lincoln's cabinet? These questions were unanswerable until the publication of the private papers of Secretary Chase, which shed ample light on them. Why Mr. Stanton revealed Mr. Chase's secret to McClellan, and enabled the latter to defeat the plot, can be conjectured. Willing to be made War Secretary by Mr. Chase's intrigues, he may not have been so willing to have McDowell, or any other general closely allied to Mr. Chase, placed in command of the army.

On the very day on which Gen. McClellan made use of Mr. Stanton's information, and left his bed to visit the President, Mr. Chase devoted himself to concentrating the plans for bringing Mr. Stanton into the cabinet. He regarded it as a matter of the highest importance, and his account, in his private diary for that day, of his method of using Secretary Cameron and Seward to accomplish his end forms a very extraordinary intermingling of piety and politics, as follows (see Warden's "Account, etc., of S. P. Chase," p. 400):

"*January* 12, 1862. - At church this morning. Wished much to join in communion, but felt myself too subject to temptation to sin. After church went to see Cameron by appointment; but being obliged to meet the President, etc., at one, could only excuse myself. At President's found Gens. McDowell, Franklin, and Meigs, and Seward and Blair. Meigs decided against dividing forces and in favor of battle in front. President said McClellan's health was much improved, and thought it best to adjourn until to-morrow, and have all then present attend with McC. at three. Home, and talk and reading. Dinner. Cameron came

My relations with Mr. Lincoln were generally very pleasant, and I seldom had trouble with him when we could meet face to face. The difficulty always arose behind my back. I believe that he liked me personally, and certainly he was always much influenced by me when we were together. During the early part of my command in Washington he often consulted with me before taking important steps or appointing general officers.

He appointed Hunter a major-general without consulting me, and a day or two afterwards explained that he did so "because the people of Illinois seemed to want somebody to be a sort of father to them, and he thought Hunter would answer that purpose."

in. . . We talked of his going to Russia, and Stanton as successor, and he proposed I should again see the President.

"I first proposed seeing Seward, to which he assented. . . He and I drove to Willard's, where I left him, and went myself to Seward's, I told him at once what was in my mind - that I thought the President and Cameron were both willing that C. should go to Russia. He seemed to receive the matter as new, except so far as suggested by me last night. Wanted to know who would succeed Cameron. I said Holt and Stanton had been named; that I feared Holt might embarrass us on the slavery question, and might not prove quite equal to the emergency; that Stanton was a good lawyer and full of energy, but I could not, of course, judge him as an executive officer as well as he (S) could, for he knew him when he was in Buchanan's cabinet. Seward replied that he saw much of him then; that he was of great force, full of expedients, and thoroughly loyal.

"Finally he agreed to the whole thing, and promised to go with me to talk with the President about it to-morrow. Just at this point Cameron came in with a letter from the President proposing his nomination to Russia in the morning! He was quite offended, supposing the letter intended as a dismissal, and therefore discourteous. We both assured him it could not be so. . We went off together, I taking him to his house.

"Before parting I told him what had passed between me and Seward concerning Stanton, with which he was gratified. I advised him to go to the President in the morning, express his thanks for the consideration with which his wishes, made known through me as well as by himself orally, had been treated, and tell him frankly how desirable it was to him that his successor should be a Pennsylvanian and should be Stanton.

"I said I thought that his wish, supported, as it would be, by Seward and myself, would certainly be gratified, and told him that the President had already mentioned Stanton in a way which indicated that no objection on his part would be made. I said also that if he wished I would see Seward, and would go to the President, after he had left him, and urge the point. He asked, why not come in when me (he) should be there, and I assented to this. We parted, and I came home.

"A day which may have - and seemingly must have-great bearing on affairs. Oh! that my heart and life were so pure and right before God that I might not hurt our great cause.

"I fear Mr. Seward may think Cameron's coming into his house prearranged, and that I was not dealing frankly. I feel satisfied, however, that I have acted right and with just deference to all concerned, and have in no respect deviated from the truth."

When he appointed, as general officers, some of the released prisoners from the first Bull Run, he afterwards explained to me that he did it as a recompense for their sufferings, unaware, no doubt, that in other armies they would have been brought before some tribunal to explain their capture.

Soon after arriving in Washington the President one day sent for me to ask my opinion of Hooker, who was urged for appointment as a brigadier-general of volunteers, and stated that he wished me to regard the conversation as strictly confidential. I told him that Hooker had been a good soldier in Mexico, but that common report stated that he had fallen in California; but that I had no personal knowledge of this, and I advised him to consult with officers who were in California with Hooker. He, however, gave him the appointment a few days later. Remembering that this conversation was sought by the President and that he desired me to regard it as confidential, it was with no little surprise that I learned, after Antietam, that Hooker had been informed of the conversation, except of its confidential nature and that it was sought by the President.

As before stated, when Stanton was made Secretary of War I knew nothing of the matter until the nomination had already gone to the Senate. Next day the President came to my house to apologize for not consulting me on the subject. He said that he knew Stanton to be a friend of mine and assumed that I would be glad to have him Secretary of War, and that he feared that if he told me beforehand "some of those fellows" would say that I had dragooned him into it.

The evening before the order appeared finally relieving me from the command of the Army of the Potomac, the elder Mr. Frank Blair drove to the Soldiers' Home to dissuade the President from relieving me, rumors being current that such a thing was in contemplation. After a long, conversation Mr. Blair left with the distinct understanding that I was not to be relieved. Next morning the order appeared in the papers, and when Mr. Blair met the President in the course of the day the latter said: "Well, Mr. Blair, I was obliged to play shut-pan with you last night." Mr. Blair was my authority for this.

Officially my association with the President was very close until the severe attack of illness in December, 1861. I was often sent for to attend formal and informal cabinet meetings, and at all hours whenever the President desired to consult with me on any subject; and he often came to my house, frequently late at night, to learn the last news before retiring. His fame as a narrator of anecdotes was fully deserved, and he always had something apropos on the spur of the moment.

Late one night, when he was at my house, I received a telegram from an officer commanding a regiment on the upper Potomac. The despatch related some very desperate fighting that had been done during the day, describing in magniloquent terms the severe nature of the contest, fierce bayonet-charges, etc., and terminated with a very small list of killed and wounded, quite out of proportion with his description of the struggle.

The President quietly listened to my reading of the telegram, and then said that it reminded him of a notorious liar, who attained such a reputation as an exaggerator that he finally instructed his servant to stop him, when his tongue was running too rapidly, by pulling his coat or touching his feet. One day the master was relating wonders he had seen in Europe, and described a building which was about a mile long and a half-mile high. Just then the servant's heel came down on the narrator's toes, and he stopped abruptly. One of the listeners asked how broad this remarkable building might be; the narrator modestly replied, "About a foot!"

I think he enjoyed these things quite as much as his listeners.

Long before the war, when vice-president of the Illinois Central Railroad Company, I knew Mr. Lincoln, for he was one of the counsel of the company. More than once I have been with him in out-of-the-way county-seats where some important case was being tried, and, in the lack of sleeping accommodations, have spent the night in front of a stove listening to the unceasing flow of anecdotes from his lips. He was never at a loss, and I could never quite make up my mind how many of them he had really heard before, and how many he invented on the spur of the moment. His stories were seldom refined, but were always to the point.

The President ignored all questions of weather, state of roads, and preparation, and gave orders impossible of execution. About the middle of Feb., 1862, the President having reluctantly consented to abandon his plan of operation for that suggested by me, preparations were begun for the collection of the necessary water transportation. On the 27th of that month Mr. John Tucker, of Philadelphia, Assistant Secretary of War, was placed in charge of the procuring of the requisite steamers, etc., and performed his task with wonderful skill and energy. The President's War Order of March 8, 1862, "that any movement as aforesaid, *en route* for a new base of operations, which may be ordered by the general-in-chief, and which may be intended to move upon the Chesapeake Bay, shall begin to move upon the bay as early as the 18th March instant, and the general-in-chief shall be responsible that it moves as early as that day," was extraordinary, in view of the fact that the furnishing of transports was in no manner under my control, and that the beginning of the movement must necessarily depend upon their arrival.

When the operation by the lower Chesapeake was finally decided upon and approved by the corps commanders, it was distinctly understood that the movement would be made by the complete four corps, consisting of twelve divisions, plus the reserve artillery, engineer brigade, regular infantry and cavalry, and several cavalry regiments not assigned to the corps, and that I was authorized to form a division of 10,000 men from the troops in and near Fort Monroe and attach it to the active army. Moreover, we were assured of the active co-operation of the navy in reducing the batteries at Yorktown and Gloucester.

As my story progresses it will appear that I was deprived of five out of the thirteen infantry divisions, with their batteries, and of nine regiments of cavalry, and that I never received the co-operation of the navy in reducing the batteries at Yorktown and Gloucester.

On the 15th of March the aggregate present and absent under my command was about 233,578, taking as a basis the return of March 1; the number present for duty, including all extra-duty men, guards, etc., etc., was 203,213. Of these I purposed to leave behind, in Baltimore, Washington, and the Shenandoah, an aggregate of 66,552, brought up by new arrivals to about 77,401 at the close of March, or, deducting Gen. Dix's command, 65,621, equal to about 57,091 present for duty, with the convalescent hospitals at hand to dram upon.

Now, the estimate made of the necessary garrison of Wash-

13

ington by the chiefs of engineers and artillery on the 24th of
Oct., 1861 was a little less than 34,000 men, including reserves,
so that a force of a little over 23,000 men would have been left
for the Shenandoah Valley - much more than enough under the
circumstances, if properly handled.

I thus expected to take with me to the Peninsula a force of
146,122 present for duty, to be increased by a division of 10,000
formed from the troops at Fort Monroe - a total of about 156,-
000 men.

But the 1st corps, Blenker's division, the expected Fort Monroe division, the cavalry, etc. (afterwards taken away), amounted
to about 63,000 for duty, and reduced my paper force to 93,000,
which, in consequence of leaving behind many men unfit for the
field, was actually reduced to 85,000 not much more than one-
half of what I expected. Making the proper deduction for extra-
duty men, etc., there remained only about 70,000 effectives.

Moreover, on the second day after I left Washington an order
was issued breaking up all the recruiting rendezvous for volunteers, and thus abruptly stopping all recruiting at the very time it
was most necessary.

I will anticipate somewhat the sequence of events, and state
the manner in which these reductions of force were accomplished.

A few days before sailing for Fort Monroe I met the President, by his appointment, on a steamer at Alexandria. He
informed me that he was most strongly pressed to remove Blenker's German division from my command and assign it to Fremont, who had just been placed in command of the Mountain
Department. He suggested several reasons against the proposed
removal of the division, to all of which I assented. He then said
that he had promised to talk to me about it, that he had fulfilled
his promise, and that he would not deprive me of the division.

On the 3Ist of March, a few hours before I sailed I was
much surprised by the receipt of the following letter:

"EXECUTIVE MANSION WASHINGTON March 31, 1862.
"*Maj.-Gen. McClellan:*

"MY DEAR SIR: This morning I felt constrained to order
Blenker's division to Fremont; and I write this to assure you
that I did so with great pain, understanding that you would wish

it otherwise. If you could know the full pressure of the case I am confident that you would justify it, even beyond a mere acknowledgment that the commander-in-chief may order what he pleases.   Yours very truly,
                                                "A. LINCOLN."

To this it might be replied that the commander-in-chief has no right to order what he pleases; he can only order what he is convinced is right. And the President had already assured me that he knew this thing to be wrong, and had informed me that the pressure was only a political one to swell Fremont's command.

I replied that I regretted the order and could ill-afford to lose 10,000 troops who had been counted upon in arranging the plan of campaign. In a conversation the same day I repeated this, and added my regret that any other than military considerations and necessities had been allowed to govern his decision.

He then assured me that he would allow no other troops to be withdrawn from my command.

Before I left for the field Fort Monroe and its dependencies had been placed under my command, and I was authorized to form a division of 10,000 men from the troops stationed there and add it to the Army of the Potomac, placing it under Mansfield. I arrived at Fort Monroe on the afternoon of the 2d of April, and on the 3d received a telegraphic order withdrawing Fort Monroe from my command and forbidding me to remove any of Gen. Ord's troops without his sanction. No reason has ever been given for this step, and I was thus not only deprived of 10,000 more troops, but also of the control of my immediate base of operations and supplies.

On the afternoon of the 5th, the right and left wings of the army being under fire from Yorktown and the works on the line of the Warwick, I received the following telegram:

"ADJUTANT-GENERAL'S OFFICE, April 4, 1862.
"*Gen. McClellan:*

"By direction of the President, General McDowell's army corps has been detached from the forces under your immediate command, and the general is ordered to report to the Secretary of War. Letter by mail.

"*L. THOMAS, Adjutant-General.*"

In addition to the forces already enumerated, at least nine regiments of cavalry were withheld from me, and the order of April 3, discontinuing recruiting for the volunteers, rendered it impossible for me to make good the inevitable losses from disease and battle.

The effect of these changes will appear as I resume the narrative of events.

CHAPTER X.

[*Oct.* 1, 1861, to *March* 12, 1862.]

Oct. -, 1861. - Yesterday rode to Chain Bridge, thence to Upton's Hill, and did not get back until after dark. . . . I can't tell you how disgusted I am becoming with these wretched politicians.

Oct. - . - . . . The enemy made some demonstrations up the river this morning, which prevented me from crossing the river until 1.30; then I rode to Munson's Hill, etc., and found everything going on well. We shall be ready by to-morrow to fight a battle there, if the enemy should choose to attack; and I don't think they will care to run the risk. I presume I shall have to go after them when I get ready; but this getting ready is slow work with such an administration. I wish I were well out of it. . . . We almost expected a little row up the river yesterday, but it amounted to nothing. The enemy fired 112 shots with artillery at our people at Great Falls, slightly grazing one man's arm and wounding a horse slightly. Fine shooting that! They must learn to do better if they hope to accomplish anything. Some of our men have been behaving most atrociously lately in burning houses; some eighteen have been burned in the last two or three days. I will issue an order to-day informing them that I will hang or shoot any found guilty of it, as well as any guards who permit it. Such things disgrace us and our cause. Our new position in advance is a fine one. It throws our camps into a fine, healthy country, with excellent drill-grounds and everything fresh and clean - an infinite improvement over our old places, where the men had been stuck down close to the river for months. It removes them also further from the city, so they will be less liable to temptation.

Oct. 2 (?)- . . . Gen. Gibson's funeral takes place this morn-

167

ing. I am becoming daily more disgusted with this administration-perfectly sick of it. If I could with honor resign I would quit the whole concern to-morrow; but so long as I can be of any real use to the nation in its trouble I will make the sacrifice. No one seems able to comprehend my real feeling - that I have no ambitious feelings to gratify, and only wish to serve my country in its trouble, and, when this weary war is over, to return to my wife. . . .

Oct. 6. - . . . I am quite sure that we shall spend some time here together after your recovery. Preparations are slow, and I have an infinite deal to do before my army is really ready to fight a great battle. Washington may now be looked upon as quite safe. They cannot attack it in front. My flanks are also safe; or soon will be. Then I shall take my own time to make an army that will be sure of success. . . . Gen. Scott did try to send some of my troops to Kentucky, but did not succeed. They shall not take any from here, if I can help it. The real fighting must be here: that in Kentucky will be a mere bagatelle. You need not be at all alarmed by any apprehensions you hear expressed. I have endeavored to treat Gen. Scott with the utmost respect, but it is of no avail. . . . I do not expect to fight a battle near Washington; probably none will be fought until I advance, and that I will not do until I am fully ready. My plans depend upon circumstances. So soon as I feel that my army is well organized and well disciplined, and strong enough, I will advance and force the rebels to a battle in a field of my own selection.

A long time must yet elapse before I can do this, and I expect all the newspapers to abuse me for delay; but I will not mind that.

No date. - . . . I *must* ride much every day, for my army covers much space. It is necessary for me to see as much as I can every day, and, more than that, to let the men see me and gain confidence in me. . . . I started out about three this afternoon and returned at ten; rode down to the vicinity of Alexandria, and on my return *(en route)* received a despatch to the effect that the rebels at 6.30 this morning were breaking up their camps at Manassas - whether to attack or retreat I do not yet know. If they attack they will in all probability be beaten, and the attack ought to take place to-morrow. I have made every possible preparation and feel ready for them. . . .

Oct. 9. - . . . I have a long ride to take to-day; will probably advance our right some three or four miles by may of getting more elbow-room and crowding G. W. up a trifle. The more room I get the more I want, until by and by I suppose I shall be so insatiable as to think I cannot do with less than the whole State of Virginia. The storm has entirely changed the weather, and I am afraid may affect the health of the men for a few days; for it is now cold and wet. The review of yesterday passed off very well; it was a superb display, by far the finest ever seen on this continent, and rarely equalled anywhere There were 104 guns in the review (a number greater than Lauriston's famous battery at Wagram) and 5,500 cavalry. The ground was wet, so I did not venture to let them pass at a trot or gallop; they passed only at a walk. . . I was tired out last night. My horse was young and mild, and nearly pulled my arm off. The cheering of the men made him perfectly frantic, and, as I had to keep my cap in my right hand, I had only my left to manage him.

Oct. (10 ?). - I have just time to write a very few lines before starting out. Yesterday I threw forward our right some four miles, but the enemy were not accommodating enough to give us a chance at them, so I took up a new position there and reinforced it by sending McCall over to that side. I am now going over again to satisfy myself as to the state of affairs, and perhaps edge up another mile or so, according to circumstances. When I returned yesterday, after a long ride, I was obliged to attend a meeting of the cabinet at eight P.M. and was bored and annoyed. There are some of the greatest geese in the cabinet I have ever seen - enough to tax the patience of Job. . . .

Oct. (11 ?). - . . . I rode all over our new positions yesterday to make some little changes and correct errors, as well as to learn the ground more thoroughly myself. It rained most of the day, which did not add to the pleasure of the trip. Secesh

keeps quiet, wonderfully so.   I presume he wants to draw me
on to Manassas to repeat the Bull Run operation; but I shan't
go until ready.   I may occupy Vienna in a few days, especially
if he does not show himself in force; but I am very well contented with our present positions, as places where we can drill
and discipline the troops to great advantage.   We have the men
now in a fine open country, high and healthy, good clean fresh
and green camp-grounds, and the *morale* of an advance,

Oct. 14. - What *do* you think I received as a present yesterday? Some poor woman away up in the middle of New York
sent me half a dozen pair of woollen socks - I beg pardon, I see
it is from Pennsylvania, not New York.   I enclose the note.

Oct. 16. - . . . Just received a telegram to the effect that the
rebels had attacked a small force we have in Harper's Ferry, and
had been handsomely repulsed with the loss of quite a number
of men and one gun. . . . In front of us the enemy remain
quiet, with the exception of occasional picket-firing.

Oct. - . - . . . I am firmly determined to force the issue with
Gen. Scott.   A very few days will determine whether his policy
or mine is to prevail.   He is for inaction and the defensive; he
endeavors to cripple me in every way; yet I see that the newspapers begin to accuse me of want of energy.   He has even com-
plained to the War Department of my making the advance of
the last few days. Hereafter the truth will be shown.

Oct. 16. - I have just been interrupted here by the President
and Secretary Seward, who had nothing very particular to say,
except some stories to tell, which were, as usual, very perti-
nent, and some pretty good. I never in my life met any one
so full of anecdote as our friend. He is never at a loss for a
story apropos of any known subject or incident.

Oct. 19. - Gen. Scott proposes to retire in favor of Halleck.
The President and cabinet have determined to accept his retirement, but not in favor of Halleck. . . . The enemy have fallen
back on Manassas, probably to draw me into the old error. I
hope to make them abandon Leesburg to-morrow.

Oct. 20 *or* 21. - . . . I yesterday advanced a division to Dranesville, some ten miles beyond its old place, and feel obliged to take advantage of the opportunity to make numerous reconnoissances to obtain information as to the country, which is very beautiful at Dranesville, where I was yesterday. The weather is delightful. The enemy has fallen back to Centreville and Manassas, expecting us to attack there. My object in moving to Dranesville yesterday and remaining there to-day was to force them to evacuate Leesburg, which I think they did last night.

Oct. 24. - Have ridden more than forty miles to-day, and have been perfectly run down ever since I returned.

Oct. 25. - . . . How weary I am of all this business! Care after care, blunder after blunder, trick upon trick. I am well-nigh tired of the world, and, were it not for you, would be fully so. That affair of Leesburg on Monday last was a horrible butchery. The men fought nobly, but were penned up by a vastly superior force in a place where they had no retreat. The whole thing took place some forty miles from here, without my orders or knowledge. It was entirely unauthorized by me, and I am in no manner responsible for it.

Col. Baker, who was killed, was in command, and violated all military rules and precautions. Instead of meeting the enemy with double their force and a good ferry behind him, he was outnumbered three to one and had no means of retreat. Cogswell is a prisoner; he behaved very handsomely. Raymond Lee is also taken. I found things in great confusion when I arrived there. In a very short time order and confidence were restored. During the night I withdrew everything and everybody to this side of the river, which, in truth, they should never have left.

Oct. 26, 1.15 A. M. - For the last three hours I have been at Montgomery Blair's, talking with Senators Wade, Trumbull, and Chandler about war matters. They will make a desperate effort to-morrow to have Gen. Scott retired at once; until that is accomplished I can effect but little good. He is ever in my way, and I am sure does not desire effective action. I want to get through with the war as rapidly as possible. . . . I go out soon after breakfast to review Porter's division, about five miles from here.

Oct. 30. - I know you will be astonished, but it is true, that I went this evening to a fandango. The regulars just in from Utah gave a little soirée to the other regulars; music, a little dancing, and some supper. I went there intending to remain ten minutes, and did stay fully an hour and a half. I met Mrs. Andrew Porter, Mrs. Palmer and her mother, Mrs. Hancock, and several other army ladies. It was very pleasant to get among old acquaintances once more.

Oct. 31. - . . . You remember my wounded friend Col. Kelly, whom we met at Wheeling? He has just done a very pretty thing at Romney - thrashed the enemy severely, taken all their guns, etc. I am very glad to hear it. . . . "Our George" they have taken it into their heads to call me. I ought to take good care of these men, for I believe they love me from the bottom of their hearts; I can see it in their faces when I pass among them. I presume the Scott war will culminate this meek. Whatever it may be, I will try to do my duty to the army and to the country, with God's help and a single eye to the right. I hope that I may succeed. I appreciate all the difficulties in my path: the impatience of the people, the venality and bad faith of the politicians, the gross neglect that has occurred in obtaining arms, clothing, etc.; and, above all, I feel in my inmost soul how small is my ability in comparison with the gigantic dimensions of the task, and that, even if I had the greatest intellect that was ever given to man, the result remains in the hands of God. I do not feel that I am an instrument worthy of the great task, but I *do* feel that I did not seek it. It was thrust upon me. I was called to it; my previous life seems. to have been unwittingly directed to this great end; and I know that God can accomplish the greatest results with the weakest instruments-therein lies my hope. I feel, too, that, much as we in the North have erred, the rebels have been far worse than we.

No date. - I have just returned from a ride over the river, where I went pretty late, to seek refuge in Fitz Porter's camp.

You would have laughed if you could have seen me dodge off.
I quietly told the duke to get our horses saddled, and then we
slipped off without escort or orderlies, and trotted away for Fitz-
John's camp, where we had a quiet talk over the camp-fire.
I saw yesterday Gen. Scott's letter asking to be placed on the
retired list and saying nothing about Halleck. The offer was
to be accepted last night, and they propose to make me at once
commander-in-chief of the army. I cannot get up any especial
feeling about it. I feel the vast responsibility it imposes upon
me. I feel a sense of relief at the prospect of having my own
way untrammelled, but I cannot discover in my own heart one
symptom of gratified vanity or ambition.

Nov. 2, 1.30 A.M. - I have been at work, with scarcely one
minute's rest, ever since I arose yesterday morning-nearly eighteen hours. I find "the army" just about as much disorganized
as was the Army of the Potomac when I assumed command;
everything at sixes and sevens; no system, no order, perfect
chaos. I can and will reduce it to order. I will soon have it
working smoothly.

Nov. 3. - I have already been up once this morning - that was
at four o'clock to escort Gen. Scott to the depot. It was pitch-
dark and a pouring rain; but with most of my staff and a
squadron of cavalry I saw the old man off. He was very polite
to me ; sent various kind messages to you and the baby; so we
parted. The old man said that his sensations were very peculiar
in leaving Washington and active life. I can easily understand
them; and it may be that at some distant day I, too, shall totter
away from Washington, a worn-out soldier, with naught to do
but make my peace with God. The sight of this morning was a
lesson to me which I hope not soon to forget. I saw there the
end of a long, active, and ambitious life, the end of the career of
the first soldier of his nation; and it was a feeble old man scarce
able to walk; hardly any one there to see him off but his successor. Should I ever become vainglorious and ambitious, remind me of that spectacle. I pray every night and every
morning that I may become neither vain nor ambitious, that I
may be neither depressed by disaster nor elated by success, and
that I may keep one single object in view - the good of my

country. At last I am the "major-general commanding the army." I do not feel in the least elated, for I do feel the responsibility of the position. And I feel the need of some support. I trust that God will aid me.

Nov. - . - . . . A deputation of thirty waited on me and presented me with that sword from the city of Philadelphia. It is certainly a very fine one. I listened meekly to a speech and replied in my usual way - *i.e.,* in very few words. I then had a collation - I abominate the word, it is so steamboaty - in the back parlor. Wormley did himself credit on the occasion, and got it up very well indeed. The President came in during the proceedings. . . . After that I came back and received quite a number of congratulatory calls; then went to dine with Andrew Porter, where I had a very pleasant time - Andrew and his wife, her brother, her sister-in-law, Seth, and myself.

Nov 7. - I am very glad to learn that my order changed Gen. Scott's feelings entirely, and that he now says I am the best man and the best general that ever existed.

No date. - Yesterday I was so busily engaged in getting Halleck off to Missouri and Buell to Kentucky that I had but little time to look about me.

Nov. 10. - Yesterday worked at the office until noon and then started to review Porter's division. Got soaked and had a chill: all right this morning. Before breakfast the President and Seward came in.

Nov. 11, 1.30 A.M. - Went to Chase's at eight P.M. to meet some New York financiers; left them in good spirits. Have just finished Halleck's instructions.

Nov. - , 1861. - You will have heard the glorious news from Port Royal. Our navy has covered itself with glory and cannot receive too much credit. The thing was superbly done and the chivalry well thrashed. They left in such haste that officers forgot even to carry away their swords. But one white man was found in Beaufort, and he drunk! The negroes came flocking down to the river with their bundles in their hands. ready to take passage. There is something inexpressibly mournful to me in that - those poor, helpless, ignorant beings, with the wide world and its uncertainties before them; the poor serf, with his little bundle, ready to launch his boat on the wide ocean of life he knows so little of. When I think of some of the features of slavery I cannot help shuddering. Just think for one moment, and try to realize that at the will of some brutal master you and I might be separated for ever! It is horrible; and when the day of adjustment comes I will, if successful, throw my sword into the scale to force an improvement in the condition of these poor blacks. I do think that some of the rights of humanity ought to be secured to the negroes. There should be no power to separate families, and the right of marriage ought to be secured to them. . . .

Nov. 12. - Last night the German division gave a grand torch-light procession and serenade. What little I saw of it was very fine, but I had to attend a pseudo cabinet meeting while it was in progress, so that I saw by no means the whole of it. Quite a party came here to see the performance.

Nov. 17 - . . . I find that to-day is not to be a day of rest for me. This unfortunate affair of Mason and Slidell has come up, and I shall be obliged to devote the day to endeavoring to get our government to take the only prompt and honorable course of avoiding a war with England and France. . . . It is sickening in the extreme, and makes me feel heavy at heart, when I see the weakness and unfitness of the poor beings who control the destinies of this great country. How I wish that God had permitted me to live quietly and unknown with you! But His will be done! I will do my best, try to preserve an honest mind, do my duty as best I may, and will ever continue to pray that He will give me that wisdom, courage, and strength that are so necessary to me now, and so little of which I possess.

The outside world envy me, no doubt. They do not know the weight of care that presses on me. . . . I will try again to write a few lines before I go to Stanton's to ascertain what the law of nations is on this Slidell and Mason seizure. . . . I went to the White House shortly after tea. I then went to the Prince de Joinville's. We went up-stairs and had a long, confidential talk upon politics. The prince is a noble character, one whom I shall be glad to have you know well. He bears adversity so well and so uncomplainingly. I admire him more than almost any one I have ever met with. He is true as steel; like all deaf men, very reflective; says but little, and that always to the point. . . . After I left the prince's I went to Seward's, where I found the President again. . . . The President is honest and means well. As I parted from him on Seward's steps he said that it had been suggested to him that it was no more safe for me than for him to walk out at night without some attendant. I told him that I felt no fear; that no one would take the trouble to interfere with me. On which he deigned to remark that they would probably give more for my scalp at Richmond than for his. . . .

Nov. - . - . . . Went to the Prince de Joinville's, where I found Barry, Dahlgren, and the family. If it would at all comfort you I might do what I have never done - carry a pistol in my pocket, especially as I received two days since a lamb-like present of four revolvers of different sizes, bringing my private armory up to something like eleven pistols of various dimensions. What more can be asked of any one?

Nov. - . - Some infatuated individual sent me, a day or two ago, a "McClellan Polka." What in the world did he expect *me* to do with it? Not to whistle or dance it, I hope.

Nov. - . - . . . I have been at work all day nearly on a letter to the Secretary of War (Cameron) in regard to future military operations. I have not been at home for some three hours, but am concealed at Stanton's to dodge all enemies in shape of "browsing" Presidents, etc. . . .

1 A.M. - I am pretty thoroughly tired out. The paper is a very important one, as it is intended to place on record that I have left nothing undone to make this army what it ought to be, and that the necessity for delay has not been my fault. I have a set of men to deal with unscrupulous and false; if possible they will throw whatever blame there is on my shoulders, and I do not intend to be sacrificed by such people. I still trust that the all-wise Creator does not intend our destruction, and that in

His own good time He will free the nation from the men who curse it, and will restore us to His favor. I know that as a nation we have grievously sinned; but I trust there is a limit to His wrath, and that ere long we will begin to experience His mercy. . . . . I cannot guess at my movements, for they are not within my control. I cannot move without more means, and I do not possess the power to control those means.

The people think me all-powerful. Never was there a greater mistake. I am thwarted and deceived by these incapables at every turn.

I am doing all I can to get ready to move before winter sets in, but it now begins to look as if we were condemned to a winter of inactivity. If it is so the fault will not be mine; there will be that consolation for my conscience, even if the world at large never knows it. . . .

I have one great comfort in all this - that is, that I did not seek this position, as you well know; and I still trust that God will support me and bear me out. He could not have placed me here for nothing. . . .

Nov. 25. - . . . After dinner yesterday rode over the river. I came back after dark in a driving snow-storm. . . . It has cleared off since last night, and is quite cold to-day. It was a very disagreeable ride last night - dark as pitch, roads bad, and the snow driving hard. . . . .

Nov. 27. - . . . Went to a grave consultation at Secretary Chase's in regard to the reopening of the Baltimore and Ohio Railroad. . . .

After the review of the regulars I went down to the river to see the volunteer pontoniers throw a bridge-train. I went through the usual routine of being presented to an infinite number of ladies. Made a close inspection of the camp and of the men, and then returned.

Nov. 30, 1861. - I was hard at work until half-past four, when I came back to dinner. Gen. Banks dined with me. When he left I had several business calls. At eight all the officers of the 4th Infantry, just returned from California, came to pay their respects. When they left I went to Com. Goldsborough, where he, Fox, Prof. Bache, and myself remained in serious consultation about naval and military movements until after midnight.

Sandy Hook, near Harper's Ferry, Monday A.M., *Feb. 27, 1862.* - . . . Here I still am. I crossed the river as soon as the bridge was finished, and watched the troops pass. It was a magnificent spectacle, one of the grandest I ever saw. As soon as my horse and escort got over I rode out to the line of pickets and saw for myself that everything was right and ready for an attack. The position is a superb one. I got over about 12 guns and 8,000 infantry before dark; also a squadron of cavalry. I heard in the afternoon a rumor that G. W. Smith was expected at Winchester with 15,000 men. Although I did not fully credit it, I nevertheless took all the military precautions necessary, and felt perfectly secure during the night. The enemy are not now in sight, but I have sent out cavalry patrols that may bring in intelligence of value. It was after dark and raining hard when I recrossed the bridge. The narrow road was so completely blocked up that it was a very difficult matter to make one's way among the wagons. It rained hard and was very cold during the night. . . . Slept in a car; I was up most of the night, telegraphing, etc. This morning it is blowing a hurricane, but the bridge stands well thus far. Burns's brigade came up during the night. I left them in the cars and crossed them this morning early. The wagons have gone over; a regiment of cavalry is now crossing, another battery will follow, and I will have everything well cleared up before the arrival of Abercrombie's brigade, which should be here by two o'clock. I will get it over before dark, also the heavy artillery and regular cavalry, if it arrives. I hope to be able to occupy Charleston tomorrow and get Lander to Martinsburg. It will then require but a short time to finish matters here. The roads on the other side are good; the country more open than near Washington. You have no idea how the wind is howling now - a perfect tornado; it makes the crossing of the river very difficult, and interferes with everything. I am anxious about our bridge. . . .

Fairfax Court-House, March 11, 1862. - . . . None of our wagons came up until after I rode out this morning, so we got along as best we could last night. Someone lent me some blankets, and somebody else a cot, so I was very well off. To-night I have my own bed. I started at about nine this morning and rode first to Centreville. We found there quite a formidable series of works, which would have been somewhat uncomfortable for new troops to carry by storm. Thence I rode over horrid roads to the celebrated Manassas, which me found also abandoned. Thence to the battle-field of last July, and over pretty much the whole of it. Thence home *via* Stone Bridge and Centreville, reaching here about half-past eight. I rode Kentuck to-day, and as he was fretful he fatigued me very much, so that it is impossible for me to go to Washington to-night, notwithstanding your father's pressing telegram. I regret that the rascals are after me again. I had been foolish enough to hope that when I went into the field they would give me some rest, but it seems otherwise. Perhaps I should have expected it. If I can get out of this scrape you will never catch me in the power of such a set again. The idea of persecuting a man behind his back! I suppose they are now relieved from the pressure of their fears by the retreat of the enemy, and that they will increase in virulence. Well, enough of that; it is bad enough for me to be bothered in that way without annoying you with it. The country which me passed to-day was very desolate. I think Manassas is the most desolate and forbidding spot I ever beheld. They have not destroyed many of their winter-quarters, which are very well built and comfortable - far more so than I expected to see them. From the great number of camps scattered about it is evident that they had a very large force here. They must have left in a great hurry, for they abandoned a great deal of baggage, tents, stores, ammunition, caissons, wagons, etc. It seems that the order was given very suddenly. They left on Sunday, except a rear-guard. It is said by "intelligent contrabands" and others that the men were very much disgusted and disheartened. . . .

14

CHAPTER XI

Events in and around Washington - Ball's Bluff - Harper's Ferry - Stanton's trick - Enemy's batteries on the Potomac.

ON the 9th of Oct. McCall's division marched from Tennallytown to Langley, on the Virginia side of the Potomac. This addition to the forces already there enabled me to push reconnoissances more actively; and as it was particularly desirable to obtain accurate information in regard to the topography of the country in front of our right, Gen. McCall was ordered to move on the 19th as far as Dranesville to cover the work of the topographical engineers directed to prepare maps of that region. On the 20th Gen. Smith pushed out strong parties to Freedom Hill, Vienna, Flint Hill, Peacock Hill, etc., with a similar object.

From his destination Gen. McCall sent the following despatch:

"DRANESVILLE, Oct. 19, 1861, 6.30 P.M.

"To *Gen. McClellan* :

"I arrived here this morning. All is quiet. No enemy seen. Country for one mile beyond Difficult creek broken and woody. Bad country to manœuvre. Nothing but skirmishing could be done by infantry. Artillery could not leave the road. One mile beyond Difficult creek the country becomes open; some pretty battle-fields. Country high. I shall bivouac here to-night. Park is with me.

"(Signed)   GEO. A. McCALL."

He remained near Dranesville during the whole of the 20th, covering the operations of the topographical engineers. On the morning of the 21st he sent me the following despatch:

"CAMP NEAR DRANESVILLE, VA.,
Oct. 21, 1861, 6.30 A.M.

" *Maj.-Gen. Geo. B. McClellan:*

"GENERAL: In a couple of hours we shall have completed the plane-table survey to the ground I first occupied one and one-
180

half miles in front, and, by odometer or by observation, all the cross-roads this side of the point where me met Gen. Smith's parties, from the Alexandria pike to the L. and H. R. R., and the more northern ones from the pike to the river.

"On the return march the plane-table will be at work on the Leesburg and Georgetown pike, and the side-roads to the river will be examined. . . .

"Very respectfully,
" GEO. A. McCALL,
"Brig.-Gen."

On the 12th of Oct. Gen. Stone telegraphed that he thought the enemy were entrenching between Conrad's Ferry and Leesburg, about one mile from the town. In the morning of the 13th he telegraphed that the enemy had strengthened their force opposite Harrison's island by one or two regiments from below, and that much work was going on in the way of new batteries and lines, and strengthening old ones. At night on the same day he telegraphed that work had been done at Smart's Hill, that the pickets near Mason's island were largely reinforced, and that he anticipated an early attempt by the enemy to secure Mason's or Harrison's island, perhaps both, but probably the latter, commanded, as it was, by the bluffs on their side.

On the 15th he telegraphed that there was considerable movement between the river and Leesburg-apparently preparations for resistance rather than attack. On the 18th, at 10.45 P.M., he telegraphed that the enemy's pickets were withdrawn from most of the posts in our front; that he had sent an officer over the river within two miles of Leesburg the same evening, and that he should push the reconnoissances farther the following day, if all remained favorable.

Such was the state of affairs when, on the morning of the 20th, I received the following telegram from Gen. Banks's headquarters:

"DARNESTOWN, Oct. 20, 1861.

"SIR: The signal station at Sugar Loaf telegraphs that the enemy have moved away from Leesburg. All quiet here.

"R. M. COPELAND,

"Gen. MARCY. *Assist. Adj.-Gen."*

Whereupon I sent to Gen. Stone, at Poolesville, the following telegram:

CAMP GRIFFIN, Oct. 20, 1861.

Gen. McClellan desires me to inform you that Gen. McCall occupied Dranesville yesterday, and is still there. Will send out heavy reconnoissances to-day in all directions from that point. The general desires that you will keep a good look-out upon Leesburg, to see if this movement has the effect to drive them away. Perhaps a slight demonstration on your part would have the effect to move them.

A. V. COLBURN,
Assist. Adj.-Gen.

Brig.-Gen. C. P. STONE, *Poolesville.*

Deeming it possible that Gen. McCall's movement to Dranesville, together with the subsequent reconnoissances, might have the effect of inducing the enemy to abandon Leesburg, and the despatch from Sugar Loaf appearing to confirm this view, I wished Gen. Stone - who had only a line of pickets on the river, the mass of his troops being out of sight of, and beyond range from, the Virginia bank - to make some display of an intention to cross, and also to watch the enemy more closely than usual. I did not direct him to cross, nor did I intend that he should cross the river in force for the purpose of fighting.

The above despatch was sent on the 20th, and reached Gen. Stone as early as eleven A.M. of that day. I expected him to accomplish all that was intended on the same day; and this he did, as will be seen from the following despatch received at my headquarters in Washington from Poolesville on the evening of Oct. 20:

"Made a feint of crossing at this place this afternoon, and at the same time started a reconnoitring party towards Leesburg from Harrison's island. The enemy's pickets retired to entrenchments. Report of reconnoitring party not yet received. I have means of crossing one hundred and twenty-five men once in ten minutes at each of two points. River falling slowly.

" C. P. STONE,
"Brig.-Gen.

"Maj.-Gen. McCLELLAN."

As it was not foreseen or expected that Gen. McCall would be needed to co-operate with Gen. Stone in any way, he had been directed to fall back from Dranesville to his original camp, near Prospect Hill, as soon as the required reconnoissances were completed.

Accordingly he left Dranesville, on his return, at about 8.30 A.M. of the 21st, reaching his old camp at about one P.M.

In the meantime I was surprised to hear from Gen. Stone that a portion of his troops were engaged on the Virginia side of the river, and at once sent instructions to Gen. McCall to remain at Dranesville, if he had not left before the order reached him.

The order did not reach him until his return to his camp at Prospect Hill. He was then ordered to rest his men, and hold his division in readiness to return to Dranesville at a moment's notice, should it become necessary. Similar instructions were given to other divisions during the afternoon.

The first intimation I received from Gen. Stone of the real nature of his movements was in a telegram, as follows:

" EDWARD'S FERRY, Oct. 21, 11.10 A.M.

"The enemy have been engaged opposite Harrison's island: our men are behaving admirably.

"C. P. STONE,
"*Brig.-Gen.*
" Maj.-Gen. McCLELLAN."

At two P.M. Gen. Banks's adjutant-general sent the following:

" DARNESTOWN, Oct. 21, 1861, 2 P.M.

"Gen. Stone safely crossed the river this morning. Some engagements have taken place on the other side of the river-how important is not known.

" R. M. COPELAND,
"*Act. Assist. Adjt.-Gen.*
"Gen. R. B. MARCY."

Gen. Stone sent the following despatches:

" EDWARD'S FERRY, Oct. 21, 1861, 2 P.M.

"There has been sharp firing on the right of our line, and our troops appear to be advancing there under Baker. The left, under Gorman, has advanced its skirmishers nearly one mile, and, if the movement continues successful, will turn the enemy's right.

"C. P. STONE,
"*Brig.-Gen.*
"To Maj.-Gen. McCLELLAN."

"EDWARD'S FERRY, Oct. 21, 1861, 2.20 P.M.
"To Gen. Marcy:
"We cross at Edward's Ferry in flat-boats - these which we
have built: capacity forty-five men each - and in one canal-boat,
capacity two hundred men; at Harrison's island in four flat-
boats and four row-boats. There is a road from Seneca to
Edward's Ferry, and from Edward's Ferry to Leesburg; also
a road from opposite Seneca to the Leesburg road.   The mounted men will be held in readiness. Firing pretty heavy on our
right. . . .
" C. P. STONE,
" *Brig.-Gen."*

This was in reply to an inquiry as to his means of crossing
and the roads, also directing him to hold mounted men ready to
transmit frequent reports.

" EDWARD'S FERRY, Oct. 21, 1861, 4 P.M.
"Nearly all my force is across the river.   Baker on the right,
Gorman on the left.   Right sharply engaged.
"C. P. STONE,
"Brig-Gen.
"To Gen. McCLELLAN."

" EDWARD'S FERRY, Oct. 21, 1861, 6 P.M.
"Have called on Banks for a brigade, and he has ordered up
Hamilton's.   I think it would be well to send up a division on
the other side of the river. I think they have been reinforced.
"C.P. STONE,
"Brig. -Gen."

The nearest division on the Virginia side (McCall's) was
more than twenty miles from the scene of action, so that it could
not have arrived before noon of the 22d - too late to be of any
service.   Moreover, its line of march would have passed not
more than eleven or twelve miles from the enemy's position at
Centreville, and it would thus have been exposed to be cut off,
unless supported by a general movement of the Army of the
Potomac, which there was nothing to justify, according to the
information at that time (5.30 P.M.) in my possession. The
orders I had already sent to Banks seemed best adapted to the
case, as the event proved.

"EDWARD'S FERRY, Oct. 21, 1861, 6.45 P.M.
"To Maj.-Gen. McClellan:
"Col Baker has been killed at the head of his brigade. I go to the right at once.
"C. P. STONE,
" *Brig.-Gen.*"

Gen. Stone was evidently misinformed, as Col. Baker had only one battalion of his brigade with him.

" EDWARD'S FERRY, Oct. 21, 1851, 9.30 P.M.
"To Gen. McClellan:
"I am occupied in preventing further disaster, and try to get into a position to redeem. We have lost some of our best commanders - Baker dead, Coggswell a prisoner or secreted. The wounded are being carefully and rapidly removed, and Gorman's wing is being cautiously withdrawn. Any advance from Dranesville must be made cautiously. All was reported going well up to Baker's death, but in the confusion following that the right wing was outflanked. In a few hours I shall, unless a night-attack is made, be in the same position as last night, save the loss of many good men.
"C. P. STONE,
" *Brig.-Gen.*"

Although not fully informed of the state of affairs, I had, during the afternoon, as a precautionary measure, ordered Gen. Banks to send one brigade to the support of the troops at Harrison's island and to move with the other two to Seneca Mills, ready to support Gen. Stone, if necessary. The 9.30 P.M. despatch of Gen. Stone did not give me entire understanding of the state of the case.

Aware of the difficulties and perhaps fatal consequences of attempting to recross such a river as the Potomac after a repulse, and from these telegrams supposing his whole force to be on the Virginia side, I sent the following telegram:

HEADQUARTERS, ARMY OF POTOMAC,
Oct. 21, 1861, 10.30 P.M.
To Gen. C. P. Stone, Edward's Ferry:
Entrench yourself on the Virginia side and await reinforcements, if necessary.
GEO. B. MCCLELLAN,
Maj.-Gen. Commanding.

Shortly after the following:

To Gen. C. P. Stone:

Hold your position on the Virginia side of the Potomac at all hazards. Gen. Banks will support you, with one brigade at Harrison's island and the other two at Seneca. Lander will be with you at daylight.

GEO. B. McCLELLAN,
Maj.-Gen. Commanding

P.S. Change the disposition of Gen. Banks's division, if you think it necessary, so as to send two brigades to Harrison's island instead of one.

About the same time I sent the following:

HEADQUARTERS ARMY OF THE POTOMAC,
Oct. 21, 1861, 10.45 P.M.

To Gen. N. P. Banks:

Push forward your command as rapidly as possible, and put as many men over the river to reinforce Gen. Stone as you can before daylight. Gen. Stone is directed to hold his command on the Virginia side of the Potomac at all hazards, and informed that you will support him. You will assume command when you join Gen. Stone.

GEO. B. McCLELLAN,
Maj.- Gen. Commanding.

The following despatches were next received:

"EDWARD'S FERRY, Oct. 21, 11 P.M.

"To Maj.-Gen. McClellan:

"We hold the ground half a mile back of Edward's Ferry on Virginia shore. Harrison's island has parts of thirteen companies, only seven hundred (700) men, and will soon be reinforced by one hundred fresh men, besides what support Hamilton brings. I cover the shore opposite this with guns, and am disposing others to help the defence of Harrison's, I think the men will fight well. Entrenchments ordered this morning.

"C. P. STONE,
" *Brig.-Gen.*"

"HEADQUARTERS, SENECA MILLS,
Oct. 21, 11 P.M.

"To *Gen. McClellan:*

"Arrived here at nine and a half o'clock. Gen. Stone telegraphs for whole division immediately. Col. Baker is killed, and some trouble exists on his right. We go at once.

"N. P. BANKS,
"Maj.-Gen. Commanding Division."

Hamilton's brigade arrived at midnight, and Gen. Banks with the remainder of his division reached Edward's Ferry at three A.M. of the 22d. He found Gen. Stone on the Maryland side, and reported that he ascertained that at no time had more than one-third of his (Gen. Stone's) troops crossed. Assuming command, and consulting with the generals present, he telegraphed me the facts, and received a reply directing him to send over men enough to hold the opposite side, with orders to entrench themselves; all of which was done. During the afternoon there was a skirmish, in the course of which Gen. Lander was wounded.

Meanwhile Gen. Banks had collected all the canal-boats to be found, in order to increase the means of transportation. I reached Edward's Ferry during the evening of the 22d and assumed command. Passing through Poolesville, I first learned the actual condition of affairs and the details of what had occurred, and sent the following:

POOLESVILLE, Oct. 22, 5.30 P M
To President Lincoln;
From what I learn here the affair of yesterday was a more serious disaster than I had supposed. Our loss in prisoners and killed was severe. I leave at once for Edward's Ferry.

GEO. B. McCLELLAN,
Maj.-Gen. Commanding.

The following extract from the evidence of Gen. Stone before the "Committee on the Conduct of the War" on the 5th of Jan., 1862, will throw further light on this occurrence:

Gen. Stone says he received the order from my headquarters to make a slight demonstration at about eleven o'clock A.M. on the 20th, and that, in obedience to that order, he made the demonstration on the evening of the same day.

In regard to the reconnoissance on the 21st, which resulted in the battle of Ball's Bluff, he was asked the following questions:

Question. "Did this reconnoissance originate with yourself, or had you orders from the general-in-chief to make it?"

To which he replied: "It originated with myself - the reconnoissance."

Question. "The order did not proceed from Gen. McClellan?"

Answer. "I was directed the day before to make a demonstration; that demonstration was made the day previous."

Question. "Did you receive an order from the general-in-chief to make the reconnoissance?"

Answer. "No, sir."

Making a personal examination on the 23d, I found that the position on the Virginia side at Edward's Ferry was not a tenable one, but did not think it wise to withdraw the troops by daylight. I therefore caused more artillery to be placed in position on the Maryland side to cover the approaches to the ground held by us, and crossed the few additional troops that the high wind permitted us to get over, so as to be as secure as possible against any attack during the day.

Up to six o'clock I kept my intention secret, all supposing that I intended to advance on Leesburg. My object was not to discourage the command in the event of their being attacked. At six o'clock I sent to Gen. Stone, then on the Virginia side of the river, the detailed instructions for the withdrawal of the troops during the night. Before nightfall all the precautions were taken to secure an orderly and quiet passage of the troops and guns.

The movement was commenced soon after dark, under the personal supervision of Gen. Stone, who received the order for the withdrawal at 7.15 P.M. By four A.M. of the 24th everything had reached the Maryland shore in safety. A few days afterwards I received information, which seemed to be authentic, to the effect that large bodies of the enemy had been ordered from Manassas to Leesburg to cut off our troops on the Virginia side. Their timely withdrawal probably prevented a still more serious disaster. Gen. Stone's report of this battle and his testimony before the Committee on the Conduct of the War furnish further details.

Gen. Banks's division deserves great credit for its rapid night-march to the relief of General Stone. On the 23th the total loss in killed, mounded, and missing was reported as 680, with stragglers constantly coming in.

The true story of the affair of Ball's Bluff is, in brief, as follows :

One of Gen. Stone's officers, Capt. Philbrick, of the 15th Mass., thought that he had discovered a camp of the enemy about one mile beyond Harrison's island in the direction of Leesburg. Having completed the feint of crossing made in the course of the 20th Gen. Stone at 10.30 P.M. of the same day issued his orders for the surprise of the supposed camp at daybreak of the 21st. Col. Devens, of the 15th Mass., was entrusted with the duty, with four companies of his regiment. Col. Lee, of the 20th Mass., was directed to replace Col. Devens in Harrison's island with four companies of his own regiment, one of which was to pass over to the Virginia shore and hold the heights there to cover Col. Devens's return. Col. Devens was directed to "attack the camp at daybreak, and, having routed, to pursue them as far as he deems prudent, and to destroy the camp, if practicable, before returning." "He will make all the observations possible on the country, will, under all circumstances, keep his command well in hand, and not sacrifice this to any supposed advantages of rapid pursuit. Having accomplished this duty, Col. Devens will return to his present position, unless he shall see one on the Virginia side near the river which he can undoubtedly hold until reinforced, and one which can be successfully held against largely superior numbers. In which case he will hold on and report."

In obedience to these orders Col. Devens crossed about midnight with five companies (instead of four), numbering about 300 men, and halted until daybreak in an open field near the bluffs bordering the shore. While there he was joined by Col. Lee with 100 men of the 20th Mass., who halted here to cover his return.

At daybreak he advanced about a mile towards Leesburg, and then discovered that the supposed camp did not exist. After examining the vicinity and discovering no traces of the enemy, he determined not to return at once, but at about half-past six A.M. sent a non-commissioned officer to report to Gen. Stone that he thought he could remain where he was until reinforced. At about seven o'clock a company of hostile riflemen were observed on the right, and a slight skirmish ensued. A company of cavalry being soon observed on the left, the skirmishers were drawn back to the woods, and, after waiting half an hour for attack, the command was withdrawn to the position held by Col. Lee; but, after again scouting, the woods, Col. Devens returned to his advanced position. About eight o'clock the messenger returned from Gen. Stone with orders for Col. Devens to remain where he was, and that he would be reinforced. The messenger was again sent back to report the skirmish that had taken place. Col. Devens then threw out skirmishers and awaited reinforcements. At about ten o'clock the messenger again returned with the information that Col. Baker would soon arrive with his brigade and take command. Between nine and eleven Col. Devens was joined by Lieut.-Col. Learned with the remainder of the 15th, bringing up his command to 28 officers and 625 men.

About midday Col. Devens learned that the enemy were gathering on his left, and about half-past twelve or one he was strongly attacked; and as he was in great danger of being outflanked, and no reinforcements had arrived, at about a quarterpast two he fell back to the bluff, where he found Col. Baker, who directed him to take the right of the position he proposed to occupy; the centre and left being composed of about 300 men of the 20th Mass., under Col. Lee, and a battalion of the California regiment about 600 strong. Two howitzers and a 6-pounder were also in line.

At about three o'clock the enemy attacked in force, the weight of his attack being on our centre and left. At about four our artillery was silenced, and Col. Devens was ordered to send two of his companies to support the left of our line; shortly after he learned that Col. Baker had been killed. Col. Coggswell then assumed command, and, after a vain attempt to cut his way through to Edward's Ferry, was obliged to give the order to retreat to the river-bank and direct the men to save themselves as best they could.

I have gone thus much into detail because at the time I was much criticised and blamed for this unfortunate affair, while I was in no sense responsible for it.

Early in 1862 it was determined to attempt the reopening of the Baltimore and Ohio Railroad as far eastward from Cumberland as circumstances would justify.

Gen. F. W. Lander was ordered to cover this operation from Cumberland towards Hancock, and on the 5th of Jan. reached Hancock *en route* to his destination. He found Jackson on the opposite bank of the Potomac, tearing up rails, etc. Shortly after his arrival Lander was summoned by Jackson to surrender; this, of course, was a mere act of bravado, for it is not probable that Jackson had the slightest intention of crossing the river. The enemy fired a few shells into Hancock, doing little or no damage.   Gen. Banks sent reinforcements to Hancock under Gen. Williams, who remained in that vicinity for some time. Jackson now moved towards Bloomery Gap and Romney, whither Lander was ordered to go.   The force at Romney being insufficient to hold the place and its communications, Lander was instructed to fall back to the mouth of Patterson's creek, where he awaited the arrival of reinforcements now on the way to him.

Finding it difficult to procure supplies, and not venturing to attack Lander in his position, Jackson fell back from Romney to Unger's Store with the mass of his force about the 23d of Jan. About the 5th of Feb. Lander obliged him to evacuate Romney entirely.

Lander now moved his headquarters to the Paw Paw Tunnel, from which position he covered the reconstruction of the Baltimore and Ohio Railroad, which was reopened from the west to Hancock on the 14th of Feb. On the 13th he made a very dashing attack upon a party of the enemy at Bloomery Gap, taking several prisoners and dispersing the rest.

Notwithstanding the severe illness from which he suffered, Lander remained at Paw Paw, covering the railroad and keeping the country - clear of the enemy, until the 28th of Feb., when he was ordered to move to Bunker Hill to co-operate with Gen. Banks, then at Charlestown, covering, the rebuilding of the railroad as he advanced. While engaged in preparing to execute this order his disease assumed a more violent form, and on the 2d of March this gallant officer breathed his last.   On some occasions during this brief campaign I was obliged to check Lander rather abruptly for attempting to assume control over troops not under his command, and for endeavoring to initiate some very rash movements when the great risk could not be counterbalanced by the very faint chances of success.   These errors arose partly from inexperience, and also, no doubt, from the effects of the malady which so soon terminated his life.

These occurrences did not change my feeling towards him, and I doubt whether they influenced his for me.

I had often observed to the President and to members of the cabinet that the reconstruction of this railway could not be undertaken until we were in a condition to fight a battle to secure it. I regarded the possession of Winchester and Strasburg as necessary to cover the railway in the rear, and it was not till the month of February that I felt prepared to accomplish this very desirable but not vital purpose.

The whole of Banks's division and two brigades of Sedgwick's division were thrown across the river at Harper's Ferry, leaving one brigade of Sedgwick's division to observe and guard the Potomac from Great Falls to the mouth of the Monocacy. A sufficient number of troops of all arms were held in readiness in the vicinity of Washington, either to march *via* Leesburg or to move by rail to Harper's Ferry, should this become necessary in carrying out the objects in view.

The subjoined Notes from a communication subsequently addressed to the War Department will sufficiently explain the conduct of these operations:

NOTES.

When I started for Harper's Ferry I plainly stated to the President and Secretary of War that the chief object of the operation would be to open the Baltimore and Ohio Railroad by crossing the river in force at Harper's Ferry; that I had collected the material for making a permanent bridge by means of canal-boats; that, from the nature of the river, it was doubtful whether such a bridge could be constructed; that if it could not I would at least occupy the ground in front of Harper's Ferry, in order to cover the rebuilding of the railroad bridge; and finally, when the communications were perfectly secure, move on Winchester.

When I arrived at the place I found the bateau bridge nearly completed; the holding-ground proved better than had been anticipated; the weather was favorable, there being no wind. I at once crossed over the two brigades which had arrived, and took steps to hurry up the other two, belonging respectively to Banks's and Sedgwick's divisions. The difficulty of crossing supplies had not then become apparent. That night I telegraphed for a regiment of regular cavalry and four batteries of heavy artillery to come up the next day (Thursday), besides directing Keyes's division of infantry to be moved up on Friday.

Next morning the attempt was made to pass the canal-boats

through the lift-lock, in order to commence at once the construction of a permanent bridge. It was then found for the first time that the lock was too small to permit the passage of the boats, it having been built for a class of boats running on the Shenandoah canal, and too narrow by some four or six inches for the canal-boats. The lift-locks, above and below, are all large enough for the ordinary boats. I had seen them at Edward's Ferry thus used. It had always been represented to the engineers by the military railroad employees and others that the lock *was* large enough, and, the difference being too small to be detected by the eye, no one had thought of measuring it or suspected any difficulty. I thus suddenly found myself unable to build the permanent bridge. A violent gale had arisen, which threatened the safety of our only means of communication; the narrow approach to the bridge was so crowded and clogged with wagons that it was very clear that, under existing circumstances, nothing more could be done than to cross over the baggage and supplies of the two brigades. Of these, instead of being able to cross both during the morning, the last arrived only in time to go over just before dark. It was evident that the troops under orders would only be in the way, should they arrive, and that it would not be possible to subsist them for a rapid march on Winchester. It was therefore deemed necessary to countermand the order, content ourselves with covering the reopening of the railroad for the present, and in the meantime use every exertion to establish, as promptly as possible, depots of forage and subsistence on the Virginia side to supply the troops and enable them to move on Winchester independently of the bridge. The next day (Friday) I sent a strong reconnoissance to Charlestown, and, under its protection, went there myself. I then determined to hold that place, and to move the troops composing Lander's and Williams's commands at once on Martinsburg and Bunker Hill, thus effectually covering the reconstruction of the railroad.

Having done this, and taken all the steps in my power to insure the rapid transmission of supplies over the river, I returned to this city, well satisfied with what had been accomplished. While up the river I learned that the President was dissatisfied with the state of affairs; but, on my return here, understood from the Secretary of War that upon learning the whole state of the case the President was fully satisfied. I contented myself, therefore, with giving to the secretary a brief statement, about as I have written it here; he did not even require that much of me. He was busy; I troubled him as little as possible, and immediately went to work at other important affairs.

The design aimed at was entirely accomplished, and the

railroad was in running order before I started for the Peninsula. As a demonstration against his left flank this movement had much to do with the enemy's evacuation of his position at Manassas on the 8th and 9th of March; and I should state that I made the movement unwillingly, because I anticipated precisely that effect, and did not wish them to move from Manassas until I had fairly commenced the movement to the lower Chesapeake. But the pressure was so strong that I could not resist it; and this was no doubt the best and easiest way to force the navigation of the lower Potomac, which the administration laid so much stress upon. They had neither the courage nor the military insight to understand the effect of the plan I desired to carry out.

Immediately upon my return from Harper's Ferry I called upon the secretary and handed him the memorandum referred to in the "Notes" just given, expressing a desire to explain the matter personally to the President. The secretary said that the President now understood the whole affair, but that he would hand him my memorandum. He told me, a day or two afterwards, that he had done so, and that the President was entirely satisfied with my conduct, and desired me not to mention the subject to the President. I was foolish enough to believe him, and acted accordingly. The following telegrams will aid in giving the true state of the case :

"WASHINGTON, Feb. 28, 1862.

" *Gen. McClellan* :

"What do you propose to do with the troops that have crossed the Potomac?

"E. M. STANTON,
"Sec. of War."

To this I replied:

SANDY HOOK, Feb. 28, 1862.

Hon. E. M. Stanton, Sec. of War:

Your despatch received. I propose to occupy Charlestown and Bunker Hill, so as to cover the rebuilding of the railway, while I throw over the supplies necessary for an advance in force. I have quite men enough to accomplish this. I could not at present supply more.

GEORGE B. McCLELLAN,
Maj.-Gen. Commanding.

On the same day I telegraphed to the President as follows:

> It is impossible for many days to do more than supply the troops now here and at Charlestown. We could not supply a movement to Winchester for many days, and had I more troops here they would have been at a loss for food on the Virginia side. I know that I have acted wisely and that you will cheerfully agree with me when I explain. I have arranged to establish depots on that side, so we can do what we please. I have secured opening road.
>
> GEORGE B. McCLELLAN,
> *Maj.-Gen. Commanding.*

On the same day I telegraphed to Gen. Lander as follows:

> We hold Charlestown. As soon as possible please occupy Bunker Hill and communicate with Banks at Charlestown. Scout well towards Winchester. Push the repairs of the railway rapidly. Get free of this business. I want. you with me in another direction.
>
> GEORGE B. McCLELLAN.
> *Maj.-Gen. Commanding.*

It was a part of Mr. Stanton's policy - only too well carried out-to prevent frequent personal interviews between the President and myself; he was thus enabled to say one thing to the President and exactly the opposite to me. A few days later, on the 8th of March, the President sent for me at an early hour in the morning, about half-past seven, and I found him in his office. He appeared much concerned about something, and soon said that he wished to talk with me about "a very ugly matter." I asked what it was; and, as he still hesitated, I said that the sooner and more directly such things were approached the better.

He then referred to the Harper's Ferry affair (the boats being too wide for the lift-locks, etc.), upon which I found that the secretary had deceived me when he said that the President was satisfied. I told him what had passed between the secretary and myself (as related above), at which he was much surprised. He told me that he had never heard of my memorandum or of any explanation on my part. I then gave him my statement of the matter, with which he expressed himself entirely satisfied.

He then adverted to the more serious - or ugly - matter, and now the effects of the intrigues by which he had been surrounded became apparent. He said that it had been repre-

15

sented to him (and he certainly conveyed to me the distinct impression that he regarded these representations as well founded) that my plan of campaign (which was to leave Washington under the protection of a sufficient garrison, its numerous well-built and well-armed fortifications, and the command of Banks, then in the Shenandoah Valley, and to throw the whole active army suddenly by water from Annapolis and Alexandria to the forts on James river, and thence by the shortest route upon Richmond) was conceived with the traitorous intent of removing its defenders from Washington, and thus giving over to the enemy the capital and the government, thus left defenceless.

It is difficult to understand that a man of Mr. Lincoln's intelligence could give ear to such abominable nonsense. I was seated when he said this, concluding with the remark that it did look to him much like treason. Upon this I arose, and, in a manner perhaps not altogether decorous towards the chief magistrate, desired that he should retract the expression, telling him that I could permit no one to couple the word treason with my name. He was much agitated, and at once disclaimed any idea of considering me a traitor, and said that he merely repeated what others had said, and that he did not believe a word of it. I suggested caution in the use of language, and again said that I would permit no doubt to be thrown upon my intentions; whereupon he again apologized and disclaimed any purpose of impugning my motives.

I then informed him that I had called a meeting of the generals of division for that day with reference to the proposed attack upon the enemy's Potomac batteries, and suggested that my plan should be laid before them in order that he might be satisfied. This was done, and I heard no more of treason in that connection.

Before leaving this subject I will call attention to the fact that my official report contained the statement that the secretary had assured me of the President's approval of my action when I returned from the upper Potomac, and that this assertion was never denied. Moreover, no other statement made in the memorandum was ever denied or objected to either by the President or the secretary; and that memorandum shows very clearly that there was no ground of dissatisfaction with my conduct, but that

I did precisely what I told them I should do under given circumstances.

In my official report I have given all necessary information as to the reasons which prevented an attack upon the enemy's batteries on the Potomac. I will here repeat only that careful reconnoissances and a full consideration of the matter led to the inevitable conclusion that although we might, at a greater or less sacrifice of life, carry and destroy any particular battery, we could prevent the construction of permanent batteries and the employment of rifled field-batteries only by a general movement of the army to drive the enemy entirely behind the Rappahannock and Rapidan, after a general action; and that it would then be necessary to hold the lines of those rivers in force or continue the campaign by the overland route.

I did not regard the inconvenience resulting from the presence of the enemy's batteries on the Potomac as sufficiently great to justify the direct efforts necessary to dislodge them, especially since it was absolutely certain that they would evacuate all their positions as soon as they became aware of the movement to the James and York rivers.

It was therefore with the greatest reluctance that I made the arrangements required to carry out the positive orders of the government, and it was with great satisfaction that I found myself relieved from the necessity of making what I knew to be a false and unnecessary movement.

When the enemy abandoned his position on the 8th and 9th of March, the roads were still in such a condition as to make the proposed movement upon the batteries impracticable. Before this time I had strongly and repeatedly urged upon the Navy Department the propriety of hastening the completion of the *Monitor,* that she might be sent to the Potomac to try her hand upon the batteries on its banks. As the reason for this I urged that it was well to try her qualities under fire, when necessary repairs and alterations could readily be made, rather than to send her immediately to New Orleans, as had been intended. It is a little singular that the effect of my urgency was to hasten her completion, so that she arrived in Hampton Roads in season to check the operations of the *Merrimac.*

CHAPTER XII.

Review of the situation - McClellan succeeds Scott in command of all the armies - Their condition; general disorganization; no plan for the war - McClellan's plans for the whole war - Simultaneous movements throughout the country - Orders to Burnside for North Carolina expedition; to Halleck and Buell for operations in the West; to Butler for the New Orleans expedition - Halleck and Grant - Correspondence of McClellan and Grant.

I DO not know that any one worthy of attention has questioned the manner in which was performed the task of converting the unorganized, defeated, and dispirited remains of Mc-Dowell's Bull Run command into the Army of the Potomac-an army which so long bore on its bayonets the life and honor of the nation.

Everything was to be done. An army was to be created *ab initio* - out of nothing. Raw material there was, but it was completely raw, and was to be fashioned into shape. Private soldiers, non-commissioned officers, officers, regiments, brigades, divisions, army corps, armies, with all their staff corps, were to be organized and instructed, not merely on paper, but in effective reality.

Small arms, field-guns, siege and garrison artillery, ammunition, equipments, camp-equipage, bridges, ambulances, baggage and supply trains, tents, clothing - all these wonderful instruments and *impedimenta* of a modern army were to be fabricated; and not only fabricated, but so made that it would be possible to use them: so strong as to withstand a heavy strain, so light that they could be handled. It added to the difficulty of the task that no army approaching in magnitude that now required had ever existed on this continent, so that our own experience was not of much avail in the crisis so suddenly upon us.

In fact, one of the greatest obstacles I encountered at this time was the difficulty of drawing some of the heads of departments out of the old ruts, and convincing them that what was eminently appropriate for five or ten thousand men was often an absurdity or impossibility for ten or twenty times those numbers. Besides all this - and going on *pari passu* with it all - was the irresistible and pressing necessity of so fortifying Washington as to provide for its immediate and future safety; so that the active army of operations should not necessarily be tied down to it as its base of operations and be unable to uncover it without endangering its security.

More yet than this, the work was to be done in the face of a victorious enemy, whose outposts were within rifle-shot of our own and in sight of the capital; the only communications of the army and the government passing, as far as to the Susquehanna, through a people of very doubtful loyalty.

Moreover, the government was utterly ignorant of military affairs and incapable of judging the necessities of the situation; too often actuated by mere motives of partisan expediency instead of patriotic resolve. The people, also, were ignorant of war, and sure to be urged to clamorous and senseless impatience by a partisan press.

Finally, I was not only unsupported, but sometimes thwarted by Gen. Scott, whose views often differed from my own. Under these circumstances I had only my own unwavering sense of right to sustain me. In spite of all threats and clamors I quietly persevered in the course I knew to be necessary for the safety of the nation, regardless of the result to my personal fortunes.

The work was accomplished, and I know of no case in history where so great a task was so thoroughly performed in so brief a period.

It certainly was not till late in Nov., 1861, that the Army of the Potomac was in any condition to move, nor even then were they capable of assaulting entrenched positions. By that time the roads had ceased to be practicable for the movement of armies, and the experience of subsequent years proved that no large operations could be advantageously conducted in that region during the winter season.

Any success gained at that time in front of Washington could not have been followed up, and a victory would have given us the barren possession of the field of battle, with a longer and more difficult line of supply during the rest of the winter. If the Army of the Potomac had been in condition to move before

winter, such an operation would not have accorded with the
general plan I had determined upon after succeeding Gen.
Scott as general in command of the armies.

On Nov. 1, 1861, the following private letter was received
from the President:

"Private.

"EXECUTIVE MANSION,
Nov. 1, 1861.

"Maj.- Gen. Geo. E. McCellan:
"MY DEAR SIR: Lieut.-Gen. Scott having been, upon his own
application, placed on the list of retired officers, with his advice,
and the concurrence of the entire cabinet, I have designated you
to command the whole army. You will, therefore, assume this
enlarged duty at once, conferring with me so far as necessary.
"Yours truly,
"A. LINCOLN.

"P.S. For the present let Gen. Wool's command be excepted.
"A. L."

Immediately after succeeding Gen. Scott in the chief command of all the armies of the United States I arranged in my
own mind the general plans for the operations of the ensuing year.
I soon ascertained that more remained to be done in the West
than in the East to bring the armies to a state of efficiency, and to
that end did all in my power during the autumn and winter.

Until my own sphere of command and responsibility was
extended from the Army of the Potomac to all the armies, I
supposed that some general plan of operations existed, but now
learned that there was none such, and that utter disorganization
and want of preparation pervaded the Western armies. I had
supposed that they were nearly, if not quite, in condition to act,
but found that I was mistaken.

Even if the Army of the Potomac had been in condition to
undertake a campaign in the, autumn of 1861, the backward state
of affairs in the West would have made it unwise to do so; for on
no sound military principle could it be regarded as proper to
operate on one line alone while all was quiescent on the others,
as such a course would have enabled the enemy to concentrate
everything on the one active army. Again, if, within a week or
two of the first Bull Run, it had been possible to advance and
defeat the Confederate army at Manassas, the moral effect might

have justified the attempt, even were it impossible to follow up
the victory; but after the lapse of some months it would have
been foolish to advance unless prepared to follow up a victory
and enter upon a campaign productive of definite results.

Early in Sept., 1861, Gens. W. T. Sherman and G. H. Thomas
had been taken from my command and ordered to report to Gen.
Robert Anderson, just placed in command of Kentucky. Before
many weeks Anderson was relieved, in consequence of failing
health, and Sherman succeeded to his duties.

In October he became very much depressed and took an
exceedingly gloomy view of the situation. He called for 200,000
men - a force entirely out of the power of the government to supply at that time. On the 2d of Nov. he requested me to order
Halleck, Buell, Stevens, and some officers of experience to Kentucky, stating that the importance of his department was beyond
all estimate.

On the 3d, after giving in detail the position of the troops,
about 25,000, he says: "Our forces are too small to do good
and too large to sacrifice."

On the 4th he telegraphed to me: "The publication of Adj.-
Gen. Thomas's report impairs my influence. I insist upon being
relieved to your army, my old brigade. Please answer."

On the 6th he telegraphed me: " . . . If Simon Buckner
crosses Green river by the practicable fords, of which there
are many at wide marks, may get in McCook's rear. Look at
map between camp and Louisville. Two roads, one by Bards-
town and other by mouth of Salt river. The great danger is in
stripping Ohio and Indiana of troops and putting them on this
side with no retreat. The enemy also threatens the lower river
at Owensboro, where I have nothing but unorganized volunteers."

I have not a copy of the telegram, but my memory is clear
that he also asked permission to fall back across the Ohio to
prevent being cut off.

I knew the condition of affairs well enough to be satisfied not
only that there was no danger that the enemy would cross the
Ohio river, but also that, if he were mad enough to do so, he
would never get back, and believed that the State could be held
with the troops then in it. Therefore I gladly and promptly
acquiesced in Sherman's request to be relieved, and sent Buell

to replace him, ordering Sherman to report to Halleck for duty. On Buell's arrival he found a complete state of disorganization; not only so, but that nothing was being done to mend the matter, and no steps being taken to prepare the troops for the field. A total lack of system prevailed, and everything was allowed to run on as best it could. The new commander at once made himself felt, and justified the propriety of his appointment by the skill and energy with which he devoted himself to the task of bringing order and efficiency out of chaos and helplessness. Buell found no difficulty in holding his own in Kentucky, and drove the enemy out of Kentucky and out of the capital of Tennessee as soon as he had received and organized the reinforcements, which were provided as rapidly as possible, and which Sherman would have received in due course; and, having accomplished the first part of his task, still found means to rescue Grant and Sherman from defeat at Shiloh with the army he had so recently created.

In my letters of instruction to Gen. Buell, Nov. 7 and 12, 1861 (hereafter given), I advised his remaining on the defensive for the moment, on the direct line to Nashville, and that he should throw the mass of his forces, by rapid marches *via* Cumberland Gap or Walker's Gap, on Knoxville, in order to occupy the railroad at that point to prevent its use by the Confederates, and to rally to us the loyal citizens of that region. Buell found it impossible to carry out these instructions, on account of the unprepared condition of the troops, the state of the roads, and lack of means of transportation.

About the same time I sent Halleck to Missouri to relieve Gen. Fremont in the command of that department. I instructed him to fortify and garrison some important points in the interior, and to concentrate the mass of his troops on or near the Mississippi for such ulterior operations as might prove necessary.

I determined to expedite the preparations of the Western armies as much as possible during the winter, and as early as practicable in the spring throw them forward; commencing their advance so much earlier than that of the Army of the Potomac as to engage all the Confederate Western forces on their own ground, and thus prevent them from reinforcing their army in front of Richmond.

As early as the beginning of Dec., 1861, I had determined not to follow the line of operations leading by land from Washington to Richmond, but to conduct a sufficient force by mater to Urbana, and thence by a rapid march to West Point, hoping thus to cut off the garrison of Yorktown and all the Confederates in the Peninsula; then, using the James river as a line of supply, to move the entire Army of the Potomac across that river to the rear of Richmond.

In pursuance of this plan I did not propose disturbing the Confederate forces at Manassas and Centreville, but, while steadily pushing forward the fortifications of Washington and the instruction and organization of the Army of the Potomac, I desired to hold them there to the last moment, and especially until the Urbana movement was well in process of execution.

There was no possible military reason for disturbing them, and it best answered my purposes to keep them where they were I was not apprehensive of any attack by them after the first few weeks. Their presence served to keep my men on the *qui vive.* The skirmishes which necessarily occurred gave experience of fire and taught watchfulness. They covered no ground in front of Richmond furnishing supplies needed by either party. They had the longest and most difficult line of supply that they could have.

Early in December this plan was so far matured that, finding Secretary Chase seriously troubled in his financial operations by the uncertainty as to military operations, I went one day to his private office in the Treasury building and of my own volition confidentially laid my plans before him. He was delighted, said it was a most brilliant conception, and thanked me most cordially for the confidence I had thus reposed in him.

Meanwhile the preparations for operations on the lower Atlantic and Gulf coasts were progressing slowly but satisfactorily. Early in January Gen. Burnside received his final instructions for the expedition to the coast of North Carolina. The general purposes of this expedition were to control the navigation of the sounds on the North Carolina coast, thus cutting off the supplies of Norfolk by water, and at the same time covering the left flank of the main army when operating against Richmond by the line of James river, the reduction of New Berne, Beaufort, and Wilmington, which would give us the double advantage of preventing blockade-running at those points and of enabling us to threaten or attack the railways near the coast, upon which Richmond largely depended for supplies. All of these objects were promptly accomplished except the capture of Wilmington. Had I remained in chief command I should have proceeded to its capture as soon as practicable after the fall of Fort Macon, which took place April 26, 1862.

Towards the end of Feb., 1863, I also gave Gen. Butler his final instructions for the capture of New Orleans. This was accomplished chiefly by the gallant action of the naval forces, about the 1st of May. Gen. Butler was ordered to secure all the approaches to New Orleans and open his communications with the column coming down the Mississippi. This being accomplished, Mobile, Pensacola, Galveston, etc., were to be attacked and occupied in turn.

About the middle of February I instructed Gen. T. W. Sherman to undertake the siege of Fort Pulaski and to occupy Fernandina, also directing him to study the problem of the reduction of Charleston and its defences.

By means of these various expeditions, carried out to their legitimate consequences, I hoped, without the employment of any very large land force, to occupy the important harbors on the coast, in order to reduce blockade-running to a minimum, and thus essentially cut off the very valuable assistance the Confederates, in return for their cotton, received from abroad in the way of arms, ammunition, clothing, and other necessary supplies which their own country produced either not at all or in wholly insufficient quantities. In addition to this most vital purpose, the possession of these important points on the coast would enable us to interfere seriously with the use of all railroads near the sea, give us new bases of operation from which either to make independent expeditions inland or to furnish new and short lines of supply to any main army moving parallel with the coast, while at the same time considerable numbers of the Confederate forces were occupied in watching them.

The following letters, and a subsequent paper addressed to the Secretary of War, sufficiently indicate the nature of those combinations:

TO THE SECRETARY OF WAR.

HEADQUARTERS, ARMY OF THE POTOMAC,
WASHINGTON, Sept. 6, 1861.

SIR: I have the honor to suggest the following proposition, with the request that the necessary authority be at once given me to carry it out: To organize a force of two brigades of five regiments each, of New England men, for the general service, but particularly adapted to coast service; the officers and men to be sufficiently conversant with boat-service to manage steamers, sailing-vessels, launches, barges, surf-boats, floating batteries, etc. To charter or buy for the command a sufficient number of propellers or tug-boats for transportation of men and supplies, the machinery of which should be amply protected by timber; the vessels to have permanent, experienced officers from the merchant service, but to be manned by details from the command. A naval officer to be attached to the staff of the commanding officer. The flank companies of each regiment to be armed with Dahlgren boat-guns, and carbines with waterproof cartridges; the other companies to have such arms as I may hereafter designate; to be uniformed and equipped as the Rhode Island regiments are. Launches and floating batteries with timber parapets of sufficient capacity to land or bring into action the entire force.

The entire management and organization of the force to be under my control, and to form an integral part of the Army of the Potomac.

The immediate object of this force is for operations in the inlets of Chesapeake bay and the Potomac. By enabling me thus to land troops at points where they are needed, this force can also be used in conjunction with a naval force operating against points on the sea-coast. This coast division to be commanded by a general officer of my selection; the regiments to be organized as other land forces; the disbursements for vessels, etc., to be made by the proper department of the army upon the requisitions of the general commanding the division, with my approval.

I think the entire force can be organized in thirty days; and by no means the least of the advantages of this proposition is the fact that it will call into the service a class of men who would not otherwise enter the army.

You will immediately perceive that the object of this force is to follow along the coast and up the inlets and rivers the movements of the main army when it advances.

I am, very respectfully, your obedient servant,

G. B. MCCLELLAN,

Maj-Gen. Commanding.

Hon. SIMON CAMERON,
Secretary of War.

Owing chiefly to the difficulty in procuring the requisite vessels and adapting them to the special purposes contemplated, this expedition was not ready for service until Jan., 1862. Then in the chief command, I deemed it best to send it to North Carolina, with the design indicated in the following letter:

TO GEN. BURNSIDE.

HEADQUARTERS OF THE ARMY,
WASHINGTON, Jan. 7, 1862.

GENERAL: In accordance with verbal instructions heretofore given you, you will, after uniting with Flag-officer Goldsborough at Fort Monroe, proceed under his convoy to Hatteras inlet, where you will, in connection with him, take the most prompt measures for crossing the fleet over the Bulkhead into the waters of the sound. Under the accompanying general order constituting the Department of North Carolina, you will assume command of the garrison at Hatteras inlet, and make such dispositions in regard to that place as your ulterior operations may render necessary, always being careful to provide for the safety of that very important station in any contingency.

Your first point of attack will be Roanoke island and its dependencies. It is presumed that the navy can reduce the batteries on the marshes and cover the landing of your troops on the main island, by which, in connection with a rapid movement of the gunboats to the northern extremity as soon as the marsh-battery is reduced, it may be hoped to capture the entire garrison of the place. Having occupied the island and its dependencies, you will at once proceed to the erection of the batteries and defences necessary to hold the position with a small force. Should the flag-officer require any assistance in seizing or holding the debouches of the canal from Norfolk, you will please afford it to him.

The commodore and yourself having completed your arrangements in regard to Roanoke island and the waters north of it, you will please at once make a descent on New Berne, having gained possession of which and the railroad passing through it, you will at once throw a sufficient force upon Beaufort and take the steps necessary to reduce Fort Macon and open that port. When you seize New Berne you will endeavor to seize the railroad as far west as Goldsborough, should circumstances favor such a movement. The temper of the people, the rebel force at hand, etc., will go far towards determining the question as to how far west the railroad can be safely occupied and held. Should circumstances render it advisable to seize and hold Raleigh, the main north and south line of railroad passing, through Goldsborough should be so effectually destroyed for considerable distances north and south of that point as to render it impossible for the rebels to use it to your disadvantage. A great point would be gained, in any event, by the effectual destruction of the Wilmington and Weldon Railroad.

I would advise great caution in moving so far into the interior as upon Raleigh. Having accomplished the objects mentioned, the next point of interest would probably be Wilmington, the reduction of which may require that additional means shall be afforded you. I would urge great caution in regard to proclamations. In no case would I go beyond a moderate joint proclamation with the naval commander, which should say as little as possible about politics or the negro; merely state that the true issue for which we are fighting is the preservation of the Union and upholding the laws of the general government, and stating that all who conduct themselves properly will, as far as possible, be protected in their persons and property.

You will please report your operations as often as an opportunity offers itself.

With my best wishes for your success, I am, etc., etc.,

GEO. B. MCCLELLAN,
Maj.-Gen. Commanding-in- Chief.
Brig.-Gen. A. E. BURNSIDE,
Commanding Expedition.

The following letters of instruction were sent to Gens. Halleck, Buell, Sherman, and Butler; and I also communicated verbally to these officers my views in full regarding the field of operations assigned to each, and gave them their instructions as much in detail as was necessary at that time:

TO GEN. HALLECK.

HEADQUARTERS OF THE ARMY,
WASHINGTON, D. C., Nov. 11, 1861.

GENERAL: In assigning you to the command of the Department of Missouri it is probably unnecessary for me to state that I have entrusted to you a duty which requires the utmost tact and decision.

You have not merely the ordinary duties of a military commander to perform, but the far more difficult task of reducing chaos to order, of changing probably the majority of the *personnel* of the staff of the department, and of reducing to a point of economy consistent with the interests and necessities of the State a system of reckless expenditure and fraud perhaps unheard of before in the history of the world.

You will find in your department many general and staff

officers holding illegal commissions and appointments not recog-
ized or approved by the President or Secretary of War. You
will please at once inform these gentlemen of the nullity of their
appointment, and see that no pay or allowances are issued to
them until such time as commissions may be authorized by the
President or Secretary of War.

If any of them give the slightest trouble, you will at once
arrest them and send them, under guard, out of the limits of
your department, informing them that if they return they will be
placed in close confinement. You will please examine into the
legality of the organization of the troops serving in the department. Then you find any illegal, unusual, or improper organizations, you will give to the officers and men an opportunity to
enter the legal military establishment under general laws and
orders from the War Department, reporting in full to these
headquarters any officer or organization that may decline.

You will please cause competent and reliable staff officers to
examine all existing contracts immediately, and suspend all payments upon them until you receive the report in each case.
Where there is the slightest doubt as to the propriety of the
contract you will be good enough to refer the matter, with full
explanation, to these headquarters, stating in each case what
would be a fair compensation for the services or materials
rendered under the contract. Discontinue at once the reception of material or services under any doubtful contract. Arrest
and bring to prompt trial all officers who have in any way violated their duty, to the government. In regard to the political
conduct of affairs, you will please labor to impress upon the
inhabitants of Missouri and the adjacent States that we are
fighting solely for the integrity of the Union, to uphold the
power of our national government, and to restore to the nation
the blessings of peace and good order.

With respect to military operations, it is probable, from the
best information in my possession, that the interests of the government will be best served by fortifying and holding in considerable strength Rolla, Sedalia, and other interior points, keeping
strong patrols constantly moving from the terminal stations, and
concentrating the mass of the troops on or near the Mississippi,
prepared for such ulterior operations as the public interests may
demand.

I would be glad to have you make as soon as possible a personal inspection of all the important points in your department,
and report the result to me. I cannot too strongly impress upon
you the absolute necessity of keeping me constantly advised of
the strength, condition, and location of your troops, together with
all facts that will enable me to maintain that general direction of
the armies of the United States which it is my purpose to exercise. I trust to you to maintain thorough organization, disci-

pline, and economy throughout your department. Please inform me as soon as possible of everything relating to the gunboats now in process of construction, as well as those completed.

The militia force authorized to be raised by the State of Missouri for its defence will be under your orders.

I am, general, etc., etc.,

GEORGE B. McCLELLAN,
Maj.-Gen. Commanding U. S. A.

Maj.-Gen. H. W. HALLECK, U. S. A.,
Commanding Department of Missouri.

TO GEN. BUELL.

HEADQUARTERS OF THE ARMY,
WASHINGTON, Nov. 7, 1861.

GENERAL: In giving you instructions for your guidance in command of the Department of the Ohio I do not design to fetter you. I merely wish to express plainly the general ideas which occur to me in relation to the conduct of operations there. That portion of Kentucky west of the Cumberland river is by its position so closely related to the States of Illinois and Missouri that it has seemed best to attach it to the Department of Missouri. Your operations there, in Kentucky, will be confined to that portion of the State east of the Cumberland river. I trust I need not repeat to you that I regard the importance of the territory committed to your care as second only to that occupied by the army under my immediate command. It is absolutely necessary that we shall hold all the State of Kentucky; not only that, but that the majority of its inhabitants shall be warmly in favor of our cause, it being that which best subserves their interests. It is possible that the conduct of our political affairs in Kentucky is more important than that of our military operations. I certainly cannot overestimate the importance of the former. You will please constantly to bear in mind the precise issue for which we are fighting; that issue is the preservation of the Union and the restoration of the full authority of the general government over all portions of our territory. We shall most readily suppress this rebellion and restore the authority of the government by religiously respecting the constitutional rights of all. I know that I express the feelings and opinion of the President when I say that we are fighting only to preserve the integrity of the Union and the constitutional authority of the general government.

The inhabitants of Kentucky may rely upon it that their domestic institutions will in no manner be interfered with, and that they will receive at our hands every constitutional protection. I have only to repeat that you will in all respects carefully regard the local institutions of the region in which you command, allowing nothing but the dictates of military necessity to cause you to depart from the spirit of these instructions.

So much in regard to political considerations. The military problem would be a simple one could it be entirely separated from political influences; such is not the case. Were the population among which you are to operate wholly or generally hostile, it is probable that Nashville should be your first and principal objective point. It so happens that a large majority of the inhabitants of Eastern Tennessee are in favor of the Union; it therefore seems proper that you should remain on the defensive on the line from Louisville to Nashville, while you throw the mass of your forces, by rapid marches by Cumberland Gap or Walker's Gap, on Knoxville, in order to occupy the railroad at that point, and thus enable the loyal citizens of Eastern Tennessee to rise, while you at the same time cut off the railway communication between Eastern Virginia and the Mississippi. It will be prudent to fortify the pass before leaving it in your rear.

Brig.-Gen. D. C. BUELL.

TO GEN. BUELL.

HEADQUARTERS OF THE ARMY,
WASHINGTON, Nov. 12, 1861.

GENERAL: Upon assuming command of the department I will be glad to have you make as soon as possible a careful report of the condition and situation of your troops, and of the military and political condition of your command. The main point to which I desire to call your attention is the necessity of entering Eastern Tennessee as soon as it can be done with reasonable chances of success, and I hope that you will, with the least possible delay, organize a column for that purpose, sufficiently guarding at the same time the main avenues by which the rebels may invade Kentucky. Our conversations on the subject of military operations have been so full, and my confidence in your judgment is so great, that I will not dwell further upon the subject, except to urge upon you the necessity of keeping me fully informed as to the state of affairs, both military and political, and your movements. In regard to political matters, bear in mind that we are fighting only to preserve the integrity of the Union and to uphold the power of the general government; as far as military necessity will permit, religiously respect the constitutional rights of all. Preserve the strictest discipline among the troops, and, while employing the utmost energy in military movements, be careful so to treat the unarmed inhabitants as to contract, not widen, the breach existing between us and the rebels.

I mean by this that it is the desire of the government to avoid unnecessary irritation by causeless arrests and persecution of individuals. Where there is good reason to believe that persons are actually giving aid, comfort, or information to the enemy, it is, of course, necessary to arrest them; but I have always found that it is the tendency of subordinates to make vexatious arrests on mere suspicion. You will find it well to direct that no arrest shall be made except by your order or that of your generals, unless in extraordinary cases, always holding the party making the arrest responsible for the propriety of his course. It should be our constant aim to make it apparent to all that their property, their comfort, and their personal safety will be best preserved by adhering to the cause of the Union.

If the military suggestions I have made in this letter prove to have been founded on erroneous data, you are, of course, perfectly free to change the plans of operations.

Brig.-Gen. D. C. BUELL,
Commanding Department of the Ohio.

TO GEN. T. W. SHERMAN.

HEADQUARTERS OF THE ARMY,
WASHINGTON, Feb. 14, 1862.

GENERAL: Your despatches in regard to the occupation of Dafuskie island, etc., were received to-day. I saw also to-day, for the first time, your requisition for a siege-train for Savannah.

After giving the subject all the consideration in my power I am forced to the conclusion that, under present circumstances, the siege and capture of Savannah do not promise results commensurate with the sacrifices necessary. When I learned that it was possible for the gunboats to reach the Savannah river above Fort Pulaski, two operations suggested themselves to my mind as its immediate results:

First. The capture of Savannah by a *coup de main,* the result of an instantaneous advance and attack by the army and navy.

The time for this has passed, and your letter indicates that you are not accountable for the failure to seize the propitious moment, but that, on the contrary, you perceived its advantages.

Second. To isolate Fort Pulaski, cut off its supplies, and at least facilitate its reduction by a bombardment.

Although we have a long delay to deplore, the second course still remains open to us; and I strongly advise the close blockade of Pulaski, and its bombardment as soon as the 13-inch mortars and heavy guns reach you. I am confident you can thus reduce it. With Pulaski you gain all that is really essential: you obtain complete control of the harbor, you relieve the blockading fleet, and render the main body of your force disposable for other operations.

I do not consider the possession of Savannah worth a siege

16

after Pulaski is in our hands.   But the possession of Pulaski is of the first importance.   The expedition to Fernandina is well, and I shall be glad to learn that it is ours.

But, after all, the greatest moral effect would be produced by the reduction of Charleston and its defences.   There the rebellion had its birth; there the unnatural hatred of our government is most intense; there is the centre of the boasted power and courage of the rebels.

To gain Fort Sumter and hold Charleston is a task well worthy of our greatest efforts and considerable sacrifices.   That is the problem I would be glad to have you study.   Some time must elapse before we can be in all respects ready to accomplish that purpose.   Fleets are *en route* and armies in motion which have certain preliminary objects to accomplish before we are ready to take Charleston in hand.   But the time will before long arrive when I shall be prepared to make that movement.   In the meantime it is my advice and wish that no attempt be made upon Savannah, unless it can be carried with certainty by a *coup de main.*

Please concentrate your attention and forces upon Pulaski and Fernandina. St. Augustine might as well be taken by way of an interlude while awaiting the preparations for Charleston. Success attends us everywhere at present.

> Very truly yours,
> GEO. B. McCLELLAN,
>   *Maj.-Gen.   Commanding.*

Gen. T. W. SHERMAN,
   Commanding at Port Royal, etc.

TO GEN. BUTLER.

> HEADQUARTERS OF THE ARMY,
> WASHINGTON, Feb. 23, 1862.

GENERAL: You are assigned to the command of the land forces destined to co-operate with the navy in the attacks upon New Orleans. You will use every means to keep your destination a profound secret, even from your staff officers, with the exception of your chief of staff and Lieut. Weitzell, of the engineers. The force at your disposal will consist of the first thirteen regiments named in your memorandum handed to me in person, the 21st Indiana, 4th Wisconsin, and 6th Michigan (old and good regiments from Baltimore).

The 21st Indiana, 4th Wisconsin, and 6th Michigan will await your orders at Fort Monroe.

Two companies of the 21st Indiana are well drilled as heavy artillery. The cavalry force already *en route* for Ship island will be sufficient for your purposes.

After full consultation with officers well acquainted with the country in which it is proposed to operate, I have arrived at the conclusion that two (2) light batteries fully equipped, and one (1) without horses, will be all that are necessary.

This will make your force about 14,400 infantry, 275 cavalry, 580 artillery; total, 15,255 men. The commanding general of the Department of Key West is authorized to loan you, temporarily, two regiments, Fort Pickens can probably give you another, which will bring your force to nearly 18,000.

The object of your expedition is one of vital importance-the capture of New Orleans. The route selected is up the Mississippi river, and the first obstacle to be encountered (perhaps the only one) is in the resistance offered by Forts St. Philip and Jackson. It is expected that the navy can reduce these works; in that case you will, after their capture, leave a sufficient garrison in them to render them perfectly secure; and it is recommended that, on the upward passage, a fern heavy guns and some troops be left at the pilot station (at the forks of the river) to cover a retreat in the event of a disaster. These troops and guns will, of course, be removed as soon as the forts are captured.

Should the navy fail to reduce the works you will land your forces and siege-train, and endeavor to breach the works, silence their fire, and carry them by assault.

The next resistance will be near the English Bend, where there are some earthen batteries. Here it may be necessary for you to land your troops and co-operate with the naval attack, although it is more than probable that the navy unassisted can accomplish the result. If these works are taken the city of New Orleans necessarily falls. In that event it will probably be best to occupy Algiers with the mass of your troops, also the eastern bank of the river above the city. It may be necessary to place some troops *in* the city to preserve order ; but if there appears to be sufficient Union sentiment to control the city, it may be best for purposes of discipline to keep your men out of the city.

After obtaining possession of New Orleans it will be necessary to reduce all the works guarding its approaches from the east, and particularly to gain the Manchac pass.

Baton Rouge, Berwick bay, and Fort Livingston will next claim your attention.

A feint on Galveston may facilitate the objects we have in view. I need not call your attention to the necessity of gaining possession of all the rolling stock you can on the different railways, and of obtaining control of the roads themselves. The occupation of Baton Rouge by a combined naval and land force should be accomplished as soon as possible after you have gained New Orleans. Then endeavor to open your communication with the northern column by the Mississippi, always bearing in mind the necessity of occupying Jackson, Mississippi as soon as you . can safely do so, either after or before you have effected the junction. Allow nothing to divert you from obtaining full possession of *all* the approaches to New Orleans. When that object is accomplished to its fullest extent it will be necessary to make a combined attack on Mobile, in order to gain possession of the harbor and works, as well as to control the railway terminus at the city. In regard to this I will send more detailed instructions as the operations of the northern column develop themselves.

I may briefly state that the general objects of the expedition are, *first* the reduction of New Orleans and all its approaches; then Mobile and its defences; then Pensacola, Galveston, etc. It is probable that by the time New Orleans is reduced it will be in the power of the government to reinforce the land forces sufficiently to accomplish all these objects. In the meantime you will please give all the assistance in your power to the army and navy commanders in your vicinity, never losing sight of the fact that the great object to be achieved is the capture and firm retention of New Orleans.

I am, etc.,

GEO. B. MCCLELLAN,
Maj.-Gen. Commanding U. S. Army.

Maj.-Gen. B. F. BUTLER,
U. S. Volunteers.

The plan indicated in the above letters comprehended in its scope the operations of all the armies of the Union, the Army of the Potomac as well. It was my intention, for reasons easy to be seen, that its various parts should be carried out simultaneously, or nearly so, and in co-operation along the whole line. If this plan was wise - and events have failed to prove that it was not- then it is unnecessary to defend any delay which would have enabled the Army of the Potomac to perform its share in the execution of the whole work.

The operations in the West began early in February, and soon resulted in the capture of Forts Henry and Donelson and the capture of Nashville. Shiloh took place on the 6th and 7th of April. It was not until May 21 that Corinth was evacuated.

I have already alluded to the very unsatisfactory condition in which Buell found his command, but he very soon satisfied himself that there was no apprehension of a dangerous offensive movement by the enemy, and steadily went to work to organize and discipline his troops. I gave him all the support and assistance in my power, sending him as much in the may of troops, arms, and supplies as the resources of the government and the necessities of other points permitted. He displayed very high qualities as an organizer, and mastered the strategical questions with marked ability; and I am satisfied that one of the very best things I did when in command was sending him to Kentucky.

About the time he went there, and for some months thereafter, immense pressure was brought to bear upon the government to do something at once for the relief of the Union men in East Tennessee. I was fully impressed by the necessity for doing this, and constantly urged Buell to send a column to that region, even at the expense of remaining temporarily on the defensive in front of Bowling Green. But Buell found it impossible to do so, in consequence of the disorganization which prevailed, the lack of transportation and supplies, and the impracticable condition of the roads in the fall and winter. My confidence in Buell's judgment and knowledge of the circumstances was such that I reluctantly acquiesced. I still regret that it was impossible to carry out this intention, for the effect of the occupation of Knoxville at that time would have been of the first importance. But I have no doubt as to the propriety of Buell's decision. He was so true and loyal a soldier that no mere obstacles would have deterred him from carrying out my clearly expressed wishes. He was the best judge as to the possibility of the expedition, and I have no doubt that he was right. Before the close of November Buell and I discussed the propriety of a movement up the Cumberland and Tennessee rivers, and concluded that it should form a necessary part of the plan of offensive operations. This was so self-evident a proposition that I had long thought of it, but I am not sure whether the actual suggestion to carry it practically into effect came first from Buell or myself - very likely from Buell; certainly it did not originate with Halleck or any of his surroundings. I will for the moment leave this subject, simply stating that by the 26th of Feb. Nashville was in our hands, and by the 3d of March Columbus, Kentucky. In the course of these operations Halleck delivered himself of several prophetic statements in regard to "good strategy," each of which proved to be ridiculous.

On the morning of Sunday, March 2, 1862, desiring to give orders for the further movements of Buell's and Halleck's commands, I went to the military telegraph-office - then in the headquarters of the Army of the Potomac at the corner of Pennsylvania avenue and Jackson square - and caused communication to be cut off from all wires except those leading to Halleck's headquarters at St. Louis and Buell's at Nashville. I then called Buell and Halleck to their respective offices, and asked for a full report of the condition of affairs, number, position, and condition of their troops, that of the enemy, etc. Buell promptly gave me the information needed.   Halleck replied the same day:

" . . . I have had no communication with Gen. Grant for more than a week. He left his command without my authority and went to Nashville. His army seems to be as much demoralized by the victory of Fort Donelson as was that of the Potomac by the defeat of Bull Run. It is hard to censure a successful general immediately after a victory, but I think he richly deserves it. I can get no returns, no reports, no information of any kind from him. Satisfied with his victory, he sits down and enjoys it without any regard to the future. I am worn out and tired with this neglect and inefficiency. C. F. Smith is almost the only officer equal to the emergency."

To this I replied:

Your despatch of last evening received.   The success of our cause demands that proceedings such as Grant's should be at once checked. Generals must observe discipline as well as private soldiers. Do not hesitate to arrest him at once, if the good of the service requires it, and place C. F. Smith in command. You are at liberty to regard this as a positive order, if it will smooth your way.   I appreciate the difficulties you have to encounter, and will be glad to relieve you from trouble as far as possible.

On the 4th Halleck telegraphed me:

"A rumor has just reached me that since the taking of Fort Donelson Grant has resumed his former bad habits. If so, it will account for his repeated neglect of my often-repeated orders. I do not deem it advisable to arrest him at present, but have placed Gen. Smith in command of the expedition up the Tennessee. I think Smith will restore order and discipline. . . ."

On the 6th Halleck telegraphed to Grant:

"Gen. McClellan directs that you report to me daily the num-

ber and position of the forces under your command. Your
neglect of repeated orders to report the strength of your command
has created great dissatisfaction and seriously interfered with military plans. Your going to Nashville without authority, and when
your presence with your troops was of the greatest importance,
was a matter of serious complaint at Washington, so much so
that I was advised to arrest you on your return."

On the 31st of March Halleck informed Grant:

"Gen. McClellan directed me to place Gen. Smith in command of the expedition until you were ordered to join it."

On the 10th of March the adjutant-general of the army, by
direction of the President, required from Halleck a report as to
Grant's unauthorized visit to Nashville and as to his general conduct.   On the 15th Halleck replied that Grant had gone to Nashville to communicate with Buell, that his motives were proper,
and advised that no further proceedings be had in the case.

Now to the story which prompts me to insert these despatches.
More than a year after the events in question Franklin wrote to   .
me that on meeting Grant at Memphis, or some such point on
the Mississippi, Grant asked what had made me hostile to him.
Franklin replied that he knew that I was not hostile but very
friendly to him.   Grant then said that that could not be so, for,
without any reason, I had ordered Halleck to relieve him from
command and arrest him soon after Fort Donelson, and that
Halleck had interfered to save him. I took no steps to unde-
ceive Grant, trusting to time to elucidate the question.

In the latter part of 1866, while I was in Europe, Gen. Grant,
through one of his staff, communicated with Gen. Marcy in regard
to papers missing from the files of the office of general-in-chief
during my tenure of the place.

In searching my papers Gen. Marcy found my retained copy-
of the despatch of March 2 from Halleck in which he reports
Grant's unauthorized absence, etc. This he forwarded to Gen.
Grant, who was thus for the first time informed of the truth.
This despatch and my reply had, with many others, disappeared
from the files in the office. So with regard to my correspondence as general-in-chief.

The military telegraph-office was first established by me, and
was located, as already stated, in the headquarters of the Army

of the Potomac. While I was absent from Washington for a
couple of days in March the Secretary of War, without any intimation to me, caused the entire office, with all the telegraphic
records, to be removed to the War Department.

I was relieved from the general command of the army while
with the front near Manassas (March 11), and never re-entered
the office of commanding general in the War Department. All
the papers there were taken possession of by the Secretary of
War, and he and Halleck are alone responsible for any gaps in
the files.

Some one abstracted the telegrams above alluded to. As to
Halleck's conduct with regard to Grant, no comment by me is
necessary. The facts speak for themselves.

[In this connection see "Personal Memoirs of U. S. Grant,"
vol. i. pp. 324-8; also, *North American Review*, Dec., 1885.
The following correspondence between Gens. Grant and McClellan is appended by the editor:]

HOTEL BYRON, VILLENEUVE, Nov. 24, 1866.
Gen. U. S. Grant, Commanding U. S. Army:

GENERAL: In a letter received yesterday from Gen. Marcy
he says: "I had a note yesterday from a member of Gen. Grant's
staff, in which he says it has been officially reported to the general that he (McClellan) had retained in his possession certain
records pertaining to the headquarters of the army which were
loaned to him while preparing his report in 1862-3."

I desire to state that I have not knowingly retained or caused
to be withheld any document whatever, whether important or
unimportant, belonging to the headquarters of the army or to
any other department of the government.

When my report was completed I caused all the original subordinate reports and all other documents belonging to the government to be boxed up, and sent them to the adjutant-general
of the army in Washington, I think at the same time with my
report. My recollection is that they were sent by the hands
of my aide-de-camp, Capt. A. McClellan. I do not think it possible that any document can have been overlooked, because in
examining my papers subsequently my attention would in all
probability have been attracted to it, and, as a matter of course,
I would at once have forwarded it to Washington. I shall be
under especial obligations to you, general, if you will cause me
to be informed what documents are alluded to in the report
referred to, also by whom the report was made to you.

To such a general statement as that made to Gen. Marcy-at least as it has reached me - I can only return a general reply, as I have already done.

Desiring the favor of an early reply, directed to the care of "Messrs. J. S. Morgan & Co., 22 Old Broad Street, London," I am, general, very truly yours,

GEO. B. MCCLELLAN.

"HEADQUARTERS, ARMIES OF THE U. S.,
"WASHINGTON, D. C., Dec. 10, 1866.

"DEAR GENERAL: I have the honor to acknowledge receipt of your letter of the 24th of Nov. In reply I enclose you copies of all letters addressed to Gen. Marcy on the subject of papers supposed to be in your possession. These letters contain a full explanation to yours, and, as you will see, do not imply an intention on your part to withhold any paper properly belonging to the headquarters of the army.

"Trusting that this letter, with enclosures, will relieve you of any misapprehension you may have felt from Gen. Marcy's letter, and with the assurance that the general kindly offered to furnish anything we might want from papers retained in your possession. I remain, very truly yours,

"U. S. GRANT.

"To Gen. G. B. MCCLELLAN."

VEVAY, SWITZERLAND,
Dec. 26, 1866.

MY DEAR GENERAL: Yours of the 10th inst. reached me yesterday, and I now fully understand what is wanted.

When called to the command of the United States armies in 1861 I left unchanged the organization of the Army of the Potomac and its headquarters, and in no manner merged them with those of the headquarters of the United States army - the staff for each being distinct, except with regard to my personal aides-de-camp. Thus Gen. Marcy, the chief of staff of the Army of the Potomac, had nothing to do with the headquarters of the army of the United States. Gen. S. Williams was adjutant-general of the Army of the Potomac, while Gen. L. Thomas was my adjutant-general in my capacity as commander of the United States army, etc. The papers and records of the two offices were entirely distinct. I had in the War Department building two rooms for my office as commanding general of the United States army, and thither Gen. Thomas brought to me all papers and matters requiring my action, received my orders thereon, carried back the papers to his own office, where they should be found, together with the orders and letters issued by him thereon in conformity with my instructions. You will the more readily comprehend the state of affairs when I remind you that my predecessor, Gen. Scott, had an office - first in New York, afterwards in Washington - entirely distinct from that of the adjutant-general of the United States army, where he had his own adjutant-general and entirely distinct records; the adjutant-general of the United States army being then simply the adjutant-general of the Secretary of War. I changed the arrangement, dispensed with the machinery of a separate office, and merged all the routine service and records of the command-in-chief with those of the adjutant-general's office. The only papers, to the best of my recollection, kept in my office were the retained copies of my own letters on subjects of an important nature requiring more or less secrecy, such as letters of instruction in regard to military movements. As the telegraph was much used, these letters were not numerous. Col. A. V. Colburn had charge of these letters, and I am not sure whether they were copied into books or simply filed.   I kept nothing for myself but the original rough drafts, either in my own handwriting or that of the aides to whom they were dictated.   All written reports received went finally to the adjutant-general's office or that of the Secretary of War; none were retained in my office, which was, after all, simply a place for the transaction of business, and not a place of record. When I left Washington in March, 1862, to accompany the Army of the Potomac on its march towards Manassas, I was still the commanding general of the United States army, had no reason whatever to suppose that any change was contemplated by the President, left at a few hours notice, and expected to return in a few days, preparatory to the final movement to the Peninsula. I therefore made no special arrangements in regard to my office in the War Department, and left everything as it happened to be, all my personal aides accompanying me. Two or three days after, while at Fairfax Court-House, I, to my complete surprise, received *through the newspapers* the orders relieving me from the command of the United States army, and never afterwards entered the office in Washington.   I was informed that it was *immediately* taken possession of by the War Department for its own uses, and have no knowledge of what disposition was made of the papers, etc., found there, further than that it was about the same time stated to me that the War Department had taken possession of everything in the office, as the functions of commanding general were assumed by the secretary. All telegraphic despatches of any importance were sent and received in cipher, and were handed to me translated; the work of deciphering, and the reverse, being executed in the telegraph-office. My recollection is that the cipher copies, at least, were recorded in books, which were kept in the chief telegraph-office; these books were never in my personal possession. This chief office, originally organized under my direction, was in the building occupied as the headquarters of the Army of the Potomac.

on Pennsylvania avenue and Jackson square. Soon after the accession of the present Secretary of War to office, and during my absence from the city on duty for two or three days, the entire establishment, with all its records, apparatus, and *personnel,* was removed to the War Department building, without my knowledge, by order of the Secretary of War; and from, that time I ceased to have the slightest control over it. When I returned to the city I found the removal accomplished, which was the first intimation I had of it. In that office should be found copies of all the messages that passed through it. With regard to the books containing the original duplicates of my messages sent, I have now no means of knowing what ones were left in my War Department office when it passed from my possession. I do not think there are any in my possession (among my papers in the United States) except that sent to you by Gen. Marcy. As that was simply my private memorandum, I would be glad to have it returned to Gen. Marcy when you have done with it. I was not aware that the telegrams of Feb. and March, 1862, from Gen. Halleck were among my papers. I have requested Gen. Marcy to forward to you whatever copies of telegrams, etc., he may find. From his letter to me I think that he has examined all my papers, for all that I know of are at Orange. I will do my best to aid him in making a thorough search. When I return to the United States-probably in the course of a few months - I will most cheerfully aid you, in any possible way, to carry out your wishes; but I am at present inclined to think that a close search in Washington will be productive of much better results than one conducted elsewhere.

I must apologize for inflicting so long a letter upon you, and am, my dear general,

Sincerely your friend,
GEO. B. MCCLELLAN.

Gen. U. S. GRANT,
Commanding U. S. Armies.

CHAPTER XIII.

Evacuation of Manassas - Army corps - McClellan removed from chief command - President's military orders - Plan of advance on Richmond - Derangement of all plans by the administration.

THE organization of army corps directed by the President's order of March 8, 1862, was the work of the President and Secretary of War, probably urged by McDowell. It was issued without consulting me and against my judgment, for from the beginning it had been my intention to postpone the formation of army corps until service in the field had indicated what general officers were best fitted to exercise those most important commands. The mistakes of an incompetent division commander may be rectified, but those of a corps commander are likely to be fatal. The President designated the senior general officers to command the corps. The day after this order was issued we received information, that seemed reliable, of the evacuation of Manassas. The President and Secretary were with me at the time, and fully approved my determination of going to Porter's headquarters, where I could receive information more readily and be better prepared to act as circumstances might require, whether to move in pursuit or not. I at once sent Averill with a brigade of cavalry to verify the news and do what he could against the enemy's rear-guard; but Gen. Johnston had, as usual, masked his retreat so well that nothing could be effected.

In the course of the evening I determined to move the whole army forward, partly with the hope that I might be able to take advantage of some accident and bring Johnston to battle under favorable circumstances, but also to break up the camps, give the troops a little experience in marching and bivouac before finally leaving the old base of supplies, to test the transportation arrangements and get rid of *impedimenta,* and thus prepare things for the movement to the Peninsula. It also seemed probable that this advance, in connection with the recent move on Harper's Ferry and Charleston, would tend to make Johnston more uncertain as to my real intentions. In the course of the evening I telegraphed to the Secretary of War:

"In the arrangements for the advance of to-morrow it is impossible to carry into effect the arrangements for the formation of army corps. I am obliged to take groups as I find them, and to move them by divisions. I respectfully ask a suspension of the order directing it until the present movement be over."

To this the secretary made the following singular reply:

"I think it is the duty of every officer to obey the President's orders. Nor can I see any reason why you should not obey them in the present instance; I must therefore decline to suspend them."

To this I at once replied at one A.M.:

"You have entirely misunderstood me, and the idea I intended to convey was simply that I could not, under the pressure of the new aspect of affairs, immediately carry out the President's order as to the formation of army corps. It is absolutely necessary that I should at once move divisions as they stand. If you require me to suspend movements until army corps can be formed, I will do so, but I regard it as a military necessity that the divisions should move to the front at once without waiting for the formation of army corps. If it is your order to wait until the corps can be formed, I will, of course, wait. I will comply with the President's order as soon as possible. I intended to do so to-morrow, but circumstances have changed. If you desire it I will at once countermand all the orders I have given for an advance until the formation of army corps is completed. I have only to add that the order I have given to-night to advance early in the morning was dictated solely by the present condition of affairs. If the leave to suspend the order be granted there will be no unreasonable delay in the formation of army corps. I await your reply here, that, if you so direct, I may countermand my orders at once. Please reply at once."

To this the secretary replied:

"I do not understand the President's order as restraining you from any military movement, by divisions or otherwise, that circumstances in your judgment may render expedient, and I certainly do not wish to delay or change any movement whatever that you have made or desire to make. I only wish to avoid giving any sanction to a suspension of a policy which the President has ordered to be pursued; but if you think that the terms of the order as it stands would operate to retard or in any way restrain movements that circumstances require to be made before the army corps are formed, I will assume the responsibility of suspending the order for that purpose, and authorize you to make any movement, by division or otherwise, to your own judgment, without stopping to form the army corps. My desire is that you should exercise every power that you think present circumstances require to be exercised without delay, but I want that you and I should not seem to be desirous of opposing any order of the President without necessity. I say, therefore, move just as you think best now, and let the other matter stand until it can be done without impeding movements."

To this I replied at 2.40 A.M.:

Your reply received. The troops are in motion. I thank you for your despatch: it relieves me much, and you will be convinced that I have not asked too much of you.

It was only by throwing the responsibility of delay upon the secretary that he withdrew his quite unnecessary opposition. My order for the formation of the corps was given on the 13th, as soon as circumstances permitted.

McDowell was very anxious to have the reserve artillery, the cavalry, and the regular infantry attached to his corps; fortunately, I kept them by themselves, or I should, no doubt, have lost them as well as McDowell's own corps.

On the 10th I reached Fairfax Court-House and established headquarters there. It was now evident, from the information received, that it would be impossible to reach the enemy within a reasonable distance from Washington. The various divisions were therefore halted where they stood, at convenient distances from headquarters, and the preparations pushed for embarking for the Peninsula. I threw forward Sumner with two divisions and Stoneman with a cavalry command to proceed as far as the Rapidan and Rappahannock, to secure the crossings and still further deceive the enemy as to my intentions.

While here I learned through the public newspapers that I was displaced in the command of the United States armies. It may be well to state that no one in authority had ever expressed to me the slightest disapprobation of my action in that capacity, nor had I received any information of a purpose to change my position.

President's War Order, No. 3,

"EXECUTIVE MANSION, WASHINGTON,
"March 11, 1862.

"Maj.-Gen. McClellan having personally taken the field at the head of the Army of the Potomac, until otherwise ordered he is relieved from the command of the other military departments, he retaining command of the Department of the Potomac.

"*Ordered, further,* That the departments now under the respective commands of Gens. Halleck and Hunter, together with so much of that under Gen. Buell as lies west of a north and south line indefinitely drawn through Knoxville, Tennessee, be consolidated and designated the Department of the Mississippi; and that, until otherwise ordered, Maj.-Gen. Halleck have command of said department.

"*Ordered, also,* That the country west of the Department of the Potomac and east of the Department of the Mississippi be a military department to be called the Mountain Department, and that the same be commanded by Maj.-Gen. Fremont.

"That all the commanders of departments, after the receipt of this order by them, respectively report severally and directly to the Secretary of War, and that prompt, full, and frequent reports will be expected of all and each of them.

"ABRAHAM   LINCOLN."

The intelligence took me entirely by surprise, and the order proved to be one of the steps taken to tie my hands in order to secure the failure of the approaching campaign. Elsewhere I state the effect of this change in altering the condition of affairs, and breaking that unity of action which it was my purpose to enforce in the operations of the different armies in the field, as well as its effect upon operations in Virginia.

Though unaware of the President's intention to remove me from the position of general-in-chief, I cheerfully acceded to the disposition he saw fit to make of my services, and so informed him in a note on the 12th of March:

Unofficial.

FAIRFAX COURT-HOUSE,
March 12, 1862.

His Excellency A. Lincoln, President:

MY DEAR SIR: I have just seen Gov. Dennison, who has

detailed to me the conversation he held with you yesterday and to-day.

I beg to say that I cordially endorse all he has said to you in my behalf, and that I thank you most sincerely for the official confidence and kind personal feelings you entertain for me.

I believe I said to you some weeks since, in connection with some Western matters, that no feeling of self-interest or ambition should ever prevent me from devoting myself to your service. I am glad to have the opportunity to prove it, and you will find that, under present circumstances, I shall work just as cheerfully as before, and that no consideration of self will in any manner interfere with the discharge of my public duties. Again thanking you for the official and personal kindness you have so often evinced towards me,

I am, most sincerely your friend,

GEO. B. McCLELLAN.

While at Fairfax Court-House an order arrived assigning Gen. Wadsworth to the command of Washington. The secretary had spoken to me on the subject some days before, whereupon I objected to the selection for the reason that Gen. Wadsworth was not a soldier by training. I said that one of the very best soldiers in the army was necessary for the command of Washington, which was next in importance to the command of the Army of the Potomac - an officer fully posted in all the details of the profession; and that, much as I should dislike sparing him, I would give up Franklin for the place. The secretary replied that Wadsworth had been selected because it was necessary, for political reasons, to conciliate the agricultural interests of New York, and that it was useless to discuss the matter, because it would in no event be changed.

When Gen. Wadsworth parted from me at Fairfax he professed the greatest devotion and friendship for me, but at once became an enemy, probably because Stanton informed him of the objections I had made to his appointment, without giving him the real grounds of my opposition.

My memorandum of Aug. 2, 1861, shows that even then I regarded Virginia as the most important portion of the immense theatre of operations. Gen. Scott differed from me, and thought the valley of the Mississippi more vital. While fully recognizing the importance and necessity of operations in the valley of the Mississippi, Tennessee, and Cumberland rivers, and of coast expeditions, I always held the eastern line to be the true theatre of decisive operations.

If I had been retained in chief command, untrammelled as to time and means, I should, in the early spring of 1862, have pushed with all energy the operations against Wilmington, Charleston, and New Orleans, as well as in the Mississippi, Tennessee, and Cumberland valleys, and against the Knoxville and Lynchburg Railroad, *via* Cumberland Gap, and early in May have thrown the Army of the Potomac to the James river with a strength of over 150,000 for duty. I intended to transport by water to Urbana, on the lower Rappahannock, four divisions of infantry with their batteries, the regular infantry, one bridge-train, a few squadrons of cavalry, and a small number of wagons; with them to push by a forced march to the vicinity of West Point, and then cross the Mattapony and Pamunkey rivers, thus compelling the evacuation of Yorktown, and perhaps cutting off Magruder's force in the Peninsula. Meanwhile the reserve artillery, the remaining cavalry, bridge-trains, and necessary wagons were to be concentrated in the vicinity of Point Lookout, and, simultaneously with the landing at Urbana, ferried across the Potomac on North river ferry-boats, marched to the Rappahannock - the movement covered by an infantry force near Heathsville - then ferried over the Rappahannock and moved rapidly to unite with the force first landed. Prior to the evacuation of Yorktown the remaining portions of the army would have been landed at Urbana, and, subsequently to that, at West Point or on the James, as circumstances required.

As soon as the leading divisions of infantry crossed the Pamunkey they would have moved on Richmond, covered by cavalry on both flanks. My letters of Feb. 3 and March 19, 1862, to the Secretary of War, show that, under certain circumstances, I contemplated crossing the James river and attacking Richmond from the south.

The fears of the administration and their inability to comprehend the merits of the scheme, or else the determination that I should not succeed in the approaching campaign, induced them to prohibit me from carrying out the Urbana movement. They gave me the choice between the direct overland route via Manassas, and the route with Fort Monroe as a base. Of course I

17

selected the latter. My report gives all the most important correspondence on this subject, and the arguments I used in support of the plan of campaign which commended itself to my judgment.

Let me here call attention to the President's orders of Jan. 27 and Jan. 31, 1862, and his letter to me of Feb. 3, answered in mine of the same day to the Secretary of War:

President's General War Order, No. 1.

"EXECUTIVE MANSION,
"WASHINGTON, Jan. 27, 1862.

"*Ordered,* That the 22d day of Feb., 1862, be the day for a general movement of the land and naval forces of the United States against the insurgent forces. That especially the army at and about Fortress Monroe, the Army of the Potomac, the Army of Western Virginia the army near Munfordville, Kentucky, the army and flotilla at Cairo, and a naval force in the Gulf of Mexico be ready to move on that day.

"That all other forces, both land and naval, with their respective commanders, obey existing orders for the time, and be ready to obey additional orders when duly given.

"That the heads of departments, and especially the Secretaries of War and of the Navy, with all their subordinates, and the general-in-chief, with all other commanders and subordinates of land and naval forces, will severally be held to their strict and full responsibilities for prompt execution of this order.

"ABRAHAM LINCOLN."

The order of Jan. 31, 1862, was as follows:

President's Special Way Order, No. 1.

"EXECUTIVE MANSION,
"WASHINGTON, Jan. 31, 1862.

"*Ordered,* That all the disposable force of the Army of the Potomac, after providing safely for the defence of Washington, be formed into an expedition for the immediate object of seizing and occupying a point upon the railroad southwestward of what is known as Manassas Junction, all details to be in the discretion of the commander-in-chief, and the expedition to move before or on the 22d day of Feb. next.

"ABRAHAM LINCOLN."

I asked his excellency whether this order was to be regarded as final, or whether I could be permitted to submit in writing my objections to his plan and my reasons for preferring my own. Permission was accorded, and I therefore prepared the letter to the Secretary of War which is given below.

Before this had been submitted to the President he addressed me the following not:

EXECUTIVE MANSION
"WASHINGTON Feb. 3, 1862.

"MY DEAR SIR: You and I have distinct and different plans for a movement of the Army of the Potomac: yours to be done by the Chesapeake, up the Rappahannock to Urbana, and across land to the terminus of the railroad on the York river; mine to move directly to a point on the railroad southwest of Manassas.

"If you will give satisfactory answers to the following questions I shall gladly yield my plan to yours:

"1st. Does not your plan involve a greatly larger expenditure of *time* and *money* than mine?

"2d. Wherein is a victory *more certain* by your plan than mine?

"3d. Wherein is a victory *more valuable* by your plan than mine?

"4th. In fact, would it not be less valuable in this: that it would break no great line of the enemy's communications, while mine would?

"5th. In case of disaster would not a retreat be more difficult by your plan than mine?

"Yours truly,

"ABRAHAM LINCOLN.

"Maj.-Gen. McCLELLAN."

These questions were substantially answered by the following letter of the same date to the Secretary of War:

HEADQUARTERS OF THE ARMY,
WASHINGTON, Feb. 3, 1862.

SIR: I ask your indulgence for the following papers, rendered necessary by circumstances.

I assumed command of the troops in the vicinity of Washington on Saturday, July 27, 1861, six days after the battle of Bull Run.

I found no army to command - a mere collection of regiments cowering on the banks of the Potomac, some perfectly raw, others dispirited by the recent defeat.

Nothing of any consequence had been done to secure the southern approaches to the capital by means of defensive works; nothing whatever had been undertaken to defend the avenues to the city on the northern side of the Potomac.

The troops were not only undisciplined, undrilled, and dispirited; they were not even placed in military positions. The city was almost in a condition to have been taken by a dash of a regiment of cavalry.

Without one day's delay I undertook the difficult task assigned to me. That task the honorable secretary knows was given to me without solicitation or foreknowledge. How far I have accomplished it will best be shown by the past and the present.

The capital is secure against attack; the extensive fortifications erected by the labor of our troops enable a small garrison to hold it against a numerous army; the enemy have been held in check; the State of Maryland is securely in our possession, the detached counties of Virginia are again within the pale of our laws, and all apprehension of trouble in Delaware is at an end; the enemy are confined to the positions they occupied before the disaster of the 21st July. More than all this, I have now under my command a well-drilled and reliable army, to which the destinies of the country may be confidently committed. This army is young and untried in battle, but it is animated by the highest spirit and is capable of great deeds.

That so much has been accomplished and such an army created in so short a time from nothing will hereafter be regarded as one of the highest glories of the administration and the nation.

Many weeks - I may say many months - ago this Army of the Potomac was fully in condition to repel any attack; but there is a vast difference between that and the efficiency required to enable troops to attack successfully an army elated by victory and entrenched in a position long since selected, studied, and fortified.

In the earliest papers I submitted to the President I asked for an effective and movable force far exceeding the aggregate now on the banks of the Potomac. I have not the force I asked for.

Even when in a subordinate position I always looked beyond the operations of the Army of the Potomac. I was never satisfied in my own mind with a barren victory, but looked to combined and decisive operations.

When I was placed in command of the armies of the United States I immediately turned my attention to the whole field of operations, regarding the Army of the Potomac as only one, while the most important, of the masses under my command.

I confess that I did not then appreciate the total absence of a general plan which had before existed, nor did I know that utter disorganization and want of preparation pervaded the Western armies.

I took it for granted that they were nearly, if not quite, in

condition to move towards the fulfilment of my plans. I acknowledge that I made a great mistake.

I sent at once, with the approval of the executive, officers I
considered competent to command in Kentucky and Missouri.
Their instructions looked to prompt movements. I soon found
that the labor of creation and organization had to be performed
there; transportation, arms, clothing, artillery, discipline - all
were wanting. These things required time to procure them.

The generals in command have done their work most credi-
tably, but we are still delayed. I had hoped that a general advance could be made during the good weather of December; I
was mistaken.

My wish was to gain possession of the Eastern Tennessee
Railroad as a preliminary movement, then to follow it up immediately by an attack on Nashville and Richmond, as nearly at the
same time as possible.

I have ever regarded our true policy as being that of fully
preparing ourselves, and then seeking for the most decisive
results. I do not wish to waste life in useless battles, but prefer
to strike at the heart.

Two bases of operations seem to present themselves for the
advance of the Army of the Potomac:

1st. That of Washington - its present position - involving a
direct attack upon the entrenched positions of the enemy at
Centreville, Manassas, etc., or else a movement to turn one or
both flanks of those positions, or a combination of the two
plans.

The relative force of the two armies will not justify an attack
on both flanks; an attack on his left flank alone involves a long
line of wagon communication, and cannot prevent him from collecting for the decisive battle all the detachments now on his
extreme right and left.

Should we attack his right flank by the line of the Occoquan,
and a crossing of the Potomac below that river and near his
batteries, we could perhaps prevent the junction of the enemy's
right with his centre (we might destroy the former); we would
remove the obstructions to the navigation of the Potomac, reduce
the length of wagon transportation by establishing new depots at
the nearest points of the Potomac, and strike more directly his
main railway communication.

The fords of the Occoquan below the mouth of the Bull Run
are watched by the rebels; batteries are said to be placed on the
heights in the rear (concealed by the woods), and the arrangement of his troops is such that he can oppose some considerable
resistance to a passage of that stream. Information has just been
received to the effect that the enemy are entrenching a line of
heights extending from the vicinity of Sangster's (Union Mills)
towards Evansport. Early in January Spriggs's ford was occu-

pied by General Rhodes with 3,600 men and eight (8) guns; there are strong reasons for believing that Davis's ford is occupied. These circumstances indicate or prove that the enemy anticipates the movement in question, and is prepared to resist it. Assuming for the present that this operation is determined upon, it may be well to examine briefly its probable progress. In the present state of affairs our column (for the movement of so large a force must be made in several columns, at least five or six) can reach the Accotink without danger; during the march thence to the Occoquan our right flank becomes exposed to an attack from Fairfax Station, Sangster's, and Union Mills. This danger must be met by occupying in some force either the two first-named places, or, better, the point of junction of the roads leading thence to the village of Occoquan; this occupation must be continued so long as we continue to draw supplies by the roads from this city, or until a battle is won.

The crossing of the Occoquan should be made at all the fords from Wolf's Run to the mouth, the points of crossing not being necessarily confined to the fords themselves. Should the enemy occupy this line in force we must, with what assistance the flotilla can afford, endeavor to force the passage near the mouth, thus forcing the enemy to abandon the whole line or be taken in flank himself.

Having gained the line of the Occoquan, it would be necessary to throw a column by the shortest route to Dumfries, partly to force the enemy to abandon his batteries on the Potomac, partly to cover our left flank against an attack from the direction of Acquia, and, lastly, to establish our communications with the river by the best roads, and thus give us new depots. The enemy would by this time have occupied the line of the Occoquan above Bull Run, holding Brentsville in force, and perhaps extending his lines somewhat further to the southwest.

Our next step would then be to prevent the enemy from crossing the Occoquan between Bull Run and Broad Run, to fall upon our right flank while moving on Brentsville. This might be effected by occupying Bacon Race church and the cross-roads near the mouth of Bull Run, or still more effectually by moving to the fords themselves and preventing, him from debouching on our side.

These operations would possibly be resisted, and it would require some time to effect them, as, nearly at the same time as possible, we should gain the fords necessary to our purposes above Broad Run. Having secured our right flank, it would become necessary to carry Brentsville at any cost, for we could not leave it between the right flank and the main body. The final movement on the railroad must be determined by circumstances existing at the time.

This brief sketch brings out in bold relief the great advantage possessed by the enemy in the strong central position he occupies, with roads diverging in every direction, and a strong line of defence enabling him to remain on the defensive, with a small force on one flank, while he concentrates everything on the other for a decisive action.

Should we place a portion of our force in front of Centreville, while the rest crosses the Occoquan, we commit the error of dividing our army by a very difficult obstacle, and by a distance too great to enable the two parts to support each other, should either be attacked by the masses of the enemy while the other is held in check.

I should perhaps have dwelt more decidedly on the fact that the force left near Sangster's must be allowed to remain somewhere on that side of the Occoquan until the decisive battle is over, so as to cover our retreat in the event of disaster, unless it should be decided to select and entrench a new base somewhere near Dumfries - a proceeding involving much time.

After the passage of the Occoquan by the main army this covering force could be drawn into a more central and less exposed position - say Brimstone Hill or nearer the Occoquan. In this latitude the weather will for a considerable period be very uncertain, and a movement commenced in force on roads in tolerably firm condition will be liable, almost certain, to be much delayed by rains and snow. It will, therefore, be best to impossible to surprise the enemy or take him at a disadvantage by rapid manœuvres. Our slow progress will enable him to divine our purposes and take his measures accordingly. The probability is, from the best information we possess, that the enemy has improved the roads leading to his lines of defence, while we have to work as we advance.

Bearing in mind what has been said, and the present unprecedented and impassable condition of the roads, it will be evident that no precise period can be fixed upon for the movement on this line. Nor can its duration be closely calculated; it seems certain that many weeks may elapse before it is possible to commence the march. Assuming the success of this operation, and the defeat of the enemy as certain, the question at once arises as to the importance of the results gained. I think these results would be confined to the possession of the field of battle, the evacuation of the line of the upper Potomac by the enemy, and the moral effect of the victory - important results, it is true, but not decisive of the war, nor securing the destruction of the enemy's main army, for he could fall back upon other positions and fight us again and again, should the condition of his troops permit. If he is in no condition to fight us again out of the range of the entrenchments at Richmond, we would find it a very difficult and tedious matter to follow him up there, for he would destroy his railroad bridges and otherwise impede our progress through a region where the roads are as bad as they well can be, and we would probably find ourselves forced at last to change the whole theatre of war, or to seek a shorter land route to Richmond, with a smaller available force and at an expenditure of much more time, than were we to adopt the short line at once. We would also have forced the enemy to concentrate his forces and perfect his defensive measures at the very points where it is desirable to strike him when least prepared.

2d. The second base of operations available for the Army of the Potomac is that of the lower Chesapeake bay, which affords the shortest possible land route to Richmond and strikes directly at the heart of the enemy's power in the east.

The roads in that region are passable at all seasons of the year.

The country now alluded to is much more favorable for offensive operations than that in front of Washington (which is *very* unfavorable): much more level, more cleared land, the woods less dense, the soil more sandy, and the spring some two or three weeks earlier. A movement in force on that line obliges the enemy to abandon his entrenched position at Manassas, in order to hasten to cover Richmond and Norfolk. He *must* do this; for should he permit us to occupy Richmond his destruction can be averted only by entirely defeating us in a battle in which he must be the assailant. This movement, if successful, gives us the capital, the communications, the supplies of the rebels; Norfolk would fall; all the waters of the Chesapeake would be ours; all Virginia would be in our power, and the enemy forced to abandon Tennessee and North Carolina. The alternative presented to the enemy would be, to beat us in a position selected by ourselves, disperse, or pass beneath the Caudine Forks.

Should we be beaten in a battle we have a perfectly secure retreat down the Peninsula upon Fort Monroe, with our flanks perfectly covered by the fleet.

During the whole movement our left flank is covered by the water. Our right is secure, for the reason that the enemy is too distant to reach us in time; he can only oppose us in front. We bring our fleet into full play.

After a successful battle our position would be - Burnside forming our left; Norfolk held securely: our centre connecting Burnside with Buell, both by Raleigh and Lynchburg; Buell in Eastern Tennessee and North Alabama; Halleck at Nashvilie and Memphis.

The next movement would be to connect with Sherman on the left by reducing Wilmington and Charleston; to advance our centre into South Carolina and Georgia; to push Buell either towards Montgomery or to unite with the main army in Georgia; to throw Halleck southward to meet the naval expedition from New Orleans.

We should then be in a condition to reduce at our leisure all the Southern seaports; to occupy all the avenues of communication; to use the great outlet of the Mississippi; to re-establish our government and arms in Arkansas, Louisiana, and Texas; to force the slaves to labor for our subsistence instead of that of the rebels; to bid defiance to all foreign interference. Such is the object I have ever had in view; this is the general plan which I hope to accomplish.

For many long months I have labored to prepare the Army of the Potomac to play its part in the programme; from the day when I was placed in command of all our armies I have exerted myself to place all the other armies in such a condition that they, too, could perform their allotted duties.

Should it be determined to operate from the lower Chesapeake, the point of landing which promises the most brilliant result is Urbana, on the lower Rappahannock. This point is easily reached by vessels of heavy draught; it is neither occupied nor observed by the enemy; it is but one march from West Point, the key of that region, and thence but two marches to Richmond. A rapid movement from Urbana would probably cut off Magruder in the Peninsula and enable us to occupy Richmond before it could be strongly reinforced. Should we fail in that we could, with the co-operation of the navy, cross the James and throw ourselves in rear of Richmond, thus forcing the enemy to come out and attack us, fur his position would be untenable with us on the southern bank of the river.

Should circumstances render it not advisable to land at Urbana we can use Mobjack bay, or, the worst coming to the worst, me can take Fort Monroe as a base and operate with complete security, although with less celerity and brilliancy of results, up the Peninsula.

To reach whatever point may be selected as a base, a large amount of cheap water transportation must be collected, consisting mainly of canal-boats, barges, mood-boats, schooners, etc., towed by small steamers, all of a very different character from those required for all previous expeditions. This can certainly be accomplished within thirty days from the time the order is given. I propose, as the best possible plan that can, in my judgment, be adopted, to select Urbana as a landing-place for the first detachments; to transport by water four divisions of infantry with their batteries, the regular infantry, a fern wagons, one bridge-train, and a few squadrons of cavalry, making the vicinity of Hooker's position the place of embarkation for as many as possible; to move the regular cavalry and reserve artillery, the remaining bridge-trains and wagons, to a point somewhere near Cape Lookout, then ferry them over the river by means of North river ferry-boats, march them over to the Rappahannock (covering the movement by an infantry force near Heathsville), and to cross the Rappahannock in a similar way. The expense and difficulty of the movement will then be very much diminished (a saving of transportation of about 10,000 horses) and the result none the less certain.

The concentration of the cavalry, etc., on the lower counties of Maryland can be effected without exciting suspicion, and the movement made without delay from that cause.

This movement, if adopted, will not at all expose the city of Washington to danger.

The total force to be thrown upon the new line would be, according to circumstances, from 110,000 to 140,000. I hope to use the latter number by bringing fresh troops into Washington and still leaving it quite safe. I fully realize that in all projects offered time will probably be the most valuable consideration. It is my decided opinion that, in that point of view, the second plan should be adopted. It is possible, nay, highly probable, that the weather and state of the roads may be such as to delay the direct movement from Washington, with its unsatisfactory results and great risks, far beyond the time required to complete the second plan. In the first case we can fix no definite time for an advance. The roads have gone from bad to worse. Nothing like their present condition was ever known here before; they are impassable at present. We are entirely at the mercy of the weather. It is by no means certain that we can beat them at Manassas. On the other line I regard success as certain by all the chances of war. We demoralize the enemy by forcing him to abandon his prepared position for one which we have chosen, in which all is in our favor, and where success must produce immense results.

My judgment, as a general, is clearly in favor of this project. Nothing is certain in war, but all the chances are in favor of this movement. So much am I in favor of the southern line of operations that I would prefer the move from Fortress Monroe as a base, as a certain though less brilliant movement than that from Urbana, to an attack upon Mannssas.

I know that his excellency the President, you, and I all agree in our wishes; and that these wishes are, to bring this war to a close as promptly as the means in our possession will permit. I believe that the mass of the people have entire confidence in us—I am sure of it. Let us, then, look only to the great result to be accomplished, and disregard everything else.

I am, very respectfully, your obedient servant,

GEO. B. MCCLELLAN,
Maj.-Gen. Commanding.

Hon. E. M. STANTON,
Secretary of War.

This letter must have produced some effect upon the mind of

the President, since the execution of his order was not required, although it was not revoked as formally as it had been issued. Many verbal conferences ensued, in which, among other things, it was determined to collect as many canal-boats as possible, with a view to employ them largely in the transportation of the army to the lower Chesapeake. The idea was at one time entertained by the President to use them in forming a bridge across the Potomac near Liverpool Point, in order to throw the army over at that point; but this was subsequently abandoned. It was also found by experience that it would require much time to prepare the canal-boats for use in transportation to the extent that had been anticipated.

Finally, on the 27th of Feb., 1862, the Secretary of War, by the authority of the President, instructed Mr. John Tucker, Assistant Secretary of War, to procure at once the necessary steamers and sailing craft to transport the Army of the Potomac to its new field of operations.

The following extract from the report of Mr. Tucker, dated April 5, will show the nature and progress of this well-executed service:

.   .   .   .

"I was called to Washington by telegraph, on 17th Jan. last, by Assistant Secretary of War Thomas A. Scott. I was informed that Maj.-Gen. McClellan wished to see me. From him I learned that he desired to know if transportation on smooth water could be obtained to move at one time, for a short distance, about 50,000 troops, 10,000 horses, 1,000 wagons, 13 batteries, and the usual equipment of such an army. He frankly stated to me that he had always supposed such a movement entirely feasible until two experienced quartermasters had recently reported it impracticable, in their judgment. A few days afterwards I reported to Gen. McClellan that I was entirely confident the transports could be commanded, and stated the mode by which his object could be accomplished. A week or two afterwards I had the honor of an interview with the President and Gen. McClellan, when the subject was further discussed, and especially as to the time required.

"I expressed the opinion that as the movement of the horses and wagons would have to be made chiefly by schooners and barges, that as each schooner would require to be properly fitted for the protection of the horses, and furnished with a supply of water and forage, and each transport for the troops provided with water, I did not deem it prudent to assume that such an expedition could start within thirty days from the time the order was given.

"The President and Gen. McClellan both urgently stated the vast importance of an earlier movement. I replied that if favorable winds prevailed, and there was great despatch in loading, the time might be materially diminished.

"On the 14th Feb. you (Secretary of War) advertised for transports of various descriptions, inviting bids on the 27th Feb. I was informed that the proposed movement by water was decided upon. That evening the quartermaster-general was informed of the decision. Directions were given to secure the transportation; any assistance was tendered. He promptly detailed to this duty two most efficient assistants in his department. Col. Rufus Ingalis was stationed at Annapolis, where it was then proposed to embark the troops, and Capt. Henry C. Hodges was directed to meet me in Philadelphia to attend to chartering the vessels. With these arrangements I left Washington on the 28th Feb.

"I beg to hand herewith a statement, prepared by Capt. Hodges, of the vessels chartered, which exhibits the prices paid and parties from whom they were taken:

113 steamers, at an average price per day,	$215 10
188 schooners, " " "	24 45
88 barges, " " "	14 27

"In thirty-seven days from the time I received the order in Washington (and most of it was accomplished in thirty days), these vessels transported from Perryville, Alexandria, and Washington to Fort Monroe (the place of departure having been changed, which caused delay) 121,500 men, 14,592 animals, 1,150 wagons, 44 batteries, 74 ambulances, besides pontoon bridges, telegraph materials, and the enormous quantity of equipage, etc., required for an army of such magnitude. The only loss of which I have heard is eight mules and nine barges, which latter went ashore in a gale within a few miles of Fort Monroe, the cargoes being saved. With this trifling exception not the slightest accident has occurred, to my knowledge.

"I respectfully, but confidently, submit that, for economy and celerity of movement, this expedition is without a parallel on record.

"JOHN TUCKER,
"Assistant Secretary of War."

The same order which confined my command to the Department of the Potomac placed Buell under Halleck, and created the Mountain Department, extending from the western limits of the Department of the Potomac to the eastern boundary of Halleck's command."

The Department of the Potomac then included all that part of Virginia east of the Alleghanies and north of the James river, with the exception of Fortress Monroe and the country within sixty miles thereof; also the District of Columbia and the States of Maryland, Delaware, Pennsylvania, and New Jersey. During the latter part of March, as I have already stated, Fortress Monroe and its dependencies were added to my command (but the order was countermanded on the 3d of April). Thus, when about to start for the Peninsula it was my duty to provide for the security of Washington and the Shenandoah Valley, and all operations in that region were under my direction.

It was very clear to me that the enemy did not abandon their positions on the Potomac and near Manassas without some good reason. I knew that they could not intend to return immediately, that they would never undertake the assault of the works around Washington, and that from the moment the operations by the lower Chesapeake were developed they would be tied down to the vicinity of Richmond so long as the Army of the Potomac remained anywhere near the James river. All they could attempt would be a raid in the Shenandoah. I therefore

---

*The following memoranda were found lying with the manuscript at this point:

MEMORANDA. - On the 5th of March there were no transports of importance at Annapolis, some at Perryville and Washington, and many engaged and fitting up in New York.

On March 12 there were at Alexandria transports for 15,000 infantry and one squadron, but they were not coaled or ready to receive the troops. The pontoon trains and engineers' tools were loaded up.

March 17 the leading division - Hamilton's - embarked.

March 20 there were eight to ten horse-transports at the wharves of Alexandria and as many more at anchor. Artillery - transports ready at the wharves.

March 21 - Porter's artillery in Alexandria, but no sufficient accommodation for the horses and no arrangement of vessels for infantry and artillery.

March 22 - Porter's division moved off in splendid style and well provided; reached Fortress Monroe on the 23d.

March 23 - Only 150 horses fit for artillery in Alexandria depot; 300 expected next day.

March 24 - Many new regiments arriving from the North. No additional transportation. Hunt and Averill can embark.

regarded a full garrison for Washington and 20,000 men for the Shenandoah as more than enough under existing circumstances.

The instructions I gave on the 16th of March were to the effect that Manassas Junction should be strongly entrenched, using the enemy's works as far as possible, and that Gen. Banks should put the mass of his forces there, with grand guards at Warrenton or Warrenton Junction, and, if possible, as far out as the Rappahannock; the country to be thoroughly scouted by cavalry, the railway from Washington to Manassas and thence to Strasburg to be at once repaired and put in running order, all the bridges to be protected by block-houses; as soon as the railway was in operation a brigade of infantry with two batteries to be strongly entrenched at or near the point where the railroad crosses the Shenandoah; Chester Gap to be also occupied by an infantry detachment well entrenched; two regiments of cavalry to be added to this brigade to scour the valley thoroughly. Under this arrangement the immediate approaches to Washington would be covered by a strong, force well entrenched, and able to fall back upon the city if overpowered; while if the enemy advanced down the Shenandoah the force entrenched at Strasburg would be able to hold him in check until assistance could reach them by rail from Manassas. If these measures had been carried into effect Jackson's subsequent advance down the Shenandoah would have been impracticable; but, unfortunately, as soon as I started for the Peninsula this region was withdrawn from my command, and my instructions were wholly disregarded.

Again, with Manassas entrenched as I directed, Pope would have had a secure base of operations from which to manœuvre, and the result of his campaign might have been very different. Certainly, if I had resumed command at Manassas instead of within the defences of Washington, Lee would not have ventured to cross the Potomac.

On the 1st of April, in view of what had occurred meanwhile, I temporarily changed the arrangements to the extent of leaving Banks in the Shenandoah. I placed Abercrombie in command at Warrenton and Manassas, under Banks's general orders, with 7,780 men at the former and 10,859 men at the latter place, and 18,000 men in Washington so that if Abercrombie was obliged to retire upon Washington there would be concentrated there 36,639 men, besides 1,350 on the lower Potomac and 35,467 under Banks in the Shenandoah.

In the event of an advance of the enemy in force in the Shenandoah Valley, Banks could have withdrawn to his aid at least 10,000 men from Abercrombie's command, or, in the reverse case, could hare gone to the latter's assistance with at least 30,000 men, leaving his Strasburg entrenchments well guarded. Had I remained in command I would have seen to it that the entrenchments referred to were promptly executed.

To say that the force I left behind me was, under the circumstances of the case, insufficient is an untruth which proves either complete ignorance or wilful malevolence. The quality of the troops I left was amply good for the purposes in view.

The administration actually retained about 134,000 for the defence of Washington, leaving me but 85,000 for operations.

Gen. Wadsworth received clear instructions as to his duties. On the 4th of April the Valley of the Shenandoah was formed into a department under Gen. Banks, while the Department of the Rappahannock was constituted for McDowell. This department embraced "that portion of Virginia east of the Blue Ridge and west of the Potomac and the Fredericksburg and Richmond Railroad, including the District of Columbia and the country between the Potomac and the Patuxent."

Thus, instead of operating with an army of 156,000 men under my immediate command, with control of all the forces, supplies, and operations from the Atlantic to the Alleghanies and from the North Carolina line to New York, I was reduced to 85,000 men and a little strip of ground bounded on the west by the railroad from Fredericksburg to Richmond, on the south by the James from Richmond to the mouth of the Appomattox, on the east by a curved line running from the mouth of the Appomattox to a point on the Chickahominy between Long's and Bottom's bridges, thence to the White House on the Pamunkey, thence through King and Queen Court-House to a point on the Rappahannock about ten miles above Urbana, and thence to the mouth of the Potomac, the northern boundary being the Potomac from the mouth of Acquia creek downward. My bases of operations at Washington and Fortress Monroe were both removed from my control, and I remained simply with my 85,000 men, and not even the ground they occupied until I passed beyond White House.

Add to this consideration that I had now only too good reason to feel assured that the administration, and especially the Secretary of War, were inimical to me and did not desire my success, and some conception may be formed of the weight upon my mind at a time when whatever hopefulness and vigor I possessed were fully needed to overcome the difficulties in my path.

CHAPTER XIV.

Letters and despatches relating to subjects treated in the foregoing and following chapters.

HALLECK TO McCLELLAN.

"ST. LOUIS, March 10, 8 P.M.

"GEN. MCCLELLAN: Reserves intended for Gen. Curtis will now be drawn in as rapidly as possible and sent to the Tennessee river. I purpose going there in a few days. That is now the great strategic line of the Western campaign, and I am surprised that Gen. Buell should hesitate to reinforce me. He was too late at Fort Donelson, as Gen. Hunter has been in Arkansas. I am obliged to make my calculations independent of both. Believe me, general, you make a serious mistake in having three independent commands in the West. There never will and never can be any co-operation at the critical moment; all military history proves it. You will regret your decision against me on this point. Your friendship for individuals has influenced your judgment. Be it so. I shall soon fight a great battle on the Tennessee river, unsupported it seems; but if successful it will settle the campaign in the West.

"H. W. HALLECK,
"Maj.-Gen."

By the time this reached me I was no longer the general-in-chief. It may suffice to say that I had never been intimate with Buell, and that my friendship for him grew out of my admiration for his excellent character and high soldierly qualities. I regarded him as a far better soldier than Halleck, and the subsequent course of events did not modify my views. If I had placed any one in command of all the operations in the West it would have been Buell and not Halleck. I could not then place Buell in that position, and was consequently obliged to do the best I could with a divided command.

BURNSIDE TO McCLELLAN.

Unofficial letter.

ROANOKE ISLAND, March 5, 1862.

MY DEAR MAC.: My official report will be short to-day, as

nothing of importance has transpired since my last. It is due to me to say confidentially to you that we are waiting on the naval ammunition, our supplies having arrived some time since in sufficient quantities to move. I am embarking my men as fast as possible. All Reno's brigade is on board, half of Parke's, and half of Foster's; and I hope to get them all on board to-morrow, leaving Col. Hawkins, with three regiments, in command of the island. I hope to get off to-morrow night, and will move at once upon New Berne; but I am not sure of it, as we cannot calculate upon more than one good day in the week. But we are getting used to storms, so that we don't mind them. How we have escaped with so little loss of life is to me a miracle. I feel thankful enough.

During our delay here I came very near moving upon [illegible], making my headquarters there, and rushing some columns up to burn the bridges on the Black Water, Nottoway, and Menheim, and then rush with my entire force upon Weldon and Gaston. But it is a risky move with my small force, and your orders are to go to New Berne. The same move can be made after we get New Berne (if we succeed), if you will send me men enough - say double the force. I feel sure that I can cut the enemy's communications at Weldon and Gaston with an additional force of even two regiments. In case you decide to send them you must not hesitate to send any division you like, as I am quite willing to serve under any other officer. You know, Mac., what I want, and that is peace and quietness at home. If I succeed in taking New Berne and Fort Macon I shall at once return to this place, unless otherwise ordered by you. I shall send off another mail very soon. If we move in the interior we will need more wagons - say 150 - and teams. Please let me know fully as to your wishes, and I'll follow them out to the letter.

"It must be a great gratification to you to see all your plans in all parts of the army succeed. Hold on, old fellow, and don't let the politicians drive you. You know old Davy Crockett's saying: 'Be sure you're right, then go ahead.' . . . I have two parties out to burn the bridges over the Trent at New Berne and the Tar at Washington, the result of which I hoped to report by this mail, but the bad weather has doubtless delayed them.

"Your old friend,

"BURNSIDE."

SAME TO SAME.

Unofficial.

"NEW BERNE, March 15, 1862.

"MY DEAR MAC. : We've got New Berne, and I hope to have Fort Macon before long.

"I've followed your instructions to the letter, and have succeeded.

"You'll come out all right. You know my faith in you. Hope you'll soon wipe them out. . . . If I had 40,000 men like these I could do almost anything.
"Your old friend,
"BURNSIDE."

SAME TO SAME.

Unofficial.   "NEW BERNE, May 5, 1862.

"MY DEAR MAC.: We're now in a state of 'stand still.' Fort Macon has been reduced, and I am ordering Parke up to this place with his men. We have more sickness than I like to acknowledge; but we are improving, and are not weak now. If you want us to do anything within our strength we'll do it. Don't fail to command me. . . . When you start the rebels from Yorktown please let me know at once, and I'll give them a kick in the flank that will make them see stars.

"Stick to them, old fellow, and don't allow the politicians to get you into a controversy. You have acted wisely, and you'll come out all right. In God is our trust. Tell me what to do, and I'll try to do it. . . . You know as well as I that it is easier to turn a flank than force a front. God bless you!
"Your old friend,
"BURNSIDE."

MEMORANDA.

Supposing Burnside's force 15,000 :

In event of movement on [illegible*], etc., would probably have to leave at least 5,000 in New Berne, 1,000 as railway guards, 1,000 Beaufort and Fort Macon, 500 Hatteras Inlet, 1 ,000 Roanoke - 8,500 in all, leaving not over 6,000 or 6,500 for active operations; too small to do much good. While by operating on Goldsborough would have to leave, say, 1,000 at Roanoke, 500 Beaufort, 1,000 New Berne, leaving 12,500 available in the field.

I would therefore think that a cautious yet bold advance on Goldsborough as soon as transportation arrives would produce a better effect than anything else that can be done, and would have the effect to neutralize a large portion of the enemy's force.
G. B. McCLELLAN.

*The word resembles Wynton.

BARNARD TO McCLELLAN.

"WASHINGTON, March 19, 1862,
2.30 P.M.

"DEAR GENERAL: Fox didn't like the propeller plan; thinks the channel could not be effectually obstructed in that way. I told him you and I both objected to the other (landing plan), which I consider an exact parallel to the expedition of Hooker's to capture the Potomac batteries, and where he would have got captured himself; or, more truly, to the last plan, to make a campaign merely to take batteries as preliminary to a campaign. I just saw Stanton, and was must gratified by what he said. It was: 'Gen. McClellan has no firmer friend than myself; but I may not be where I am long.' 'I think Gen, McClellan ought not to move till he is *fully ready.*'

" I told him that the *Mystic* would be in Hampton Roads in ten days, and then we could certainly control the *Merrimac* and have a big steamer or two for Yorktown. He repeated: 'He ought not to put a man afloat till he is ready.'

"In great haste,

"J. G. BARNARD.

"Gen. McCLELLAN."

SAME TO SAME

"STEAMSHIP Minnesota, 3 P.M.,
"Gen. G. B. McClellan;   "Thursday, March 20, 1862.

"DEAR GENERAL: Woodbury left day before yesterday, I wonder I did not hear of him yesterday in town. I had an interview with Gen. Wool this morning. He was very friendly, and said he would do everything; but it is a great drawback, this having two commanders. For instance, there are several bridges over Back river that ought to be rebuilt. General Wool said that he was going out to-day to direct one on the principal road to be rebuilt, but Houston told me that they expected Hamilton's division to do such things. Now, Hamilton is perfectly ignorant of localities, and his division in the confusion of arrival. If Wool's force is to co-operate it is a. great misfortune that it can't be *ordered* what to do. That letter expressing readiness to do everything amounts to nothing. Houston is here getting information, but I have not had time to see what he has done.

"Now for Goldsborough. He is very much in favor of reinforcing Burnside and taking Norfolk from the Chowan and Currituck; but if this is not done his ideas are essentially coincident with yours - landing on Back bay or York river or the Poquosin, at the same time with an advance from here, carrying Yorktown, then marching on Richmond, and then taking Norfolk.

"He is opposed and pronounces impracticable the operation proposed by Fox on Sewell's Point, and also considers any operation on Norfolk *from here* impracticable while the *Merrimac* is extant. He says he is responsible to the country for keeping down the *Merrimac,* and has perfect confidence that he can do it, but cannot spare from here anything except the following:

"*Victoria* - two eight-inch guns and one thirty-two-pound Parrott ;

"*Anacostia, Freeborn, Island Belle* - Potomac fleet;

"*Octoroon* - not yet arrived; Fox calls her a regular gunboat of four guns;

"*Currituck* - merchant steamer like the Potomac gunboats, I suppose;

"*Daylight* - merchant steamer like the Potomac gunboats, I suppose; and two regular gunboats - the *Chocorua,* not yet arrived, and the *Penobscot,* here - these two carrying each two eleven-inch guns.

"He says he can't furnish vessels to attack Yorktown simultaneously, but he thinks what you propose is easily done; that the vessels he mentions are fully adequate to cover a landing, and that, with a landing and an advance from here, Yorktown will fall.

"He recommends - and it may be a good idea - a landing in the Severn simultaneously, taking Gloucester in the rear, and from there battering Yorktown. Yorktown and Gloucester taken, the small gunboats, regular and irregular, will be enough to command the navigation of the York river. He thinks, and Gen. Wool thinks, that the whole attention of the enemy is concentrated on Norfolk; that they are reinforcing that place and increasing their batteries day and night, and that Magruder is not reinforced. Wool thinks that some troops passed over from north to south side of James river recently to reinforce Huger.

"This is all I can write now. I must stay a little longer to get some definite information about the places where we propose to land. There are 20,000 available men (nearly) here now (including Wool's, Mansfield's, etc.), and 20,000 men for the landing ought to be enough for the first operations. . . . .

"Very truly yours,

"J. G. BARNARD."

BARNARD TO COLRURN, A. A. G.

"WASHINGTON, March 23, 10 P.M.

"*Col. A. V. Colburn, A. A. G.:*

"I have endeavored to get some plan arranged and means procured for the most important part of our enterprise - viz., a landing. The only means we have now are the bateaux. These

I had intended to go with Capt. Duane's command and with McDowell's corps. I learned to-day that the Annapolis bateaux had been ordered to Fortress Monroe. The trestles or the india-rubber or the canvas boats will answer for crossing the creeks, and all the bateaux should be with the landing corps - McDowell's. To-day I had a consultation with McDowell, and it was decided to place the whole matter of providing means of landing under Gen. Woodbury, and to put temporarily Capt. Duane under his command; to have the necessary scows, canal-boats, etc., prepared immediately; and the bateaux are to form an essential part of the means. The orders have been issued by Gen. McDowell for that purpose. Unless the arrangements are made now it is out of the question to think of landing any considerable force as a tactical or strategical operation. One company of Duane's command might go with the land forces to put down trestle-bridges - perhaps two companies; but he himself and all the bateaux should go with McDowell, and Woodbury will furnish the additional men necessary and see to the getting-up of arrangements. Answer as soon as possible.

"J. G. BARNARD."

SAME TO SAME.

"WASHINGTON, March 24, 1862.

"Col. A. V. Colburn, A. A. G.:

"The general's telegram received. Gen. Woodbury will go to headquarters to-day and concert matters so that there shall be no misunderstanding. The streams on the Peninsula are narrow where crossed by the road - forty to eighty feet wide - and the Newport News road requires no bridges. It is desirable to know - for the constant uncertainty about this has embarrassed us - whether Capt. Duane or any portion of his command is to leave before McDowell's corps; if so, how much of it, and when. Let me know when to join headquarters. . . .

"J. G. BARNARD,
"Brig-Gen., etc."

McCLELLAN TO FOX.

FAIRFAX COURT-HOUSE, March 12.

Hon. G. O. Fox, Assist. Sec. Navy:

Can I rely on the *Monitor* to keep the *Merrimac* in check, so that I can take Fortress Monroe as a base of operation?

G. B. McCLELLAN,
Maj.-Gen.

FOX TO McCLELLAN.

"WASHINGTON, March 13.

"Gen. McClellan:

"The Monitor is more than a match for the *Merrimac,* but she might be disabled in the next encounter. I cannot advise so great dependence to be placed upon her. Burnside and Goldsborough are very strong for the Chorvan river route to Norfolk, and I brought up maps, explanations, etc. It turns everything, and is only twenty-seven miles to Norfolk by two good roads. Burnside will have New Berne this week. The Merrimac must go into dock for repairs. The *Monitor* may, and I think will, destroy the *Merrimac* in the next fight; but this is hope, not certainty.

"G. O. Fox,
"Assist. Sec. Navy.

"P. S. - In my opinion the *Merrimac* does not intend to pass by Fort Monroe. I am also of the opinion that we shall take her if she does so pass. I think the above is sure enough to make any movement upon.

"G. O. Fox,
"Assist. Sec. Navy."

WISE TO McCLELLAN.

"WASHINGTON, March 13.

Gen. McClellan:

"In reply to your telegram I am clearly of opinion that the Monitor will be fully able to hold the *Merrimac* in check should she attempt to pass Fortress Monroe.

"H. A. WISE."

WOOL TO McCLELLAN.

"FORT MONROE, March 12.

"Gen. McClellan:

"It is thought the *Monitor* is a match for the *Merrimac.* The former has two guns, the latter eight. The *Monitor* is our chief dependence. If any accident should befall her Newport News would be taken, probably depending on the land force.

"It is said Magruder has from 15,000 to 18,000 men extending from James river to Yorktown. I have almost 12,500 effective troops, including the garrison of Fortress Monroe, and only about 110 regulars artillery. I do not believe the channel could be blocked between Sewell's Point and Craney island without first taking Sewell's battery, consisting of from 25 to 30 guns, several of which are 10-inch.

"JOHN E. WOOL,
"*Maj.-Gen.*"

HEINTZELMAN TO McCLELLAN.

"FORT LYON, March 13.

"*Gen. McClellan:*

"Allow me to recommend to you to have a complete survey made, by the engineers, of the enemy's works at Centreville and Manassas, with a memoir to meet the false statements that will be made to your prejudice.

"S. P. HEINTZELMAN,
"*Brig.-Gen.*"

DENNISON TO McCLELLAN.

"WASHINGTON, March 14.

"*Gen. McClellan:*

"Have just left the President. He is very much gratified with your letter, and says my construction of the order as I gave it to you is exactly correct. You command the Army of the Potomac wherever it may go. Everything is right. Move quick as possible.

"W. DENNISON."

McCLELLAN TO MARCY.

FAIRFAX COURT-HOUSE,
March 13, 1.30 P.M.

Gen. Marcy:

Direct the barges at Perryville and Annapolis containing wagons to be ready to move at one hour's notice. Have the teams loaded up at the same place at once.

G. B. McCLELLAN.

SAME TO SAME.

FAIRFAX COURT-HOUSE,
March 13.

Gen. Marcy:

Prepare to embark Hunt's reserve artillery, together with all the reserve ammunition belonging to it. When will the transportation be ready?

G. B. McCLELLAN.

McCLELLAN TO TUCKER.

FAIRFAX COURT-HOUSE,
March 13, 10.30 P.M.

Hon. John Tucker, Assist. Sec. of War

. . . What transports are certainly on hand at Alexandria and Washington for troops, horses, and guns, and how many of each kind? I cannot make my arrangements for details of movement until I know exactly what is on hand. It is absolutely necessary that I should be kept constantly informed. I wish to move so that the men can move directly on board ship.

G. B. McCLELLAN, *Maj.-Gen.*

McCLELLAN TO VAN VLIET.

FAIRFAX COURT-HOUSE,
March 13, 10.50 P.M.

Gen. Van Vliet:

Arrange to send to Fort Monroe at once the wagons and horses at Perryville and Annapolis. Send to same destination rations as promptly as practicable for my 140,000 men and forage for my 15,000 animals. See Shiras about the rations. A quartermaster should be sent to Fort Monroe to receive these stores and keep them separate. They should all be landed at once. Please inform me to-night what transports are on hand, and keep me informed as fast as they arrive. I will make it Col. Astor's business to keep the run of it, so that I may be constantly posted.

G. B. McCLELLAN.

McCLELLAN TO McDOWELL.

FAIRFAX COURT-HOUSE,
March 13, 11.30 P.M.

Maj.-Gen. McDowell, Washington:

Please make your arrangements to go to Fort Monroe very soon to receive troops, stores, etc. Try to complete your staff arrangements at once. I shall, of course, wish to see you before you go. I am perfectly willing that you should have Ingalls and Beckwith, merely remembering the special duty Ingalls is doing. See Heintzelman about Richardson. He will explain to the President.

G. B. McCLELLAN.

McCLELLAN TO STANTON.

HEADQUARTERS, ARMY OF THE POTOMAC,
March 16, 1862.

Hon. E. M. Stanton, Sec. of War:

SIR: In order to carry out the proposed object of this army

it has now become necessary that its commander should have the entire control of affairs around Fortress Monroe. I would respectfully suggest that the simplest method of effecting this would be to merge the Department of Virginia with that of the Potomac, the name of which might properly be changed to that of the Department of the Chesapeake. In carrying this into effect I would respectfully suggest the present commander of the Department of Virginia be assigned to some other command.

Gen. Mansfield can take temporary charge of Fortress Monroe and its dependencies until the army arrive there.

I am, very respectfully, your obedient servant,

GEO. B. McCLELLAN.

McCLELLAN TO HEINTZELMAN.

SEMINARY, March 28.

Brig.-Gen. Heintzelman, Fort Monroe:

Your telegram of yesterday morning received only last night. I hope the movement on Big Bethel was well considered in view of my wish not to prematurely develop our plan to the enemy. If the destruction of their batteries, and your subsequent return, confirms the idea that we are after Norfolk, ail is well, except the mere fact of falling back. If this reaches you in time it would be well to hold the position of Big Bethel, if its occupation by the enemy can give us any trouble. You, on the ground, can best judge of this.

G. B. McCLELLAN,
Maj.-Gen. Commanding.

McCLELLAN TO BLENKER.

"HEADQUARTERS, ARMY OF POTOMAC,
"STEAMER *Commodore,* March 29, 1862.

"Gen. L. Blenker, Warrenton Junction:

"The commanding general desires that you will hold your division in readiness to move at short notice to Alexandria for embarkation. It is his design to have your command join the active army the moment it can be spared from the service upon which it is now employed. He is anxious to afford your division an opportunity to meet the enemy, feeling well assured that it will prove itself conspicuous for valor on the battle-field and fully realize the high anticipations he had formed with respect to your command.

"S. WILLIAMS, A. A. G."

CHAPTER XV.

The Peninsular Campaign - Landing at Fortress Monroe - That place removed from his command - Secretary Stanton stops all recruiting - Advance on Richmond - Columns under fire - First corps withdrawn from the army.

IN the course of description of the operations preliminary to the siege of Yorktown, attention is necessarily directed to the erroneous maps in our possession, and on which certain orders were based. This was but a single instance among many. In fact, it may be broadly stated that we had no military maps of any value. This was one of our greatest difficulties, and always seriously interfered with our movements in the early part of the war. When in presence of the enemy it was necessary to reconnoitre under fire, the accidents of the ground being entirely unknown to us.

It was a peculiar feature of our staff departments before the war that no measures were taken to collect topographical information about our own or any neighboring country. I do not know to what extent this has now been rectified, but there certainly should be some bureau charged with the collection and arrangement of topographical and statistical information in regard to our own and adjacent countries. It is true that the Confederates were no better off for correct maps than ourselves, but they possessed the inestimable advantage of operating on their own ground, which they knew perfectly well; they had plenty of good guides; and as they usually conducted a defensive campaign, they had plenty of time to construct maps and acquaint themselves thoroughly with the ground in the interests of active operations. Moreover, the white people, at least, were usually in their favor and acted as scouts, guides, and spies. Even when the negroes were favorable to us they seldom possessed the intelligence required to give any value to their information. They rarely knew more of the country than the plantations on which they had passed their lives, could give no accurate or intelligible description of roads or accidents of the ground, and their estimates of numbers were almost always ridiculously inaccurate. If a negro were asked how many Confederates he had seen at a certain point his answer was very likely to be: "I dunno, massa, but I guess about a million."

I went on board the steamer *Commodore* on the afternoon of the 1st of April, off Alexandria, and remained at anchor until an early hour next morning, being engaged all night in giving the necessary orders for the conduct of affairs in front of Washington, the movements of troops, supplies, etc.

I reached Fort Monroe on the afternoon of the 2d, still under the delusion that I should have an active army of 146,000 and the full control of my base of operations, and that I should receive efficient support from the navy.

According to the best information in our possession in regard to the Peninsula, our main road extended from Fortress Monroe, through Hampton and Big Bethel, to Yorktown; while another existed from Newport News, nearly parallel with the James river, and passing through Warwick Court-House to the Halfway House, where it met the main road from Yorktown to Williamsburg. Both of these roads between Yorktown and the point of the Peninsula were intersected by many streams, and we had information to the effect that many of these crossings - as, for example, Big Bethel, Young's Mill, Howard's bridge, Cockletown, etc. - were strongly entrenched and would be obstinately defended.

Our information seemed also to be clear that the Warwick river ran alongside of the Newport News road, which crossed only an insignificant branch, and that it presented no obstacle to a march on the Halfway House in rear of Yorktown.

After the Fort Monroe movement was decided upon my first intention was to inaugurate the operation by despatching the 1st corps in mass to the Sand-Box, three or four miles south of Yorktown, in order to turn all the entrenched crossings referred to, and receive a base of supplies as near as possible to Yorktown; or else, should the condition of affairs at the moment render it desirable, to land it on the Gloucester side of the York river at the mouth of the Severn, and throw it upon West Point. But transports arrived so slowly, and the pressure of the administration for a movement was so strong and unreasonable, that I felt obliged to embark the troops by divisions as fast as trans-

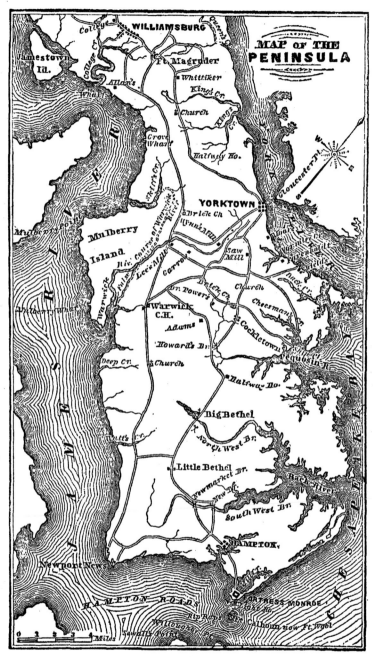

ports arrived, and then determined to hold the 1st corps to the last, and land it as a unit whenever the state of affairs promised the best results.   A few hours after I had determined to act upon this determination McDowell telegraphed me from Washington, suggesting that the troops should be embarked by divisions: according to convenience, instead of awaiting the arrival of sufficient transports to move his whole corps.   Soon after this I was more than once informed that Gen. McDowell and others in Washington had instanced this decision to embark the troops by divisions as a proof that I had disobeyed the President's order as to the formation of army corps, and that I intended to throw obstacles in the way of its fulfilment.

Considerable delay occurred in the arrival of the sailing transports for horses, in consequence of an order being given, without my knowledge, for the steamers to come to Alexandria without them.

The first division which had embarked was Hamilton's, formerly Heintzelman's, of the 3d corps, which sailed on the 17th of March; it was followed by Gen. F. J. Porter's division of the same corps on the 22d of March.   Gen. Heintzelman accompanied Porter's division, and was instructed to get his corps in condition for an advance without delay.   He was also ordered to encamp his two divisions some three or four miles out from Fort Monroe, in good defensive position, and to push out strong reconnoissances to ascertain the position and the strength of the enemy, without going so far out as to destroy the impression that our movements might be intended against Norfolk.

On the 27th he sent Porter towards Big Bethel and Howard's bridge, and Smith towards Young's Mill, on the James river road.

Porter occupied Big Bethel and pushed one brigade four miles further, sending skirmishers on to Howard's bridge, where they saw entrenchments occupied.   Deserters reported Magruder at the place with 800 men.   Smith went as far as Watt's Creek, where he found no entrenchments, and gained information that the enemy held Young's Mill in strong force.   Both divisions returned to their camps after completing the reconnoissance. Heintzelman reported that, from the best information, Magruder had from 15,000 to 20,000 men, and gave not the slightest indication that he thought he could take or invest Yorktown.

On the 3d of April there were of my command in the vicinity of Fort Monroe the 3d Penn. Cavalry, the 2d, 5th, and a part of the 1st U. S. Cavalry, a part of the reserve artillery, two divisions each of the 3d and 4th corps ready to move, one division of the 2d corps, Sykes's brigade of U. S. Infantry. Casey's division of the 4th corps was at Newport News, but totally unprovided with transportation. Richardson's division of the 2d corps and Hooker's of the 3d had not yet arrived. The troops ready to advance numbered about 53,000 men and 100 guns-less than 45,000 effectives. The amount of wagon-transportation arrived was altogether insufficient for a long movement, and it became necessary to advance in order to establish new depots on the shore more to the front. It was evident that to await any considerable accession of force and transportation would involve a delay of many days; I therefore determined to advance on the 4th of April.

The following telegram of April 3 to Mr. Stanton requires no explanation:

I expect to move from here to-morrow morning on Yorktown, where a force of some 15,000 of the rebels are in an entrenched position, and I think it quite probable they will attempt to resist us. No appearance of the *Merrimac* as yet. Commodore Goldsborough is quite confident he can sink her when she comes out.

Before I left Washington an order had been issued by the War Department placing Fort Monroe and its dependencies under my control, and authorizing me to draw from the troops under Gen. Wool a division of about 10,000 men, which was to be assigned to the 1st corps.

During the night of the 3d I received a telegram from the adjutant-general of the army stating that, by the President's order, I was deprived of all control over Gen. Wool and the troops under his command, and forbidden to detach any of his troops without his sanction.

This order left me without any base of operations under my own control.

On my arrival at Fortress Monroe I was informed that the enemy had been very active for some days past in crossing troops over the James river on the line of communication between Yorktown and Norfolk. Reports were conflicting as to the direction of this movement, but in any event it seemed proper under the circumstances to move on Yorktown as promptly as possible with the troops in hand, in order to invest the place before further reinforcements and supplies could reach it.

On the same day, on the very eve of the advance of the Army of the Potomac into the enemy's country, with the certainty of heavy losses by battle and disease, was issued the order putting a complete stop to the recruiting, service for the volunteers and breaking up all the recruiting stations:

General Order No. 33.

"ADJUTANT-GENERAL'S OFFICE, U. S. A.,
"WASHINGTON, April 3, 1862.

"III. The recruiting service for volunteers will be discontinued in every State from this date. The officers detached on the Volunteer Recruiting Service will join their regiments without delay, taking with them the parties and recruits at their respective stations.

"The superintendents of the Volunteer Recruiting Service will disband their parties and close their offices, after having taken the necessary steps to carry out these orders. The public property belonging to the Volunteer Recruiting Service will be sold to the best advantage possible, and the proceeds credited to the fund for collecting, drilling, and organizing volunteers.

"By order of the Secretary of War.

"L. THOMAS,
"Adj.-Gen. U. S. A."

Common sense and the experience of all wars prove that when an army takes the field every possible effort should be made at home to collect recruits and establish depots, whence the inevitable daily losses may be made good with instructed men as fast as they occur, so that the fighting force may be kept up to their normal strength. Failure to do this proves either a desire for the failure of the campaign or entire incompetence. Between the horns of this dilemma the friends of Mr. Stanton must take their choice.

During the preceding autumn I advocated a system of drafting, but was not listened to. Had it been adopted at that time, when recruiting was rapid and easy, it could have been established and well regulated without difficulty and without any shock to the country. The system as finally adopted was as bad as bad could be, and cannot be defended. It was unneces-

sary to disturb all the relations of society and the business interests of the country, and the numbers called out were absurdly
large.

The numbers of troops on foot in April, 1862, in the various
parts of the country, were ample for the suppression of the rebellion, if they had been properly handled and their numbers made
good by a constant stream of recruits poured into the old regiments, so as to keep them always at their full strength. Instead
of this, spasmodic calls for large numbers of men were made, and
the general rule was to organize them into new regiments, often
allowing the invaluable old regiments to die out. This system
was infinitely more expensive, but gave the opportunity to pro-
mote personal or political favorites. The new regiments required
a long time to make them serviceable, while the same men placed
in the old regiments, under experienced officers and surrounded
by veterans, would in a few days become efficient soldiers.
Another grave defect of this system was the destructive effects
on the esprit de corps of the old officers and men-an invaluable
adjunct in war.

Out of these wholesale drafts grew the system of substitutes
and bounties, which cost so many unnecessary millions to the
country, and so seriously affected the quality of the troops in the
latter years of the war.

Never in the whole history of nations was anything more
absurdly and recklessly managed than the whole system of recruiting, drafting, and organization under the regime of Secretary
Stanton. When his actions are coolly criticised, apart from the
influence of party feeling, his administration will be regarded as
unparalleled in history for blunders and ignorant self-assertion.
He unnecessarily prolonged the war at least two years, and at
least tripled its cost in blood and treasure.

The movement was made by the two roads already mentioned: the two divisions of the 4th corps from Newport News
via Warwick Court-House; the two divisions of the 3d, supported by Sedgwick's division of the 2d corps, Sykes's brigade,
and the reserve artillery, by the road from Hampton and Big
Bethel to Yorktown. The advance on Big Bethel would turn
the works at Young's Mill and open the way for the 4th corps;
while, in turn, the advance of the latter corps on Warwick Court-
House would turn the works at Howard's bridge and Ship Point,

19

and open the road of the right column to the immediate vicinity of Yorktown.

Smith's division (4th corps) encamped on the 4th of April at Young's Mill, with one brigade in advance on the road from Big Bethel to Warwick; Couch's division on Fisher's creek.

Porter, on the same day, occupied Cockletown with Morell's division and a battery, his pickets a mile in advance near Pavis's house; the other brigades of the division less than two miles in rear of Morell. Averill's cavalry found the Ship Point batteries abandoned. They were strong and well constructed, with deep wet ditches; they had platforms and magazine for siege-guns, all the guns withdrawn; there were excellent quarters for three regiments of ten companies each. Hamilton's division encamped about two miles in rear of Howard's creek. The reserve cavalry, artillery, and infantry bivouacked with headquarters at Big Bethel. Gen. Heintzelman learned during the evening that there were no batteries between Porter and Yorktown; that Yorktown was strongly fortified; that its garrison until recently consisted of 10,000 men, but was then increased to 20,000 or 25,000; that there were more troops at Williamsburg, and batteries about two miles south of it, and that reinforcements were said to have come from Richmond. Gen. Heintzelman concluded that the enemy had no idea of abandoning Yorktown. During the same afternoon Gen. Keyes, commanding the left column, received information that from 5,000 to 8,000 of the enemy were strongly entrenched at Lee's Mill. Still ignorant of the true course of the Warwick and of its relations to the entrenchments at Lee's Mill, and alive to the necessity of preventing further reinforcements to the garrison at Yorktown, I, on the evening of the 4th, ordered the movements for the 5th as follows:

Smith's division to move at six A.M. *via* Warwick Court-House to the Halfway House on the Yorktown and Williamsburg road; Couch's division to move at the same hour and close up on Smith at the Halfway House; any positions of the enemy met with on the may to be carried by assault without delay; on reaching the Halfway House the corps to occupy the narrow dividing ridge at that point, so as to prevent the escape or reinforcement of the garrison of Yorktown.

Porter's division to close up on its advanced guard at six A.M., and more forward to an intersection of roads about two and three-quarter miles from Yorktown, there to halt and send out reconnoitring parties, to cover the reconnoissances of the engineer officers, etc.

Hamilton's division to move at the same hour and close up on Porter. Sedgwick, temporarily attached to headquarters, to move with the reserves to Dr. Pavis's house, where the road to Lee's Mill diverged, and there await orders.

If Heintzelman found it possible to assault the works at Yorktown immediately, the reserves were in position to support him; if he found an assault impracticable, and Keyes needed assistance in carrying out his orders, the reserves were in position to move at once to his support. If Keyes had succeeded in passing Lee's Mill and reaching the Halfway House, I should at once have gone to his support with all the reserves and one of Heintzelman's divisions, thus holding the key-point of the operation with four divisions of infantry, the brigade of regulars, the cavalry and artillery reserves.

In consequence of the heavy rains the roads were very bad and the troops moved with difficulty, so that little of Keyes's artillery and none of the ammunition, forage, and provision trains could be brought up. Heintzelman early in the day came under the artillery-fire of the works of Yorktown, and soon saw that an assault was impracticable. Keyes also found himself brought to a halt by the artillery-fire of the Lee's Mill works, and discovered that they were covered by the Warwick river, rendering any attempt at assault utterly out of the question.

It was at this moment, with the leading division of each column under a hot artillery-fire, and the skirmishers of the 3d corps engaged, being myself with Porter's division, that I received the telegram informing me of the withdrawal of the 1st corps (McDowell's) from my command:

"ADJUTANT-GENERAL'S OFFICE,

"Gen. McClellan: "April 4, 1862.

"By directions of the President Gen. McDowell's army corps has been detached from the force under your immediate command, and the general is ordered to report to the Secretary of War; letter by mail.

" L. THOMAS,
"Adj.-Gen."

CHAPTER XVI.

Effects of reduction of the army - Overthrow of the campaign - New campaign with reduced army - Siege of Yorktown.

Soon after receiving the telegram I sent the following to the Secretary of War, dated April 5:

The enemy are in large force along our front, and apparently intend making a determined resistance. A reconnoissance just made by Gen. Barnard shows that their line of works extends across the entire Peninsula from Yorktown to Warwick river. Many of them are formidable. Deserters say that they are being reinforced daily from Richmond and from Norfolk. Under the circumstances I beg that you will reconsider the order detaching the 1st corps from my command.

In my deliberate judgment the success of our cause will be imperilled by so greatly reducing my force when it is actually under the fire of the enemy and active operations have commenced. Two of my divisions have been under fire of artillery during most of the day. I am now of the opinion that I shall have to fight all the available force of the rebels not far from here. Do not force me to do so with diminished ranks; but whatever your decision may be, I will leave nothing undone to obtain success.

If you cannot leave me the whole of the 1st corps, I urgently ask, as a military necessity, that I may not lose Franklin and his division.

On the same day, at ten P.M., I sent the following to Secretary Stanton:

Since Gen. Woodbury's brigade of volunteer engineer troops was only temporarily attached to the 1st corps for special service, and is much needed here, I have directed Gen. Woodbury to bring it here at once. Their services are indispensable.

The following letter was written during the evening of April 5:

HEADQUARTERS, ARMY OF POTOMAC,
CAMP NEAR YORKTOWN, April 5, 1862.

Brig.-Gen. L. Thomas, Adj.-Gen. U. S. A.:

GENERAL: I have now a distinct knowledge of the general position of the enemy in my front. His left is in Yorktown; his

262

line thence extends along and in rear of the Warwick river to its mouth. That stream is an obstacle of great magnitude. It is fordable at only one point (so far as I yet know) below its head, which is near Yorktown; is for several miles unfordable, and has generally a very marshy valley. His batteries and entrenchments render this line an exceedingly formidable one, entirely too much so (so far as I now understand it) to be carried by a simple assault. I shall employ to-morrow in reconnoissances, repairing roads, establishing a depot at Ship's Point, and in bringing up supplies.

Porter, the head of the right column, has moved as close upon the town as the enemy's guns will permit; he is encamped there, supported by Hamilton's division. Porter has been under fire all the afternoon. But five men killed. His rifled field-guns and sharpshooters have caused some loss to the enemy. Keyes, with two divisions, is in front of Lee's Mill, where the road from Newport News to Williamsburg crosses Warwick river. He has been engaged in an artillery combat of several hours' duration, losing some five killed. At Lee's Mill we have a causeway covered by formidable batteries. The information obtained at Fort Monroe in regard to the topography of the country and the position and strength of the enemy has been unreliable. He is in strong force and very strong position. If the reconnoissances of to-morrow verify the observations of to-day, we shall be obliged to use much heavy artillery before we can force their lines and isolate the garrison of Yorktown. I omitted to state that I hold the reserves in a central position until I can learn more of the condition of affairs. The present aspect of affairs renders it exceedingly unfortunate that the 1st corps has been detached from my command. It is no longer in my power to make a movement from the Severn river upon Gloucester and West Point. I am reduced to a front attack upon a very strong line. I still hope that the order detaching the 1st corps may be reconsidered. I do not feel that without it I have force sufficient to accomplish the objects I have proposed in this campaign with that certainty, rapidity, and completeness which I had hoped to obtain. The departments will, I trust, realize that more caution will be needed on my part after having been so unexpectedly deprived of so very large a portion of my force when actually having my troops under fire. I have frankly stated what I now consider to be the strength of the enemy's position; the reconnoissances of to-morrow may modify my opinion. Whatever the facts may be, I shall make the best use I can of the force at my disposal, determined to gain my point as completely and as rapidly as may be.

Very respectfully, your obedient servant,

GEO. B. MCCLELLAN,
Maj.-Gen. Commanding.

P. S. All my movements up to this evening were predicated upon the expectation that no more troops would be detached from my command. I have involved my troops in actual conflict upon that supposition, and calculating upon the prompt arrival of the 1st corps as a part of the programme. It has just occurred to me to say that the maps of the Peninsula I sent to the President and secretary are perfectly unreliable; the roads are wrong, and the Warwick river crosses the Newport News and Williamsburg road some three miles above Warwick Court-House, which latter place is about one mile from the road.

GEO. B. McCLELLAN,
Maj.-Gen.

This, then, was the situation in which I found myself on the evening of April 5: Flag-Officer Goldsborough had informed me that it was not in his power to control the navigation of the James river so as to enable me to use it as a line of supply, or to cross it, or even to cover my left flank; nor could he, as he thought, furnish any vessels to attack the batteries of Yorktown and Gloucester, or to run by them in the dark and thus cut off the supplies of the enemy by water and control their land-communication. I was thus deprived of the co-operation of the navy and left to my own resources.

I had been deprived of five infantry divisions, and out of the four left to me there were present at the front five divisions of volunteer regiments, the weak brigade of regulars, Hunt's artillery reserve, and a small cavalry force.

Owing to the lack of wagons Casey did not reach Young's Mill until the 16th. Richardson's division reached the front on the same day. Hooker's division commenced arriving at Ship's Point on the 10th. The roads were so bad and wagons so fern that it was with the utmost difficulty supplies could be brought up, and the field-artillery moved with great difficulty. Even the headquarters wagons could not get up, and I slept in a deserted hut with my saddle-blanket for a bed.

My telegram of April 7 to the President shows that only 53,000 men had joined me, so that I had not more than 44,000 effectives, and found myself in front of a position which apparently could not be carried by assault. The force was too small to attempt any movement to turn Gloucester without the assistance of the navy, and I was obliged to abandon the plan of rapid turning movements which I had intended to carry out.

All that could be done was to halt where we were, and by close reconnoissances ascertain whether there were any weak points which we could assault, or, failing in that, determine what could be effected with the aid of siege-artillery to cover the attack.

Next day, April 6, I sent the following telegram to his excellency the President:

The order forming new departments, if rigidly enforced, deprives me of the power of ordering up wagons and troops absolutely necessary to enable me to advance to Richmond. I have by no means the transportation I must have to move my army even a few miles. I respectfully request I may not be placed in this position, but that my orders for wagons, trains, and ammunition, and other material that I have prepared and necessarily left behind me, as well as Woodbury's brigade, may at once be complied with. The enemy is strong in my front, and I have a most serious task before me, in the fulfilment of which I need all the aid the government can give me. I again repeat the urgent request that Gen. Franklin and his division may be restored to my command.

I received the following reply from Secretary Stanton:

"The President directs me to say that your despatch to him has been received. Gen. Sumner's corps is on the road to you and will go forward as fast as possible. Franklin's division is now on the advance towards Manassas. There is no means of transportation here to send it forward in time to be of service in your present optrations. Telegraph frequently, and all in the power of the government shall be done to sustain you as occasion may require."

And this from the President:

"Yours of eleven A.M. to-day received. Secretary of War informs me that the forwarding of transportation, ammunition, and Woodbury's brigade under your order has not and will not be interfered with. You now have over one hundred thousand troops with you, independent of Gen. Wool's command. I think you had better break the enemy's line from Yorktown to Warwick river at once. This will probably use time as advantageously as you can.

"A. LINCOLN
"President. "

To this I replied, April 7, to the President:

Your telegram of yesterday received. In reply I have the honor to state that my entire force for duty only amounts to about eighty-five thousand (85,000) men. Gen. Wool's command, as you will observe from the accompanying order, has been taken out of my control, although he has most cheerfully co-operated with me. The only use that can be made of his command is to protect my communications in rear of this point. At this time only fifty-three thousand (53,000) men have joined me, but they are coming up as rapidly as my means of transportation will permit. Please refer to my despatch to the Secretary of War of to-night for the details of our present situation.

I find on the back of my retained copy of this despatch the following memorandum made at the time by myself:

Return of March 31, 1862, shows men present for duty 171,602
Deduct 1st corps, infantry and artillery,   32,119
"   Blenker,   8,616
"   Banks,   21,739
"   Wadsworth,   19,318
"   Cavalry of 1st corps, etc.,   1,600
"   "   " Blenker,   800
         Van Alen and Wyndham,   1,600

                                               85,792   85,792
                                                         ───────
                                                         85,810

Officers, about 3,900.
Total absent from whole command, 23,796.

As this memorandum was a calculation to ascertain only the number of troops left under my command, it did not take into consideration all the troops left behind which did not compose parts of the total of 171,602 for duty. My letters of April 1, show that many more were left in addition to those mentioned in this memorandum.

The telegram referred to in my despatch to the President was the following, of April 7, to Secretary Stanton:

Your telegram of yesterday arrived here while I was absent examining the enemy's right, which I did pretty closely. . . . The whole line of the Warwick, which really heads within a mile of Yorktown, is strongly defended by detached redoubts and other fortifications, armed with heavy and light guns. The approaches, except at Yorktown, are covered by the Warwick, over which there is but one, or at most two, passages, both of which are covered by strong batteries. It will be necessary to resort to the use of heavy guns and some siege operations before we assault. All the prisoners state that Gen. J. E. Johnston arrived at Yorktown yesterday with strong reinforcements. It seems clear that I shall have the whole force of the enemy on my hands - probably not less than (100,000) one hundred thousand men, and possibly more. In consequence of the loss of Blenker's division and the 1st corps my force is possibly less than that of the enemy, while they have all the advantage of position.

I am under great obligations to you for the offer that the whole force and material of the government will be as fully and as speedily under my command as heretofore, or as if the new departments had not been created.

Since my arrangements were made for this campaign at least (50,000) fifty thousand men have been taken from my command. Since my despatch of the 5th instant five divisions have been in close observation of the enemy, and frequently exchanging shots. When my present command all joins I shall have about (85,000) eighty-five thousand men for duty, from which a large force must be taken for guards, scouts, etc. With this army I could assault the enemy's works, and perhaps carry them. But were I in possession of their entrenchments, and assailed by double my numbers, I should have no fears as to the result.

Under the circumstances that have been developed since we arrived here, I feel fully impressed with the conviction that here is to be fought the great battle that is to decide the existing contest. I shall, of course, commence the attack as soon as I can get up my siege-train, and shall do all in my power to carry the enemy's works; but to do this with a reasonable degree of certainty requires, in my judgment, that I should, if possible, have at least the whole of the 1st corps to land upon the Severn river and attack Gloucester in the rear.

My present strength will not admit of a detachment sufficient for this purpose without materially impairing the efficiency of this column. Flag-Officer Goldsborough thinks the works too strong for his available vessels unless I can turn Gloucester. I send by mail copies of his letter and one of the commander of the gunboats here.

Gen. Keyes, commanding 4th army corps, after the examination of the enemy's defences on the left, addressed the following letter to the Hon. Ira Harris, U. S. Senate, and gave me a copy. It describes the situation at that time in some respects so well that I introduce it here:

"HEADQUARTERS, 4TH CORPS,
"WARWICK COURT-HOUSE, Va., April 7, 1862.

"MY DEAR SENATOR: The plan of campaign on this line was
2 0

made with the distinct understanding that *four* army corps should be employed, and that the navy should co-operate in the taking of Yorktown, and also (as I understood it) support us on our left by moving gunboats up James river.

"To-day I have learned that the 1st corps, which by the President's order was to embrace four divisions, and one division (Blenker's) of the 2d corps, have been withdrawn altogether from this line of operations and from the Army of the Potomac. At the same time, as I am informed, the navy has not the means to attack Yorktown, and is afraid to send gunboats up James river for fear of the Merrimac.

"The above plan of campaign was adopted unanimously by Maj.-Gen. McDowell and Brig.-Gens. Sumner, Heintzelman, and Keyes, and was concurred in by Maj.-Gen. McClellan, who first proposed Urbana as our base.

"This army being reduced by forty-five thousand troops, some of them among the best in the service, and without the support of the navy, the plan to which we are reduced bears scarcely any resemblance to the one I voted for.

"I command the James river column, and I left my camp near Newport News the morning of the 4th instant. I only succeeded in getting my artillery ashore the afternoon of the day before, and one of my divisions had not all arrived in camp the day I left, and for the want of transportation has not yet joined me. So you will observe that not a day was lost in the advance, and in fact we marched so quickly and so rapidly that many of our animals were twenty-four and forty-eight hours without a ration of forage. But, notwithstanding the rapidity of our advance, we were stopped by a line of defence nine or ten miles long, strongly fortified by breastworks, erected nearly the whole distance behind a stream or succession of ponds, nowhere fordable, one terminus being Yorktown and the other ending in the James river, which is commanded by the enemy's gunboats. Yorktown is fortified all around with bastioned works, and on the water-side it and Gloucester are so strong that the navy are afraid to attack either.

"The approaches on one side are generally through low, swampy, or thickly wooded ground, over roads which we are obliged to repair or to make before we can get forward our carriages. The enemy is in great force, and is constantly receiving reinforcements from the two rivers. The line in front of us is therefore one of the strongest ever opposed to an invading force in any country.

"You will, then, ask why I advocated such a line for our operations? My reasons are few but, I think, good.

"With proper assistance from the navy we could take Yorktown, and then with gunboats on both rivers we could beat any force opposed to us on Warwick river, because the shot and shell from the gunboats would nearly overlap across the Peninsula; so that if the enemy should retreat - and retreat he must - he would have a long way to go without rail or steam transportation, and every soul of his army must fall into our hands or be destroyed.

"Another reason for my supporting the new base and plan was that this line, it was expected, would furnish water-transportation nearly to Richmond.

"Now, supposing we succeed in breaking through the line in front of us, what can we do next? The roads are very bad, and if the enemy retains command of James river, and we do not first reduce Yorktown, it would be impossible for us to subsist this army three marches beyond where it is now. As the roads are at present, it is with the utmost difficulty that we can subsist it in the position it now occupies.

"You will see, therefore, by what I have said, that the force originally intended for the capture of Richmond should be all sent forward. If I thought the four army corps necessary when I supposed the navy would co-operate, and when I judged of the obstacles to be encountered by what I learned from maps and the opinions of officers long stationed at Fort Monroe, and from all other sources, how much more should I think the full complement of troops requisite now that the navy cannot co-operate, and now that the strength of the enemy's lines and the number of his guns and men prove to be almost immeasurably greater than I had been led to expect! The line in front of us, in the opinion of all the military men here who are at all competent to judge, is one of the strongest in the world, and the force of the enemy capable of being increased beyond the numbers we now have to oppose to him. Independently of the strength of the lines in front of us, and of the force of the enemy behind them, we cannot advance until we get command of either York river or James river. The efficient co-operation of the navy is, therefore, absolutely essential, and so I considered it when I voted to change our base from the Potomac to Fort Monroe.

"An iron-clad boat must attack Yorktown; and if several strong gunboats could be sent up James river also, our success will be certain and complete, and the rebellion will soon be put down.

"On the other hand, we must butt against the enemy's works with heavy artillery and a great waste of time, life, and material.

"If we break through and advance, both our flanks will be assailed from two great water-courses in the hands of the enemy; our supplies would give out, and the enemy, equal, if not superior, in numbers, would, with the other advantages, beat and destroy this army.

"The greatest master of the art of war has said that 'if you would invade a country successfully, you must have one line of operations and one army, under one general.' But what is our

270 McCLELLAN'S OWN STORY.

condition? The State of Virginia is made to constitute the command, in part or wholly, of some six generals, viz.: Fremont, Banks, McDowell, Wool, Burnside, and McClellan, besides the scrap, over the Chesapeake, in the care of Dix.

"The great battle of the war is to come off here. If we win it the rebellion will be crushed. If we lose it the consequences will be more horrible than I care to foretell. The plan of campaign I voted for, if carried out with the means proposed, will certainly succeed. If any part of the means proposed are withheld or diverted, I deem it due to myself to say that our success will be uncertain.

"It is no doubt agreeable to the commander of the 1st corps to have a separate department, and, as this letter advocates his return to Gen. McClellan's command, it is proper to state that I am not at all influenced by personal regard or dislike to any of my seniors in rank. If I were to credit all the opinions which have been poured into my ears, I must believe that, in regard to my present fine command, I owe much to Gen. McDowell and nothing to Gen. McClellan. But I have disregarded all such officiousness, and I have from last July to the present day supported Gen. McClellan and obeyed all his orders with as hearty a good-will as though he had been my brother or the friend to whom I owed most. I shall continue to do so to the last and so long as he is my commander, and I am not desirous to displace him, and would not if I could. He left Washington with the understanding that he was to execute a definite plan of campaign with certain prescribed means. The plan was good and the means sufficient, and, without modification, the enterprise was certain of success. But, with the reduction of force and means, the plan is entirely changed, and is now a bad plan, with means insufficient for certain success.

"Do not look upon this communication as the offspring of despondency. I never despond; and when you see me working the hardest you may be sure that fortune is frowning upon me. I am working *now* to my utmost.

"Please show this letter to the President, and I should like also that Mr. Stanton should know its contents. Do me the honor to write to me as soon as you can, and believe me, with perfect respect,
"Your most obedient servant,
"E. D. KEYES,
" *Brig.-Gen. Commanding 4th Army Corps.*
"Hon. IRA HARRIS,
"U. S. Senate."

The reconnoissances of the 6th and 7th and following days, pushed with great vigor and with some loss, confirmed the impressions gained on the 5th. I verified all these reconnois-

GENERAL McCLELLAN RECONNOITRING AT YORKTOWN.

sances in person, going everywhere beyond our lines of pickets, and resuming my old trade of reconnoitring officer, so anxious was I to find a practicable point of attack. In fact, during the whole siege I exposed myself more in this way than was proper for a general commanding an army; but I had had far more personal experience in sieges than any of those under my command, and trusted more to my own knowledge and experience than I then could to theirs.

It was found that the Warwick valley headed within two thousand yards of the *enciente* of Yorktown, and within half that distance of the White Redoubt, or Fort Magruder, a strong work, essentially a part of the main works at Yorktown, which were so strong-having ditches from eight to ten feet deep, and more than fifteen feet wide at the top - and so heavily armed with siege and garrison guns, as to render an assault hopeless. The interval between Yorktown and the Warwick was occupied by strong works, and all the open ground in front, as well as the direct approaches to the town itself, so thoroughly swept by the direct fire of more than fifty guns of the heaviest calibres then known as to render it an act of madness to assault without first silencing the fire of the enemy's artillery. From its head to Lee's Mill the Warwick was flooded by means of artificial inundations, which rendered it unfordable. The dams constructed for this purpose were all covered by strong works so situated as to be unassailable until their artillery-fire was reduced. Below Lee's Mill the river was a tidal stream, not fordable at any stage of the tide. That portion, moreover, was controlled by the fire of the Confederate gunboats in the James river. The valley of the Warwick was generally low and swampy, the approaches to the dams were through dense forests and deep swamps, and every precaution had been taken by the enemy, in the may of felling timber and constructing works, to make a crossing as difficult as possible.

In his report of the 6th of May, immediately after the occupation of Yorktown, Gen. Barnard, chief-engineer of the Army of the Potomac, says:

"They (referring to the groups of works covering the Warwick) are far more extensive than may be supposed from the mention of them I make, and every kind of obstruction which the country affords, such as abattis, marsh, inundation, etc., was skilfully used. The line is certainly one of the most extensive

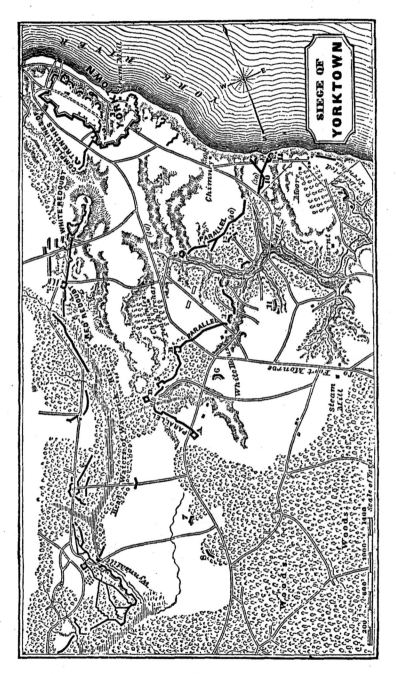

273

known to modern times. The country on both sides the Warwick from near Yorktown down is a dense forest with few clearings. It was swampy, and the roads impassable during the heavy
rains we have constantly had, except where our own labors had
corduroyed them. If we could have broken the enemy's line
across the isthmus we could have invested Yorktown, and it
must, with its garrison, have soon fallen into our hands. It was
not deemed practicable? considering the strength of that line and
the difficulty of handling our forces (owing to the impracticable
character of the country), to do so. If we could take Yorktown
or drive the enemy out of that place, the enemy's line was no
longer tenable. This we could do by siege operations. It was
deemed too hazardous to attempt the reduction of the place by
assault. The operations of the siege required extensive preparations.

"I regret that there is not time and means to prepare a complete plan of this enormous system of defences. They should
form part of the record of the operations of the Army of the
Potomac. The forcing of such a line with so little loss is in itself
an exploit, less brilliant, perhaps, but more worthy of study, than
would have been a murderous assault, even had it proved successful."

I need only add to this that Gen. Barnard never expressed to
me any opinion that an assault was practicable upon any part of
the enemy's defences. From his first reconnoissances he was
decidedly of the opinion that the use of heavy guns was necessary. More than this, I never, at the time, heard of any contrary
opinion from any one, and, so far as I know, there was entire
unanimity on the part of the general officers and chiefs of staff
departments that the course pursued was the only one practicable under the circumstances.

From Lee's Mill a line of works extended to the enemy's rear
to Skiff's creek, se that if we had forced the passage of the Warwick below that point we would have found a new line of
defence in front of us, completely covering the enemy's communications.

During the progress of these reconnoissances every effort was
made to bring up supplies and ammunition. A violent storm
beginning on the 6th, and continuing without cessation for three
or four days, almost entirely interrupted the water-communica-
tion between Fortress Monroe and Ship Point, and made the
already bad roads terrible beyond description. In those days
I more than once thought of a reply made to me by an old gen-

eral of Cossacks, who had served in all the Russian campaigns against Napoleon. I had asked how the roads were in those days, to which he replied: "My son, the roads are always bad in war."

It was not until the 10th that we were able to establish a new depot on Cheeseman's creek, which shortened the haul about three miles. The rains continued almost incessantly, and it was necessary not only to detail large working parties to unload supplies, but details of some thousands of men were required to corduroy the roads, as the only means of enabling us to get up supplies.

As illustrating the condition of things, I insert the following despatch from Mr. John Tucker, Assistant Secretary of War, dated near Yorktown, April 10, to Hon. E. M. Stanton, Secretary of War:

"I reached Gen. McClellan's headquarters at seven this evening, having had an accident to the steamer on the way from Fortress Monroe to Ship Point. I was five hours on horseback (making about five miles), the roads being almost impassable and so entirely occupied with army wagons I frequently had to leave the road and take to the woods. The severe storm at Fortress Monroe prevented transports from leaving for several days. The facilities for landing at Ship Point are very poor, and for several days it must have been next to impossible to move artillery over such roads. I learn that twelve thousand men are engaged in repairing and building new roads. The difficulties of transportation have been so great that some of the cavalry horses had to be sent back to keep them from starving. I will report my observations of army movements to-morrow, but I see an earnest determination to lose no time in attacking the enemy.

"JOHN TUCKER,
"Assistant Secretary of War."

The following telegram was sent as indicated, on April 10, to Brig.-Gen. Thomas, adjutant-general:

I examined the works on enemy's left very carefully to-day. They are very strong, the approaches difficult; enemy in force and confident. Water-batteries at York and Gloucester said to be much increased; have not seen them myself. Have not yet received reports of engineer officers. I go to-morrow to examine our left. Sharp firing on our right for some time to-day while I was there; no harm done, although their shells burst handsomely.

21

Am receiving supplies from Ship Point, repairing roads, getting up siege artillery, etc.

It seems now almost certain that we must use mortars and heavy guns freely before assaulting. The naval officers urge an attack in rear of Gloucester; I think they are right, but am now too weak to attempt it, unless new circumstances come to my knowledge. The affair will be protracted in consequence of the diminution of my force.

The following was sent to Hon. E. M. Stanton, Secretary of War, on April 8:

Weather terrible; raining heavily last twenty-eight hours; roads and camps in awful condition; very little firing to-day. Reconnoissances being continued under disadvantageous circumstances. Gen. Sumner has arrived. Most of Richardson's division at Ship Point. I cannot move it from there in present condition of roads until I get more wagons. I need more force to make the attack on Gloucester.

To Brig.-Gen. L. Thomas on April 9:

Weather still execrable; country covered with water; roads terrible. It is with the utmost difficulty that I can supply the troops. We are doing an immense deal of work on the roads. Cannot land siege-tram until wind moderates. Reconnoissances being pushed and point of attack pretty well determined. Rebels have thrown ten-inch and twelve-inch shells yesterday and to-day without effect. I have now placed all the troops in bivouac just out of shell-range, holding all our advanced positions with strong detachments well sheltered. I shall not lose an unnecessary hour in placing our heavy guns in battery, and will assault at the earliest practicable moment. The conduct of the troops is excellent.

At this time I received the following letter from the President:

"WASHINGTON, April 9, 1862.

"MY DEAR SIR: Your despatches complaining that you are not properly sustained, while they do not offend me, do pain me very much.

"Blenker's division was withdrawn from you before you left here, and you know the pressure under which I did it, and, as I thought, acquiesced in it - certainly not without reluctance.

"After you left I ascertained that less than 20,000 unorganized men, without a single field-battery, were all you designed to be left for the defence of Washington and Manassas Junction, and part of this even was to go to Gen. Hooker's old position. Gen. Banks's corps, once designed for Manassas Junction, was diverted and tied up on the line of Winchester and Strasburg, and could not leave it without again exposing the upper Potomac and the Baltimore and Ohio Railroad. This presented, or would present when McDowell and Sumner should be gone, a great temptation to the enemy to turn back from the Rappahannock and sack Washington. My implicit order that Washington should, by the judgment of all the commanders of army corps, be left entirely secure, had been neglected. It was precisely this that drove me to detain McDowell.

"I do not forget that I was satisfied with your arrangement to leave Banks at Manassas Junction; but when that arrangement was broken up, and nothing was substituted for it, of course I was constrained to substitute something for it myself. And allow me to ask, Do you really think I should permit the line from Richmond *via* Manassas Junction to this city to be entirely open, except what resistance could be presented by less than 20,000 unorganized troops? This is a question which the country will not allow me to evade.

"There is a curious mystery about the number of troops now with you. When I telegraphed you on the 6th, saying you had over a hundred thousand with you, I had just obtained from the Secretary of War a statement, taken, as he said, from your own returns, making 108,000 then with you and *en route* to you. You now say you will have but 85,000 when all en route to you shall have reached you. How can the discrepancy of 23,000 be accounted for?

"As to Gen. Wool's command, I understand it is doing for you precisely what a like number of your own would have to do if that command was away.

"I suppose the whole force which has gone forward for you is with you by this time. And if so, I think it is the precise time for you to strike a blow. By delay the enemy will relatively gain upon you - that is, he will gain faster by fortifications and reinforcements than you can by reinforcements alone. And once more let me tell you, it is indispensable to you that you strike a blow. I am powerless to help this. You will do me the justice to remember I always insisted that going down the bay in search of a field, instead of fighting at or near Manassas, was only shifting, and not surmounting, a difficulty; that we would find the same enemy and the same or equal entrenchments at either place. The country will not fail to note, is now noting, that the present hesitation to move upon an entrenched enemy is but the story of Manassas repeated.

"I beg to assure you that I have never written you or spoken to you in greater kindness of feeling than now, nor with a fuller purpose to sustain you, so far as, in my most anxious judgment, I consistently can. But you must act.

"Yours very truly,

"A. LINCOLN."

The portions of this letter referring to the arrangements for the defence of Washington and the Shenandoah have already been fully answered and need not be alluded to again in this place.

As regards the discrepancy of 23,000 men, it is sufficient to say that my estimate was made from the actual latest returns of the men present for duty, and was correct. I have no doubt that the number furnished the President was the aggregate present and absent - a convenient mistake not unfrequently made by the Secretary of War.

The number I gave was correct; that furnished the President was incorrect.

In regard to the employment of Wool's command, the authorities in Washington failed to perceive the irony of my remark in my telegram of April 7, to the effect that the only use that could be made of his command was to protect my communications in rear of the point I then occupied. There were no communications to protect beyond Ship Point, and there was no possibility of the roads to Fortress Monroe being troubled by the enemy. Wool's troops were of no possible use to me beyond holding Fortress Monroe, and would have been of very great use if the surplus had been incorporated with the Army of the Potomac.

The whole force sent forward had not joined me at the date of this letter; it was not until seven days later that Casey, Hooker, and Richardson reached the front line; they could not be brought up earlier. I have already shown the impossibility of attacking earlier or otherwise than we actually did.

When in front of Sebastopol in 1855 I asked Gen. Martimprey, chief of staff of the French army in the Crimea, how he found that the cable worked which connected the Crimean with the European lines of telegraph. He said that it worked admirably *from* the Crimea to Paris, but very badly in the opposite direction; and by way of explanation related the following anecdote: He said that immediately after the failure of the assault of June, 1855, the emperor telegraphed Pélissier to renew the assault immediately. Pélissier replied that it was impossible without certain preliminary preparations which required several weeks. The emperor repeated the peremptory order to attack at once. Pélissier repeated his reply. After one or two more interchanges of similar messages Pélissier telegraphed: "I will not renew the attack until ready; if you wish it done, come and do it yourself." That ended the matter.

Referring for a moment to the President's despatch of April 6, it is well to recall the facts that at that time, instead of 100,000 men, I had - after deducting guards and working parties - much less than 40,000 for attack, and that the portion of the enemy's lines which he thought I had better break through at once was about the strongest of the whole, except, perhaps, the town itself.

The impatience displayed at that time, after so greatly reducing my force, is in remarkable contrast with the patience which permitted Grant to occupy months in front of the lines of Petersburg, far inferior in strength to those of Yorktown.

On the 22d of March I had prepared the following:

CONFIDENTIAL MEMORANDUM.

For the operations against Yorktown, Richmond, etc., where we will probably find extensive earthworks heavily garrisoned, we shall require the means of overwhelming them by a vertical fire of shells.

I should therefore be glad to have disposable at Fortress Monroe:

    I. 1st. 20 10-inch mortars complete.
       2d. 20 8-inch mortars complete.
    II.   20 8-inch siege-howitzers.
    III.   20 4½-inch wrought-iron siege-guns.
    IV.   40 20-pounder Parrotts.
    V.   - 24-pounder siege-guns.

The 24-pounder Parrotts with the batteries will, of course, be counted as available.

I do not know the number of 4½-inch guns available; if not so many as I have indicated, something else should be substituted. I wish Gen. Barry and Col. Kingsbury to consult with Gen. Marcy, to make such suggestions as occur to them, and ascertain at once to what extent this memorandum can be filled. It is possible we cannot count upon the navy to reduce Yorktown by their independent efforts; we must therefore be prepared to do it by our own means. There are said to be at Yorktown from 27 to 32 heavy guns, at Gloucester 14 Columbiads. The probable armament of Yorktown, when exterior guns are drawn in, will be from 40 to 50 heavy guns, from 24-pounders to 8-inch and perhaps 10-inch Columbiads."

Before leaving Washington I detailed Col. Robert Tyler's 1st Conn. regiment as heavy artillery, and placed the siege-train in their charge; it will be seen, as the narrative proceeds, how admirably this splendid regiment performed their most important duties at all times and under the most trying circumstances.

As soon as it became clear that no aid was to be had from the navy, and that we must reduce Yorktown by a front attack, I took steps to increase the number of heavy guns and mortars to the extent shown by the statement of batteries given hereafter. The number of officers of the corps of engineers and of the topographical engineers at my disposal was so small that it was necessary to supplement them by civilian employees kindly furnished by Prof. Bache, of the U. S. Coast Survey, and by details from the line.   These civilian employees vied with the officers of the army in the courage, devotion, and intelligence with which they performed the dangerous and important duties devolving upon them, There were but twelve officers of the engineers, including four on duty with the three companies of engineer troops, and six of the topographical engineers.   These officers at once proceeded to ascertain by close reconnoissances the nature and strength of the enemy's defences and the character of the ground, in order to determine the points of attack and the nature of the necessary works of attack.   Meanwhile the troops were occupied in constructing roads to the depots.   Gen. Sumner reached the front on the 9th of April, and was placed in command of the left wing, consisting of his own and the 4th corps.   He was in front of the line of the Warwick, while the 3d corps was charged with the operations against Yorktown itself. The following despatch to Secretary Stanton shows the condition of affairs at its date, April 11:

The reconnoissances of to-day prove that it is necessary to invest and attack Gloucester Point. Give me Franklin's and McCall's divisions under command of Franklin, and I will at once undertake it. If circumstances of which I am not aware make it impossible for you to send me two divisions to carry out the final plan of campaign, I will run the risk and hold myself responsible for the results if you will give me Franklin's division.

If you still confide in my judgment I entreat that you will grant this request. The fate of our cause depends upon it. Although willing, under the pressure of necessity, to carry this through with Franklin alone, I wish it to be distinctly understood that I think two divisions necessary. Franklin and his division are indispensable to me. Gen. Barnard concurs in this view. I have determined upon the point of attack, and am at this moment engaged in fixing the position of the batteries.

The same day the following reached me:

"By direction of the President, Franklin's division has been ordered to march back to Alexandria and immediately embark for Fortress Monroe.

"L. THOMAS,
"Adj.-Gen."

I replied to the secretary: "I am delighted with Franklin's orders, and beg to thank you."

I insert the following letter from my venerable friend, Francis P. Blair, as an indication of the state of feeling at the time:

"WASHINGTON, April 12, 1862.

"Maj.-Gen. *G. B. McClellan:*

"MY DEAR SIR: There is a prodigious cry of 'On to Richmond!' among the carpet-knights of our city, who will not shed their blood to get there. I am one of those who wish to see you lead a triumph in the capital of the Old Dominion, but am not so eager as to hazard it by hurrying on too fast. The veterans of Waterloo filled the trenches of Gen. Jackson at New Orleans with their bodies and their blood. If you can accomplish your object of reaching Richmond by a slower process than storming redoubts and batteries in earthworks, the country will applaud the achievement which gives success to its arms with greatest parsimony of the blood of its children. The envious Charles Lee denounced his superior, Washington, as gifted too much with that 'rascally virtue prudence.' Exert it and deserve his fame.
Your friend,

"F. P. BLAIR,
"Silver Springs."

My retained copy of the following letter is not dated, but it must have been written somewhere about the 20th of April:

HEADQUARTERS, ARMY OF THE POTOMAC,
BEFORE YORKTOWN.

Hon. E. M. Stanton, Secretary of War:

SIR: I received to-day a note from Assistant Secretary Watson enclosing an extract from a letter the author of which is not mentioned. I send a copy of the extract with this. I hope that a copy has also been sent to Gen. McDowell, whom it concerns more nearly, perhaps, than it does me.

At the risk of being thought obtrusive I will venture upon some remarks which perhaps my position does not justify me in making, but which I beg to assure you are induced solely by my intense desire for the success of the government in this struggle.

You will, I hope, pardon me if I allude to the past, not in a captious spirit, but merely so far as may be necessary to explain my own course and my views as to the future.

From the beginning I had intended, so far as I might have the power to carry out my own views, to abandon the line of Manassas as the line of advance. I ever regarded it as an improper one; my wish was to adopt a new line, based upon the waters of the lower Chesapeake. I always expected to meet with strong opposition on this line, the strongest that the rebels could offer, but I was well aware that upon overcoming this opposition the result would be decisive and pregnant with great results.

Circumstances, among which I will now only mention the uncertainty as to the power of the Merrimac, have compelled me to adopt the present line, as probably safer, though far less brilliant, than that by Urbana. When the movement was commenced I counted upon an active and disposable force of nearly 150,000 men, and intended to throw a strong column upon West Point either by York river or, if that proved impracticable, by a march from the mouth of the Severn, expecting to turn in that manner all the defences of the Peninsula. Circumstances have proved that I was right, and that my intended movements would have produced the desired results.

After the transfer of troops had commenced from Alexandria to Fort Monroe, but before I started in person, the division of Blenker was detached from my command - a loss of near 10,000 men. As soon as the mass of my troops were fairly started I embarked myself. Upon reaching Fort Monroe I learned that the rebels were being rapidly reinforced from Norfolk and Richmond. I therefore determined to lose no time in making the effort to invest Yorktown, without waiting for the arrival of the divisions of Hooker and Richardson and the 1st corps, intending to employ the 1st corps in mass to move upon West Point, reinforcing it as circumstances might render necessary.

The advance was made on the morning of the second day after I reached Fort Monroe. When the troops reached the immediate vicinity of Yorktown the true nature of the enemy's position was for the first time developed. While my men were under fire I learned that the 1st corps was removed from my command. No warning had been given me of this, nor was any reason then assigned. I should also have mentioned that the evening before I left Fort Monroe I received a telegraphic despatch from the War Department informing me that the order placing Fort Monroe and its dependent troops under my command was rescinded. No reason was given for this, nor has it been to this day. I confess that I have no right to know the reason. This order deprived me of the support of another division which I had been authorized to form for active operations from among the troops near Fort Monroe.

Thus when I came under fire I found myself weaker by five divisions than I had expected when the movement commenced. It is more than probable that no general was ever placed in such a position before.

Finding myself thus unexpectedly weakened, and with a powerful enemy strongly entrenched in my front, I was compelled to change my plans and become cautious. Could I have retained my original force I confidently believe that I would now have been in front of Richmond instead of where I now am. The probability is that that city would now have been in our possession.

But the question now is in regard to the present and the future rather than the past.

The enemy, by the destruction of the bridges of the Rappahannock, has deprived himself of the means of a rapid advance on Washington. Lee will never venture upon a bold movement on a large scale.

The troops I left for the defence of Washington, as I fully explained to you in the letter I wrote the day I sailed, are ample for its protection.

Our true policy is to concentrate our troops on the fewest possible lines of attack; we have now too many, and an enterprising enemy could strike us a severe blow.

I have every reason to believe that the main portion of the rebel forces are in my front. They are *not* "drawing off" their troops from Yorktown.

Give me McCall's division and I will undertake a movement on West Point which will shake them out of Yorktown. As it is, I will win, but I must not be blamed if success is delayed. I do not feel that I am answerable for the delay of victory.

I do not feel authorized to venture upon any suggestions as to the disposition of the troops in other departments, but content myself with stating the least that I regard as essential to prompt success here. If circumstances render it impossible to give what I ask, I still feel sure of success, but more time will be required to achieve the result.

Very respectfully, your obedient servant,

GEO. B. MCCLELLAN,

Maj.-Gen. Commanding.

The affair known as the one-gun battery is explained by the following instructions and statement:

HEADQUARTERS, ARMY OF THE POTOMAC,
CAMP WINFIELD SCOTT, April 15, 1862.

Brig.-Gen. W. F. Smith, Commanding Division.

SIR: You will please advance to-morrow morning to stop the work now being carried on by the enemy near and in rear of the "one-gun battery." This can probably be most readily accomplished by throwing sharpshooters well forward to the edge of the stream, leaving in front of the work a clear interval through which four to six guns can shell the working parties and adjacent woods. Your flank towards Lee's Mill should be carefully watched, also towards Wynn's Mill, communicating with Gen. Gorman, who will have orders to prevent an attack upon your right flank from Wynn's Mill. It is probable that by placing your guns near the burned chimneys, as well under cover as possible, they will accomplish the result.

If the enemy are driven entirely away, advance cautiously a fern skirmishers across the dam to penetrate the woods and ascertain whether there is any clearing near at hand where you can hold your own. In this event cross over and send for immediate assistance, which will be promptly afforded. If you find the position across the stream dangerous and untenable, cut the dam.

In any event exercise the utmost caution before crossing the stream. The great object is to stop the work, and merely to take advantage after that of any opportunity that may offer itself to push the advantage. I should prefer stopping the work and attacking when our preparations elsewhere are more advanced. I would prefer making the attack at the one-gun battery a part of a more general plan involving the use of batteries against Lee's Mill and other contiguous points. From the statement of Capt. Hope (had since I wrote the foregoing) I imagine a position can be found on the road at a distance of some twelve hundred yards, whence their works can be shelled with 10-pound Parrotts and probably spherical case from the Napoleon guns. I would be glad to learn that the work is stopped and the enemy taught a lesson.

Please inform Gen. Gorman of your instructions, and inform me as early as possible of your arrangements.

Very truly yours,
GEO. B. MCCLELLAN,
Maj- Gen. Commanding.

P.S. I send this direct to you for the reason that it is too late to communicate it through the commander of the 4th army corps

and give time to execute the movement at a sufficiently early
hour.

Upon reflection I think it will, under present circumstances,
be wiser to confine the operation to forcing the enemy to discontinue work.

In compliance with these instructions Gen. Smith placed two
brigades and three batteries on his left to guard against any
attack from Lee's Mill, and commenced operations with his
remaining brigade and battery. He posted Mott's battery opposite the dam at a distance of about eleven hundred yards
from the works, sent in one regiment through the woods on the
right with instructions to open fire on any working parties they
might observe, another regiment on the left with similar orders,
and held the remaining three regiments in reserve. As soon as
our infantry opened fire the enemy replied with shell, upon which
Mott opened and kept up a sharp fire for about an hour until
he silenced the enemy.

About three o'clock Gen. Smith had placed eighteen guns in
position about five hundred yards from the works, supported
on either flank by Brooks's Vermont brigade, Hancock's being
brought up in support. Our guns then opened, the enemy
replying for some time with rapidity; when their fire slack-
ened Smith ordered four companies of the 3d Vermont to cross
the dam and feel the enemy. On arriving at the crest of the
work they were met by the enemy in force, who had lain secreted, and were forced to retire with a loss of about 20 killed
and wounded, after having held the work for some minutes.

Later in the day, after I had left the ground, another reconnoissance was made, under cover of the artillery-fire, by the 4th
Vermont on the right, the 5th and 6th on the left, but it was
found impracticable to push further than to the dam, which
ground was held. During the night strong entrenchments were
thrown up, on the right for four guns within three hundred yards
of the work, on the left one with eight embrasures, and in the
centre one with four embrasures, the last two within five hundred yards' range. This reconnoissances was conducted with skill
and great gallantry, the Vermont troops thus early giving earnest
of the high qualities they so often displayed during all the
war.

The losses in killed, wounded, and missing amounted to about

150. The objects of the operation mere completely achieved: we prevented further work at this point, prevented the enemy from using the crossing, and ascertained that the line could not be broken there without further preparation in the way of artillery, etc.

The general plan of operations determined upon was to establish batteries of heavy guns and mortars bearing upon Yorktown and Gloucester, their water-batteries, a line of works between Yorktown and the Warwick river, Wynn's Mill, and the "one-gun battery" about a mile lower down the Warwick.

The general order regulating the details of the siege operations: as well as the instructions issued by Gen. Fitz-John Porter, who, on the 25th of April, was assigned to duty as director of the siege, are for the present omitted. I issued all orders relating to the siege through him, making him commandant of the siege operations, and at the same time chief of staff for that especial work. Under the circumstances of the case some such arrangement was necessary to relieve me of too much personal labor, and it worked admirably.

Ground was broken on the night of the 17th of April upon batteries 1, 2, and 3, it being only at that date that the necessary roads and bridges mere completed and the requisite material collected. The first parallel was commenced on the morning of the 25th.

The work was pushed with so much energy that by the night of May 3 all the batteries were completed and nearly all armed; the armament would have been completed on the night of the 5th, and fire opened the next morning.

In all sixteen batteries were constructed, their full armament being two 200-pounder rifled guns, twelve 100-pounder rifled, ten 13-inch mortars, twenty-five 10-inch mortars, seven 8-inch mortars, twelve 4½-inch rifled siege-guns, twelve 30-pounder rifled guns, thirty-two 20-pounder rifled guns, and two 8-inch siege-howitzers, being 114 heavy guns and mortars in all.

In order to conceal our purposes and complete the work with the least possible exposure, none of the batteries were opened, except No. 1, which on the 30th of April opened with excellent effect upon the wharves of Yorktown and Gloucester, in order to prevent the landing of supplies and men.

It was intended to open with all the 114 guns and mortars at once, in order to create the greatest possible moral and physical effect.

Towards the close of the siege it was apparent that the works at Gloucester could not be carried by assault from the rear without some preliminary work in the way of reducing the fire of their batteries on the land side - a matter requiring a good deal of time, and force greater than a single division.

With the force at my disposal it was impossible to reinforce Franklin for that purpose, and I determined, late on the 2d of May, to disembark that division and move it to the front, in order to employ all my force in the assault about to be given, and thus render the result as sure as human foresight could make it. On the 3d, then, Franklin's division was disembarked, and was to have moved to the front on the 4th.

As soon as the fire of the water-batteries was silenced the gunboats, reinforced by the *Galena* under the gallant John Rodgers, were to run by and take up a position in rear, whence they could get a nearer fire on the defences and control the road leading from Yorktown to Williamsburg.

When this was effected, the artillery of the land defences silenced, and the garrison demoralized by the shell-fire, the columns of assault were to advance from the nearest cover.

The principal assault was to have been upon the line between the Warwick and Yorktown, a column being ready to assault the latter if the effect of the batteries justified it. The enfilading and two counter batteries were prepared against Wynn's Mill, which, with the dam next above it, would also have been assaulted at the same time with the main attack.

The counter batteries against Wynn's Mill enfiladed the lines stretching thence towards the "one-gun" battery, against which latter a mortar battery was also prepared; under cover of these and the fire of the field-batteries an assault was also to be made on the "one-gun" battery. Under cover of the field-guns of the 4th corps a feint was to be made upon Lee's Mill, to be converted into a real attack if the effect of the operations at other points opened the way thereto.

The fire of our batteries would probably have enabled us to assault about noon. As the enemy were practically without bomb-proof shelters, the fire of our forty-two mortars, ten of which were 13-inch and twenty-five 10-inch, should in five or six hours have blown up their magazines and rendered the works untenable for the garrisons. As many of their guns, all in the water-batteries, were *en barbette,* the fire of our seventy-two heavy guns should in the same space of time have dismounted most of their guns; and as the mortars could well continue their fire until the assaulting columns had reached the immediate vicinity of the works, the success of the assault, with very little loss, was reasonably certain.

In order to diminish the risk to the gunboats as much as possible, I proposed to Flag-Officer Goldsborough and to Capt. Smith, commanding the gunboats, that the gunboats and the *Galena* should run the batteries the night after we opened fire. If the effect of our fire had equalled our expectations so as to justify an assault during the first day's firing, I am very sure that Capt. Smith would have run by the batteries in broad daylight, without awaiting the cover of darkness. I have no doubt whatever that at the latest the dawn of the second day would have seen the gunboats in the rear of the defences, and the assault delivered with entire success and without any heavy loss on our side.

Gen. Johnston told me in Washington, during the winter of 1882 and 1883, that one of his strong objections to holding York-town was his apprehension that the gunboats would force the batteries at night and thus render the position untenable. Other Confederate general officers serving there have told me that in their opinion, at the time, the gunboats could easily have effected this on any dark night.

Early in the morning of the 4th of May it was found that the enemy had during the night evacuated all his positions, very wisely preferring to avoid the experiment of withstanding a bombardment and assault. We captured in the works, including Gloucester, seventy-seven guns and mortars, supplied with the ordinary complements, and seventy-six rounds of ammunition to each.

The captured pieces were as follows: one 10-inch Columbiad, thirteen 9-inch Dahlgren guns, sixteen 8-inch Columbiads, two 7-inch heavy guns, one 6½-inch rifle, one 4½-inch rifle, one 2 8/10-inch rifle, two rifled 32-pounders, one 8-inch siege-howitzer, three 64-pounders, eight 42-pounders, seventeen 32-pounders, four

24-pounders, one 42-pound carronade, two 8-inch mortars, two 12-pounders, one 6-pounder.

They had evidently removed such guns as they could, probably light guns.

I have been much criticised for not assaulting Yorktown immediately. Perhaps the point has been made clear enough, but at the risk of repetition I will say something more on the subject.

Before starting from Fortress Monroe the best information in our possession clearly indicated that the Warwick river ran nearly parallel with the James, instead of heading at Yorktown, and it seemed certain that the road from Newport News to Williamsburg did not cross that stream, at least any important branch of it, and that it presented no obstacle to an advance. Upon these data were predicated the orders of April 4 (for the march of the next day, the 5th), according to which Heintzelman was to move into position close to Yorktown, while Keyes was to take up a position in rear of Yorktown at the Halfway House; Keyes was also ordered to attack and carry whatever he found in front of him. Now, let it be observed that at all points (on the right, centre, and left) we found the enemy's works fully garrisoned and provided with artillery, and that Keyes and his general officers reported that they found the position in their front so strong and so well provided with troops and artillery that it was impossible to assault with any hope of success. The same state of things was clearly the case in front of the right column, where I was. Now, it is very certain that the only thing to be done was to make close reconnoissancess of the enemy's position, in order to discover a vulnerable point. This course was followed, and the unanimous opinion of all was that certain preliminary siege operations were necessary. I assert without fear of contradiction that no one *at that time* thought an assault possible; moreover, that when we saw the works abandoned by the enemy *it* remained the conviction of all that, with the raw troops we had, an assault would have resulted in simply an useless butchery with no hope of success. The statements made long afterwards by such men as Barnard were simply *ex-post-facto* opinions, gotten up for political purposes, and never could have been really entertained by them. The only fault to be found with the operations at Yorktown is in regard to the slowness with which some of the engineer officers operated. I was often obliged to make just such reconnoissancess as I did at Vera Cruz (when a brevet second lieutenant of engineers) to expedite matters. Had Duane been chief-engineer, operations would have progressed much more rapidly. The co-operation of the navy amounted to little or nothing.

CHAPTER XVII.

Despatches and letters relating to subjects treated in the foregoing and following chapters.

" APRIL 6, Sunday, 4 P.M.

"MY DEAR GENERAL: I have received your favor of this date by Col. Key, and hasten to say that I have already written you - *via* Shipping Point - in reply, giving my reason for not having joined you. The time you proposed to proceed with me had elapsed, and particularly the difficulties of my leaving my vessel owing to the want of officers of experience to take care of her.

"I have explained in my note of to-day, and have repeated to Col. Key, the greatly increased strength of the fortifications as seen from this position. The forts at Gloucester are very formidable indeed, and the water-batteries of Yorktown have evidently been increased in dimensions within a few days, as indicated by the new earth.

"As I pointed out to you in our interview, the works to be most apprehended (though they all are too formidable for our vessels, or three or four times their numbers and class) are the guns in mask about one-quarter to one-half of a mile this side of Yorktown, which position I point out to Col. Key.

"The enemy are still on Gloucester Point - how strong I cannot say. So long as he holds that formidable work (or, indeed, upper and lower work) we surely cannot command the York river. All the gunboats of the navy would fail to take it, but would be destroyed in the attempt. Yet I will not hesitate to try the experiment, if required to do so, with this force, however inadequate.

"I have explained to Col. Key that if you turn the masked work, which I fired on to-day and received its fire in return, the guns would command the next water-battery, which is about one-fifth of a mile from it towards Yorktown, as it appears from this ship.

"With those two batteries carried, this force might approach near enough to shell Yorktown at long range, but nothing more. These vessels of this class are not calculated for closer or heavier work.

"As I could not go in time to reach you to-day, as requested, I sent, after despatching my letter to you, the second in rank, Lieut.-Com. Clitz, to confer with you. And now, with Col. Key,

I proceed to Wormsley's creek to meet you or Gen. Heintzelman.

"Very truly yours,

"J. F. MISSROOM,

"*Com.*

"To Maj.-Gen. MCCLELLAN."

"*Wachusett,* April 10, 1862.

"MY DEAR GENERAL: Enclosed is the report upon the landing from this part of the river at 'Sand-Box,' where it was intended to land troops. Capt. Nicholson says he found a good picket-guard house for cavalry, stables, etc., within the Box, and some cattle near Too's Point. A steamer also penetrated a mile up Back creek to-day-which is within the Sand-Box, and whose entrance is to the eastward of Too's Point, as shown by the chart, and over which is good eight feet - to within one and a half miles of Wormsley's creek.

"It has been observed to-day that large numbers of infantry have been transported from Yorktown to Gloucester Point. And this afternoon a number of what seemed to be laborers with entrenching tools went to the same point; we conclude either to strengthen the works there or to throw up works opposite to and within long rifle-range of this anchorage. I have been expecting some such movement, and wondering why they did not try it from some point back from the beach so far that our guns (shell) could not reach them. It cannot be prevented by us.

"Very truly yours,

"J. F. MISSROOM.

"To Maj.-Gen. MCCLELLAN."

" APRIL 11, 6 A.M.

"The enemy very busy last night between Yorktown and Gloucester Point. Schooners observed to be going continually. Enemy may have notice of intention to land troops at Severn and are fortifying its entrance. Ten schooners now in sight.

"J. F. MISSROOM.

"To Maj.-Gen. G. B. MCCLELLAN."

HEADQUARTERS, ARMY OF POTOMAC,
NEAR YORKTOWN, April 8, 1862.

MY DEAR FLAG-OFFICER: Your kind letter received. From the information received thus far I am inclined to think that the "masked battery" on the river-bank below Yorktown is not in existence, but that the gun fired upon Missroom was upon the advanced bastion of the place itself. Porter thinks that he has found a place from which we can enfilade their water-batteries.

I go there in a few minutes to look at it. Should it prove to be so, we can enable the gunboats to take an effective part in the contest. The weather is infamous (has been raining hard for the last eighteen hours, and still continues), the roads are horrid, and we have the devil's own time about supplies.

I have made strong representations as to the withdrawal of the 1st corps, which has forced me to abandon the turning morement, and hope that the President may be induced to change his order. . . . The position of the enemy is immensely strong, but we are learning more of it every hour. Our men behave splendidly - brave and patient as men can be. . . .

G. B. McClellan,
Maj.-Gen. Commanding.

Flag-Officer L. M. Goldsborough, *Minnesota.*

"To Gen. McClellan: "Washington, April 16

"Good for the first lick! Hurrah for Smith and the one-gun battery! Let us have Yorktown, with Magruder and his gang, before the 1st of May, and the job will be over.

"Edwin M. Stanton,
"Secretary of War."

"U.S. Steamer *Wachusett,*
"York River, April 17, 1862.

"My dear General: In accordance with your request to have shell thrown into Yorktown yesterday, the *Sebago* (side-wheel) was ordered on that service, she being the only vessel here provided with a long-range rifle.

"Her fire was returned by two guns of equal range from the enemy with surprising accuracy. One shell passed directly between the 'smoke-stack' and mainmast, a few feet above her deck, and another within a few feet of the wheel-house, throwing the water over the vessel, and both within a short distance of her boilers and machinery, which are altogether exposed. Had she been crippled the attempt to withdraw her might, and probably would, have caused the sacrifice of other vessels also.

"The *Sebago* is the vessel capable of rendering the most important service in covering the landing of troops, and I submit whether it would not be advisable to defer any attempt to throw shell in Yorktown till night, while she can operate on Gloucester with impunity at any time. She draws six feet of water. A single shot in the midship section of that vessel especially, or indeed of either of these gunboats, disables if it do not destroy her.

"Would it not be possible for your cannon to dismount those two rifles with which the enemy fired at the *Sebago* yesterday?

They will inflict much damage on our people when Gloucester is held by them, as well as on our vessels.

"The *Sebago* threw shells into Gloucester last night three several times. I am advised that another light-draught steamer, similar to the *Sebago* is to come here. We cannot have the accuracy of fire from a vessel that the enemy exhibited yesterday.

"Many thanks for the loan of fuses.

"I am, very truly, your obedient servant,

"J. F. MISSROOM, *Com.*

"To Maj.-Gen. G. B. MCCLELLAN."

"WASHINGTON, April 18.

"To Gen. G. B. McClellan:

"Your despatch of this morning received and communicated to the President. He directs me to ask you whether the indications do not show that they are inclined to take the offensive. Banks has moved to Mount Jackson yesterday, and to New Market to-day; has taken some locomotives and prisoners.

"EDWIN M. STANTON,
"Secretary of War"

HEADQUARTERS, ARMY OF THE POTOMAC,
April 18, 10 P.M.

Hon. E. M Stanton, Secretary of War:

Despatch received. I cannot hope such good-fortune as that the enemy will take the offensive. I am perfectly prepared for any attack the enemy may make. He will do nothing more than sorties. I beg that the President will be satisfied that the enemy cannot gain anything by attacking me; the more he does attack the better I shall be contented. All is well. I am glad to hear of Banks's good-fortune.

G. B. MCCLELLAN,
Maj.-Gen.

Confidential.

HEADQUARTERS, ARMY OF THE POTOMAC,
April 18, 11.30 P.M.

His Excellency the President:

If compatible with your impressions as to the security of the capital, and not interfering with operations of which I am ignorant, I would be glad to have McCall's division, so as to be enabled to make a strong attack upon West Point to turn the position of the enemy. After all that I have heard of things which have occurred since I left Washington and before, I would prefer that Gen. McDowell should not again be assigned to duty with me.

G. B. McCLELLAN,
Maj.- Gen. Commanding.

"Maj.-Gen. McClellan: "WASHINGTON, April 27, 1862.

"I am rejoiced to learn that your operations are progressing so rapidly and with so much spirit and success, and congratulate you, and the officers and soldiers engaged, upon the brilliant affair mentioned in your telegram, repeating the assurance that everything in the power of the department is at your service. I hope soon to congratulate you upon a splendid victory that shall be the finishing stroke of the war in every quarter. The work goes bravely on.

"Yours   truly,
"EDWIN M. STANTON,
"Secretary of War"

"WASHINGTON, May 1, 2 P.M.
"Maj.-Gen. G. B. McClellan:
"Your call for Parrott guns from Washington alarms me. chiefly because it aims indefinite procrastination. Is anything to be done?

"A. LINCOLN,
" President. "

HEADQUARTERS, ARMY OF THE POTOMAC,
May 1, 9.30 P.M.
His Excellency the President:
I asked for the Parrott guns from Washington for the reason that some expected had been two weeks, nearly, on the way and could not be heard from. They arrived last night. My arrangements had been made for them, and I thought time might be saved by getting others from Washington. My object was to hasten, not procrastinate. All is being done that human labor can accomplish.

G. B. McCLELLAN,
Maj.-Gen.

HEADQUARTERS, ARMY OF THE POTOMAC,
May *3,* 1862.
Hon. E. M. Stanton, Secretary of War:
I regret to learn that Col. Campbell, 5th Penn. Cavalry, has been placed in arrest by Maj.-Gen. McDowell for endeavoring to comply with my positive order to him to report with his regiment for duty at this place. This regiment was never assigned to Gen.

McDowell's army corps, but was detailed by me to Gen. Keyes's corps. I, of course, expected it to follow me as soon as transportation could be provided, and am not a little surprised to learn that my instructions have been interfered with and my force diminished by the action of the commanding officer of the Department of the Rappahannock, in violation of G. O. No. 29, War Department, adjutant-general's office, March 22, 1862. Under these circumstances I beg the immediate interposition of the War Department to relieve from arrest a meritorious officer, against whom there appears to be no complaint save that of obedience to the orders of his rightful superior. I also ask that the regiment, as well as the 1st N. J., Col. Wyndham, may be permitted to join the army under my command without further delay.

G. B. McCLELLAN,
Maj.-Gen. Commanding.

"Wachusett, YORK RIVER,
"April 22, 1862.

"MY DEAR GENERAL: The carriage on board the *Sebago* is weak. Two carriage-makers are coming to us from Washington; I fear not in time. I am promised, if she comes in time, a steamer with 100-pounder rifle.

"The *Corwin* has no battery but a 10-pounder and two sixes, being only a surveying-craft.

When you commence attack the 100-pounder rifle can assist from the beginning. But I fear our stock of ammunition, especially shell and 'thirty' fuses, will fail us soon.

"I have failed to get what I have asked for from Hampton Roads. Can you loan us some 100-pounder shell and some more 'thirty' fuses for the *Sebago?* She has only about thirty-six fuses of that kind now. Our stock at Hampton Roads was sent to North Carolina.

"Please see the despatch I have just sent to Com. Poor. I sent a steamer to land your mortars at two A.M, with tackle.

"I ought to see you once more before you open fire on Yorktown, to have a clear understanding. Say when I shall go to you, and I will do so any time, at any day, after four P.M.

"The enemy's troops showing themselves now near spot last driven from, abreast anchorage.

"Yours very truly,

"J. F. MISSROOM.

"To Maj.-Gen. G. B. McCLELLAN."

"We got eleven-inch shell into Yorktown and Gloucester last night.

"J. F. MISSROOM.

PEACE ON EARTH

PATRISHA

LURA

EZRA

"FORTRESS MONROE, May 4.
"Maj.-Gen. McClellan:
"With my whole heart I do most cordially congratulate you on your brilliant and important achievement. The gunboats shall accompany you up York river.
"L. M. GOLDSBOROUGH,
"Flag-Officer."

"WASHINGTON, May 4, 1862.
"Maj.-Gen. McClellan:
"Accept my cordial congratulations upon the success at York-town, and I am rejoiced to hear that your forces are in active pursuit. Please favor me with the details as far as they are acquired, and I hope soon to hear your arrival at Richmond.
"EDWIN M. STANTON,
"Secretary of War."

"FORT MONROE, May 5, 1862
"Maj.-Gen. McClellan:
"The Secretary of War telegraphs me to inform him how many transports of all descriptions I can command. Please place at my disposal all you can release, except such as are required for the transportation of stores. . . .
"JOHN TUCKER,
"Assistant Secretary of War."

"CAMP NEAR YORKTOWN, May 5.
"J. Tucker, Assistant Secretary of War, Fortress Monroe:
"In reply to a part of your despatch which the time for the departure of the boat did not admit of answering, and in the absence of Gen. McClellan to the front, I have to inform *you* that the general has ordered all the available transports to carry troops to West Point, and a part of them have started for Cheese-man's creek. Your despatch will be laid before the general this evening.
"R. B. MARCY,
"Chief of Staff."

NEAR WILLIAMSBURG, May 5, 11.45 P.M.
Hon. E. M. Stanton, Secretary of War:
Mr. Tucker's telegram relating to the vessels was received after Franklin's division had embarked and on the way to West Point. Another division goes in the morning, and the last is absolutely necessary to support the first. This movement is of the greatest importance. I will release the vessels just as soon

as the troops are landed.   Nothing new except what I told you
in my last despatch.

GEO. B. MCCLELLAN,
Maj.-Gen. Commanding.

P. S. Some of the main works of the enemy are in our possession, and I am pushing troops forward, but the roads are horrible.

G. B. MCCLELLAN,
Maj.-Gen. Commanding.

WILLIAMSBURG, May 6, 3 P.M.

A portion of the army has left for the upper York, and it
would be destruction to deprive me of the water-transportation
now.   It is absolutely necessary that I should complete the
movement now commenced, or the consequences will be fatal.

G. B. MCCLELLAN,
Maj.-Gen. Commanding.

Hon. E. M. STANTON,
Secretary of War.

HEADQUARTERS, ARMY OF THE POTOMAC,
CAMP WINFIELD SCOTT, May 4, 1862.

Brig-.Gen. Heintzelman, Commanding 3d Corps :

I have received information from Gen. Smith that the enemy
are still in front of him in some force of infantry and cavalry.
Gen. Stoneman has been ordered to move as rapidly as possible
to the Halfway House, and to take possession of the cross-road
near that place, to cut off this command, and also to send a
strong reconnoissance towards Blen's wharf.

I wish Hooker to follow this movement with the utmost
rapidity. When he reaches the point where the road branches
off near the Halfway House, to leave a portion of his force
there, and with the rest to gain the Lee's Mill and Williamsburg
road, so as to support Stoneman and aid him in cutting off the
retreat of the enemy.   The division should move simply with its
ambulances and some reserve ammunition, with not more than
two days' rations. Should further information from Smith render it necessary to move Kearny's division also, I would be glad
to have you take control of the entire movement. Smith is in
possession of their works, and the enemy referred to are some
distance in rear of them-how far I do not yet know.

GEO. B. MCCLELLAN,
Maj.-Gen. Commanding.

"MAY 4, 1862.

"Col. A. V. Colburn:

"SIR: Smith has reported that the enemy is in some force in

his front. Keyes has advanced two brigades and a regiment of horse, with three batteries. They have seen no enemy, but have had a few men injured by the bursting of shells left by the enemy.

"I leave immediately to take command on the left. Telegraph me at Smith's, with duplicates for me at Keyes's headquarters.

"Very respectfully,
" E. O. SUMNER,
"Brig.-Gen. Commanding the Left Wing."

"TWO MILES BEYOND YORKTOWN.
"Gen. Marcy, Chief of Staff:

"Gen. Stoneman has met the enemy about three miles beyond the Halfway House, and has sent back for the infantry to support him. Two brigades are ahead of me.

"Yours, etc.,
"S. V. HEINTZELMAN,
"Brig.-Gen. Commanding 3d Corps."

"HEADQUARTERS, 3D CORPS, IN SIGHT OF WILLIAMSBURG,
"6 P.M., Sunday, May 4, 1862.
"Gen. R. E. Marcy:

"I have just arrived here, and find Gens. Sumner and Smith here. We will soon have three divisions, and are preparing to attack the rebels, who are entrenched in our front with two pieces of artillery, a regiment or so of cavalry, four or five regiments of infantry. Our cavalry have been repulsed with a loss of near 40 men and horses killed and wounded. We will soon carry the works. The infantry are only halting a moment to take a bite and rest.

"Yours, etc.,
"S. V. HEINTZELMAN,
" *Brig.-Gen."*

The following is a fragment of a letter of instructions sent to Gen. Sumner on the morning of the 4th, when he went to assume command on the left; and the condition of affairs then was that the enemy's infantry and cavalry were reported by Smith to be about one and one-half miles in his front in force. I had ordered Stoneman, supported by Hooker, to gain the Halfway House by a rapid march, and thus cut off the retreat of this force in front of Smith. Sumner was ordered to repair the bridges over the Warwick, etc., as quickly as possible, and then to:

"Cross the stream with the 5th Cavalry, Smith's and Couch's divisions, and Casey's if necessary. It is possible that Sedgwick's and Richardson's divisions may be needed to reinforce the right. Please hold them subject to the general's orders for that purpose. Should you be informed that they are not needed here you will be at liberty to substitute one of them for Couch's or Casey's division. It is hoped to get Stoneman's command in rear of the enemy before you attack. Watch the enemy closely with your cavalry, and should he retreat attack him without further instructions. The gunboats have gone up the York river, and Franklin's, and perhaps one other division, will follow up to-day. As soon as the bridges are finished you can cross your command and bring them into position, but do not attack unless the enemy retreat or you receive orders from me. "A. V. COLBURN,
"A. A. G."

It is unnecessary to say that the object of forbidding an attack unless the enemy retreated was to enable Stoneman to get in their rear and thus cut off the entire command.

After the orders to Stoneman, Sumner, and Heintzelman had been issued and were being carried out I received the following:

"HEADQUARTERS, SMITH'S DIVISION, May 4.
"Gen. McClellan:

"Gen. Hancock is in front, and, from what I have learned, presume it is nothing but the rear-guard. I will obey his orders as far as engaging them is concerned. The enemy is one and a half miles in front, and it is probably nothing but cavalry covering the retreat.
"W. F. SMITH,
" Brig.- Gen."

"HEADQUARTERS, SMITH'S DIVISION,
"May 5, 10.30 P.M.
"Gen. McClellan:

"There is a direct road from here to Williamsburg behind the big fort. If you send a good man to command, and these men don't leave to-night, we can capture them all in the morning and be at Williamsburg by eight o'clock. If they don't leave to-night they will give us a big fight in the morning, and we shall whip them.

"Don't risk yourself any more, or your commanders, and don't send Richardson to command this column. As far as I can see it is open country for cavalry, but the rain has made the ground soft. I have more troops - or shall have with Brooks-than I need to defend myself, but it is my earnest opinion that your advance up the James should be this way.

"W. F. SMITH."

On the back of a pencil-sketch of the ground is the following:

"Two companies garrison each fort. Fort Magruder is the far one from here-one and a quarter miles; second fort occupied; third fort, near York, is yet unfinished. They seem to be quiet now. Please order Brooks and Ayres to me in the morning at daylight. I have plenty of troops, but wish our own.

"W. F. S."

"MOUNT ZION CHURCH,
"May 5, 3 P.M.

"Gen. McClellan:

"Owing to delays in the troops coming forward, I have come down here to hasten their march, by direction of Gen. Sumner. Within the last thirty minutes he has sent me two messengers to say that the enemy was gaining ground on him. I fear nothing except a panic amongst our troops, for I am certain we are vastly superior in strength to the enemy. I went myself with a brigade of my corps, which took possession of two works on the left of the enemy. I convinced myself that the enemy commenced his audacious attack upon us to cover a retreat, but, finding that he forces us back, he may convert his feint into something more serious than was at first intended. It may be advisable, if you have troops to spare, to set some of them in motion for this point; but, above all, come yourself.

"The rear of Gen. Kearny has just passed this point on his way to reinforce Gen. Hooker, and the head of his column has probably reached the scene of action; and the firing has ceased for the last ten minutes.

"I write this note because the badness of the road, preventing the rapid concentration of troops, makes me anxious to take precaution against the possibility of reverses. As the roads must soon become absolutely impassable for supplies, our troops must starve unless you can send provisions by boats to skirt the shore, and to be put ashore in small boats. Our position is accessible to York river. The men can live on bread and bacon.

"In haste, your obedient servant,

"E. D. KEYES,
" *Brig.-Gen 4th Corps.*

"P.S. An officer from Gen. Hooker's division reports this moment that three of his batteries have been taken by the pieces miring and the horses being killed. This officer reports that the men are exhausted for want of proper food."

"In Front of Williamsburg,
"May 5, 1862, 11.20 A.M.
"Capt. Chauncey McKeever, A. A. G.:
"I have had a hard contest all the morning, but do not despair of success. My men are hard at work, but a good deal exhausted. It is reported to me that my communication with you by the Yorktown road is clear of the enemy. Batteries, cavalry, and infantry can take front by the side of mine to whip the enemy.
"Very respectfully, your obedient servant,
"HOOKER,
"Brig.-Gen."

"MAY 5, late at night.

"MY DEAR GENERAL: I did the best I could after getting your order, which was after dark some time. I sent a brigade (Martindale's) to occupy the front of York. The roads were horrible and blocked up by wagons, so that they were impassable. The brigade reached York. I sent some of Hunt's batteries; they got there and halted. The remainder I kept ready to march at two o'clock, or as soon as light enough. All are rested and fresh. Sykes's and my other brigades are in camp, also Blake. Franklin, I think, got off. I hope you have got order out of chaos. Capt. Norton says Ingalls told him he had received an order from the secretary to fit out a sea expedition, which would derange his plans considerably. A telegram can always reach me from York. We are ready to more quickly. I have directed Martindale to camp at York.
"Yours ever,
"F. J. PORTER."

HEADQUARTERS, ARMY OF THE POTOMAC,
WILLIAMSBURG, May 7, 1862, 12.30 P.M.
Gen. R. B. Marcy, Chief of Staff, Camp Winfield Scott:
GENERAL: Headquarters will be moved at once to this place; wagons light. Porter will complete his embarkation as rapidly as possible and join Franklin. The artillery of the divisions Franklin, Sedgwick, and Porter will proceed by water with the least possible delay to join their divisions, also Franklin's cavalry and as many wagons as possible. Hunt's heavy batteries will move to Brick House landing by mater. I will give orders in regard to the rest of Hunt's batteries, the regular infantry, Roach's and Gregg's cavalry shortly.
Please send me last news from Franklin, and, if necessary, send a fast special boat to learn state of affairs, and communicate on return with signal party at Queen's creek, as well as *via* Yorktown by telegraph. The orders for Sumner and Richard-

son will be given today; in the meantime let neither embark
without special orders from me: this is imperative.

How soon can the artillery of Franklin, Sedgwick, and Porter be embarked? How soon Franklin's cavalry? How soon
will transports be ready for the regular infantry and Richardson? How soon can water-transportation be furnished for
Duane and his train? For Woodbury and his trains? How
soon for Gregg and Rush? How many wagons has Van Vliet
in reserve for general purposes? If you send steamer to Franklin, inform him that Stoneman was some fourteen miles from
here a couple of hours ago, and will try to communicate with
him *via* Hockaday's Spring this evening. I start Smith's division this evening, and hope to get most of the column in motion by the morning. Will move in person to-morrow morning.
Would like to have a gunboat examine Moody's wharf, to see
whether burned.

G. B. MCCLELLAN,
Maj.-Gen. Commanding.

"BRICK HOUSE POINT, May 6, 1862.

"Gen. G. B. McClellan:

I am landing at Brick House Point. It is, however, a bad
landing; the water shoal for a long distance out - a quarter of a
mile from shore. One brigade is landed. The enemy is said to
be in force on the road, watching this point; I do not believe it,
however. I hope to get the artillery and two other brigades off
before morning.

"W. B. FRANKLIN,
"Brig.-Gen."

"BRICK HOUSE, May 7, A.M.

"Gen. G. B. McClellan:

"All of my division has landed except the cavalry. The
night passed with nothing unusual except the killing of one
picket. We have two prisoners, taken when we first arrived;
they belong to a Texan regiment, are very intelligent, but lie,
I think. I send them to Yorktown by the *Spaulding.* Dana's
brigade is here and will be landed this morning. The indications are that the enemy is in the vicinity.

"W. B. FRANKLIN,
"Brig.-Gen."

"BRICK HOUSE, May 7, 1862.

"Gen. G. B. McClellan:

"The road from Brick House Point to the main road is not
as laid down on the photographic or C. S. maps. The right

flank and rear are surrounded by a creek, and the left flank has
another creek, leaving a small opening through which the road
winds. I have ordered an examination to determine more accu-
rately these points, but it is a slow business on account of want
of cavalry. I still think it may be an open question between
this point and West Point.

"W. B. FRANKLIN,
                                    "Brig.-Gen."

"HEADQUARTERS,   FRANKLIN'S   DIVISION,
"BRICK HOUSE, May 7, 1862.

"Gen. R. B. Marcy, Chief of Staff:

"GENERAL: I have the honor to report that this morning,
about seven o'clock, our pickets were driven in on our left flank,
and that after skirmishing for about two hours the action became
quite sharp at the right extremity of that flank.   Our reserves
were driven in several times, but returned to their position each
time with ardor. Finally we held the position which we had
taken in the morning, and at several points of the line advanced
our position.

"Wherever we advanced the enemy was found in rifle-pits.
The day has been a success, and but for the extreme want of
forage and provisions, owing to the deficiency of transportation
and the difficulty of landing, we might have followed it up. As
it is, I congratulate myself that we have maintained our position.
Gen. Newton's command was most severely engaged, and his
conduct and that of Gen. Slocum, who had charge respectively
of the left and right wings, was admirable.   All of the officers
and men behaved admirably, and with transportation and forage
we could move on to-morrow.

"I respectfully request that instructions may be given to send
up forage and transportation immediately, as me are entirely tied
down for want of them. Gen. Sedgwick's infantry has arrived.
The killed and wounded amount to nearly a hundred. A more
detailed report will be given as soon as possible.

"Very respectfully,

"W. B. FRANKLIN,
                                    "Brig.-Gen."

CAMP 19 MILES FROM WILLIAMSBURG,
May 11, 1862.

Hon. E. M. Stanton, Secretary of War, Fortress Monroe:

Without waiting for further official reports which have not
yet reached me, I wish to bear testimony to the splendid conduct
of Hooker's and Kearny's divisions, under command of Gen.
Heintzelman, in the battle of Williamsburg. Their bearing was
worthy of veterans. Hooker's division for hours gallantly with-

stood the attack of greatly superior numbers, with very heavy loss. Kearny's arrived in time to restore the fortunes of the day, and came most gallantly into action. I shall probably have occasion to call attention to other commands, and do not wish to do injustice to them by mentioning them now. If I had had the full information I now have in regard to the troops above-named when I first telegraphed, they would have been specially mentioned and commended. I spoke only of what I knew at the time, and shall rejoice to do full justice to all engaged.

G B. McCLELLAN,
Maj.-Gen. Commanding.

CHAPTER XVIII.

PRIVATE LETTERS.

[*April* 1 to *May* 5, 1862]

Steamer "Commodore," April 1, 1862 *Potomac River,* 4.15 P.M. - As soon as possible after reaching Alexandria I got the *Commodore* under way and "put off." I did not feel safe until I could fairly see Alexandria behind us. I have brought a tug with us to take back despatches from Budd's Ferry, where I shall stop a few hours for the purpose of winding up everything. I found that if I remained at Alexandria I would be annoyed very much, and perhaps be sent for from Washington. . . . Officially speaking, I feel very glad to get away from that sink of iniquity. . .

8 P.M. - I have just returned from a trip in one of the naval vessels with Capt. Seymour to take a look at the rebel batteries (recently abandoned) at Shipping Point, etc. They were pretty formidable, and it would have given us no little trouble to take possession of them had they held firm. It makes only the more evident the propriety of my movements, by which Manassas was forced to be evacuated and these batteries with it. The trip was quite interesting. . . .

Steamer "Commodore," April 3, *Hampton Roads,* 1.30 P.M.- . . . I have been up to my eyes in business since my arrival. We reached here about four yesterday P.M.; ran into the wharf and unloaded the horses, then went out and anchored. Marcy and I at once took a tug and ran out to the flag-ship *Minnesota* to see Goldsborough, where we remained until about nine, taking tea with him.

On our return we found Gen. Heintzelman, soon followed by Porter and Smith, all of whom remained here all night. I sat up very late arranging movements, and had my hands full. I have been hard at work all the morning, and not yet on shore. Dine with Gen. Wool to-day at four, and go thence to our camp.

We move to-morrow A.M. Three divisions take the direct road to Yorktown, and will encamp at Howard's Bridge. Two take the James River road and go to Young's Mill. The reserve goes to Big Bethel, where my headquarters will be to-morrow night.

My great trouble is in the want of wagons - a terrible drawback; but I cannot wait for them. I hope to get possession, before to-morrow night, of a new landing-place some seven or eight miles from Yorktown, which will help us very much. It is probable that we shall have some fighting to-morrow; not serious, but we may have the opportunity of drubbing Magruder. The harbor here is very crowded; facilities for landing are bad. I hope to get possession of Yorktown day after to-morrow. Shall then arrange to make the York river my line of supplies. The great battle will be (I think) near Richmond, as I have always hoped and thought. I see my way very clearly, and, with my trains once ready, will move rapidly. . . .

Telegram - *Great Bethel, April 4,* 1862, 6 P.M. - My advanced guard five miles from Yorktown. Some slight skirmishing to-day. Our people driving rebels. Hope to invest Yorktown to-morrow. All well and in good spirits.

Big Bethel, April 5, 2 A.M. - . . . Have just got through with the orders for to-morrow; have been working very hard, and have sent off officers and orderlies in every direction. I feel sure of to-morrow. I have, I think, provided against every contingency, and shall have the men well in hand if we fight to-morrow. . . . I saw yesterday a wonderfully cool performance. Three of our men had gone close down to the enemy's position after a sheep, which they killed, skinned, and started off with. They were, of course, fired at frequently, and in the course of their travels a 12-pound shot struck directly by them. They quietly picked up the shot, held on to the sheep, and brought the shot to me, yet warm. I never saw so cool and gallant a set of men; they do not seem to know what fear is.

Near Yorktown, April 6, 1 A.M. - . . . I find the enemy in strong force and in a very strong position, but will drive him out, Fitz-John is in the advance on the right, Baldy on the

23

left; they are doing splendidly. Their divisions have been under fire all the afternoon; have lost only about five killed in each, and have punished secesh badly. Thus far it has been altogether an artillery affair.

While listening this P.M. to the sound of the guns I received an order detaching McDowell's corps from my command. It is the most infamous thing that history has recorded. I have made such representations as will probably induce a revocation of the order, or at least save Franklin to me. The idea of depriving a general of 35,000 troops when actually under fire!

To-morrow night I can tell you exactly what I intend doing. We have no baggage to-night, our wagons being detained by the bad roads. I have taken possession of a hut in a deserted secesh camp; found a table therein, and sleep on a horse-blanket, if I find time to "retire." Colburn is copying a long letter; Seth, standing by the fire, looking very sleepy. He wakes up and sends his kindest regards, in which Colburn asks to participate. I am sorry to say that your father is snoring loudly in a corner.

April 6, 1.40 P.M. - . . . Did not get to bed until 3.30, and then my bed was a rather rough one, as our wagons did not arrive. Things quiet to-day; very little firing; our people are pushing their reconnoissancess and getting up supplies. I shall take the place, but may be some time in effecting it. . . .

April 8, 8 A.M. - Raining hard all night, and still continues to do so. Am now encamped about five miles from Yorktown: have been here two or three days. Have now visited both the right and left, and, in spite of the heavy rain, must ride to Ship Point and our right immediately after breakfast. All I care for about the rain is the health and comfort of the men. They are more fond of me than ever; more enthusiastic than I deserve; wherever I go it seems to inspire the fullest confidence. . . .

I have raised an awful row about McDowell's corps. The President very coolly telegraphed me yesterday that he thought I had better break the enemy's lines at once! I was much tempted to reply that he had better come and do it himself.

April 9, near Yorktown, 8 A.M. - . . . . Last night returned late and was fully occupied with reports of reconnoissancess, etc., until very late.

It rained nearly every moment yesterday, all the night before: all last night, but has now stopped, though likely to commence again at any moment. It is execrable weather; everything knee-deep in mud; roads infamous: but we will get through it. I have had great difficulty in arranging about supplies - so few wagons and such bad roads. Rode down to Ship Point yesterday morning. . . .

9 A.M. - Interrupted and unable to finish. Have been bothered all the evening, but am getting things straightened out. . . . Start for the Point in a few minutes. . . .

April 10, 10 P.M. - Have had a pretty long ride to-day. Secretary Fox spent last night with me. As soon as he had gone I rode to Porter's camp, thence to the river-bank to meet Capt. Missroom, commanding the gunboats. Have had an excellent view of the water defences of Yorktown, as well as of Gloucester. The enemy is very strong and is adding to his works and the number of his men. I could see them coming in on schooners. But as my heavy guns are not yet landed, and the navy do not feel strong enough to go at them, I can only hurry forward our preparations and trust that the more they have the more I shall catch. . . .

Yesterday I also spent on the right, taking, under cover of the heavy rain, a pretty good look at the ground in front of York and its defences. I got back about dark, pretty wet and tired out. . . To-morrow we move headquarters to a much better and more convenient camp further to the front. . . . The present camp is a little too far from the scene of the most important operations.

April 11 - I am just recovering from a terrible scare. Early this morning I was awakened by a despatch from Fitz-John's headquarters stating that Fitz had made an ascension in the balloon this morning, and that the balloon had broken away and come to the ground some three miles southwest, which would be within the enemy's lines. You can imagine how I felt. I at once sent off to the various pickets to find out what they knew and try to do something to save him, but the order had no sooner gone than in walks Mr. Fitz just as cool as usual. He had luckily come down near my own camp after actually passing over that of the enemy. You may rest assured of one thing: you won't catch me in the confounded balloon, nor will I allow any other generals to go up in it. . . .

Don't worry about the wretches; they have done nearly their worst, and can't do much more. I am sure that I will win in the end, in spite of all their rascality. History will present a sad record of these traitors who are willing to sacrifice the country and its army for personal spite and personal aims. The people will soon understand the whole matter.

April 14, 11 P.M., *Camp Winfield Scott.*- . . . I believe I now know who instigated the attack upon me and the country. . . . So Fox told you all about our troubles. They were severe for some time, but we are pretty well over the worst of them. . . . I do not expect to lose many men, but to do the work mainly with artillery, and so avoid much loss of life. Several brave fellows have already gone to their long home, but not a large number.

I can't tell you how soon I will attack, as it will depend upon the rapidity with which certain preliminary work can be done and the heavy guns brought up. I do not fear a repulse. I shall not quit the camps until I do so to continue the march on Richmond. If I am repulsed once, will try it again, and keep it up until we succeed, But I do not anticipate a repulse; am confident of success. . . . I received to-day a very kind letter from old Mr. Blair, which I enclose for you to keep for me. . . . Remained at home this morning, doing office-work, but rode out all the afternoon; rode to the front and took another look at secesh. . . .

8.30 A.M., 15th - Am about starting for the gunboats, which are anchored near here, to take a better look at the opposite shore. . . . It is raining a little this morning - not much more than a drizzle. . . .

April 18, 1.15 A.M.- . . . About a half-hour ago the accustomed intermittent sound of artillery was varied in its monotony

by a very heavy and continued rattle of musketry, with the ac-
companiment of a very respectable firing of artillery. I started
at once for the telegraph-office, and endeavored in vain for some
ten or fifteen minutes to arouse the operators at the stations in
the direction of the firing. So I ordered twenty of the escort
to saddle up, and started off Hudson, Sweitzer, and the Duc de
Chartres to learn the state of the case. The firing has ceased
now for some minutes, and I am still ignorant as to its whereabouts and cause. Of course I must remain up until I know
what it is. I had had Arthur, Wright, Hammerstein, Radowitz,
and the Comte de Paris, as well as Colburn, also up, with some
of the escort ready to move or carry orders, as the case may
be, but just now told them to lie down until I sent for them. It
is a beautiful moonlight night, clear and pleasant - almost too
much so for sleeping. . . . Poor Wagner, of the Topogs, lost an
arm this afternoon by the bursting of a shell; he is doing well,
however.

Merrill was severely but not dangerously wounded in the arm
yesterday. In Smith's affair yesterday we lost, I fear, nearly
200 killed and wounded. The object I proposed had been fully
accomplished with the loss of about 20, when, after I left the
ground, a movement was made in direct violation of my orders,
by which the remainder of the loss was uselessly incurred. I
do not yet know the details nor who is responsible. We have
a severe task before us, but we will gain a brilliant success. . . .
Colburn is my stand-by-so true and faithful. Many of my aides
are excellent. No general ever labored under greater disadvantages, but I will carry it through in spite of everything. I hope
Franklin will be here to-morrow or next day. I will then invest
Gloucester and attack it at the same time I do York. When the
Galena arrives I will cause it to pass the batteries, take them in
reverse, and cut off the enemy's communications by York river.
As I write I hear our guns constantly sounding and the bursting
of shells in Secession.

9 P.M. - The firing of last night was caused by the attempt of
a part of the enemy to cross the stream in Smith's front. They
were repulsed at once; tried it later, and were again driven back.

April 19, 10.30 P.M. - . . . To-day it has been very quiet;
our batteries have merely fired enough to keep the enemy en-

tirely silent at his works in front of Smith and at Wynn's Mill. Last night we commenced a battery, at Farnholdt's house, for five 100-pounder Parrotts and one 200-pounder Parrott; also one for fifteen heavy guns about two thousand yards from the enemy's main defences; another for six and one for five close by. Another for six was armed to-day, and kept down the enemy's fire at Wynn's Mill. To-morrow evening we commence batteries for thirteen mortars. About Monday night we will construct the first parallel and several other batteries in exposed positions, leaving those already commenced to cover the work and render it more safe. We shall soon be raining down a terrible tempest on this devoted place. To-day the enemy sent a flag of truce to Smith, asking a suspension of hostilities to bury the killed of the 16th. The officer who met with Sweitzer acknowledged that their loss was very severe and the bearing of our men admirable. I received to-day a letter from Burnside, which I enclose. . .

Franklin arrived yesterday and spent the night in my tent. He is at Ship Point to-night; I expect his division to-morrow. . . . Don't be at all discouraged; all is going well. I know exactly what I am about. I can't go "with a rush" over strong posts. I must use heavy guns and silence their fire; all that takes much time, and I have not been longer than the usual time for such things-much less than the usual, in truth. . . .

I can't tell you when Yorktown is to be attacked, for it depends on circumstances that I cannot control. It shall be attacked the first moment I can do it successfully. But I don't intend to hurry it; I cannot afford to fail. I may have the opportunity of carrying the place next week, or may be delayed a couple of weeks; much, of course, depends on the rapidity with which the heavy guns and ammunition arrive. Never mind what such people as - say; they are beneath contempt.

I will put in a leaf of holly from the bower some of the men have made in front of my tent to-day. They have made quite an artistic thing of it - holly and pine; it adds much, too, to my comfort, as it renders the tent more private and cool.

April 20, 7.30 A.M. - . . It has been raining more or less all night, and if it were not for the men I would enjoy the rain, for I rather like to hear it patter on the tent.

I have a fire in my stove this morning, so it is quite comfortable. My tent is the same the aides use for an office; it has a floor of pine boughs - a carpet of boughs, I suppose I ought to say-a table in the middle, a desk in one corner, my bed in another, my saddle in another, a wood-pile, etc., in the last. I have a splendid two-legged washstand which Charles's mechanical ingenuity devised. Then I have a clothes-rack, consisting of a sapling with the stumps of the branches projecting. So you see I am living quite *en prince.*

April 21. - Yesterday was rather unpleasant; rained a good deal. To-day about the same; not raining much yet, but a kind of drizzle. Had a letter yesterday from Francis B. Cutting, of New York, hoping that I would not allow these treacherous hounds to drive me from my path. Have just replied to it.

April 22, 11.15 P.M. - . . . The enemy has been blazing away a good deal to-day, but hurt nothing, however; he tried his best at a skirmish with some of Smith's men this morning, but was repulsed with loss. It is said that some of his troops were blacks. I do not, however, give full credit to this. It seems too improbable to be true. The navy have been firing this morning at long range.

April 23, 7 A.M. - . . . Some few shots fired already, but not many: secesh don't mean to get up very early. I am rather anxious to hear the result of last night's work; for I am in hopes that I can get all the batteries that have been commenced well aimed to-night, so that the first parallel may be commenced at once. The weather has cleared off beautifully again, so that I am in strong hopes we shall have no more rain for some time. You have no idea of the effect of a couple of days' rain in this country; roads, camps, etc., become impassable. . . .

11.30 P.M. - . . Have been working hard all day, but not in the saddle; it has been head-work in my tent to-day. I am getting on splendidly with my "slow preparations." The prince is delighted and thinks my work gigantic. I do believe that I am avoiding the fault of the Allies at Sebastopol, and quietly preparing the way for great success. I have brought forty heavy guns in battery; to-morrow night I hope to have twelve new guns and five to ten heavy mortars in battery. I begin in the morning the redoubts to cover the flank of the first parallel, which will be constructed to-morrow night. I will not open fire unless the enemy annoys us, hoping to get all the guns in battery and the trenches well advanced before meeting with serious opposition. We have done much more than they suspect. Have ordered a forced reconnoissances of a dangerous point in the morning; it may cost several lives, but I have taken all possible precautions, and hope to gain the information necessary with but little loss. There is no other choice than to run the risk. . . . Everything is as quiet now as if there were no enemy within a hundred miles of us The *Galena,* under Rodgers, will be here by day after to-morrow.

April 26. - Again raining, and has been all the morning. Grover carried a redoubt of the rebels most handsomely this morning. It was one from which they had it in their power to annoy the left of our parallels, and it was an object to get rid of it. The work was handsomely done; the work carried by assault, and then so much destroyed that it can be of no further use to the rebels. Fifteen prisoners were taken in the affair. We lost three killed, one mortally and about ten others slightly wounded; have not all the details yet. We got eight immense mortars up by water last night; but a canal-boat loaded with empty shells ran aground in sight of secesh, who has been blazing away at them; sent one shot through. He has stopped firing now, probably because he cannot see on account of the rain. To-night we complete the first parallel, which will be nearly four thousand yards long-an immense work. From the manner in which our men pitched into the little redoubt this morning it is clear that the *morale* is on our side. The men found quite a deep and broad ditch in front of the affair, but over it they went without a moment's hesitation!

April 27, *midnight.* - . . . . Was engaged with Barnard, Porter, etc., until about one, when I rode to the trenches. Then, of course, had to walk; a good deal was muddy, so it was tiresome. Went over the whole extent and saw everything with care. The enemy have fired a good deal to-day, but the men are now so well covered that no one has been hurt to-day. Commenced to-day batteries for fifteen 10-inch mortars, and to-night another battery for heavy guns; another for ten mortars to-morrow morning; an extension of the parallel on the left commenced to-night. By to-morrow night the parallel shall be finished in all its details, as well as the two covering redoubts on the left. Some time day after to-morrow I hope to have thirty-five mortars in battery. To-morrow night will open a tuyau in advance leading to a new gun-battery fast getting ready to blow secesh up. He will have a bad time of it when we open. Have news this evening *via* Richmond that New Orleans is in our possession. I presume it is true. So the work goes bravely on. . . . Yesterday made Fitz Porter "Director of the Siege"- a novel title, but made necessary by the circumstances of the case. I give all my orders relating to the siege through him, making him at the same time commandant of the siege operations and a chief of staff for that portion of the work. This new arrangement will save me much trouble, and relieve my mind greatly, and save much time. In going over the line of trenches yesterday I found so many blunders committed that I was very thankful to put Porter on duty at once. . . . The good fellow (Colburn) never leaves me; wherever I ride he sticks close after me. He is one of the very best men I ever knew, so thoroughly honest and reliable. His judgment is excellent and he is perfectly untiring. Day and night are about the same to him, and he will start out on a long ride at midnight in a pitch-dark or rainy night with as much good-humor as at midday. "Rentuck" (horse) is still at Fort Monroe sick; will rejoin in a few days, I hope. Marsh is with him, and I am sometimes half-wicked enough to suspect that Marsh finds Fort Monroe more comfortable than camp would be.

April 28, 11.45 P.M. - . . . Rode out this P.M., and went over most of the ground from right to left. Commenced some new work still more to the front to-night; as it was exposed and dangerous, and required noiseless and rapid working, I as usual gave it to the regulars to do. Have this moment heard that although the rebels have been firing a great deal (there goes another gun), they have wounded but one man; the men should be well covered by this time, so I fancy the work is safe. I have also (there goes another gun) ordered a lot of rifle-pits for sharpshooters to be pushed out well to the front; we will, I hope, gain a good deal of ground to-night. Am getting on nicely. Will have some more batteries ready for their guns by to-morrow P.M. and will very shortly be able to open on secesh. He tried to annoy one of our working parties this morning with a couple of guns; I sent out a field-battery and silenced him after four rounds.

8 A.M. - Colburn came back from the trenches after midnight, and reported all going on well; the regulars had covered themselves well by that time, and the fire of the enemy had only wounded one man, and that not badly. Clitz was in command of the working party last night. To-day weather good; will not rain. Hope to make good progress this morning. Good deal of firing going on now.

April 30, A.M. - Had a quiet night; very little firing; drove them out of an orchard whence they had been annoying us, and pushed them still further in towards their works. A good deal of firing on their part yesterday; did very little harm, killing some three and wounding four or five of our people. Scarcely a gun fired to-day as yet; we are working like horses and will soon be ready to open. It will be a tremendous affair when we do begin, and will, I hope, make short work of it. . . . Have put the regulars on the exposed portions of the work, they work so much better. A raw, disagreeable day; I fear it will rain-unless it snows; wind from east. . . .

10.30 P.M. - After I got through my morning work went down to see the opening of Battery No. 1. It worked handsomely; drove all the rebel schooners away from the wharf, and made a general scatteration. The effect was excellent. Shall not open the general fire for some four days - I hope on Monday A.M.

Next morning (May 1) - Another wet, drizzly, uncomfortable sort of a day. Good deal of firing during the night. I shall be very glad when we are really ready to open fire, and then finish this confounded affair. I am tired of public life; and even now, when I am doing the best I can for my country in the field, I know that my enemies are pursuing me more remorselessly than ever, and "kind friends" are constantly making themselves agreeable by informing me of the pleasant predicament in which I am - the rebels on one side, and the abolitionists and other scoundrels on the other. I believe in my heart and conscience, however, that I am walking on the ridge between the two gulfs, and that all I have to do is to try to keep the path of honor and truth, and that God will bring me safely through. At all events I am willing to leave the matter in His hands, and will be content with the decision of the Almighty.

May 3, 12.30 A.M. - After the hot firing of to-day everything is so unusually still that I am a little suspicious that our friends may intend a sortie; so I have taken all the steps necessary to be ready for them, and am sitting up for a while to await developments. I feel much better satisfied when they are firing than when they are silent. To-day they have wasted about a thousand rounds and have done us no harm worth speaking of, except (Irish) bursting one of their own guns. We are now nearly ready to open; shall begin, I think, on Monday morning, certainly by Tuesday. If all works well it is not impossible that we shall have Yorktown by Wednesday or Thursday. The task is a difficult one, yet I am sure we have taken the right way to accomplish our purpose, and that we will soon win. I fear that me are to have another storm to-night. We want no more rain, but will make the best of it if it comes. Had plenty of work to do at home all the morning, and in the afternoon rode down to "Shield's House" to meet the new commander of the flotilla, Capt. Smith. . . . I don't half like the perfect quietness which reigns now. I have given orders to take advantage of it and push our approaches as far forward as possible. It don't seem natural. It looks like a sortie or an evacuation. If either, I hope it may be the former. I do not want these rascals to get away from me without a sound drubbing, which they richly deserve and will be sure to get if they remain. . . . I feel that the fate of a nation depends upon me, and I feel that I have not one single friend at the seat of government. Any day may bring an order relieving me from command. If they will simply let me alone I feel sure of success; but will they do it?

May 5, 9.30 A.M. - . . . You will have learned ere this that Yorktown is ours. It is a place of immense strength, and was very heavily armed. It so happened that our preparation for the attack was equally formidable, so that Lee, Johnston, and Davis confessed that they could not hold the place. They evacuated it in a great hurry, leaving their heavy guns, baggage, etc. I sent the cavalry after them at once, and our advance is now engaged with them at Williamsburg. The weather is infamous; it has been raining all night, and is still raining heavily; no signs of stopping; roads awful.   I hope to get to West Point to-day, although the weather has delayed us terribly.   It could not well be worse, but we will get through nevertheless. The villains (secesh) have scattered torpedoes everywhere - by springs, wells, etc. It is the most murderous and barbarous thing I ever heard of.

CHAPTER XIX.

Confederate retreat - Pursuit towards Williamsburg - Battle of Williamsburg - The horse Dan Webster.

IT appears that Gen. Johnston, the Confederate commander, regarded the position of Yorktown and the Warwick as easily held against a simple assault, but as untenable against siege operations, or when we could pass up the York or James rivers; therefore he withdrew as soon as satisfied that we were on the point of using our heavy guns.

He directed the movement to commence at dusk on the 4th of May, Magruder's command to move by the Lee's Mill road, to halt at the junction of roads on the Yorktown side of Williamsburg, and occupy the line of fortifications; Longstreet's division to follow Magruder's; D. H. Hill's and G. W. Smith's divisions to march by the Yorktown road. Longstreet, Hill, and Smith were to pass through Williamsburg, Smith halting on the Barhamsville road far enough out to leave room for the other troops between himself and the town. It was expected that Magruder and Hill would clear the way to enable Longstreet and Smith to start at nine P.M., so that the whole army could reach Williamsburg soon after midnight; but it was sunrise of the 5th before Smith's road was clear, and his rear reached the fortifications near Williamsburg about noon. He found that the fortifications were unoccupied; and as skirmishing was taking place about two miles back, he halted a small body whom he found between the works and Williamsburg, and reported the state of affairs to Gen. Johnston, who ordered back McLaws's brigade and Stuart's cavalry.

Early in the morning of the 4th of May, the moment I learned that our troops were in possession of Yorktown and the line of the Warwick, I ordered Gen. Stoneman in pursuit with all the available force of cavalry and horse-artillery, supported by infantry, on both the Lee's Mill and Yorktown roads to Williamsburg.

The next, and by far the most important, step was to throw Franklin's division, supported promptly and strongly, as rapidly as possible up the York river by water, to land on its right bank opposite West Point, in order to take in reverse whatever works might exist between that point and Yorktown, and to cut off, if possible, the enemy's trains and troops still south of the mouth of the Pamunkey.

While keeping steadily in view Stoneman's operations and his proper support, I at once turned my attention to expediting the movement up the York river by water. The weather was so bad and the wharf facilities at Yorktown so deficient that it was very difficult to bring order out of chaos, and Franklin's division did not reach its destination until the 6th of May.

On the morning of the 4th, then, Stoneman moved out of Yorktown with four batteries of horse-artillery, the 1st and 6th U. S. Cavalry, the 8th Ill. Cavalry, and Barker's squadron of Ill. cavalry. Hooker's division was ordered to move as rapidly as possible by the same road in support, and Heintzelman was ordered to hold himself in readiness to follow with Kearny's division if necessary.

Smith having reported the enemy's infantry and cavalry in force about one and a half miles in rear of Lee's Mill, Stoneman was ordered to cut off their retreat in the vicinity of the Half-way House. At the same time Sumner, in command of the left, was ordered to restore the bridges over the Warwick and place Smith's and Couch's divisions of the 4th corps, and Casey's if necessary, in front of the reported hostile force, endeavoring to hold them where they were until Stoneman could gain their line of retreat; but attacking if they fell back. His pursuit was to be by the Lee's Mill road, with Smith leading. The remaining divisions - those of Porter, Sedgwick, Richardson, and Sykes- were held in readiness to support either Keyes, Heintzelman, or Franklin, as might prove most advantageous. Stoneman was thus ordered not only to pursue and harass the enemy's rear-guard, but also to endeavor to cut off those on the Lee's Mill road in front of Sumner.

About six miles from Yorktown Stoneman came upon the enemy's pickets; two miles further on he came up with their rear-guard, a regiment of cavalry, posted on the further bank of a difficult ravine. Gibson's battery soon drove them out of this position. At this point he sent Gen. Emory, with Benson's battery, the 3d Penn., and Barker's squadron, across to the Lee's Mill road to cut off the force in front of Sumner, who was supposed to be advancing by that road. With the remainder of his force Stoneman pushed on as rapidly as safety permitted to occupy the junction of the Yorktown and Lee's Mill roads, about two miles south of Williamsburg. Before detaching Emory, Stoneman had communicated with Sumner's advanced guard, and had also learned that Hooker was close behind on the Yorktown road. Gen. P. St. G. Cooke, commanding the advanced guard, consisting of a section of Gibson's battery and a part of the 1st U. S. Cavalry, upon debauching from the wood found himself at the junction of the two roads immediately in front of a strong earthwork (Fort Magruder) flanked by redoubts, and in presence of a strong rear-guard, consisting of a regiment of cavalry, one battery, and three regiments of infantry. With his small force Cooke made immediate dispositions to attack, and Stoneman hastened up the remainder of the 1st Cavalry and of Gibson's battery.

The cleared ground available for the operations of cavalry and artillery was here so limited that only about three hundred cavalry and one battery could be brought into action. Foreseeing that he must soon retreat unless promptly supported by the infantry-some two miles in rear at last accounts-Stoneman formed the remainder of his force in a clearing half a mile in rear, in order to cover the withdrawal of his advanced guard when that became necessary, and sent to hurry up the infantry. With great difficulty, so deep was the mud and so thick the abattis, Gibson got his battery in position, and Col. W. A. Grier formed his regiment (1st U. S.) to support it. Meanwhile the enemy, strongly reinforced from his main body, had thrown himself into the abandoned works, and several regiments of infantry were seen moving in a direction threatening to turn Stoneman's right, on which he directed Maj. L. Williams, commanding the 6th U. S. Cavalry, to make a demonstration through the woods on the right in order to check the enemy until the infantry could arrive.

The fire of Fort Magruder upon Cooke's command was producing serious effects, and the 6th Cavalry had come upon a strong force of infantry and cavalry, and was saved from destruction by a gallant charge made by Capt. Saunders, commanding the rear squadron, during the withdrawal of the regiment.

Col. Grier had made two brilliant charges; men and horses were falling rapidly, and the enemy was receiving reinforcements every moment. After having held the position for about three-quarters of an hour Stoneman learned that Hooker could not get up for two hours. Under these circumstances, having done all in his power to hold his position, he fell back upon the clearing already occupied by his reserves, prepared to hold it to the utmost. He at least held the enemy to their works, and gave us the opportunity of fighting the battle of the next day.

As already stated, Gen. Emory was detached at the Halfway House, and on reaching the Lee's Mill road encountered an equal force of the enemy, whom he drove back on the Lee's Mill road, whence they escaped by a circuitous route along the banks of the James. Their escape was accounted for by the fact that Emory could not follow them without abandoning the road he was ordered to hold, and leaving his battery there unprotected, as he had no infantry. Smith's advance reached Skiff's creek at about 11.30, to find the bridge in flames and the road impassable. He therefore, by direction of Gen. Sumner, moved across to the Yorktown road, and, following it, reached Stoneman's position at about 5.30 o'clock, Gen. Sumner arriving with him and assuming command of all the troops at the front.

Hooker's division had encountered Smith's filing into the Yorktown road, and was obliged to halt for some three or four hours until it had passed. Subsequently, on its arrival at Chesapeake Church, Gen. Heintzelman turned it off by a cross-road into the Lee's Mill road, thus changing places with Smith. Marching part of the night, he came in sight of Fort Magruder early on the 5th. As soon as Smith reached the front his division was deployed and directed by Gen. Sumner to attack the works in front of him; but confusion arising in the dense forest, and darkness coming on, the attempt was deferred to the next day.

The troops bivouacked in the woods, and a heavy rain began, which lasted till the morning of the 6th, and made the roads, already terribly cut up by the enemy's troops and trains, almost impassable. Early in the evening of the 4th I learned that Smith had reached the front, and that at six P.M. two more divi-

sions would soon be ready, and were only waiting to rest the
men and let them take a little food before attacking; and that
the works would soon be carried, as they were then reported to
be held only by a rear-guard of a regiment of cavalry, two guns,
and four or five regiments of infantry.

I therefore pushed with redoubled energy the arrangements
to throw a force by water to the mouth of the Pamunkey, and
had not the slightest reason to suppose that my presence was at
all necessary at the front.

The position is about four miles in extent, the right resting
on College creek, and the left on Queen's creek; nearly three-
fourths of its front being covered by tributaries of these two
creeks, upon which there are ponds.

The ground between the heads of the boundary streams is a
cultivated plain, across which a line of detached works had been
constructed, consisting of Fort Magruder, a large work in the
centre with a bastion front, and twelve other redoubts and epaul-
ments for field-guns.

The parapet of Fort Magruder is about six feet high and
nine feet thick; the ditch nine feet wide and nine feet deep,
filled with water. The length of the interior crest is about six
hundred yards. The redoubts have strong profiles, but are of
small dimensions, having faces of about forty yards. The woods
in front of the position were felled, and the open ground in front
of the works was dotted with numerous rifle-pits.

The roads leading from the lower part of the Peninsula
towards Williamsburg, one along the York river (the Yorktown
road) and the other along the James (the Lee's Mill road), unite
between the heads of the tributary streams a short distance in
front of Fort Magruder, by which they are commanded, and
debouch from the woods just before uniting. A branch from
the James river road leaves it about one and three-fourths of a
mile below Fort Magruder and unites with the road from Allen's
landing to Williamsburg, which crosses the tributary of College
creek over a dam at the outlet of the pond, and passes just in
rear of the line of works, being commanded by the three redoubts on the right of the line. At about the same distance
from Fort Magruder a branch leaves the York river road and
crosses the tributary of Queen's creek on a dam, and, passing
over the position and through the woods in its rear, finally enters

24

Williamsburg. This road was commanded by redoubts on the left of the line of works.

On the morning of the 5th the position of our troops was as follows: On the extreme left, Emory, holding the road to Allen's farm; next, on his right, Hooker's division; next, in the centre, Stoneman, holding the main road; on his right Smith's division. Kearny, Couch, and Casey were still in rear, having bivouacked where the night overtook them. Couch and Casey were ordered to march at daylight to support Smith; at about nine o'clock Kearny was ordered up in support of Hooker.

The battle of Williamsburg was an accident, brought about by the rapid pursuit of our troops. The enemy were very anxious to get beyond West Point before we could reach it by water. Late in the afternoon of the 4th Gen. G. W. Smith was ordered to march at 2.30 A.M. of the 5th, and place his position north of Barhamsville to check any attempt on the Confederate line of retreat from the upper York river. Longstreet and Hill were to follow Smith on the Barhamsville road for about six miles, and then turn off at the Burned Tavern and take the Charles City road to Richmond *via* Long bridge. Magruder was to move by New Kent Court-House and Bottom bridge. From Barhamsville Smith was to follow Magruder. Smith commanded the troops on the New Kent Court-House road, Longstreet those on the Charles City road. The rain made the roads so bad that when we caught up with their rear-guard they were forced to reinforce it from their main body, and hold the works as long as possible, in order to enable their trains to escape.

On the afternoon of the 4th Longstreet's division, six brigades, had halted near Williamsburg, four brigades at or in rear of the line of works, two brigades, Wilcox and Colston, on the Richmond side. About seven next morning Wilcox was ordered to return to the line of works and report to Gen. Anderson. Wilcox was placed on the right and about one thousand yards in front of Fort Magruder, and at the time held the right of the Confederate line, posted in the pine-woods with occasional clearings. He supposed that there was nothing but cavalry in his front, but, sending two companies into the woods, they captured three of our infantry soldiers; whereupon he sent in a Mississippi regiment, deployed as skirmishers, with orders to advance

until forced to halt, and to find out what was in front.   Up to
this time there had been merely a dropping fire of skirmishers,
giving the impression that the woods were held by dismounted
cavalry; but now heavy firing followed, and the report came
back to Wilcox that three United States brigades were there in
position. These brigades composed Hooker's division. And all
this must have taken place between nine and ten A.M.

Wilcox immediately sent for reinforcements, and the rest of
Longstreet's division gradually came up to his support, mostly
being placed on his right, Gen. Richard Anderson finally taking command.   Early in the afternoon, being apprehensive for
his right, Anderson again attacked, took five guns of Webber's
battery, and brought Hooker to a standstill, inflicting heavy
losses.

Between three and four o'clock Kearny reached the front.
He had received the order to advance at nine o'clock, but, from
the condition of the roads and their being blocked with troops,
with all his energy and exertions he was unable to reach Hooker
until the time mentioned. He at once relieved Hooker's exhausted troops, and, promptly attacking, drove back the enemy
at every point. Hooker's losses were severe, and when I next
saw him, a day or two afterwards, he was much depressed and
thought that he had accomplished nothing, so much so that I
felt it necessary to encourage him.   It was not until some time
afterwards that he came to the conclusion that he had accomplished a brilliant feat of arms.

Emory had been left to guard the road leading to Allen's
farm, near the James. Being informed on the morning of the
5th that the enemy's right could be turned, he called upon Gen.
Heintzelman for infantry to enable him to make the attempt.
Late in the afternoon one of Kearny's brigades and two batteries were sent to him for that purpose, "but that was found
impracticable from the nature of the locality, the lateness of the
evening, and the want of a guide."

While all this was going on on our left Sumner reconnoitred
the position in the centre and on our right. Finding that one
of the redoubts on the Confederate left was unoccupied, he,
at about eleven o'clock, ordered Hancock's brigade, of Smith's
division, to cross by a dam at the foot of one of the large ponds
and take possession of it. This he did with five regiments of

the division, and, finding the next redoubt also unoccupied, he promptly seized it, and sent for reinforcements to enable him to advance further and take the next redoubt, which commanded the plain between his position and Fort Magruder, and would have enabled him to take in reverse and cut the communication of the troops engaged with Gens. Hooker and Kearny.

The enemy soon began to show himself in strength before him, and, as his rear and right flank were somewhat exposed, he repeated his request for reinforcements. Gen. Smith was twice ordered to join him with the rest of his division, but each time the order was countermanded at the moment of execution, Gen. Sumner not being willing to weaken the centre. At length, in reply to Gen. Hancock's repeated messages for more troops, Gen. Sumner sent him an order to fall back to his first position, the execution of which Gen. Hancock deferred as long as possible, being unwilling to give up the advantage already gained, and fearing to expose his command by such a movement.

As the head of Couch's division did not arrive until one o'clock, it was entirely proper for Gen. Sumner to hesitate about weakening his centre until that hour. The remaining brigades of Couch followed the first immediately, Casey arriving early in the afternoon. Couch's 1st brigade, Peck's, was deployed on Hooker's right, and promptly repulsed the attack made upon it, thus affording Hooker sensible relief. Soon after it was relieved by the other two brigades, who remained undisturbed.

As already stated, as soon as our troops were in possession of the enemy's works, on the morning of the 4th, I gave the necessary orders for the pursuit, and, when all that was accomplished, drove into Yorktown in an ambulance. The enemy had made a free distribution of torpedoes in the roads, within the works, and in places where our men would be apt to go - for instance, near wells and springs, telegraph-offices, and store-houses, so that some of our men were killed. To place mines or torpedoes in the path of assaulting columns is admissible under the customs of war, but such use of them as was made here is barbarous in the extreme. When I entered Yorktown our progress was much delayed by the caution made necessary by the presence of these torpedoes. I at once ordered that they should be discovered and removed by the Confederate prisoners. They objected very strenuously, but were forced to do the work. After Williamsburg one of the Confederate surgeons, sent in to offer to take care of their wounded in our hands, told me that these torpedoes were planted at the close of the evacuation, and mentioned the name of an officer whom he saw engaged in this work.

As soon as we had possession of Yorktown the gunboats started up the York river to ascertain whether the transports with Franklin's division could safely ascend, and to capture any of the enemy's transports they could find.

If the condition of affairs near Williamsburg justified it, I intended going to West Point by water myself. Early on the 5th I sent Col. Sweitzer and Maj. Hammerstein, of my staff, to the front, to keep me informed of the condition of affairs and the progress of events. I went to Yorktown to expedite the movement by water, and to provide for the transportation of supplies to the troops in advance.

Until about one P.M. I learned nothing indicating that the affair at Williamsburg was more than a simple attack upon a rear-guard, but at that hour I received intelligence that the state of the contest was unfavorable and that my presence was urgently required. Sedgwick's division was then held ready to embark in support of Franklin. But I ordered him to move beyond Yorktown a short distance, ready to move to the front if ordered. Porter and Richardson mere also instructed to be ready to obey whatever orders they might receive.

I returned at once to my camp to give these and other necessary orders, and, remaining there only a few minutes, started with half a dozen aides and a few orderlies for the front. The distance was more than fourteen miles, over terrible roads, much obstructed by trains; but as I had my most trustworthy horse, Dan Webster, I made better progress than was agreeable to the escort, most of whom had been left behind when I reached the field of battle.

Dan was one of those horses that could trot all day long at a very rapid gait which kept all other horses at a gallop. I think it was on this ride that he earned from the aides the title of "that Devil Dan" - a name which he justified on many another long and desperate ride before I gave up the command of the Army of the Potomac.

Dan was the best horse I ever had; he never was ill for an hour, never fatigued, never disturbed under fire, and never lost his equanimity or his dignity, except on one occasion. That was when we abandoned the position at Harrison's Bar under the orders to return to Washington. From a very natural feeling I remained there until all the trains and troops had left, and, sending forward all the escort and staff, remained alone in the works for a little time, my mind full of the fatal consequences of the order I was forced to carry into execution. At length I mounted and rode out to join the escort; as I passed through the abandoned works Dan, for the first time in his life, gave vent to his feelings by a series of most vicious plunges and kicks. It was possible that the flies, who had enjoyed a whole army to feed upon, concentrated all their energies upon Dan; but I have always more than suspected that, in his quiet way, Dan understood the condition of affairs much better than the authorities at Washington, and merely wished to inform me in his own impressive manner that he fully agreed with my views as to the folly of abandoning the position, and that he, at least, had full confidence in his master.

Dan and I never quarrelled, and the dear old fellow survived the war for many years, dying at a ripe old age in 1879. No matter how long we might be parted - once for nearly four years - he always recognized me the moment we met again, and in his own way showed his pleasure at seeing me. Even on the day of his death, which was a painless one from old age, whenever I entered his stall he tried to rise and greet me, but, unable to do that, would lean his head against me and lick my hand. No soldier ever had a more faithful or better horse than I had in Dan Webster.

Riding through mud and water, often obliged to turn into the woods, but never slackening the pace when the road permitted, I reached the front between four and five o'clock. I found everything in a state of chaos and depression. Even the private soldiers saw clearly that, with force enough in hand to gain a victory, we, the pursuers, were on the defensive and content with repulsing attacks, and that there was no plan of action, no directing head. The front line was formed along the nearer edge of the woods, and the rest massed inactive in the clearings. The troops were weary and discouraged; but my pre-

"DAN WEBSTER," GEN. McCLELLAN'S WAR-HORSE.

sence at once restored their confidence, and, as they recognized me passing rapidly through their ranks, their wild and joyful cheers told the enemy, as well as our own people, that something unusual had occurred, and that the period of uncertainty and inaction was at an end.

I at once gathered the general officers around me, called upon them for a brief statement of affairs, and promptly made up my mind as to what should be done. This occurred in the clearing, close to the Whittaker House. I found that, owing, to some marshy ground, there was no direct communication with the two divisions under Heintzelman on our left; the troops forming the front of our centre were on the hither edge of the woods intervening between us and the enemy, and no one knew whether the enemy were in the woods, and, if so, in what force. Hancock, with his unsupported brigade, was. still in possession of the abandoned works on the enemy's left; one of Smith's remaining brigades was in line on our right centre, the other and Casey's division massed in rear; two of Couch's brigades formed the centre, with one in reserve.

I ordered a party to move in to the left to reopen communication with Heintzelman. Just then heavy firing began at Hancock's position, which was two miles from the nearest support, and, grasping at once the fact that he held the key of the field of battle, I ordered Smith, who was chafing like a caged lion, to move as rapidly as possible to Hancock's support with his two remaining brigades and Naglee's. Within five minutes of the time I reached the field Smith was off as rapidly as his men could move; Naglee, with his brigade of Casey's division, following the leading regiment of Smith's division. As soon as the head of Smith's column started I ordered the centre to advance into the woods and gain the more distant edge, driving out any of the enemy who might be there. This was promptly done, and I rode in with them, and into the cleared ground in front, in close view of the enemy's works. There were none of the enemy in the woods, but they held the works in considerable force.

Their position was so strong that when my reconnoissance was completed I did not think proper to attack without making arrangements to use our artillery and carefully arrange our columns of attack.

I therefore returned to the Whittaker House, quickly gave orders for the proper posting of the troops in the centre, and started rapidly for Hancock's position. A little before reaching the dam by which he had crossed I met the column of prisoners whom he had just taken.

Before Gens. Smith and Naglee could reach the field of Gen. Hancock's operations, although they moved with great rapidity, he had been confronted by a superior force. Feigning to retreat slowly, he awaited their onset, and then turned upon them, and, after some terrific volleys of musketry, he charged them with the bayonet, routing and dispersing their whole force, killing, mounding, and capturing from 500 to 600 men, he himself losing only 31 men.

This was one of the most brilliant engagements of the war, and Gen. Hancock merited the highest praise for the soldierly qualities displayed and his perfect appreciation of the vital importance of his position.

Hancock's command consisted of the 5th Wis., 6th Me., and 49th Penn. regiments of volunteers of his own brigade, and the 7th Me. and 30th N.Y. of Davidson's brigade. Keeping on to Hancock's brigade, I remained there long enough to thank them for their gallant conduct, to appreciate the importance of the position and the value of the success gained. I sent some of the approaching reinforcements to occupy a dangerous mass of woods on the right, and, there being no indication of any new attack by the enemy, I left as soon as Smith arrived with sufficient troops to render the position perfectly secure. By the time Smith's troops all arrived and were properly posted it was too dark to attempt any new operations until the next morning.

It was raining heavily and nearly dark when I returned to the Whittaker House, so that nothing more could be done than to arrange for security during the night and a prompt resumption of operations in the morning. All the troops slept on the muddy field, in the rain, with what protection their shelter-tents gave them, and many without food. I was not much better off, for, with the exception of a piece of biscuit for breakfast on the morning of the 6th, I had nothing to eat from the early morning of the 5th until late in the day on the 6th. The night was a horrible one. The little Whittaker House was crowded

25

with several general officers and their staffs, so that sleep or rest was impossible. It rained hard, and I passed much of the evening among the men, by way of encouraging them, who think little of hardship when their general shares it with them.

It was unfortunate that the absolute necessity of expediting the movement of troops and supplies up the York river detained me so long at Yorktown, and that I did not receive earlier information of the necessity for my presence at the front. All the reports, up to those that took me so rapidly to the field, represented the affair as simply one against an ordinary rear-guard, and with good reason I expected every moment to learn that the enemy was defeated and his works occupied, as the troops on the field of battle were more than enough for the purpose. Could I have arrived at one o'clock it is very certain that Smith, supported by Couch and afterwards by Casey, would have at once debauched from Hancock's ground, and have cut off the retreat of the greater part of the troops engaged against Hooker. Up to the time of Couch's arrival it would probably have been imprudent to move the whole of Smith's division in support of Hancock, but the moment the head of Couch's column appeared near the front it was proper to push Smith forward as rapidly as possible. In fact, Hooker's repulse was of no consequence, except for the loss of life it involved, and his falling back somewhat would only facilitate the decisive advance by our right. When I reached the field the commanding generals gave me the impression that, far from our having a simple rear-guard to deal with, the enemy was present in very heavy force. Therefore, to guard against all eventualities, I sent back orders to Porter to occupy Yorktown, and to Sedgwick and Richardson to advance by land in the morning.

During the night Heintzelman reported to me that Hooker's division had suffered so much that it could not be relied on for the next day, and that Kearny could do no more than hold his own unless reinforced. But, after fully considering the state of affairs during the evening, I was so confident of the advantage to be derived from Smith's possession of the decisive point that I determined to carry on our operations with the force then in hand, even were the enemy superior in numbers. If the enemy held their ground and were not superior in numbers, it was certain that an advance by Smith and Casey, with the cavalry, direct on Williamsburg, supported by Couch as the centre was cleared, would cut off all the troops in front of Heintzelman. Even if the enemy proved to be superior in numbers this advance would no doubt cause them to withdraw their right and thus enable Hooker and Kearny to come into line on Smith's left, and I could perfectly well hold my own and keep the enemy in position while the movement to West Point was being carried out. Therefore, during the night, I countermanded the orders to Sedgwick and Richardson, and directed them to return to Yorktown and, together with Porter, embark as rapidly as possible in support of Franklin.

Early on the morning of the 6th it was found that the enemy had abandoned his positions during the night; we at once occupied them and the town of Williamsburg, which was filled with the enemy's wounded, for whose assistance eighteen of the Confederate surgeons were sent by Gen. J. E. Johnston, the Confederate commander.

CHAPTER XX.

Advance from Williamsburg - Franklin's movement - Alarm of prisoners in Williamsburg - Plan of the campaign - Orders to move towards north of Richmond - Fatal to the campaign - Movements on this line.

IT became clear that we had been opposed by only a portion of the Confederate army, at first by a single rear-guard, which was subsequently considerably reinforced by troops brought back during the first night and the next day to hold the works as long as possible and enable their trains to escape. Longstreet's and D. H. Hill's divisions, more than half their army, were engaged. Their losses were heavy, and we captured eight guns and many caissons and wagons, which the deep mud prevented them from carrying off.

Wilcox's Confederate brigade, having received no orders, found itself at half-past ten P.M. of the 5th entirely alone, and moved back beyond Williamsburg, being the last to leave the field. It has been stated that G. W. Smith had been ordered to move at half-past two A.M. of the 5th and take a position north of Barhamsrille. He moved at the hour designated, just as a heavy rain commenced. The roads soon became axle-deep in mud, and extraordinary efforts were required to get the wagons along. Late in the afternoon, when the head of the column had nearly reached Barhamsville, Smith received an order from Gen. Johnston to suspend the movement, as a heavy attack had been made on the fortifications at Williamsburg, in which Longstreet's and D. H. Hill's divisions had been engaged. On the two following days Gen. Johnston, learning of Franklin's disembarkation at Brick House, concentrated the greater part of his army near Barhamsville.

It has already been stated that Franklin's division was disembarked on the 3d of May to take part in the approaching assault of Yorktown. Gen. Franklin passed the night of the 3d at general headquarters, his division remaining at Cheeseman's landing. As soon as the evacuation was known I instructed him to re-embark his division immediately and bring it by water to

Yorktown, where he would receive further orders. He at once returned to it and commenced the work, which he carried on with all possible speed, completing it about one o'clock on the 5th. The embarkation was much delayed by the atrocious weather; by the facts that all the ordinary means for loading and unloading were fully occupied with putting supplies ashore for the rest of the army, so that Gen. Franklin was obliged to improvise his own means; that forage and provision for several days had to be reloaded; but most of all by the difficulty of re-embarking the artillery, all the carriages of which had to be unlimbered and floated out on rafts and then hoisted upon the transports. Gen. Franklin's letter explains this subject in detail, and I need only say that the delay was unavoidable and that Gen. Franklin did not lose an unnecessary moment in carrying his order into effect:

"HARTFORD, Feb. 8, 1884.
"Gen. G. B. McClellan, New York:

"MY DEAR GENERAL: It so happens that I have just had a correspondence with Howard about the West Point landing in May, 1862, and, as it covers the greater part of the ground indicated in your letter of the 5th inst., I enclose it with this.

"The long time taken to re-embark my division at Poquosin, or Cheeseman's creek, was due—

"1st. To the weather, which, you will remember, was atrocious;

"2d. To the fact that such landing facilities as were at hand were fully occupied with getting supplies ashore for the army at Yorktown, leaving me to my own crude devices for getting things aboard; and,

"3d. To the absolute necessity there was for unlimbering all artillery vehicles, in order to pack them in the limited deckspace of the transports that were available.

"This loading the artillery was the great cause of delay. Getting the carriages on to the transports was a tedious and exasperatingly slow process. They had to be floated on rafts from the shore to the transports and then lifted several feet to the deck. I do not now remember how the horses were got aboard, but I know that everything was done as quickly as it could be done.

"Then, too, the provisions and forage for several days had to be reloaded in the infantry transports - a tedious process under the circumstances. Towing the artillery transports was a very slow process. These transports mere each made of two canal barges placed about as far apart as the width of beam of a single barge, the whole space being decked over, thus. They had been 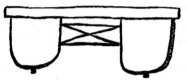 so arranged for the landing that it was contemplated I was to make when I first arrived. They made excellent transports for a short run in smooth water, but they would not steer and were heart-breaking to tow. So we finally started for Yorktown, when another unlooked-for delay occurred by the grounding of many of the transports, which were of all draughts of water. I stayed by until I saw that all would get off, and then started for Yorktown, where I met you in the afternoon and received my instructions. Of course, after arriving at West Point, the landing was slow, although not nearly so slow as the loading. The infantry and artillery were got off during the night, and a line was formed which was rectified and strengthened after daylight. I returned to my headquarters boat to hurry off the transports, which were very slow in moving, and while I was engaged in this business an attack was made on Newton's brigade. I hurried ashore and found that a sharp attack had been made, by Hampton's brigade, I think. They drove Newton out of the woods at first, but the brigade soon retook its position, driving the enemy back; and as the gunboats were in position to shell the woods in front of our line, a few shots from them drove the enemy off and ended the fight. Both lines, however, remained within musket-shot of each other until well on in the afternoon, when the transports returned, bringing Sedgwick's division, I think it was. As my orders only directed me to hold my position, and as my right flank was necessarily in the air and ought to have been turned by the enemy, I was in no condition to have advanced into the interior, and, in fact, under your orders I had no business to make the attempt.

> "Truly your friend,
> "Wм. B. Franklin."

The flotilla experienced great difficulty in reaching Yorktown, which it effected about four o'clock on the 5th. Meanwhile Gen. Franklin, when the greatest difficulties had been overcome, preceded it, and must have reached Yorktown before one o'clock, where he received his final instructions from me.

When the flotilla arrived Gen. Franklin visited Com. Missroom on his flagship and informed him that he was ready to start. The commodore replied that he would not consent to go up the river on a night as dark as that approaching (it was then raining in torrents), and the joint expedition, therefore, waited until next morning. The commodore was entirely correct in this decision to await the morning, for I have not the slightest doubt that the result of an effort to move on such a night would have been the loss of many transports and lives, and the disorganization of the whole expedition.

The flotilla started at daybreak of the 6th; the infantry transports arrived off West Point about noon, and the landing commenced at once. The artillery transports did not arrive until nearly night, and were unloaded without wharves during the night and early in the morning of the 7th. The process of landing was necessarily slow, but not so much so as that of loading up.

At about seven A.M. of the 7th the pickets of Newton's brigade, forming the left of the line, were driven in, but soon regained the ground.

Skirmishing continued for a couple of hours, when a sharp attack was made by Whiting's division; this was repulsed, and everything then became quiet, our people having regained their original positions, and at some points having made considerable advances.

Franklin's orders were simply to hold his position until reinforced sufficiently to justify an advance. That this was a wise decision is shown by the fact that G. W. Smith witnessed the disembarkation, and, refraining from opposing it, suggested to Gen. Johnston to take measures to cut him off if he advanced beyond the protection of the gunboats. G. W. Smith's entire division, much stronger than Franklin's, was in his front, and soon after the greater part of the Confederate army, ready to overwhelm Franklin had he advanced.

By the time Sedgwick's division was in position to support him, the morning of the 8th, the enemy's rear had passed on towards Richmond; but Franklin's movement had fully served its purpose in clearing our front to the banks of the Chickahominy.

On my way into Williamsburg on the morning of the 6th I passed a cluster of barracks, and, seeing some men lying in them, I dismounted to see who they were. They were filled with our own and the enemy's wounded. The first man I spoke to was one of ours. I asked him who the men around him were. "Oh! that's a secesh; that is one of our men; that's a secesh," and so on. In reply to my question as to how they had been treated by the enemy he said: "Just like their own men." Here were these poor fellows lying together in perfect amity who had met in mortal combat the day before.

The College and other large buildings in Williamsburg were crowded with wounded, almost all Confederates. While in one of the larger hospitals one of my aides came to me and said that a wounded Confederate desired to speak to me. I went there and found a wounded private soldier belonging to a Virginia regiment, an intelligent, honest-looking man, who said that he had been deputed by his comrades to beg me to spare their lives. I told him that I did not understand him, whereupon he repeated his petition, and I again said that I could not imagine what he meant. He then said that they had been told that we Northern men had come down there to destroy and slay, and that our intention was to kill all the prisoners, wounded and unwounded alike; but that they had been told that I had treated kindly the prisoners I had taken in West Virginia the year before, and thought that perhaps I might be induced to spare their lives. I then relieved his mind by telling him that, although I was perhaps the most brutal among the Northern generals, I would treat them precisely as I did my own wounded.

The poor fellows stretched on the floor around him followed the conversation with keen interest, and I saw by the expression of their faces that they felt much relieved when my final answer came. I was told, after the battle of Fair Oaks, that when the Confederates were for a time in possession of the camp of Casey's division Gen. Roger Pryor went around among the wounded, giving them whiskey and water, and that he told them it was a repayment of the kindness with which their wounded were treated at Williamsburg.

During the forenoon of the 6th Confederate surgeons came in (as before stated), under a flag of truce, to offer their services in tending their own wounded. I entertained them as well as could be done without baggage or supplies, and found them to be very agreeable gentlemen. Their services were not needed.

Having gained possession of Williamsburg, the first thing to be done was to get up supplies for the troops, to care for the wounded, to hasten supports to Franklin by water, and to force the pursuit by land in order to open direct communication with

Franklin, or to bring the enemy to battle if he halted south of the mouth of the Pamunkey. The frightful condition of the roads rendered the supply question very difficult, but by repairing the nearest landings on the York river, and by the energy of the quartermaster's department, that task was soon accomplished.

So great were the difficulties of land-transportation that even the headquarters wagons did not reach Williamsburg until the forenoon of the 9th, up to which time I was absolutely without baggage of any kind. Sedgwick's division reached Franklin during the 7th; one brigade of Porter's division got off from Yorktown by water on the afternoon of the 7th, the rest on the 8th, without cavalry or artillery; two brigades of Richardson's division got off on the 11th, the remaining brigade on the 12th. The regular infantry, Duane's engineer battalion, and the light batteries of the reserve artillery marched from Yorktown on the 8th.

Immediately upon our arrival in Williamsburg Gen. Averill was sent forward with a cavalry force to push the enemy's rear-guard. He found several guns abandoned, and captured a number of stragglers. But the roads were so bad and his supplies so scanty that he was obliged to return after marching a few miles. On the next day, the 7th, Stoneman moved with the advanced guard, consisting of the cavalry, horse-batteries, and two regiments of infantry, the 2d R. I. and the 98th Penn.

At ten A.M. his artillery and cavalry had reached a point only two and a half to three miles from Williamsburg; the infantry had not yet joined him. At half-past one P.M. he had come up with the enemy's rear-guard, at about six miles from Williamsburg, and while here he heard heavy firing in the direction of Franklin's position. Stoneman's infantry joined him here, coming up at the double-quick.

He encamped for the night at a church about ten miles from Williamsburg, having been delayed by the condition of the roads and the necessity of procuring and cooking meat for the infantry, who were almost in a famished condition.

At nine A.M. of the 8th he had reached a point fourteen miles from Williamsburg. At half-past three P.M. he reached with his main body Hockaday's Springs, about six miles and a half from Franklin's position, and there learned that his advanced guard had communicated with Franklin's pickets.

Stoneman learned here that a Confederate force of ten regiments of infantry, one battery, and some cavalry had encamped the night before at Hockaday's Springs, and left that morning *via* Diascund Bridge, and that the enemy were in full retreat upon the Chickahominy. He sent cavalry in pursuit to harass the enemy until dark. This detachment found the enemy at dark strongly posted at New Kent Court-House, and, in accordance with instructions, then returned to the main body of the advanced guard.

On the 9th Stoneman occupied and held the junction of the West Point and Williamsburg roads, about three miles from New Kent Court-House. The occupation of this place occurred as the result of a brisk skirmish in which a portion of the 6th U. S. Cavalry, under Maj. Williams, and Robinson's battery took part; one squadron of the 6th, under the personal command of Maj. Williams, made two very handsome charges.

On the 10th Stoneman sent Farnsworth's 8th Ill. Cavalry some six miles beyond New Kent Court-House, and with his main body moved to Cumberland, leaving New Kent Court-House occupied by two New Jersey regiments and four guns from Franklin's division.

On the 11th he sent Maj. Williams with six companies of cavalry to occupy the railroad-crossing at White House and scout the surrounding country. He was again delayed on the 11th by the necessity of awaiting provisions from Franklin. Stoneman says: "The men have had no sugar or coffee since leaving Williamsburg, and but a very limited amount of hard bread and pork. We have lived principally on fresh meat, sometimes without salt, for the past week; but I have not heard a complaint or murmur."

D. R. Jones's division constituted the rear-guard of the enemy. It consisted of ten regiments of infantry, sixteen pieces of artillery, and the 1st Va. Cavalry. The rear of the rear-guard consisted of one regiment of infantry, three pieces of artillery, and three squadrons, with which they would check us at every difficult place and then leave. Owing to the peculiar nature of the country, admirably adapted for the operations of an active and vigorous rear-guard, which we had in our front, we could get but one chance to attack him and make it tell - this at Slatesville, from which he was driven with loss. Three miles from Slatesville, at New Kent Court-House, the whole division was drawn up in line of battle: and I thought it expedient to retain with me the New Jersey brigade (two regiments and four guns) and Farnsworth's cavalry.

As soon as a reasonable amount of supplies were received and the roads improved somewhat I resumed the movement by land from Williamsburg. Smith's division marched on the afternoon of the 8th, Couch, Casey, and Kearny on the morning of the 9th. The reserves came up to Williamsburg on the morning of the same day. During the night of the 9th headquarters were four miles in front of Williamsburg with the regulars, the other four divisions just mentioned in advance, Hooker still at Williamsburg.

On the evening of the 10th headquarters were at Roper's Church, nineteen miles beyond Williamsburg, in easy communication with Franklin; the regulars, Smith, Couch, Casey, and Kearny near headquarters. We now began to draw supplies from Elthan.

Headquarters remained at Roper's Church until the morning of the 13th, while the troops were moving in such a manner that at the close of that day the disposition was as follows: headquarters, with the divisions of Porter, Franklin, Sykes (regulars), and the artillery reserves, at Cumberland, now a temporary depot; Couch and Casey at New Kent Court-House; Hooker and Kearny near Roper's Church; Richardson and Sedgwick near Elthan.   Gen. Van Alen was left, with a small force, as military governor of Yorktown; Col. Campbell with his regiment, the 5th Pa. Cavalry, at Williamsburg.

On the 14th and 15th it rained heavily and continuously, and somewhat on the 16th. On the 15th and 16th the divisions of Porter, Franklin, and Smith were with great difficulty advanced to White House.   The roads were so bad, narrow, and infrequent as to render the movements of large masses very slow and difficult; so much so that in the movement to White House on the 15th and 16th it required forty-eight hours to move two divisions and their trains five miles.

On the 16th headquarters advanced to White House; and on that day and the next Sykes and the reserve artillery moved up to the same point with no little difficulty, and a permanent depot was established.   The weather changed on the night of the 16th, so that the 17th and 18th were clear, warm days.

The 17th and 18th were occupied, while the roads were drying, in closing up all the troops and trains, with the final preparations to advance, and in numerous and extensive reconnoissances pushed in all directions.

It was at this moment, May 18, 1862, that, in consequence of my earnest representations, the President authorized me to organize two provisional army corps, the 5th and 6th, which soon became permanent corps, and the organization of the Army of the Potomac was now as follows :

2d Corps - Gen. Sumner. Consisting of the divisions Sedgwick and Richardson.
3d Corps - Gen. Heintzelman.   Consisting of the divisions Kearny and Hooker.
4th Corps - Gen. Keyes.   Consisting of the divisions Couch and Casey.
5th Corps - Gen. Fitz-John Porter. Consisting of the divisions Morell Sykes, and Hunt's reserve artillery.
6th Corps - Gen. Franklin.   Consisting of the divisions W. F. Smith and Slocum.

The organization of the cavalry remained unchanged, and, as no new regiments were assigned to the Army of the Potomac except Col. Campbell's, which remained at Williamsburg, we suffered very much during the subsequent operations from the glaring deficiency of the cavalry force in point of numbers.

On the 18th of May headquarters were at White House; the advanced guard held the country nearly to the Chickahominy and well to the north of the railway. The 5th and 6th corps were at White House; the 2d, 3d, and 4th corps were near New Kent Court-House.

The enemy had withdrawn across the Chickahominy, having his main force between New bridge and Richmond.   Bottom's, Long, and Jones's bridges were merely watched by small cavalry patrols, and there were no indications even of this with regard to the last two.

The necessity of following the enemy until he was fairly across the Chickahominy, and the question of supplies, had naturally brought the Army of the Potomac into the positions just described, for the James river was not open until the 12th, when the *Merrimac* was destroyed.

The question was now to be decided as to the ultimate line of operations of the army.

Two courses were to be considered: first, to abandon the line of the York, cross the Chickahominy in the lower part of its course, gain the James, and adopt that as the line of supply; second, to use the railroad from West Point to Richmond as the line of supply, which would oblige us to cross the Chickahominy somewhere north of White Oak Swamp. The army was perfectly placed to adopt either course.

Masking the movement by the advanced guard, the army could easily have crossed the Chickahominy by Jones's bridge, and at Coles's ferry and Barret's ferry by pontoon bridges, while the advanced guard, and probably one or two corps, could have followed the movement by Long bridge and under cover of the White Oak Swamp, and the army would have been concentrated at Malvern Hill, ready either to advance upon Richmond by the roads near the left bank of the James, or to cross that river and place itself between Richmond and Petersburg.

With all the aid of the gunboats and water-transportation I am sure that I could have occupied Petersburg and placed the army in position between that place and Richmond, so that the enemy would have been obliged to abandon his capital or to come out to attack in a position of my own choosing, where, with the whole army concentrated, success would not have been doubtful and Richmond would have been the prize of victory.

Moreover, the water line of transportation would have insured the prompt and safe arrival of the 1st corps, or such other reinforcements as might have been sent to me.

It is needless to state that the army was well placed to follow the second line of operations indicated.

Up to the 18th my repeated and urgent demands for reinforcements by water had been met in such a way as to render it probable that if the 1st corps were ordered up to my support at all, the overland route would be selected by the authorities in Washington. Among other despatches calling for reinforcements I sent the following:

CAMP AT CUMBERLAND, May 14, 1862.

I have more than twice telegraphed to the Secretary of War, stating that, in my opinion, the enemy were concentrating all their available force to fight this army in front of Richmond, and that such ought to be their policy. I have received no reply whatever to any of these telegrams. I beg leave to repeat their substance to your excellency, and to ask that kind consideration which you have ever accorded to my representations and views. All my information from every source accessible to me establishes the fixed purpose of the rebels to defend Richmond against this army by offering us battle with all the troops they can collect from east, west, and south, and my own opinion is confirmed by that of all my commanders whom I have been able to consult.

Casualties, sickness, garrisons, and guards have much weakened my force, and will continue to do so. I cannot bring into actual battle against the enemy more than 80,000 men at the utmost, and with them I must attack in position, probably entrenched, a much larger force, perhaps double my numbers. It is possible that Richmond may be abandoned without a serious struggle; but the enemy are actually in great strength between here and there, and it would be unwise, and even insane, for me to calculate upon anything but a stubborn and desperate resistance. If they should abandon Richmond it may well be that it is done with the purpose of making the stand at some place in Virginia south or west of there, and we should be in condition to press them without delay. The Confederate leaders must employ their utmost efforts against this army in Virginia, and they will be supported by the whole body of their military officers, among whom there may be said to be no Union feeling, as there is also very little among the higher class of citizens in the seceding States.

I have found no fighting men left in this Peninsula. All are in the ranks of the opposing foe.

Even if more troops than I now have should prove unnecessary for purposes of military occupation, our greatest display of imposing force in the capital of the rebel government will have the best moral effect. I most respectfully and earnestly urge upon your excellency that the opportunity has come for striking a fatal blow at the enemies of the Constitution, and I beg that you will cause this army to be reinforced without delay by all the disposable troops of the government. I ask for every man that the War Department can send me. Sent by water they will soon reach me. Any commander of the reinforcements whom your excellency may designate will be acceptable to me, whatever expression I may have heretofore addressed to you on that subject.

I will fight the enemy, whatever their force may be, with whatever force I may have; and I firmly believe that we shall beat them, but our triumph should be made decisive and complete. The soldiers of this army love their government, and will fight well in its support. You may rely upon them. They have confidence in me as their general, and in you as their President. Strong reinforcements will at least save the lives of many of them. The greater our force the more perfect will be our combinations and the less our loss.

For obvious reasons I beg you to give immediate consideration to this communication, and to inform me fully at the earliest moment of your final determination.

GEO. B. MCCLELLAN,
Major-General.

His Excellency ABRAHAM LINCOLN,
President of the United States.

To which, on the 18th of May, I received this reply:

"WASHINGTON, May-18, 2 P.M.

"GENERAL: Your despatch to the President, asking reinforcements, has been received and carefully considered.

"The President is not willing to uncover the capital entirely; and it is believed that, even if this were prudent, it would require more time to effect a junction between your army and that of the Rappahannock by the way of the Potomac and York river than by a land march. In order, therefore, to increase the strength of the attack upon Richmond at the earliest moment, Gen. McDowell has been ordered to march upon that city by the shortest route.

"He is ordered, keeping himself always in position to save the capital from all possible attack, so to operate as to put his left wing in communication with your right wing, and you are instructed to co-operate so as to establish this communication as soon as possible, by extending your right wing to the north of Richmond.

"It is believed that this communication can be safely established either north or south of the Pamunkey river.

"In any event you will be able to prevent the main body of the enemy's forces from leaving Richmond and falling in overwhelming force upon Gen. McDowell. He will move with between thirty-five (35) and forty thousand (40,000) men.

"A copy of the instructions to Gen. McDowell are with this. The specific task assigned to his command has been to provide against any danger to the capital of the nation.

"At your earnest call for reinforcements he is sent forward to co-operate in the reduction of Richmond, but charged, in attempting this, not to uncover the city of Washington, and you will give no order, either before or after your junction, which can put him out of position to cover this city. You and he will communicate with each other, by telegraph or otherwise, as frequently as may be necessary for sufficient co-operation. When Gen. McDowell is in position on your right his supplies must be drawn from West Point, and you will instruct your staff-officers to be prepared to supply him by that route.

"The President desires that Gen. McDowell retain the command of the Department of the Rappahannock and of the forces with which he moves forward.

"By order of the President.
                                          "EDWIN M. STANTON,
                                               "Secretary of War.
"Maj.-Gen. GEO. B. MCCLELLAN."

This order rendered it impossible for me to use the James river as a line of operations, forced me to establish our depots on the Pamunkey, and to approach Richmond from the north.

Herein lay the failure of the campaign.

The order obliged me to extend and expose my right in order to secure the junction. As it was impossible to get at Richmond and the enemy's army covering it without crossing the Chickahominy, I was obliged to divide the Army of the Potomac into two parts, separated by that stream. As the order for Gen. McDowell's advance was soon suspended, I incurred great risk, of which the enemy finally took advantage and frustrated the plan of campaign.

Had Gen. McDowell joined me by water I could have approached Richmond by the James, and thus have avoided the delays and losses incurred in bridging the Chickahominy, and could have had the army united in one body instead of being necessarily divided by that stream.

McDowell's movement by water would not have jeopardized Washington in the slightest degree. There mere troops enough without him to hold the works against anything that the enemy could have sent against them, and the more they sent the easier would my task have been in front of Richmond. But Jackson's movement was merely a feint, and if McDowell had joined me on the James the enemy would have drawn in every available man from every quarter to make head against me. A little of the nerve at Washington which the Romans displayed during the campaign against Hannibal would have settled the fate of Richmond in very few weeks.

The following telegram was received at headquarters, Army of the Potomac, May 24, 1862:

"HEADQUARTERS DEPARTMENT OF RAPPAHANNOCK, OPPOSITE FREDERICKSBURG, May 22, 1862.

"Maj.-Gen. G. B. McClellan:

"I have received the orders of the President to move with the army under my command and co-operate with yours in the reduction of Richmond, and also a copy of his instructions to you in relation to that co-operation. Maj.-Gen. Shields will join me to-day.

"As far (soon) as the necessary preparations for the march can be completed, which I think will be by the twenty-fourth (24th) inst., we shall set forth as (in) the general direction ordered. There is in front of us to impede our advance the secession Army of the Rappahannock, so called, under the command of Joseph R. Anderson, of the Tredegar Iron-Works.

"His force is from 12,000 to 15,000 men, mostly South Carolina and Georgia troops. We shall engage this force on our first day's march, as they are within from six to eight miles of us, posted on and to the right and left of the Fredericksburg and Richmond Railroad, and in a position of considerable strength. It is my purpose to try and turn this position by throwing a force on their left flank, and cut off their opportunity of receiving any reinforcements from the direction of Gordonsville, and at the same time endeavor to save the railroad bridges. If this can be done another channel of supply can be had for the forces going against Richmond that cannot fail to give great relief to the quartermaster's and commissary departments of your army, and thus facilitate your operations. We cannot rely on this at first, because they now occupy the line, and, I am told, are prepared to destroy the bridges if they are forced to fall back. I beg to ask to what extent can I rely on co-operation from you in my present movement in the way of your cutting off the retreat of the enemy upon Richmond, where they would add 12,000 to the forces against you, and in saving the railroad bridge across the Pamunkey, and to what point on the Pamunkey can you extend your right to join me, and to what point can you cause supplies to be placed for my command, and by what date can I count on finding them ready for me? I shall require subsistence for thirty-eight thousand (38,000) men, and forage for eleven thousand (11,000) animals.

"IRWIN MCDOWELL,
"Maj.-Gen."

The following is a copy of the instructions to Gen. McDowell:

"WAR DEPARTMENT,
"WASHINGTON, May 17, 1862.

"GENERAL: Upon being joined by Gen. Shields's division

26

you will move upon Richmond by the general route of the Richmond and Fredericksburg Railroad, co-operating with the forces under Gen. McClellan, now threatening Richmond from the line of the Pamunkey and York rivers.

"While seeking to establish as soon as possible a communication between your left wing and the right wing of Gen. McClellan, you will hold yourself always in such position as to cover the capital of the nation against a sudden dash of any large body of the rebel forces.

"Gen. McClellan will be furnished with a copy of these instructions, and will be directed to hold himself in readiness to establish communication with your left wing, and to prevent the main body of the enemy's army from leaving Richmond and throwing itself upon your column before a junction of the two armies is effected.

"A copy of his instructions in regard to the employment of your force is annexed.

"By order of the President.

"EDWIN M. STANTON,
"*Secretary of War.*

"Gen. McDOWELL,
" *Commanding Department of Rappahannock.* "

Having some doubts, from the wording of the foregoing orders, as to the extent of my authority over the troops of Gen. McDowell, and as to the time when I might anticipate his arrival, on the 21st of May I sent this despatch to President Lincoln:

MAY 21, 1862, 11 P.M.

Your despatch of yesterday respecting our situation and the batteries of Fort Darling was received while I was absent with the advance where I have been all this day. I have communicated personally with Capt. Goldsborough, and by letter with Capt. Smith. The vessels can do nothing without co-operation on land, which I will not be in condition to afford for several days. Circumstances must determine the propriety of a land-attack.

It rained again last night, and rain on this soil soon makes the roads incredibly bad for army transportation. I personally crossed the Chickahominy to-day at Bottom's bridge ford, and went a mile beyond, the enemy being about half a mile in front. I have three regiments on the other bank guarding the rebuilding of the bridge. Keyes's corps is on the New Kent road, near Bottom's bridge. Heintzelman is on the same road, within supporting distance. Sumner is on the railroad, connecting right with left. Stoneman, with advanced guard, is within one mile of New bridge. Franklin, with two divisions, is about two miles this side of Stoneman. Porter's division, with the reserves of infantry and artillery, is within supporting distance. Headquarters will probably be at Cold Harbor to-morrow, one mile this side of Franklin. All the bridges over the Chickahominy are destroyed. The enemy are in force on every road leading to Richmond, within a mile or two west of the stream. Their main body is on the road from New bridge, encamped along it for four or five miles, spreading over the open ground on both sides. Johnson's headquarters are about two miles beyond the bridge.

All accounts report their numbers as greatly exceeding our own. The position of the rebel forces, the declaration of the Confederate authorities, the resolutions of the Virginia legislature, the action of the city government, the conduct of the citizens, and all other sources of information accessible to me, give positive assurance that our approach to Richmond involves a desperate battle between the opposing armies.

All our divisions are moving towards the foe. I shall advance steadily and carefully, and attack them according to my best judgment, and in such manner as to employ my greatest force.

I regret the state of things as to Gen. McDowell's command. We must beat the enemy in front of Richmond. One division added to this army for that effort would do more to protect Washington than his whole force can possibly do anywhere else in the field. The rebels are concentrating from all points for the two battles at Richmond and Corinth. I would still, most respectfully, suggest the policy of our concentrating here by movements on water. I have heard nothing as to the probabilities of the contemplated junction of McDowell's force with mine. I have no idea when he can start, what are his means of transportation, or when he may be expected to reach this vicinity. I fear there is little hope that he can join me overland in time for the coming battle. Delays on my part will be dangerous. I fear sickness and demoralization. This region is unhealthy for Northern men, and, unless kept moving, I fear that our soldiers may become discouraged. At present our numbers are weakening from disease, but our men remain in good heart.

I regret also the configuration of the Department of the Rappahannock. It includes a portion even of the city of Richmond. I think that my own department should embrace the entire field of military operations designed for the capture and occupation of that city.

Again, I agree with your excellency that one bad general is better than two good ones.

I am not sure that I fully comprehend your orders of the 17th instant addressed to myself and Gen. McDowell. If a junction is effected before me occupy Richmond it must necessarily be east of the railroad to Fredericksburg and within my department. This fact, my superior rank, and the express language of the sixty-second Article of War will place his command under my orders, unless it is otherwise specially directed by your excellency; and I consider that he will be under my command, except that I am not to detach any portion of his forces, or give any orders which can put him out of position to cover Washington. If I err in my construction I desire to be at once set right. Frankness compels me to say, anxious as I am for an increase of force, that the march of McDowell's column upon Richmond by the shortest route will, in my opinion, uncover Washington, as to any interposition by it, as completely as its movement by water. The enemy cannot advance by Fredericksburg on Washington.

Should they attempt a movement which to me seems utterly improbable, their route would be by Gordonsville and Manassas. I desire that the extent of my authority over McDowell may be clearly defined, lest misunderstandings and conflicting views may produce some of those injurious results which a divided command has so often caused. I would respectfully suggest that this danger can only be surely guarded against by explicitly placing Gen. McDowell under my orders in the ordinary way, and holding me strictly responsible for the closest observance of your instructions. I hope, Mr. President, that it is not necessary for me to assure you that your instructions would be observed in the utmost good faith, and that I have no personal feelings which could influence me to disregard them in any particular.

I believe that there is a great struggle before this army, but I am neither dismayed nor discouraged. I wish to strengthen its force as much as I can, but in any event I shall fight it with all the skill, caution, and determination that I possess, and I trust that the result may either obtain for me the permanent confidence of my government or that it may close my career.

GEORGE B. McCLELLAN,
Maj.-Gen. Commanding.

His Excellency ABRAHAM LINCOLN,
President of the United States.

On the 24th I received the following reply:

"MAY 24, 1862 (from Washington, 24th).

"I left Gen. McDowell's camp at dark last evening. Shields's command is there, but it is so worn that he cannot move before Monday morning, the twenty-sixth (26th). We have so thinned our line to get troops for other places that it was broken yesterday at Front Royal, with a probable loss to us of one (1) regiment infantry, two (2) companies cavalry, putting Gen. Banks in some peril.

"The enemy's forces, under Gen. Anderson, now opposing Gen. McDowell's advance have, as their line of supply and retreat, the road to Richmond.

"If, in conjunction with McDowell's movement against Anderson, you could send a force from your right to cut off the enemy's supplies from Richmond, preserve the railroad bridges across the two (2) forks of the Pamunkey, and intercept the enemy's retreat, you will prevent the army now opposed to you from receiving an accession of numbers of nearly fifteen thousand (15,000) men; and if you succeed in saving the bridges you will secure a line of railroad for supplies in addition to the one you now have. Can you not do this almost as well as not while you are building the Chickahominy bridges? McDowell and Shields both say they can, and positively will, move Monday morning. *I wish you to move cautiously and safely.*

"You will have command of McDowell, after he joins you, precisely as you indicated in your long despatch to us of the twenty-first (21st).

"A. LINCOLN,
"President."

This information, that McDowell's corps would march for Fredericksburg on the following Monday (the 26th), and that he would be under my command, as indicated in my telegram of the 21st, was cheering news, and I now felt confident that we would on his arrival be sufficiently strong to overpower the large army confronting us.

At a later hour on the same day I received the following:

"MAY 24, 1862 (from Washington, 4 P.M.)

"In consequence of Gen. Banks's critical position I have been compelled to suspend Gen. McDowell's movements to join you. The enemy are making a desperate push upon Harper's Ferry, and we are trying to throw Gen. Fremont's force and part of Gen. McDowell's in their rear.

"A. LINCOLN,
"President."

"Maj.-Gen. GEO. B. MCCLELLAN."

From which it will be seen that I could not expect Gen. McDowell to join me in time to participate in immediate operations in front of Richmond, and on the same evening I replied to the President that I would make my calculations accordingly.

CHAPTER XXI.

[*May* 6 *to May* 18, 1862.]

Williamsburg, May 6, 1862. - I telegraphed you this morning that we had gained a battle. Every hour its importance is proved to be greater. On Sunday I sent Stoneman in pursuit with the cavalry and four batteries of horse-artillery. He was supported by the divisions of Hooker, Smith, Couch, Casey, and Kearny, most of which arrived on the ground only yesterday. Unfortunately I did not go with the advance myself, being obliged to remain to get Franklin and Sedgwick started up the river for West Point. Yesterday I received pressing private messages from Smith and others begging me to go to the front. I started with half a dozen aides and some fifteen orderlies, and found things in a bad state. Hancock was engaged with a vastly inferior force some two miles from any support. Hooker fought nearly all day without assistance, and the mass of the troops were crowded together where they were useless. I found everybody discouraged, officers and men; our troops in wrong positions, on the wrong side of the woods; no system, no co-operation, no orders given, roads blocked up. As soon as I came upon the field the men cheered like fiends, and I saw at once that I could save the day. I immediately reinforced Hancock and arranged to support Hooker, advanced the whole line across the woods, filled up the gaps, and got everything in hand for whatever might occur. The result was that the enemy saw that he was gone if he remained in his position, and scampered during the night. His works were very strong, but his loss was very heavy. The roads are in such condition that it is impossible to pursue except with a few cavalry. It is with the utmost difficulty that I can feed the men, many of whom have had nothing to eat for twenty-four hours and more. I had no dinner yesterday, no supper; a cracker for breakfast, and no dinner yet. I have no baggage; was out in the rain all day and until late at night; slept

352

in my clothes and boots, and could not even wash my face and hands. I, however, expect my ambulance up pretty soon, when I hope for better things. I have been through the hospitals, where are many of our own men and of the rebels. One Virginian sent for me this morning and told me that I was the only general from whom they expected any humanity. I corrected this mistake. This is a beautiful little town; several very old houses and churches, pretty gardens. I have taken possession of a very fine house which Joe Johnston occupied as his headquarters. It has a lovely flower-garden and conservatory. If you were here I should be much inclined to spend some weeks here. G. W. was one of the whipped community, also Joe Johnston, Cadmus Wilcox, A. P. Hill, D. H. Hill, Longstreet, Jeb Stuart, Early (badly wounded) ; and many others that we know. We have all their mounded; eight guns so far. In short, we have given them a tremendous thrashing, and I am not at all ashamed of the conduct of the Army of the Potomac.

Telegram - *Williamsburg, May* 6, 1862, 11 P.M. - The battle of Williamsburg has proved a brilliant victory. None of your friends injured, though our loss considerable. That of the enemy severe. The Quaker army is doing very well. Hancock was superb yesterday.

Williamsburg, May 6, *midnight.* - . . . Am very tired; had but little sleep last night, and have not had my clothes off; besides, was pretty well wet last night. I have not a particle of baggage with me; nothing but a buffalo-robe and horse-blanket, not even a hair-brush or tooth-brush. . . .

Monday, 1 P.M. *(8th).*- . . . I hope to get Smith's division off this afternoon, followed by others in the morning. Stoneman is some fifteen miles in advance, and will, I hope, communicate with Franklin to-night, although I am not yet sure that the enemy may not still be between the two. I shall start to-morrow morning and overtake Smith. I have ordered up headquarters and the accompanying paraphernalia at once, so I hope to get within a few miles of my tooth-brush in a day or two. It is not very pleasant, this going entirely without baggage, but it could not be helped. I find that the results of my operations are beginning to be apparent. The rebels are evacuating Norfolk, I learn. Your two letters of Sunday and Monday reached me last night. It would have been easy for me to have sacrificed 10,000 lives in taking Yorktown, and I presume the world would have thought it more brilliant. I am content with what I have done. The battle of Williamsburg was more bloody. Had I reached the field-three hours earlier I could have gained far greater results and have saved a thousand lives. It is, perhaps, well as it is, for officers and men feel that I saved the day. . . .

I don't know where the next battle will occur; I presume on the line of the Chickahominy, or it may be to-morrow in effecting a junction with Franklin. It may suit the views of the masses better, as being more bloody. I hope not, and will make it as little so as possible. . . .

Williamsburg, May 9, 2 P.M - . . . I have moved four divisions already. The reserves have arrived. My wagons have arrived, and in an hour or two I will move myself. . . . I rather think that we have a very severe battle to fight before reaching Richmond, but the men are just in the humor for it. . . . Carpet-bag has at last arrived.

Camp No. 1, *May* 9, 8.30 P.M. - We are fairly started on the march again; my camp is only about four miles from Williamsburg. The road was so much blocked up with wagons that I did not start till late. Smith, Couch, Casey, and Kearny are all in front of me, the regulars close by. To-morrow headquarters start at five A.M., and will pass all but Smith, encamping with or just in rear of him. I hope to see Franklin to-morrow night and learn more of the enemy. . . . The secesh prisoners strongly protested against being obliged to remove the torpedoes at Yorktown, but without avail, for they had to do it. I think they may be more careful next time. I heard this afternoon from Stoneman that they (secesh) had murdered some of our men after they were taken prisoners. I have given orders to hold all their people we have responsible for it. If it is confirmed to-morrow I will send a flag to Joe Johnston and quietly inform him that I will hang two of his officers for every one of our men thus murdered; and I will carry the threat into execution. I will pay them in their own coin, if they wish to carry on war in that manner. I hope there is some mistake about the murders, for I do not wish to make reprisals. It is a sad business at best. . .

May 10, *Saturday,* 11.45 P.M., *camp* 19 *miles from Williamsburg.* - . . . Am encamped now at an old wooden church, and am in easy communication with Franklin, Porter, etc. Fitz came over to see me this afternoon, and I go over to see him and Franklin to-morrow. To-morrow being Sunday, I give the men a rest, merely closing up some of the troops in rear. I begin to find some Union sentiment in this country. . . . I expect to fight a very severe battle on the Chickahominy, but feel no doubt as to the result. I saw the effect of my presence the other day in front of Williamsburg. The men behaved superbly, and will do better, if possible, next time. To-morrow I will get up supplies, reorganize, arrange details, and get ready for the great fight, feeling that I shall lose nothing by respecting Sunday as far as I can. Secesh is gathering all he can in front of me. So much the better. I have implicit confidence in my men, and they have in me. What more can I ask? . . .

Sunday, 8 A.M. (same letter *as last*) .- . . As I told you last night, I am giving my men some rest to-day. They need it much, for they have for some time been living on long marches, short rations, and rainy bivouacs. . . . My cavalry were within six miles of the upper Chickahominy yesterday. Norfolk is in our possession, the result of my movements. . . .

May 12, *Monday* P.M. *(same letter-).* - . . While I write the 2d Dragoons' band is serenading, and about fifty others are playing tattoo at various distances - a grand sound in this lovely moonlight night. My camp is at an old frame church in a grove. I differ from most of the generals in preferring a tent to a house. I hope not to sleep in a house again until I see you. . . . Are you satisfied now with my bloodless victories? Even the Abolitionists seem to be coming round; judging, at least, from the very handsome resolutions offered by Mr. Lovejoy in the House. I look upon that resolution as one of the most complimentary I know of, and that, too, offered by my bitterest persecutors. But the union of civic merit with military success is what pleases me most; to have it recognized that I have saved the lives of my

27

men and won success by my own efforts is to me the height of glory. I hope that the result in front of Richmond will cause still greater satisfaction to the country. I still hope that the God who has been so good to me will continue to smile upon our cause, and enable me to bring this war to a speedy close, so that I may at last have the rest I want so much. . . . I do need rest. You know I have had but little in my life. But the will of God be done! What is given me to do I will try to do with all my might. . . . I think one more battle here will finish the work. I expect a great one, but feel that confidence in my men and that trust in God which makes me very sanguine as to the result. They will fight me in front of Richmond, I am confident. Defeat there is certain destruction to them, and I think will prove the ruin of their wretched cause. They are concentrating everything for the last death-struggle. My government, alas! is not giving me any aid. But I will do the best I can with what I have, and trust to God's mercy and the courage of my men for the result. . . . We march in the morning to Cumberland, gradually drawing nearer to Richmond.

May 15, *Cumberland*, 2.30 P.M. - Another wet, horrid day! It rained a little yesterday morning, more in the afternoon, much during the night, and has been amusing itself in the same manner very persistently all day. I had expected to move headquarters to White House to-day; but this weather has put the roads in such condition that I cannot do more than get Franklin and Porter there to-day. Headquarters cavalry and Hunt will move there to-morrow; perhaps one or two other divisions as well, We had quite a visitation yesterday in the shape of Secretary Seward, Gideon Welles, Mr. Bates, F. Seward, Dahlgren, Mrs. Goldsborough and one of her daughters, Mrs. F. Seward, and some other ladies whose names I did not catch. I went on board their boat; then had some ambulances harnessed up and took them around camps. We are just about twenty-five miles from Richmond here, the advance considerably nearer. I don't yet know what to make of the rebels. I do not see how they can possibly abandon Virginia and Richmond without a battle; nor do I understand why they abandoned and destroyed Norfolk and the *Merrimac,* unless they also intended to abandon all of Virginia. There is a puzzle there somewhere which will soon be solved. . . . I am heartily tired of this life I am leading - always some little absurd thing being done by those gentry in Washington. I am every day more and more tired of public life, and earnestly pray that I may soon be able to throw down my sword and live once more as a private gentleman. . . . I confess I find it difficult to judge whether the war will soon be at an end or not. I think that the blows the rebels are now receiving and have lately received ought to break them up; but one can do no more than speculate. Yes, I can imagine peace and quietness reigning once more in this land of ours. It is just *that* I am fighting for! . . . Still raining hard and dismally; an awful time for the men; the only comfort is that they all have plenty to eat.

9 P.M. *(same day).-* . . . Have received to-day the official copy of the resolutions of the House. I learn that the Abolitionists begin to think that I am not such a wretch after all, or else that it is best to say so.

It was all a humbug about my being struck by a piece of a shell at Williamsburg. That reminds me of a joke some of the youngsters played upon - at Yorktown. They sent him to see an immense "shell" that had fallen in our headquarters camp. He found a large oyster-shell. . . .

I send you a photograph which I have just received from Gen. Blume, chief of artillery in the Prussian army. I knew him abroad, and the old gentleman writes to me occasionally.

Telegram - *May* 16, 1862, *White House.* - Have just arrived over horrid roads. No further movement possible until they improve. This house is where Washington's courtship took place and where he resided when first married. I do not permit it to be occupied by any one, nor the grounds around. It is a beautiful spot directly on the banks of the Pamunkey. All well and in fine spirits. Hope to get our baggage up by water, otherwise will fare badly to-night.

May 16, 11.30 P.M., *White House.* - . . . I rode over a horrid road to this place this morning; spent some time at Washington's house, or at least his wife's, and afterwards rode to the front, visiting in the course of my ride the old church (St. Peter's) where he was married. It is an old brick church with a rather pretentious tower, more remarkable for its situation than for anything else   The situation is very fine, on a commanding hill. A tablet in the interior records the death of some one in 1690. As I happened to be there alone for a few moments, I could not help kneeling at the chancel and praying that I might serve my country as truly as he did. . . .

May 17, 8.30 A.M. *(same letter).* - . . . We have a change in the weather. It is clear and very hot, so I presume the roads will improve much to-day.   I am pushing on the advanced guard and reconnoissances in various directions. We gain some ground every day; but our progress has been slow on account of the execrable nature of the roads, as well as their extreme narrowness and fewness in number, making it a very difficult matter to move large masses of men with any rapidity or convenience. I expect to have our advanced parties near enough to Bottom's bridge to-day to ascertain whether the enemy is there in much force or not, and by to-morrow or next day to obtain similar information about the other bridges-all of which, by the bye, are burned, I believe.   But the river is fordable, so the difficulty is not insuperable by any means.   It is very difficult to divine whether secesh will fight a great battle in front of Richmond or not; I still think they ought to, but there are some circumstances which look somewhat as if they would evacuate.   Time only will show, and the trial cannot be long deferred. I am very sorry that we could not have advanced more rapidly ; my only consolation is that it has been impossible. Just think of its requiring forty-eight hours to move two divisions with their trains five miles!   Nothing could be much worse than that. The fastest way to move is never to move in wet weather.

Midnight. - . . . I am now at this present moment involved in a great many different orders for parties to move out at daybreak on reconnoissances. . .

May 18, Sunday, 6 P.M., *White House.* - . . . We leave here in the morning. Porter and Franklin march at four and eight A.M., headquarters at seven. We will go to Tunstall's, or perhaps a little beyond it, and will now soon close up on the Chickahominy and find out what secesh is doing.   I think he will fight us there, or between that and Richmond; and if he is badly thrashed (as I trust he will be), incline to believe that he will begin to cry *peccavi* and say that he has enough of it, especially if Halleck beats him at Corinth. . . .

Midnight (same letter). - . . . I start early in the morning. . . . Those hounds in Washington are after me again.

CHAPTER XXII.

White House - The Chickahominy river - Bridges - Battle of Hanover
Court-House - Porter's victory - Neglect at Washington - McDowell's
retention useless.

WHITE HOUSE was a very fine plantation belonging to Mrs.
Gen. Lee. It was the residence of Mrs. Custis when she was
married to Washington. The ceremony took place in St. Peter's
Church, a lonely old building beautifully placed on a commanding hill. I observed within it a tablet commemorating a death
which took place in 1690. Finding one's self alone within that
historic building, it was a natural impulse to invoke the aid of
God to enable me to serve the country as unselfishly and truly
as did the great man who had often worshipped there.

The residence at White House was not the original building
of the time of Washington - that had been destroyed by fire; but
the existing one was constructed on the same foundations.

I neither occupied it myself nor permitted any others to do
so, but placed a guard to preserve it. For this natural act of
respect for the memory of the greatest man our country has produced I was most violently attacked and maligned by the extreme radicals. I am willing that posterity shall judge between
them and myself.

On the 19th headquarters and the 5th and 6th corps advanced to Tunstall's Station, six miles from White House. The
rain recommenced on this day, and through it I rode to Bottom's bridge and made a short reconnoissance. The enemy were
there, but not in great force. The advanced guard was near
New bridge.

The camp at Tunstall's was the most beautiful we occupied
during the campaign. Headquarters were on the summit of a
hill, commanding a superb view in all directions. The country
was highly cultivated, being covered with fine plantations. Towards Richmond large masses of troops were bivouacked, while
towards the Pamunkey there were no signs of an army. The
contrast between war and peace was vivid and most impressive.

360

At night when the countless bivouac-fires were lighted the scene was grand and brilliant beyond description. But he must have been devoid of feeling who could regard this magnificent spectacle without a sentiment of most sincere regret that human madness and folly should have made it necessary to march armies through this fair and peaceful land. The Army of the Potomac was mainly composed of good men, who took up arms from the noblest motives; and I doubt whether any troops ever did so little needless damage in a hostile country. But at best a large

McCLELLAN AT WHITE HOUSE.

army leaves a wide swath in its rear, and cannot move without leaving the marks of its passage.

On the 20th it again rained heavily. On the evening of the 21st the army was posted as follows:

The advanced guard within a mile of New bridge; the 6th corps three miles from New bridge, with the 5th corps at supporting distance in its rear; the ad corps on the railway, about three miles from the Chickahominy, connecting the right with the left; the 4th corps on the New Kent road, near Bottom's bridge, having three regiments across the stream covering the rebuilding of the bridge; the 3d corps within easy supporting distance of the 4th corps.

On the 22d headquarters were advanced to Cold Harbor, and on the 26th the railway was in operation as far as the Chickahominy, and the railway bridge across the stream nearly completed.

The Chickahominy river rises some fifteen miles to the northward of Richmond, and unites with the James about forty miles below that city. Our operations embraced the part of the river between Meadow's and Bottom's bridges, covering the approaches to Richmond from the east. In this vicinity the river, in its ordinary stage, is about forty feet wide, fringed with a dense growth of heavy forest trees, and bordered by low, marshy bottom-lands varying from half a mile to a mile in width.

Within the limits above-mentioned the firm ground lying above high-water mark seldom approaches the river on either bank, and no place was found, within this section, where the high ground came near the stream on both banks.

It was subject to frequent, sudden, and great variations in the volume of water, and a single violent rain-storm of brief duration would cause a rise of water which overflowed the bottom-lands on both sides, and for many days made the river absolutely impassable without bridges.

When our light troops approached the river on the 20th of May it was found that all the bridges had been destroyed by the enemy on our approach, except that at Mechanicsville, and it became necessary not only to rebuild the old bridges, but also to construct several additional ones. The west bank of the river, opposite New, Mechanicsville, and Meadow bridges, was bordered by high bluffs, which afforded the enemy commanding positions on which to establish his batteries, to enfilade the approaches by the principal roads leading to Richmond on our right, and to prevent the reconstruction of these important bridges. We were thus obliged to select other less exposed points for our crossings.

Had the 1st corps effected its promised junction we might have turned the head-waters of the Chickahominy and attacked Richmond from the north and northwest, while we preserved our line of supply from West Point; but with the force actually at my disposal such an attempt would simply have exposed the Army of the Potomac to destruction in detail, and the total loss of its communications. It is hardly necessary to say that the country in which we operated could supply nothing for the wants of the army, and that were our communications with the depots cut and held by the enemy nothing but starvation awaited us.

When we arrived opposite Bottom's bridge on the 20th the enemy was there in only small force, and, as it was of the utmost importance to secure a lodgment on the right bank before he could concentrate his forces and resist the passage of the stream, I ordered Casey's division of the 4th corps to ford the river at once and occupy the heights on the further bank. This was promptly done, and reconnoissances were immediately pushed forward, while instant steps were taken to rebuild the bridge. The troops were directed to throw up defences to secure our left flank, and the 3d corps was moved up in support.

Meanwhile our centre and right were advanced to the river, and on the 24th Mechanicsville was carried, the enemy being driven out by our artillery and forced across the bridge, which they destroyed. Gen. Naglee, of Casey's division of the 4th corps, on the same day dislodged a force of the enemy from the vicinity of Seven Pines, and the advance of our left secured a strong position near that place. All the information obtained from negroes, deserters, prisoners, and spies indicated that the enemy occupied in force all the approaches to Richmond from the east, and that he intended to dispute every step of our advance beyond the Chickahominy on our left, and to resist the passage of the stream opposite our right. That their army was superior to ours in numbers seemed certain. Strong entrenchments had been constructed around the city. Up to this time I had every reason to expect that McDowell would commence his march from Fredericksburg on the morning of the 26th, and it was only during the evening of the 24th that I received from the President the telegram, already given, announcing the suspension of his movement.

So far, then, as immediate operations were concerned, it only remained for me to make the best use of the forces at my disposal, and to avail myself of all possible artificial auxiliaries, to compensate as far as possible for the inadequacy of numbers.

28

I concurred fully with the President in his injunction, contained in his telegram of the 24th, that it was necessary, with my limited force, to move "cautiously and safely,"

In view of the peculiar character of the Chickahominy, and the liability to sudden inundations, it became necessary to construct eleven bridges, all long and difficult, with extensive logway approaches, and often built under fire.

It will be remembered that the order for the co-operation of McDowell was only suspended, not revoked; and, therefore, I could not abandon the northern approach and my communications with West Point. To cover these communications, and be prepared to effect the junction with the 1st corps when it advanced, it was necessary to retain a portion of the army on the left bank of the Chickahominy, and I could not make any serious movement with the forces on the right bank until the communications between the two parts of the army were firmly and securely established by strong and sufficiently numerous bridges.

As the entrenchments around Richmond were strong and heavily garrisoned, it would have been an act of madness and folly had I temporarily abandoned my communications and thrown the entire army across the stream, trusting to the chances of carrying the place by assault before the troops had exhausted the supplies carried with them.

I was not responsible for the fact that I was obliged to select a faulty and dangerous plan as the least objectionable of those from which I could choose.

On the 24th a very spirited and successful reconnoissance took place near New bridge, which first brought Lieut. (afterwards Gen.) Custer to my notice. His commanding officers commended him highly for his conduct, and I sent for him to thank him. He was then a slim, long-haired boy, carelessly dressed. I thanked him for his gallantry, and asked what I could do for him. He replied very modestly that he had nothing to ask, and evidently did not suppose that he had done anything to deserve extraordinary reward. I then asked if he would like to serve on my personal staff as an aide-de-camp. Upon this he brightened up and assured me that he would regard such service as the most gratifying he could perform; and I at once gave the necessary orders. He continued on my staff until I was relieved from the command.

In those days Custer was simply a reckless, gallant boy, undeterred by fatigue, unconscious of fear; but his head was always clear in danger, and he always brought me clear and intelligible reports of what he saw when under the heaviest fire. I became much attached to him. In the later days of the war, when he commanded cavalry troops, he displayed a degree of prudence and good sense, in conducting the most dangerous expeditions, that surprised many who thought they knew him well.

In the battle of the Rosebud, against the Sioux, where he lost his life and the whole of his immediate command was destroyed, no one survived to tell the story of the disaster. On that fatal day he simply repeated the tactics that he had so often successfully used against large bodies of Indians; and it is probable that he was deceived as to the strength and fighting capacity of his opponents, and that, from his want of knowledge of the details of the ground where the tragedy occurred, he was suddenly surrounded by overwhelming masses of well-armed warriors, against whom the heroic efforts of his command wasted themselves in vain.

Those who accused him of reckless rashness would, perhaps, have been the first to accuse him of timidity if he had not attacked, and thus allowed the enemy to escape unhurt. He died as he had lived, a gallant soldier; and his whole career was such as to force me to believe that he had good reasons for acting as he did.

With the exception of the 25th, it rained heavily every day from the 22d to the battle of Fair Oaks, and during the day and night of the 30th an unusually violent storm occurred, accompanied by torrents of rain. The valley of the Chickahominy was flooded more than ever; all work on the bridges was suspended, and they became well-nigh impracticable.

The enemy seized the occasion and determined to attack the part of the army that had crossed the Chickahominy, when it would be very difficult or impossible to support it. Exposure and fatigue had brought upon me a violent attack of illness, which confined me to my bed on the 30th and the morning of the 31st. I left my bed to go to the field of battle as soon as I was satisfied of the importance of the crisis. Two corps, the 3d and the 4th, were across the Chickahominy, three on the left bank.

The 4th corps was in position near Fair Oaks and Seven Pines. Kearny's division of the 3d corps was on and near the railroad in advance of Savage's Station. Hooker's division was on the left, near White Oak Swamp. The 2d corps was on the left bank of the Chickahominy, at and near the Grapevine bridge, in position to support either wing of the army.

The 5th and the 6th corps were also on the left bank, between Mechanicsville and New bridge.

Having been informed late on the 24th that McDowell's advance was suspended, I caused work upon the bridges to be commenced immediately and pushed forward with the greatest vigor; but heavy rains continued to fall from day to day, which flooded the valley and raised the water to a greater height than had been known for twenty years.

The bridges first made, together with their approaches, which were not arranged for such unprecedented high water, were carried away or rendered impassable. It thus became necessary, with immense labor, to build others much larger, more elevated and stable. Our men worked in the mater, exposed to the fire of the enemy from the opposite bank.

On the 25th of May I received the following telegram:

"Your despatch received. Gen. Banks was at Strasburg with about six thousand (6,000) men, Shields having been taken from him to swell a column for McDowell to aid you at Richmond, and the rest of his force scattered at various places. On the 23d a rebel force of from 7,000 to 10,000 fell upon one regiment and two companies guarding the bridge at Front Royal, destroying it entirely; crossed the Shenandoah, and on the 24th - yesterday - pushed on to get north of Banks on the road to Winchester. Gen. Banks ran a race with them, beating them into Winchester yesterday evening. This morning a battle ensued between the two forces, in which Gen. Banks was beaten back into full retreat towards Martinsburg, and probably is broken up into a total rout. Geary, on the Manassas Gap Railroad, just now reports that Jackson is now near Front Royal with 10,000 troops, following up and supporting, as I understand, the force now pursuing Banks. Also, that another force of 10,000 is near Orleans, following on in the same direction. Stripped bare, as we are here, I will do all we can to prevent them crossing the Potomac at Harper's Ferry or above. McDowell has about 20,000 of his forces moving back to the vicinity of Front Royal, and Fremont, who was at Franklin, is moving to Harrisonburg; both these movements intended to get in the enemy's rear.

"One more of McDowell's brigades is ordered through here to Harper's Ferry; the rest of his forces remain for the present at Fredericksburg. We are sending such regiments and dribs from here and Baltimore as we can spare to Harper's Ferry, supplying their places in some sort, calling in militia from the adjacent States. We also have eighteen cannon on the road to Harper's Ferry, of which arm there is not a single one at that point. This is now our situation.

"If McDowell's force was now beyond our reach we should be entirely helpless. Apprehensions of something like this, and no unwillingness to sustain you, has always been my reason for withholding McDowell's forces from you.

"Please understand this, and do the best you can with the forces you have.

"A. LINCOLN,
"President."

On the 25th the following was also received:

"The enemy is moving north in sufficient force to drive Gen. Banks before him; precisely in what force we cannot tell. He is also threatening Leesburg, and Geary on the Manassas Gap Railroad, from both north and south; in precisely what force we cannot tell. I think the movement is a general and concerted one, such as would not be if he was acting upon the purpose of a very desperate defence of Richmond. I think the time is near when you must either attack Richmond or give up the job and come to the defence of Washington. Let me hear from you instantly.

"A. LINCOLN,
"President."

To which I replied as follows:

Telegram received. Independently of it, the time is very near when I shall attack Richmond. The object of the movement is probably to prevent reinforcements being sent to me. All the information obtained from balloons, deserters, prisoners, and contrabands agrees in the statement that the mass of the rebel troops are still in the immediate vicinity of Richmond, ready to defend it. I have no knowledge of Banks's position and force, nor what there is at Manassas; therefore cannot form a definite opinion as to the force against him.

I have two corps across Chickahominy, within six mile of Richmond; the others on this side at other crossings within same distance, and ready to cross when bridges are completed.

On the 26th I received the following:

"We have Gen. Banks's official report. He has saved his

army and baggage, and has made a safe retreat to the river, and is probably safe at Williamsport. He reports the attacking force at fifteen thousand (15,000).

"A. LINCOLN,
"*President.*"

Also the following:

"Can you not cut the Acquia Creek Railroad? Also, what impression have you as to entrenched works for you to contend with in front of Richmond? Can you get near enough to throw shells into the city?

" A. LINCOLN,
"*President*"

On the same day I sent the following:

Have cut the Virginia Central Road in three places between Hanover Court-House and the Chickahominy. Will try to cut the other. I do not think Richmond entrenchments formidable; but am not certain. Hope very soon to be within shelling distance. Have railroad in operation from White House to Chickahominy. Hope to have Chickahominy bridge repaired to-night. Nothing of interest to-day.

The interruption of the railroad here referred to was effected by the command of Brig.-Gen. Stoneman, and was intended to prevent the enemy from drawing supplies by that route or from sending reinforcements to Anderson or Jackson. At ten A.M. I telegraphed to the President:

I am glad to know affairs are not so bad as might have been. I would earnestly call your attention to my instructions to Gen. Banks of March 16, to Gen. Wadsworth of same date, and to my letter of April 1 to the adjutant-general. I cannot but think that a prompt return to the principles there laid down would relieve all probability of danger. I will forward copies by mail. I beg to urge the importance of Manassas and Front Royal in contradistinction to Fredericksburg.

On the same day I received intelligence that a very considerable force of the enemy was in the vicinity of Hanover Court-House, to the right and rear of our army, thus threatening our communications, and in a position either to reinforce

Jackson or to impede McDowell's junction, should he finally move to unite with us. On the same day I also received information from Gen. McDowell, through the Secretary of War, that the enemy had fallen back from Fredericksburg towards Richmond, and that Gen. McDowell's advance was eight miles south of the Rappahannock.

"WASHINGTON, May 26, 1862.
"Gen. McClellan:

"Following despatch received late last night:

"'*Falmouth,* 25th - *To Hon. E. M. Stanton:* I have just examined a lieutenant, three sergeants, and a corporal who came in from the army as deserters this morning. They are, with the exception of one Frenchman, from the North, pressed into service. They are all men of fine intelligence. The lieutenant and the sergeants, who came from the same battery, are positive the army has fallen back to Richmond. The first order was to go at 1.30 P.M. to Hanover Junction, they having heard of McClellan's right wing being at Hanover Court-House and having destroyed the railroad to Gordonsville at that place, which made them fear for their communications.

"'This was suddenly revoked, and an order was read on parade directing the command back to Richmond to take part in the great battle now about to take place there. Two other men thought that the force was going to join Jackson, who was going to get in the rear of my army, and was going into Maryland. This was only surmise; the order for Richmond was written and published. My advance is eight miles beyond Fredericksburg. I hope soon to be able to tell you more precisely where the enemy is. One thing is certain: that, whether they left here to join Jackson or not, they have not done so yet, and that all the grand masses Geary reports must have come from some other place than here. They left here by stealth, and with dread of being attacked. They went at night, and for a distance by railroad. They thought I had sixty thousand men. - (Signed) IRWIN MCDOWELL.'

"E. M. STANTON,
"Secretary of War."

It was thus imperative to dislodge or defeat this force, independently even of the wishes of the President as expressed in his telegram of the 26th. I entrusted this task to Brig.-Gen. Fitz-John Porter, commanding the 5th corps, with orders to move at daybreak on the 27th.

Through a heavy rain and over bad roads that officer moved his command as follows:

Brig.-Gen. W. H. Emory led the advance with the 5th and 6th regiments U. S. Cavalry and Benson's horse-battery of the 2d U. S. Artillery, taking the road from New bridge *via* Mechanicsville to Hanover Court-House.

Gen. Morell's division, composed of the brigades of Martindale, Butterfield, and McQuade, with Berdan's regiment of sharpshooters and three batteries under Capt. Charles Griffin, 5th U. S. Artillery, followed on the same road.

Col. G. K. Warren, commanding a provisional brigade composed of the 5th and 13th N. Y., the 1st Conn. Artillery acting as infantry, the 6th Penn. Cavalry, and Weeden's R. I. Battery, moved from his station at Old Church by a road running to Hanover Court-House, parallel to the Pamunkey.

After a fatiguing march of fourteen miles through the mud and rain, Gen. Emory at noon reached a point about two miles from Hanover Court-House, where the road forks to Ashland, and found a portion of the enemy formed in line across the Hanover Court-House road.

Gen. Emory had, before this, been joined by the 25th N. Y. (of Martindale's brigade) and Berdan's sharpshooters; these regiments were deployed with a section of Benson's battery, and advanced slowly towards the enemy until reinforced by Gen. Butterfield with four regiments of his brigade, when the enemy was charged and quickly routed, one of his guns being captured by the 17th N. Y., under Col. Lansing, after having been disabled by the fire of Benson's battery. The firing here lasted about an hour. The cavalry and Benson's battery were immediately ordered in pursuit, followed by Morell's infantry and artillery, with the exception of Martindale's brigade. Warren's brigade, having been delayed by repairing bridges, etc., now arrived, too late to participate in this affair; a portion of this command was sent to the Pamunkey to destroy bridges, and captured quite a number of prisoners; the remainder followed Morell's division. In the meantime Gen. Martindale, with the few remaining regiments of his brigade and a section of artillery, advanced on the Ashland road, and found a force of the enemy's infantry, cavalry, and artillery in position near Beake's Station on the Virginia Central Railroad; he soon forced them to retire towards Ashland.

The 25th N. Y. having been ordered to rejoin him, Gen. Martindale was directed to form his brigade and move up the railroad to rejoin the rest of the command at Hanover Court-House.

He sent one regiment up the railroad, but remained with the 2d Me., afterwards joined by the 25th N. Y., to guard the rear of the main column.

The enemy soon returned to attack Gen. Martindale, who at once formed the 2d Me., 25th N. Y., and a portion of the 44th N. Y., with one section of Martin's battery, on the New bridge road, facing his own position of the morning, and then held his ground for an hour against large odds until reinforced.

Gen. Porter was at Hanover Court-House, near the head of his column, when he learned that the rear had been attacked by a large force. He at once faced the whole column about, recalled the cavalry sent in pursuit towards Ashland, moved the 13th and 14th N. Y. and Griffin's battery direct to Martindale's assistance, pushed the 9th Mass. and 62d Penn., of Mc-Quade's brigade, through the woods on the right (our original left), and attacked the flank of the enemy, while Butterfield, with the 83d Penn. and 16th Mich., hastened towards the scene of action by the railroad and through the woods, further to the right, and completed the rout of the enemy. During the remainder of this and the following day our cavalry was active in the pursuit, taking a number of prisoners.

Capt. Harrison, of the 5th U. S. Cavalry, with a single company, brought in as prisoners two entire companies of infantry with their arms and ammunition. A part of Rush's lancers also captured an entire company with their arms.

The immediate results of these affairs were some 200 of the enemy's dead buried by our troops, 730 prisoners sent to the rear, one 12-pound howitzer, one caisson, a large number of small arms, and 2 railroad trains captured.

Our loss amounted to 53 killed, 344 wounded and missing.

Their camp at Hanover Court-House was taken and destroyed.

Having reason to believe that Gen. Anderson, with a strong force, was still at Ashland, I ordered Gen. Sykes's division of regulars to move on the 28th from New bridge towards Hanover Court-House, to be in position to support Gen. Porter. They reached a point within three miles of Hanover Court-House, and remained there until the evening of the 29th, when they returned to their original camp.

On the 28th Gen. Stoneman's command of cavalry, horse-artillery, and two regiments of infantry were also placed under Gen. Porter's orders.

On the same day I visited Hanover Court-House, whence I sent the following despatch to the Secretary of War:

MAY 28, 2 P.M.

Porter's action of yesterday was truly a glorious victory; too much credit cannot be given to his magnificent division and its accomplished leader. The rout of the rebels was complete; not a defeat, but a complete rout. Prisoners are constantly coming in; two companies have this moment arrived with excellent arms.

There is no doubt that the enemy are concentrating everything on Richmond. I will do my best to cut off Jackson, but am doubtful whether I can.

It is the policy and duty of the government to send me by water all the well-drilled troops available. I am confident that Washington is in no danger. Engines and cars in large numbers have been sent up to bring down Jackson's command.

I may not be able to cut them off, but will try; we have cut all but the Fredericksburg and Richmond Railroad. The real issue is in the battle about to be fought in front of Richmond. All our available troops should be collected here-not raw regiments, but the well-drilled troops. It cannot be ignored that a desperate battle is before us; if any regiments of good troops remain unemployed it will be an irreparable fault committed.

Having ascertained the state of affairs, instructions were given for the operations of the following day.

On the 28th a party under Maj. Williams, 6th U. S. Cavalry, destroyed the common road bridges over the Pamunkey, and Virginia Central Railroad bridge over the South Anna.

On the 29th he destroyed the Fredericksburg and Richmond Railroad bridge over the South Anna, and the turnpike bridge over the same stream.

On the same day, and mainly to cover the movement of Maj. Williams, Gen. Emory moved a column of cavalry towards Ashland from Hanover Court-House. The advance of this column, under Capt. Chambliss, 5th U. S. Cavalry, entered Ashland, driving out a party of the enemy, destroyed the railroad bridge over Stony creek, broke up the railroad and telegraph.

Another column of all arms, under Col. Warren, was sent on the same day by the direct road to Ashland, and entered it shortly after Gen. Emory's column had retired, capturing a small party there.

Gen. Stoneman on the same day moved on Ashland by Leach's Station, covering well the movements of the other columns.

The objects of the expedition having been accomplished, and it being certain that the 1st corps would not join us at once, Gen. Porter withdrew his command to their camps with the main army on the evening of the 29th.

On the night of the 27th and 28th I sent the following despatch to the Secretary of War:

Porter has gained two complete victories over superior forces, yet I feel obliged to move in the morning with reinforcements to secure the complete destruction of the rebels in that quarter. In doing so I run some risk here, but I cannot help it. The enemy are even in greater force than I had supposed. I will do all that quick movements can accomplish, but you must send me all the troops you can, and leave to me full latitude as to choice of commanders. It is absolutely necessary to destroy the rebels near Hanover Court-House before I can advance.

In reply to which I received the following from the President:

"WASHINGTON May 28, 1862.
"I am very glad of Gen. F. J. Porter's victory; still, if it was a total rout of the enemy, I am puzzled to know why the Richmond and Fredericksburg Railroad was not seized again, as, you say you have all the railroads but the Richmond and Fredericksburg. I am puzzled to see how lacking that, you can have any, except the scrap from Richmond to West Point. The scrap of the Virginia Central from Richmond to Hanover Junction, without more, is simply nothing. That the whole of the enemy is concentrating on Richmond I think cannot be certainly known to you or me. Saxton, at Harper's Ferry, informs us that large forces, supposed to be Jackson's and Ewell's, forced his advance from Charlestown to-day. Gen. King telegraphs us from Fredericksburg that contrabands give certain information that 15,000 left Hanover Junction Monday morning to reinforce Jackson. I am painfully impressed with the importance of the struggle before you, and shall aid you all I can consistently with my view of due regard to all points."

In regard to this telegram of the President it may be re-marked that it would have been dangerous and foolish in the extreme to leave Porter at Ashland and Hanover Court-House to hold the railways. I knew that McDowell would not advance for some time, if at all. I could not reinforce Porter sufficiently to enable him to remain in his advanced position without draw-ing so largely from the main army as to endanger its safety and reduce it to inaction. Moreover, there was no object in running this risk. I had broken the direct line of communication be-tween Richmond and Jackson; had cleared the front of Freder-icksburg, so that McDowell could advance unopposed, and had relieved my own right flank and rear from immediate danger.

At 6 P.M. of the 29th I telegraphed the Secretary of War:

Gen. Porter has gained information that Gen. Anderson left his position in vicinity of Fredericksburg at four A.M. Sunday with the following troops: 1st S. C., Col. Hamilton; one battal-ion S. C. Rifles, 34th and 38th N. C., 45th Ga., 12th, 13th, and 14th S. C., 3d La., two batteries of four guns each-namely, Letcher's Va. and McIntosh's S. C. batteries. Gen. Anderson and his command passed Ashland yesterday evening *en route* for Richmond, leaving men behind to destroy bridges over the tele-graph road which they travelled. This information is reliable. It is also positively certain that Branch's command was from Gordonsville, bound for Richmond, whither they have now gone.

It may be regarded as positive, I think, that there is no rebel force between Fredericksburg and Junction.

The following was also sent on the same day by Gen. Marcy :

"A detachment from Gen. F. J. Porter's command, under Maj. Williams, 6th Cavalry, destroyed the South Anna railroad bridge at about nine A.M. to-day; a large quantity of Confederate public property was also destroyed at Ashland this morning."

In reply to which the following was received from the Pre-sident:

"Your despatch as to the South Anna and Ashland being seized by our forces this morning is received. Understanding these points to be on the Richmond and Fredericksburg Rail-road, I heartily congratulate the country, and thank Gen. Mc-Clellan and his army for their seizure."

On the 30th I sent the following to Secretary Stanton:

From the tone of your despatches and the President's I do not think that you at all appreciate the value and magnitude of Porter's victory. It has entirely relieved my right flank, which was seriously threatened; routed and demoralized a considerable portion of the rebel forces; taken over 750 prisoners; killed and wounded large numbers; one gun, many small arms, and much baggage taken. It was one of the handsomest things in the war, both in itself and in its results. Porter has returned, and my army is again well in hand. Another day will make the probable field of battle passable for artillery. It is quite certain that there is nothing in front of McDowell at Fredericksburg. I regard the burning of South Anna bridges as the least important result of Porter's movement.

The results of this brilliant operation of Gen. Porter were the dispersal of Gen. Branch's division and the clearing of our right flank and rear. It was rendered impossible for the enemy to communicate by rail with Fredericksburg, or with Jackson *via* Gordonsville, except by the very circuitous route of Lynchburg, and the road was left entirely open for the advance of McDowell had he been permitted to join the Army of the Potomac. His withdrawal towards Front Royal was, in my judgment, a serious and fatal error; he could do no good in that direction, while, had he been permitted to carry out the orders of May 17, the united forces would have driven the enemy within the immediate entrenchments of Richmond before Jackson could have returned to its succor, and probably would have gained possession promptly of that place.

It is very clear that the arrangements I directed in March and on the 1st of April for the defence of Washington and the Shenandoah would have proved ample to check Jackson without delaying the advance of McDowell. The total disregard of these instructions led to the actual condition of affairs.

On the 25th of May McDowell's advance was eight miles beyond Fredericksburg. If he had marched on the 26th, as first ordered, he would have found no enemy in his front until he reached the South Anna, on the 27th or early on the 28th. For his telegram of the 25th shows that they had hastily fallen back during the night of the 24th and 25th, and Porter found them at Hanover Court-House and Ashland on the 27th; so that, as things were, Porter's division alone would have insured McDowell's junction with the Army of the Potomac without the slightest difficulty.

Had McDowell advanced, however, my own movements would naturally have been modified.

I would have placed the 3d corps in position to hold Bottom's bridge and the railroad bridge, and to guard our left and communications with West Point. The 4th corps would have been placed near New Cold Harbor, with one division a couple of miles to the westward to watch the crossings of the Chickahominy from Grapevine bridge to Beaver Dam creek, ready to support either the 4th or the 2d corps, as might be necessary.

The 2d corps near Mechanicsville, to hold the crossing opposite thereto and that at Meadow bridge, and prepared to move instantly to the support of the 5th and 6th corps.

The 6th corps through Atlee's Station to the Fredericksburg and Richmond turnpike, to occupy the Virginia Central Railroad and Winston's bridge, and, leaving a sufficient force to hold that point, to move either direct upon the line of the Fredericksburg and Richmond Railroad south of Ashland, or to support the 5th corps in the direction of Hanover Court-House, as circumstances might have required.

The 5th corps would have followed the line of march which Morell's division pursued on the 27th, sending a detached brigade direct from Old Church to Hanover Court-House; and having reached the Central Railroad and the Fredericksburg turnpike about four miles south of Hanover Court-House, the mass of the corps would either have moved on Hanover Court-House or in conjunction with the 6th corps on Ashland, as the movements of the enemy might have required. Thus our old positions would have been securely held, McDowell's junction would have been secured in spite of any movements of the enemy, and the chances would have been in favor of our destroying any force of the enemy between the Chickahominy and the South Anna.

The moment these objects mere accomplished the 5th and 6th corps would have returned to the vicinity of Mechanicsville. It would then have been easy for McDowell to advance by the Fredericksburg turnpike far enough to turn the batteries covering the Mechanicsville crossings, so that the two armies could unite on the right bank of the Chickahominy, and the capture of Richmond could have been accomplished long before Jackson could return to reinforce the garrison.

CHAPTER XXIII.

Operations on the Chickahominy - Battle of Fair Oaks - McDowell's corps is coming - Still stretching the right wing - Floods of the Chickahominy - Movement on Old Tavern.

ON the 20th of May a reconnoissance had been ordered on the south side of the Chickahominy towards James river. This was accomplished by Brig. Gen. H. M. Naglee, who crossed his brigade near Bottom's bridge and pushed forward to within two miles of James river without serious resistance or finding the enemy in force. The rest of the 4th corps, commanded by Gen. E. D. Keyes, crossed the Chickahominy on the 23d of May.

On the 24th, 25th, and 26th a very gallant reconnoissance was pushed by Gen. Naglee, with his brigade, beyond the Seven Pines, and on the 25th the 4th corps was ordered to take up and fortify a position in the vicinity of the Seven Pines. The order was at once obeyed, a strong line of rifle-pits opened, and an abatis constructed a little in the rear of the point where the nine-mile road comes into the Williamsburg road.

On the same day Gen. Heintzelman was ordered to cross with his corps (the 3d) and take a position two miles in advance of Bottom's bridge, watching the crossing of White Oak Swamp, and covering the left and the rear of the left wing of the army. Being the senior officer on that side of the river, he was placed in command of both corps and ordered to hold the Seven Pines at all hazards, but not to withdraw the troops from the crossings of White Oak Swamp unless in an emergency.

On the 28th Gen. Keyes was ordered to advance Casey's division to Fair Oaks, on the Williamsburg road, some three-quarters of a mile in front of the Seven Pines, leaving Gen. Couch's division at the line of rifle-pits. A new line of rifle-pits and a small redoubt for six field-guns were commenced, and much of the timber in front of this line was felled on the two days following. The picket-line was established, reaching from the Chickahominy to White Oak Swamp.

On the 30th Gen. Heintzelman, representing that the advance had met with strong opposition in taking up their position, and that he considered the point a critical one, requested and obtained authority to make such a disposition of his troops as he saw fit to meet the emergency. He immediately advanced two brigades of Kearny's division about three-fourths of a mile in front of Savage's Station, thus placing them within supporting distance of Casey's division, which held the advance of the 4th corps.

On the 30th the troops on the south side of the Chickahominy were in position as follows: Casey's division on the right of the Williamsburg road, at right angles to it, the centre at Fair Oaks; Couch's division at the Seven Pines; Kearny's division on the railroad, from near Savage's Station towards the bridge; Hooker's division on the borders of White Oak Swamp. Constant skirmishing had been kept up between our pickets and those of the enemy. While these lines were being taken up and strengthened large bodies of Confederate troops were seen immediately to the front and right of Casey's position.

During the day and night of the 30th of May a very violent storm occurred. The rain falling in torrents rendered work on the rifle-pits and bridges impracticable, made the roads almost impassable, and threatened the destruction of the bridges over the Chickahominy.

The enemy, perceiving the unfavorable position in which we were placed, and the possibility of destroying that part of our army which was apparently cut off from the main body by the rapidly rising stream, threw an overwhelming force (grand divisions of Gens. D. H. Hill, Huger, Longstreet, and G. W. Smith) upon the position occupied by Casey's division.

It appears from the official reports of Gen. Keyes and his subordinate commanders that at ten o'clock A.M. on the 31st of May an aide-de-camp of Gen. J. E. Johnston was captured by Gen. Naglee's pickets. But little information as to the movements of the enemy was obtained from him, but his presence so near our lines excited suspicion and caused increased vigilance, and the troops were ordered by Gen. Keyes to be under arms at eleven o'clock. Between eleven and twelve o'clock it was reported to Gen. Casey that the enemy were approaching in considerable force on the Williamsburg road. At this time

Casey's division was disposed as follows: Naglee's brigade extending from the Williamsburg road to the Garnett field, having one regiment across the railroad; Gen. Wessells's brigade in the rifle-pits, and Gen. Palmer's in the rear of Gen. Wessells's; one battery of artillery in advance with Gen. Naglee; one battery in rear of rifle-pits to the right of the redoubt; one battery in rear of the redoubt, and another battery unharnessed in the redoubt. Gen. Couch's division, holding the second line, had Gen. Abercrombie's brigade on the right, along the nine-mile road, with two regiments and one battery across the railroad near Fair Oaks Station; Gen. Peck's brigade on the right and Gen. Devens's in the centre.

On the approach of the enemy Gen. Casey sent forward one of Gen. Palmer's regiments to support the picket-line; but this regiment gave way without making much, if any, resistance. Heavy firing at once commenced, and the pickets were driven in. Gen. Keyes ordered Gen. Couch to move Gen. Peck's brigade to occupy the ground on the left of the Williamsburg road, which had not before been occupied by our forces, and thus to support Gen. Casey's left, where the first attack was the most severe. The enemy now came on in heavy force, attacking Gen. Casey simultaneously in front and on both flanks. Gen. Keyes sent to Gen. Heintzelman for reinforcements, but the messenger was delayed, so that orders were not sent to Gens. Kearny and Hooker until nearly three o'clock, and it was nearly five P.M. when Gens. Jameson's and Berry's brigades of Gen. Kearny's division arrived on the field. Gen. Birney was ordered up the railroad, but by Gen. Kearny's order halted his brigade before arriving at the scene of action. Orders were also despatched for Gen. Hooker to move up from White Oak Swamp, and he arrived after dark at Savage's Station.

As soon as the firing was heard at headquarters orders were sent to Gen. Sumner to get his command under arms and be ready to move at a moment's warning. His corps, consisting of Gens. Richardson's and Sedgwick's divisions, was encamped on the north side of the Chickahominy some six miles above Bottom's bridge. Each division had thrown a bridge over the stream opposite to its own position.

At one o'clock Gen. Sumner moved the two divisions to their respective bridges, with instructions to halt and await further

29

orders. At two o'clock orders were sent from headquarters to cross these divisions without delay and push them rapidly to Gen. Heintzelman's support. This order was received and communicated at half-past two, and the passage was immediately commenced. In the meantime Gen. Naglee's brigade, with the batteries of Gen. Casey's division, which Gen. Naglee directed, struggled gallantly to maintain the redoubt and rifle-pits against the overwhelming masses of the enemy. They were reinforced by a regiment from Gen. Peck's brigade. The artillery, under command of Col. G. D. Bailey, 1st N. Y. Artillery, and afterwards of Gen. Naglee, did good execution on the advancing column. The left of this position was, however, soon turned, and a sharp cross-fire opened upon the gunners and men in the rifle-pits. Col. Bailey, Maj. Van Valkenberg, and Adj. Ramsey, of the same regiment, were killed; some of the guns in the redoubt were taken, and the whole line was driven back upon the position occupied by Gen. Couch. The brigades of Gens. Wessells and Palmer, with the reinforcements which had been sent them from Gen. Couch,, had also been driven from the field with heavy loss, and the whole position occupied by Gen. Casey's division was taken by the enemy.

Previous to this time Gen. Keyes ordered Gen. Couch to advance two regiments to relieve the pressure upon Gen. Casey's right flank, In making this movement Gen. Couch discovered large masses of the enemy pushing towards our right and crossing the railroad, as well as a heavy column which had been held in reserve and which was now making its way towards Fair Oaks station. Gen. Couch at once engaged this column with two regiments; but, though reinforced by two additional regiments, he was overpowered, and the enemy pushed between him and the main body of his division. With these four regiments and one battery Gen. Couch fell back about half a mile towards the Grapevine bridge, where, hearing that Gen. Sumner had crossed, he formed line of battle facing Fair Oaks Station and prepared to hold the position.

Gens. Berry's and Jameson's brigades had by this time arrived in front of the Seven Pines. Gen. Berry was ordered to take possession of the woods on the left and push forward so as to have a flank-fire on the enemy's lines. This movement was executed brilliantly, Gen. Berry pushing his regiments forward through the woods until their rifles commanded the left of the camp and works occupied by Gen. Casey's division in the morning. Their fire on the pursuing columns of the enemy was very destructive, and assisted materially in checking the pursuit in that part of the field. He held his position in these woods against several attacks of superior numbers, and after dark, being cut off by the enemy from the main body, he fell back towards White Oak Swamp, and by a circuit brought his men into our lines in good order.

Gen. Jameson, with two regiments (the other two of his brigade having been detached-one to Gen. Peck and one to Gen. Birney), moved rapidly to the front on the left of the Williamsburg road, and succeeded for a time in keeping the abatis clear of the enemy. But large numbers of the enemy pressing past the right of his line, he too was forced to retreat through the woods towards White Oak Swamp, and in that way gained camp under cover of night.

Brig.-Gen. Devens, who had held the centre of Gen. Couch's division, had made repeated and gallant efforts to regain portions of the ground lost in front, but each time was driven back, and finally withdrew behind the rifle-pits near Seven Pines.

Meantime Gen. Sumner had arrived with the advance of his corps, Gen. Sedgwick's division, at the point held by Gen. Couch with four regiments and one battery. The roads leading from the bridge were so miry that it was only by the greatest exertion Gen. Sedgwick had been able to get one of his batteries to the front.

The leading regiment (1st Minn., Col. Sully) was immediately deployed to the right of Couch to protect the flank, and the rest of the division formed in line of battle, Kirby's battery near the centre in an angle of the woods. One of Gen. Couch's regiments was sent to open communication with Gen. Heintzelman. No sooner were these dispositions made than the enemy came in strong force. and opened a heavy fire along the line. He made several charges, but was each time repulsed with great loss by the steady fire of the infantry and the splendid practice of the battery. After sustaining the enemy's fire for a considerable time Gen. Sumner ordered five regiments (the 34th N. Y., Col. Sinter; 82d N. Y., Lieut.-Col. Hudson; 15th Mass., Lieut.-Col. Kimball; 20th Mass., Col. Lee; 7th Mich., Maj. Richardson - the three former of Gen. Gorman's brigade, the two latter of Gen. Dana's brigade) to advance and charge with the bayonet. This charge was executed in the most brilliant manner. Our troops, springing over two fences which were between them and the enemy, rushed upon his lines and drove him in confusion from that part of the field. Darkness now ended the battle for that day.

During the night dispositions were made for its early renewal. Gen. Couch's division, and so much of Gen. Casey's as could be collected together, with Gen. Kearny's, occupied the rifle-pits near Seven Pines. Gen. Peck, in falling back on the left, had succeeded late in the afternoon in rallying a considerable number of stragglers, and was taking them once more into the action, when he was ordered back to the entrenched camp by Gen. Kearny. Gen. Hooker brought up his division about dark, having been delayed by the heaviness of the roads and the throng of fugitives from the field, through whom the colonel of the leading regiment (Starr) reports he "was obliged to force his way with the bayonet." This division bivouacked for the night in rear of the right of the rifle-pits on the other side of the railroad. Gen. Richardson's division also came upon the field about sunset. He had attempted the passage of the Chickahominy by the bridge opposite his own camp, but it was so far destroyed that he was forced to move Gens. Howard and Meagher's brigades, with all his artillery, around by Gen. Sedgwick's bridge, while Gen. French's brigade with the utmost difficulty crossed by the other. Gen. Sedgwick's division, with the regiments under Gen. Couch, held about the same position as when the fight ceased, and Gen. Richardson on his arrival was ordered to place his division on the left to connect with Gen. Kearny. Gen. French's brigade was posted along the railroad, and Gens. Howard's and Meagher's brigades in second and third lines. All his artillery had been left behind, it being impossible to move it forward through the deep mud as rapidly as the infantry pushed towards the field, but during the night the three batteries of the division were brought to the front.

About five o'clock on the morning of the 1st of June skirmishers and some cavalry of the enemy were discovered in front of Gen. Richardson's division. Capt. Pettit's battery (B, 1st N. Y.), having come upon the ground, threw a few shells among them, when they dispersed. There was a wide interval between

Gen. Richardson and Gen. Kearny. To close this Gen. Richardson's line was extended to the left and his first line moved over the railroad. Scarcely had they gained the position when the enemy, appearing in large force from the woods in front, opened a heavy fire of musketry at short range along the whole line. He approached very rapidly, with columns of attack formed on two roads which crossed the railroad. These columns were supported by infantry in line of battle on each side, cutting Gen. French's line. He threw out no skirmishers, but appeared determined to carry all before him by one crushing blow. For nearly an hour the first line of Gen. Richardson's division stood and returned the fire, the lines of the enemy being reinforced and relieved time after time, till finally Gen. Howard was ordered with his brigade to go to Gen. French's assistance. He led his men gallantly to the front, and in a few minutes the fire of the enemy ceased and his whole line fell back on that part of the field. On the opening of the firing in the morning Gen. Hooker pushed forward on the railroad with two regiments (5th and 6th N. J.), followed by Gen. Sickles's brigade. It was found impossible to move the artillery of this division from its position on account of the mud. On coming near the woods, which were held by the enemy in force, Gen. Hooker found Gen. Birney's brigade, Col. J. Hobart Ward in command, in line of battle. He sent back to hasten Gen. Sickles's brigade, but ascertained that it had been turned off to the left by Gen. Heintzelman to meet a column advancing in that direction. He at once made the attack with the two New Jersey regiments, calling upon Col. Ward to support him with Gen. Birney's brigade. This was well done, our troops advancing into the woods under a heavy fire, and pushing the enemy before them for more than an hour of hard fighting. A charge with the bayonet was then ordered by Gen. Hooker with the 5th and 6th N. J., 3d Me., and 38th and 40th N. Y., and the enemy fled in confusion, throwing down arms and even clothing in his flight. Gen. Sickles, having been ordered to the left, formed line of battle on both sides of the Williamsburg road and advanced under a sharp fire from the enemy, deployed in the woods in front of him. After a brisk interchange of musketry-fire while crossing the open ground, the Excelsior Brigade dashed into the timber with the bayonet and put the enemy to flight.

On the right the enemy opened fire after half an hour's cessation, which was promptly responded to by Gen. Richardson's division. Again the most vigorous efforts were made to break our line, and again they were frustrated by the steady courage of our troops. In about an hour Gen. Richardson's whole line advanced, pouring in their fire at close range, which threw the line of the enemy back in some confusion. This was followed up by a bayonet-charge, led by Gen. French in person, with the 57th and 66th N. Y., supported by two regiments sent by Gen. Heintzelman, the 71st and 73d N. Y., which turned the confusion of the enemy into precipitate flight. One gun captured the previous day was retaken.

Our troops pushed forward as far as the lines held by them on the 31st before the attack. On the battle-field there were found many of our own and the Confederate wounded, arms, caissons, wagons, subsistence stores, and forage, abandoned by the enemy in his rout. The state of the roads and impossibility of manœuvring artillery prevented further pursuit. On the next morning a reconnoissance was sent forward, which pressed back the pickets of the enemy to within five miles of Richmond; but again the impossibility of forcing even a few batteries forward precluded our holding permanently this position. The lines held previous to the battle were therefore resumed.

On the 31st, when the battle of Fair Oaks commenced, we had two of our bridges nearly completed; but the rising waters flooded the log-way approaches and made them almost impassable, so that it was only by the greatest efforts that Gen. Sumner crossed his corps and participated in that hard-fought engagement. The bridges became totally useless after this corps had passed, and others on a more permanent plan were commenced.

On my way to headquarters, after the battle of Fair Oaks, I attempted to cross the bridge where Gen. Sumner had taken over his corps on the day previous. At the time Gen. Sumner crossed this was the only available bridge above Bottom's bridge. I found the approach from the right bank for some four hundred yards submerged to the depth of several feet, and, on reaching the place where the bridge had been, I found a great part of it carried away, so that I could not get my horse over, and was obliged to send him to Bottom's bridge, six miles below, as the only practicable crossing.

The approaches to New and Mechanicsville bridges were

also overflowed, and both of them were enfiladed by the enemy's batteries established upon commanding heights on the opposite side. These batteries were supported by strong forces of the enemy, having numerous rifle-pits in their front, which would have made it necessary, even had the approaches been in the best possible condition, to have fought a sanguinary battle, with but little prospect of success, before a passage could have been secured.

The only available means, therefore, of uniting our forces at Fair Oaks for an advance on Richmond soon after the battle was to march the troops from Mechanicsville and other points on the left bank of the Chickahominy down to Bottom's bridge, and thence over the Williamsburg road to the position near Fair Oaks, a distance of about twenty-three miles. In the condition of the roads at that time this march could not have been made with artillery in less than two days, by which time the enemy would have been secure within his entrenchments around Richmond. In short, the idea of uniting the two wings of the army in time to make a vigorous pursuit of the enemy, with the prospect of overtaking him before he reached Richmond, only five miles distant from the field of battle, is simply absurd, and was, I presume, never for a moment seriously entertained by any one connected with the Army of the Potomac. An advance involving the separation of the two wings by the impassable Chickahominy would have exposed each to defeat in detail. Therefore I held the position already gained, and completed our crossings as rapidly as possible.

In the meantime the troops at Fair Oaks were directed to strengthen their positions by a strong line of entrenchments, which protected them while the bridges were being built, gave security to the trains, liberated a larger fighting force, and offered a safer retreat in the event of disaster.

On June 2 the Secretary of War telegraphed: "The indications are that Fremont or McDowell will fight Jackson to-day, and as soon as he is disposed of another large body of troops will be at your service."

On the 3d the President telegraphed: "With these continuous rains I am very anxious about the Chickahominy - so close in your rear, and crossing your line of communication. Please look to it."

To which I replied: "Your despatch of five P.M. just received. As the Chickahominy has been almost the only obstacle in my way for several days, your excellency may rest assured that it has not been overlooked. Every effort has been made, and will continue to be, to perfect the communications across it."

My views of the condition of our army on the 4th were explained to the President as follows:

Terrible rain-storm during the night and morning; not yet cleared off. Chickahominy flooded; bridges in bad condition. Are still hard at work at them. I have taken every possible step to insure the security of the corps on the right bank, but I cannot reinforce them here until my bridges are all safe, as my force is too small to insure my right and rear, should the enemy attack in that direction, as they may probably attempt. I have to be very cautious now. Our loss in the late battle will probably exceed (5,000) five thousand. I have not yet full returns. On account of the effect it might have on our own men and the enemy, I request that you will regard this information as confidential for a few days. I am satisfied that the loss of the enemy was very considerably greater; they were terribly punished. I mention these facts now merely to show you that the Army of the Potomac has had serious work, and that no child's play is before it.

You must make your calculations on the supposition that I have been correct from the beginning in asserting that the serious opposition was to be made here.

And to the Secretary of War on the same day:

June 4. - Please inform me at once what reinforcements, if any, I can count upon having at Fortress Monroe or White House within the next three days, and when each regiment may be expected to arrive. It is of the utmost importance that I should know this immediately. The losses in the battle of the 31st and 1st will amount to (7,000) seven thousand. Regard this as confidential for the present.

If I can have five new regiments for Fort Monroe and its dependencies, I can draw three more old regiments from there safely. I can well dispose of four more raw regiments on my communications. I can well dispose of from fifteen to twenty well-drilled regiments among the old brigades in bringing them up to their original effective strength. Recruits are especially necessary for the regular and volunteer batteries of artillery, as well as for the regular and volunteer regiments of infantry. After the losses in our last battle I trust that I will no longer be regarded as an alarmist.   I believe we have at least one more desperate battle to fight.

On the 5th the Secretary telegraphed me:

"I will send you five (5) new regiments as fast as transportation can take them; the first to start to-morrow from Baltimore. I intend sending you a part of McDowell's force as soon as it can return from its trip to Front Royal, probably as many as you want. The order to ship the new regiments to Fort Monroe has already been given. I suppose that they may be sent directly to the fort. Please advise me if this be as you desire."

On the 7th of June I telegraphed as follows:

In reply to your despatch of two P.M. to-day, I have the honor to state that the Chickahominy river has risen so as to flood the entire bottoms to the depth of three and four feet. I am pushing forward the bridges in spite of this, and the men are working night and day, up to their waists in water, to complete them.

The whole face of the country is a perfect bog, entirely impassable for artillery, or even cavalry, except directly in the narrow roads, which renders any general movement, either of this or the rebel army, entirely out of the question until we have more favorable weather.

I am glad to learn that you are pressing forward reinforcements so vigorously.

I shall be in perfect readiness to move forward and take Richmond the moment McCall reaches here and the ground will admit the passage of artillery.   I have advanced my pickets about a mile to-day, driving off the rebel pickets and securing a very advantageous position.

The rebels have several batteries established, commanding the debouches from two of our bridges, and fire upon our working parties continually; but as yet they have killed but very few of our men.

As I did not think it probable that any reinforcements would be sent me in time for the advance on Richmond, I stated in the foregoing despatch that I should be ready to move when Gen. McCall's division joined me; but I did not intend to be understood by this that no more reinforcements were wanted, as will be seen from the following despatch:

June 10. - I have again information that Beauregard has arrived, and that some of his troops are to follow him. No great reliance - perhaps none whatever-can be attached to this; but it is possible, and ought to be their policy.

I am completely checked by the weather. The roads and fields are literally impassable for artillery, almost so for infantry. The Chickahominy is in a dreadful state; we have another rainstorm on our hands.

I shall attack as soon as the weather and ground will permit; but there will be a delay, the extent of which no one can foresee, for the season is altogether abnormal.

In view of these circumstances, I present for your consideration the propriety of detaching largely from Halleck's army to strengthen this; for it would seem that Halleck has now no large organized force in front of him, while we have. If this cannot be done, or even in connection with it, allow me to suggest the movement of a heavy column from Dalton upon Atlanta. If but the one can be done it would better conform to military principles to strengthen this army. And even although the reinforcements might not arrive in season to take part in the attack upon Richmond, the moral effect would be great, and they would furnish valuable assistance in ulterior movements.

I wish to be distinctly understood that, whenever the weather permits, I will attack with whatever force I may have, although a larger force would enable me to gain much more decisive results.

I would be glad to have McCall's infantry sent forward by water at once, without waiting for his artillery and cavalry.

If Gen. Prim returns *via* Washington, please converse with him as to the condition of affairs here.

Our work upon the bridges continued to be pushed forward vigorously until the 20th, during which time it rained almost every day, and the exposure of the men caused much sickness.

On the 11th the Secretary of War telegraphed:

"Your despatch of three-thirty (3.30) yesterday has been received. I am fully impressed with the difficulties mentioned, and which no art or skill can avoid, but only endure, and am striving to the uttermost to render you every aid in the power of the government. . . . McCall's force was reported yesterday as having embarked and on its way to join you. It is intended to send the residue of McDowell's force also to join you as speedily as possible.

"Fremont had a hard fight, day before yesterday, with Jackson's force at Union Church, eight miles from Harrisonburg. He claims the victory, but was pretty badly handled. It is clear that a strong force is operating with Jackson for the purpose of detaining the forces here from you. I am urging as fast as possible the new levies.

"Be assured, general, that there never has been a moment when my desire has been otherwise than to aid you with my whole heart, mind, and strength, since the hour we first met; and whatever others may say for their own purposes, you have never had, and never can have, any one more truly your friend, or more anxious to support you, or more joyful than I shall be at the success which I have no doubt will soon be achieved by your arms."

On the 12th and 13th Gen. McCall's division arrived.

On the 13th of June two squadrons of the 5th U. S. Cavalry, under the command of Capt. Royall, stationed near Hanover Old Church, were attacked and overpowered by a force of the enemy's cavalry numbering about 1,500 men, with four guns. They pushed on towards our depots, but at some distance from our main body, and, though pursued very cleverly, made the circuit of the army, repassing the Chickahominy at Long bridge. The burning of two schooners laden with forage and fourteen government wagons, the destruction of some sutlers' stores, the killing of several of the guard and teamsters at Garlick's landing, some little damage done at Tunstall's Station, and a little *éclat,* were the precise results of this expedition.

On the 14th I telegraphed to the Secretary of War:

June 14, *midnight* - All quiet in every direction. The stampede of last night has passed away. Weather now very favorable. I hope two days more will make the ground practicable. I shall advance as soon as the bridges are completed and the ground fit for artillery to move. At the same time I would be glad to have whatever troops can be sent to me. I can use several new regiments to advantage.

It ought to be distinctly understood that McDowell and his troops are completely under my control. I received a telegram from him requesting that McCall's division might be placed so as to join him immediately on his arrival.

That request does not breathe the proper spirit. Whatever troops come to me must be disposed of so as to do the most good. I do not feel that, in such circumstances as those in which I am now placed, Gen. McDowell should wish the general interests to be sacrificed for the purpose of increasing his command.

If I cannot fully control all his troops I want none of them, but would prefer to fight the battle with what I have, and let others be responsible for the results.

The department lines should not be allowed to interfere with me; but Gen. McD., and all other troops sent to me, should be placed completely at my disposal, to do with them as I think best. In no other way can they be of assistance to me. I therefore request that I may have entire and full control. The stake at issue is too great to allow personal considerations to be entertained; you know that I have none.

On the 20th I telegraphed to the President:

There is not the slightest reason to suppose that the enemy intends evacuating Richmond; he is daily increasing his defences. I find him everywhere in force, and every reconnoissance costs many lives, yet I am obliged to feel my way, foot by foot, at whatever cost, so great are the difficulties of the country; by to-morrow night the defensive works covering our position on this side of the Chickahominy should be completed. I am forced to this by my inferiority in numbers, so that I may bring the greatest possible numbers into action and secure the army against the consequences of unforeseen disaster.

All the information I could obtain, previous to the 24th of June, regarding the movements of Gen. Jackson led to the belief that he was at Gordonsville, where he was receiving reinforcements from Richmond *via* Lynchburg and Staunton; but what his purposes were did not appear until the date specified, when a young man, very intelligent but of suspicious appearance, was brought in by our scouts from the direction of Hanover Court-House. He at first stated that he was an escaped prisoner from Col. Kenley's Maryland regiment, captured at Front Royal, but finally confessed himself to be a deserter from Jackson's command, which he left near Gordonsville on the 21st. Jackson's troops were then, as he said, moving to Frederick's Hall, along the Virginia Central Railroad, for the purpose of attacking my rear on the 28th. I immediately despatched two trusty negroes to proceed along the railroad and ascertain the truth of the statement. They were unable, however, to get beyond Hanover Court-House, where they encountered the enemy's pickets, and were forced to turn back without obtaining the desired information. On that day I sent the following despatch to Secretary Stanton:

June 24. - A very peculiar case of desertion has just occurred from the enemy. The party states that he left Jackson, Whiting, and Ewell (fifteen brigades) at Gordonsville on the 21st; that they were moving to Frederick's Hall, and that it was intended to attack my rear on the 28th. I would be glad to learn, at your earliest convenience, the most exact information you have as to the position and movements of Jackson, as well as the sources from which your information is derived, that I may the better compare it with what I have.

G. B. McCLELLAN,
Maj.-Gen.

The following is his reply:

"*June* 25. - We have no definite information as to the numbers or position of Jackson's force. Gen. King yesterday reported a deserter's statement that Jackson's force was, nine days ago, 40,000 men. Some reports place 10,000 rebels under Jackson at Gordonsville; others, that his force is at Port Republic, Harrisonburg, and Luray. Fremont yesterday reported rumors that Western Virginia was threatened, and Gen. Kelley that Ewell was advancing to New creek, where Fremont has his depots. The last telegram from Fremont contradicts this rumor. The last telegram from Banks says the enemy's pickets are strong in advance at Luray; the people decline to give any information as to his whereabouts. Within the last two (2) days the evidence is strong that for some purpose the enemy is circulating rumors of Jackson's advance in various directions, with a view to conceal the real point of attack. Neither McDowell, who is at Manassas, nor Banks and Fremont, who are at Middletown, appear to have any accurate knowledge of the subject. A letter transmitted to the department yesterday, purported to be dated Gordonsville on the fourteenth (14th) instant, stated that the actual attack was designed for Washington and Baltimore as soon as you attacked Richmond, but that the report was to be circulated that Jackson had gone to Richmond, in order to mislead, This letter looked very much like a blind, and induces me to suspect that Jackson's real movement now is towards Richmond. It came from Alexandria, and is certainly designed, like the numerous rumors put afloat, to mislead. I think, therefore, that while the warning of the deserter to you may also be a blind, that it could not safely be disregarded. I will transmit to you any further information on this subject that may be received here."

On the 25th, our bridges and entrenchments being at last completed, an advance of our picket-line of the left was ordered, preparatory to a general forward movement.

Immediately in front of the most advanced redoubt on the

Williamsburg road was a large, open field; beyond that a swampy belt of timber, some five hundred yards wide, which had been disputed ground for many days. Further in advance was an open field, crossed by the Williamsburg road and the railroad, and commanded by a redoubt and rifle-pits of the enemy.

It was decided to push our lines to the other side of these moods, in order to enable us to ascertain the nature of the ground, and to place Gens. Heintzelman and Sumner in position to support the attack intended to be made on the Old Tavern, on the 26th or 27th, by Gen. Franklin, by assailing that position in the rear.

Between eight and nine o'clock on the morning of the 25th the advance was begun by Gen. Heintzelman's corps. The enemy were found to be in strong force all along the line, and contested the advance stubbornly, but by sunset our object was accomplished.

The following telegram was sent to the Secretary of War on the same day:

25th 6.15 P.M. - I have just returned from the field, and found your despatch in regard to Jackson.

Several contrabands just in give information confirming supposition that Jackson's advance is at or near Hanover Court-House, and that Beauregard arrived with strong reinforcements in Richmond yesterday.

I incline to think that Jackson will attack my right and rear. The rebel force is stated at two hundred thousand, including Jackson and Beauregard. I shall have to contend against vastly superior odds if these reports be true. But this army will do all in the power of men to hold their position and repulse any attack.

I regret my great inferiority in numbers, but feel that I am in no way responsible for it, as I have not failed to represent repeatedly the necessity of reinforcements; that this was the decisive point, and that all the available means of the government should be concentrated here. I will do all that a general can do with the splendid army I have the honor to command, and, if it is destroyed by overwhelming numbers, can at least die with it and share its fate.

But if the result of the action, which will probably occur to-morrow or within a short time, is a disaster, the responsibility cannot be thrown on my shoulders; it must rest where it belongs.

Since I commenced this I have received additional intelligence confirming the supposition in regard to Jackson's movements and Beauregard's arrival. I shall probably be attacked to-morrow, and now go to the other side of the Chickahominy to arrange for the defence on that side.

I feel that there is no use in my again asking for reinforcements.

CHAPTER XXIV.

PRIVATE LETTERS.

[*May* 20 to *June* 26, 1862.]

May 20, 12.30 A.M., *Tunstall's Station.-* . . . I moved head-quarters and four divisions here to-day, about six miles from the White House. I rode myself to Bottom's bridge in the rain, and made a short reconnoissance of it. Found the enemy there, though not in great force. The engineers will make a close examination to-morrow morning, driving the enemy's pickets. The advanced guard also is near New bridge. We are gradually drawing near the rascals. I think they intend to fight us in front of Richmond; if they do it will be a decisive battle. Our camp here is one of the most beautiful I ever saw. The country is lovely, and the view from the high hill on which are headquarters is really magnificent. This evening, when the bivouac-fires were lighted, the scene was grand beyond description. There are some very fine plantations in this vicinity. What fools their owners are to submit themselves to the necessity of being overrun and devastated! An army leaves a wide swath in its rear, but my men are generally behaving very well.

May 21, 1.30 A.M., *Tunstall's Station.* - . . . Headquarters will move to-morrow some seven or eight miles more to the front. . . .

Wednesday morning (same letter). - . . . Porter's troops have been marching past for a couple of hours, and the rumbling of wagons has been going on for some time. . . .
A little later. - I have just learned that some of our troops have succeeded in crossing the Chickahominy at Bottom's bridge. . .

May 22, 6.30 P.M., *camp near Chickahominy.* - . . . I have
394

just returned from a ride to the front, where I have taken a good look at the rebel lines. I suppose I must have ridden some thirty miles or less to-day.

Some one just brought me a bouquet of wild white flowers-a negro at that. I clutched it most eagerly, as reminding me of one who two years ago became my wife. It is on the table in front of me as I write; in a tin tumbler, to be sure, but none the less pure and white.

May 23, P.M. *(continuation of same letter).* - Soon after I finished the last page I was taken quite sick, and continued so most of the night. I have remained in my tent all day, feeling quite miserable, but will be all right and able to ride out in the morning. . . . The occurrences of the next few days are quite uncertain. I have secured one passage of the Chickahominy, and hope to get two more to-morrow. I have been within six miles of the rebel capital, and our balloonists have been watching it all day. The intentions of the enemy are still doubtful. I go on prepared to fight a hard battle, but I confess that the indications are not now that he will fight. Unless he has some deep-laid scheme that I do not fathom, he is giving up great advantages in not opposing me on the line of the Chickahominy. He could give me a great deal of trouble and make it cost me hundreds or thousands of lives. . . . God knows that I am sick of this civil war, although no feeling of the kind unsteadies my hand or ever makes me hesitate or waver. It is a cruel necessity. I am very glad that the President has come out as he did about Hunter's order. . . . If I succeed in getting the two additional passages of the river to-morrow I will move next day. In fact, I hope to have a strong advanced guard within a couple of miles of Richmond to-morrow evening. Then I shall be able to examine the enemy's position and arrange for the battle. I will not fight on Sunday if I can help it. If I am obliged to do so I will still have faith that God will defend the right, and trust that we have the right on our side. How freely I shall breathe when my long task of months is over and Richmond is ours! I know the uncertainty of all human events. I know that God may even now deem best to crush all the high hopes of the nation and this army. I will do the best I can to insure success, and will do my best to be contented, with whatever result God sees fit to terminate our efforts. I am here on the eve of one of the great historic battles of the world - one of those crises in a nation's life that occur but seldom. Far more than my fate is involved in the issue. I have done the best I could; I have tried to serve my country honestly and faithfully. All I can now do is to commit myself to the hands of God and pray that the country may not be punished for my sins and shortcomings.

11 P.M. - . . . Have had some skirmishes and cannonading to-day. Successful in all.

May 25, Sunday, 3.30 P.M., *Cold Harbor.* - . . . Have been rather under the weather the last three days. Had to ride out in the rain yesterday, and was kept up very late last night, so I was not so well as I might have been this morning. . . . It cleared off about sunset yesterday, and to-day has been bright and pleasant, drying up the roads rapidly. They have been so cut and bad as to prevent any movements in force or with rapidity. Fortunately the ground dries rapidly here, and will soon be in such condition that we can move anywhere. I have this moment received a despatch from the President, who is terribly scared about Washington, and talks about the necessity of my returning in order to save it. Heaven save a country governed by such counsels! I must reply to his telegram, and finish this by and by. . . . I feel much better this afternoon - quite myself again. , . . If I should find Washington life as bad after the war as it was when I was there, I don't think I could be induced to remain in the army after peace.

10 P.M. *(same letter).* - It seems, from some later despatches I have received, that Banks has been soundly thrashed, and that they are terribly alarmed in Washington. A scare will do them good, and may bring them to their senses. . . . I have a fire in my tent to-night.

May 26, 8 P.M., *camp near New bridge.* - . . . We broke up the last camp about two and moved to this place, which is quite on the banks of the Chickahominy and very near New bridge. It, of course, commenced raining about an hour after we started; but as it was not a very heavy rain, we got on very well. . . . I have been troubled by the old Mexican complaint, brought on, I suppose, by exposure to the wet, but I am really substantially well again. . . . Fitz starts off in the morning on a trip that will take a day to go and one to return; the object being to cut off and disperse a force of the enemy threatening my right and rear, also to destroy the railroad bridges. When this is done I will feel very comfortable in that direction, and shall be quite ready to attack. My men are in such excellent condition and such good spirits that I cannot doubt the result. The people here have not much Union feeling, but are becoming heartily tired of the war, especially as they now feel its evils in their midst-a fate from which I pray that God may deliver our own Northern States. My camp is about four and a half to five miles from Richmond. . . . Had the instructions I left for Banks and Wadsworth been complied with we should have been spared the shame of Banks's stampede. . . . I feared last night that I would be ordered back for the defence of Washington!

May 27, 11.45 P.M. - . . . I sent Fitz-John out this morning to "pick up" a large force of the enemy who were threatening my right and rear, also to burn the bridges of the two railways of the South Anna. The old fellow has done splendidly. Thrashed 13,000 badly, and I am momentarily expecting to hear the details of his second attack. We are getting on splendidly. I am quietly clearing out everything that could threaten my rear and communications, providing against the contingency of disaster, and so arranging as to make my whole force available in the approaching battle. The only fear is that Joe's heart may fail him. . . .

New bridge, May 29, 8 P.M. - . . . I rode some forty-odd miles yesterday, got wet, had nothing to eat all day, and returned to camp about two o'clock this morning, noble old Dan taking me through most splendidly. Found myself quite sick this morning - my old Mexican enemy. I had been fighting against it for several days with more or less success. But this morning I gave up and sent for the doctor, in whose hands I placed myself. . . . Feel a great deal better to-night; the pain gone and my head clearer. . . . Fitz did his work nobly, as I expected. I rode to his battle-field yesterday and several miles beyond it. The railroad bridge across the South Anna was burned yesterday and to-day, thus effectually cutting off railroad communication between Richmond and the North. Lawrence Williams arranged both affairs very handsomely. The country around Hanover Court-House is very beautiful. . . .

June 2, 8 P.M., *New bridge.* - It has been impossible for me to write to you for the last two or three days. I was quite sick on Friday and Saturday; on the last day rose from my bed and went to the field of battle; remained on horseback most of the time until Sunday evening. I came back perfectly worn out and exhausted; lay down at once, and, though I could not sleep much I got some rest. I think to-night will bring me quite up again; I am not anxious. The Chickahominy is now falling, and I hope we can complete the bridges to-morrow. I can do, nothing more until that is accomplished. The enemy attacked on Saturday and Sunday with great ferocity and determination; their first attack alone was successful. Casey's division broke. As the other divisions came up they checked the enemy, and we gradually got the better of him; he was badly handled before night. On Sunday morning he renewed the attack and was everywhere repulsed in disorder and with heavy loss. We had regained all the ground lost, and more, last night; to-day we are considerably in advance of the field of battle. It is certain that me have gained a glorious victory; I only regret that the rascals were smart enough to attack when the condition of the Chickahominy was such that I could not throw over the rest of the troops to follow up the success; but the weather now seems. settled, and I hope the river will be low enough to-morrow to enable me to cross. I am tired of the sickening sight of the battle-field, with its mangled corpses and poor suffering wounded! Victory has no charms for me when purchased at such cost. I shall be only too glad when all is over and I can return where I best love to be. . . . Your father is quite well; so are all the staff. I don't think any of your friends were hurt in the battle; several colonels killed and some wounded.

June 3, 10 A.M., *New bridge.* - . . . . There has been some heavy cannonading within the last hour, and I learned that the enemy were advancing on Sumner. I am awaiting further news before going to the front; in the meantime working hard at the bridges over the confounded Chickahominy. We may have another fight at any hour now; I can't tell when or where. I expect some 5,500 troops from Fortress Monroe to-night, which will go some ways towards replacing my losses; hope that one regiment arrived last night. If the enemy will give me time to get these fresh troops in line I will be obliged to them exceedingly; I am none too strong, I can assure you. But all will go well. . . .

June 5, 9 A.M. (Thursday), *New bridge.* - We have had a terrible time during the last few days: torrents of rain constantly falling; ground a sea of mud; the Chickahominy a booming river; bridges swept away; the railroad pretty much used up- in short, about all the troubles that armies fall heir to, except defeat! But I am so grateful that God gave us the victory that I will not complain of minor evils. The enemy must have been very badly whipped not to have renewed his attack under the very favorable circumstances of the last few days.

P.M. - Have been, as usual, interrupted. . . . The enemy has opened from two or three batteries, and is blazing away upon our working parties at the bridges; some of our heavy batteries have opened upon him, and will, I hope, soon silence them. I feel much better to-day, and if secesh will permit me to remain quiet until to-morrow morning I am sure that I shall be quite well. My head feels clearer to-day, and I feel generally better, though somewhat weak. My report of the battle (telegraphic) was incorrectly printed in some respects in the papers, and, of course, raises a tempest in a teapot. I never saw so much selfishness and petty feeling in my life as I have seen developed during this unhappy war. . . . This camp-life in the mud is becoming tedious; yet here, I am tied up, the confounded river running like mad, and no present chance of crossing the rest of the troops, although we are doing all that can be done. . . . The artillery still keeps up its firing. I must send again for news. . . .

June 6. - . . . The bad weather still continues, horrid in the extreme. . . . It seems that Joe Johnston was seriously, if not dangerously, wounded in the last battle. I had occasion to write him some letters to-day which ought to be answered, so I can probably tell by the reply how it really is. . . . I am receiving

reinforcements now which will soon repair our losses and enable
me to act with freedom of motion. . . .

10 P.M. - . . . Have been, as usual, very quiet to-day, lying
down almost all the time, and leaving my tent scarcely at all,
. . . It has at last cleared up, and for some days, I think. . . .
It is now quite certain that Joe Johnston was severely wounded
last Saturday - now said to be in the shoulder by a rifle-ball. I
think there is very little doubt that it is so. That places Smith,
G. W., in command. I have drawn nine regiments from Fort
Monroe - the first use I made of the command given me of that
place; the last of them will be up to-morrow. These will go far
towards filling our ranks. The losses in the late battle were
about 5,500; of course we have lost many by disease. I am promised either McCall's or King's division in a very few days. If
I learn to-morrow that they will surely be here in three or four
days I will wait for them, as it would make the result certain and
less bloody. I can't afford to have any more men killed than
can be avoided. . . .

June 7, 8.30 A.M. *(same letter).* - . . . The sun is struggling
very hard this morning with the clouds; thus far the latter has
rather the better of him, but I hope the old fellow will persevere
and beat them out in an hour or two. I presume the mystery of
the two telegraphic messages has been cleared up before this. I
said that none of your acquaintances were killed. The operator
must have been unmanned by excitement, for my official despatches were terribly bungled in many ways. One of the two
similar despatches must have been sent on the operator's own
account. I think I sent you but two altogether that day. Did
not that solution occur to you?

June 8, 1862. - Gen. Prim and staff, some nine or ten in
number, have arrived. They went direct to the battle-field from
the railway, so I will be spared until evening, when I shall be in
for it. How Charles will make out I cannot imagine. It is a
terrible nuisance to take care of these parties in camp. They
always come entirely unprovided, and it puts every one to great
inconvenience to take care of them. I had sense enough, when I
went to the Crimea, to take tents, messing apparatus, servants,

horses, etc., so that I was perfectly independent. But none of these foreigners seem to follow so good an example. . . .

I had occasion day before yesterday to send a letter to Joe Johnston in reply to a request of us for permission to send in and get the bodies of a couple of generals and half a dozen colonels supposed to be killed. An answer came yesterday apologizing for the delay in replying to my communication (which involved other matters), and also apologizing for some of his people firing at Sweitzer, who carried the flag of truce. Well, whom do you think the letter came from? From no one else than A. P. Hill, major-general commanding the Light Division. . . . I hope we shall have clear weather for a few days, so that it will be possible to move and use artillery, as well as to get it over the river. You have no idea of the state of the ground now ; just as much as a horse can do to make his way! We have pretty quiet times; a little artillery-firing and picket-skirmishing by way of breaking the monotony - *voilà tout!* I suppose both sides are gathering for the great battle. I have received ten regiments since the battle, nine of which from Fort Monroe, one from Baltimore; and one from Washington will arrive to-night. I am also promised McCall's division at once. If the promise is kept I shall be quite strong again. . . . Am much better to-day-quite myself.

June 9. - . . . A large dose of Spaniards yesterday. Gen. Prim and staff arrived and are quartered on us, some seven in all - a rather inconvenient addition to the mess. On the other hand, however, they are very gentlemanly and a very nice set of people. Gen. Prim speaks only French and Spanish. He is a dark-faced, black-haired, bright, young-looking man of forty-five. I like him much. His chief of staff, Gen. Milans, is a perfect old trump, who speaks English and looks for all the world like a French marquis of the stage. His hair and beard are iron gray; his moustache of the most approved pattern of the Spanish cavaliers of old; a cane suspended to his button-hole; red pants tucked in high boots; a loose green coat covered with silver embroidery; the funniest little hat imaginable - on the whole a most peculiar picture, such as I never saw before. They are delighted with what they have seen (I hear the funny little fellow's voice now: "G'd-mornin', sir; hope yo' well"), fully appreciate the great difficulties under which we have been laboring, and will do much, I think, towards giving a just idea in Europe of the difficulties we have to contend against in this most singular of all campaigns. . . . I had a telegram from McDowell last evening stating that he was ordered down here with his command, and assuring me that he received the order with great satisfaction. The secretary and President are becoming quite amiable of late; I am afraid that I am a little cross to them, and that I do not quite appreciate their sincerity and good feeling. *"Timeo Danaos et dona ferentes."* How glad I will be to get rid of the whole lot! I had another letter from our friend A. P. H. yesterday in reply to mine to Joe Johnston; so I am now confident that Joe is badly wounded. In my reply sent this morning I ignore Hill entirely, and address mine to the" Commanding General, etc.," so G. W. will have to come out this time. I hope to arrange for a general exchange of prisoners, and thus relieve our poor fellows who have been so long confined. I must do secesh the justice to say that they now treat our wounded and prisoners as well as they can. . . .

June 10, 7.30 A.M. - . . . It is again raining hard, and has been for several hours! I feel almost discouraged - that is, I would do so did I not feel that it must all be for the best, and that God has some great purpose in view through all this. It is certain that there has not been for years and years such a season; it does not come by chance. I am quite checked by it. First, the Chickahominy is so swollen and the valley so covered with water that I cannot establish safe communications over it; then, again, the ground is so muddy that we cannot use our artillery: the guns sink up to their axle-trees. I regret all this extremely, but take comfort from the thought that God will not leave so great a struggle as this to mere chance. If He ever interferes with the destinies of men and nations, this would seem to be a fit occasion for it. So whenever I feel discouraged by adverse circumstances I do my best to fall back on this great source of confidence, and always find that it gives me strength to bear up against anything that may occur. I do not see how any one can fill such a position as I do without being constantly forced to think of higher things and the Supreme Being. The great responsibility, the feeling of personal weakness and incompetency, of entire dependence on the will of God, the thousand circumstances entirely beyond our control that may defeat our best-laid plans, the sight of poor human suffering - all these things *will* force the mind to seek rest above. . . . I feel quite well to-day, by far better than at any time before. I think that if I can stand the test of this rainy day all must be right. I will not go out while it rains, if I can help it. . . The Spaniards are still here, and I fear will remain some time, unless this rain drives them off. Prim is very well, but it is a nuisance to be obliged to be polite when one's head is full of more important things. . . . Still raining very hard. I don't know what *will* become of us!

June 11, *New bridge,* A.M. - . . . Am very well to-day, and the weather is good. . . . Will start in half an hour or so for the other side of the river. It threatens rain again, so that I do not believe I can make the entire tour - probably only on Smith and Sumner; do the rest to-morrow. Besides, I do not care to ride too far to-day, as I have not been on horseback before since the day of the battle. I *must* be careful, for it would be utter destruction to this army were I to be disabled so as not to be able to take command.

Burnside left yesterday; thinks there is a great deal of Union feeling in North Carolina, and that our gaining possession of Richmond will at once bring North Carolina back into the Union. . . . I half-doubt whether there is much Union feeling south of North Carolina. . . . McCall's division has commenced arriving; some of them reached the White House last night. This relieves me very much.

June 12, 8 A.M., *New bridge* - . . . Am about to break up this camp and move over the Chickahominy to Dr. Trent's house; to the vicinity, at least, for I abominate houses when on the field. In addition have to take a farewell ride some seven or eight miles up this side of the river to look again at the ground and give the last instructions to Porter and Franklin for their guidance on this side of the river. I took quite a ride yesterday, the first since the battle, and got through with it nicely. I am about as nearly well now as I expect to be in this climate; bright and strong enough to fight a much better battle than any yet. I had a wonderful telegram from the Secretary of War last night; he declares that he is and ever has been my best friend!

June 14, *camp at Dr. Trent's Saturday* A.M.. - . . . . Your letters reached me yesterday morning just as I was starting out on a hot ride around the lines. Did not return until late, and then they got up, a stampede on the other side of the Chickahominy which kept me busy until bed-time. Some of the enemy's cavalry got in to the railroad, cut the telegraph-wires, and burned some wagons. I do not know particulars yet, but the cavalry and some infantry are out after them, and will, I hope, repay secesh for his impudence. As it is, the telegraph is broken and may not be re-established for several hours. . . . It is terribly hot, so much so that one can hardly exist. I was up before six this morning, and even then found it overpowering; the sun bakes down. I have the best possible place for a camp, right on the summit of a high hill, under the shade of a couple of large walnut-trees, but the trouble this morning is that no air whatever is stirring. Am quite well now; took a long ride in the hot sun yesterday and did not feel it very much; am not quite strong yet, and have to be a little careful. . . . Yesterday morning secesh commenced a very warm fire of artillery quite early, but killed only one man. By and by, however, Smith got some of his sharpshooters near their guns, drove off the gunners and kept them off all day, so that there was no more firing. There has been none to-day. I learn that the enemy moved away their guns during the night; this is probably true. A couple of days more of this weather will dry the roads and fields so as to render them practicable and enable me to try it again. I am heartily tired of inactivity, and shall be only too glad to settle this matter, have the battle, and get through with our work. . . . Senator Rice was here this morning. . . .

June 15, 10.15 P.M., *Camp Lincoln.* - . . . We have had several skirmishes. The rebels have attacked our pickets on several points, but were everywhere beaten back with the loss of several killed and a respectable number of prisoners. . . .

The worst interruption of all was a "party" of ladies and gentlemen that - had no more sense than to insist upon coming up here, Senator - and a lot of others. All of whom

I was really glad to see, although this was no place for them. I am sorry to say that when I heard of their arrival I "swore" a little internally, and sent Russell flying out of my tent, declaring that I would not see any of them. But soon afterwards Senator - came here, and he was so kind and friendly that I was at once mollified. I talked with him some time, and he went back to Van Vliet's tent. I then gave to Averill my orders for a surprise-party to-morrow, to repay secesh for his raid of day before yesterday. Then went over to call on Mrs. —. There I was in for it. I was presented to all the ladies, listened to Mrs. —'s version of her trip to Richmond, and very rapidly beat a retreat, giving business as an excuse. Charles got up a lunch for the party, a rainstorm coming on in the meanwhile. When they were nearly through I took Averill over and talked with them for a while. Then they adjourned to my tent. The two dear old mesdames were just as good as they could be; can I say more? When they left they asked me to give them sprigs from the bower in front of my tent, so I send you one, too. . . . I do not think our rain of to-day will do much harm, The chances now are that I will make the first advance on Tuesday or Wednesday. By that time I think the ground will be fit for the movements of artillery and that all our bridges will be completed. I think the rebels will make a desperate fight, but I feel sure that we will gain our point. Look on the maps I sent you a day or two ago, and find "Old Tavern," on the road from New bridge to Richmond; it is in that vicinity that the next battle will be fought. I think that they see it in that light, and that they are fully prepared to make a desperate resistance. I shall make the first battle mainly an artillery combat. As soon as I gain possession of the "Old Tavern" I will push them in upon Richmond and behind their works; then I will bring up my heavy guns, shell the city, and carry it by assault. I speak very confidently, but if you could see the faces of the troops as I ride among them you would share my confidence. They will do anything I tell them to do. I could not help laughing when, on the day of the last battle, I was riding along in front, a man jumped out in an interval of the cheering and addressed me quite familiarly, saying: "Halloo, George! how are you? You are the only one of the whole crowd of generals that is worth a—."

I won't fill up the last word, but the whole command shouted, "That's so!" . . I think there is scarcely a man in this whole army who would not give his life for me, and willingly do whatever I ask. I have tried them more than once, and whenever I am near they never fail me. The next battle will doubtless be a desperate one, but I think that I can so use our artillery as to make the loss of life on our side comparatively small. . . .

June 17, 4 P.M. - The weather yesterday and to-day has been splendid. It is clear and bright, but a delightfully cool breeze has been blowing constantly. The roads and fields are drying beautifully. The river is falling rapidly; our bridges are nearly finished, and we shall soon be on the move.

Camp at Trent's house, June 21, 1862, 10 A.M. - . . We have had good weather for the last few days, and have been improving it as best we could. Both parties are active, but the nature of the country is such as to make our progress difficult in the extreme. I hope to knock secesh out of Old Tavern and its vicinity within a couple of days; shall try it, at all events. . . . I see the Abolitionists have got a new dodge in my behalf-the White House business! In the first place, I never saw Col. Lee in my life, and, of course, never made any arrangement with him. The house was guarded simply from motives of respect for the memory of Washington, which I thought would be appreciated by every honest person in the country. The adjacent property has been freely used for all necessary purposes. The house has never been needed for a hospital, and would not accommodate over thirty or forty persons anyhow. The "spring" alluded to is one of a great many. There are plenty there, and this one is prohibited only because access to it brings people too near the house. I was not even sure that it was guarded, and do not even now know whether it is anything more than the guard placed over all springs near camps to prevent them from being misused by the men. So you have the truth of the White House story, all of which was in the possession of the secretary some ten days ago. I yesterday sent Tripler down to investigate the whole matter, and when I receive his report will nail the lie to the counter, - wrote a letter to the secretary, in which he repeats the spring story as of his own knowledge; that is, he asserts it as a fact! One thing is certain: I will some day or other repay some of these people with interest, and make them feel ashamed of themselves, if there is such a thing in their composition, which I rather doubt. I can't tell you how sick I am of this kind of life. I suppose it is the "cross" that it is my lot to bear, and that I should not repine. I know it is wrong, and I do my best to bear everything contentedly; but sometimes the old, impatient spirit will break out and I lose my temper. But I will keep on trying to do my best. . . .

June 22, *Sunday,* 3 P.M. - . . . By an arrival from Washington to-day I learn that Stanton and Chase have fallen out; that McDowell has deserted his friend C. and taken to S.! Alas! poor country that should have such rulers. I tremble for my country when I think of these things; but still can trust that God in His infinite wisdom will not punish us as we deserve, but will in His own good time bring order out of chaos and restore peace to this unhappy country. His will be done, whatever it may be! I am as anxious as any human being can be to finish this war. Yet when I see such insane folly behind me I feel that the final salvation of the country demands the utmost prudence on my part, and that I must not run the slightest risk of disaster, for if anything happened to this army our cause would be lost. I got up some heavy guns to-day, and hope to give secesh a preliminary pounding to-morrow and to make one good step next day. The rascals are very strong, and outnumber me very considerably; they are well entrenched also, and have all the advantages of position, so I must be prudent; but I will yet succeed, notwithstanding all they do and leave undone in Washington to prevent it. I would not have on my conscience what those men have for all the world. I am sorry that I shall lose the dear old Prince de Joinville in a few days; he is obliged to return to Europe. Gen. Prim has sent me his photograph. . . .

It is quite hot this afternoon. . . . It is almost time for our evening skirmish, Secesh has been very quiet to-day; scarcely fired a shot. I am very glad of it, as it has enabled me to give my men a good, quiet rest for Sunday.

June 23, 3 P.M. - I am delighted that you are so much pleased at Orange. It must be a lovely place from your description. Will the doctor invite me to pay you a visit there, do you think? How do you occupy yourself? Or are you contented just to rest and be quiet? That is my idea of happiness now - rest with you and the baby. We have had rather an exciting day of it. The enemy has been making some rather mysterious movements, and I have taken advantage of them to push forward our pickets considerably on the left. I don't yet know exactly what it means, but so far it has been of advantage to us, and you may be sure that I won't be caught in any trap. We have had a sharp thunder-shower this afternoon, and it will be of benefit by cooling and clearing the air. There has not been rain enough to do any harm yet.

10.30 P.M. - . . . You may be sure that no man in this army is so anxious as its general to finish the campaign. Every poor fellow that is killed or wounded almost haunts me! My only consolation is that I have honestly done my best to save as many lives as possible, and that many others might have done less towards it.

I have had a rather anxious day, the movements of the enemy being mysterious; but I have gained something, and am ready for any eventuality, I think. I have a kind of presentiment that to-morrow will bring forth *something-what* I do not know. We will see when the time arrives. I expect to be able to take a decisive step in advance day after to-morrow, and, if I succeed, will gain a couple of miles towards Richmond. It now looks to me as if the operations would resolve themselves into a series of partial attacks rather than a general battle.

24th, 10 A.M. - I was interrupted just here by some stampede telegrams that kept me up until 1.30 or 2 this morning. In the meantime a terrible storm came up and blew this unhappy sheet into the mud and rain. I send it as it is, however, as a slight specimen of the "sacred soil," also because I am about starting out on a ride, from which I am not likely to return before the mail leaves camp. Nothing of interest this morning; all quiet; weather cloudy, and may rain to-day again.

Telegram - *June* 26, 1862. - . . . Did not write yesterday; was on the battle-field all day. Have been up and in the saddle all night, and do not expect to be able to write more than a line to-day. Will probably be up all night again. . . . Our affair yesterday perfectly successful.

CHAPTER XXV.

Beginning of the Seven Days - Mcdowell coming, but not yet - Mc-Clellan resolves on flank movement to the James river - Preparations - Battle of Gaines's Mill - The movement goes on - McClellan charges Stanton with intent to sacrifice the army.

ON the 26th, the day upon which I had decided as the time for our final advance, the enemy attacked our right in strong force, and turned my attention to the protection of our communications and depots of supply.

The event was a bitter confirmation of the military judgment which had been reiterated to my superiors from the inception and through the progress of the Peninsular campaign.

I notified the Secretary of War in the following despatch:

12 M. - I have just heard that our advanced cavalry pickets on the left bank of Chickahominy are being driven in. It is probably Jackson's advanced guard. If this be true you may not hear from me for some days, as my communications will probably be cut off. The case is perhaps a difficult one, but I shall resort to desperate measures, and will do my best to out-manœuvre, outwit, and outfight the enemy. Do not believe reports of disaster, and do not be discouraged if you learn that my communications are cut off, and even Yorktown in possession of the enemy. Hope for the best, and I will not deceive the hopes you formerly placed in me.

On the same day I received the following despatches from the Secretary of War:

"6 P.M. - Arrangements are being made as rapidly as possible to send you five thousand (5,000) men as fast as they can be brought from Manassas to Alexandria and embarked, which can be done sooner than to wait for transportation at Fredericksburg. They will be followed by more, if needed. McDowell, Banks, and Fremont's force will be consolidated as the Army of Virginia, and will operate promptly in your aid by land. Nothing will be spared to sustain you, and I have undoubting faith in your success. Keep me advised fully of your condition."

"11.20 P.M. - Your telegram of 6.15 has just been received.
410

The circumstances that have hitherto rendered it impossible for the government to send you any more reinforcements than has been done, have been so distinctly stated to you by the President that it is needless for me to repeat them.

"Every effort has been made by the President and myself to strengthen you. King's division has reached Falmouth; Shields's division and Ricketts's division are at Manassas. The President designs to send a part of that force to aid you as speedily as it can be done."

The following was sent at 2.30 P.M.:

Your despatch and that of the President received. Jackson is driving in my pickets, etc., on the other side of the Chickahominy. It is impossible to tell where reinforcements ought to go, as I am yet unable to predict result of approaching battle. It will probably be better that they should go to Fort Monroe, and thence according to state of affairs when they arrive.

It is not probable that I can maintain telegraphic communication more than an hour or two longer.

But 5,000 of the reinforcements spoken of in these communications came to the Army of the Potomac, and these reached us at Harrison's Bar after the Seven Days.

In anticipation of a speedy advance on Richmond, to provide for the contingency of our communications with the depot at the White House being severed by the enemy, and at the same time to be prepared for a change of the base of our operations to James river, if circumstances should render it advisable, I had made arrangements more than a week previous (on the 18th) to have transports with supplies of provisions and forage, under a convoy of gunboats, sent up James river. They reached Harrison's Landing in time to be available for the army on its arrival at that point. Events soon proved this change of base to be, though most hazardous and difficult, the only prudent course.

Early on the 25th Gen. Porter was instructed to send out reconnoitring parties towards Hanover Court-House to discover the position and force of the enemy, and to destroy the bridges on the Tolopotamy as far as possible.

Up to the 26th of June the operations against Richmond had been conducted along the roads leading to it from the east and northeast. The superiority of the James river route, as a line of attack and supply, is too obvious to need exposition.

31

My own opinion on that subject had been early given. The dissipation of all hope of the co-operation by land of Gen. McDowell's forces, deemed to be occupied in the defence of Washington, their inability to hold or defeat Jackson, disclosed an opportunity to the enemy, and a new danger to my right, and to the long line of supplies from the White House to the Chickahominy, and forced an immediate change of base across the Peninsula. To that end, from the evening of the 26th, every energy of the army was bent.

Such a change of base, in the presence of a powerful enemy, is one of the most difficult undertakings in war, but I was confident in the valor and discipline of my brave army, and knew that it could be trusted equally to retreat or advance, and to fight the series of battles now inevitable, whether retreating from victories or marching through defeats; and, in short, I had no doubt whatever of its ability, even against superior numbers, to fight its way through to the James, and get a position whence a successful advance upon Richmond would be again possible. Their superb conduct through the next seven days justified my faith.

On the same day (26th) Gen. Van Vliet, chief-quartermaster of the Army of the Potomac, by my orders telegraphed to Col. Ingalls, quartermaster at the White House, as follows:

"Run the cars to the last moment, and load them with provisions and ammunition. Load every wagon you have with subsistence, and send them to Savage's Station by way of Bottom's bridge. If you are obliged to abandon White House burn everything that you cannot get off. You must throw all our supplies up the James river as soon as possible, and accompany them yourself with all your force. It will be of vast importance to establish our depots on James river without delay, if we abandon White House. I will keep you advised of every movement so long as the wires work; after that you must exercise your own judgment."

All these commands were obeyed. On the 26th orders were sent to all the corps commanders on the right bank of the Chickahominy to be prepared to send as many troops as they could spare on the following day to the left bank of the river. Gen. Franklin received instructions to hold Gen. Slocum's division in readiness, by daybreak of the 27th, and, if heavy firing

GEN. MORELL.   COL. COLBURN.   GEN. MCCLELLAN.   COL. SWEITZER.   PRINCE   COMTE
                                                                   DE JOINVILLE. DE PARIS.

GEN. MCCLELLAN AT GEN. MORELL'S HEADQUARTERS, MINOR'S HILL, VA.

should at that time be heard in the direction of Gen. Porter, to move at once to his assistance without further orders.

At noon on the 26th the approach of the enemy, who had crossed above Meadow bridge, was discovered by the advanced pickets at that point, and at 12.30 P.M. they were attacked and driven in. All the pickets were now called in, and the regiment and battery at Mechanicsville withdrawn.

Meade's brigade was ordered up as a reserve in rear of the line, and shortly after Martindale's and Griffin's brigades, of Morell's division, were moved forward and deployed on the right of McCall's division, towards Shady Grove church, to cover that flank. Neither of these three brigades, however, were warmly engaged, though two of Griffin's regiments relieved a portion of Reynolds's line just at the close of the action.

The position of our troops was a strong one, extending along the left bank of Beaver Dam creek, the left resting on the Chickahominy and the right in thick woods beyond the upper road from Mechanicsville to Cold Harbor The lower or river road crossed the creek at Ellison's Mill. Seymour's brigade held the left of the line from the Chickahominy to beyond the will, partly in woods and partly in clear ground, and Reynolds's the right, principally in the woods and covering the upper road. The artillery occupied positions commanding the roads and the open ground across the creek.

Timber had been felled, rifle-pits dug, and the position generally prepared with a care that greatly contributed to the success of the day. The passage of the creek was difficult along the whole front, and impracticable for artillery, except by the two roads where the main efforts of the enemy were directed.

At three P.M. he formed his line of battle, rapidly advanced his skirmishers, and soon attacked our whole line, making at the same time a determined attempt to force the passage of the upper road, which was successfully resisted by Gen. Reynolds. After a severe struggle he was forced to retire with very heavy loss.

A rapid artillery-fire, with desultory skirmishing, was maintained along the whole front, while the enemy massed his troops for another effort at the lower road about two hours later, which was likewise repulsed by Gen. Seymour with heavy slaughter.

The firing ceased and the enemy retired about nine P.M., the action having lasted six hours, with entire success to our arms. But few, if any, of Jackson's troops were engaged on this day. The portion of the enemy encountered were chiefly from the troops on the right bank of the river, who crossed near Meadow bridge and at Mechanicsville.

The information in my possession soon after the close of this action convinced me that Jackson was really approaching in large force. The position on Beaver Dam creek, although so successfully defended, had its right flank too much in the air and was too far from the main army to make it available to retain it longer. I therefore determined to send the heavy guns at Hogan's and Gaines's houses over the Chickahominy during the night, with as many of the wagons of the 5th corps as possible, and to withdraw the corps itself to a position stretching around the bridges, where its flanks would be reasonably secure and it would be within supporting distance of the main army. Gen. Porter carried out my orders to that effect.

It was not advisable at that time, even had it been practicable, to withdraw the 5th corps to the right bank of the Chickahominy. Such a movement would have exposed the rear of the army, placed as between two fires, and enabled Jackson's fresh troops to interrupt the movement to James river by crossing the Chickahominy in the vicinity of Jones's bridge before we could reach Malvern Hill with our trains. I determined then to resist Jackson with the 5th corps, reinforced by all our disposable troops in the new position near the bridge-heads, in order to cover the withdrawal of the trains and heavy guns, and to give time for the arrangements to secure the adoption of the James river as our line of supplies in lieu of the Pamunkey.

The greater part of the heavy guns and wagons having been removed to the right bank of the Chickahominy, the delicate operation of withdrawing the troops from Beaver Dam creek was commenced shortly before daylight and successfully executed.

Meade's and Griffin's brigades were the first to leave the ground. Seymour's brigade covered the rear, with the horse-batteries of Capts. Robertson and Tidball; but the withdrawal was so skilful and gradual, and the repulse of the preceding day so complete, that, although the enemy followed the retreat closely and some skirmishing occurred, he did not appear in front of the new line in force till about noon of the 27th, when we were prepared to receive him.

About this time Gen. Porter, believing that Gen. Stoneman would be cut off from him, sent him orders to fall back on the White House and afterwards rejoin the army as best he could.

On the morning of the 27th of June, during the withdrawal of his troops from Mechanicsville to the selected position already mentioned, Gen. Porter telegraphed as follows:

"I hope to do without aid, though I request that Franklin or some other command be held ready to reinforce me. The enemy are so close that I expect to be hard pressed in front. I hope to have a portion in position to cover the retreat. This is a delicate movement, but, relying on the good qualities of the commanders of divisions and brigades, I expect to get back and hold the new line."

This shows how closely Porter's retreat was followed.

Notwithstanding all the efforts used during the entire night to remove the heavy guns and wagons, some of the siege-guns were still in position at Gaines's house after sunrise, and were finally hauled off by hand. The new position of the 5th corps was about an arc of a circle, covering the approaches to the bridges which connected our right wing with the troops on the opposite side of the river.

Morell's division held the left of the line in a strip of woods on the left bank of the Gaines's Mill stream, resting its left flank on the descent to the Chickahominy, which was swept by our artillery on both sides of the river, and extending into open ground on the right towards New Cold Harbor. In this line Gen. Butterfield's brigade held the extreme left; Gen. Martindale's joined his right, and Gen. Griffin, still further to the right, joined the left of Gen. Sykes's division, which, partly in woods and partly in open ground, extended in rear of Cold Harbor.

Each brigade had in reserve two of its own regiments; McCall's division, having been engaged on the day before, was formed in a second line in rear of the first; Meade's brigade on the left, near the Chickahominy; Reynolds's brigade on the right, covering the approaches from Cold Harbor and Despatch Station to Sumner's bridge, and Seymour's in reserve to the second line still further in rear. Gen. P. St. G. Cooke, with five companies of the 5th Regular Cavalry, two squadrons of the 1st Regular Cavalry, and three squadrons of the 1st Penn. Cavalry (lancers), were posted behind a hill in rear of the position, and near the Chickahominy, to aid in watching the left flank and defending the slope to the river.

The troops were all in position by noon, with the artillery on the commanding ground, and in the intervals between the divisions and brigades. Besides the division batteries there were Robertson's and Tidball's horse-batteries from the artillery reserve; the latter posted on the right of Sykes's division, and the former on the extreme left of the line, in the valley of the Chickahominy.

Shortly after noon the enemy was discovered approaching in force, and it soon became evident that the entire position was to be attacked. His skirmishers advanced rapidly, and soon the fire became heavy along our whole front. At two P.M. Gen. Porter asked for reinforcements. Slocum's division of the 6th corps was ordered to cross to the left bank of the river by Alexander's bridge, and proceed to his support.

Gen. Porter's first call for reinforcements, through Gen. Barnard, did not reach me, nor his demand for more axes through the same officer. By three P.M. the engagement had become so severe, and the enemy were so greatly superior in numbers, that the entire second line and reserves had been moved forward to sustain the first line against repeated and desperate assaults along the whole front.

At 3.30 Slocum's division reached the field, and was immediately brought into action at the weak points of our line.

On the left the contest was for the strip of woods running almost at right angles to the Chickahominy, in front of Adams's house, or between that and Gaines's house. The enemy several times charged up to this wood, but were each time driven back with heavy loss. The regulars of Sykes's division, on the right, also repulsed several strong attacks.

But our own loss under the tremendous fire of such greatly superior numbers was very severe, and the troops, most of whom had been under arms more than two days, were rapidly becoming exhausted by the masses of fresh men constantly brought against them.

When Gen. Slocum's division arrived on the ground it increased Gen. Porter's force to some 35,000, who were probably contending against about 70,000 of the enemy. The line was severely pressed in several points; and as its being pierced at any one would have been fatal, it was unavoidable for Gen. Porter, who was required to hold his position until night, to divide Slocum's division, and send parts of it, even single regiments, to the points most threatened.

About five P.M., Gen. Porter having reported his position as critical, French's and Meagher's brigades, of Richardson's division (3d corps), were ordered to cross to his support. The enemy attacked again in great force at six P.M., but failed to break our lines, though our loss was very heavy.

About seven P.M. they threw fresh troops against Gen. Porter with still greater fury, and finally gained the woods held by our left. This reverse, aided by the confusion that followed an unsuccessful charge by five companies of the 5th Cavalry, and followed, as it was, by more determined assaults on the remainder of our lines, now outflanked, caused a general retreat from our position to the hill in rear overlooking the bridge.

French's and Meagher's brigades now appeared, driving before them the stragglers who were thronging towards the bridge.

These brigades advanced boldly to the front, and by their example, as well as by the steadiness of their bearing, reanimated our own troops and warned the enemy that reinforcements had arrived. It was now dusk. The enemy, already repulsed several times with terrible slaughter, and hearing the shouts of the fresh troops, failed to follow up their advantage. This gave an opportunity to rally our men behind the brigades of Gens. French and Meagher, and they again advanced up the hill, ready to repulse another attack. During the night our thin and exhausted regiments mere all withdrawn in safety, and by the following morning all had reached the other side of the stream. The regular infantry formed the rear-guard, and about six o'clock on the morning of the 28th crossed the river, destroying the bridge behind them.

Although we were finally forced from our first line after the enemy had been repeatedly driven back, yet the objects sought for had been obtained. The enemy was held at bay. Our siege-guns and material were saved, and the right wing had now joined the main body of the army.

The number of guns captured by the enemy at this battle was twenty-two, three of which were lost by being run off the bridge during the final withdrawal.

Great credit is due for the efficiency and bravery with which this important arm of the service (the artillery) was fought, and it was not until the last successful charge of the enemy that the cannoneers were driven from their pieces or struck down and the guns captured. Dietrich's, Kauerhem's, and Grimm's batteries took position during the engagement in the front of Gen. Smith's line on the right bank of the stream, and, with a battery of siege-guns served by the 1st Conn, Artillery, helped to drive back the enemy in front of Gen. Porter.

So threatening were the movements of the enemy on both banks of the Chickahominy that it was impossible to decide until the afternoon where the real attack would be made. Large forces of infantry were seen during the day near the Old Tavern, on Franklin's right, and threatening demonstrations were frequently made along the entire line on this side of the river, which rendered it necessary to hold a considerable force in position to meet them.

On the 26th a circular had been sent to the corps commanders on the right bank of the river, asking them how many of their troops could be spared to reinforce Gen. Porter after retaining sufficient to hold their positions for twenty-four hours.

Gen. Heintzelman replied:

"I think I can hold the entrenchments with four brigades for twenty-four hours. That would leave two brigades disposable for service on the other side of the river, but the men are so tired and worn out that I fear they would not be in a condition to fight after making a march of any distance. . . ."

Telegrams from Gen. Heintzelman on the 25th and 26th had indicated that the enemy was in large force in front of Gens. Hooker and Kearny, and on the Charles City road (Longstreet, Hill, and Huger), and Gen. Heintzelman expressed the opinion on the night of the 25th that he could not hold his advanced position without reinforcements.

Gen. Keyes telegraphed:
32

"As to how many men will be able to hold this position for twenty-four hours, I must answer, All I have, if the enemy is as strong as ever in front, it having at all times appeared to me that our forces on this flank are small enough."

On the morning of the 27th the following despatch was sent to Gen. Sumner: "Gen. Smith just reports that 'six or eight regiments have moved down to the woods in front of Gen. Sumner.' " At eleven o'clock A.M. Gen. Sumner telegraphed: "The enemy threatens an attack on my right near Smith." At 12.30 P.M. he telegraphed: "Sharp shelling on both sides." At 2.45 P.M. : "Sharp musketry-firing in front of Burns. We are replying with artillery and infantry. The man on the look-out reports some troops drawn up in line of battle about opposite my right and Smith's left; the number cannot be made out."

In accordance with orders given on the night of the 26th, Gen. Slocum's division commenced crossing the river, to support Gen. Porter, soon after daybreak on the morning of the 27th; but, as the firing in front of Gen. Porter ceased, the movement was suspended. At two P.M. Gen. Porter called for reinforcements. I ordered them at once, and at 3.25 P.M. sent him the following:

"Slocum is now crossing Alexander's bridge with his whole command. Enemy has commenced an infantry attack on Smith's left. I have ordered down Sumner's and Heintzelman's reserves, and you can count on the whole of Slocum's. Go on as you have begun."

During the day the following despatches were received, which will show the condition of affairs on the right bank of the Chickahominy:

Gen. Franklin telegraphed: "Gen. Smith thinks the enemy are massing heavy columns in the clearings to the right of James Garnett's house and on the other side of the river opposite it. Three regiments are reported to be moving from Sumner's to Smith's front. The arrangements are very good made by Smith."

Afterwards he telegraphed: "The enemy has begun an attack on Smith's left with infantry. I know no details." Afterwards the following: "The enemy has opened on Smith from a battery of three pieces to the right of the White House. Our shells are bursting well, and Smith thinks Sumner will soon have a cross-fire upon them that will silence them."

Afterwards (at 5.50 P.M.) the following was sent to Gen. Keyes: "Please send one brigade of Couch's division to these headquarters without a moment's delay. A staff officer will be here to direct the brigade where to go."

Subsequently the following was sent to Gens. Sumner and Franklin: "Is there any sign of the enemy being in force in your front? Can you spare any more force to be sent to Gen. Porter? Answer at once."

At 5.15 P.M. the following was received from Gen. Franklin: "I do not think it prudent to take any more troops from here at present."

Gen. Sumner replied: "If the general desires to trust the defence of my position to my front line alone, I can send French with three regiments and Meagher, with his brigade, to the right; everything is so uncertain that I think it would be hazardous to do it."

These two brigades were sent to reinforce Gen. Porter, as has been observed.

At 5.25 P.M. I sent the following to Gen. Franklin:

Porter is hard pressed; it is not a question of prudence, but of possibilities. Can you possibly maintain your position until dark with two brigades? I have ordered eight regiments of Sumner's to support Porter; one brigade of Couch's to this place.

Heintzelman's reserve to go in rear of Sumner. If possible, send a brigade to support Porter. It should follow the regiments ordered from Sumner.

At 7.35 P.M. the following was sent to Gen. Sumner: "If it is possible, send another brigade to reinforce Gen. Smith; it is said three heavy columns of infantry are moving on him."

From the foregoing despatches it will be seen that all disposable troops were sent from the right bank of the river to reinforce Gen. Porter, and that the corps commanders were left with smaller forces to hold their positions than they deemed adequate. To have done more, even though Porter's reverse had been pre-

vented, would have had the still more disastrous result of imper-
illing the whole movement across the Peninsula.

The operations of this day proved the numerical superiority
of the enemy, and made it evident that while he had a large army
on the left bank of the Chickahominy, which had already turned
our right and was in position to intercept the communications
with our depot at the White House, he was also in large force
between our army and Richmond. I therefore effected a junction
of our forces.

This might probably have been executed on either side of the
Chickahominy, and if the concentration had been effected on the
left bank it is possible we might, with our entire force, have defeated the enemy there; but at that time they held the roads leading to the White House, so that it would have been impossible to
have sent forward supply-trains in advance of the army in that
direction, and the guarding of those trains would have seriously
embarrassed our operations in the battle we would have been
compelled to fight, if concentrated on that bank of the river.
Moreover, we would at once have been followed by the enemy's
forces upon the Richmond side of the river operating upon our
rear; and if, in the chances of war, we had been ourselves defeated in the effort, we would have been forced to fall back to
the White House, and probably to Fort Monroe; and, as both
our flanks and rear would then have been entirely exposed, our
entire supply-train, if not the greater part of the army itself,
might have been lost.

The movements of the enemy showed that they expected
this, and, as they themselves acknowledged, they were prepared
to cut off our retreat in that direction.

I therefore concentrated all our forces on the right bank of
the river.

During the night of the 26th and morning of the 27th all
our wagons, heavy guns, etc., were gathered there.

It may be asked why, after the concentration of our forces
on the right bank of the Chickahominy, with a large part of the
enemy drawn away from Richmond upon the opposite side, I did
not, instead of striking for James river, fifteen miles below that
place, at once march directly on Richmond.

It will be remembered that at this juncture the enemy was
on our rear, and there was every reason to believe that he would

sever our communications with the supply-depot at the White House.

We had on hand but a limited amount of rations, and if we had advanced directly on Richmond it would have required considerable time to carry the strong works around that place, during which our men would have been destitute of food; and even if Richmond had fallen before our arms the enemy could still have occupied our supply communications between that place and the gunboats, and turned the disaster into victory. If, on the other hand, the enemy had concentrated all his forces at Richmond during the progress of our attack, and we had been defeated, we must in all probability have lost our trains before reaching the flotilla.

The battles which continued day after day in the progress of our flank movement to the James, with the exception of the one at Gaines's Mill, were successes to our arms, and the closing engagement at Malvern Hill was the most decisive of all.

On the evening of the 27th of June I assembled the corps commanders at my headquarters, and informed them of the plan, its reasons, and my choice of route and method of execution.

Gen. Keyes was directed to move his corps, with its artillery and baggage, across the White Oak Swamp bridge, and to seize strong positions on the opposite side of the swamp, to cover the passage of the other troops and trains.

This order was executed on the 28th by noon. Before daybreak on the 28th I went to Savage's Station, and remained there during the day and night, directing the withdrawal of the trains and supplies of the army.

Orders were given to the different commanders to load their wagons with ammunition and provisions, and the necessary baggage of the officers and men, and to destroy all property which could not be transported with the army. Orders were also given to leave with those of the sick and wounded who could not be transported a proper complement of surgeons and attendants, with a bountiful supply of rations and medical stores.

The large herd of 2,500 beef cattle was, by the chief commissary, Col. Clark, transferred to the James river without loss.

On the morning of the 28th, while Gen. Franklin was withdrawing his command from Golding's farm, the enemy opened upon Gen. Smith's division from Garnett's Hill, from the valley

above, and from Gaines's Hill on the opposite side of the Chickahominy, and shortly afterwards two Georgia regiments attempted
to carry the works about to be evacuated, but this attack was
repulsed by the 23d N.Y., and the 49th Penn. Volunteers on
picket, and a section of Mott's battery.

Porter's corps was moved across White Oak Swamp during
the day and night, and took up positions covering the roads leading from Richmond towards White Oak Swamp and Long bridge.
McCall's division was ordered, on the night of the 28th, to move
across the swamp and take a proper position to assist in covering
the remaining troops and trains.

During the same night the corps of Sumner and Heintzelman and the division of Smith were ordered to an interior line,
the left resting on Keyes's old entrenchments and curving to
the right so as to cover Savage's Station.

General Slocum's division, of Franklin's corps, was ordered to
Savage's Station in reserve.

They were ordered to hold this position until dark of the 29th,
in order to cover the withdrawal of the trains, and then to fall
back across the swamp and unite with the remainder of the army.

On the 28th I sent the following to the Secretary of War:

HEADQUARTERS, ARMY OF THE POTOMAC,
SAVAGE'S STATION, June 28, 1862, 12.20 A.M.
Hon. E. M. Stanton, Secretary of War:
I now know the full history of the day. On this side of the
river (the right bank) we repulsed several strong attacks. On the
left bank our men did all that men could do, all that soldiers
could accomplish, but they were overwhelmed by vastly superior
numbers, even after I brought my last reserves into action. The
loss on both sides is terrible. I believe it will prove to be the
most desperate battle of the war. The sad remnants of my men
behave as men. Those battalions who fought most bravely and
suffered most are still in the best order. My regulars were
superb, and I count upon what are left to turn another battle in
company with their gallant comrades of the volunteers. Had I
twenty thousand (20,000), or even ten thousand (10,000), fresh
troops to use to-morrow, I could take Richmond; but I have
not a man in reserve, and shall be glad to cover my retreat and
save the material and *personnel* of the army.

If we have lost the day we have yet preserved our honor, and no one need blush for the Army of the Potomac. I have lost this battle because my force was too small.

I again repeat that I am not responsible for this, and I say it with the earnestness of a general who feels in his heart the loss of every brave man who has been needlessly sacrificed to-day. I still hope to retrieve our fortunes; but to do this the government must view the matter in the same earnest light that I do. You must send me very large reinforcements, and send them at once. I shall draw back to this side of the Chickahominy, and think I can withdraw all our material. Please understand that in this battle we have lost nothing but men, and those the best we have.

In addition to what I have already said, I only wish to say to the President that I think he is wrong in regarding me as ungenerous when I said that my force was too weak. I merely intimated a truth which to-day has been too plainly proved. If, at this instant, I could dispose of ten thousand (10,000) fresh men, I could gain the victory to-morrow.

I know that a few thousand more men would have changed this battle from a defeat to a victory. As it is, the government must not and cannot hold me responsible for the result.

I feel too earnestly to-night. I have seen too many dead and wounded comrades to feel otherwise than that the government has not sustained this army. If you do not do so now the game is lost.

If I save this army now, I tell you plainly that I owe no thanks to you or to any other persons in Washington.

You have done your best to sacrifice this army.

G. B. McCLELLAN.

CHAPTER XXVI.

Continuation of the Seven Days' battles - Allen's field - Savage's Station - White Oak Swamp - Charles City cross-roads - Glendale - Malvern Hill - The army at Harrison's Landing.

THE headquarters camp at Savage's Station was broken up early on the morning of the 29th and moved across White Oak Swamp. As the essential part of this day's operation was the passage of the trains across the swamp, and their protection against attack from the direction of New Market and Richmond, as well as the immediate and secure establishment of our communications with the gunboats, I passed the day in examining the ground, directing the posting of troops, and securing the uninterrupted movement of the trains.

In the afternoon I instructed Gen. Keyes to move during the night to James river and occupy a defensive position near Malvern Hill, to secure our extreme left flank.

Gen. F. J. Porter was ordered to follow him and prolong the line towards the right. The trains were to be pushed on towards James river in rear of these corps, and placed under the protection of the gunboats as they arrived.

A sharp skirmish with the enemy's cavalry early this day on the Quaker road showed that his efforts were about to be directed towards impeding our progress to the river, and rendered my presence in that quarter necessary.

The difficulty was not at all with the movement of the troops, but with the immense trains, that were to be moved virtually by a single road and required the whole army for their protection. With the exception of the cavalry affair on the Quaker road, we were not troubled during this day south of the swamp, but there was severe fighting north of it.

Gen. Sumner vacated his works at Fair Oaks on June 29, at daylight, and marched his command to Orchard Station, halting at Allen's field, between Orchard and Savage's Stations.

The divisions of Richardson and Sedgwick were formed on

the right of the railroad, facing towards Richmond, Richardson holding the right, and Sedgwick joining the right of Heintzelman's corps. The first line of Richardson's division was held by Gen. French, Gen. Caldwell supporting in the second. A log building in front of Richardson's division was held by Col. Brooks with one regiment (53d Penn. Volunteers), with Hazzard's battery on an elevated piece of ground a little in rear of Col. Brooks's command.

At nine A.M. the enemy commenced a furious attack on the right of Gen. Sedgwick, but were repulsed. The left of Gen. Richardson was next attacked, the enemy attempting in vain to carry the position of Col. Brooks. Capt. Hazzard's battery, and Pettit's battery, which afterwards replaced it, were served with great effect, while the 53d Penn. kept up a steady fire on the advancing enemy, compelling them at last to retire in disorder. The enemy renewed the attack three times, but were as often repulsed.

Gen. Slocum arrived at Savage's Station at an early hour on the 29th, and was ordered to cross White Oak Swamp and relieve Gen. Keyes's corps. As soon as Gen. Keyes was thus relieved he moved towards James river, which he reached in safety, with all his artillery and baggage, early on the morning of the 30th, and took up a position below Turkey creek bridge.

During the morning Gen. Franklin heard that the enemy, after having repaired the bridges, was crossing the Chickahominy in large force and advancing towards Savage's Station. He communicated this information to Gen. Sumner, at Allen's farm, and moved Smith's division to Savage's Station. A little after noon Gen. Sumner united his forces with those of Gen. Franklin and assumed command.

I had ordered Gen. Heintzelman, with his corps, to hold the Williamsburg road until dark, at a point where were several field-works, and a skirt of timber between these works and the railroad.

Through a misunderstanding of his orders, and being convinced that the troops of Sumner and Franklin at Savage's Station were ample for the purpose in view, Heintzelman withdrew his troops during the afternoon, crossed the swamp at Brackett's ford, and reached the Charles City road with the rear of his column at ten P.M.

On reaching Savage's Station Sumner's and Franklin's commands were drawn up in line of battle in the large open field to the left of the railroad, the left resting on the edge of the woods and the right extending down to the railroad. Gen. Brooks, with his brigade, held the wood to the left of the field, where he did excellent service, receiving a wound, but retaining his command.

Gen. Hancock's brigade was thrown into the woods on the right and front. At four P.M. the enemy commenced his attack in large force by the Williamsburg road. It was gallantly met by Gen. Burns's brigade, supported and reinforced by two lines in reserve, and finally by the N. Y. 69th, Hazzard's and Pettit's batteries again doing good service. Osborn's and Bramhall's batteries also took part effectively in this action, which was continued with great obstinacy until between eight and nine P.M., when the enemy were driven from the field.

Immediately after the battle the orders were repeated for all the troops to fall back and cross White Oak Swamp, which was accomplished during the night in good order. By midnight all the troops were on the road to White Oak Swamp bridge, Gen. French, with his brigade, acting as rear-guard, and at five A.M. on the 30th all had crossed and the bridge was destroyed.

On the afternoon of the 29th I gave to the corps commanders their instructions for the operations of the following day. Porter's corps was to move forward to James river, and, with the corps of Gen. Keyes, to occupy a position at or near Turkey Bend, on a line perpendicular to the river, thus covering the Charles City road to Richmond, opening communication with the gunboats, and covering the passage of the supply-trains, which were pushed forward as rapidly as possible upon Haxall's plantation. The remaining corps were pressed onward, and posted so as to guard the approaches from Richmond, as well as the crossings of the White Oak Swamp over which the army had passed. Gen. Franklin was ordered to hold the passage of White Oak Swamp bridge, and cover the withdrawal of the trains from that point. His command consisted of his own corps, with Gen. Richardson's division and Gen. Naglee's brigade, placed under his orders for the occasion. Gen. Slocum's division was on the right of the Charles City road.

On the morning of the 30th I again gave to the corps commanders within reach instructions for posting their troops. I found that, notwithstanding all the efforts of my personal staff and other officers, the roads were blocked by wagons, and there was great difficulty in keeping the trains in motion.

The engineer officers whom I had sent forward on the 28th to reconnoitre the roads had neither returned nor sent me any reports or guides. Gens. Keyes and Porter had been delayed-one by losing the road, and the other by repairing an old road-and had not been able to send any information. We then knew of but one road for the movement of the troops and our immense trains.

It was therefore necessary to post the troops in advance of this road as well as our limited knowledge of the ground permitted, so as to cover the movement of the trains in the rear.

I then examined the whole line from the swamp to the left, giving final instructions for the posting of the troops and the obstruction of the roads towards Richmond, and all corps commanders were directed to hold their positions until the trains had passed, after which a more concentrated position was to be taken up near James river.

Our force was too small to occupy and hold the entire line from the White Oak Swamp to the river, exposed, as it was, to be taken in reverse by a movement across the lower part of the swamp, or across the Chickahominy below the swamp. Moreover, the troops were then greatly exhausted, and required rest in a more secure position.

I extended my examinations of the country as far as Haxall's, looking at all the approaches to Malvern, which position I perceived to be the key to our operations in this quarter, and was thus enabled to expedite very considerably the passage of the trains and to rectify the positions of the troops.

Everything being then quiet, I sent aids to the different corps commanders to inform them what I had done on the left, and to bring me information of the condition of affairs on the right. I returned from Malvern to Haxall's, and, having made arrangements for instant communication from Malvern by signals, went on board of Com. Rodgers's gunboat, lying near, to confer with him in reference to the condition of our supply-vessels and the state of things on the river. It was his opinion that it would be necessary for the army to fall back to a position below City

Point, as the channel there was so near the southern shore that it would not be possible to bring up the transports, should the enemy occupy it. Harrison's Landing was, in his opinion, the nearest suitable point. Upon the termination of this interview I returned to Malvern Hill, and remained there until shortly before daylight.

On the morning of the 30th Gen. Sumner was ordered to march with Sedgwick's division to Glendale ("Nelson's farm"). Gen. McCall's division (Pennsylvania reserves) was halted during the morning on the New Market road, just in advance of the point where the road turns off to Quaker church. This line was formed perpendicularly to the New Market road, with Meade's brigade on the right, Seymour's on the left, and Reynolds's brigade, commanded by Col. S. G. Simmons, of the 5th Penn., in reserve; Randall's regular battery on the right, Kern's and Cooper's batteries opposite the centre, and Dietrich's and Kauerhem's batteries of the artillery reserve on the left-all in front of the infantry line. The country in Gen. McCall's front was an open field, intersected towards the right by the New Market road and a small strip of timber parallel to it; the open front was about eight hundred yards, its depth about one thousand yards.

On the morning of the 30th Gen. Heintzelman ordered the bridge at Brackett's ford to be destroyed, and trees to be felled across that road and the Charles City road. Gen. Slocum's division was to extend to the Charles City road; Gen. Kearny's left to connect with Gen. Slocum's left; Gen. McCall's position was to the left of the Long bridge road, in connection with Gen. Kearny's left; Gen. Hooker was on the left of Gen. McCall. Between twelve and one o'clock the enemy opened a fierce cannonade upon the divisions of Smith and Richardson and Naglee's brigade at White Oak Swamp bridge. This artillery-fire was continued by the enemy through the day, and he crossed some infantry below our position. Richardson's division suffered severely. Captain Ayres directed our artillery with great effect. Capt. Hazzard's battery, after losing many cannoneers, and Capt. Hazzard being mortally wounded, was compelled to retire. It was replaced by Pettit's battery, which partially silenced the enemy's guns.

Gen. Franklin held his position until after dark, repeatedly driving back the enemy in their attempts to cross the White Oak Swamp.

At two o'clock in the day the enemy were reported advancing in force by the Charles City road, and at half-past two o'clock the attack was made down the road on Gen. Slocum's left, but was checked by his artillery. After this the enemy, in large force, comprising the divisions of Longstreet and A. P. Hill, attacked Gen. McCall, whose division, after severe fighting, was compelled to retire.

Gen. McCall, in his report of the battle, says:

"About half-past two my pickets were driven in by a strong advance, after some skirmishing, without loss on our part.

"At three o'clock the enemy sent forward a regiment on the left centre and another on the right centre to feel for a weak point. They were under cover of a shower of shells and boldly advanced, but were both driven back-on the left by the 12th regiment, and on the right by the 7th regiment.

"For nearly two hours the battle raged hotly here. . . . At last the enemy was compelled to retire before the well-directed musketry-fire of the reserves. The German batteries were driven to the rear, but I rode up and sent them back. It was, however, of little avail, and they were soon after abandoned by the cannoneers. . . .

"The batteries in front of the centre were boldly charged upon, but the enemy was speedily forced back. . . .

"Soon after this a most determined charge was made on Randall's battery by a full brigade, advancing in wedge-shape, without order, but in perfect recklessness. Somewhat similar charges had, I have stated, been previously made on Cooper's and Kern's batteries by single regiments, without success, they having recoiled before the storm of canister hurled against them. A like result was anticipated by Randall's battery, and the 4th regiment was requested not to fire until the battery had done with them.

"Its gallant commander did not doubt his ability to repel the attack,, and his guns did, indeed, mow down the advancing host; but still the gaps were closed, and the enemy came in upon a run to the very muzzles of his guns.

"It was a perfect torrent of men, and they were in his battery before the guns could be removed. Two guns that were, indeed, successfully limbered had their horses killed and wounded, and were overturned on the spot, and the enemy, dashing past, drove the greater part of the 4th regiment before them.

"The left company (B), nevertheless, stood its ground, with its captain, Fred. A. Conrad, as did likewise certain men of other companies. I had ridden into the regiment and endeavored to check them, but with only partial success. . . .

"There was no running. But my division, reduced by the previous battles to less than six thousand (6,000), had to contend with the divisions of Longstreet and A. P. Hill, considered two of the strongest and best among many of the Confederate army, numbering that day 18,000 or 20,000 men, and it was reluctantly compelled to give way before heavier force accumulated upon them. . . ."

Gen. Heintzelman states that about five o'clock P.M. Gen. McCall's division was attacked in large force, evidently the principal attack; that in less than an hour the division gave way, and adds:

"Gen. Hooker, being on his left, by moving to his right repulsed the rebels in the handsomest manner with great slaughter. Gen. Sumner, who was with Gen. Sedgwick in McCall's rear, also greatly aided with his artillery and infantry in driving back the enemy. They now renewed their attack with vigor on Gen. Kearny's left, and were again repulsed with heavy loss. . . .

"This attack commenced about four P.M., and was pushed by heavy masses with the utmost determination and vigor. Capt. Thompson's battery, directed with great precision, firing double charges, swept them back. The whole open space, two hundred paces wide, was filled with the enemy; each repulse brought fresh troops. The third attack was only repulsed by the rapid volleys and determined charge of the 63d Penn., Col. Hays, and half of the 37th N. Y. Volunteers."

Gen. McCall's troops soon began to emerge from the woods into the open field. Several batteries were in position and began to fire into the woods over the heads of our men in front. Capt. De Russy's battery was placed on the right of Gen. Sumner's artillery, with orders to shell the woods. Gen. Burns's brigade was then advanced to meet the enemy, and soon drove him back. Other troops began to return from the White Oak Swamp. Late in the day, at the call of Gen. Kearny, Gen. Taylor's 1st N. J. brigade, Slocum's division, was sent to occupy a portion of Gen. McCall's deserted position, a battery accompanying the brigade. They soon drove back the enemy, who shortly after gave up the attack, contenting themselves with keeping up a desultory firing till late at night. Between twelve and one o'clock at night Gen. Heintzelman commenced to withdraw his corps, and soon after daylight both of his divisions, with Gen. Slocum's division and a portion of Gen. Sumner's command, reached Malvern Hill. On the morning of the 30th Gen. Sumner, in obedience to orders, had moved promptly to Glendale, and upon a call from Gen. Franklin for reinforcements sent him two brigades, which returned in time to participate and render good service in the battle near Glendale. Gen. Sumner says of this battle:

"The battle of Glendale was the most severe action since the battle of Fair Oaks. About three o'clock P.M. the action commenced, and after a furious contest, lasting till after dark, the enemy was routed at all points and driven from the field."

The rear of the supply-trains and the reserve artillery of the army reached Malvern Hill about four P.M. At about this time the enemy began to appear in Gen. Porter's front, and at five o'clock advanced in large force against his left flank, posting artillery under cover of a skirt of timber, with a view to engage our force on Malvern Hill, while with his infantry and some artillery he attacked Col. Warren's brigade. A concentrated fire of about thirty guns was brought to bear on the enemy, which, with the infantry-fire of Col. Warren's command, compelled him to retreat, leaving two guns in the hands of Col. Warren. The gunboats rendered most efficient aid at this time, and helped to drive back the enemy.

It was very late at night before my aides returned to give me the results of the day's fighting along the whole line and the true position of affairs. While waiting to hear from Gen. Franklin, before sending orders to Gens. Sumner and Heintzelman, I received a message from the latter that Gen. Franklin was falling back; whereupon I sent Col. Colburn, of my staff, with orders to verify this, and, if it were true, to order in Gens. Sumner and Heintzelman at once. He had not gone far when he met two officers sent from Gen. Franklin's headquarters with the information that he was falling back. Orders were then sent to Gens. Sumner and Heintzelman to fall back also, and definite instructions were given as to the movement which was to commence on the right. The orders met these troops already en route to Malvern. Instructions were also sent to Gen. Franklin as to the route he was to follow.

Gen. Barnard then received full instructions for posting the troops as they arrived.

I then returned to Haxall's, and again left for Malvern soon after daybreak. Accompanied by several general officers, I once more made the entire circuit of the position, and then returned to Haxall's, whence I went with Com. Rodgers to select the final location for the army and its depots. I returned to Malvern before the serious fighting commenced, and after riding along the lines, and seeing most cause to feel anxious about the right, remained in that vicinity.

The position selected for resisting the further advance of the enemy on the 1st of July was with the left and centre of our lines resting on Malvern Hill, while the right curved backwards through a wooded country towards a point below Haxall's, on James river. Malvern Hill is an elevated plateau about a mile and a half by three-fourths of a mile in area, well cleared of timber, and with several converging roads running over it. In front are numerous defensible ravines, and the ground slopes gradually towards the north and east to the woodland, giving clear ranges for artillery in those directions. Towards the northwest the plateau falls off more abruptly into a ravine which extends to James river. From the position of the enemy his most obvious lines of attack would come from the direction of Richmond and White Oak Swamp, and would almost of necessity strike us upon our left wing. Here, therefore, the lines were strengthened by massing the troops and collecting the principal part of the artillery. Porter's corps held the left of the line (Sykes's division on the left, Morell's on the right), with the artillery of his two divisions advantageously posted, and the artillery of the reserve so disposed on the high ground that a concentrated fire of some sixty guns could be brought to bear on any point in his front or left. Col. Tyler also had, with great exertion, succeeded in getting ten of his siege-guns in position on the highest point of the hill.

Couch's division was placed on the right of Porter; next came Kearny and Hooker; next Sedgwick and Richardson; next Smith and Slocum; then the remainder of Keyes's corps, extending by a backward curve nearly to the river. The Pennsylvania reserve corps was held in reserve, and stationed behind Porter's and Couch's position. One brigade of Porter's was thrown to the left on the low ground to protect that flank from any movement direct from the Richmond road. The line was

GENERAL McCLELLAN POSTING THE BATTERIES AT MALVERN HILL.

very strong along the whole front of the open plateau, but from thence to the extreme right the troops were more deployed. This formation was imperative, as an attack would probably be made upon our left. The right was rendered as secure as possible by slashing the timber and by barricading the roads. Com. Rodgers, commanding the flotilla on James river, placed his gunboats so as to protect our flank and to command the approaches from Richmond.

Between nine and ten A.M. the enemy commenced feeling along our whole left wing, with his artillery and skirmishers, as far to the right as Hooker's division.

About two o'clock a column of the enemy was observed moving towards our right, within the skirt of woods in front of Heintzelman's corps, but beyond the range of our artillery. Arrangements were at once made to meet the anticipated attack in that quarter; but, though the column was long, occupying more than two hours in passing, it disappeared and was not again heard of. The presumption is that it retired by the rear, and participated in the attack afterwards made on our left.

About three P.M. a heavy fire of artillery opened on Kearny's left and Couch's division, speedily followed up by a brisk attack of infantry on Couch's front. The artillery was replied to with good effect by our own, and the infantry of Couch's division remained lying on the ground until the advancing column was within short musket-range, when they sprang to their feet and poured in a deadly volley which entirely broke the attacking force and drove them in disorder back over their own ground. This advantage was followed up until we had advanced the right of our line some seven or eight hundred yards, and rested upon a thick clump of trees, giving us a stronger position and a better fire.

Shortly after four o'clock the firing ceased along the whole front, but no disposition was evinced on the part of the enemy to withdraw from the field. Caldwell's brigade, having been detached from Richardson's division, was stationed upon Couch's right by Gen. Porter, to whom he had been ordered to report. The whole line was surveyed by the general, and everything held in readiness to meet the coming attack. At six o'clock the enemy suddenly opened upon Couch and Porter with the whole strength of his artillery, and at once began pushing forward his columns of attack to carry the hill. Brigade after brigade, formed under cover of the woods, started at a run to cross the open space and charge our batteries, but the heavy fire of our guns, with the cool and steady volleys of our infantry, in every case sent them reeling back to shelter and covered the ground with their dead and wounded. In several instances our infantry withheld their fire until the attacking column, which rushed through the storm of canister and shell from our artillery, had reached within a few yards of our lines. They then poured in a single volley and dashed forward with the bayonet, capturing prisoners and colors, and driving the routed columns in confusion from the field.

About seven o'clock, as fresh troops were accumulating in front of Porter and Couch, Meagher and Sickles were sent with their brigades, as soon as it was considered prudent to withdraw any portion of Sumner's and Heintzelman's troops, to reinforce that part of the line and hold the position. These brigades relieved such regiments of Porter's corps and Couch's division as had expended their ammunition, and batteries from the reserve were pushed forward to replace those whose boxes were empty. Until dark the enemy persisted in his efforts to take the position so tenaciously defended; but, despite his vastly superior numbers, his repeated and desperate attacks were repulsed with fearful loss, and darkness ended the battle of Malvern Hill, though it was not until after nine o'clock that the artillery ceased its fire. The result was complete victory.

During the whole battle Com. Rodgers added greatly to the discomfiture of the enemy by throwing shell among his reserves and advancing columns.

It was necessary to fall back still further, in order to reach a point where our supplies could be brought to us with certainty. As before stated, in the opinion of Com. Rodgers, commanding the gunboat flotilla, this could only be done below City Point; concurring in his opinion, I selected Harrison's Bar as the new position of the army. The exhaustion of our supplies of food, forage, and ammunition made it imperative to reach the transports immediately.

The greater portion of the transportation of the army having been started for Harrison's Landing during the night of the 30th of June and 1st of July, the order for the movement of the troops was at once issued upon the final repulse of the enemy at Malvern Hill. The order prescribed a movement by the left and rear, Gen. Keyes's corps to cover the manœuvre. It was not carried out in detail as regards the divisions on the left, the roads being somewhat blocked by the rear of our trains. Porter and Couch were not able to move out as early as had been anticipated, and Porter found it necessary to place a rearguard between his command and the enemy. Col. Averill, of the 3d Penn. Cavalry, was entrusted with this delicate duty. He had under his command his own regiment and Lieut.-Col. Buchanan's brigade of regular infantry and one battery. By a judicious use of the resources at his command he deceived the enemy so as to cover the withdrawal of the left wing without being attacked, remaining himself on the previous day's battlefield until about seven o'clock of the 2d of July. Meantime Gen. Keyes, having received his orders, commenced vigorous preparations for covering the movement of the entire army and protecting the trains. It being evident that the immense number of wagons and artillery-carriages pertaining to the army could not move with celerity along a single road, Gen. Keyes took advantage of every accident of the ground to open new avenues and to facilitate the movement. He made preparations for obstructing the roads after the army had passed, so as to prevent any rapid pursuit, destroying effectually Turkey bridge, on the main road, and rendering other roads and approaches temporarily impassable by felling trees across them. He kept the trains well closed up, and directed the march so that the troops could move on each side of the roads, not obstructing the passage, but being in good position to repel an attack from any quarter. His dispositions were so successful that, to use his own words, "I do not think more vehicles or more public property were abandoned on the march from Turkey bridge than would have been left, in the same state of the roads, if the army had been moving towards the enemy instead of away from him. And when it is understood that the carriages and teams belonging to this army, stretched out in one line, would extend not far from forty miles, the energy and caution necessary for their safe withdrawal from the presence of an enemy vastly superior in numbers will be appreciated." The last of the wagons did not reach the site selected at Harrison's Bar until after dark on the

3d of July, and the rear-guard did not move into their camp until everything was secure. The enemy followed up with a small force, and on the 3d threw a few shells at the rear-guard, but were quickly dispersed by our batteries and the fire of the gunboats.

Great credit must be awarded to Gen. Keyes for the skill and energy which characterized his performance of the important and delicate duties entrusted to his charge.

High praise is also due to the officers and men of the 1st Conn. Artillery, Col. Tyler, for the manner in which they withdrew all the heavy guns during the Seven Days and from Malvern Hill. Owing to the crowded state of the roads the teams could not be brought within a couple of miles of the position, but these energetic soldiers removed the guns by hand for that distance, leaving nothing behind.

So long as life lasts the survivors of those glorious days will remember with quickened pulse the attitude of that army when it reached the goal for which it had striven with such transcendent heroism. Exhausted, depleted in numbers, bleeding at every pore, but still proud and defiant, and strong in the consciousness of a great feat of arms heroically accomplished, it stood ready to renew the struggle with undiminished ardor whenever its commander should give the word. It was one of those magnificent episodes which dignify a nation's history and are fit subjects for the grandest efforts of the poet and the painter.*

This movement was now successfully accomplished, and the Army of the Potomac was at last in position on its true line of operations, with its trains intact, no guns lost save those taken in battle when the artillerists had proved their heroism and devotion by standing to their guns until the enemy's infantry were in their midst.

During the Seven Days the Army of the Potomac consisted of 143 regiments of infantry, 55 batteries, and less than 8 regiments of cavalry all told. The opposing Confederate army con-

*In the evening, before his sudden death in the night, Gen. McClellan had been occupied in preparing, from his memoirs, an article for the *Century Magazine.* Among the manuscript, which we found next morning lying as he left it, the paragraph above, commencing with the words, "So long as life lasts," appeared to be the last work of his pen. The last words he wrote were thus this final expression of his admiration for the Army of the Potomac. I have thought fit to insert them here.

W . C . P .

sisted of 187 regiments of infantry, 79 batteries, and 14 regiments of cavalry. The losses of the two armies from June 25 to July 2 were:

	Killed	Wounded	Missing.	Total
Confederate Army,	2,823	13,703	3,223	19,749
Army of the Potomac,	1,734	8,062	6,053	15,849

The Confederate losses in killed and wounded alone were greater than the total losses of the Army of the Potomac in killed, wounded, and missing.

No praise can be too great for the officers and men who passed through these seven days of battle, enduring fatigue without a murmur, successfully meeting and repelling every attack made upon them, always in the right place at the right time, and emerging from the fiery ordeal a compact army of veterans, equal to any task that brave and disciplined men can be called upon to undertake. They needed now only a few days of well-earned repose, a renewal of ammunition and supplies, and reinforcements to fill the gaps made in their ranks by so many desperate encounters, to be prepared to advance again, with entire confidence, to meet their worthy antagonists in other battles. It was, however, decided by the authorities at Washington, against my earnest remonstrances, to abandon the position on the James, and the campaign. The Army of the Potomac was accordingly withdrawn.

It was not until two years later that it again found itself under its last commander at substantially the same point on the bank of the James. It was as evident in 1862 as in 1865 that there was the true defence of Washington, and that it was on the banks of the James that the fate of the Union was to be decided.

CHAPTER XXVII.

PRIVATE LETTERS.

[*June* 26 to *Aug.* 23, 1862.]

June 26, 2 P.M., *Trent's.* - . . Yesterday I wished to advance our picket-line, and met with a good deal of opposition. We succeeded fully, however, and gained the point with but little loss. The enemy fought pretty hard, but our men did better. I was out there all day taking a personal direction of affairs, and remained until about 5.30 P.M., when I returned to camp, and met on my way the news that Stonewall Jackson was on his way to attack my right and rear. I rode over to Porter's soon after I reached camp, and returned about 2.30 A.M. At three I started off again and went to the front, where an attack was expected by some Finding all quiet, I rode all along the lines and returned here. You may imagine that I am rather tired out. I think that Jackson will attempt to attack our rear. . . .

Have just received the positive information that Jackson is *en route* to take us in rear. You probably will not hear for some days; but do not be at all worried. . . .

Gen. McClellan's headquarters, June 26, 1862 -Telegram, *in cipher, care of Mr. Eckert, who will regard it as private and strictly confidential, and forward it privately to my wife.* - DEAR NELL: I may not be able to telegraph or write to you for some days. There will be a great stampede, but do not be alarmed. There will be severe fighting in a day or two, but you may be sure that your husband will not disgrace you, and I am confident that God will smile upon my efforts and give our arms success. You will hear that we are pursued, annihilated, etc. Do not believe it, but trust that success will crown our efforts. I tell you this, darling, only to guard against the agony you would feel if you trusted the newspaper reports. . . .

Telegram - *June* 27, 1.15 P.M. - Heavy firing in all directions.

441

So far we have repulsed them everywhere. I expect wire to be cut any moment. All well and very busy. Cannot write to-day.

Telegram - *McClellan's Headquarters, June* 27. - Have had a terrible fight against vastly superior numbers. Have generally held our own, and we may thank God that the Army of the Potomac has not lost its honor. It is impossible as yet to tell what the result is. I am well, but tired out; no sleep for two nights, and none to-night. God bless you!

Telegram - *McClellan's Headquarters, June* 28. - We are all well to-night. I fear your uncle has been seriously hurt in the terrible tight of yesterday. They have outnumbered us everywhere, but we have not lost our honor. This army has acted magnificently. I thank my friends in Washington for our repulse.

June 29, 3 P.M., *in the field.* - I send you only a line to say that I still think God is with us. We have fought a terrible battle against overwhelming numbers. We held our own, and history will show that I have done all that man can do. . . .

June 30, 7 P.M., *Turkey bridge.* - Well, but worn out; no sleep for many days. We have been fighting for many days, and are still at it. . . . We have fought every day for five days. . . .

July 1, *Haxall's Plantation.*- . . . The whole army is here; worn out and war-worn, after a week of daily battles. I have still very great confidence in them, and they in me. The dear fellows cheer me as of old as they march to certain death, and I feel prouder of them than ever.

July 2, . . . *Berkley, James river.* - . . . I have only energy enough left to scrawl you a few lines to say that I have the whole army here, with all its material and guns. We are all worn out and haggard. . . . My men need repose, and I hope will be allowed to enjoy it to-morrow. . . . Your poor uncle was killed at the battle of Gaines's Mills on Friday last. We are well, but very tired. . . .

July 2, 11 P.M. - I will now take a few moments from the rest which I really need, and write at least a few words. . . . We have had a terrible time. On Wednesday the serious work commenced. I commenced driving the enemy on our left, and, by hard fighting, gained my point. Before that affair was over I received news that Jackson was probably about to attack my right. I galloped back to camp, took a fresh horse, and went over to Porter's camp, where I remained all night making the best arrangements I could, and returned about daybreak to look out for the left. On Thursday afternoon Jackson began his attack on Mc-Call, who was supported by Porter. Jackson being repulsed, I went over there in the afternoon and remained until two or three A.M. I was satisfied that Jackson would have force enough next morning to turn Porter's right, so I removed all the wagons, heavy guns, etc., during the night, and caused Porter to fall back to a point nearer the force on the other side of the Chickahominy. This was most handsomely effected, all our material being saved. The next day Porter was attacked in his new position by the whole force of Jackson, Longstreet, Ewell, Hill, and Whiting. I sent what supports I could, but was at the same time attacked on my own front, and could only spare seven brigades. With these we held our own at all points after most desperate fighting. It was on this day that your poor uncle [Col. Rossell] was killed, gallantly leading his regiment. He was struck in the breast, and died in a few hours. Clitz fell that day also. John Reynolds was taken prisoner. I was forced that night to withdraw Porter's force to my side of the Chickahominy, and therefrom to make a very dangerous and difficult movement to reach the James river. I *must* say goodnight now, for I am very tired, and may require all my energies to-morrow.

July 4, *Berkley* .- . . . You will understand before this reaches you the glorious yet fearful events which have prevented me from writing. We have fine weather to-day, which is drying the ground rapidly. I was quite stampeded yesterday just before your father left. A report came to me that the enemy were advancing in overwhelming numbers, and that none of my orders for placing the troops in position and reorganizing them had been carried out. I at once rode through the

34

camps, clear in front of them, to let them see that there was
no danger. They began to cheer as usual, and called out that
they were all right and would fall to the last man "for Little
Mac "! I saw where the trouble was, halted all the commands,
looked at the ground, and made up my mind what the true position was. Started Smith at a double-quick to seize the key-
point, followed by a battery of horse-artillery at a gallop. They
went up most beautifully, opened on the enemy, drove him off
after eighteen rounds, and finally held the place. I pushed Slocum's division up in support, hurried off Heintzelman's corps
to take its position on Franklin's left, supported by Keyes still
further to the left, and came back to camp a little before dark
with a light heart for the first time in many days. I am ready
for an attack now, give me twenty-four hours even, and I will
defy all secession. The movement has been a magnificent one;
I have saved all our material, have fought every day for a week,
and marched every night. You can't tell how nervous I became;
everything seemed like the opening of artillery, and I had no
rest, no peace, except when in front with my men. The duties
of my position are such as often to make it necessary for me to
remain in the rear. It is an awful thing.

I have re-established the playing of bands, beating the calls,
etc., by way of keeping the men in good spirits, and have ordered the national salute to be fired to-day at noon from the
camp of each corps. I have some more official letters to write,
so I must close this, and must soon start to ride around the
lines.

July -, Monday, 7.30 A.M. - I have had a good, refreshing
night's sleep. . . . We are to have another very hot day; it
is already apparent. I am writing in my shirt-sleeves and with
tent-walls raised, etc. . . . Our army has not been repulsed;
we fought every day against greatly superior numbers, and
were obliged to retire at night to new positions that we could
hold against fresh troops. The army behaved magnificently;
nothing could have been finer than its conduct. . . .

July 8. - . . . The day is insufferably hot, intense, so much
so that I have suspended all work on the part of the men. I
have written a strong, frank letter to the President, which I

send by your father. If he acts upon it the country will be saved. I will send you a copy to-morrow, as well as of the other important letters which I wish you to keep as my record. They will show, with the others you have, that I was true to my country, that I understood the state of affairs long ago, and that had my advice been followed we should not have been in our present difficulties. . . . I have done the best I could. God has disposed of events as to Him seemed best. I submit to His decrees with perfect cheerfulness, and as sure as He rules I believe that all will yet be for the best. . . .

Midnight. - Everything is quiet now; none awake save the sentinels. I am alone with you and the Almighty, whose good and powerful hand has saved me and my army. The terrible moments I have undergone of late I regard as a part of the cross I have to bear, and, with God's help, will endure to the end when my task is finished. I place myself. in His hands, and with a sincere heart say His will be done. Oh! how ardently I pray for rest   Rest with you. I care not where, only that I may be alone with you. We are to have service at headquarters to-morrow morning, and I will endeavor to have it every Sunday hereafter."

July 9, 9.30 P.M., *Berkley.* - I telegraphed you briefly this

* The following order will be read with interest in this connection :

General Orders, No. 7.

HEADQUARTERS, ARMY OF THE POTOMAC, WASHINGTON, Sept. 6, 1861.

The major-general commanding desires and requests that in future there may be a more perfect respect for the Sabbath on the part of his command.

We are fighting in a holy cause, and should endeavor to deserve the benign favor of the Creator.

Unless in the case of an attack by the enemy, or some other extreme military necessity, it is commended to commanding officers that all work shall be suspended on the Sabbath; that no unnecessary movements shall be made on that day; that the men shall, as far as possible, be permitted to rest from their labors; that they shall attend divine service after the customary Sunday morning inspection, and that officers and men shall alike use their influence to insure the utmost decorum and quiet on that day. The general commanding regards this as no idle form; one day's rest in seven is necessary to men and animals; more than this, the observance of the holy day of the God of Mercy and of Battles is our sacred duty.

GEORGE B. MCCLELLAN.
Maj.-Gen. Commanding.

afternoon that I thought Secesh had retired. This opinion seems to be fully confirmed, at least to the extent of his having fallen back a certain distance. He is not within six or seven miles of us even with his cavalry, and considerably further with his infantry. I am not sorry, on the whole, that he has gone, for the reason that it will enable my men to rest tranquilly - just what they need. I do not expect to receive many reinforcements for some time. Even Burnside's men are halted at Fortress Monroe by order of the President. His excellency was here yesterday and left this morning. He found the army anything but demoralized or dispirited; in excellent spirits. I do not know to what extent he has profited by his visit ; not much, I fear. I will enclose with this a copy of a letter I handed him, which I would be glad to have you preserve carefully as a very important record. . . . My camp is now immediately on the banks of the James river, in the woods. . . .

7 A.M. (10th).- . . . Rose a little before six. . . . I do not know what paltry trick the administration will play next. . . . I have honestly done the best I could. I shall leave it to others to decide whether that was the best that could have been done, and, if they find any one who can do better, am perfectly willing to step aside and give way. I would not for worlds go through that horrid work again, when, with my heart full of care, I had to meet everybody with a cheerful smile and look as light-hearted as though nothing were at stake. . . .

Telegram - *Berkley, July* 10, 1862. - We are all very well and in good spirits. Secesh has gone off and left us for the present. Clitz is certainly in Richmond, recovering from his wounds. If properly supported I will yet take Richmond. Am not in the least discouraged; am in better health than for many months. Your father returned to Washington two days ago.

July 12.- I am sure that God will bring us together again in this world; but, whether so or not, we will try so to live that me may be reunited in that world where we can be happy for ever and never again be parted. . . . In this weary world I have seen but little happiness save what I have enjoyed with you. How very happy our first year of married life was, when

we were together! So the baby has more teeth! I suppose
when I come back I shall find her handling a knife and fork.
When will she begin to say a word or two? I hope she will
not begin to do much before I come home. I want to have the
fun and satisfaction of matching her progress in life and the
development of her accomplishments. . . . I enclose with this
a letter from Stanton and my reply, which I want you to preserve very carefully with my other "archives," as it may be
important. . . .

July 13, *Sunday,* 7.45 A.M. - I have ordered all labor suspended to-day to give the men a chance to think of all they
have gone through. We are to have service to-day by the
chaplain of Gregg's regiment Penn. cavalry. Next Sunday I
think I will invite Mr. Neal to preach for us, provided there is
any attendance to-day.

I enclose this in an envelope with some letters I send you,
one from Bishop McIlvaine, which will gratify you, I know;
another from some poor fellow in Indiana who has named his
child after me. If you choose to send out some little present
to it, well and good.

1.30 P.M. - . . . Had service this morning by the chaplain of
Gregg's regiment, the Rev. Mr. Egan, an Episcopal clergyman
of Philadelphia. . . . There never was such an army; but there
have been plenty of better generals. When I spoke about being
repulsed I meant our failure to take Richmond. In no battle
were we repulsed. We always at least held our own on the field,
if we did not beat them. . . . I still hope to get to Richmond this
summer, unless the government commits some extraordinarily
idiotic act; but I have no faith in the administration, and shall
cut loose from public life the very moment my country can dis-
pense with my services. Don't be alarmed about the climate.
It is not at all bad yet, and we are resting splendidly. The men
look better every day. So you want to know how I feel about
Stanton, and what I think of him now? I will tell you with the
most perfect frankness. I think . . . I *may* do the man injustice. God grant that I may be wrong! For I hate to think that
humanity can sink so low. But my opinion is just as I have told
you. He has deceived me once: he never will again. Are you
satisfied now, lady mine? I ever will hereafter trust your judg-

ment about men. Your woman's tact and your pure heart make you a better judge than my dull apprehension. I remember what you thought of Stanton when you first saw him. I thought you were wrong. I now know you were right. Enough of the creature!

Since I reached here I have received about 8,500 or 9,000 fresh troops. My losses in the battles will not be over 12,000. Burnside has 8,000 (about) at Fortress Monroe, where he was detained by order of the President. He has been in Washington and will probably be here himself to-night, when I will know the views of the President. The probability is that I will attack again very soon - as soon as some losses are supplied. I also wish first to get off all the sick and wounded.

11.30 P.M. - Have just been at work dictating my report of the recent operations; got as far as bringing Porter back across the Chickahominy. . . . Please reply to Mr. - and say that I thank him and feel deeply grateful for his trust and kind feeling, and that I am glad to say that there is no reason for despondency on account of my present position. I flatter myself that this army is a greater thorn in the side of the rebellion than ever, and I most certainly (with God's blessing) intend to take Richmond with it. . . . I trust that we have passed through our darkest time, and that God will smile upon us and give us victory. . . .

July 15, 7.30 A.M. - . . . I was amused at a couple of telegrams yesterday urging me to the offensive - as if I were unwilling to take it myself! It is so easy for people to give advice-it costs nothing! But it is a little more difficult for poor me to create men and means, and to wipe out by mere wishes the forces of the enemy. I confess that I sometimes become provoked.

. . . I had quite an adventure in a small way last night that was rather ludicrous. I yesterday sent a flag of truce after some wounded men, Sweitzer going on the boat. Well, it appears that he and the doctor on board, between them, allowed a young English nobleman to come down with them, and Raymond was discreet enough to bring him up to headquarters, and was apparently quite proud of his prize; wished me to see him. Upon inquiry I found that he came from Richmond, had no papers or passports, save a pass from the secesh Secretary of

War, and acknowledged that he had surreptitiously slipped into Richmond a couple of weeks ago. This was a pretty kettle of fish. I did not like to hang the young rascal for a spy, for fear of getting up a row with England. I determined he should not go through; so I this morning sent him back to Secessia, and told him to try it again at his peril The young man was exceedingly disgusted, and has, I presume, by this time come to the conclusion that the fact of being an Englishman is not everywhere a sufficient passport.

July 17, A.M. - Gens. Dix and Burnside are both here. . . . Burnside is very well, and, if the President permits, will bring me large (respectably) reinforcements. . . . Am quite well to-day; a little disgusted at the stupidity of the people in Washington. You need not be at all alarmed as to my being deceived by them. I know that they are ready to sacrifice me at any moment. I shall not be at all surprised to have some other general made commander of the whole army, or even to be superseded here.

7 P.M. -. . . You ask me when I expect to reach Richmond and whether I shall act on the offensive this summer. I am at the mercy of the government. After the first 9,000 or 10,000 men sent to me they have withheld all further reinforcements. Burnside is halted at Fortress Monroe. With his own troops and those of Hunter he can bring me some 20,000 troops; but I have no idea of the intentions of the government. If I am reinforced to that extent I will try it again with the least possible delay. I am not at all in favor of baking on the banks of this river, but am anxious to bring matters to an issue. . . . You need not be at all alarmed lest any of these people flatter me into the belief that they are my friends. It's mighty little flattery or comfort I get out of any of them in these days, I assure you. . . .

So you like my letter to the President? I feel that I did my duty in writing it, though I apprehend it will do no good whatever; but it clears my conscience to have spoken plainly at such a time. You do not feel one bit more bitterly towards those people than I do. I do not say much about it, but I fear they have done all that cowardice and folly can do to ruin our poor country, and the blind people seem not to see it. It makes my blood boil when I think of it. I cannot resign so long as the fate of the Army of the Potomac is entrusted to my care. I owe a great duty to this noble set of men, and that is the only feeling that retains me. I fear that my day of usefulness to the country is past - at least under this administration. I hope and trust that God will watch over, guide, and protect me. I accept most resignedly all He has brought upon me. Perhaps I have really brought it on myself; for while striving conscientiously to do my best, it may well be that I have made great mistakes that my vanity does not permit me to perceive. When I see so much self-blindness around me I cannot arrogate to myself greater clearness of vision and self-examination. I *did* have a terrible time during that week, for I stood alone, without any one to help me. I felt that on me rested everything, and I felt how weak a thing poor, mortal, erring man is! I felt it sincerely, and shall never, I trust, forget the lesson; it will last me to my dying day. . . I am very well now, perfectly well, and ready for any amount of fatigue that can be imagined.

July 18, 7.45 A.M. - . . . We are to have another very hot day, I fancy; no air stirring, and the atmosphere close and murky. I don't at all wish to spend the summer on the banks of this river; we will fry or bake! If our dear government will show some faint indication of brains or courage we can finish the work in a short time. . . . I am so sorry that poor Prince is going blind. It is a great pity. I flattered myself that when I became a poor blind soldier, a second Belisarius, Prince would probably lead me about.

9 P.M. - I am inclined now to think that the President will make Halleck commander of the army, and that the first pretext will be seized to supersede me in command of this army. Their game seems to be to withhold reinforcements, and then to relieve me for not advancing, well knowing that I have not the means to do so. If they supersede me in the command of the Army of the Potomac I will resign my commission at once. If they appoint Halleck commanding general I will remain in command of this army as long as they will allow me to, provided the army is in danger and likely to play an active part. I cannot remain as a subordinate in the army I once commanded any longer than the interests of my own Army of the Potomac require. I owe no gratitude to any but my own soldiers here; none to the govern-

ment or to the country. I have done my best for the country; I expect nothing in return; they are my debtors, not I theirs. . . . If things come to pass as I anticipate I shall leave the service with a sad heart for my country, but a light one for myself. But one thing keeps me at my work-love for my country and my army. Surely no general had ever better cause to love his men than I have to love mine.

Confidential - To William H. Aspinwall, Esq.-Berkley, July 19, 1862.

MY DEAR MR. ASPINWALL: I again find myself in a position such that I may ere long have to tax your friendship for me. I have reason to believe that Gen. Halleck is to be made commander-in-chief of the army, and, if I am not mistaken, I think I detect the premonitory symptoms of still further changes.   I can get no replies from Washington to any of my despatches. Burnside and his troops are taken out of my hands.   I receive no reinforcements, and no hope of them is held out to me.   The game apparently is to deprive me of the means of moving, and then to cut my head off for not advancing. In other words, it is my opinion that I will be removed from the command of this army in a short time.   The present feeling is, I think, merely a continuation of the inveterate persecution that has pursued me since I landed on the Peninsula-weakening my command so as to render it inadequate to accomplish the end in view, and then to hold me responsible for the result. I am quite weary of this. If I am superseded in the command of the army of the Potomac I shall resign my commission in the service, feeling that I can no longer be of use; on the contrary, only in the way.

Looking forward to that event, my main object in writing to you is to ask you to be kind enough to cast your eyes about you to see whether there is anything I can do in New York to earn a respectable support for my family.   I have no exaggerated ideas or expectations. All I wish is some comparatively quiet pursuit, for I really need rest. Pretty much everything I had has been sacrificed in consequence of my re-entering the service, and when I leave it I must commence anew and work for my support. That I am quite willing to do.

I know that I need not apologize for troubling you in regard

to this matter. Please regard this as confidential, except with
Mr. Alsop and Mr. Bartlett.

I am, my dear sir, most sincerely your friend,

GEO. B. MCCLELLAN.

July 20, A.M. - . . . Went on the hospital-steamer to see Clitz
yesterday.   He is doing very well. . . . I saw all the officers and
men on board, and tried to cheer them up.   The visit seemed to
do them a great deal of good, and it would have done you good
to see how the poor, suffering fellows brightened up when they
saw me. . . . I wonder whether the baby will know me.   I fear
that she will be afraid of me and won't come to me.   Would not
that be mortifying?   I hope the dear little thing will take to me
kindly.   I should feel terribly if she should refuse to have anything to do with me.   Bless her sweet little ladyship!   She must
be a great comfort to you; and we will be happier than any kings
and queens on earth, if we three are permitted to be together
again, and that before May changes much.   I want so much to
see her again while she is a baby, before she begins to talk and
walk and be human. . . .

P.M. - Which despatch of mine to Stanton do you allude to?
The telegraphic one in which I told him that if I saved the army
I owed no thanks to any one in Washington, and that he had
done his best to sacrifice my army?   It was pretty frank and
quite true.   Of course they will never forgive me for that.   I
knew it when I wrote it; but as I thought it possible that it
might be the last I ever wrote, it seemed better to have it exactly
true.   The President, of course, has not replied to my letter, and
never will.   His reply may be, however, to avail himself of the
first opportunity to cut my head off.   I see it reported in this
evening's papers that Halleck is to be the new general-in-chief.
Now let them take the next step and relieve me, and I shall once
more be a free man. . . .

Later. - . . . I believe it is now certain that Halleck is commander-in-chief.   I have information this evening from Washington, from private sources, which seems to render it quite certain.
You will have to cease directing your letters to me as commanding United States army, and let the address be, "Commanding
the Army of the Potomac"- quite as proud a title as the other,
at all events. I shall have to remove the three stars from my

shoulders and put up with two. *Eh bien!* it is all for the best, I doubt not. I hope Halleck will have a more pleasant time in his new position than I did when I held it. This, of course, fixes the future for us. I cannot remain permanently in the army after this slight. I must, of course, stick to this army so long as I am necessary to it. . . . I have tried to do my best, honestly and faithfully, for my country. That I have to a certain extent failed I do not believe to be my fault, though my self-conceit probably blinds me to many errors that others see. But one useful lesson I have learned - to despise earthly honors and popular favor as vanities. I am content. I have not disgraced my name, nor will my child be ashamed of her father. Thank God for that! I shall try to get something to do which will make you comfortable; and it will be most pleasant and in the best taste for me that we should lead hereafter a rather quiet and retired life. It will not do to parade the tattered remnants of my departed honors to the gaze of the world. Let us try to live for each other and our child, and to prepare for the great change that sooner or later must overtake us all. I have had enough of earthly honors and place. I believe I can give up all and retire to privacy once more, a better man than when me gave up our dear little home with wild ideas of serving the country. I feel that I have paid all that I owe her. I am sick and weary of all this business. I am tired of serving fools God help my country! He alone can save it. It is grating to have to serve under the orders of a man whom I know by experience to be my inferior. But so let it be. God's will be done! All will turn out for the best. My trust is in God, and I cheerfully submit to His will. . . .

July 22, 7.30 A.M. - . . . While I think of it, be very careful what you telegraph, and tell your father the same thing. I have the proof that the secretary reads all my private telegrams. If he has read my private letters to you also his ears must have tingled somewhat. I am about doing a thing to-day which will, I suppose, cause the abolitionists and my other friends to drive the last nail in my official coffin. You know that our sick and wounded in Richmond are suffering terribly for want of proper food, medicines, and hospital supplies. I have ordered a boatload of all such things - lemons, tea, sugar, brandy, underclothing, lint, bandages, chloroform, quinine, ice, etc., etc. - to be sent up to Gen. Lee to-day, to be used at his discretion for the sick and wounded of both armies. I know he would not, and could not, receive them for our men alone, therefore I can only do it in the way I propose, and trust to his honor to apply them properly-half and half. I presume I will be accused now of double-dyed treason - giving aid and comfort to the enemy, etc. What do you think of it? Am I right or wrong? . . . I see that the Pope bubble is likely to be suddenly collapsed. Stonewall Jackson is after him, and the young man who wanted to teach me the art of war will in less than a week either be in full retreat or badly whipped. He will begin to learn the value of "entrenchments, lines of communication and of retreat, bases of supply," etc.

July 22. - It is a lovely afternoon, bright and sunny, a pleasant breeze blowing, and everything charming to the eye. The old river looks beautiful to-day, as bright as when John Smith, Esq., and my dusky ancestress, Madam Pocahontas Rolfe, *née* Powhatan, paddled her canoe and children somewhere in this vicinity. If it were not for the accompaniments and present surroundings it would delight me beyond measure to have you here to see the scenery and some of the fine old residences which stud its banks. The men of two or three generations ago must have lived in great state and comfort here. I suspect they had a pretty good time, interrupted only by the chills and fever, bad luck in gambling and horse-racing, and the trouble of providing for their woolly-headed dependants.

July 23. - . . . . There is now no doubt about Halleck being made commander-in-chief. The other change will, I feel sure, follow in a very few days, perhaps a week. . . .
Popularity, Nell, is a humbug. What good has been done to me or to the country by my "popularity" in the North? It has not prevented my enemies from withholding all support from me ; it did not hinder them from almost ruining my army; it brings me not a man; it will not be worth a breath of air to prevent Halleck being put in my place.

July 24. - . . . . Your father arrived this evening. . . .
Took a long ride in the sun to-day. . . Our men look better

than ever; like real veterans now-tough, brown, and fearless.
. . . I hear nothing yet from Washington, and must confess that
I am as indifferent as possible to what they do. If they reinforce me I am ready to fight harder than ever, and will give
Secesh a sharp rub for his capital. If they make it necessary
for me to resign I am quite ready to do so. . . . I presume I
shall learn something to-morrow about the destination of Burnside. I can then enable you to guess how matters will go. I
am yet in complete ignorance, being no longer taken into the
confidence of the "powers that be." . . . You ask me whether
my self-respect will permit me to remain longer in the service
after Halleck's appointment? It will permit me to remain only
so long as the welfare of the Army of the Potomac demands-
no longer. Don't mind these things; I bide my time. Whatever
God sends me, be it defeat and loss of rank, or be it success and
honor, I will cheerfully submit to, May God help me in this!

July 25. - . . . . Started out early in the morning to review
Porter's corps, and spent several hours at it in the hot sun.
Then I went to visit the wounded from Richmond. Then I
heard that Halleck was here, and was obliged to return to see
"my master." I think Halleck will support me and give me the
means to take Richmond. . . . I am not to be relieved from the
command of this army - at least that does not seem to be the
present intention. . . .

July 26, 9 P.M. - . . . . From nine this morning until 6.30 this
evening I have been among the sick and wounded. More than
a thousand came from Richmond last night and were in the
steamer. I saw every one of the poor fellows; talked to them
all; heard their sorrows; tried to cheer them up, and feel
that I have done my duty towards them. If you could have
seen how the poor, maimed, brave fellows, some at the point of
death, brightened up when they saw me and caught my hand, it
would have repaid you for much of our common grief and
anxiety. It has been the most harrowing day I ever passed, yet
a proud one for me, too. I realized how these men love and
respect me, and I trust that many a poor fellow will sleep more
soundly and feel more happily to-night for my visit to them. It
makes them feel that they are not forgotten or neglected when

their general comes to see them and console them. My men love me very much. What a terrible responsibility this imposes upon me! I pray that God will give me strength to bear it and the wisdom to do what is best. It is an awful load that is imposed upon me by the trust and affection of these poor fellows. . . .

July 27.- . . . I can't tell you how glad I am that I went to see all those poor wounded men yesterday. Another batch will come to-night, and I will, if possible, go to see all of them to-morrow morning. I regard it as a duty I owe the poor fellows-rather a hard one to perform, but still one that cannot be neglected. . . . You ask me whether I advised the President to appoint Halleck. The letter of which I sent you a copy is all that ever passed on the subject, either directly or indirectly; not another word than is there written. We never conversed on the subject; I was never informed of his views or intentions, and even now have not been officially informed of the appointment. I only know it through the newspapers. In all these things the President and those around him have acted so as to make the matter as offensive as possible. . . . Fitz Porter has stuck through it all most nobly, He is all that I thought him, and more. Nothing has depressed him; he is always cheerful, active, and ready.

July 28, 9.15 A.M. - . . . Some 500 wounded came down last night, and this morning I am going out to the boats to see them. I have collected an armful of papers to give the poor fellows. . . .

9.30 P.M. - . . . Am very tired, for I saw and talked to every one of the wounded men to-day, being occupied all day at it. Between the closeness of the cabins and being on my feet so long I am quite weary. . . .

I enclose with this some "Lines" a poor wounded fellow handed me yesterday and begged me to accept; they were written while he was lying wounded and under fire. I don't know that the poetry possesses any peculiar merit, but the incident is interesting. My friend was of the *Hibernian* persuasion. Queer fellows those Irish are. There is a vein of humor in everything they do, even when suffering from wounds and sickness. I sometimes can hardly keep from laughing when talking with some poor fellow who is desperately wounded so strangely and peculiarly do they describe things. . . . I think I will go to the general hospital to-day and see how those poor fellows are getting on. . . . I am still "on my back" awaiting a decision from Washington. Burnside is still kept from me. I am getting no reinforcements, and presume that Burnside will be ordered to Washington the first thing I know. Then I shall be in a pretty predicament - too strong to remain here and too weak to advance. . . .

P.M. -. . . . I hear nothing as yet from Washington, and begin to believe that they intend and hope that I and my army may melt away under the hot sun. . . . Secesh is very quiet of late-scarcely even a cavalry skirmish. He is almost too quiet for good, and must be after some mischief. May be me *will* have a visit from *Merrimac* No. 2. What a row it would create among the transports! I am in hopes that I will receive orders of some kind from Washington this evening. I am getting dreadfully tired of doing nothing. I begin to feel the want of a little quiet excitement. I could rest at home away from my men, but the idea of remaining quietly in camp, with an army about me and an active enemy at some mischief or other, is a very different thing.

10.30 P.M. - . . . Nothing to-night from Washington, so that I am yet completely in the dark as to the intentions of our benign government.

July 29. - What do you think I have been doing for the last half-hour? Guess, guess ! ! I have been sewing on buttons and patching my woollen shirts. I have waited in vain for Charles to do anything of the kind, or to have it done, and have been nearly scratched to pieces by the numberless pins that were necessary to keep myself together. So I dove into the pocket of my carpet-bag, and, to my intense delight, found a needle and a spool of sewing-silk. Off came my shirt, and at it I went *con amore.* I was so delighted with the result of that operation that I pulled out of my trunk a clean one that I had been casting sheep's eyes at but found too ragged to wear. That I fixed up, and I am now as grand as any king, with two shirts to my name that I can wear. My friend Charles has no idea of the advantages of mending clothes, and, as he has a very short memory, it is not of much use to tell him. So you see "how the mighty are fallen" - the general of a hundred thousand men sewing on buttons and mending his own clothes. It carried me back to the unhappy days of my miserable bachelorhood. Thank Heaven that that epoch of my existence is past and gone! . . By the way, did I tell you of that gorgeous smoking-cap that was sent to me the other day? I must take the first opportunity to send it home; it is entirely too magnificent for camp, and I fear too much so for me under any circumstances. Should I take a fancy to go to a fancy-ball as the Doge of Venice or the King of Persia, it might make a first-rate head-dress, but would hardly do for anything short of that. We might make a look at it a standing reward for the baby whenever she is particularly good. I have no doubt it would make her open her eyes.

July 30, 10.15 P.M. - Another day elapsed and nothing from Washington. I have positive information to-day that the command of this army was pressed upon Burnside, and that he peremptorily refused it. I learn that Meigs is very anxious for it; much good may it do him! I still think, from all that comes to me, that the chances are at least that I will be superseded. . . . We are relieved to-day by a little excitement. The gunboats reported that six rebel gunboats (including *Mr. Merrimac* No. 2) were on the way down. So we were for some hours considerably brightened up by the prospect of seeing a shindy; but it turned out to be a false report. . . . I see, among other lies, that the papers say that the enemy drove off five hundred of our beef cattle the other day - a lie out of whole cloth. . . . I am sorry to say that I learn that too much faith must not be rested in Halleck. I hope it is not so, but will be very careful how far I trust him, or any other man in these days. He has done me no good yet.

July 31 - . . . This morning I visited the general hospital not far from here, and went through it all, finding the patients comfortable and all improving in health. They are nearly all in hospital-tents and are well provided for; in truth, they are about as well off as they could be away from home, and many of them doubtless better off than they would be there.   I find the men more contented than the officers.   I confess that the men enlist my sympathies much more warmly than the officers.   They are so patient and devoted.   They have generally entered the service, too, from higher and more unselfish motives.   Poor fellows! I can never willingly break the link that unites me to them, and shall always be very proud of them and of their love for me, even if it is not decreed by Providence that I am to lead them to Richmond. After the long time that has elapsed without my hearing anything from Washington I can hardly hope to learn anything by to-day's mail; but I assure you that we are all becoming very impatient at the long delay here, so unnecessary, as it seems to us. I commenced turning over a new leaf to-day; that is, neither writing nor telegraphing to Washington, and have about determined to draw back into my shell until the oracle deigns to speak.   I have said all I well can; I have told them about all I think and know; have pointed out to them what I regard as the general effects of the course I fear they are likely to adopt. Words can no further go. By saying more, and repeating what has been already said, I should only render myself ridiculous and a bore.   So I will be silent, and if they send me the order I dread (that of withdrawing this army) I will make one last, desperate appeal, and then let matters take their course, confident that I have honestly endeavored to do the best I could, although I may not have done as well as others could.   There is a great consolation in feeling that one has tried to do right and not been actuated by selfish motives.   Of the last I *know* that I am free, and would say so were I now on my death-bed. . . . Don't feel at all discouraged.   If I have to begin the world anew and work as hard as ever, it is doubtless all for the best.   When I return to civil life I shall have the consolation of knowing that I am working for you and the baby.   I don't know what rest is, and probably never shall; but as long as God gives me health and strength, and my mind remains clear, it is better that I should work. I am not so fond of it but that I should like to rest; but if that cannot be, I will do my best and try to do my duty ever. . . . I told you the result of the interview with Halleck; thus far practically nothing. Not a word have I heard from Washington since his return there. I shall not write or telegraph another word until I hear from them, unless something

of great importance occurs. I shall stand on what is left of
my dignity now!

1 A.M. - . . . As I was just about comfortably asleep,
about three-quarters of an hour ago, I was awakened by a tremendous shelling. The rascals opened on us with field-guns
from the other side of the river, and kept up a tremendous fire.
It is now pretty much over, but still going on; no shells have
burst nearer than three hundred or four hundred yards from my
camp. It took me about five minutes to awaken Marcy; he did
not hear a single shot. . . . Still some firing-now heavy again;
gunboats at work - they were very slow in getting ready. A
queer thing this, writing a letter to my wife, at this time of night,
to the music of shells! I fear they must have done some harm.
Now they are quiet again; there goes a whopper from the gunboats! Queer times these!

1.30 A.M. - Pretty quiet now; only an occasional shot, apparently from the gunboats-there goes one! Now another! Marcy
and I have just been discussing (another) people in Washington,
and conclude that they are "a mighty trifling set." Indeed, it is
evry criminal to leave me thus without one word of information
as to their plans and purposes. If any lives have been lost
to-night the guilt (another shot) is on their shoulders, for I told
them that I desired to occupy with Burnside's troops the very
point whence this firing has come to-night (another shot); but
I begin to believe that they wish this army to be destroyed. . . .

2.45. . - Tired of waiting for Hammerstein's return with the
news of the damage done. . . . Well, he has just returned. It
was so dark that no one could tell what the damage was; one
man at Fitz Porter's headquarters had his leg shot off; no vessels set on fire; the camps all quiet.

Aug. 1, *midnight.* - . . . Everything quiet since I went to
bed last night; not a shot fired. We had ten men killed, twelve
wounded, half a dozen horses killed; vessels not hurt a bit.
One shell did fall in my camp. Fitz Porter caught the most of
the storm, but had only one man killed. This afternoon I sent
a party across the river to where most of the firing came from,
to cut down some timber that obstructs the view and burn some
houses that the enemy had been using as observatories and
to screen their pickets; it was all done successfully without

opposition. It turned out, as I supposed, that the guns used were field-guns, with which they ran away as soon as they found the gunboats and our own guns were getting troublesome. . . . I had a very friendly letter from Halleck this morning. . . .

Aug. 2. - . . . Circumstances have made it unavoidable for me to send out two important expeditions and a large working party, although it is Sunday. One of the expeditions goes to Malvern, the other on the south side of the James river. . . . I had quite an interesting visit on the other side to-day. The place we burned up yesterday was a very handsome one. It was a rather hard case to be obliged to do it, but it could not be avoided. . . .

I had (as usual) not a single word from Washington to-day from any one, nor anything from Burnside. If the latter is really under orders for the Rappahannock there is something very strange in his failure to communicate with me, not even giving me the slightest hint of it; therefore I am disposed to discredit Com Wilkes's report, and to think that he must be mistaken in regard to it. . . . If he is ordered to the Rappahannock I believe that this army will be withdrawn from here. . . . When you contrast the policy I urge in my letter to the President with that of Congress and of Mr. Pope, you can readily agree with me that there can be little natural confidence between the government and myself. We are the antipodes of each other; and it is more than probable that they will take the earliest opportunity to relieve me from command and get me out of sight. I shall endeavor to pursue the plain path of duty. As I have often told you, my mind is prepared to endure anything that a man of honor can. But I shall consult my own sense of right and my own judgment, not deferring to that of others when my own convictions are strong. There are some things to which I cannot submit and to which nothing can induce me to yield. . . .

7.30 A.M., *Aug.* 3 (same letter).- . . . One of my expeditions of last night failed: had to come back because the guides lost the way; will try it again to-night or to-morrow. The other one not yet heard from, but has, I hope, met with better luck than the first. . . . Everything quiet during the night; no firing and no stampede of any kind. . . .

Berkley, Aug. 4, 6.30 P.M.- . . . I was off on the other side of the river all day yesterday, where I had a hot and fatiguing tramp on foot, besides getting a little damp in the rain. Our enterprises on that side of the river were quite successful. I found a splendid position to cover that bank, so as to enable us to cross the army if necessary, as well as to prevent any more midnight serenades like that of last week. I now hold the other shore with a sufficient number of troops to prevent a surprise. Averill went out with three squadrons, met and thrashed an entire regiment, drove them to and through their camp, which he captured and leisurely destroyed, thus rendering the 13th Va. Cavalry exceedingly uncomfortable last night, for all their tents, provisions, cooking utensils, and baggage were effectually burned up. He got some prisoners and sabred a respectable number, having only two wounded himself. The 5th Regular Cavalry and the 3d Penn. Cavalry did the work. . . .

11.30 P.M. - I had a note from Burnside this evening. He has been ordered to the Rappahannock, and has, I presume, started. Not one word have I heard on that subject from Washington. Halleck has begun to show the cloven foot already. . . . I have a large expedition out to-night-a couple of divisions of infantry and some 2,000 cavalry - to try to catch the secesh who are at Malvern Hill. Shall not hear from them before to-morrow noon. Colburn has gone with them. . . .

7 A.M. - Pretty sharp cannonading has been going on in my front this morning - Hooker's command at Malvern; they are still cracking away pretty sharply. Have not heard details, but will ride out in that direction. . .

Aug. 5, *Malvern Hill,* 1 P.M. *(to Gen. Marcy).* - . . . Hooker has been entirely successful in driving off the enemy; took about one hundred prisoners, killed and wounded several. The mass escaped under cover of a thick fog. Hooker's dispositions were admirable, and nothing but the fog prevented complete success. We have lost three killed and eleven wounded, among the latter two officers. I shall retain the command here to-night. Keep all things ready to move out should we be attacked. I shall not return before dark, and may remain all night; will send in for my blankets and ambulance if I stay. I am now starting to look over the ground. I have sent a party to communicate with

Averill, directing him to take post to-night near Nelson's farm. Will send in again as soon as I return from my ride. Excuse the illegibility of this, as it is written on horseback, and the flies trouble Dan. The enemy in strong force at New Market. Better send a special despatch to Halleck and tell him that I hate to give up this position. Secesh is under cover, and, though he is in strong force, I can beat him if they will give me rein-forcements. Send this to Nell if I do not get back in time for mail.

Aug. 7, 11 P.M. - . . . I have been so situated for the last two days that I could not write to you. Spent night before last at Malvern, and had no means of writing. I came in from there yesterday, and was up nearly all night giving orders and securing reports in regard to the abandonment of the position. . . . Was not very well off at Malvern. My ambulance lost the road, came near being bagged by the enemy, and did not make its appear-ance until late next day, so I had nothing. I got some coffee and some bread from one of the companies, used my saddle-blanket and saddle for a bed, and got through the night without mishap.

Aug. 8, *Berkley.* - I can't convey any idea of the heat to-day. It has been intense; not a breath of air stirring. . . . Received some reports from Pleasonton that the enemy are pressing him hard near Malvern Hill, and gave the necessary orders. . . . I am in strong hopes that the enemy will be foolish enough to drive Pleasonton in and attack me in this position. I have ordered P. to draw them on, if possible, and if they come in sight will try to keep my men concealed and do my best to induce them to attack me. Should they be so foolish as to do that I will surely beat them and follow them up to Richmond; but I fear they are too smart for that. I can hardly hope for so much good luck. If it is a possible thing to humbug them into an attack I will do it. I will issue to-morrow an order giving my comments on Mr. John Pope. I will strike square in the teeth of all his infamous orders, and give directly the reverse instructions to my army: forbid all pillaging and stealing, and take the highest Christian ground for the conduct of the war. Let the government gainsay it if they dare. I am willing to fall in such a cause. I will not permit this army to degenerate into a mob of thieves, nor will I return these men of mine to their families as a set of wicked and demoralized robbers. I will never have that sin on my conscience. . . . I have received my orders from Halleck; I cannot tell you what they are, but if you will bear in mind what I have already written to you, you can readily guess them when I say that they are as bad as they can be, and that I regard them as almost fatal to our cause. I have remonstrated as warmly as I know how to do, but to no avail. My only hope is that I can induce the enemy to attack me. I shall, of course, obey the orders, unless the enemy give me a very good opening, which I should at once avail myself of. I have learned through private sources that they have not yet determined how to dispose of me personally. Their game is to force me to resign; mine will be to force them to place me on leave of absence, so that when they begin to reap the whirlwind that they have sown I may still be in position to do something to save my country. With all their faults, I do love my countrymen, and if I can save them I will yet do so. . . .

I had another letter from Halleck to-night, I strongly suspect him.

Aug. - . - . . . Shortly after that a wind-storm set in with great violence; it knocked over my desk and broke it. The desk fell on the table and broke one leaf off; it broke my "monkey" (did you know I had a menagerie ?), * scattered my papers to the four corners of the-tent, and brought all the orderlies in with a terrific rush. Finally they righted and gathered everything together, so that I am now comfortable again, except damages and the flies. The gust has cooled the air, however, so we are gainers. No rain has fallen here, but the wind is from our dear old North, and is therefore doubly pleasant to me. The fact is, I don't like the South; it is entirely too hot to suit me, and I am sure I don't envy the possessors of it in the least. I wish you could see what a business I am doing, as I write, in the way of spearing flies; every time, nearly, that I dip the pen in the inkstand out comes a defunct fly. I am so glad you

---

* In the Gulf States a "monkey" is the name given to a porous pottery jug or large bottle of water, which hangs by a cord and cools the water by evaporation.

visited that hospital.   I thank you for it from the bottom of my heart.   I know it did them infinite good, and I am sure that you will never meet one of the Army of the Potomac without a kind word and your brightest smile.

Aug 10, 8 A.M. - . . . Halleck is turning out just like the rest of the herd. The affair is rapidly developing itself, and I see more clearly every day their settled purpose to force me to resign. I am trying to keep my temper. I have no idea that I will be with this army more than two or three weeks longer, and should not be surprised any day or hour to get my "walking-papers." . . .

4. P.M. - . . . The absurdity of Halleck's course in ordering the army away from here is that it cannot possibly reach Washington in time to do any good, but will necessarily be too late. I am sorry to say that I am forced to the conclusion that H. is very dull and very incompetent.   Alas, poor country! I hope to be ready to-morrow afternoon to move forward in the direction of Richmond.   I will try to catch or thrash Longstreet, and then, if the chance offers, follow in to Richmond while they are lamming away at Pope.   It is in some respects a desperate step, but it is the best I can do for the nation just now, and I would rather even be defeated than retreat without an effort to relieve Washington in the only way at all possible.   If I fail, why well and good. I will fall back. If I win I shall have saved my country, and will then gracefully retire to private life. . . . I am getting the sick away quite rapidly now, but they are in large numbers, and it is at best a slow process.   The heavy baggage is all being stored on board ship, so that in whatever direction we move we will be comparatively unencumbered.   I shall send off all that I have, except a carpet-bag and pair of blankets, change my large tent for a "wall-tent," and go about as light as any of them. I half apprehend that they will be too quick for me in Washington, and relieve me before I have the chance of making the dash. If so, well and good. I am satisfied that the dolts in Washington are bent on my destruction, if it is possible for them to accomplish it. . . .

Midnight.- . . . I received a very harsh and unjust telegram from Halleck this morning, and a very *friendly private* letter from the same individual - blows hot and cold.   I replied to his telegram, closing by quietly remarking: "The present moment is probably not the proper one for me to refer to the unnecessarily harsh and unjust tone of your telegrams of late. It will, however, make no difference in my official action." Under the circumstances I feel compelled to give up the idea of my intended attack upon Richmond, and must retrace my steps. Halleck writes that all the forces in Virginia, including Pope, Burnside, etc., are to be placed under my command; I doubt it. They are committing a fatal error in withdrawing me from here, and the future will show it. I think the result of their machination will be that Pope will be badly thrashed within ten days, and that they will be very glad to turn over the redemption of their affairs to me. . . .

Aug. 11 .- I am free to chat with you for a few minutes, at least until the impetuous Hatter rushes in and asks "the general to be good enough to come to breakfast." Our breakfasts are not very splendid or tempting just now; probably a little ham or beefsteak, coffee, bread and butter; never any ice for breakfast - that is, very seldom, if ever; and hot as blazes. In this climate one needs cool and light food, fruit, etc.; but we don't get much of that sort of thing.

. . . Have been hard at work all day, and expect to keep at it until I get this army away from Fortress Monroe, unless my head is chopped off in the meantime - a circumstance I am in the daily expectation of occurring, and can't say that I much dread. . . . I presume Pope is having his hands quite full to-day; is probably being hard pressed by Jackson. I cannot help him in time, as I have not the means of transportation; but I foresee that the government will try to throw upon me the blame of their own delays and blunders. So be it. I have learned to endure, and shall continue to as long as the good of the country requires that I shall do so; but not one moment longer than that.

P.M.- . . . You see that Halleck has done otherwise than to reinforce me; quite the reverse. Burnside is at Acquia. I strongly suspect that one reason for their not imparting their plans to me is that they have very few to impart; they are drifting, not steering the poor Ship of State, and I fear they will be wrecked ere long. . . . If they do read our letters in Washington they must feel one ear tingle occasionally! . . . You need not dread any engagement at present. The "powers" won't let me go after the enemy, and I am quite sure they won't be kind enough to come after me. It is scarcely possible that we can have anything more than a mere affair of rear-guards. I don't think now that will occur; so make your mind quite easy. . . .

Cherrystone Inlet, Aug. 14, 2 A.M. - Left camp yesterday morning at seven o'clock in a gunboat to go to the telegraph-station at Jamestown island, so that I could talk with Halleck with less loss of time. On arriving there I found that the wires were not working through, and went straight on to Fortress Monroe, arriving there about 8.30 P.M. There I ascertained that the cable to this place was broken, so I took a steamer and came over here, arriving at eleven P.M. Halleck came to the Washington office about one and a half or two hours ago, I have sent him several telegrams, and his first reply is just arriving in cipher. I presume I am in for sitting up all night. The steamer is about two miles from here; came that distance in a row-boat. This is an abandoned secesh city, consisting of one house in the wilderness; so I am not likely to be disturbed. Porter, Ingalls, Colburn, and Key are with me. They are all sound asleep, so I have no one to distract my attention. I must confess, however, that as I went to bed very late last night, and have had no sleep since the morning, I am rather sleepy myself; but I can't just now indulge in the luxury.

3.30 A.M. - . . . We have just got back to the steamer, and I am getting under way to return to Fort Monroe, where I go direct to camp in a fast boat. My communication with Halleck was unsatisfactory in the extreme. He did not even behave with common politeness; he is a *bien mauvais sujet* - he is not a gentleman. . . . I am writing by a dim light, and confess that I am very tired and very much disgusted. I fear that I am very mad, and think I have a perfect right to be so. . . . Every day convinces me more and more that it is the intention of Halleck and the government to drive me off, and I begin to feel that I cannot preserve my self-respect and remain in the service much longer. I think the crisis will soon arrive. . . .

Berkley, Aug. 14. - Returned about noon. On my way down I stopped at the site of the old settlement of Jamestown. There is nothing left of it but the brick tower of the church and the churchyard. The oldest tombstone I could decipher was of 1698. I saw one of a poor young wife, only sixteen years and eleven months. I plucked a couple of poor little flowers from the site of the church and enclose them in this, only to show you that you are *sometimes* in my thoughts. . . . Porter's corps starts this evening, Franklin in the morning, the remaining three to-morrow and next day. Headquarters will remain here until nearly the last. We are going, not to Richmond, but to Fort Monroe, I am ashamed to say! . . . It is a terrible blow to me, but I have done all that could be done to prevent it, without success, so I must submit as best I can and carry it out. I shall, of course, conduct the march to Fortress Monroe and attend to the embarkation thence; my mind is pretty much made up to try hard to break off at that point.

Aug. 17, 3 P.M., *Barrett's Ferry, Chickahominy.* - . . . I have the greater part of the army now over, and if we are not disturbed for six hours more all will be well. I have abandoned neither men nor material, and the "retreat" has been conducted in the most orderly manner, and is a perfect success, so far as so disgusting an operation can be. I learn that all the troops in Virginia are to be placed under my command. Burnside came down to assure me from Halleck that he (H.) is really my friend -*qu'il soit!* . . . I hope to get everything over to-night, and will be at my old headquarters at Williamsburg to-morrow evening; next day at Yorktown. If all is then quiet I will go thence by water to Fortress Monroe and complete the arrangements for embarking. . . . I took a savage satisfaction in being the last to leave my camp at Berkley yesterday! . . .

Aug. 18, P.M., *Williamsburg.* - . . . Am pretty well tired out, for I have been much in the saddle lately, besides having slept very little. . . . I crossed the Chickahominy yesterday and remained there to-day until all the troops had crossed and moved several miles in advance. When I left, the bridge was taken up and nothing but a few worthless stragglers left behind. They will all be brought over to-night, I think; though, so far as they are concerned individually, I would much prefer that secesh should capture them all. I have made a remarkably successful retreat; left absolutely nothing behind. Secesh can't find one dollar's worth of property if he hunts a year for it. I have not seen the enemy since we started, and I rather doubt whether he knows where we are now. . . . It will take a long time to embark this army and have it ready for action on the banks of the Potomac. . . . The men all know that I am not responsible. I have remained constantly with the rear-guard; was the very last one to leave our camp at Berkley; remained on the Chickahominy until the bridge was removed, and still have the proud satisfaction of hearing the cheers of the men as I pass, seeing their faces brighten up. . . . Strange as it may seem, they have not, I think, lost one particle of confidence in me, and love me just as much as ever. Pleasonton has done splendidly. I placed him in command of the rear-guard of the main column, and nothing could have been better than his performance; he is really a fine officer, cool, collected, and intelligent. . . . I have felt every moment that I was conducting a false movement, and which was altogether against my own judgment and that of the army. I have done it without demoralizing the army. . . .

Fortress Monroe, Aug. 20, A.M. - Arrived here yesterday afternoon. The "retreat" is successfully accomplished and the troops have commenced embarking; a good many have left already.

Aug. 21, 4 P.M. *(Fort Monroe).* - Have just returned from an examination of this fort and the Rip Raps. . . . The whole of Porter's corps got off last night. Heintzelman from Yorktown to-day. Franklin commences to embark here and at Newport News to-morrow. Sumner will reach here to-morrow and commence embarking as soon as transports are ready, probably in a couple of days. I do not know what they intend doing with me. I still think they will place me on the shelf or do something disagreeable to get me out of the way. I shall be glad of anything that severs my connection with such a set. . . . I have had nothing from Washington to-day. As they do not see fit to give me any information either as to their intentions or their situation, I shall ask no more questions, nor will I make any more suggestions. They may go to the deuce in their own way, and I think are moving in that direction with sufficient rapidity to gratify secesh exceedingly. . .

Met with a terrible misfortune to-day. In entering the ambulance I tore the last uniform coat I had, except that one an inch thick, which I cannot well wear in this hot weather. So I am in citizen's dress. I shall be in a terrible predicament for citizen's clothes when I come home, and will have to remain *perdu* in the daytime until I get some clothes to wear, for it will not do for me to appear in uniform.

8 P.M. - Just received a telegram from Halleck stating that Pope and Burnside are very hard pressed, urging me to push forward reinforcements and to *come myself* as soon as *I possibly can!* I am going to the Fortress now to hurry on my arrangements; shall put headquarters on board a vessel to-morrow morning, and probably go myself in a fast boat to-morrow afternoon. Now they are in trouble they seem to want the "Quaker," the "procrastinator," the "coward," and the "traitor"! *Bien,* my ambulance is ready and I must go.

Aug. 22, 10 A.M. - . . . I did not get back from the Fort until some time after midnight, and too tired to write. . . . I shall go to the Fort pretty soon, and as soon as the tents are dry move everything on board the vessels, so that I shall be ready to start at a moment's notice. I have two corps off and away. . . . I think they are all pretty well scared in Washington, and probably with good reason. I am confident that the disposition to be made of me will depend entirely upon the state of their nerves in Washington. If they feel safe there I will, no doubt, be shelved; perhaps placed in command here *vice* Gen. Dix. I don't care what they do; would not object to being kept here for a while, because I could soon get things in such condition that I could have you here with me. . . . Their sending for me to go to Washington only indicates a temporary alarm. If they are at all reassured you will see that they will soon get rid of me. I shall be only too happy to get back to quiet life again; for I am truly and heartily sick of the troubles I have had, and am not fond of being a target for the abuse and slander of all the rascals in the country. Well, we will continue to trust in God and feel certain that all is for the best. It is often difficult to understand the ways of Providence; but I have faith enough to believe that nothing is done without some great purpose. . . .

Aug. 23, 9.30 P.M., *Steamer "City of Hudson."* - I am off at last and on the way to Acquia.

We are pounding along up the Potomac now, and, as the boat is a fast one, are passing everything we find. . . . We will reach Acquia some time after midnight. Early in the morning I will telegraph to Halleck informing him of my arrival and asking for orders. I have no idea what they will be, nor do I know what has been happening on the Rappahannock yesterday and to-day. I take it for granted that my orders will be as disagreeable as it is possible to make them, unless Pope is beaten, in which case they will want me to save Washington again. Nothing but their fears will induce them to give me any command of importance or to treat me otherwise than with discourtesy.

CHAPTER XXVIII.

Letters of Gen. Halleck and Gen. Burnside - Correspondence with Secretary Stanton - His professions of devotion - The truth.

BURNSIDE TO McCLELLAN.

"OLD POINT, July 15, 1862.

"MY DEAR MAC: I've just arrived from Washington and have not time to get ready to go up this morning, but will to-morrow. I've much to say to you and am very anxious to see you. . . . The President has ordered me to remain here for the present, and when I asked him how long he said five or six days. I don't know what it means; but I do know, my dear Mac, that you have lots of enemies. But you must keep cool; don't allow them to provoke you into a quarrel. You must come out all right; I'll tell you all to-morrow.

"Your old friend,
"BURN."

BURNSIDE TO McCLELLAN.

"FORT MONROE, Aug. 2, 1862.

"MY DEAR MAC: I'm laid up with a lame leg, and besides am much worried at the decision they have chosen to make in regard to your army. From the moment I reached Washington I feared it would be so, and I am of the opinion that your engineers had much to do with bringing about the determination. When the conclusion was arrived at I was the only one who advocated your forward movement. I speak now as if a positive decision had been arrived at, which I do not know, and you, of course, do; my present orders indicate it. But you know what they are, and all about it, so I will accept it as something that is ordered for the best. Let us continue to give our undivided support to the cause, and all will be well. It looks dark sometimes, but a just God will order everything for the best. We can't expect to have it all as we wish. I'm off for my desti-

472

nation and will write you a long letter from there. The troops
are nearly all embarked. Good-by. God bless you!
"Your old friend,

"A. E. BURNSIDE."

HALLECK TO McCLELLAN.

Unofficial.

"WASHINGTON, July 30, 1862.
*"Maj.-Gen. G. B. McClellan, Commanding, etc., Army of the
Potomac:*

"MY DEAR GENERAL: You are probably aware that I hold
my present position contrary to my own wishes, and that I did
everything in my power to avoid coming to Washington, But
after declining several invitations from the President I received
the order of the 11th instant, which left me no option.

"I have always had strong personal objections to mingling
in the politico-military affairs of Washington. I never liked the
place, and I like it still less at the present time.   But, aside from
personal feelings, I really believed that I could be much more
useful in the West than here. I had acquired some reputation
there, but here I could hope for none, and I greatly feared that,
whatever I might do, I should receive more abuse than thanks.
There seemed to be a disposition in the public press here to cry
down any one who attempted to serve the country instead of
party.   This was particularly the case with you, as I understand,
and I could not doubt that it would be in a few weeks the case
with me. Under these circumstances I could not see how I
could be of much use here.   Nevertheless, being ordered, I was
obliged to come.

"In whatever has occurred heretofore you have had my full
approbation and cordial support.   There was no one in the army
under whom I could serve with greater pleasure.   And I now
ask of you that same support and co-operation, and that same
free interchange of opinion, as in former days. If we should
disagree in opinion I know that we will do so honestly and
without unkind feelings. The country demands of us that we
act together and with cordiality.   I believe that we can and will
do so. Indeed, we *must* do so if we expect to put down this
rebellion.   If we permit personal jealousies to interfere for a

single moment with our operations we shall not only injure the cause but ruin ourselves. But I am satisfied that neither of us will do this, that we will work together with all our might to bring the war to an early termination.

"I have written to you frankly, assuring you of my friendship and confidence, believing that my letter would be received with the same kind feelings in which it is written,

"Yours truly,

" H. W. HALLECK."

HALLECK TO McCLELLAN.

"HEADQUARTERS OF THE ARMY,
"WASHINGTON, Aug. 7, 1862.

"Maj.-Gen. McClellan, Berkley:

"MY DEAR GENERAL: Your private letter of the 1st instant was received a day or two ago, but I have been too busy to answer it sooner.

"If you still wish it I will order Barnard here; but I cannot give you another engineer officer (unless you will take Benham), for you already have a larger proportion than any one else. I had most of the time in the West only two, and you, with no larger force, have a dozen engineer officers.

"I fully agree with you in regard to the manner in which the war should be conducted, and I believe the present policy of the President to be conservative. I think some of Gen. Pope's orders very injudicious, and have so advised him; but as I understand they were shown to the President before they were issued, I felt unwilling to ask him to countermand them. An oath of allegiance taken through force is not binding, and to put over the lines those who do not take it is only adding numbers to the rebel army. What he has made the general rule should only be the exceptions, and I have so advised him.

"I deeply regret that you cannot agree with me as to the necessity of reuniting the old Army of the Potomac. I, however, have taken the responsibility of doing so, and am willing to risk my reputation on it. As I told you when at your camp, it is my intention that you shall command all the troops in Virginia as soon as we can get them together, and with the army thus concentrated I am certain that you can take Richmond.

"I must beg of you, general, to hurry along this movement; your reputation as well as mine may be involved in its rapid execution. I cannot regard Pope and Burnside as safe until you reinforce them. Moreover, I wish them to be under your immediate command, for reasons which it is not necessary to specify. As things now are, with separate commands, there will be no concert of action, and we daily risk being attacked and defeated in detail.

"I would write you more fully, but nearly all my time is occupied with the new drafts and enlistments. They are doing well, but several weeks must elapse before we can get the troops into the field.

"Bragg seems to be concentrating a large force against Buell, and the latter is asking for reinforcements. When he will reach Chattanooga is a problem I am unable to solve.*

"Yours truly,

"H. W. HALLECK "

SECRETARY STANTON TO GEN. McCLELLAN.
Telegram; Cipher.

"HEADQUARTERS, DEPARTMENT OF WAR,
"WASHINGTON, July 5, 1862, 2.20 P.M.
" *Maj.-Gen. G. B. McClellan, Commanding, etc., Army of the Potomac:*
"I have nominated for promotion Gen. E. V. Sumner as brevet major-general of the regular service and major-general of volunteers; Gens. Heintzelman, Keyes, and Porter as brevet brigadiers in the regular service and major-generals of volun-

Note by the Editor.- In his private diary, Aug. 15 (Warden, p. 452), Mr. Secretary Chase writes: "Went to War Department. Stanton said Halleck had sent Burnside to James river to act as second in command, or as adviser of McClellan-in reality to control him."

Writing Sept. 2, Mr. Chase (Schuckers, p. 448) says that he saw Gen. Halleck on his return from visiting McClellan, and proceeds: "I cannot fix the date. It was late in July. He unreservedly condemned McClellan's whole military operations, and especially the conduct of the engagement before Richmond and the subsequent retreat to the James." "About this time I saw a good deal of Gen. Pope. . . . He condemned Gen. McClellan's conduct more and in stronger terms than Gen. Halleck. and said that in conversation he found Halleck quite agreed with him, but averse to precipitate action."

36

teers. The gallantry of every officer and man in your noble army shall be suitably acknowledged.

"Gen. Marcy is here and will take you cheering news.

"Be assured you shall have the support of this department and the government as cordially and faithfully as was ever rendered by man to man, and if we should ever live to see each other face to face you will be satisfied that you have never had from me anything but the most confiding integrity.

"EDWIN M. STANTON,
"Secretary of War."

SECRETARY STANTON TO GEN. MARCY.

"WAR DEPARTMENT,
"WASHINGTON CITY, D. C., July 5, 1862.

"DEAR GENERAL : I have to hasten to the country on account of the illness of one of my children, and must therefore forego the pleasure of your company.

"I leave a brief note for the general, having intended to write him at large. But you can explain to him much that I would say.

"Yours truly,
"EDWIN M. STANTON."

The following is the "brief note" referred to in the foregoing :

SECRETARY STANTON TO GEN. McCLELLAN.

"WAR DEPARTMENT,
"WASHINGTON CITY, D. C., July 5, 1862.

"DEAR GENERAL: I have had a talk with Gen. Marcy, and meant to have written you by him, but am called to the country, where Mrs. Stanton is with her children, to see one of them die.

"I can therefore only say, my dear general, in this brief moment, that there is no cause in my heart or conduct for the cloud that wicked men have raised between us for their own base and selfish purposes. No man had ever a truer friend than I have been to you and shall continue to be. You are seldom absent from my thoughts, and I am ready to make any sacrifice to aid you. Time allows me to say no more than that I pray Almighty God to deliver you and your army from all peril and lead you on to victory.*

"Yours truly,

"EDWIN M. STANTON."

GEN. McCLELLAN TO SECRETARY STANTON.

HEADQUARTERS, ARMY OF THE POTOMAC,
CAMP NEAR HARRISON'S LANDING, VA., July 8, 1862.

DEAR SIR: Your letter of the 5th instant by Gen. Marcy has made a deep impression on my mind. Let me, in the first place, express my sympathy with you in the sickness of your child, which I trust may not prove fatal.

I shall be better understood by you, and our friendly relations will become more fixed, if I am permitted to recur briefly to the past.

When you were appointed Secretary of War I considered you my intimate friend and confidential adviser. Of all men in the nation you were my choice for that position.

It was the unquestionable prerogative of the President to determine the military policy of the administration and to select the commanders who should carry out the measures of the government. To any action of this nature I could, of course, take no personal exception.

But from the time you took office your official conduct towards me as commander-in-chief of the army of the United States, and afterwards as commander of the Army of the Potomac, was marked by repeated acts done in such manner as to be deeply offensive to my feelings and calculated to affect me injuriously in public estimation.

After commencing the present campaign your concurrence in the withholding of a large portion of my force, so essential to the success of my plans, led me to believe that your mind was warped by a bitter personal prejudice against me.

Your letter compels me to believe that I have been mistaken in regard to your real feelings and opinions, and that your conduct, so unaccountable to my own fallible judgment, must have

*See note at end of the chapter.

proceeded from views and motives which I did not understand. I have made this frank statement because I thought that it would best accord with the spirit of your communication.

It is with a feeling of great relief that I now say to you that I shall at once resume on my part the same cordial confidence which once characterized our intercourse.

You have more than once told me that together we could save this country. It is yet not too late to do so.

To accomplish this there must be between us the most entire harmony of thought and action, and such I offer you.

The crisis through which we are passing is a terrible one.

I have briefly given in a confidential letter to the President my views (please ask to see it) as to the policy which ought to govern this contest on our part.

You and I during last summer so often talked over the whole subject that I have only expressed the opinions then agreed upon between us.

The nation will support no other policy. None other will call forth its energies in time to save our cause. For none other will our armies continue to fight.

I have been perfectly frank with you. Let no cloud hereafter arise between us.

Very respectfully, your obedient servant,

GEORGE B. McCLELLAN,

Maj.- Gen. Commanding.

Hon. E. M. STANTON,
Secretary of War.

Note by the Editor. - There is no more sorrowful page in the story of men and of peoples than this, in which it becomes necessary, for the truth of history, to bring together the evidence of a war secretary's private treason to the general in the field, fighting his country's battles. It is unnecessary to draw on the countless sources of private evidence which exist, since the testimony of Secretaries Chase and Welles, and Postmaster-General Blair, his associates in Mr. Lincoln's cabinet, suffice, without extending the miserable record of Mr. Stanton's falsehood and shame, to show his continuous personal hostility to Gen. McClellan from the time of his entering the cabinet in January, at the precise date of writing the above telegram and letter of July 5, and during the rest of McClellan's campaigns.

Mr. Gideon Welles, Secretary of the Navy in the cabinet with Mr. Stanton, in his work, "Lincoln and Seward," New York, 1874, says:

(P. 190) "With the change in the War Department in Jan., 1862, came the *hostility of Secretary Stanton to McClellan, then general-in-chief.*"

(P. 191) "This unwise letter [the Harrison's Bar letter] and the *reverses of the army,* with the *active hostility* of Stanton, brought Halleck, a vastly inferior man, to Washington. . . . On coming to Washington, Pope, who was ardent and, I think, courageous, though not always discreet, very naturally fell into the views of Secretary Stanton, *who improved every opportunity to denounce McClellan* and his hesitating policy. Pope also reciprocated the commendations bestowed on him by Halleck, by uniting with Stanton and Gen. Scott in advising that McClellan should be superseded and Halleck placed in charge of military affairs at Washington. This, combined with the movements and the disasters before Richmond, and his own imprudent letter, *enabled Stanton to get rid of McClellan at headquarters.*

(P. 193) "But Pope was defeated, and the army, sadly demoralized, came retreating to the Potomac. The War Department, and especially Stanton and Halleck, became greatly alarmed. On the 30th August, in the midst of these disasters, and before the result had reached us, though most damaging information in regard to McClellan, who lingered at Alexandria, was current, the Secretary of the Treasury, Mr. Chase, called upon me with a protest, *signed by himself and Stanton, denouncing the conduct of McClellan and demanding his immediate dismissal.* Two other members were ready to append their names after mine. I declined to sign the paper, *which was in the handwriting of Stanton;* not that I did not disapprove of the course of the general, but because the combination was improper and disrespectful to the President. . . . I had doubted the wisdom of recalling the Army of the Potomac from Richmond, therein differing from Chase and Stanton. *The object in bringing that army back to Washington, in order to start a new march overland and regain the abandoned position, I did not understand unless it was to get rid of McClellan. . . .* The President never knew of this paper, but was not unaware of the popular feeling against that officer, in which he sympathized, and of the sentiments of the members of the cabinet, aggravated by the hostility and *strong if not exaggerated rumors sent out by the Secretary of War.* Both Stanton and Halleck were, however, filled with apprehensions beyond others, as the army of stragglers and broken battalions, on the last of August and first of September, came rushing toward Washington."

Mr. S. P. Chase, Secretary of the Treasury in the same cabinet, writing shortly after Sept. 2, 1862, says:

"From the day the President told me McClellan was beaten, and I saw his despatches announcing his retreat towards the James river, I never entertained a doubt of the necessity of withdrawing the army altogether, if it was to remain under his command, and I expressed this opinion at once to the President. The military men said that to attempt to withdraw the army would involve the loss of all its material, ammunition, guns, provisions, and stores."

Mr. Chase then refers to the visit of Gen. Marcy at Washington (on which occasion Mr. Stanton's letter of July 5 was written), and what Gen. Marcy had said, and continues:

"The danger of withdrawal; the impossibility of strengthening the army for an advance on Richmond from the position to which it had retreated; the certainty that no vigorous effort would be made by

McClellan, by unexpected blows south of the James, to retrieve the disasters north of it; the possibility of the loss of the entire army-convinced me, and *convinced the Secretary of War,* that the command of the Army of the Potomac should be given to some more active officer. *We proposed to the President to send Pope to the James,* and give Mitchell the command of the army in front of Washington, which . . . had been placed under Pope. The President was not prepared for anything so decisive, and sent for Halleck and made him commander-in-chief" (Schuckers's "Life, etc., of S. P. Chase," p. 447).

After Pope's defeat Mr. Chase says:

"The President . . . himself gave the command of the fortifications and the troops for the defence of Washington to McClellan. It was against my protest and that of the Secretary of War" (ibid. p. 450).

Aug. 29 Mr. Chase writes:

"The Secretary of War called on me in reference to Gen. McClellan. He has long believed, and so have I, that Gen. McClellan ought not to be trusted with the command of any army of the Union, and the events of the last few days have greatly strengthened our judgment. We called on . . . Gen. Halleck and remonstrated against Gen. McClellan commanding. Secretary wrote and presented to Gen. H. a call for a report touching McC.'s disobedience of orders and consequent delay of support to Army of Virginia; Gen. H. promised answer to-morrow morning" (Warden's "Account, etc., of S. P. Chase," p. 456).

On Aug. 30 Mr. Chase states that he and Mr. Stanton prepared and signed a paper expressing their judgment of McClellan (ibid. p. 456).

Sept. 1 Mr. Chase states: "On suggestion of Judge Bates, the remonstrance against McClellan, which had been previously signed by Smith, was modified; and, having been further slightly altered on my suggestion, was signed by Stanton, Bates, and myself, and afterward by Smith. Welles declined to sign it, on the ground that it might seem unfriendly to the President, though this was the exact reverse of its intent. He said he agreed in opinion, and was willing to express it personally. This determined us to await the cabinet meeting to morrow" (ibid. p, 458).

The testimony of Postmaster-General Blair will be found further on in connection with accounts of the cabinet meeting on Sept. 2, as given by Secretaries Chase and Welles. When Mr. Stanton had succeeded, as he supposed, in depriving McClellan of command by his ironical order of Aug. 30, and when the peril of the capital and country led Mr. Lincoln on Sept. 2 to appeal to McClellan to save them, Mr. Stanton openly declared, says Mr. Blair, that he would rather see the capital lost than McClellan restored to command.

CHAPTER XXIX.

The army at Harrison's Bar - Indecision at Washington - The Harrison's Bar letter - Army ordered home - Protests of McClellan - On the bank of the James river the fate of the Union should be decided - Transportation not provided - Withdrawal of the army - Transfer to front of Washington.

WHEN the troops reached the James the first want of the men was something to eat and drink, and the next a bath in the river. As I rode among the men they would cry to me for their supper, and upon my assuring them that they should have it they would give their usual cheers and be perfectly content. For two or three days after we reached Harrison's Bar the banks of the river were crowded all day long with the men bathing.

It should be understood that in time of action every army reduces itself into two of unequal strength - one, the fighting men, who stick by their colors as long as life and strength last, and are ever ready to meet the enemy; the other consisting of the weaker men, and those prone to straggle, and those not too fond of unnecessary combat. The better the discipline of the army, the larger the first category, and *vice versa.* It must be confessed that the contingent of stragglers was pretty large on our arrival at the James, but after a day or two all had rejoined their colors and were ready for work again.

A very few days sufficed to give the men the necessary rest, and the army was then in condition to make any movement justified by its numbers, and was in an admirable position for an offensive movement. It was at last upon its true line of operations, which I had been unable to adopt at an earlier day in consequence of the Secretary of War's peremptory order of the 18th of May requiring the right wing to be extended to the north of Richmond in order to establish communication with Gen. McDowell. Gen. McDowell was then under orders to advance from Fredericksburg, but never came, because, in spite of his earnest protest, these orders were countermanded from

481

Washington, and he was sent upon a fruitless expedition towards the Shenandoah instead of being permitted to join me, as he could have done, at the time of the affair of Hanover Court-House.

I urged in vain that the Army of the Potomac should remain on the line of the James, and that it should resume the offensive as soon as reinforced to the full extent of the means in possession of the government. Had the Army of the Potomac been permitted to remain on the line of the James I would have crossed to the south bank of that river, and, while engaging Lee's attention in front of Malvern, have made a rapid movement in force on Petersburg, having gained which I would have operated against Richmond and its communications from the west, having already gained those from the south.

Subsequent events proved that Lee did not move northward from Richmond with his army until assured that the Army of the Potomac was actually on its way to Fort Monroe, and they also found that, so long as the Army of the Potomac was on the James, Washington and Maryland would have been entirely safe under the protection of the fortifications and a comparatively small part of the troops then in that vicinity; so that Burnside's troops and a large part of the Union Army of Virginia might, with entire propriety, have been sent by water to join the army under my command, which - with detachments from the West - could easily have been brought up to more than 100,000 men disposable on the actual field of battle.

In spite of my most pressing and oft-repeated entreaties, the order was insisted upon for the abandonment of the Peninsula line and the return of the Army of the Potomac to Washington in order to support Gen. Pope, who was in no danger so long as the Army of the Potomac remained on the James. With a heavy heart I relinquished the position gained at the cost of so much time and blood.

As an evidence of my good faith in opposing this movement it should be mentioned that Gen. Halleck had assured me, verbally and in writing, that I was to command all the troops in front of Washington, including those of Gens. Burnside and Pope - a promise which was not carried into effect.

On the 1st of July I received the following from the President:

"It is impossible to reinforce you for your present emergency. If we had a million of men we could not get them to give you in time. We have not the men to send. If you are not strong enough to face the enemy you must find a place of security and wait, rest, and repair.

"Maintain your ground if you can, but save the army at all events, even if you fall back to Fort Monroe. We still have strength enough in the country, and will bring it out."

In a despatch from the President to me on the 2d of July he says:

"If you think you are not strong enough to take Richmond just now, I do not ask you to. Try just now to save the army material and personnel, and I will strengthen it for the offensive again as fast as I can.

"The governors of eighteen (18) States offer me a new levy of 300,000, which I accept."

On the 2d of July the following was received from Gen. Barnard:

Private.

"HEADQUARTERS, July 2, 1862.

"DEAR GENERAL: It seems to me the only salvation is for this army to be ready promptly to reassume the offensive.

"For this we must immediately push our forces further forward, or we are bagged. Besides being able to shell us out, the enemy will entrench us in, and, shutting us up here with a small force, be off for Washington.

"The fresh troops (how many?) now here or on the river ought to enable us to push out at once and to assume an offensive as soon as our old army can be rested.

"But we need large reinforcements. The state of affairs is concealed in Washington to hide their own blunders, and the country will not respond to the crisis unless it is known. We need 200,000 more men to fill up the ranks and form new regiments.

"A large part of Halleck's force, all that can be withdrawn, should come from the West.

"There is no use in writing. Should you not send at once an officer who will not be afraid to speak? And though such a messenger does not open his lips except to Lincoln and Stanton, the public will soon know that there is something concealed. It should be done by all means.

"To-day we must get ourselves enough out to save being

shut in. There is no use in entrenching a line of no real utility, and what Duane can do to-day will only wear out his men for nothing.

"It is troops alone that can help us to-day. By to-morrow we will be able to know where to entrench.

"We must have fresh troops immediately in large numbers, and I would, if necessary, abandon Norfolk and New Berne to get them, and all the useless coast of South Carolina and Georgia, holding only Fort Pulaski.

"Pensacola is of no use, but I suppose may be held with few troops.

"Yours, etc.,

"J. G. BARNARD."

On the 3d of July the following was received from the President:

"... Yours of 5.30 yesterday is just received. I am satisfied that yourself, officers, and men have done the best you could. All accounts say better fighting was never done. Ten thousand thanks for it. . . ."

On the 4th I sent the following to the President:

JULY 4, 1862.

I have the honor to acknowledge the receipt of your despatch of the 2d instant.

I shall make a stand at this place, and endeavor to give my men the repose they so much require.

After sending my communication on Tuesday the enemy attacked the left of our lines, and a fierce battle ensued, lasting until night; they were repulsed with great slaughter. Had their attack succeeded, the consequences would have been disastrous in the extreme. This closed the hard fighting which had continued from the afternoon of the 26th ultimo, in a daily series of engagements wholly unparalleled on this continent for determination and slaughter on both sides.

The mutual loss in killed and wounded is enormous; that of the enemy certainly greatest. On Tuesday morning, the 1st, our army commenced its movement from Haxall's to this point, our line of defence there being too extended to be maintained by our weakened forces. Our train was immense, and about four P.M. on the 2d a heavy storm of rain began, which continued during the entire day and until the forenoon of yesterday.

The roads became horrible. Troops, artillery, and wagons moved on steadily, and our whole army, men and material. was finally brought safe into this camp.

The last of the wagons reached here at noon yesterday. The exhaustion was very great, but the army preserved its morale, and would have repelled any attack which the enemy was in condition to make.

We now occupy a line of heights about two miles from the James, a plain extending from there to the river; our front is about three miles long. These heights command our whole position, and must be maintained. The gunboats can render valuable support upon both flanks. If the enemy attack us in front we must hold our ground as we best may and at whatever cost.

Our positions can be carried only by overwhelming numbers. The spirit of the army is excellent; stragglers are finding their regiments, and the soldiers exhibit the best results of discipline. Our position is by no means impregnable, especially as a morass extends on this side of the high ground from our centre to the James on our right. The enemy may attack in vast numbers, and if so our front will be the scene of a desperate battle, which, if lost, will be decisive. Our army is fearfully weakened by killed, wounded, and prisoners.

I cannot now approximate to any statement of our losses, but we were not beaten in any conflict.

The enemy were unable, by their utmost efforts, to drive us from any field. Never did such a change of base, involving a retrograde movement, and under incessant attacks from a most determined and vastly more numerous foe, partake so little of disorder. We have lost no guns except 25 on the field of battle, 21 of which were lost by the giving way of McCall's division under the onset of superior numbers.

Our communications by the James river are not secure. There are points where the enemy can establish themselves with cannon or musketry and command the river, and where it is not certain that our gunboats can drive them out. In case of this, or in case our front is broken, I will still make every effort to preserve at least the *personnel* of the army; and the events of the last few days leave no question that the troops will do all that their country can ask. Send such reinforcements as you can; I will do what I can. We are shipping our wounded and sick, and landing supplies. The Navy Department should co-operate with us to the extent of its resources. Com. Rodgers is doing all in his power in the kindest and most efficient manner.

When all the circumstances of the case are known it will be acknowledged by all competent judges that the movement just completed by this army is unparalleled in the annals of war. Under the most difficult circumstances we have preserved our trains, our guns, our material, and, above all, our honor.

To which I received the following reply from the President:

"A thousand thanks for the relief your two despatches of twelve and one P.M. yesterday gave me. Be assured the heroism and skill of yourself, officers, and men is and for ever will be appreciated.

"If you can hold your present position we shall have the enemy yet."

The following letter was received from his Excellency the President:

"*July* 4. - I understand your position, as stated in your letter, and by Gen. Marcy. To reinforce you so as to enable you to resume the offensive within a month, or even six weeks, is impossible. In addition to that arrived and now arriving from the Potomac (about 10,000 I suppose), and about 10,000 I hope you will have from Burnside very soon, and about 5,000 from Hunter a little later, I do not see how I can send you another man within a month. Under these circumstances the defensive, for the present, must be your only care. Save the army first, where you are if you can, and, secondly, by removal if you must. You, on the ground, must be the judge as to which you will attempt, and of the means for effecting it. I but give it as my opinion that, with the aid of the gunboats and the reinforcements mentioned above, you can hold your present position, provided, and so long as, you can keep the James river open below you. If you are not tolerably confident you can keep the James river open, you had better remove as soon as possible. I do not remember that you have expressed any apprehension as to the danger of having your communication cut on the river below you, yet I do not suppose it can have escaped your attention.

"P.S. If at any time you feel able to take the offensive, you are not restrained from doing so."

The following telegram was sent on the 7th to the President:

As boat is starting, I have only time to acknowledge receipt of despatch by Gen. Marcy. Enemy have not attacked. My position is very strong, and daily becoming more so. If not attacked to-day I shall laugh at them. I have been anxious about my communications. Had long consultation about it with Flag-Officer Goldsborough last night; he is confident he can keep river open. He should have all gunboats possible. Will see him again this morning. My men in splendid spirits, and anxious to try it again.

Alarm yourself as little as possible about me, and don't lose confidence in this army.

While general-in-chief, and directing the operations of all our armies in the field, I had become deeply impressed with the importance of adopting and carrying out certain views regarding the conduct of the war which, in my judgment, were essential to its objects and its success.

During an active campaign of three months in the enemy's country these were so fully confirmed that I conceived it a duty, in the critical position we then occupied, not to withhold a candid expression of the more important of these views from the commander-in-chief, whom the Constitution places at the head of the armies and navies, as well as of the government, of the nation.

Mr. Lincoln visited me at Harrison's Bar. I handed him myself, on board of the steamer in which he came, the letter of July 7, 1862. He read it in my presence, but made no comments upon it, merely saying, when he had finished it, that he was obliged to me for it, or words to that effect. I do not think that he alluded further to it during his visit, or at any time after that.

THE HARRISON'S BAR LETTER.

HEADQUARTERS, ARMY OF THE POTOMAC,
CAMP NEAR HARRISON'S LANDING, VA., July 7, 1862.

MR. PRESIDENT: You have been fully informed that the rebel army is in the front, with the purpose of overwhelming us by attacking our positions or reducing us by blocking our river communications. I cannot but regard our condition as critical, and I earnestly desire, in view of possible contingencies, to lay before your excellency, for your private consideration, my general views concerning the existing state of the rebellion, although they do not strictly relate to the situation of this army or strictly come within the scope of my official duties. These views amount to convictions, and are deeply impressed upon my mind and heart. Our cause must never be abandoned; it is the cause of free institutions and self-government. The Constitution and the Union must be preserved, whatever may be the cost in time, treasure, and blood. If secession is successful other dissolutions are clearly to be seen in the future. Let neither military disaster, political faction, nor foreign war shake your settled purpose to enforce the equal operation of the laws of the United States upon the people of every State.

The time has come when the government must determine

upon a civil and military policy covering the whole ground of our national trouble.

The responsibility of determining, declaring, and supporting such civil and military policy, and of directing the whole course of national affairs in regard to the rebellion, must now be assumed and exercised by you, or our cause will be lost. The Constitution gives you power sufficient even for the present terrible exigency.

This rebellion has assumed the character of war; as such it should be regarded, and it should be conducted upon the highest principles known to Christian civilization. It should not be a war looking to the subjugation of the people of any State in any event. It should not be at all a war upon population, but against armed forces and political organizations. Neither confiscation of property, political executions of persons, territorial organization of States, or forcible abolition of slavery should be contemplated for a moment. In prosecuting the war all private property and unarmed persons should be strictly protected, subject only to the necessity of military operations. All private property taken for military use should be paid or receipted for; pillage and waste should be treated as high crimes; all unnecessary trespass sternly prohibited, and offensive demeanor by the military towards citizens promptly rebuked. Military arrests should not be tolerated, except in places where active hostilities exist, and oaths not required by enactments constitutionally made should be neither demanded nor received. Military government should be confined to the preservation of public order and the protection of political rights. Military power should not be allowed to interfere with the relations of servitude, either by supporting or impairing the authority of the master, except for repressing disorder, as in other cases. Slaves contraband under the act of Congress, seeking military protection, should receive it. The right of the government to appropriate permanently to its own service claims to slave labor should be asserted, and the right of the owner to compensation therefor should be recognized.

This principle might be extended, upon grounds of military necessity and security, to all the slaves within a particular State, thus working manumission in such State; and in Missouri, perhaps in Western Virginia also, and possibly even in Maryland, the expediency of such a measure is only a question of time.

A system of policy thus constitutional and conservative, and pervaded by the influences of Christianity and freedom, would receive the support of almost all truly loyal men, would deeply impress the rebel masses and all foreign nations, and it might be humbly hoped that it would commend itself to the favor of the Almighty.

Unless the principles governing the future conduct of our struggle shall be made known and approved, the effort to obtain requisite forces will be almost hopeless. A declaration of radical views, especially upon slavery, will rapidly disintegrate our present armies. The policy of the government must be supported by concentrations of military power. The national forces should not be dispersed in expeditions, posts of occupation, and numerous armies, but should be mainly collected into masses and brought to bear upon the armies of the Confederate States. Those armies thoroughly defeated, the political structure which they support would soon cease to exist.

In carrying out any system of policy which you may form you will require a commander-in-chief of the army, one who possesses your confidence, understands your views, and who is competent to execute your orders by directing the military forces of the nation to the accomplishment of the objects by you proposed. I do not ask that place for myself. I am willing to serve you in such position as you may assign me, and I will do so as faithfully as ever subordinate served superior.

I may be on the brink of eternity; and as I hope forgiveness from my Maker, I have written this letter with sincerity towards you and from love for my country.*

Very respectfully, your obedient servant,

GEO. B. McCLELLAN,

Maj.- Gen. Commanding.

His Excellency A. LINCOLN,

President.

*Note by the Editor. - It has been frequently intimated that this letter was written, in consultation with friends at the North, as a political document. It was the misfortune of McClellan that civilians at Washington, judging him in their own lights, could not conceive it possible that he or any man could render honest, unselfish service to country and cause without some concealed purpose of benefit to himself. Pure devotion to duty, without thought of self, is incomprehensible to the average politician. I think it proper to say, therefore, that no one of McClellan's most intimate personal friends at the North knew even of the existence of this letter until rumors about it came from members of Mr. Lincoln's cabinet. None of them saw it until after the general was finally relieved from command. Meantime it had been discussed thoroughly by those to whom the President showed it, and it cannot be doubted that a general inability to appreciate the sincere motives in which it was written did much to determine the future conduct of the administration towards McClellan. Mr. Chase, with startling innocence of mind, avows (Warden, p. 440) that on July 22 he urged Mr. Lincoln to remove McClellan, on the ground "that I did not regard Gen. McClellan as *loyal to the administration, although I did not question his general loyalty to the country."* This is the confession of a motive in the conduct of a great war which is universally regarded as infamous. It is an avowal that the controlling consideration of such leaders as Mr. Chase, in the use of the blood and treasure of the people, was the supremacy of

I telegraphed the President on the 11th: "We are very strong here now, so far as defensive is concerned. Hope you will soon make us strong enough to advance and try it again. All in fine spirits."

Telegrams were sent to the President on the 12th, 17th, and 18th:

12th. - I am more and more convinced that this army ought not to be withdrawn from here, but promptly reinforced and thrown again upon Richmond. If we have a little more than half a chance we can take it. I dread the effects of any retreat upon the *morale* of the men.

17th. - I have consulted fully with Gen. Burnside, and would commend to your favorable consideration the general's plan for bringing (7) seven additional regiments from North Carolina, by leaving New Berne to the care of the gunboats. It appears manifestly to be our policy to concentrate here everything we can possibly spare from less important points, to make sure of crushing the enemy at Richmond, which seems clearly to be the most important point in rebeldom. Nothing should be left to chance here. I would recommend that Gen. Burnside, with all his troops, be ordered to this army, to enable it to assume the offensive as soon as possible.

18th. - Am anxious to have determination of government, that no time may be lost in preparing for it. Hours are very precious now, and perfect unity of action necessary.

The following was telegraphed to Gen. Halleck on the 28th:

My opinion is more and more firm that here is the defence of Washington, and that I should be at once reinforced by all available troops to enable me to advance. Retreat would be disastrous to the army and the cause. I am confident of that.

On the 30th to Gen. Halleck:

I hope that it may soon be decided what is to be done by this army, and that the decision may be to reinforce it at once. We are losing much valuable time, and that at a moment when energy and decision are sadly needed.

party, and not the success of country. Neither the President nor Gen. McClellan had any such impure ideas. And it is beyond doubt that the radical difference between his own views and those of the self-seeking men who surrounded him led Mr. Lincoln to the despairing state of mind in which, a few weeks later, he desired to resign.

About half an hour after midnight on the morning of Aug. 1 the enemy brought some light batteries to Coggins's Point and the Coles House, on the right bank of James river directly opposite Harrison's Landing, and opened a heavy fire upon our shipping and encampments. It was continued rapidly for about thirty minutes, when they were driven back by the fire of our guns.

To prevent another demonstration of this character, and to insure a debouch on the south bank of the James, it became necessary to occupy Coggins's Point, which was done on the 3d, and the enemy driven back towards Petersburg.

On the 1st of Aug. I received the following despatches from Gen. Halleck:

"Washington, July 30, 1862, 8 P.M. - A despatch just received from Gen. Pope says that deserters report that the enemy is moving south of James river, and that the force in Richmond is very small. I suggest that he be pressed in that direction, so as to ascertain the facts of the case."

"Washington, July 30, 1862, 8 P.M. - In order to enable you to move in any direction it is necessary to relieve you of your sick. The surgeon-general has therefore been directed to make arrangements for them at other places, and the quartermaster-general to provide transportation. I hope you will send them away as quickly as possible, and advise me of their removal."

It is clear that the general-in-chief attached some weight to the report received from Gen. Pope, and I was justified in supposing that the order in regard to removing the sick contemplated an offensive movement rather than a retreat, as I had no other data than the telegrams just given from which to form an opinion as to the intentions of the government. The following telegram from him strengthened me in that belief:

"Washington, July 31, 1862, 10 A.M. - Gen. Pope again telegraphs that the enemy is reported to be evacuating Richmond, and falling back on Danville and Lynchburg.

"H. W. HALLECK,
"*Maj.-Gen.*"

In occupying Coggins's Point I was influenced by the necessity of possessing a secure debouch on the south of the James, in order to enable me to move on the communications of Rich-

37

mond in that direction, as well as to prevent a repetition of midnight cannonades.

To carry out Gen. Halleck's first order, of July 30, it was necessary first to gain possession of Malvern Hill, which was occupied by the enemy, apparently in some little force, and controlled the direct approach to Richmond. Its temporary occupation at least was equally necessary in the event of a movement upon Petersburg, or even the abandonment of the Peninsula. Gen. Hooker, with his own division and Pleasonton's cavalry, was therefore directed to gain possession of Malvern Hill on the night of the 2d of Aug.

He failed to do so on account of the incompetency of guides.

On the 4th Gen. Hooker was reinforced by Gen. Sedgmick's division, and, having obtained a knowledge of the roads, he succeeded in turning Malvern Hill and driving the enemy back towards Richmond.

The following is my report of this affair at the time:

Malvern Hill, Aug. 5, 1862, 1 P.M. - Gen. Hooker at 5.30 this morning attacked a very considerable force of infantry and artillery stationed at this place, and carried it handsomely, driving the enemy towards New Market, which is four miles distant, and where it is said they have a large force. We have captured 100 prisoners, killed and wounded several, with a loss on our part of only three killed and eleven wounded; among the latter two officers.

I shall probably remain here to-night, ready to act as circumstances may require after the return of my cavalry reconnoissances.

The mass of the enemy escaped under the cover of a dense fog; but our cavalry are still in pursuit, and I trust may succeed in capturing many more.

This is a very advantageous position to cover an advance on Richmond, and only fourteen and three-quarter miles distant; and I feel confident that, with reinforcements, I would march this army there in five days.

I this instant learn that several brigades of the enemy are four miles from here on the Quaker road, and I have taken steps. to prepare to meet them.

Gen. Hooker's dispositions were admirable, and his officers and men displayed their usual gallantry.

On the same day I telegraphed to Gen. Halleck:

Our troops have advanced twelve miles in one direction

and seventeen in another towards Richmond to-day. We have secured a strong position at Coggins's Point, opposite our quartermaster's depot, which will effectually prevent the rebels from using artillery hereafter against our camps.

I learn this evening that there is a force of 20,000 men about six miles back from this point, on the south bank of the river; what their object is I do not know, but will keep a sharp lookout on their movements.

I am sending off sick as rapidly as our transports will take them. I am also doing everything in my power to carry out your orders to push reconnoissances towards the rebel capital, and hope soon to find out whether the reports regarding the abandonment of that place are true.

To the despatch of one P.M., Aug. 5, the following answer was received Aug. 6:

"I have no reinforcements to send you.
"H. W. HALLECK,
" *Maj.-Gen.*"

And soon after the following, also from Gen. Halleck:

"You will immediately send a regiment of cavalry and several batteries of artillery to Burnside's command at Acquia creek. It is reported that Jackson is moving north with a very large force."

On the 4th I had received Gen. Halleck's order of the 3d (which appears below), directing me to withdraw the army to Acquia, and on the same day sent an earnest protest against it.

A few hours before this Gen. Hooker had informed me that his cavalry pickets reported large bodies of the enemy advancing and driving them in, and that he would probably be attacked at daybreak. Under these circumstances I had determined to support him; but as I could not get the whole army in position until the next afternoon, I concluded, upon the receipt of the above telegram from the general-in-chief, to withdraw Gen. Hooker, that there might be the least possible delay in conforming to Gen. Halleck's orders. I therefore sent to Gen. Hooker:

. . . Under advices I have received from Washington, I think it necessary for you to abandon the position to-night, getting everything away before daylight.

Five batteries, with their horses and equipments complete, were embarked on the 7th and 8th. Simultaneously with Gen. Hooker's operations upon Malvern I despatched a cavalry force under Col. Averill towards Savage's Station to ascertain if the enemy were making any movements towards our left flank. He found a rebel cavalry regiment near the White Oak Swamp bridge, and completely routed it, pursuing well towards Savage's Station.

These important preliminary operations assisted my preparations for the removal of the army to Acquia creek, and the sending off our sick and supplies was pushed both day and night as rapidly as the means of transportation permitted.

On the subject of the withdrawal of the army from Harrison's Landing the following correspondence passed between the general-in-chief and myself while the reconnoissances towards Richmond were in progress.

On the 2d of Aug. I received the following from Gen. Halleck:

"You have not answered my telegram [of July 30, 8 P.M.] about the removal of your sick. Remove them as rapidly as possible, and telegraph me when they will be out of your way. The President wishes an answer as early as possible."

To which I sent this reply:

3d, 11 P.M. - Your telegram of (2d) second is received. The answer [to despatch of July 30] was sent this morning. We have about 12,500 sick, of whom perhaps 4,000 might make easy marches. We have here the means to transport 1,200, and will embark to-morrow that number of the worst cases. With all the means at the disposal of the medical director the remainder could be shipped in from seven to ten days. It is impossible for me to decide what cases to send off, unless I know what is to be done with this army.

Were the disastrous measures of a retreat adopted all the sick who cannot march and fight should be despatched by mater. Should the army advance many of the sick could be of service at the depots. If it is to remain here any length of time, the question assumes still a different phase.

Until I am informed what is to be done I cannot act understandingly or for the good of the service. If I am kept longer in ignorance of what is to be effected I cannot be expected to accomplish the object in view. In the meantime I will do all in my power to carry out what I conceive to be your wishes.

The moment I received the instructions for removing the sick I at once gave the necessary directions for carrying them out.

With the small amount of transportation at hand the removal of the severe cases alone would necessarily take several days, and, in the meantime, I desired information to determine what I should do with the others.

The order required me to send them away as quickly as possible, and to notify the general-in-chief *when they were removed.*

Previous to the receipt of the despatch of the 2d of Aug., not having been advised of what the army under my command was expected to do, or which way it was to move, if it moved at all, I sent the following despatch to Gen. Halleck:

Berkley, Aug. 3 - I hear of sea-steamers at Fort Monroe; are they for removing my sick? If so, to what extent am I required to go in sending them off? There are not many who need go.

As I am not in any way informed of the intentions of the government in regard to this army, I am unable to judge what proportion of the sick should leave here, and must ask for specific orders.

If the army was to retreat to Fort Monroe it was important that it should be unencumbered with any sick, wounded, or other men who might at all interfere with its mobility; but if the object was to operate directly on Richmond from the position we then occupied, there were many cases of slight sickness which would speedily be cured and the patients returned to duty.

As the service of every man would be important in the event of a forward offensive movement, I considered it to be of the utmost consequence that I should know what was to be done. It was to ascertain this that I sent the despatch of eleven P.M. on the 3d, before receiving the following telegram from Gen. Halleck:

"*Washington, Aug.* 3, 1862, 7.45 P.M. - I have waited most anxiously to learn the result of your forced reconnoissance towards Richmond, and also whether all your sick have been sent away, and I can get no answer to my telegram.

"It is determined to withdraw your army from the Peninsula to Acquia creek. You will take immediate measures to effect this, covering the movement the best you can.

"Its real object and withdrawal should be concealed even from your own officers.

"Your material and transportation should be removed first. You will assume control of all the means of transportation within your reach, and apply to the naval forces for all the assistance they can render you. You will consult freely with the commander of these forces. The entire execution of the movement is left to your discretion and judgment.

"You will leave such forces as you may deem proper at Fort Monroe, Norfolk, and other places, which we must occupy."

I proceeded to obey this order with all possible rapidity, firmly impressed, however, with the conviction that the withdrawal of the Army of the Potomac from Harrison's Landing, where its communications had, by the co-operation of the gunboats, been rendered perfectly secure, would at that time have the most disastrous effect upon our cause.

I did not, as the commander of that army, allow the occasion to pass without distinctly setting forth my views upon the subject to the authorities in the following telegram:

Aug. 4. - Your telegram of last evening is received. I must confess that it has caused me the greatest pain I ever experienced, for I am convinced that the order to withdraw this army to Acquia creek will prove disastrous to our cause.

I fear it will be a fatal blow.

Several days are necessary to complete the preparations for so important a movement as this; and while they are in progress I beg that careful consideration may be given to my statements.

This army is now in excellent discipline and condition. We hold a debouch on both banks of the James river, so that we are free to act in any direction, and, with the assistance of the gunboats, I consider our communications as now secure. We are twenty-five miles from Richmond, and are not likely to meet the enemy in force sufficient to fight a battle until we have marched fifteen to eighteen miles, which brings us practically within ten miles of Richmond. Our longest line of land-transportation would be from this point twenty-five miles; but with the aid of the gunboats we can supply the army by water, during its advance, certainly to within twelve miles of Richmond.

At Acquia creek we would be seventy-five miles from Richmond, with land-transportation all the way.

From here to Fort Monroe is a march of about seventy miles; for I regard it as impracticable to withdraw this army and its material except by land.

The result of the movement would thus be a march of one hundred and forty-five miles to reach a point now only twenty-five miles distant, and to deprive ourselves entirely of the powerful aid of the gunboats and water-transportation. Add to this the certain demoralization of this army which would ensue, the terribly depressing effect upon the people of the North, and the strong probability that it would influence foreign powers to recognize our adversaries, and there appear to me sufficient reasons to make it my imperative duty to urge, in the strongest terms afforded by our language, that this order may be rescinded, and that, far from recalling this army, it be promptly reinforced to enable it to resume the offensive.

It may be said that there are no reinforcements available. I point to Burnside's force, to that of Pope - not necessary to maintain a strict defensive in front of Washington and Harper's Ferry - to those portions of the Army of the West not required for a strict defensive there. Here, directly in front of this army, is the heart of the rebellion; it is here that all our resources should be collected to strike the blow which will determine the fate of the nation. All points of secondary importance elsewhere should be abandoned and every available man brought here; a decided victory here, and the military strength of the rebellion is crushed, it matters not what partial reverses we may meet with elsewhere.

Here is the true defence of Washington; it is here, on the banks of the James, that the fate of the Union should be decided.

Clear in my convictions of right, strong in the consciousness that I have ever been, and still am, actuated solely by love of my country, knowing that no ambitious or selfish motives have influenced me from the commencement of this war, I do now what I never did in my life before - I entreat that this order may be rescinded.

If my counsel does not prevail I will, with a sad heart, obey your orders to the utmost of my power, directing to the movement, which I clearly foresee will be one of the utmost delicacy and difficulty, whatever skill I may possess.

Whatever the result may be - and may God grant that I am mistaken in my forebodings - I shall at least have the internal satisfaction that I have written and spoken frankly, and have sought to do the best in my power to avert disaster from my country.

G. B. McCLELLAN,
Maj-Gen. Commanding.

Maj.-Gen. H. W. HALLECK,
Commanding U. S. Army.

Soon after sending this telegram I received the following from Gen. Halleck in reply to mine of eleven P.M. of the 3d:

"My telegram to you of yesterday will satisfy you in regard to future operations; it was expected that you would have sent off your sick, as directed, without waiting to know what were or would be the intentions of the government respecting future movements.

"The President expects that the instructions which were sent you yesterday, with his approval, will be carried out with all possible despatch and caution. The quartermaster-general is sending to Fort Monroe all the transportation he can collect."

To which the following is my reply:

Your telegram of yesterday received, and is being carried out as promptly as possible. With the means at my command no human power could have moved the sick in the time you say you expected them to be moved. . . .

My efforts for bringing about a change of policy were unsuccessful. On the 7th I received the following telegram from Gen. Halleck:

"You will immediately report the number of sick sent off since you received my order; the number still to be shipped, and the amount of transportation at your disposal; that is, the number of persons that can be carried on all the vessels which by my order you were authorized to control."

To which I made this reply:

Aug. 7. - In reply to your despatch of 10 A.M. to-day I report the number of sick sent off since I received your order as follows: 3,740, including some that are embarked to-night and will leave to-morrow morning. The number still to be shipped is, as nearly as can be ascertained, 5,700.

The embarkation of five batteries of artillery! with their horses, wagons, etc., required most of our available boats, except the ferry-boats. All the transports that can ascend to this place have been ordered up: they will be here to-morrow evening. Col. Ingalls reports to me that there are no transports now available for cavalry, and will not be for two or three days. As soon as they can be obtained I shall send off the 1st N. Y. Cavalry.

After the transports with sick and wounded have returned, including some heavy-draught steamers at Fort Monroe that cannot come to this point, we can transport 25,000 men at a time. We have some propellers here, but they are laden with commissary supplies and are not available.

The transports now employed in transporting sick and wounded will carry 12,000 well infantry soldiers. Those at Fort Monroe, and of too heavy draught to come here, will carry 8,000 or 10,000 infantry. Several of the largest steamers have been used for transporting prisoners of war, and have only become available for the sick to-day.

The report of my chief-quartermaster upon the subject is as follows:

"HEADQUARTERS, ARMY OF THE POTOMAC,
"OFFICE OF CHIEF-QUARTERMASTER,
"HARRISON'S LANDING, August 7, 1862.

"GENERAL: I have the honor to return the papers herewith which you sent me, with the following remarks:

"We are embarking five batteries of artillery, with their horses, baggage, etc., which requires the detailing of most of our available boats, except the ferry-boats. The medical department has ten or twelve of our largest transport vessels, which, if disposable, could carry 12,000 men. Besides, there are some heavy-draught steamers at Fort Monroe that cannot come to this point, but which can carry 8,000 or 10,000 infantry.

"I have ordered all up here that can ascend to this depot. They will be here to-morrow evening. As it now is, after the details already made we cannot transport from this place more than 5,000 infantry.

"There are no transports now available for cavalry. From and after to-morrow, if the vessels arrive, I could transport 10,000 infantry. In two or three days a regiment of cavalry can be sent, if required. If you wait, and ship from Yorktown or Fort Monroe after the sick and mounded transports are at my disposal, we can transport 25,000 at a time. The number that can be transported is contingent on circumstances referred to.

"Most of the propellers here are laden with commissary or other supplies, and most of the tugs are necessary to tow off sail-craft also laden with supplies.

"I am, very respectfully, your most obedient servant,
"RUFUS INGALLS,
"Chief-Quartermaster.

"Gen. R. B. MARCY,
"Chief of Staff."

On the 9th I received this despatch from Gen. Halleck:

"I am of the opinion that the enemy is massing his forces in front of Gens. Pope and Burnside, and that he expects to crush them and move forward to the Potomac.

"You must send reinforcements instantly to Acquia creek.

"Considering the amount of transportation at your disposal, your delay is not satisfactory. You must move with all possible celerity."

To which I sent the following reply:

Telegram of yesterday received. The batteries sent to Burnside took the last available transport yesterday morning. Enough have since arrived to ship one regiment of cavalry to-day. The sick are being embarked as rapidly as possible. There has been no unnecessary delay, as you assert - not an hour's - but everything has been and is being pushed as rapidly as possible to carry out your orders.

The following report, made on the same day by the officer then in charge of the transports, exposes the injustice of the remark in the despatch of the general-in-chief, that, "considering the amount of transportation at your disposal, your delay is not satisfactory":

"ASSISTANT QUARTERMASTER'S OFFICE,
"ARMY OF THE POTOMAC,
"HARRISON'S LANDING, VIRGINIA, Aug. 10, 1862.

"Col. Ingalls, being himself ill, has requested me to telegraph to you concerning the state and capacity of the transports now here. On the night of the 8th I despatched eleven steamers, principally small ones, and six schooners, with five batteries of heavy horse-artillery, none of which have yet returned.

"Requisition is made this morning for transportation of 1,000 cavalry to Acquia creek. All the schooners that had been chartered for carrying horses have been long since discharged or changed into freight-vessels.

"A large proportion of the steamers now here are still loaded with stores, or are in the floating hospital service engaged in removing the sick. To transport the 1,000 cavalry to-day will take all the available steamers now here not engaged in the service of the harbor. These steamers could take a large number of infantry, but are not well adapted to the carrying of horses, and much space is thus lost. Several steamers are expected here to-day, and we are unloading schooners rapidly; most of these are not chartered, but are being taken for the service required, at same rates of pay as other chartered schooners. If you could cause a more speedy return of the steamers sent away from here it would facilitate matters.

"C. G. SAWTELLE,
"*Capt. and Assist. Quartermaster, commanding Depot.*"

Our wharf facilities at Harrison's Landing were very limited, admitting but few vessels at one time. These were continually in use as long as there were disposable vessels, and the officers of the medical and quartermaster's departments, with all their available forces, were incessantly occupied, day and night, in embarking and sending off the sick men, troops, and material.

Notwithstanding the repeated representations I made to the general-in-chief that such were the facts, on the 10th I received the following from Gen. Halleck:

"The enemy is crossing the Rapidan in large force. They are fighting Gen. Pope to-day; there must be no further delay in your movements. That which has already occurred was entirely unexpected and must be satisfactorily explained. Let not a moment's time be lost, and telegraph me daily what progress you have made in executing the order to transfer your troops."

To which I sent this reply:

Your despatch of to-day is received. I assure you again that there has not been any unnecessary delay in carrying out *your* orders. You are probably laboring under some great mistake as to the amount of transportation available here. I have pushed matters to the utmost in getting off our sick and the troops you ordered to Burnside.

Col. Ingalls has more than once informed the quartermaster-general of the condition of our water-transportation. From the fact that you directed me to keep the order secret I took it for granted that you would take the steps necessary to provide the requisite transportation. A large number of transports for all arms of service and for wagons should at once be sent to Yorktown and Fort Monroe. I shall be ready to move the whole army by land the moment the sick are disposed of. You may be sure that not an hour's delay will occur that can be avoided. I fear you do not realize the difficulty of the operation proposed. The regiment of cavalry for Burnside has been in course of embarkation to-day and to-night. Ten steamers were required for the purpose. 1,258 sick loaded to-day and to-night. Our means exhausted, except one vessel returning to Fort Monroe in the morning, which will take some 500 cases of slight sickness.

The present moment is probably not the proper one for me to refer to the unnecessarily harsh and unjust tone of your telegrams of late. It will, however, make no difference in my official action.

On the 11th this report was made:

The embarkation of 850 cavalry and one brigade of infantry will be completed by two o'clock in the morning; 500 sick were embarked to-day; another vessel arrived to-night, and 600 more sick are now being embarked. I still have some 4,000 sick to dispose of. You have been grossly misled as to the amount of transportation at my disposal. Vessels loaded to their utmost capacity with stores, and others indispensable for service here, have been reported to you as available for carrying sick and well. I am sending off all that can be unloaded at Fort Monroe, to have them return here. I repeat that I have lost no time in carrying out your orders.

On the 12th I received the following from Gen. Halleck:

"The quartermaster-general informs me that nearly every available steam-vessel in the country is now under your control. It was supposed that 8,000 or 10,000 of your men could be transported daily. In addition to steamers there is a large fleet of sailing-vessels which could be used as transports. The bulk of your material on shore, it was thought, could be sent to Fort Monroe covered by that part of the army which could not get water-transportation. Such were the views of the government here. Perhaps me were misinformed as to the facts; if so, the delay could be explained. Nothing in my telegram was intentionally harsh or unjust; but the delay was so unexpected that an explanation was required. There has been and is the most urgent necessity for despatch, and not a single moment must be lost in getting additional troops in front of Washington."

I telegraphed the following reply at eleven P.M.:

Your despatch of noon to-day received. It is positively the fact that no more men could have embarked hence than have gone, and that no unnecessary delay has occurred. . . .
I am sure that you have been misinformed as to the availability of vessels on hand. We cannot use heavily loaded supply-vessels for troops or animals; and such constitute the mass of those here, which have been represented to you as capable of transporting this army. . .
There shall be no unnecessary delay, but I cannot manufacture vessels. I state these difficulties from experience, and because it appears to me that we have been lately working at cross-purposes, because you have not been properly informed by those around you, who ought to know - the inherent difficulties of such an undertaking. It is not possible for any one to place this army where you wish it, ready to move, in less than a month.
If Washington is in danger now this army can scarcely arrive in time to save it; it is in much better position to do so from here than from Acquia.
"Our material can only be saved by using the whole army to cover it if me are pressed. If sensibly weakened by detachments the result might be the loss of much material and many men. I will be at the telegraph-office to-morrow morning.

It will be seen by the concluding paragraph of the foregoing despatch that in order to have a more direct, speedy, and full explanation of the condition of affairs in the army than I could by sending a single despatch by steamer to the nearest tele-graph-office at Jamestown island, some seventy miles distant, and waiting ten hours for a reply, I proposed to go in person to the office. This I did.

On my arrival at Jamestown island there was an interruption in the electric current, which rendered it necessary for me to continue on to Fort Monroe, and across the Chesapeake bay to Cherry Stone inlet, on the "Eastern Shore," where I arrived late in the evening, and immediately sent the two annexed despatches:

13th 11.30 P.M. - Please come to office; wish to talk to you. What news from Pope?

14th 12.30 A.M. - Started to Jamestown island to talk with

you; found cable broken and came here.   Please read my long
telegram [of Aug: 12, 11 P.M.]   All quiet at camp.   Enemy burned
wharves at City Point yesterday.   No rebel pickets within eight
(8) miles of Coggins's Point yesterday.

Richmond prisoners state that large force with guns left
Richmond northward on Sunday.

To which the following reply was received:

"1.40 A.M. - I have read your despatch.   There is no change
of plans.   You will send up your troops as rapidly as possible.
There is no difficulty in landing them.   According to your own
accounts there is now no difficulty in withdrawing your forces.
Do so with all possible rapidity.

"H. W. HALLECK,
"*Maj.- Gen.*"

Before I had time to decipher and reply to this despatch, the
telegraph operator in Washington informed me that Gen. Halleck had gone out of the office immediately after writing this
despatch, without leaving any intimation of the fact for me or
waiting for any further information as to the object of my jour-
ney across the bay.   As there was no possibility of other communication with him at that time, I sent the following despatch
and returned to Harrison's Landing:

1.40 A.M. - Your orders will be obeyed.   I return at once.
I had hoped to have had a longer and fuller conversation with
you, after travelling so far for the purpose.

On the 14th and 15th, and before we had been able to
embark all our sick men, two army corps were put in motion
towards Fort Monroe. This was reported in the annexed
despatch:

Aug. 16, 11 P.M. - Movement has commenced by land and
water.   All sick will be away to-morrow night.   Everything
being done to carry out your orders.   I don't like Jackson's
movements; he will suddenly appear where least expected.
Will telegraph fully and understandingly in the morning.

The phrase "movement has commenced," it need not be
remarked, referred obviously to the movement of the main
army after completing the necessary preliminary movements
of the sick, etc.

The perversion of the term to which the general-in-chief saw fit to give currency, in a letter to the Secretary of War, should have been here rendered impossible by the despatches which precede this of the 14th, which show that the movement really began immediately after the receipt of the order of Aug. 4.*

After the commencement of the movement it was continued with the utmost rapidity until all the troops and material were en route, both by land and water, on the morning of the 16th.

Late in the afternoon of that day, when the last man had disappeared from the deserted camps, I followed with my personal staff in the track of the grand Army of the Potomac, bidding farewell to the scene still covered with the marks of its presence, and to be for ever memorable in history as the vicinity of its most brilliant exploits.

Previous to the departure of the troops I had directed Capt. Duane, of the engineer corps, to proceed to Barrett's Ferry, near the mouth of the Chickahominy, and throw across the river at that point a pontoon-bridge. This was executed promptly and satisfactorily, under the cover of gunboats, and an excellent bridge of about 2,000 feet in length was ready for the first arrival of troops. The greater part of the army, with its artillery, wagon-trains, etc., crossed it rapidly, and in perfect order and safety, so that on the night of the 17th everything was across the Chickahominy, except the rear-guard, which crossed early on the morning of the 18th, when the pontoon-bridge was immediately removed.

Gen. Porter's corps, which was the first to march from Harrison's Landing, had been pushed forward rapidly, and on the 16th reached Williamsburg, where I had directed him to halt until the entire army was across the Chickahominy.

On his arrival at Williamsburg, however, he received an intercepted letter, which led to the belief that Gen. Pope would have to contend against a very heavy force then in his front. Gen. Porter, therefore, very properly took the responsibility of continuing his march directly on to Newport News, which place he reached on the morning of the 18th of August, having marched

* In a letter to the Secretary of War, Aug. 30, 1862, Gen Halleck said: "It will be seen from my telegraphic correspondence that Gen. McClellan protested against the movement, and that it was not actually commenced till the 14th inst."

his corps sixty miles in the short period of three days and one night, halting one day at the crossing of the Chickahominy.

The embarkation of this corps commenced as soon as transports were ready, and on the 20th it had all sailed for Acquia creek from Barrett's Ferry.

On the 18th and 19th our march was continued to Williamsburg and Yorktown, and on the 20th the remainder of the army was ready to embark at Yorktown, Fortress Monroe, and Newport News.

From the commencement to the termination of this most arduous campaign the Army of the Potomac always evinced the most perfect subordination, zeal, and alacrity in the performance of all the duties required of it.

The amount of severe labor accomplished by this army in the construction of entrenchments, roads, bridges, etc., was enormous; yet all the work was performed with the most gratifying cheerfulness and devotion to the interests of the service.

During the campaign ten severely contested and sanguinary battles had been fought, besides numerous smaller engagements, in which the troops exhibited the most determined enthusiasm and bravery. They submitted to exposure, sickness, and even death, without a murmur. Indeed, they had become veterans in their country's cause and richly deserved the warm commendation of the government.

It was in view of these facts that this seemed to me an appropriate occasion for the general-in-chief to give, in general orders, some appreciative expression of the services of the army while upon the Peninsula. Accordingly, on the 18th I sent him the following despatch:

HEADQUARTERS, ARMY OF THE POTOMAC,
Aug. 18, 1862, 11 P.M.

Please say a kind word to my army that I can repeat to them in general orders in regard to their conduct at Yorktown, Williamsburg, West Point, Hanover Court-House, and on the Chickahominy, as well as in regard to the Seven Days and the recent retreat.

No one has ever said anything to cheer them but myself. Say nothing about me. Merely give my men and officers credit for what they have done. It will do you much good, and will strengthen you much with them, if you issue a handsome order to them in regard to what they have accomplished. They deserve it.

G. B. McCLELLAN,
Maj.-Gen.

Maj.-Gen. HALLECK,
Washington, D. C.

As no reply was received to this communication, and no order was issued by the general-in-chief, I conclude that the suggestion did not meet with his approbation.

All the *personnel* and material of the army had been transferred from Harrison's Landing to the different points of embarkation in the very brief period of five days without the slightest loss or damage. Porter's troops sailed from Newport News on the 19th and 20th. Heintzelman's corps sailed from Yorktown on the 21st. On that day I received the following telegram from the general-in-chief:

"Leave such garrisons in Fortress Monroe, Yorktown, etc., as you may deem proper. They will be replaced by new troops as rapidly as possible.

"The forces of Burnside and Pope are hard pushed, and require aid as rapidly as you can send it. Come yourself as soon as you can. . . ."

38

CHAPTER XXX.

The army reaches Alexandria; sent forward to Pope - Pope's campaign - McClellan's work at Alexandria - The last man sent forward - Stanton's ironical order - McClellan commands a hundred men - Halleck in despair - McClellan's volunteer services.

ON the evening of Aug. 23 I sailed with my staff for Acquia creek, where I arrived at daylight on the following morning, reporting to Gen. Halleck as follows:

Acpuia creek, Aug. 24, 1862. - I have reached here, and respectfully report for orders.

I also telegraphed as follows to Gen. Halleck:

Morell's scouts report Rappahannock Station burned and abandoned by Pope without any notice to Morell or Sykes. This was telegraphed you some hours ago. Reynolds, Reno, and Stevens are supposed to be with Pope, as nothing can be heard of them to-day. Morell and Sykes are near Morrisville Post-office, watching the lower fords of Rappahannock, with no troops between there and Rappahannock Station, which is reported abandoned by Pope.

Please inform me immediately exactly where Pope is and what doing; until I know that, I cannot regulate Porter's movements. He is much exposed now, and decided measures should be taken at once. Until I know what my command and position are to be, and whether you still intend to place me in the command indicated in your first letter to me, and orally through Gen. Burnside at the Chickahominy, I cannot decide where I can be of most use. If your determination is unchanged I ought to go to Alexandria at once. Please define my position and duties.

To which I received the following reply from Gen. Halleck:

"*Aug.* 24. - You ask me for information which I cannot give. I do not know either where Gen. Pope is or where the enemy in force is. These are matters which I have all day been most anxious to ascertain."

On the 26th I received the following from Gen. Halleck:

"There is reason to believe that the enemy is moving a large force into the Shenandoah Valley. Reconnoissances will soon determine. Gen. Heintzelman's corps was ordered to report to Gen. Pope, and Kearny's will probably be sent to-day against the enemy's flank. Don't draw any troops down the Rappahannock at present; we shall probably want them all in the direction of the Shenandoah. Perhaps you had better leave Gen. Burnside in charge at Acquia creek and come to Alexandria, as very great irregularities are reported there. Gen. Franklin's corps will march as soon as it receives transportation."

On receipt of this I immediately sailed for Alexandria, and reported as follows to Gen. Halleck:

Aug. 27, 8 A.M. - I arrived here last night, and have taken measures to ascertain the state of affairs here, and that proper remedies may be applied. Just received a rumor that railway bridge over Bull Bun was burned last night.

Aug. 27, 9.40 A.M. . - The town is quiet, although quite full of soldiers, who are said to be chiefly convalescents.

The affairs of the quartermaster's department are reported as going on well.

It is said that the Bull Run bridge will be repaired by to-morrow. The disembarkation of Sumner's corps commenced at Acquia yesterday afternoon. I found that he could reach Rappahannock Station earlier that way than from here.

On the same day I received the following from Gen. Halleck:

"*Aug:* 27. - Telegrams from Gen. Porter to Gen Burnoide, just received, say that Banko is at Fayetteville; McDowell, Sigel, and Ricketts near Warrenton; Reno on his right. Porter is marching on Warrenton Junction to reinforce Pope. Nothing said of Heintzelman. Porter reports a general battle imminent. Franklin's corps should move out by forced marches, carrying three or four days' provisions, and to be supplied, as far as possible, by railroad. Perhaps you may prefer some other road than to Centreville. Col. Haupt has just telegraphed about sending out troops. Please see him and give him your directions. There has been some serious neglect to guard the railroad, which should be immediately remedied."

I replied as follows:

Aug. 27, 10 A.M. - Telegram this moment received. I have

sent orders to Franklin to prepare to march with his corps at once, and to repair here in person to inform me as to his means of transportation.

Kearny was yesterday at Rappahannock Station; Porter at Bealeton, Kellip, Barnell's, etc. Sumner will commence reaching Falmouth to-day. Williams's Mass. Cavalry will be mostly at Falmouth to-day.

I loaned Burnside my personal escort (one squadron 4th regulars), to scout down Rappahannock.

I have sent for Couch's division to come at once. As fast as I gain any information I will forward it, although you may already have it.

I also received the following telegrams from Gen. Halleck :

"*Aug.* 27. - Direct Gen. Casey to furnish you about 5,000 of the new troops under his command.

"Take entire direction of the sending-out of the troops from Alexandria.

"Determine questions of priority in transportation and the places they shall occupy. Pope's headquarters are near Warrenton Junction, but I cannot ascertain the present position of his troops."

"*Aug.* 27. - I can get no satisfactory information from the front, either of the enemy or of our troops. There seems to have been great neglect and carelessness about Manassas. Franklin's, corps should march in that direction as soon as possible. A competent officer should be sent out to take direction of affairs in that vicinity."

Upon the receipt of these I immediately sent the following telegram to Gens. Heintzelman and Porter:

Alexandria, Aug. 27, 1862, 10.30 A.M. - Where are you, and what is state of affairs? What troops in your front, right, and left? Sumner is now landing at Acquia. Where is Pope's left, and what of enemy? Enemy burned Bull Run bridge last night with cavalry force.

Maj.-Gen. HEINTZELMAN, Warrenton.
Maj.-Gen. PORTER, Bealeton.

P.S. If these general officers are not at the places named, nearest operator will please have message forwarded.

I also telegraphed to the general-in-chief the following despatches:

Aug. 27, 10.50 A.M. - I have sent all the information I possess to Burnside, instructing him to look out well for his right flank, between the Rappahannock and Potomac, and to send no trains to Porter without an escort. I fear the cavalry who dashed at Bull Run last night may trouble Burnside a little. I have sent to communicate with Porter and Heintzelman *via* Falmouth, and hope to give you some definite information in a few hours. I shall land the next cavalry I get hold of here, and send it out to keep open the communication between Pope and Porter, also to watch vicinity of Manassas. Please send me a number of copies of the best maps of present field of operations. I can use fifty to advantage.

Aug. 27, 11.20 A.M. - In view of Burnside's despatch, just received, would it not be advisable to throw the mass of Sumner's corps here, to move out with Franklin to Centreville or vicinity? If a decisive battle is fought at Warrenton, a disaster would leave any troops on lower Rappahannock in a dangerous position.

They would do better service in front of Washington.

Alexandria, Aug. 27, 12 M. - I have just learned through Gen. Woodbury that it was stated in your office last night that it was very strange that, with (20,000) twenty thousand men here, I did not prevent the raid upon Manassas. This induces me to ask whether your remark in your telegram to-day, that there had been great neglect about Manassas, was intended to apply to me. I cannot suppose it was, knowing, as you do, that I arrived here without information and with no instructions beyond pushing the landing of my troops. The bridge was burned before my arrival; I knew nothing of it until this morning. I ask as a matter of justice that you will prevent your staff from making statements which do me such gross injustice at a time when the most cordial co-operation is required.

Aug. 27, 12.5 P.M. - My aide has just returned from Gen. Franklin's camp; reports that Gens. Franklin, Smith, and Slocum are all in Washington. He gave the order to the next in rank to place the corps in readiness to move at once. I learn that heavy firing has been heard this morning at Centreville, and have sent to ascertain the truth. I can find no cavalry to send out on the roads. Are the works garrisoned and ready for defence?

Aug. 27, 12.20 P.M. - What bridges exist over Bull Run? Have steps been taken to construct bridges for the advance of troops to reinforce Pope, or to enable him to retreat if in trouble?

There should be two gunboats at Acquia creek at once. Shall I push the rest of Sumner's corps here, or is Pope so strong as to be reasonably certain of success? I have sent to inspect the works near here and their garrisons.

As soon as I can find Gen. Casey, or some other commanding officer, I will see to the railway, etc. It would be well to have them report to me, as I do not know where they are. I am trying to find them, and will lose no time in carrying out your orders. Would like to see Burnside.

Aug. 27, 1.15 P.M. - Franklin's artillery have no horses, except for (4) four guns without caissons. I can pick up no cavalry. In view of these facts, will it not be well to push Sumner's corps here by water as rapidly as possible, to make immediate arrangements for placing the works in front of Washington in an efficient condition of defence? I have no means of knowing the enemy's force between Pope and ourselves.

Can Franklin, without his artillery or cavalry, effect any useful purpose in front?

Should not Burnside take steps at once to evacuate Falmouth and Acquia, at the same time covering the retreat of any of Pope's troops who may fall back in that direction?

I do not see that we have force enough in hand to form a connection with Pope, whose exact position we do not know. Are we safe in the direction of the valley?

Aug. 27, 1.35 P.M. - I learn that Taylor's brigade, sent this morning to Bull Run bridge, is either cut to pieces or captured; that the force against them had many guns and about (5,000) five thousand infantry, receiving reinforcements every minute; also, that Gainesville is in possession of the enemy. Please send some cavalry, out towards Dranesville *via* Chain bridge, to watch Lewinsvllle and Dranesville, and go as far as they can. If you will give me even one squadron of good cavalry here I will ascertain the state of the case. I think our policy now is to make these works perfectly safe, and mobilize a couple of corps as soon as possible, but not to advance them until they can have their artillery and cavalry. I have sent for Col. Tyler to place his artillerymen in the works.

Is Fort Marcy securely held?

Aug. 27, 2.30 P.M. - Sumner has been ordered to send here all of his corps that are within reach. Orders have been sent to Couch to come here from Yorktown with the least possible delay. But one squadron of my cavalry has arrived; that will be disembarked at once and sent to the front.

If there is any cavalry in Washington it should be ordered to report to me at once.

I still think that we should first provide for the immediate defence of Washington on both sides of the Potomac.

I am not responsible for the past, and cannot be for the future unless I receive authority to dispose of the available troops according to my judgment. Please inform me at once what my position is. I do not wish to act in the dark.

Aug. 27, 6 P.M. - I have just received the copy of a despatch from Gen. Pope to you, dated ten A.M. this morning, in which he says : "All forces now sent forward should be sent to my right at Gainesville."

I now have at my disposal here about (10,000) ten thousand men of Franklin's corps, about (2,800) twenty-eight hundred of Gen. Tyler's brigade, and Col. Tyler's 1st Conn. Artillery, which I recommend should be held in hand for the defence of Washington.

If you wish me to order any part of this force to the front, it is in readiness to march at a moment's notice to any point you may indicate.

In view of the existing state of things in our front, I have deemed it best to order Gen. Casey to hold his men for Yorktown in readiness to move, but not to send them off till further orders.

On the 28th I telegraphed as follows to Gen. Halleck:

Aug. 28, 4.10 P.M - Gen. Franklin is with me here. I will know in a few minutes the condition of artillery and cavalry.

We are not yet in condition to move; may be by to-morrow morning.

Pope must cut through to-day or adopt the plan I suggested. I have ordered troops to garrison the works at Upton's Hill. They must be held at any cost. As soon as I can see the may to spare them I will send a corps of good troops there. It is the key to Washington, which cannot be seriously menaced as long as it is held.

I received the following from the general-in-chief:

"*Aug.* 28, 1862. - I think you had better place Sumner's corps, as it arrives, near the guns, and particularly at the Chain bridge.

"The principal thing to be feared now is a cavalry raid into this city, especially in the night-time.

"Use Cox's and Tyler's brigades and the new troops for the same object, if you need them.

"Porter writes to Burnside from Bristoe, 9.30 A.M. yesterday, that Pope's forces were then moving on Manassas, and that Burnside would soon hear of them by way of Alexandria.

"Gen. Cullum has gone to Harper's Ferry, and I have only a single regular officer for duty in the office.

"Please send some of your officers to-day to see that every precaution is taken at the forts against a raid, also at the bridge. Please answer."

On the 29th the following despatch was telegraphed to Gen. Halleck:

Aug. 29, 10.30 A.M. - Franklin's corps is in motion; started about (6) six A.M. I can give him but two squadrons of cavalry. I propose moving Gen. Cox to Upton's Hill, to hold that important point with its works, and to push cavalry scouts to Vienna via Freedom Hill and Hunter's Lane. Cox has (2) two squadrons of cavalry. Please answer at once whether this meets your approval. I have directed Woodbury, with the engineer brigade, to hold Fort Lyon. Sumner detached last night two regiments to vicinity of Forts Ethan Allen and Marcy. Meagher's brigade is still at Acquia. If he moves in support of Franklin it leaves us without any reliable troops in and near Washington. Yet Franklin is too weak alone. What shall be done? No more cavalry arrived; have but (3) three squadrons. Franklin has but (40) forty rounds of ammunition, and no wagons to move more. I do not think Franklin is in condition to accomplish much if he meets with serious resistance. I should not have moved him but for your pressing order of last night. What have you from Vienna and Dranesville?

To which the following is a reply from Gen. Halleck:

"*Aug.* 29, 12 M. - Upton's Hill arrangement all right. We must send wagons and ammunition to Franklin as fast as they arrive.

"Meagher's brigade ordered up yesterday. Fitz-Hugh Lee was, it is said on good authority, in Alexandria on Sunday last for three hours. I have nothing from Dranesville."

On the same day the following was received from his Excellency the President:

"*Washington, Aug.* 29, 1862, 2.30 P.M. - What news from direction of Manassas Junction? What generally?

"A. LINCOLN.

"Maj.-Gen. MCCLELLAN."

To which I replied as follows:

Aug. 29, 1862, 2.45 P.M. - The last news I received from the direction of Manassas was from stragglers, to the effect that the enemy were evacuating Centreville and retiring towards Thoroughfare Gap. This by no means reliable.

I am clear that one of two courses should be adopted: 1st, to concentrate all our available forces to open communications with Pope; 2d, to leave Pope to get out of his scrape, and at once use all our means to make the capital perfectly safe.

No middle ground will now answer. Tell me what you wish me to do, and I will do all in my power to accomplish it. I wish to know what my orders and authority are. I ask for nothing, but will obey whatever orders you give. I only ask a prompt decision, that I may at once give the necessary orders. It will not do to delay longer.

GEO. B. MCCLELLAN,
Maj.-Gen.

A. LINCOLN, *President.*
And copy to Gen. Halleck.

To which the following is a reply:

"*Washington, Aug.* 29, 1862, 4.10 P.M. - Yours of to-day just received. I think your first alternative, to wit, "to concentrate all our available forces to open communication with Pope," is the right one, but I wish not to control. That I now leave to Gen. Halleck, aided by your counsels.

"A. LINCOLN.

"Maj.-Gen. MCCLELLAN."

It had been officially reported to me from Washington that the enemy, in strong force, was moving through Vienna in the direction of the Chain bridge, and had a large force in Vienna. This report, in connection with the despatch of the general-in-chief on the 28th, before noted, induced me to direct Franklin to halt his command near Annandale until it could be determined, by Reconnoissances to Vienna and towards Manassas, whether these reports were true. Gen. Cox was ordered to send his small cavalry force from Upton's Hill towards Vienna and Dranesville in one direction, and towards Fairfax Court-House in the other, and Franklin to push his two squadrons as far towards Manassas as possible, in order to ascertain the true position of the enemy.

With the enemy in force at Vienna and towards Lewinsville, it would have been very injudicious to have pushed Franklin's small force beyond Annandale. It must be remembered that at that time we were cut off from direct communication with Gen. Pope; that the enemy was, by the last accounts, at Manassas in strong force, and that Franklin had only from 10,000 to 11,000 men, with an entirely insufficient force of cavalry and artillery.

In order to represent this condition of affairs in its proper light to the general-in-chief, and to obtain definite instructions, from him, I telegraphed to him as follows:

Aug. 29, 12 M. - Have ordered most of the (12th) Twelfth Penn. Cavalry to report to Gen. Barnard for scouting duty towards Rockville, Poolesville, etc.

If you apprehend a raid of cavalry on your side of river, I had better send a brigade or two of Sumner's to near Tennally-town, where, with two or three old regiments in Forts Allen and Marcy, they can watch both Chain bridge and Tennallytown.

Would it meet your views to post the rest of Sumner's corps. between Arlington and Fort Corcoran, whence they can either support Cox, Franklin, or Chain bridge, and even Tennallytown?

Franklin has only between (10,000) ten thousand and (11,000) eleven thousand for duty.

How far do you wish this force to advance?

Also the following:

Aug. 29, 1 P.M. - I anxiously await reply to my last despatch. in regard to Sumner. Wish to give the order at once.

Please authorize me to attach new regiments permanently to my old brigades. I can do much good to old and new troops in that way. I shall endeavor to hold a line in advance of Forts Allen and Marcy, at least with strong advanced guards. I wish to hold the line through Prospect Hill, Mackall's, Minor's, and Hall's Hills. This will give us timely warning. Shall I do as seems best to me with all the troops in this vicinity, including Franklin, who I really think ought not, under present circum-- stances, to advance beyond Annandale?

On the same day I received a despatch from the general-in-chief, in which he asks me why I halted Franklin in Annandale, to which I replied as follows:

Aug. 29, 10.30 A.M. - By referring to my telegrams of 10.30. A.M., 12 M., and 1 P.M., together with your reply of 2.48 P.M., you will see why Franklin's corps halted at Annandale. His small cavalry force - all I had to give him - was ordered to push on as far as possible towards Manassas.

It was not safe for Franklin to move beyond Annandale, under the circumstances, until we knew what was at Vienna.

Gen. Franklin remained here until about one P.M., endeavoring to arrange for supplies for his command. I am responsible for both these circumstances, and do not see that either was in disobedience to your orders.

Please give distinct orders in reference to Franklin's movements of to-morrow, I have sent to Col. Haupt to push out construction and supply trains as soon as possible.

Gen. Tyler to furnish the necessary guards.

I have directed Gen. Banks's supply-trains to start out tonight at least as far as Annandale, with an escort from Gen. Tyler.

In regard to to-morrow's movements I desire definite instructions, as it is not agreeable to me to be accused of disobeying orders when I have simply exercised the discretion you committed to me.

On the same evening I sent the following despatches to Gen. Halleck:

Aug. 29, 10 P.M. - Not hearing from you, I have sent orders. to Gen. Franklin to place himself in communication with Gen. Pope as soon as possible, and at the same time cover the transit of Pope's supplies.

Orders have been given for railway and wagon trains to move to Pope with least possible delay.

I am having inspections made of all the forts around the city by members of my staff, with instructions to give all requisite-orders.

I inspected Worth and Ward myself this evening; found them in good order.

Reports, so far as heard from, are favorable as to condition of works.

Aug. 29, 10 P.M. - Your despatch received. Franklin's corps. has been ordered to march at six o'clock to-morrow morning. Sumner has about 14,000 infantry, without cavalry or artillery, here. Cox's brigade of four regiments is here, with two batteries of artillery. Men of two regiments, much fatigued, came in to-day. Tyler's brigade of three new regiments, but little drilled, is also here; all these troops will be ordered to hold themselves ready to march to-morrow morning, and all except Franklin's to await further orders.

If you wish any of them to move towards Manassas, please inform me.

Col. Wagner, 2d N. Y. Artillery, has just come in from the

front. He reports strong infantry and cavalry force of rebels near Fairfax Court-House; reports rumors from various sources that Lee and Stuart, with large forces, are at Manassas; that the enemy, with 120,000 men, intend advancing on the forts near Arlington and Chain bridge, with a view of attacking Washington and Baltimore.

Gen. Barnard telegraphs me to-night that the length of the line of fortifications on this side of the Potomac requires 2,000 additional artillerymen, and additional troops to defend intervals, according to circumstances; at all events, he says an old regiment should be added to the force at Chain bridge, and a few regiments distributed along the lines to give confidence to our new troops. I agree with him fully, and think our fortifications along the upper part of our line on this side the river very unsafe with their present garrisons, and the movements of the enemy seem to indicate an attack upon those works.

Aug. 30, 11.30 A.M. - Your telegram of 9 A.M. received. Ever since Gen. Franklin received notice that he was to march from Alexandria he has been endeavoring to get transportation from the quartermaster at Alexandria, but he has uniformly been told that there was none disposable, and his command marched without wagons. After the departure of his corps he procured twenty wagons, to carry some extra ammunition, by unloading Banks's supply-train.

Gen. Sumner endeavored, by application upon the quartermaster's department, to get wagons to carry his reserve ammunition, but without success, and was obliged to march with what he could carry in his cartridge-boxes.

I have this morning directed that all my headquarters wagons that are landed be at once loaded with ammunition for Sumner and Franklin; but they will not go far towards supplying the deficiency.

Eighty-five wagons were got together by the quartermasters last night, loaded with subsistence, and sent forward at one A.M. with an escort *via* Annandale. Every effort has been made to carry out your orders promptly. The great difficulty seems to consist in the fact that the greater part of the transportation on hand at Alexandria and Washington has been needed for current supplies of the garrisons. Such is the state of the case as represented to me by the quartermasters, and it appears to be true.

I take it for granted that this has not been properly explained to you.

On the morning of the 30th heavy artillery-firing was heard in the direction of Fairfax Court-House, which I reported to the general-in-chief:

Aug. 30, 9.15 A.M. - Heavy artillery firing is now in progress in direction of Fairfax Court-House; there has been a good deal of it for two or three hours. I hear it so distinctly that I should judge it to be this side of Fairfax. Have not yet been able to ascertain the cause. It seems that the garrisons in the works on north side of Potomac are altogether too small.

At eight A.M. the following was sent to Gen. J. G. Barnard in Washington:

Aug. 30, 8 A.M. - I yesterday sent nearly a regiment of cavalry to report to you for scouting on north bank of Potomac. Three brigades of Sumner's are on both sides of Chain bridge, and thence to Tennallytown. The rest of this corps near Arlington and Corcoran. I have nothing in hand here at all-not a man. You had better ask for some more raw troops on north side.

At 8.20 A.M. the following was sent to Gen. Burnside at Falmouth:

Aug. 30, 8.20 A.M. - Telegram of midnight received. Use your discretion about the cavalry. I have only three squadrons, two of which with Franklin. I expect some, to-day. Do not strip yourself of anything. Your information about Pope substantially confirmed from this side. His troops are at Centreville. Supplies have gone to him by rail and by wagon. Secesh has missed his first *coup.* We will soon see what his second is to be.

At eleven A.M. the following telegram was sent to Gen. Halleck:

Aug. 30, 11 A.M. - Have ordered Sumner to leave (1) one brigade in vicinity of Chain bridge, and to move the rest *via* Columbia pike on Annandale and Fairfax Court-House.
Is this the route you wish them to take? He and Franklin are both instructed to join Pope as promptly as possible.
Shall Couch move out also when he arrives?

On the same day I received the following from Gen. Halleck:

"*Aug.* 30, 1.45 P.M. - Ammunition, and particularly for artillery, must be immediately sent forward to Centreville for Gen. Pope. It must be done with all possible despatch."

To which this reply was made:

Aug. 30, 2.10 P.M. - I know nothing of the calibres of Pope's artillery. All I can do is to direct my ordnance officer to load up all the wagons sent to him. I have already sent all my headquarters wagons. You will have to see that wagons are sent from Washington. I can do nothing more than give the order that every available wagon in Alexandria shall be loaded at once.

The order to the brigade of Sumner that I directed to remain near Chain bridge and Tennallytown should go from your headquarters to save time. I understand you to intend it also to move. I have no sharpshooters except the guard around my camp. I have sent off every man but those, and will now send them with the train, as you direct. I will also send my only remaining squadron of cavalry with Gen. Sumner. I can do no more. You now have every man of the Army of the Potomac who is within my reach.

The War Department now issued the following order:

"WAR DEPARTMENT, Aug. 30, 1862.

"The following are the commanders of the armies operating in Virginia :

"Gen. Burnside commands his own corps, except those that have been temporarily detached and assigned to Gen. Pope.

"Gen. McClellan commands that portion of the Army of the Potomac that has not been sent forward to Gen. Pope's command.

"Gen. Pope commands the Army of Virginia and all the forces temporarily attached to it.

"All the forces are under the command of Maj.-Gen. Halleck, general-in-chief.

"E. D. TOWNSEND,
"*Assist. Adj.-Gen.*"

I was informed by Col. Townsend that the above order was published by order of the Secretary of War. The following despatch was sent to Gen. Barnard at Washington the same day:

Aug. 30, 3.20 P.M. - Your telegram to Gen. Williams received. Of course everything is under your charge as usual. Upon arriving here and finding the state of things uncertain in my front, I took all the means in my power to place affairs in a safe condition. At the request of Gen. Halleck I sent some of my staff officers to inspect the works. I have placed Tyler's regiment in garrison near here, and ordered the (14th) Fourteenth Mass. to duty again as heavy artillery. I have merely used my authority as the senior general officer for duty to assist you, having failed to find you. The whole of Sumner's corps has been ordered to the front by Gen. Halleck. Couch's division will take the same direction as soon as it arrives. I am now sending off my camp-guard and escort-the last I can do. Tyler will, of course, be under your orders so long as he remains in the works.

I have no more troops to give you, and, as I have no command nor any position, I shall not regard it as my duty to take any further steps in regard to the works, except that I shall always be glad to confer with you in regard to any point about which you may be in doubt. I shall try to see Gen. Cox at Upton's Hill to-day or to-morrow. I think he ranks you, but his command was, the only one available for the purpose.

The following were sent to Gen. Halleck the same afternoon :

Aug. 30, 5.15 P.M. - Despatch just received from Gen. Cox, at Upton's Hill, reports that his cavalry have been to Fairfax Court-House, Vienna, Freedom Hill, and Lewinsville, and found all quiet and no enemy heard of in immediate neighborhood. Has a party out to go to Dranesville, if practicable. States that at four P.M. Lieut.-Col. Fowler, of 14th Brooklyn, passed him in an ambulance? wounded, who states that the fighting was north of Little River pike, between it and Thoroughfare Gap. Longstreet had passed through the Gap, which was subsequently partially obstructed by our troops, so that it would hardly be practicable as a retreat for artillery. Reports general result of fighting in our favor, but cannot give particulars.

Gen. Cox states that firing at four P.M. was more rapid and continuous than before. I still hear it.

Aug. 30, 7.45 P. M. - I am glad to report the arrival of Col. Gregg with about (450) four hundred and fifty of his regiment, the (8th) Eighth Penn. Cavalry. Col. Gregg will disembark during the night and lose no time in getting his men ready to march. More of Gen. Couch's division have arrived. I have ordered them to disembark during the night. Have you any special orders for Gregg? Couch's infantry are almost [too] good to use as railway guards. It is an excellent division of veterans. Will you permit new troops to be used for the purpose ?

At 10.30 P.M. the following telegram was sent to Gen. Halleck:

Aug. 30, 10.30 P.M. - I have sent to the front all my troops,

TELEGRAM.

Head Quarters, Army of the Potomac,

Camp near Alexandria   1862.
        Aug. 30   10 30 Pm

I have sent to the front all
my troops with the exception of
Couch's Division & have given the orders
necessary to ensure its being disposed
of as you directed. I hourly expect
the return of one of my aides also will
for authentic news from the field
of battle. I cannot express to you the
pain & mortification I have experienced
today in listening to the distant sound
of the firing of my men. As I can be
of no further use here I respectfully
ask that if there is a probability of
the conflict being renewed tomorrow I
may be permitted to go to the scene of
battle with my staff merely to be with
my own men if nothing more — they
will fight none the worse for my

bring with them

If it is not deemed best to
entrust me with the command
even of my own army I simply
ask to be permitted to share
their fate on the field of battle.
Please reply to this tonight.

I have been engaged for the last
few hours in doing what I can
to make arrangements for the
wounded. I have started out all
the ambulances now landed

G B McClellan
Maj Gen

Maj Gen Halleck
Comdg USA
Washington

As I have sent my escort to the
front I would be glad to take some
of Gregg's cavalry with me if allowed

with the exception of Couch's division, and have given the orders necessary to insure its being disposed of as you directed. I hourly expect the return of one of my aides, who will give authentic news from the field of battle.

I cannot express to you the pain and mortification I have experienced to-day in listening to the distant sound of the firing of my men. As I can be of no further use here, I respectfully ask that, if there is a probability of the conflict being renewed to-morrow, I may be permitted to go to the scene of battle with my staff, merely to be with my own men, if nothing more; they will fight none the worse for my being with them. If it is not deemed best to entrust me with the command even of my own army, I simply ask to be permitted to share their fate on the field of battle.

Please reply to this to-night.

I have been engaged for the last few hours in doing what I can to make arrangements for the wounded. I have started out all the ambulances now landed.

As I have sent my escort to the front, I would be glad to take some of Gregg's cavalry with me, if allowed to go.

To which, on the following day, I received this answer:

"*Aug.* 31, 9.18 A.M. - I have just seen your telegram of 11.5 last night. The substance was stated to me when received, but I did not know that you asked for a reply immediately. I cannot answer without seeing the President, as Gen. Pope is in command, by his orders, of the department.

"I think Couch's division should go forward as rapidly as possible and find the battle-field."

On the same day the following was received from Gen. Halleck:

" *Aug.* 31, 12.45 P.M. - The subsistence department are making Fairfax Station their principal depot. It should be well guarded. The officer in charge should be directed to secure the depot by abatis against cavalry. As many as possible of the new regiments should be prepared to take the field. Perhaps some more should be sent to the vicinity of Chain bridge."

At 2.30 P.M. the following despatch was telegraphed to Gen. Halleck:

Aug. 31, 2.30 P.M. - Maj. Haller is at Fairfax Station with my provost and headquarters guard and other troops. I have requested (4) four more companies to be sent at once, and the precautions you direct to be taken.

Under the War Department order of yesterday I have no control over anything except my staff, some one hundred men in my camp here, and the few remaining near Fort Monroe. I have no control over the new regiments - do not know where they are, or anything about them, except those near here. Their commanding officers and those of the works are not under me.

Where I have seen evils existing under my eye I have corrected them. I think it is the business of Gen. Casey to prepare the new regiments for the field, and a matter between him and Gen. Barnard to order others to the vicinity of Chain bridge. Neither of them is under my command, and by the War Department order I have no right to give them orders.

To which the following was the answer from Gen. Halleck:

"*Aug.* 31, 10.7 P.M. - Since receiving your despatch relating to command, I have not been able to answer any not of absolute necessity. I have not seen the order as published, but will write to you in the morning. You will retain the command of everything in this vicinity not temporarily belonging to Pope's army in the field.

"I beg of you to assist me in this crisis with your ability and experience. I am entirely tired out."

The following reply was sent to Gen. Halleck that night:

Aug. 31, 10.25 P.M.- I am ready to afford you any assistance in my power, but you will readily perceive how difficult an undefined position such as I now hold must be.

At what hour in the morning can I see you alone, either at your own house or the office?

At 7.30 P.M. the following was sent to Gen. Halleck:

Aug. 31, 7.30 P.M. - Having been informed that there were some twenty thousand stragglers from Pope's army between this and Centreville, all of Gregg's cavalry have been sent to endeavor to drive them back to their regiments. Two hundred of 8th Ill. Cavalry will be ready in the morning, and two hundred and fifty more as soon as disembarked. The armament of Forts Buffalo and Ramsay is very incomplete.

At 11.30 P.M. I telegraphed the following to Gen. Halleck:

Aug. 31, 11.30 P.M. - The squadron of 2d Regular Cavalry

that I sent with Gen. Sumner was captured to-day about two P.M. some three miles from Fairfax Court-House, beyond it on the Little River pike, by Fitz-Hugh Lee with 3,000 cavalry and three light batteries.

I have conversed with the first sergeant, who says that when he last saw them they were within a mile of Fairfax. Pope had no troops on that road, this squadron getting there by mistake. There is nothing of ours on the right of Centreville but Sumner's corps. There was much artillery-firing during the day. A rebel major told the sergeant that the rebels had driven in our entire left to-day. He says the road is filled with wagons and stragglers coming towards Alexandria.

It is clear from the sergeant's account that we were badly beaten yesterday, and that Pope's right is entirely exposed.

I recommend that no more of Couch's division be sent to the front, that Burnside be brought here as soon as practicable, and that everything available this side of Fairfax be drawn in at once, including the mass of the troops on the railroad. I apprehend that the enemy will or have by this time occupied Fairfax Court-House and cut off Pope entirely, unless he falls back to-night *via* Sangster's and Fairfax Station.

I think these orders should be sent at once. I have no confidence in the dispositions made as I gather them. To speak frankly-and the occasion requires it - there appears to be a total absence of brains, and I fear the total destruction of the army. I have some cavalry here that can carry out any orders you may have to send. The occasion is grave, and demands grave measures. The question is the salvation of the country. I learn that our loss yesterday amounted to 15,000. We cannot afford such losses without an object,

It is my deliberate opinion that the interests of the nation demand that Pope should fall back to-night, if possible, and not one moment is to be lost.

I will use all the cavalry I have to watch our right. Please answer at once. I feel confident that you can rely upon the information I give you.

I shall be up all night, and ready to obey any orders you give me.

To which this reply was received from Gen. Halleck:

"*Sept.* 1, 1.30 A.M. - Burnside was ordered up very early yesterday morning. Retain remainder of Couch's forces, and make arrangements to stop all retreating troops in line of works, or where you can best establish an entire line of defence. My news from Pope was up to four P.M.; he was then all right. I must wait for more definite information before I can order a retreat, as the falling back on the line of works must necessarily be directed in case of a serious disaster. Give me all additional news that is reliable.

"I shall be up all night, and ready to act as circumstances may require. I am fully aware of the gravity of the crisis, and have been for weeks."

It will be seen from what has preceded that I lost no time in moving the Army of the Potomac from the Peninsula to the support of the Army of Virginia; that I spared no effort to hasten the embarkation of the troops at Fort Monroe, Newport News, and Yorktown, remaining at Fort Monroe myself until the mass of the army had sailed ; and that after my arrival at Alexandria I left nothing in my power undone to forward supplies and reinforcements to Gen. Pope. I sent with the troops that moved all the cavalry I could get hold of-even my personal escort was sent out upon the line of the railway as a guard, with the provost and camp-guard at headquarters-retaining less than 100 men, many of whom were orderlies, invalids, members of bands, etc. All the headquarters teams that arrived were sent out with supplies and ammunition, none being retained even to move the headquarters camp. The squadron that habitually served as my personal escort was left at Falmouth with Gen. Burnside, as he was deficient in cavalry.

CHAPTER XXXI.

PRIVATE LETTERS.

[*Aug.* 24 to *Sept.* 2, 1862.]

Aug. 24, Sunday, 9.30 A.M., *Acpuia creek.* - We reached here during the night. Sent a despatch about six to Halleck, informing him that I had arrived here and awaited orders; also sent one to Burnside. . . . I have no reply as yet to my despatches, and am not at all impatient. I learn that all my troops are ordered to Alexandria for embarkation, so I presume they will be merged in Pope's army. If this is the case I will (if I find it proper) try for a leave of absence. . . . I learn nothing whatever of the state of affairs, not even whether Pope is still falling back or whether there has been any fighting. So I suppose it is all right. I fancy that Pope is in retreat, though this is only a guess of mine, without anything to base it on. I don't see how I can remain in the service if placed under Pope; it would be too great a disgrace, and I can hardly think that Halleck would permit it to be offered me. . . . I expect Porter and Burnside here in a few minutes, and then will know something of the state of affairs, I hope. This is a wretched place, utterly unfit for the landing and supplying of a large body of troops. They have at last found it out, though H. insisted upon it that there were ample facilities here for all purposes. . . .

12.15 P.M. - I have seen Burnside and Porter, and gained some information from them. I have not one word yet from Washington, and am quietly waiting here for something to turn up. I presume they are discussing me now, to see whether they can get along without me. . . . They will suffer a terrible defeat if the present state of affairs continues. I *know* that with God's help I can save them. . . .

Aug. 25, 1 P.M. - . . . Was at Falmouth pretty much all night. . . .

Aug. 27, A.M., *Alexandria.* - We arrived here last night. Rose early; reported to Washington that I had arrived, and am waiting for something to turn up. It seems that some 500 of the enemy's cavalry made a dash last night and burned the Bull Run railroad bridge. I fear this will cause much inconvenience, as the troops in front are mainly dependent on the railroad for supplies. My troops are getting pretty well into position: Porter between Fredericksburg and the Rappahannock Station; Heintzelman at Rappahannock Station; Franklin near this place; Sumner landing at Acquia creek. I have heard nothing new to-day, and don't know what is going on in front; am terribly ignorant of the state of affairs, and therefore somewhat anxious to know. . . . I find all going on well enough here. Davis has just returned from selecting a camp for headquarters; he has picked out a place between the Seminary (our old camp) and the river, about one-half or three-quarters of a mile from the Seminary. I shall go into my tent this time and not trouble a house. With the exception of the two or three days I passed at Williamsburg on our upward march, and one night at Fort Monroe, I have not slept in a house since I left you. I know nothing definite yet in regard to my fate. . . .

10.30. - Have been again interrupted by telegrams requiring replies. Halleck is in a disagreeable situation: can get no information from the front, either as to our own troops or the enemy. I shall do all I can to help him loyally and will trouble him as little as possible, but render all the assistance in my power without regard to myself or my own position. . . . Our affairs here are much tangled up, and I opine that in a day or two your old husband will be called upon to unravel them. In the meantime I shall be very patient, do to the best of my ability whatever I am called upon to do, and wait my time. I hope to have my part of the work pretty well straightened out to-day. In that case I shall move up to Washington this evening. . . . Have just heard that it is probable that a general engagement will be fought to-day or to-morrow near Warrenton. . . .

Aug. 28, 9.30 A.M., *steamer "Ariel."* - I am just about starting back for Alexandria. I came up here (Washington) last night; reached Halleck's house about midnight, and remained talking with him until three. . . . I have a great deal of hard work before me now, but will do my best to perform it. I find Halleck well disposed; he has had much to contend against. I shall keep as clear as possible of the President and cabinet; endeavor to do what must be done with Halleck alone; so I shall get on better. Pope is in a bad way; his communication with Washington cut off, and I have not yet the force at hand to relieve him. He has nearly all the troops of my army that have arrived. I hope to hear better news when I reach Alexandria.

Aug. 29, 3 P.M. - . . . I was awake all last night, and have not had one moment until now to write to you. I have a terrible task on my hands now-perfect imbecility to correct. No means to act with, no authority, yet determined, if possible, to save the country and the capital. I find the soldiers all clinging to me; yet I am not permitted to go to the post of danger! Two of my corps will either save Pope or be sacrificed for the country. I do not know whether I shall be permitted to save the capital or not. I have just telegraphed very plainly to the President and Halleck what I think ought to be done. I expect merely a contemptuous silence. . . . I am heart-sick with the folly and ignorance I see around me. God grant that I may never pass through such a scene again! . . .

9.30 P.M.- . . Late yesterday afternoon a violent gale arose and blew over my tent, soaking everything I had, including this note and myself. . . . I have been terribly busy since reaching here; not a moment have I had to myself. I found everything in the most terrible confusion-apparently inextricably so; but affairs are now better. The works on this side of the river are in condition for defence. . . . I see the evening paper states that I have been placed in command of all the troops in Virginia. This is not so. I have no command at present-that is to say, I have none of the Army of the Potomac with me, and have merely " turned in" on my own account to straighten out whatever I catch hold of. By to-morrow evening I hope to have the works, etc., in fair condition of defence. . . . Pope has been in a tight place, but from the news received this evening I think the danger is pretty much over. To-morrow will tell the story. I am terribly crippled by the want of cavalry. None of mine have arrived except three small squadrons. I hope for more to-night. There was a terrible scare in Washington last night. A rumor got out that Lee was advancing rapidly on the Chain bridge with 150,000 men. And such a stampede! I did not get five minutes consecutive sleep all night, so thick were the telegrams. . . . I have seen neither the President nor the secretary since I arrived here; have been only once to Washington, and hope to see very little of the place. I abominate it terribly. . . . I have no faith in any one here, and expect to be turned loose the moment their alarm is over. I expect I got into a row with Halleck to-night. He sent me a telegram I did not like, and I told him so very plainly. He is not a refined person at all, and probably says rough things when he don't mean them. . . .

Aug. 30, 8 A.M. - . . . Was awakened last night by a few scattering shots that, no doubt, came from some of those very raw troops that are about here. Shall start soon after breakfast and ride to Upton's Hill, thence to the Chain bridge and along the line of forts. I want to see all on this side of the river to-day, if I can. No one in Washington appears to know the condition of matters, and I have a fancy for finding them out for myself. If I once get matters reasonably straight I shall not trouble myself much more. What I am doing now is rather a volunteer affair - not exactly my business; but you know that I have a way of attending to most other things than my own affairs. . . .

1.30 P.M., *camp near Alexandria.* - . . . I expected to start out on a long ride, but have thus far been detained by various matters which have kept me very busy. . . . There has been heavy firing going on all day long somewhere beyond Bull Run. I have sent up every man I have, pushed everything, and am left here on the flat of my back without any command whatever. It is dreadful to listen to this cannonading and not be able to take any part in it. But such is my fate. . . .

9.15 P.M. - . . . I feel too blue and disgusted to write any more now, so I will smoke a cigar and try to get into a better humor. They have taken all my troops from me! I have even sent off my personal escort and camp-guard, and am here with a few orderlies and the aides. I have been listening to the sound of a great battle in the distance. My men engaged in it and I away! I never felt worse in my life.

Sunday (31st), 9.30 A.M. - . . . There was a severe battle yesterday, and almost exactly on the old Bull Run battle-ground.
Pope sent in accounts during the day that he was getting on
splendidly, driving the enemy all day, gaining a glorious victory,
etc., etc.   About three this morning Hammerstein returned from
the field (where I had sent him to procure information), and told
me that we were badly whipped, McDowell's and Sigel's corps
broken, the corps of my own army that were present (Porter and
Heintzelman) badly cut up but in perfect order.   Banks was not
engaged. Franklin had arrived and was in position at Centreville. Sumner must have got up by this time. Couch's division
is about starting. It is probable that the enemy are too much
fatigued to renew the attack this morning, perhaps not at all to-
day; so that time may be given to our people to make such
arrangements as will enable them to hold their own.   I telegraphed last evening asking permission to be with my troops;
received a reply about half an hour ago from Halleck that he
would have to consult the President first! If they refuse to let
me go out I think I shall feel obliged to insist upon a leave, or
something of the kind, the moment the question of the existing
battle is settled.   I feel like a fool here, sucking my thumbs and
doing nothing but what ought to be done by junior officers. I
leave it all in the hands of the Almighty. I will try to do my
best in the position that may be assigned to me, and be as patient
as I can. . . .

10.45. - . . . I feel in that state of excitement and anxiety
that I can hardly keep still for a moment.   I learn from Hammerstein that the men in front are all anxious for me to be with
them. It is too cruel!

12.30 P.M. - A short time since I saw the order defining commands.   Mine is that part of the Army of the Potomac not sent
to Pope.   As all is sent there, I am left in command of *nothing*-
a command I feel fully competent to exercise, and to which I can
do full justice.   I am going to write a quiet, moderate letter to
Mr. - presently, explaining to him the exact state of the case,
without comment, so that my friends in New York may know all.
. . . Everything is too uncertain and unsafe around Washington
at present for you to dream of going there. As a matter of self-
respect, I cannot go there. . . . I do not regard Washington as
safe against the rebels. If I can quietly slip over there I will

send your silver off. There is an order forbidding any one going there without permission from the War Department, and I do not care to ask them for so slight a favor as that. . . .

Sept. 1, *Washington,* 2 P.M. - I have only time to tell you that I have been placed in command of Washington and all the garrisons, etc., in the vicinity, to do the best I can with it. The decisive battle will be fought to-day near Fairfax Court-House. My headquarters are to be in town. If the squall passes over, and Washington is a safe place, you shall come on to see me, if I can't get off to see you. . . .

CHAPTER XXXII.

Recalled to save the capital - Pope defeated - The President appeals to McClellan - He accepts command - Alarm in Washington - Enthusiasm of the army - The capital safe - The order of Sept. 2 - Halleck's testimony - Stormy cabinet meeting.

LATE at night of Aug. 31, I think, Maj. Hammerstein - one of my aides, whom I had sent to the front to bring me news as to the real state of affairs - returned, bringing a despatch from Pope, which was to be sent to Halleck by telegraph. The information Hammerstein brought proved that Pope's despatch was false throughout.

On the 1st of Sept. I met Gen. Halleck at his office in Washington, who by verbal order directed me to take charge of Washington and its defences, but expressly prohibited me from exercising any control over the active troops under Gen. Pope.

At this interview I told him what I had every reason to know to be the true state of affairs. He doubted the accuracy of my information and believed the statements of Pope. I then told him that he ought to go to the front in person and see what the true condition of affairs was. He said that he was so much occupied with office-duty that it was impossible for him to leave. I told him that there could be no duty so important for the general-in-chief of the armies as to know the condition of the chief army of the country, then actually fighting for the defence of the capital, and that his first duty was to go out and see for himself how matters stood, and, if need be, assume command in person. He merely repeated his reply, and I urged him as strongly as possible to follow my advice. He still refused, and I then urged him to send out his chief of staff, Gen. Cullum, who just then entered the room, but Cullum said that he could not go. Then I asked that Kelton, his adjutant-general, might be sent. Kelton cheerfully offered to go, and it was determined that he should start immediately. I took Kelton to one side and

534

advised him not to content himself with merely seeing Pope, but also to make it a point to converse freely with the general officers and learn their individual opinions. Next morning while I was at breakfast, about 7 or 7.30 o'clock, the President and Gen. Halleck came to my house.

The President informed me that Col. Kelton had returned and represented the condition of affairs as much worse than I had stated to Halleck on the previous day; that there were 30,000 stragglers on the roads; that the army was entirely defeated and falling back to Washington in confusion. He then said that he regarded Washington as lost, and asked me if I would, under the circumstances, as a favor to him, resume command and do the best that could be done.

Without one moment's hesitation, and without making any conditions whatever, I at once said that I would accept the command and would stake my life that I would save the city. Both the President and Halleck again asserted that it was impossible to save the city, and I repeated my firm conviction that I could and would save it. They then left, the President verbally placing me in entire command of the city and of the troops falling back upon it from the front.

He instructed me to take steps at once to stop and collect the stragglers, to place the works in a proper state of defence, and to go out to meet and take command of the army when it approached the vicinity of the works; then to put the troops in the best position for defence-committing everything to my hands. The President left me with many thanks and showing much feeling.

I immediately went to work, collected my staff, and started them in all directions with the necessary orders to the different fortifications; some to the front with orders for the disposition of such corps as they met, others to see to the prompt forwarding of ammunition and supplies to meet the retreating troops.

In the course of the morning I signed a requisition for small arms and ammunition upon the commandant of the arsenal. After a time it was brought back to me with the statement that it could not be filled for the reason that the contents of the arsenal were all being put, or about being put, on board ship for transportation to New York, or some safe place, in accordance with the orders of the Secretary of War and general-in-chief, in order to save the stores from the enemy. I at once started out and succeeded in having the order countermanded. At the same time there was a war-steamer anchored off the White House, with steam up, ready to take off the President, cabinet, etc., at a moment's notice.

The only published order ever issued in regard to the extent of my command after my interview with the President on the morning of the 2d was the following: *

> "WAR DEPARTMENT, ADJUTANT-GENERAL'S OFFICE,
> "WASHINGTON, Sept. 2, 1862.
>
> "Maj.-Gen. McClellan will have command of the fortifications, of Washington and of all the troops for the defence of the capital.
> "By order of Maj.-Gen. Halleck.
> > "E. D. TOWNSEND,
> > " *Assist. Adj.-Gen.* "

I sent an aide to Gen. Pope with the following letter:

> HEADQUARTERS, WASHINGTON, Sept. 2, 1862.
>
> *Maj.-Gen. John Pope, Commanding Army of Virginia:*
>
> GENERAL: Gen. Halleck instructed me to repeat to you the order he sent this morning to withdraw your army to Washington without unnecessary delay. He feared that his messenger might miss you, and desired to take this double precaution.
>
> In order to bring troops upon ground with which they are already familiar, it would be best to move Porter's corps upon Upton's Hill, that it may occupy Hall's Hill, etc.; McDowell's to Upton's Hill; Franklin's to the works in front of Alexandria; Heintzelman's to the same vicinity; Couch to Fort Corcoran, or, if practicable, to the Chain bridge; Sumner either to Fort Albany or to Alexandria, as may be most convenient.
>
> In haste, general, very truly yours,
> > GEO. B. MCCLELLAN,
> > *Maj.-Gen. U. S. A.*

In a very short time I had made all the requisite preparations and was about to start to the front in person to assume command as far out as possible, when a message came to me from Gen. Halleck informing me that it was the President's order that I should not assume command until the troops had reached the immediate vicinity of the fortifications.

---

* See note A at end of this chapter.

I therefore waited until the afternoon, when I rode out to the most advanced of the detached works covering the capital.

I had with me Colburn, Key, and some other aides, with a small cavalry escort, and rode at once to Munson's Hill. About the time I reached there the infantry of King's division of McDowell's corps commenced arriving, and I halted them and ordered them into position. Very soon - within twenty minutes - a regiment of cavalry appeared, marching by twos, and sandwiched in the midst were Pope and McDowell with their staff officers. I never saw a more helpless-looking headquarters. About this time rather heavy artillery-firing was heard in the distance. When these generals rode up to me and the ordinary salutations had passed, I inquired what that artillery-firing was. Pope replied that it was no doubt that of the enemy against Sumner, who formed the rear-guard and was to march by the Vienna and Langley road. He also intimated that Sumner was probably in a dilemma. He could give me no information of any importance in relation to the whereabouts of the different corps, except in a most indefinite way; had evidently not troubled his head in the slightest about the movements of his army in retreat, and had coolly preceded the troops, leaving them to get out of the scrape as best they could. He and McDowell both asked my permission to go on to Washington, to which I assented, remarking at the same time that I was going to that artillery-firing. They then took leave and started for Washington. I have never since seen Pope.

Immediately I despatched all my aides and orderlies with instructions to the troops coming in by the Alexandria and Central roads, retaining only Colburn with me. I borrowed three orderlies from some cavalry at hand, and, accompanied by them and Colburn, started across country as rapidly as possible to reach the Langley road. By the time I reached that road the firing had ceased, with the exception of perhaps a dropping shot occasionally. It was after dark - I think there was moonlight - by the time I met the first troops, which were, I think, of Morell's division, 5th corps; Porter had gone on a little while before to make arrangements for the bivouac of his troops. I was at once recognized by the men, upon which there was great cheering and excitement; but when I came to the regular division (Sykes's) the scene was the most touching I had

up to that time experienced.   The cheers in front had attracted
their attention, and I have been told since by many that the men
at once pricked up their ears and said that it could only be
for "Little Mac."   As soon as I came to them the poor fellows
broke through all restraints, rushed from the ranks and crowded
around me, shouting, yelling, shedding tears, thanking God that
they were with me again, and begging me to lead them back to
battle.   It was a wonderful scene, and proved that I had the
hearts of these men."

I next met Sigel's corps, and soon satisfied myself that
Sumner was pursuing his march unmolested, so I sent on to
inform him that I was in command, and gave him instructions
as to his march. I then returned by the Chain bridge road,
having first given Sigel his orders; and at a little house beyond
Langley I found Porter, with whom I spent some time, and at
length reached Washington at an early hour in the morning.
Before the day broke the troops were all in position to repulse
attack, and Washington was safe.

* See note B.

A. *Note by the Editor.* - This order of Sept. 2, 1862, was the last order
ever issued to Gen. McClellan giving him any command.   He seems
never to have known that it actually appeared in two forms within twenty-
four hours, first as an order from the President by direction of the Secretary of War, second as a simple order of Gen. Halleck. The history of its
origin and modification is obscure.   The purposes of Secretary Stanton
and Gen. Halleck in its issue and the change of its form must be left to
conjecture, with what light can be thrown on it from the events of the time.
When these events are seen in close relation every honest mind must be
filled with amazement at the duplicity with which McClellan was surrounded.

The War Department had occupied itself in giving out what Secretary
Welles called "exaggerated rumors," but which were pure fabrications,
designed to convince the public that McClellan had been the cause of
Pope's defeat by delay in forwarding reinforcements. Mr. Stanton and
Gen. Halleck had assumed the responsibility of recalling the Army of the
Potomac from before Richmond, thus releasing the enemy to fall on Pope.
Every military and common-sense consideration had been violated. The
paramount purpose was to take the army away from McClellan, since they
had been unable to persuade Mr. Lincoln to take McClellan from the
army.   McClellan had been ordered to return, for the purpose, as he was
told, of taking the command of all the forces of Pope and his own troops
combined.

Having ordered the withdrawal of the Army of the Potomac, Halleck and Stanton had made the fearful error of not providing transportation for it, and, when aware of their blunder, threw the blame on McClellan. He arrived at Alexandria on the 26th Aug., under Halleck's direct command, who assumed the responsibility of everything, and declined to give McClellan any specific position. From day to day the country was informed, by telegrams inspired at the War Department, that McClellan was delaying the advance of troops to Pope. Meantime McClellan, doing his own work, was also doing Halleck's work for him as a pure volunteer, while the latter was in a hopeless condition of mind, semi-paralyzed. The work done by McClellan was herculean, in sending forward his own troops, in volunteer inspection and adjustment of the defences of Washington, in aiding and advising Halleck, who was powerless. The despatches in chapter xxx., which indicate all this, are but a small portion of McClellan's orders and despatches, during the five days after his arrival at Alexandria, which he left as part of his memoirs. I have exercised the discretion given me and reserved the remainder of these for future publication, leaving here only such and so many as will outline what the general did from Aug. 26 to Aug. 31. If no one else saw, it is clear from Mr. Lincoln's despatches to McClellan, and his acts on Sept. 2, that he saw and knew what Halleck did not do, and what McClellan was doing, in those eventful days.

Gen. Halleck had written to McClellan on the Peninsula, asking frank co-operation. McClellan had promised it heartily, and now gave it gallantly. Ignoring this, and seeking with others to throw on McClellan all the responsibilities of the five days, Gen. Halleck, testifying before the Committee on the Conduct of the War, stated that McClellan was placed in command of the fortifications of Washington and all the troops for its defence *on the day he arrived at Alexandria,* and that the order of Sept. 2 was only the reduction to writing of that command. The following is Halleck's testimony:

"On his [Gen. McClellan's] arrival at Alexandria he was told to take immediate command of all the troops in and about Washington, in addition to those which properly belonged to the Army of the Potomac. Some days after he had been verbally directed to take such command he asked for a formal order, which was issued from the adjutant-general's office. The order issued from the adjutant-general's office was after Gen. Pope's army commenced falling back, and was dated Sept. 2, but Gen. McClellan had been in command ever since his arrival in Alexandria. He arrived at Alexandria on the 26th of Aug. The formal order was issued that he might have no difficulty with Gen. Pope's forces; that they might not question his authority."

That this testimony of Gen. Halleck was distinctly false is now demonstrated beyond any dispute by the publication of his own correspondence with McClellan during the period Aug. 26 to Aug. 31, and by other proofs. It is charity to Gen. Halleck to suppose that his mind and memory were muddled by the fearful catastrophe he and Secretary Stanton had brought on the army and country, so that, when before the committee, he had forgotten the countless facts which prove his statement untrue.

40

From the 26th to the 30th Aug. his despatches to McClellan recognized that officer as in command of his own Army of the Potomac. On the 24th McClellan, arrived at Acquia, had telegraphed him: "Until I know what my command and position are to be, and whether you still intend to place me in the command indicated in your first letter to me, and orally through Gen. Burnside at the Chickahominy, I cannot decide where I can be of most use. If your determination is unchanged I ought to go to Alexandria at once. Please define my position and duties." Halleck made no reply to this; and from what followed it is evident that he had no intention of giving McClellan any command, it being his and Mr. Stanton's plan to order all of the Army of the Potomac, piece by piece, away from McClellan's command, and discharge him.

On the 27th Halleck telegraphed McClellan: "Take entire direction of the sending out troops from Alexandria."

On the same day McClellan telegraphed Halleck: "Please inform me at once what my position is. I do not wish to act in the dark." To this Halleck made no reply.

On the 29th McClellan telegraphed both the President and Gen. Halleck: "Tell me what you wish me to do, and I will do all in my power to accomplish it. I wish to know what my orders and authority are. I ask for nothing, but will obey whatever orders you give. I only ask a prompt decision." To this he received no reply, except that the President, replying to another part of the same despatch, said: "I wish not to control. That I leave to Gen. Halleck, aided by your counsels."

The unexplained and embarrassing position in which Halleck kept McClellan at this time is illustrated by many despatches which are omitted from the present volume. Thus, on the 29th of Aug. Gen. S. Williams, A. A. G. at McClellan's camp near Alexandria, telegraphed Brig.-Gen. James S. Wadsworth, military governor of Washington: "It is important that these headquarters should receive the countersign issued to the guards at the Long bridge. I was stopped late night before last, returning to camp, and compelled to go to your office for the countersign. Lieut.-Col. Colburn, going to the city last night on important business requiring despatch, was stopped at this end of the bridge and had to go back to Fort Albany. On both occasions the officers of the guards, though aware of our positions, said they had no discretion."

On the 30th, Assist. Adj.-Gen. Williams telegraphs Gen. Wadsworth: "In the absence of orders defining the limits of his command Gen. McClellan issues a countersign to-day to the troops of the Army of the Potomac in this vicinity. It is 'Malvern.' If yours is different he will be obliged to you to communicate it, and also to instruct the guards at the Long bridge to recognize ours. Do you know what command furnishes the guard for the Virginia end of the Long bridge?"

A duplicate of the first part of this same despatch was sent the same day to Gen. John P. Slough, military governor of Alexandria, where Gen. McClellan's own headquarters then were. Obviously McClellan was not at this time "in command of all the troops in and about Washington," Gen. Halleck's testimony that he was notwithstanding.

On the 30th Gen. McClellan telegraphed Gen. Barnard, who was in command of the military defences of Washington: "I have no more troops to give you, and, as I have no command nor any position, I shall not regard it as my duty to take any further steps in regard to the works."

On the same day McClellan telegraphed Halleck: "You now have every man of the Army of the Potomac who is within my reach." This despatch announced to Gen. Halleck and Mr. Stanton the completion of their purpose in recalling the Army of the Potomac - namely, to remove it from McClellan's command. Their response was now prompt; and McClellan received the first reply to his repeated requests to know what his position was, in these words: "Gen. McClellan commands that portion of the Army of the Potomac that has not been sent forward to Gen. Pope's command." McClellan's command was thus reduced to less than a hundred men, many of whom were maimed or sick soldiers, around his tent at Alexandria. Secretary Stanton himself issued this order, which was, of course, intended to be insulting to McClellan, and which was received with much exultation in Washington by those who had desired McClellan's dismissal. At this moment it was believed in Washington that Pope was victorious and McClellan finally crushed. Of course, when McClellan's command was thus defined by this order, in terms whose exactness was intended to be contemptuous, he was not in command of any fortifications or any troops for the defence of anything.

On the night of the 30th McClellan made a vain appeal to Halleck to be allowed to go to the front and be with his troops in battle.

On the afternoon of the 31st, in reply to an order from Halleck, McClellan telegraphed him: "Under the War Department order of yesterday I have no control over anything except my staff, some one hundred men in my camp here, and the few remaining near Fort Monroe. I have no control over the new regiments. . . . Their commanding officers, and those of. the works, are not under me."

At ten P.M. of the 31st Halleck replied to this: "I have not seen the order as published" (implying that he had seen it in Stanton's draft form), and adds: "You will retain command of everything in this vicinity not temporarily to be Pope's army in the field. I beg of you to assist me in this crisis with your ability and experience. I am entirely tired out."

This indefinite despatch was the first hint of any order placing McClellan in command of the fortifications. On the same day McClellan had telegraphed to Gens. Wadsworth, Barnard, and Slough: "Gen. McClellan commands so few troops that he declines issuing a countersign, but he will be obliged if you will furnish him daily with yours, as he may have occasion to send to Washington during the night."

At 10.25 P.M., on receipt of Halleck's despairing telegram, McClellan replied: "I am ready to afford you any assistance in my power, but you will readily perceive how difficult an undefined position such as I now hold must be. At what hour in the morning can I see you alone?"

On the morning of Sept. 1 McClellan went up from Alexandria to Washington, and now Halleck verbally placed him in charge of the defences of Washington, but expressly forbade him to exercise any control over the troops of the Army of the Potomac or the Army of Virginia.

The untruthfulness of Gen. Halleck's testimony before the Committee on the Conduct of the War is thus demonstrated. He, and he alone, was in command and responsible from Aug. 26 to Sept. 1.

Gen. Halleck's verbal orders to Gen. McClellan on Sept. 1 gave the latter no control over the active army. Halleck was now encouraged about Pope, and discredited McClellan's bad news from the front.

Pope had telegraphed that he had fought a terrific battle, which lasted from daylight to dark, by which time the enemy was driven from the field, which we now occupy." "The enemy is still in our front, but badly used up." "We have made great captures, but I am not able yet to form an idea of their extent." The urgency of McClellan, who discredited Pope's statements, alone induced Halleck to send Col. Kelton to the front for information. The return of that officer in the night of Sept. 1 - 2 revealed the truth, which brought terror to Washington.

Without dwelling on the condition of alarm into which the War Department was now plunged, it is important to note that it continued certainly till Sept. 8, when Mr. Hiram Barney, Collector of the Port of New York, told Mr. Chase "that Stanton and Wadsworth had advised him to leave for New York this evening, as communication with Baltimore might be cut off before to-morrow" (Warden, p. 415). Secretary Welles says Stanton and Halleck were "filled with apprehensions beyond others." They gave up the capital as lost, and issued orders to empty the arsenal preparatory to the occupation of Washington by the enemy.

Early in the morning of Sept. 2 the President, accompanied by Gen. Halleck, went to Gen. McClellan's house, and found him alone. They told him the capital was lost. The President asked him if "under the circumstances" (to wit, the recent treatment of Stanton and Halleck, and the insulting general order of Aug. 30) he would "resume command and do the best that could be done." The instant acceptance of this vast responsibility by McClellan puts at rest a falsehood published on the authority of Gen. Burnside, that McClellan proposed to make conditions, took time to consider, and finally only yielded to the persuasions of others in accepting the command. This story was a pure fabrication - one of thousands which were directed against McClellan, and which a deluded public widely accepted as true.

Gen. McClellan has contented himself with a brief account of this remarkable interview, in which Mr. Lincoln, with deep emotion, threw himself and the salvation of the capital and the Union on the general whom his subordinates had cajoled, slandered, deceived, and represented to the people as disgraced. The terms of the trust reposed in him were unlimited. The simple words "resume command" were ample. Two honest minds were in contact, and each trusted the other. Mr. Lincoln then intended to give to McClellan discretionary powers over military matters, and neither of them stopped to choose words.

Gen. McClellan went swiftly to work. Gen. Halleck went to inform Secretary Stanton of the overthrow of their plans by the recall of McClellan to command.

It may here be noted that Mr. Chase was in error when, on Sept. 19, he said (Warden, p. 480) that Halleck's telegram of Aug. 31, asking McClellan to help him, "announced Halleck's surrender to McClellan." While Mr. Chase was right enough in thus confessing the existence of a war against McClellan, he might well have spared his criticisms, since it will appear in the progress of McClellan's narrative that Halleck maintained the war with much vigorous disregard of truth, to the end which was sought. The events of Sept. 2, which must be pursued, amply attest his position in the conflict. which now became more serious when the President appeared to stand firmly for McClellan.

Hitherto no one has appreciated the state of mind of Mr. Lincoln at this appalling moment, when he realized the condition into which he and the country had been brought by the conspiracy of Mr. Stanton and his associate politicians against the army and its commander. Mr. Lincoln was a sagacious man. He knew thoroughly the character of the men who were around him; had always known it. He had felt the importance of avoiding an open rupture with Congress, which was under the control of the extreme radical wing of the party. He had yielded much to this consideration.

Now, when he heard from Mr. Stanton and Gen. Halleck that the capital was lost, and that they had issued orders for the abandonment of the arsenal and flight of the administration, he scouted their attempts to transfer their responsibility for the catastrophe to McClellan, and went at once to the general, with unbounded confidence in him. The quiet assurances he received from the man who had never deceived him relieved his apprehensions of the loss of the capital, and he went away better prepared to meet his cabinet, who were expecting the enemy around and in the city. He still shrank from an open rupture with Mr. Chase, Mr. Stanton, the majority of the Committee on the Conduct of the War, and Congress which had become subservient to their leadership. He had hither-to prevented a division of the party, which was always imminent. Doubtless his avowed principle of "not swapping horses while crossing a stream" influenced him to his present determination to go on with the same cabinet officers in council and the same general in command.

But when he left McClellan, the simple, loyal soldier and servant of the people, he had to face men of a very different character. The cabinet meeting which now followed was in many respects the most remarkable ever held in Washington. Mr. Lincoln entered it knowing his men. He knew that Mr. Chase and Mr. Stanton were Presidential candidates, guiding, each in his own peculiar way, their official conduct and acts as his rivals for the next nomination. He was perfectly aware that in this critical time they were ready to throw on him all the responsibility of the impending ruin, the loss of the capital, if that were to be, the end of the Union itself which might possibly follow. That they would seek to save their own reputations at any cost to his was a matter of course with such men. He had this advantage in meeting them, that McClellan's confidence had reassured him, while they were still in a state of wild alarm.

Believing the loss of Washington and Maryland inevitable, and anticipating the judgment of the people of the North, they forgot all respect for their chief and became insolent in their treatment of him. Stanton reproached him with giving personal orders to McClellan, creating confusion, making neither Halleck nor McClellan responsible, and then disavowed any responsibility of the War Department for the position. Chase told him that any engineer officer would have done as well as the general he had selected, and boldly added that by placing McClellan in command he had given the capital to the enemy.

It was plain that the two Presidential candidates in the cabinet had determined on their course - to assure the country that Mr. Lincoln was alone responsible for the ruin they believed inevitable.

The President retained his dignity and maintained at first a calm attitude. He had been accustomed for months to the nagging policy of the secretaries; but it now became so personal and bitter that he was at last driven to the exclamation, never before or since uttered by a President of the United States, that he would gladly resign his high office.

The history of this tempestuous cabinet meeting forms an important part of the history of the war, and throws strong light on the story of McClellan and the Army of the Potomac.

In his private diary (Warden, p. 459) Mr. Chase thus describes it:

"The Secretary of War came in. In answer to some inquiry the fact was stated by the President or the secretary that McClellan had been placed in command of the forces to defend the capital - or rather, to use the President's own words, 'he had set him to putting these troops into the fortifications about Washington,' believing that he could do that thing better than any other man.

"I remarked that this could be done equally well by the engineer who constructed the forts. . . .

"The Secretary of War said that no one was now responsible for the defence of the capital: that the order to McClellan was given by the President direct to McClellan, and that Gen. Halleck considered himself relieved from responsibility, although he acquiesced and approved the order; that McClellan could now shield himself, should anything go wrong, under Halleck, while Halleck could and would disclaim all responsibility for the order given.

"The President thought Gen. Halleck as much responsible as before, and repeated that the whole scope of the order was simply to direct McClellan to put the troops into the fortifications and command them for the defence of Washington.

"I remarked . . . that I could not but feel that giving command to him was equivalent to giving Washington to the rebels. *This and more I said.* . . .

"The President said it distressed him exceedingly to find himself differing on such a point from the Secretary of War and the Secretary of the Treasury; *that he would gladly resign his place;* but that he could not

see who could do the work wanted as well as McClellan. I named
Hooker, or Sumner, or Burnside, either of whom would do the work better."

Mr. Gideon Welles, Secretary of the Navy, in his book, "Lincoln
and Seward," New York, 1874, page 194, says:

"At the stated cabinet meeting on Tuesday, the 2d of Sept, while the
whole community was stirred up and in confusion, and affairs were growing beyond anything that had previously occurred, Stanton entered the
council-room a few moments in advance of Mr. Lincoln, and said, with
great excitement, he had just learned from Gen. Halleck that the President had placed McClellan in command of the forces in Washington.
The information was surprising, and, in view of the prevailing excitement
against that officer, alarming. The President soon came in, and, in answer
to an inquiry from Mr. Chase, confirmed what Stanton had stated. General regret was expressed, and Stanton, with some feeling, remarked that
no order to that effect had issued from the War Department. The President, calmly but with some emphasis, said the order was his, and he
would be responsible for it to the country. . . . Before separating the
Secretary of the Treasury expressed his apprehension that the reinstate-
ment of McClellan would prove a national calamity."

Mr. Montgomery Blair, Postmaster-General, in private letters, from
which, now in the hands of the editor, the following extracts are taken,
says :

Under date April 22. 1870: "The bitterness of Stanton on the rein-
statement of McClellan you can scarcely conceive. He preferred to see
the capital fall. . . . McClellan was bound to go when the emergency was
past, and Halleck and Stanton furnished a pretence."

Under date April 3, 1879: "The folly and disregard of public interests thus exhibited would be incredible but that the authors of this intrigue,
Messrs. Stanton and Chase, when the result of it came, and I proposed the
restoration of McClellan to command, and to prevent the completion of
ruin by the fall of this capital, *actually declared that they would prefer the
loss of the capital to the restoration of McClellan to command.* Yet these are
the men who have been accounted by a large portion of our countrymen as
the civil heroes of the war, whilst McClellan, who saved the capital, was
dismissed. . . ."

Whatever changes of mind Mr. Lincoln, subsequently underwent may
with probability be attributed to the causes already indicated - his personal
confidence in McClellan on one hand, and his desire to avoid a rupture
with the radical wing of his party on the other hand. His adherence at
this moment to his adopted plan, in face of the violence of the secretaries,
was a notable exhibition of firmness.

Meantime McClellan, heedless of the renewed war in his rear, devoted
his attention to the enemy in front. But when, acting on the trust imposed
by the President, he was about to go out to meet the retreating army, Halleck stopped him with the information that the President had limited his
command to the fortifications. Under all the circumstances we may take
leave to doubt whether any such order came from the President. It was

contradictory to the spirit of the morning interview, and merciless to an army pursued by a victorious enemy.

At some time during the early part of the day the order of Sept. 2 was prepared by Gen. Halleck and telegraphed throughout the country in the following form:

> "HEADQUARTERS OF THE ARMY,
> "ADJUTANT - GENERAL'S OFFICE,
> "WASHINGTON, Sept. 2, 1862.

"By direction of the President, Maj.-Gen. McClellan will have command of the fortifications of Washington and of all the troops for the defence of the capital.
> "By order of the Secretary of War.
> "E. D. TOWNSEND,
> *"A. A. Gen."*

It will be remembered that Mr. Stanton had declared with "some feeling," as Mr. Welles puts it, that no such order had issued from the War Department. But this order had issued, as from the Secretary of War.

Later in the day, and of course after Gen. Halleck's interview with Secretary Stanton, it reappeared in the form following:

> "WAR DEPARTMENT,
> "ADJUTANT - GENERAL'S OFFICE,
> "WASHINGTON, Sept. 2, 1862.

" Maj.-Gen. McClellan will have command of the fortifications of Washington and of all the troops for the defence of the capital.
> " By order of Maj.-Gen. Halleck.
> "E. D. TOWNSEND,
> *" A. A. Gen."*

The history of its origin and modification is certainly obscure. Little light is thrown on it by the following, which is an extract from an official letter from the adjutant-general's office, dated March 1, 1886, and signed J. C. Kelton, Assist. Adj.-Gen. Col. Kelton was the officer on Gen. Halleck's staff who had brought the intelligence of the condition of Gen. Pope's command on the morning of Sept. 2. It is therefore clear that the first draft of the order was made that morning; but whether before or after Gen. Halleck had consulted with Mr. Stanton does not appear. Col. Kelton says:

"It appears from the records that a draft of General Order No. 122 was written by Col. J. C. Kelton, then assistant adjutant-general, headquarters of the army, Sept. 2, 1862, with request that Col. E. D. Townsend number and issue the same. and have it published in the *Star*. The general order was prepared accordingly by Col. E. D. Townsend, Assist. Adj.-Gen., and, having been submitted to Gen. Halleck, was the same day returned by Col. Kelton to Col. Townsend, amended as it now stands."

Whether McClellan, when he received Halleck's message forbidding him to go beyond the fortifications, recognized an intent to interfere between him and the President's unlimited trust we cannot know. He obeyed the instruction. But when in the afternoon, at Upton's Hill, the farthest - out fortification, he met Pope and McDowell leading the retreat into Washington, and heard the sound of artillery-firing on the Army of the Potomac, abandoned to their fate without a commander, he left the fortifications and the orders of Gen. Halleck behind him, and crossed country to the sound of the enemy's cannon.

From that time he acted on his own judgment, as seemed to him best for the country, and, "with the halter around his neck," led the army on the swiftest and most brilliant campaign in its history, to the victories of South Mountain and Antietam.

The order of Sept. 2 remained in force thereafter. It perhaps explains some differences between the reports of officers in the field and those in Washington in regard to supplies, as all horses, ammunition, and supplies furnished to troops in and around Washington could properly be charged and reported as furnished to McClellan's command.

It is not probable that Mr. Lincoln's attention was ever called to the existence of this order. For it is a remarkable fact than, when he finally consented to displace McClellan, he gave the order that he "be relieved from the command of the Army of the Potomac" - a command which Gen. McClellan had not held by any authority since Aug. 30.

B. - Capt. William H. Powell, of the 4th Regular Infantry, in a letter to the *Century*, dated Fort Omaha, Neb., March 12, 1885, thus describes this scene [Century, January, 1886, p. 473]:

"About four o'clock on the next afternoon, from a prominent point, we descried in the distance the dome of the Capitol. We would be there at least in time to defend it. Darkness came upon us, and still we marched. As the night wore on we found at each halt that it was more and more difficult to arouse the men from the sleep they would fall into apparently as soon as they touched the ground. During one of these halts, while Col. Buchanan, the brigade commander, was resting a little off the road, some distance in advance of the head of the column, it being starlight, two horsemen came down the road towards us. I thought I observed a familiar form, and, turning to Col. Buchanan, said:

"'Colonel, if I did not know that Gen. McClellan had been relieved of all command, I should say that he was one of that party,' adding immediately, 'I do really believe it is he!'

"Nonsense!' said the colonel; 'what would Gen. McClellan be doing out in this lonely place, at this time of night, without an escort?'

"The two horsemen passed on to where the column of troops was lying, standing, or sitting, as pleased each individual, and were lost in the shadowy gloom. But a few moments had elapsed, however, when Capt. John D. Wilkins, of the 3d Infantry (now colonel of the 5th), came running towards Col. Buchanan, crying out:

"'Colonel! Colonel! Gen. McClellan is here!'

"The enlisted men caught the sound Whoever was awake aroused his neighbor. Eyes were rubbed, and those tired fellows, as the news passed down the column, jumped to their feet and sent up such a hurrah as the Army of the Potomac had never heard before. Shout upon shout went out into the stillness of the night; and, as it was taken up along the road and repeated by regiment, brigade, division, and corps, we could hear the roar dying away in the distance. The effect of this man's presence upon the Army of the Potomac - in sunshine or rain, in darkness or in daylight, in victory or defeat - was ever electrical, and too wonderful to make it worth while attempting to give a reason for it.   Just two weeks from this time this defeated army, under the leadership of McClellan, won the battles of South Mountain and Antietam, and had to march ten days out of the two weeks in order to do it."

CHAPTER XXXIII.

Maryland invaded - McClellan not to command in the field - Halleck declines advice about Harper's Ferry - The North in danger - McClellan assumes command - The halter around his neck - McClellan unrestrained - Marching, and reorganizing the army on the march - Harper's Ferry lost - McClellan relieves it, but Miles surrenders - Franklin's victory at Crampton's Gap.

NEXT day I rode to the front of Alexandria, and was engaged in rectifying the positions of the troops and giving orders necessary to secure the issuing of the necessary supplies, etc.

On the 3d the enemy had disappeared from the front of Washington, and the information which I received induced me to believe that he intended to cross the upper Potomac into Maryland. This materially changed the aspect of affairs and enlarged the sphere of operations; for, in case of a crossing in force, an active campaign would be necessary to cover Baltimore, prevent the invasion of Pennsylvania, and clear Maryland.

I therefore, on the 3d, ordered the 2d and 12th corps to Tennallytown, and the 9th corps to a point on the Seventh street road near Washington, and sent such cavalry as was available to the fords near Poolesville, to watch and impede the enemy in any attempt to cross in that vicinity.

As soon as this was done I reported the fact to Gen. Halleck, who asked what general I had placed in command of those three corps. I replied that I had made no such detail, as I should take command in person if the enemy appeared in that direction. He then said that my command included only the defences of Washington, and did not extend to any active column that might be moved out beyond the line of works; that no decision had yet been made as to the commander of the active army. He repeated the same thing on more than one occasion before the final advance to South Mountain and Antietam took place.

Before I went to the front Secretary Seward came to my

quarters one evening and asked my opinion of the condition of affairs at Harper's Ferry, remarking that he was not at ease on the subject. Harper's Ferry was not at that time in any sense under my control, but I told Mr. Seward that I regarded the arrangements there as exceedingly dangerous; that in my opinion the proper course was to abandon the position and unite the garrison (ten thousand men, about) to the main army of operations, for the reason that its presence at Harper's Ferry would not hinder the enemy from crossing the Potomac; that if we were unsuccessful in the approaching battle Harper's Ferry would be of no use to us, and its garrison necessarily lost; that if we were successful we would immediately recover the post without any difficulty, while the addition of 10,000 men to the active army would be an important factor in insuring success. I added that if it were determined to hold the position the existing arrangements were all wrong, as it would be easy for the enemy to surround and capture the garrison, and that the garrison ought, at least, to be withdrawn to the Maryland Heights, where they could resist attack until relieved.

The secretary was much impressed by what I said, and asked me to accompany him to Gen. Halleck and repeat my statement to him. I acquiesced, and we went together to Gen. Halleck's quarters, where we found that he had retired for the night. But he received us in his bed-room, when, after a preliminary explanation by the secretary as to the interview being at his request, I said to Halleck precisely what I had stated to Mr. Seward.

Halleck received my statement with ill-concealed contempt; said that everything was all right as it was; that my views were entirely erroneous, etc., and soon bowed us out, leaving matters at Harper's Ferry precisely as they were.

On Sept. 5 the 2d and 12th corps were moved to Rockville, and Couch's division (the only one of the 4th corps that had been brought from the Peninsula) to Offutt's cross-roads.

On the 6th the 1st and 9th corps were ordered to Leesburg; the 6th corps and Sykes's division of the 5th corps to Tennally-town.

On the 7th the 6th corps was advanced to Rockville, to which place my headquarters were moved on the same day.

All the necessary arrangements for the defence of the city under the new condition of things had been made, and Gen.

Banks was left in command, having received his instructions from me.

As the time had now arrived for the army to advance, and I had received no orders to take command of it, but had been expressly told that the assignment of a commander had not been decided, I determined to solve the question for myself, and when I moved out from Washington with my staff and personal escort I left my card, with P. P. C. written upon it, at the White House, War Office, and Secretary Seward's house, and went on my way.

I was afterwards accused of assuming command without authority, for nefarious purposes, and, in fact, fought the battles of South Mountain and Antietam with a halter around my neck; for if the Army of the Potomac had been defeated and I had survived I would, no doubt, have been tried for assuming authority without orders, and, in the state of feeling which so unjustly condemned the innocent and most meritorious Gen. F. J. Porter, I would probably have been condemned to death. I was fully aware of the risk I ran, but the path of duty was clear and I tried to follow it.

It was absolutely necessary that Lee's army should be met, and, in the state of affairs I have briefly described, there could be no hesitation on my part as to doing it promptly.

Very few in the Army of the Potomac doubted the favorable result of the next collision with the Confederate army, but in other quarters not a little doubt prevailed, and the desire for very rapid movements, so loudly expressed after the result was gained, did not make itself heard during the movements preceding the battles; quite the contrary was the case, as I was more than once cautioned that I was moving too rashly and exposing the capital to an attack from the Virginia side.

As is well known, the result of Gen. Pope's operations had not been favorable, and when I finally resumed command of the troops in and around Washington they were weary, disheartened, their organization impaired, their clothing, ammunition, and supplies in a pitiable condition.

The Army of the Potomac was thoroughly exhausted and depleted by its desperate fighting and severe marches in the unhealthy regions of the Chickahominy and afterwards during the second Bull Run campaign. Its trains, administration services, and supplies were disorganized or lacking, in consequence of the rapidity and manner of its removal from the Peninsula, as well as from the nature of its operations during the second Bull Run campaign. In the departure from the Peninsula, trains, supplies, cavalry, and artillery were often necessarily left at Fort Monroe and Yorktown for lack of vessels, as the important point was to move the infantry divisions as rapidly as possible to the support of Gen. Pope. The divisions of the Army of Virginia were also exhausted and weakened, and their trains and supplies disorganized and deficient by the movements in which they had been engaged."

Had Gen. Lee remained in front of Washington it would have been the part of wisdom to hold our own army quiet until its pressing wants were fully supplied, its organization restored, and its ranks filled with recruits - in brief, prepared for a campaign. But as the enemy maintained the offensive and crossed the upper Potomac to threaten or invade Pennsylvania, it became necessary to meet him at any cost, notwithstanding the condition of the troops; to put a stop to the invasion, save Baltimore and Washington, and throw him back across the Potomac.

Nothing but sheer necessity justified the advance of the Army of the Potomac to South Mountain and Antietam in its then condition, and it is to the eternal honor of the brave men who composed it that under such adverse circumstances they gained those victories; for the work of supply and reorganization was continued

* The "Army of Virginia," which had been under the command of Gen. Pope, ceased to exist on the 2d of Sept., 1862, by force of circumstances, and, so far as appears, without any order issued. The following correspondence is the only known record:

"ARLINGTON. Sept. 5, 12.05 P.M.
"Maj.-Gen. Halleck, Gen.-in-Chief:
"I have just received an order from Gen. McClellan to have my command in readiness to march with three days' rations, and further details of the march. What is my command, and where is it? McClellan has scattered it about in all directions, and has not informed me of the position of a single regiment. Am I to take the field, and under McClellan's orders?
"JNO. POPE,
" *Maj.- Gen.* "

"WASHINGTON D.C., Sept. 5, 1862.
"Maj.-Gen. Pope, Arlington.
"The armies of the Potomac and Virginia being consolidated, you will report for orders to the Secretary of War.
"H. W. HALLECK,
"Gen.-in-chief."

as best we might while on the march, and after the close of the battles so much remained to be done to place the army in condition for a campaign that the delay which ensued was absolutely unavoidable, and the army could not have entered upon a new campaign one day earlier than it did.

The purpose of advancing from Washington was simply to meet the necessities of the moment by frustrating Lee's invasion of the Northern States, and, when that was accomplished, to push with the utmost rapidity the work of reorganization and supply, so that a new campaign might be promptly inaugurated with the army in condition to prosecute it to a successful termination without intermission.

The advance from Washington was covered by the cavalry, under Gen. Pleasonton, pushed as far to the front as possible, and soon in constant contact with the enemy's cavalry, with whom several well-conducted and successful affairs occurred.

Partly in order to move men freely and rapidly, partly in consequence of the lack of accurate information as to the exact position and intention of Lee's army, the troops advanced by three main roads that near the Potomac by Offutt's crossroads and the mouth of the Seneca, that by Rockville to Frederick, and that by Brookeville and Urbana to New Market. We were then in condition to act according to the development of the enemy's plans, and to concentrate rapidly in any position. If Lee threatened our left flank by moving down the river road or by crossing the Potomac at any of the forks from Coon's Ferry upward, there were enough troops on the river road to hold him in check until the rest of the army could move over to support them; if Lee took up a position behind the Seneca near Frederick, the whole army could be rapidly concentrated in that direction to attack him in force; if he moved upon Baltimore the entire army could rapidly be thrown in his rear and his retreat cut off; if he moved by Gettysburg or Chambersburg upon York or Carlisle we were equally in position to throw ourselves in his rear.

The first thing was to gain accurate information as to Lee's movements, and meanwhile to push the work of supply and reorganization as rapidly as possible.

Gen. Lee and I knew each other well in the days before the war. We had served together in Mexico and commanded against each other in the Peninsula. I had the highest respect for his ability as a commander, and knew that he was not a general to be trifled with or carelessly afforded an opportunity of striking a fatal blow. Each of us naturally regarded his own army as the better, but each entertained the highest respect for the endurance, courage, and fighting qualities of the opposing army; and this feeling extended to the officers and men. It was perfectly natural under these circumstances that both of us should exercise a certain amount of caution: I in my endeavors to ascertain Lee's strength, position, and intentions before I struck the final blow; he to abstain from any extended movements of invasion, and to hold his army well in hand until he could be satisfied as to the condition of the Army of the Potomac after its second Bull Run campaign, and as to the intentions of its commander.

The right wing, consisting of the 1st and 9th corps, under the command of Maj.-Gen. Burnside, moved on Frederick; the 1st corps *via* Brookeville, Cooksville, and Ridgeville, and the 9th corps *via* Damascus and New Market.

The 2d and 12th corps, forming the centre, under the command of Gen. Sumner, moved on Frederick; the former *via* Clarksburg and Urbana, the 12th corps on a lateral road between Urbana and New Market, thus maintaining the communication with the right wing and covering the direct road from Frederick to Washington. The 6th corps, under the command of Gen. Franklin, moved to Buckeystown *via* Darnestown, Dawsonville, and Barnesville, covering the road from the mouth of the Monocacy to Rockville, and being in a position to connect with and support the centre, should it have been necessary (as was supposed) to force the line of the Monocacy.

Couch's division moved by the river road, covering that approach, watching the fords of the Potomac, and ultimately following and supporting the 6th corps.

The following extracts from telegrams received by me after my departure from Washington will show how little was known there about the enemy's movements, and the fears which were entertained for the safety of the capital. On the 9th of Sept. Gen. Halleck telegraphed me as follows:

"Until we can get better advices about the numbers of the enemy at Dranesville, I think we must be very cautious about stripping too much the forts on the Virginia side. It may be the enemy's object to draw off the mass of our forces and then attempt to attack from the Virginia side of the Potomac. Think of this."

Again, on the 11th of Sept., Gen. Halleck telegraphed me as follows:

"Why not order forward Keyes or Sigel? I think the main force of the enemy is in your front. More troops can be spared from here."

This despatch, as published by the Committee on the Conduct of the War, and furnished by the general-in-chief, reads as follows:

"Why not order forward Porter's corps or Sigel's? *If the main force of the enemy* is in your front, more troops can be spared from here."

I remark that the original despatch, as received by me from the telegraph operator, is in the words quoted above: "I *think the main force of the enemy,*" etc.

In accordance with this suggestion I asked, on the same day, that all the troops that could be spared should at once be sent to reinforce me ; but none came.

On the 12th I received the following telegram from his Excellency the President: "Governor Curtin telegraphs me: 'I have advices that Jackson is crossing the Potomac at Williamsport, and probably the whole rebel army will be drawn from Maryland.'" The President adds: "Receiving nothing from Harper's Ferry or Martinsburg to-day, and positive information from Wheeling that the line is cut, corroborates the idea that the enemy is recrossing the Potomac. Please do not let him get off without being hurt."

On the 13th Gen. Halleck telegraphed as follows: "Until you know more certainly the enemy's force south of the Potomac you are wrong in thus uncovering the capital. I am of the opinion that the enemy will send a small column towards Pennsylvania to draw your forces in that direction, then suddenly move on Washington with the forces south of the Potomac and those he may cross over." Again, on the 14th, Gen. Halleck telegraphed
41

me that "scouts report a large force still on the Virginia side of the Potomac. If so I fear you are exposing your left and rear."

Again, as late as the 16th, after we had the most positive evidence that Lee's entire army was in front of us, I received the following from him:

"Yours of seven A.M. is this moment received. As you give me no information in regard to the position of your forces, except that at Sharpsburg, of course I cannot advise. I think, however, you will find that the whole force of the enemy in your front has crossed the river. I fear now more than ever that they will recross at Harper's Ferry or below, and turn your left, thus cutting you off from Washington. This has appeared to me to be a part of their plan, and hence my anxiety on the subject. A heavy rain might prevent it."

The importance of moving with all due caution, so as not to uncover the national capital until the enemy's position and plans were developed, was, I believe, fully appreciated by me; and as my troops extended from the Baltimore and Ohio Railroad to the Potomac, with the extreme left flank moving along that stream, and with strong pickets left in rear to watch and guard all the available fords, I did not regard my left or rear as in any degree exposed. But it appears from the foregoing telegrams that the general-in-chief was of a different opinion, and that my movements were, in his judgment, too precipitate, not only for the safety of Washington, but also for the security of my left and rear.

The precise nature of these daily injunctions against a precipitate advance may now be perceived. The general-in-chief, in his testimony before the Committee on the Conduct of the War, says:

"In respect to Gen. McClellan going too fast, or too far from Washington, there can be found no such telegram from me to him. He has mistaken the meaning of the telegrams I sent him. I telegraphed him that he was going too far, not from Washington, but from the Potomac, leaving Gen. Lee the opportunity to come down the Potomac and get between him and Washington. I thought Gen. McClellan should keep more on the Potomac, and press forward his left rather than his right, so as the more readily to relieve Harper's Ferry."

As I can find no telegram from the general-in-chief recommending me to keep my left flank nearer the Potomac, I am compelled to believe that when he gave this testimony he had forgotten the purport of the telegrams above quoted, and had also ceased to remember the fact, well known to him at the time, that my left, from the time I left Washington, always rested on the Potomac, and that my centre was continually in position to reinforce the left or right, as occasion might require. Had I advanced my left flank along the Potomac more rapidly than the other columns marched upon the roads to the right, I should have thrown that flank out of supporting distance of the other troops and greatly exposed it; and if I had marched the entire army in one column along the banks of the river, instead of upon five different parallel roads, the column, with its trains, would have extended about fifty miles, and the enemy might have defeated the advance before the rear could have reached the scene of action. Moreover, such a movement would have uncovered the communications with Baltimore and Washington on our right, and exposed our left and rear.

I presume it will be admitted by every military man that it was necessary to move the army in such order that it could at any time be concentrated for battle, and I am of opinion that this object could not have been accomplished in any other way than the one employed. Any other disposition of our forces would have subjected them to defeat in detached fragments.

On the 10th of Sept. I received from my scouts information which rendered it quite probable that Gen. Lee's army was in the vicinity of Frederick, but whether his intention was to move towards Baltimore or Pennsylvania was not then known.

On the 11th I ordered Gen. Burnside to push a strong reconnoissance across the National Road and the Baltimore and Ohio Railroad towards New Market, and, if he learned that the enemy had moved towards Hagerstown, to press on rapidly to Frederick, keeping his troops constantly ready to meet the enemy in force. A corresponding movement of all the troops in the centre and on the left was ordered in the direction of Urbana and Poolesville.

On the 12th a portion of the right wing entered Frederick, after a brisk skirmish at the outskirts of the city and in the streets. On the 13th the main bodies of the right wing and centre passed through Frederick.

In the report of a military commission, of which Maj.-Gen. D. Hunter was president, which convened at Washington for the purpose of investigating the conduct of certain officers in connection with the surrender of Harper's Ferry, I find the following:

"The commission has remarked freely on Col. Miles, an old officer, who has been killed in the service of his country, and it cannot, from any motives of delicacy, refrain from censuring those in high command when it thinks such censure deserved.

"The general-in-chief has testified that Gen. McClellan, after having received orders to repel the enemy invading the State of Maryland, marched only six miles per day, on an average, when pursuing this invading enemy.

" The general-in-chief also testifies that, in his opinion, he could and should have relieved and protected Harper's Ferry; and in this opinion the commission fully concur."

This commission, in its investigations, never called upon me, nor upon any officer of my staff, nor, so far as I know, upon any officer of the Army of the Potomac able to give an intelligent statement of the movements of that army.   But another paragraph in the same report makes testimony from such sources quite superfluous. It is as follows:

"By a reference to the evidence it will be seen that at the very moment Col. Ford abandoned Maryland Heights his little army *was in reality relieved* by Gens. Franklin's and Sumner's corps at Crampton's Gap, within seven miles of his position."

The corps of Gens. Franklin and Sumner were a part of the army which I at that time had the honor to command, and they were acting under my orders at Crampton's Gap and elsewhere; and if, as the commission states, Col. Ford's "little army was in reality relieved" by those officers, it was relieved by me.

I had, on the morning of the 10th, sent the following despatch in relation to the command at Harper's Ferry to Gen. Halleck:

Sept. 10, 9.45 A.M. - Col. Miles is at or near Harper's Ferry, as I understand, with 9,000 troops. He can do nothing where he is, but could be of great service if ordered to join me.   I suggest that he be ordered to join me by the most practicable route.

To this I received the following reply from Gen. Halleck:

"There is no way for Col. Miles to join you at present; his only chance is to defend his works till you can open communication with him."

It seems necessary, for a distinct understanding of this matter, to state that I was directed on the 12th to assume command of the garrison of Harper's Ferry as soon as I should open communications with that place, and that when I received this order all communication from the direction in which I was approaching was cut off. Up to that time, however, Col. Miles could, in my opinion, have marched his command into Pennsylvania by crossing the Potomac at Williamsport or above; and this opinion was confirmed by the fact that Col. Davis marched the cavalry part of Col. Miles's command from Harper's Ferry on the 14th, taking the main road to Hagerstown, and he encountered no enemy except a small picket near the mouth of the Antietam.

Before I left Washington, and when there certainly could have been no enemy to prevent the withdrawal of the forces of Col. Miles, I recommended to the proper authorities that the garrison of Harper's Ferry should be withdrawn *via* Hagerstown, to aid in covering the Cumberland valley; or that, taking up the pontoon bridge and obstructing the railroad bridge, it should fall back to the Maryland Heights and there hold out to the last.

In this position it ought to have maintained itself for many days. It was not deemed proper to adopt either of these suggestions; and when the matter was left to my discretion it was too late for me to do anything but endeavor to relieve the garrison. I accordingly directed artillery to be fired by our advance at frequent intervals as a signal that relief was at hand. This was done, and, as I afterwards learned, the reports of the cannon were distinctly heard at Harper's Ferry. It was confidently expected that Col. Miles would hold out until we had carried the mountain-passes and were in condition to send a detachment to his relief. The left was therefore ordered to move through Crampton's Pass in front of Burkittsville, while the centre and right marched upon Turner's Pass in front of Middletown.

It may be asked, by those who are not acquainted with the topography of the country in the vicinity of Harper's Ferry, why

Franklin, instead of marching his column over the circuitous road from Jefferson *via* Burkittsville and Brownsville, was not ordered to move along the direct turnpike to Knoxville, and thence up the river to Harper's Ferry.

It was for the reason that I had received information that the enemy were anticipating our approach in that direction, and had established batteries on the south side of the Potomac which commanded all the approaches to Knoxville. Moreover, the road from that point winds directly along the river-bank at the foot of a precipitous mountain, where there was no opportunity of forming in line of battle, and where the enemy could have placed batteries on both sides of the river to enfilade our narrow approaching columns.

The approach through Crampton's Pass, which debouches into Pleasant Valley in rear of Maryland Heights, was the only one which afforded any reasonable prospect of carrying that formidable position; at the same time the troops upon that road were in better relation to the main body of our forces.

On the morning of the 14th a verbal message reached me from Col. Miles, which was the first authentic intelligence I had received as to the condition of things at Harper's Ferry. The messenger informed me that on the preceding afternoon Maryland Heights had been abandoned by our troops after repelling an attack of the rebels, and that Col. Miles's entire force was concentrated at Harper's Ferry, the Maryland, Loudon, and Bolivar Heights having been abandoned by him and occupied by the enemy. The messenger also stated that there was no apparent reason for the abandonment of the Maryland Heights, and that Col. Miles instructed him to say that he could hold out with certainty two days longer.

I directed him to make his way back, if possible, with the information that I was approaching rapidly and felt confident I could relieve the place.

On the same afternoon I wrote the following letter to Col. Miles, and despatched three copies by three different couriers on different routes. I did not, however, learn that any of these men succeeded in reaching Harper's Ferry:

MIDDLETOWN, Sept. 14, 1862.

COLONEL: The army is being rapidly concentrated here.

We are now attacking the pass on the Hagerstown road over the Blue Ridge. A column is about attacking the Burkittsville and Boonsborough Pass. You may count on our making every effort to relieve you. You may rely upon my speedily accomplishing that object. Hold out to the last extremity. If it is possible, reoccupy the Maryland Heights with your whole force. If you can do that I will certainly be able to relieve you. As the Catoctin valley is in our possession, you can safely cross the river at Berlin or its vicinity, so far as opposition on this side of the river is concerned. Hold out to the last.

GEORGE B. McCLELLAN,
Maj.-Gen. Commanding.

Col. D. S. MILES.

On the previous day I had sent Gen. Franklin the following instructions:

HEADQUARTERS, ARMY OF THE POTOMAC,
CAMP NEAR FREDERICK, Sept. 13, 1862, 6.20 P.M.

GENERAL: I have now full information as to movements and intentions of the enemy. Jackson has crossed the upper Potomac to capture the garrison at Martinsburg and cut off Miles's retreat towards the west. A division on the south side of the Potomac was to carry Loudon Heights and cut off his retreat in that direction. McLaws, with his own command and the division of R. H. Anderson, was to move by Boonsborbugh and Rohrersville to carry the Maryland Heights. The signal officers inform me that he is now in Pleasant Valley. The firing shows that Miles still holds out. Longstreet was to move to Boonsborough, and there halt with the reserve corps; D. H. Hill to form the rear-guard; Stuart's cavalry to bring up stragglers, etc. We have cleared out all the cavalry this side of the mountains and north of us. The last I heard from Pleasonton he occupied Middletown, after several sharp skirmishes. A division of Burnside's command started several hours ago to support him. The whole of Burnside's command, including Hooker's corps, march this evening and early to-morrow morning, followed by the corps of Sumner and Banks, and Sykes's division, upon Boonsborough to carry that position. Couch has been ordered to concentrate his division and join you as rapidly as possible. Without waiting for the whole of that division to join, you will move at daybreak in the morning by Jefferson and Burkittsville upon the road to Rohrersville. I have reliable information that the mountain-pass by this road is practicable for artillery and wagons. If this pass is not occupied by the enemy in force, seize it as soon as practicable, and debouch upon Rohrersville in order to cut off the retreat of or destroy McLaws's command. If you find this pass held by the enemy in large force, make all your dispositions for the attack and commence it about half an hour after you hear severe firing at the pass on the Hagerstown pike, where the main body will attack. Having gained the pass, your duty will be first to cut off, destroy, or capture McLaws's command and relieve Col. Miles. If you effect this you will order him to join you at once with all his disposable troops, first destroying the bridges over the Potomac, if not already done; and, leaving a sufficient garrison to prevent the enemy from passing the ford, you will then return by Rohrersville on the direct road to Boonsborough, if the main column has not succeeded in its attack. If it has succeeded, take the road to Rohrersville, to Sharpsburg and Williamsport, in order either to cut off the retreat of Hill and Longstreet towards the Potomac, or prevent the repassage of Jackson. My general idea is to cut the enemy in two and beat him in detail. I believe I have sufficiently explained my intentions. I ask of you, at this important moment, all your intellect and the utmost activity that a general can exercise.

GEO. B. MCCLELLAN,
Maj.-Gen. Commanding.

Maj.-Gen. W. B. FRANKLIN,
Commanding 6th Corps.

Again, on the 14th, I sent him the following:

HEADQUARTERS, ARMY OF THE POTOMAC,
FREDERICK, Sept. 14, 1862, 2 P.M.

Your despatch of 12.30 just received. Send back to hurry up Couch. Mass your troops and carry Burkittsville at any cost. We shall have strong opposition at both passes. As fast as the troops come up I will hold a reserve in readiness to support you. If you find the enemy in very great force at any of these passes let me know at once, and amuse them as best you can so as to retain them there. In that event I will probably throw the mass of the army on the pass in front of here. If I carry that it will clear the way for you, and you must follow the enemy as rapidly as possible.

GEORGE B. MCCLELLAN,
Maj.-Gen. Commanding.

Maj.-Gen. FRANKLIN.

Gen. Franklin pushed his corps rapidly forward towards Crampton's Pass, and at about twelve o'clock on the 14th arrived at Burkittsville, immediately in rear of which he found the enemy's infantry posted in force on both sides of the road, with artillery in strong positions to defend the approaches to the pass.   Slocum's division was formed upon the right of the road leading through the gap, and Smith's upon the left. A line formed of Bartlett's and Torbert's brigades, supported by Newton, whose activity was conspicuous, advanced steadily upon the enemy at a charge on the right.   The enemy were driven from their position at the base of the mountain, where they were protected by a stone wall, steadily forced back up the slope until they reached the position of their battery on the road, well up the mountain.   There they made a stand.   They were, however, driven back, retiring their artillery in echelon, until, after an action of three hours, the crest was gained, and the enemy hastily fled down the mountain on the other side.

On the left of the road Brooks's and Irvin's brigades, of Smith's division, formed for the protection of Slocum's flank, charged up the mountain in the same steady manner, driving the enemy before them until the crest was carried.   400 prisoners from seventeen different organizations, 700 stand of arms, 1 piece of artillery, and 3 colors were captured by our troops in this brilliant action.   It was conducted by Gen. Franklin in all its details.   These details are given in a report of Gen. Franklin, and due credit awarded to the gallant officers and men engaged.

The loss in Gen. Franklin's corps was 115 killed, 416 wounded, and 2 missing. The enemy's loss was about the same. The enemy's position was such that our artillery could not be used with any effect.   The close of the action found Gen. Franklin's advance in Pleasant Valley on the night of the 14th, within three and a half miles of the point on Maryland Heights where he might, on the same night or on the morning of the 15th, have formed a junction with the garrison of Harper's Ferry had it not been previously withdrawn from Maryland Heights, and within six miles of Harper's Ferry.

On the night of the 14th the following despatch was sent to Gen. Franklin:

BOLIVAR, Sept. 15, 1 A.M.

GENERAL:

The commanding general directs that you occupy with your command the road from Rohrersville to Harper's Ferry, placing a sufficient force at Rohrersville to hold that position in case it

should be attacked by the enemy from Boonsborough. Endeavor
to open communication with Col. Miles at Harper's Ferry, attacking and destroying such of the enemy as you may find in
Pleasant Valley. Should you succeed in opening communication with Col. Miles, direct him to join you with his whole command, with all the guns and public property he can carry with
him. The remainder of the guns will be spiked or destroyed;
the rest of the public property will also be destroyed.   You will
then proceed to Boonsborough - which place the commanding
general intends to attack to-morrow - and join the main body of
the army at that place.   Should you find, however, that the enemy has retreated from Boonsborough towards Sharpsburg, you
will endeavor to fall upon him and cut off his retreat.
    By command of Maj.-Gen. McClellan.

                                    GEO. D. RUGGLES,
                                        Col. and A. B. C.
Gen. FRANKLIN.

On the 15th the following were received from Gen. Franklin:

   "AT THE FOOT OF THE MOUNTAIN IN PLEASANT VALLEY,
         "THREE MILES FROM ROHRERSVILLE,
              "Sept. 15, 8.50 A.M.

    "GENERAL: My command started at daylight this morning,
and I am waiting to have it closed up here.   Gen. Couch arrived
about ten o'clock last night.   I have ordered one of his brigades
and one battery to Rohrersville, or to the strongest point in its
vicinity. The enemy is drawn up in line of battle about two
miles to our front - one brigade in sight.   As soon as I am sure
that Rohrersville is occupied I shall move forward to attack the
enemy. This may be two hours from now. If Harper's Ferry
is fallen - and the cessation of firing makes me fear that it has
- it is my opinion that I should be strongly reinforced.

                           " W. B. FRANKLIN,
                      " *Maj.-Gen. Commanding 6th. Corps.*
"Gen. G. B. MCCLELLAN.

                                    "SEPT. 15, 11 A.M.
    "GENERAL: I have received your despatch by Capt. O'Keefe.
The enemy is in large force in my front, in two lines of battle
stretching across the valley, and a large column of artillery and
infantry on the right of the valley looking towards Harper's
Ferry. They outnumber me two to one. It of course will not
answer to pursue the enemy under these circumstances.   I shall
communicate with Burnside as soon as possible.   In the meantime I shall wait here until I learn what is the prospect of rein-

forcement. I have not the force to justify an attack on the force I see in front. I have had a very close view of it, and its position is very strong.

"Respectfully,

"W. B. FRANKLIN,

"Maj.-Gen.

"Maj.-Gen. G. B. McCLELLAN,

"Commanding."

Col. Miles surrendered Harper's Ferry at eight A.M. on the 15th, as the cessation of the firing indicated, and Gen. Franklin was ordered to remain where he was, to watch the large force in front of him and protect our left and rear, until the night of the 16th, when he was ordered to join the main body of the army at Keedysville, after sending Couch's division to Maryland Heights.

While the events which have just been described were taking place at Crampton's Gap, the troops of the centre and right wing, which had united at Frederick on the 13th, were engaged in the contest for the possession of Turner's Gap.

CHAPTER XXXIV.

PRIVATE LETTERS.

[*Sept.* 2 to *Sept.* 14, 1862.]

Sept. 2, 12.30 P.M. - I was surprised this morning, when at breakfast, by a visit from the President and Halleck, in which the former expressed the opinion that the troubles now impending could be overcome better by me than any one else. Pope is ordered to fall back upon Washington, and, as he re-enters, everything is to come under my command again! A terrible and thankless task. Yet I will do my best, with God's blessing, to perform it. God knows that I need His help. I am too busy to write any more now. Pray that God will help me in the great task now imposed upon me. I assume it reluctantly, with a full knowledge of all its difficulties and of the immensity of the responsibility. I only consent to take it for my country's sake and with the humble hope that God has called me to it; how I pray that He may support me! . . . Don't be worried; my conscience is clear, and I trust in God.

Sept. 3, 11.30 A.M. - . . . I am now about to jump into the saddle, and will be off all day. I did not return from my ride last night until after midnight. I went out to meet the troops and place them in position. Colburn and I rode out several miles to the front. All is quiet to-day, and I think the capital is safe. Just as I was starting off yesterday to gather up the army, supposing that I would find it savagely followed up by the rebels, and that I might have dangerous work before me, I commenced the enclosed scrawl on a scrap of paper as a good-by; could not even finish it. It may amuse you now that the danger is over:

"Enclosure - *Sept.* 2, 4 P.M. - . . . I am just about starting out to pick up the Army of the Potomac. Don't know whether I will get back, but can't resist saying one last word to you before I start. . ."

Sept. 5, 11 A.M. - . . . Again I have been called upon to save the country. The case is desperate, but with God's help I will try unselfishly to do my best, and, if He wills it, accomplish the salvation of the nation. My men are true and will stand by me till the last. I still hope for success, and will leave nothing undone to gain it. . . . How weary I am of this struggle against adversity! But one thing sustains me - that is, my trust in God. I know that the interests at stake are so great as to justify His interference; not for me, but for the innocent thousands, millions rather, who have been plunged in misery by no fault of theirs. It is probable that our communications will be cut off in a day or two, but don't be worried. You may rest assured that I am doing all I can for my country, and that no shame shall rest upon you, wilfully brought upon you by me. . . . My hands are full, so is my heart. . . .

Sept. 5, 4 P.M.- . . . It makes my heart bleed to see the poor, shattered remnants of my noble Army of the Potomac, poor fellows! and to see how they love me even now. I hear them calling out to me as I ride among them, "George, don't leave us again!" "They sha'n't take you away from us again," etc., etc. I can hardly restrain myself when I see how fearfully they are reduced in numbers, and realize how many of them lie unburied on the field of battle, where their lives were uselessly sacrificed. It is the most terrible trial I ever experienced. Truly, God is trying me in the fire. . . .

Telegram - *Washington, Sept.* 7, 2.50 P.M. - We are all well and the entire army is now united, cheerful, and confident. You need not fear the result, for I believe that God will give us the victory. I leave here this afternoon to take command of the troops in the field. The feeling of the government towards me, I am sure, is kind and trusting. I hope, with God's blessing, to justify the great confidence they now repose in me, and will bury the past in oblivion. A victory now and we will soon be together. I send short letter to-day. God bless and reward your trust in Him, and all will be well.

Sept. 7, 2.30 P.M., *Sunday.* - . . . I leave in a couple of hours to take command of the army in the field. I shall go to Rockville to-night and start out after the rebels to-morrow. I shall have nearly 100,000 men, old and new, and hope, with God's blessing, to gain a decisive victory.

Sept. 8, camp near Rockville. - . . . You don't know what a task has been imposed upon me! I have been obliged to do the best I could with the broken and discouraged fragments of two armies defeated by no fault of mine. Nothing but a desire to do my duty could have induced me to accept the command under such circumstances. Not feeling at all sure that I could do anything, I felt that under the circumstances no one else *could* save the country, and I have not shrunk from the terrible task. McDowell's own men would have killed him had he made his appearance among them; even his staff did not dare to go among his men. I can afford to forgive and forget him. I saw Pope and McDowell for a few moments at Upton's Hill when I rode out to meet the troops and assume command. I have not seen them since; I hope never to lay eyes on them again. Between them they are responsible for the lives of many of my best and bravest men. They have done all they could (unintentionally, I hope) to ruin and destroy the country. I can never forgive them that. Pope has been foolish enough to try to throw the blame of his defeat on the Army of the Potomac. He would have been wiser to have accepted his defeat without complaint. I will probably move some four or five miles further to the front to-morrow, as I have ordered the whole army forward. I expect to fight a great battle and to do my best at it. I do not think secesh will catch me very badly.

Tuesday morning, 8.30. - . . . I hope to learn this morning something definite as to the movements of secesh, to be enabled to regulate my own. I hardly expect to equal the genius of Mr. Pope, but I hope to waste fewer lives and to accomplish something more than lame defeat. I have ordered a general advance of a few miles to-day, which will bring us on the line of the Seneca, and near enough to secesh to find out what he is doing, and take measures accordingly. I shall follow him wherever he goes and do my best to beat him. If I accomplish that the campaign will be ended.

9.30. - . . . The fact is, that commanding such an army as

this, picked up after a defeat, is no very easy thing; it does take a great deal of time and infinite labor. In coming to Rockville we arrived about midnight. Yesterday we came out to this camp, which is about a half-mile from the town. I am still uncertain whether I shall move headquarters to-day, or on which road, as that depends on the information I receive as to the enemy. I probably won't go more than four or five miles in a central direction. . . . If I can add the defeat of secesh I think I ought to be entitled to fall back into private life. . . .

Sept. 9, camp near Rockville, 5 P.M.- . . . Am going out in a few minutes to ride over to the camp of the regulars, whom I have not been to see for a long time, and who welcomed me so cordially the other night, brave fellows that they are.

It is hard to get accurate news from the front. The last reports from Pleasonton are that the enemy have 110,000 on this side of the river. I have not so many, so I must watch them closely and try to catch them in some mistake, which I hope to do. My people are mostly in front of here, some six to ten miles; moved forward to-day. They are, I think, well placed to be concentrated wherever it may be necessary, and I want now a little breathing-time to get them rested and in good order for fighting. Most of them will do well now; a few days will confirm this still further, increase my cavalry force, and put me in better condition generally. I think my present positions will check the advance into Pennsylvania and give me time to get some reinforcements that I need very much. . . . I have this moment learned that, in addition to the force on this side of the river, the enemy has also a large force near Leesburg, so McC. has a difficult game to play, but will do his best and try to do his duty.

Sept. 11, camp near Rockville. - . . . I have just time before starting to say good-by. . . I am quite tired this morning, as I did not get back from a ride to Burnside's until three A.M.; the night before I was at the telegraph office sending and receiving despatches until the same hour, and how it will be to-night is more than I can tell. . . .

Sept. 12, 3 P.M., camp near Urbana. - As our wagons are not yet up, and won't be for a couple of hours, I avail myself of the "advantages of the situation" to scrawl a few lines to you. . . . We are travelling now through one of the most lovely regions I have ever seen, quite broken with lovely valleys in all directions, and some fine mountains in the distance. From all I can gather secesh is skedaddling, and I don't think I can catch him unless he is really moving into Pennsylvania; in that case I shall catch him before he has made much headway towards the interior. I am beginning to think he is making off to get out of the scrape by recrossing the river at Williamsport, in which case my only chance of bagging him will be to cross lower down and cut into his communications near Winchester. He evidently don't want to fight me, for some reason or other. . . . I have never injured —, therefore I am not called upon to make any advances to him, as the professor seems to think I ought. As for ever having any friendly relation with him, it is simply absurd. . . .

7.30 P.M. - My tent has been pitched some time. I have given all the orders necessary for to-morrow, and they have all gone to the various camps. . . . I believe that I have done all in my power and that the arrangement of the troops is good. I learned an hour or two ago, through the signal, that our troops were entering Frederick. We certainly ought to be there in respectable force by this time. My only apprehension now is that secesh will arrange to get back across the Potomac at Williamsport before I can catch him. If he goes to Pennsylvania I think I must overhaul him before long and give him a good lesson. If he does go to Pennsylvania I feel quite confident that I can so arrange things that the chances will all be that he will never return; but I presume he is smart enough to know that and to act accordingly. . . . Interrupted here by the news that we really have Frederick. Burnside and Pleasonton both there. The next trouble is to save the garrison of Harper's Ferry, which is, I fear, in danger of being captured by the rebels. They were not placed under my orders until this afternoon, although before I left Washington I strongly urged that they should be withdrawn at once, as I feared they would be captured. But other counsels prevailed, and I am rather anxious as to the result, If they are not taken by this time I think I can save them; at all events, nothing in my power shall be left undone to accomplish this result. I feel sure of one thing now, and that is that my men will fight well. . . . The moment I hear that Harper's Ferry is safe I shall feel quite sure of the result. . . . The people cheered the troops tremendously when they entered Frederick. I have thus far found the Union sentiment much stronger in this region than I had expected. People are disposed to be very kind and polite to me; invite me into their houses, offer me dinner and various other acts of kindness that are quite unknown in the Peninsula.

Sept. 14, *Frederick,* A.M. - I have only time to say good-morning this bright, sunny Sunday, and then start to the front to try to relieve Harper's Ferry, which is sorely pressed by secesh. It is probable that we shall have a serious engagement to-day, and perhaps a general battle; if we have one at all during this operation it ought to be to-day or to-morrow. I feel as reasonably confident of success as any one well can who trusts in a higher power and does not know what its decision will be. I can't describe to you for want of time the enthusiastic reception we met with yesterday at Frederick. I was nearly overwhelmed and pulled to pieces. I enclose with this a little flag that some enthusiastic lady thrust into or upon Dan's bridle. As to flowers-they came in crowds! In truth, I was seldom more affected than by the scenes I saw yesterday and the reception I met with; it would have gratified you very much. . . .

42

CHAPTER XXXV.

Entering Frederick - The lost despatch - Advance - The battle of South Mountain - Gen. Scott hails McClellan.

IN riding into Frederick I passed through Sumner's corps, which I had not seen for some time. The men and officers were so enthusiastic as to show that they had lost none of their old feeling. During the march (from Washington up) I was much with the regulars, generally encamping with them. I never can forget their constant enthusiasm; even when I passed through them several times a day on the march they would jump up (if at a rest) and begin cheering in a way that regulars are not wont to do. Poor fellows!

Our reception at Frederick was wonderful. Men, women, and children crowded around us, weeping, shouting, and praying; they clung around old Dan's neck and almost suffocated the old fellow, decking him out with flags. The houses were all decorated with flags, and it was a general scene of joy. The secession expedition had been an entire failure in that quarter; they received no recruits of the slightest consequence and no free-will offerings of any kind.

It was soon ascertained that the main body of the enemy's forces had marched out of the city on the two previous days, taking the roads to Boonsborough and Harper's Ferry, thereby rendering it necessary to force the passes through the Catoctin and South Mountain ridges, and gain possession of Boonsborough and Rohrersville, before any relief could be extended to Col. Miles at Harper's Ferry.

On the 13th an order fell into my hands issued by Gen. Lee, which fully disclosed his plans, and I immediately gave orders for a rapid and vigorous forward movement.

The following is a copy of the order referred to:

"HEADQUARTERS, ARMY OF NORTHERN VIRGINIA,
Sept. 9, 1862.
"Special Orders, No. 191.

"The army will resume its march to-morrow, taking the Hagerstown road. Gen. Jackson's command will form the advance, and after passing Middletown, with such portion as he may select, will take the route towards Sharpsburg, cross the Potomac at the most convenient point, and by Friday night take possession of the Baltimore and Ohio Railroad, capture such of the enemy as may be at Martinsburg, and intercept such as may attempt to escape from Harper's Ferry.

"Gen. Longstreet's command will pursue the same road as far as Boonsborough, where it will halt with the reserve, supply. and baggage trains of the army.

" Gen. McLaws, with his own division and that of Gen. R. H. Anderson, will follow Gen. Longstreet; on reaching Middletown he will take the route to Harper's Ferry, and by Friday morning possess himself of the Maryland Heights and endeavor to capture the enemy at Harper's Ferry and vicinity.

"Gen. Walker, with his division, after accomplishing the object in which he is now engaged, will cross the Potomac at Cheek's ford, ascend its right bank to Lovettsville, take possession of Loudon Heights, if practicable, by Friday morning; Keys's ford on his left, and the road between the end of the mountain and the Potomac on his right. He will, as far as practicable, co-operate with Gen. McLaws and Gen. Jackson in intercepting the retreat of the enemy.

"Gen. D. R. Hill's division will form the rear-guard of the army, pursuing the road taken by the main body. The reserve artillery, ordnance and supply-trains, etc., will precede Gen. Hill.

"Gen. Stuart will detach a squadron of cavalry to accompany the commands of Gens. Longstreet, Jackson, and McLaws, and, with the main body of the cavalry, will cover the route of the army and bring up all stragglers that may have been left behind.

"The commands of Gens. Jackson, McLaws, and Walker, after accomplishing the objects for which they have been detached, will join the main body of the army at Boonsborough or Hagerstown.

"Each regiment on the march will habitually carry its axes in the regimental ordnance-wagons, for use of the men at their encampments, to procure mood, etc.

"By command of Gen. R. E. Lee.
" R. H. CHILTON,
"Assist. Adj.-Gen,

"Maj.-Gen. D. H. HILL,
"Commanding Division."

On the morning of the 13th Gen. Pleasonton was ordered to send Reynolds's brigade and a section of artillery in the direction of Gettysburg, and Rush's regiment towards Jefferson to communicate with Franklin, to whom the 6th U. S. Cavalry and a section of artillery had previously been sent, and to proceed with the remainder of his force in the direction of Middletown in pursuit of the enemy.

After skirmishing with the enemy all the morning, and driving them from several strong positions, he reached Turner's Gap of the South Mountain in the afternoon, and found the enemy in force and apparently determined to defend the pass. He sent back for infantry to Gen. Burnside, who had been directed to support him, and proceeded to make a reconnoissance of the position.

The South Mountain is at this point about one thousand feet in height, and its general direction is from northeast to southwest. The national road from Frederick to Hagerstown crosses it nearly at right angles through Turner's Gap, a depression which is some four hundred feet in depth.

The mountain on the north side of the turnpike is divided into two crests or ridges by a narrow valley, which, though deep at the pass, becomes a slight depression at about a mile to the north. There are two country roads - one to the right of the turnpike and the other to the left - which give access to the crests overlooking the main road. The one on the left, called the "Old Sharpsburg road," is nearly parallel to, and about half a mile distant from, the turnpike until it reaches the crest of the mountain, when it bends off to the left. The other road, called the "Old Hagerstown road," passes up a ravine in the mountains about a mile from the turnpike, and, bending to the left over and along the first crest, enters the turnpike at the Mountain House near the summit of the pass.

On the night of the 13th the positions of the different corps were as follows:

Reno's corps at Middletown, except Rodman's division at Frederick.

Hooker's corps on the Monocacy, two miles from Frederick.

Sumner's corps near Frederick.

Banks's corps near Frederick.

Sykes's division near Frederick.

Franklin's corps at Buckeystown.

Couch's division at Licksville.

The orders from headquarters for the march on the 14th were as follows:

13th, 11.30 P.M. - Hooker to march at daylight to Middletown.

13th, 11.30 P.M. - Sykes to move at six A.M., after Hooker, on the Middletown and Hagerstown road.

14th, 1 A.M. - Artillery reserve to follow Sykes closely.

13th, 8.45 P.M. - Turner to move at seven A.M.

14th, 9 A.M. - Sumner ordered to take the Shookstown road to Middletown. *

*By letter, dated Boston, May 19, 1884, Gen. F. A. Walker called the attention of Gen. McClellan to a statement made by the Comte de Paris in his "History of the Civil War in America," attributing delay in the advance from Frederick to Gen. Sumner and the 2d corps. The following reply, which I find among the papers relating to South Mountain, indicates Gen. McClellan's intention to embody its substance in his narrative when he should reach this point in his review:

32 WASHINGTON SQUARE, N. Y., Map 21, 1884.

MY DEAR SIR : Yours of the 19th has just reached me.

My attention was never called to the point in question.

Like yourself, I am fully satisfied as to the candor and honesty of the Comte de Paris, but his work is not free from unintentional errors, of which this is an example.

My report shows that at 8.45 P.M. of the 13th the 2d corps was ordered to move at seven A.M. on the 14th by the direct road to Middletown, following Sykes at an hour's interval.

Hooker did not move as promptly as ordered, and this delayed Sykes and Sumner. Therefore at nine A.M. I ordered Sumner to take the more circuitous road by Shookstown, that his march might be free from encumbrance.

The 2d corps made its march and arrived on the field as rapidly as circumstances permitted.

I was never dissatisfied with this march of the 2d corps, and never criticised it to any one.

I can imagine the 2d corps and its brave old commander slow in getting out of a fight, but they certainly never showed any hesitation or tardiness in getting *into* battle. The promptness and energy with which Sumner moved from Grapevine bridge to the field of Fair Oaks is simply one example of the manner in which that corps always acted while under my command. You may rest assured that no member of the 2d corps has its honor more at heart, or is more proud of its uniformly admirable conduct, whether on the march or in battle, than is the commander under whom it first served.

In my account of Antietam I will take care to correct the error of the comte.

And am always your friend,

GEO. B. MCCLELLAN.

Gen. F. A. WALKER.

13th, 6.45 P.M. - Couch ordered to move to Jefferson with his whole division.

On the 14th Gen. Pleasonton continued his reconnoissance. Gibson's battery and afterwards Benjamin's battery (of Reno's corps) were placed on high ground to the left of the turnpike, and obtained a direct fire on the enemy's position in the Gap.

Gen. Cox's division, which had been ordered up to support Gen. Pleasonton, left its bivouac near Middletown at six A.M. The 1st brigade reached the scene of action about nine A.M.. and was sent up the old Sharpsburg road by Gen. Pleasonton to feel the enemy and ascertain if he held the crest on that side in strong force. This was soon found to be the case; and Gen. Cox having arrived with the other brigade, and information having been received from Gen. Reno that the column would be supported by the whole corps, the division was ordered to assault the position. Two 20-pounder Parrotts of Simmons's battery and two sections of McMullan's battery were left in the rear in position near the turnpike, where they did good service during the day against the enemy's batteries in the Gap. Scammon's brigade was deployed, and, well covered by skirmishers, moved up the slope to the left of the road with the object of turning the enemy's right, if possible. It succeeded in gaining the crest and establishing itself there, in spite of the vigorous efforts of the enemy, who was posted behind stone walls and in the edges of timber, and the fire of a battery which poured in canister and case-shot on the regiment on the right of the brigade. Col. Crook's brigade marched in columns at supporting distance. A section of McMullan's battery, under Lieut. Croome (killed while serving one of his guns), was moved up with great difficulty, and opened with canister at very short range on the enemy's infantry, by whom (after having, done considerable execution) it was soon silenced and forced to withdraw.

One regiment of Crook's brigade was now deployed on Scammon's left and the other two in his rear, and they several times entered the first line and relieved the regiments in front of them when hard pressed. A section of Sumner's battery was brought up and placed in the open space in the woods, where it did good service during the rest of the day.

The enemy several times attempted to retake the crest, advancing with boldness, but were each time repulsed. They then withdrew their battery to a point more to the right, and formed columns on both our flanks. It was now about noon, and a lull occurred in the contest which lasted about two hours, during which the rest of the corps was coming up. Gen. Wilcox's division was the first to arrive. When he reached the base of the mountain Gen. Cox advised him to consult Gen. Pleasonton as to a position. The latter indicated that on the right afterwards taken up by Gen. Hooker. Gen. Wilcox was in the act of moving to occupy this ground when he received an order from Gen. Reno to move up the old Sharpsburg road and take a position to its right overlooking the turnpike. Two regiments were detached to support Gen. Cox at his request. One section of Cooke's battery was placed in position near the turn of the road (on the crest), and opened fire on the enemy's batteries across the Gap. The division was proceeding to deploy to the right of the road when the enemy suddenly opened (at one hundred and fifty yards) with a battery which enfiladed the road at this point, drove off Cooke's cannoneers with their Iimbers, and caused a temporary panic in which the guns were nearly lost. But the 79th N. Y. and 17th Mich. promptly rallied, changed front under a heavy fire, and moved out to protect the guns, with which Capt. Cooke had remained. Order was soon restored, and the division formed in line on the right of Cox, and was kept concealed as much as possible under the hillside until the whole line advanced. It was exposed not only to the fire of the battery in front, but also to that of the batteries on the other side of the turnpike, and lost heavily.

Shortly before this time Gens. Burnside and Reno arrived at the base of the mountain, and the former directed the latter to move up the divisions of Gens. Sturgis and Rodman to the crest held by Cox and Wilcox, and to move upon the enemy's position with his whole force as soon as he was informed that Gen. Hooker (who had just been directed to attack on the right) was well advanced up the mountain.

Gen. Reno then went to the front and assumed the direction of affairs, the positions having been explained to him by Gen. Pleasonton. Shortly before this time I arrived at the point occupied by Gen. Burnside, and my headquarters were located there until the conclusion of the action. Gen. Sturgis had left his camp at one P.M., and reached the scene of action about 3.30 P.M.

Clark's battery, of his division, was sent to assist Cox's left by order of Gen. Reno, and two regiments (2d Md. and 6th N. H.) were detached by Gen. Reno and sent forward a short distance on the left of the turnpike. His division was formed in rear of Wilcox's, and Rodman's division was divided; Col. Fairchild's brigade being placed on the extreme left, and Col. Harland's, under Gen. Rodman's personal supervision, on the right.

My order to move the whole line forward and take or silence the enemy's batteries in front was executed with enthusiasm. The enemy made a desperate resistance, charging our advancing lines with fierceness, but they were everywhere routed, and fled.

Our chief loss was in Wilcox's division. The enemy's battery was found to be across a gorge and beyond the reach of our infantry; but its position was made untenable, and it was hastily removed and not again put in position near us. But the batteries across the Gap still kept up a fire of shot and shell.

Gen. Wilcox praises very highly the conduct of the 17th Mich. in this advance - a regiment which had been organized scarcely a month, but which charged the advancing enemy in flank in a manner worthy of veteran troops; and also that of the 45th Penn., which bravely met them in front.

Cooke's battery now reopened fire. Sturgis's division was moved to the front of Wilcox's, occupying the new ground gained on the further side of the slope, and his artillery opened on the batteries across the Gap. The enemy made an effort to turn our left about dark, but were repulsed by Fairchild's brigade and Clark's battery.

At about seven o'clock the enemy made another effort to regain the lost ground, attacking along Sturgis's front and part of Cox's. A lively fire was kept up until nearly nine o'clock, several charges being made by the enemy and repulsed with slaughter, and we finally occupied the highest part of the mountain.

Gen. Reno was killed just before sunset, while making a reconnoissance to the front, and the command of the corps devolved upon Gen. Cox. In Gen. Reno the nation lost one of its best general officers. He was a skilful soldier, a brave and honest man.

There was no firing after ten o'clock, and the troops slept on their arms, ready to renew the fight at daylight; but the enemy quietly retired from our front during the night, abandoning their wounded, and leaving their dead in large numbers scattered over the field. While these operations were progressing on the left of the main column, the right, under Gen. Hooker, was actively engaged. His corps left the Monocacy early in the morning, and its advance reached the Catoctin creek about one P.M. Gen. Hooker then went forward to examine the ground.

At about one o'clock Gen. Meade's division was ordered to make a diversion in favor of Reno. The following is the order sent:

SEPT. 14, 1 P.M.

GENERAL: Gen. Reno requests that a division of yours may move up on the right (north) of the main road. Gen. McClellan desires you to comply with this request, holding your whole corps in readiness to support the movement, and taking charge of it yourself.

Sumner's and Banks's corps have commenced arriving. Let Gen. McClellan be informed as soon as you commence your movement.

GEORGE D. RUGGLES,
Col., Asst. Adj.-Gen., and Aide-de-Camp.

Maj.-Gen. HOOKER.

Meade's division left Catoctin creek about two o'clock, and turned off to the right from the main road on the old Hagers-town road to Mount Tabor church, where Gen. Hooker was, and deployed a short distance in advance, its right resting about one and a half miles from the turnpike. The enemy fired a few shots from a battery on the mountain-side, but did no conside-rable damage. Cooper's battery, "B," 1st Penn. Artillery, was placed in position on high ground at about three and a half o'clock, and fired at the enemy on the slope, but soon ceased by order of Gen. Hooker, and the position of our lines prevent-ed any further use of artillery by us on this part of the field. The 1st Mass. Cavalry was sent up the valley to the right to observe the movements, if any, of the enemy in that direction, and one regiment of Meade's division was posted to watch a road coming in the same direction. The other divisions were deployed as they came up - Gen. Hatch's on the left, and Gen. Ricketts's, which arrived at five P.M., in the rear. Gen. Gibbon's

43

brigade was detached from Hatch's division by Gen. Burnside, for the purpose of making a demonstration on the enemy's centre, up the main road, as soon as the movements on the right and left had sufficiently progressed. The 1st Penn. Rifles, of Gen. Seymour's brigade, were sent forward as skirmishers to feel the enemy, and it was found that he was in force. Meade was then directed to advance his division to the right of the road, so as to outflank them, if possible, and then to move forward and attack, while Hatch was directed to take with his division the crest on the left of the old Hagerstown road, Ricketts's division being held in reserve. Seymour's brigade was sent up to the top of the slope, on the right of the ravine through which the road runs, and then moved along the summit parallel to the road, while Col. Gallagher's and Col. Magilton's brigades moved in the same direction along the slope and in the ravine.

The ground was of the most difficult character for the movement of troops, the hillside being very steep and rocky, and obstructed by stone walls and timber. The enemy was very soon encountered, and in a short time the action became general along the whole front of the division. The line advanced steadily up the mountain-side, where the enemy was posted behind trees and rocks, from which he was gradually dislodged. During this advance Col. Gallagher, commanding 3d brigade, was severely wounded, and the command devolved upon Lieut.-Col. Robert Anderson.

Gen. Meade, having reason to believe that the enemy was attempting to outflank him on his right, applied to Gen. Hooker for reinforcements. Gen. Duryea's brigade, of Ricketts's division, was ordered up, but it did not arrive until the close of the action. It was advanced on Seymour's left, but only one regiment could open fire before the enemy retired and darkness intervened.

Gen. Meade speaks highly of Gen. Seymour's skill in handling his brigade on the extreme right, securing by his manœuvres the great object of the movement-the outflanking of the enemy.

While Gen. Meade was gallantly driving the enemy on the right, Gen. Hatch's division was engaged in a severe contest for the possession of the crest on the left of the ravine. It moved up the mountain in the following order: Two regiments of Gen.

Patrick's brigade deployed as skirmishers, with the other two regiments of the same brigade supporting them; Col. Phelps's brigade in line of battalions in mass at deploying distance, Gen. Doubleday's brigade in the same order bringing up the rear. The 21st N. Y. having gone straight up the slope, instead of around to the right as directed, the 2d U. S. Sharpshooters was sent out in its place. Phelps's and Doubleday's brigades were deployed in turn as they reached the woods, which began about half up the mountain. Gen. Patrick with his skirmishers soon drew the fire of the enemy, and found him strongly posted behind a fence which bounded the cleared space on the top of the ridge, having on his front the woods through which our line was advancing, and in his rear a cornfield full of rocky ledges, which afforded good cover to fall back to if dislodged.

Phelps's brigade gallantly advanced, under a hot fire, to close quarters, and, after ten or fifteen minutes of heavy firing on both sides (in which Gen. Hatch was wounded while urging on his men), the fence was carried by a charge, and our line advanced a few yards beyond it, somewhat sheltered by the slope of the hill.

Doubleday's brigade, now under the command of Lieut.-Col. Hoffmann (Col. Wainwright having been wounded), relieved Phelps, and continued firing for an hour and a half; the enemy, behind ledges of rocks some thirty or forty paces in our front, making a stubborn resistance and attempting to charge on the least cessation of our fire. About dusk Col. Christian's brigade of Ricketts's division came up and relieved Doubleday's brigade, which fell back into line behind Phelps's. Christian's brigade continued the action for thirty or forty minutes, when the enemy retired, after having made an attempt to flank us on the left, which was repulsed by the 75th N. Y. and 7th Ind.

The remaining brigade of Ricketts's division (Gen. Hartsuff's) was moved up in the centre, and connected Meade's left with Doubleday's right. We now had possession of the summit of the first ridge, which commanded the turnpike on both sides of the mountain, and the troops were ordered to hold their positions until further orders, and slept on their arms.

Late in the afternoon Gen. Gibbon, with his brigade and one section of Gibbon's battery ("B," 4th Artillery), was ordered to move up the main road on the enemy's centre. He advanced a regiment on each side of the road, preceded by skirmishers, and followed by the other two regiments in double column; the artillery moving on the road until within range of the enemy's guns, which were firing on the column from the gorge.

The brigade advanced steadily, driving the enemy from his positions in the woods and behind stone walls, until they reached a point well up towards the top of the pass, when the enemy, having been reinforced by three regiments, opened a heavy fire on the front and on both flanks. The fight continued until nine o'clock, the enemy being entirely repulsed; and the brigade, after having suffered severely, and having expended all its ammunition, including even the cartridges of the dead and wounded, continued to hold the ground it had so gallantly won until twelve o'clock, when it was relieved by Gen. Gorman's brigade, of Sedgwick's division, Sumner's corps (except the 6th Wis., which remained on the. field all night). Gen. Gibbon, in this delicate movement, handled his brigade with as much precision and coolness as if upon parade, and the bravery of his troops could not be excelled.

The 2d corps (Sumner's) and the 12th corps (Williams's) reached their final positions shortly after dark. Gen. Richardson's division was placed near Mount Tabor Church, in a position to support our right, if necessary; the 12th corps and Sedgwick's division bivouacked around Bolivar, in a position to support our centre and left.

Gen. Sykes's division of regulars and the artillery reserve halted for the night at Middletown. Thus on the night of the 14th the whole army was massed in the vicinity of the field of battle, in readiness to renew the action the next day or to move in pursuit of the enemy. At daylight our skirmishers were advanced, and it was found that he had retreated during the night, leaving his dead on the field and his wounded uncared for.

I had reached the front at Middletown about noon, or a little before noon, and while there received the messenger from Harper's Ferry by whom I sent the despatch to Gen. Miles before mentioned. Immediately afterwards I rode forward to a point from which I could see the Gap and the adjacent ground. About the time I started Reno sent back a message desiring that a division might be sent to the rear of the pass. I sent the order to Hooker to move at once. (Burnside had nothing to do with this.) Marcy went with him and remained there most of the day. I rather think that he really deserved most of the credit for directing the movement, but, with his usual modesty, he would say little or nothing about it.

I pushed up Sturgis to support Cox, and hurried up Sumner to be ready as a reserve. Burnside never came as near the battle as my position. Yet it was his command that was in action! He spent the night in the same house that I did. In the course of the evening, when I had prepared the telegram to the President announcing the result of the day, I showed it to Burnside before sending it off, and asked if it was satisfactory to him; he replied that it was altogether so. Long afterwards it seems that he came to the conclusion that I did not give him sufficient credit; but he never said a word to me on the subject.

On the next day I had the honor to receive the following very kind despatch from the President:

> "WAR DEPARTMENT,
> "WASHINGTON, Sept. 15, 1862, 2.45 P.M.
>
> "Your despatch of to-day received. God bless you and all with you! Destroy the rebel army, if possible.
>
> "A. LINCOLN.
>
> "To Maj.-Gen. MCCLELLAN."

The following despatch was also received on the 16th:

> "WEST POINT, 16th 1862.
> "(Received, Frederick, 16th, 1862, 10.40 A.M.)
>
> "To Maj.-Gen. McClellan:
>
> "Bravo, my dear general! Twice more and it's done.
>
> "WINFIELD SCOTT."

CHAPTER XXXVI.

Antietam - Pursuit from South Mountain - Position of the enemy - The Battle - Burnside's failure - His contradictory statements - Letters of Col. Sackett.

ON the night of the battle of South Mountain orders were given to the corps commanders to press forward their pickets. at early dawn. This advance revealed the fact that the enemy had left his positions, and an immediate pursuit was ordered; the cavalry, under Gen. Pleasonton, and the three corps under Gens. Sumner, Hooker, and Mansfield (the latter of whom had arrived that morning and assumed command of the 12th [Williams's] corps), by the national turnpike and Boonsborough; the corps of Gens. Burnside and Porter (the latter command at that time consisting of but one weak division, Sykes's) by the old Sharpsburg road; and Gen. Franklin to move into Pleasant Valley, occupy Rohrersville by a detachment, and endeavor to relieve Harper's Ferry.

Gens. Burnside and Porter, upon reaching the road from Boonsborough to Rohrersville, were to reinforce Franklin or to move on Sharpsburg, according to circumstances.

Franklin moved towards Brownsville and found there a force of the enemy, much superior in numbers to his own, drawn up in a strong position to receive him.

At this time the cessation of firing at Harper's Ferry indicated the surrender of that place.

The cavalry overtook the enemy's cavalry in Boonsborough, made a dashing charge, killing and wounding a number, and capturing 250 prisoners and 2 guns.

Gen. Richardson's division of the 2d corps, pressing the rearguard of the enemy with vigor, passed Boonsborough and Keedysville, and came upon the main body of the enemy, occupying in large force a strong position a few miles beyond the latter place.

It had been hoped to engage the enemy on the 15th. Accordingly instructions were given that if the enemy were overtaken on

584

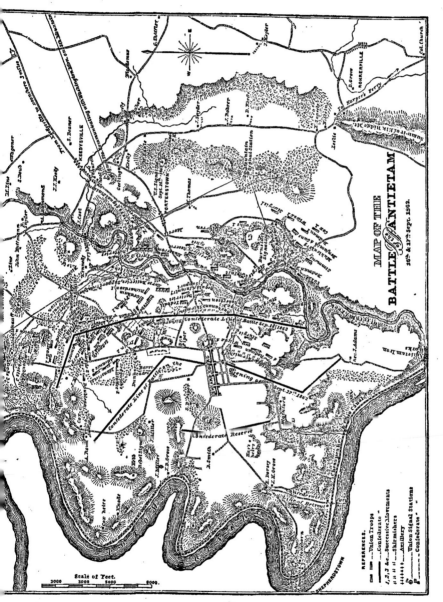

MAP OF THE
BATTLE OF ANTIETAM
16ᵗʰ & 17ᵗʰ Sept. 1862.

REFERENCES.
—— Union Troops
—— Confederate "
1,2,3 &c — Successive Movements
+++++ — Skirmishers
++++++ Artillery
⊕ Union Signal Stations
" Confederate "

Scale of Feet.
1000   2000   4000   6000.

585

the march they should be attacked at once; if found in heavy force and in position, the corps in advance should be placed in position for attack and await my arrival.

Early in the morning I had directed Burnside to put his corps in motion upon the old Sharpsburg road, but to wait with me for a time until more detailed news came from Franklin. About eight o'clock he begged me to let him go, saying that his corps had been some time in motion, and that if he delayed longer he would have difficulty in overtaking it; so I let him go. At about midday I rode to the point where Reno was killed the day before, and found that Burnside's troops, the 9th corps, had not stirred from its bivouac, and still blocked the road for the regular division. I sent for Burnside for an explanation, but he could not be found. He subsequently gave as an excuse the fatigued and hungry condition of his men.

> "HEADQUARTERS, ARMY OF POTOMAC.
> "Sept. 15, 12.30 P.M.
>
> "Gen. *Burnside:*
>
> "Gen. McClellan desires you to let Gen. Porter's go on past you, if necessary. You will then push your own command on as rapidly as possible. The general also desires to know the reason for your delay in starting this morning.
>
> "Very respectfully, your obedient servant,
> "GEO. D. RUGGLES,
> " *Col. and A. D. C.*"

After seeing the ground where Reno fell, and passing over Hooker's battle-ground of the previous day, I went rapidly to the front by the main road, being received by the troops, as I passed them, with the wildest enthusiasm. Near Keedysville I met Sumner, who told me that the enemy were in position in strong force, and took me to a height in front of Keedysville whence a view of the position could be obtained. We were accompanied by a numerous staff and escort; but no sooner had we shown ourselves on the hill than the enemy opened upon us with rifled guns, and, as his firing was very good, the hill was soon cleared of all save Fitz-John Porter and myself. I at once gave orders for the positions of the bivouacs, massing the army so that it could be handled as required. I ordered Burnside to the left. He grumbled that his troops were fatigued, but I started him off anyhow.

The first rapid survey of the enemy's position inclined me to attack his left, but the day was far gone.

He occupied a strong position on the heights, on the west side of Antietam creek, displaying a large force of infantry and cavalry, with numerous batteries of artillery, which opened on our columns as they appeared in sight on the Keedysville road and Sharpsburg turnpike, which fire was returned by Capt. Tidball's light battery, 2d U. S. Artillery, and Pettit's battery, 1st N. Y. Artillery.

The division of Gen. Richardson, following close on the heels of the retreating foe, halted and deployed near Antietam river, on the right of the Sharpsburg road. Gen. Sykes, leading on the division of regulars on the old Sharpsburg road, came up and deployed to the left of Gen. Richardson, on the left of the road.

Antietam creek, in this vicinity, is crossed by four stone bridges - the upper one on the Keedysville and Williamsport road; the second on the Keedysville and Sharpsburg turnpike, some two and a half miles below; the third about a mile below the second, on the Rohrersville and Sharpsburg road; and the fourth near the mouth of Antietam creek, on the road leading from Harper's Ferry to Sharpsburg, some three miles below the third. The stream is sluggish, with few and difficult fords. After a rapid examination of the position I found that it was too late to attack that day, and at once directed the placing of the batteries in position in the centre, and indicated the bivouacs for the different corps, massing them near and on both sides of the Sharpsburg turnpike. The corps were not all in their positions until the next morning after sunrise.

On the morning of the 16th it was discovered that the enemy had changed the position of his batteries. The masses of his troops, however, were still concealed behind the opposite heights. Their left and centre were upon and in front of the Sharpsburg and Hagerstown turnpike, hidden by woods and irregularities of the ground; their extreme left resting upon a wooded eminence near the cross-roads to the north of J. Miller's farm, their left resting upon the Potomac. Their line extended south, the right resting upon the hills to the south of Sharpsburg, near Snavely's farm.

The bridge over the Antietam near this point was strongly
44

covered by riflemen protected by rifle-pits, stone fences, etc., and enfiladed by artillery. The ground in front of this line consisted of undulating hills, their crests in turn commanded by others in their rear. On all favorable points the enemy's artillery was posted, and their reserves, hidden from view by the hills on which their line of battle was formed, could manœuvre unobserved by our army, and from the shortness of their line could rapidly reinforce any point threatened by our attack. Their position, stretching across the angle formed by the Potomac and Antietam, their flanks and rear protected by these streams, was one of the strongest to be found in this region of country, which is well adapted to defensive warfare.

On the right, near Keedysville, on both sides of the Sharpsburg turnpike, were Sumner's and Hooker's corps. In advance, on the right of the turnpike and near the Antietam river, Gen. Richardson's division of Gen. Sumner's corps was posted. Gen. Sykes's division of Gen. Porter's corps was on the left of the turnpike and in line with Gen. Richardson, protecting the bridge No. 2 over the Antietam. The left of the line, opposite to and some distance from bridge No. 3, was occupied by Gen. Burnside's corps.

Before giving Gen. Hooker his orders to make the movement which will presently be described, I rode to the left of the line to satisfy myself that the troops were properly posted there to secure our left flank from any attack made along the left bank of the Antietam, as well as to enable us to carry bridge No. 3.

I rode along the whole front, generally in front of our pickets, accompanied by Hunt, Duane, Colburn, and a couple of orderlies, and went considerably beyond our actual and eventual left. Our small party drew the enemy's fire frequently, and developed the position of most of his batteries. I threw some of the regulars a little more to the left, and observed that our extreme left was not well placed to cover the position against any force approaching from Harper's Ferry by the left bank of the Antietam; also that the ground near "Burnside's bridge" was favorable for defence on our side, and that an attack across it would lead to favorable results. I therefore at once ordered Burnside to move his corps nearer the bridge, occupy the heights in rear, as well as to watch the approach from Harper's Ferry just spoken of. I gave this order at midday; it was near night before it was executed. I also instructed him to examine all the vicinity of the bridge, as he would probably be ordered to attack there next morning.

In front of Gens. Sumner's and Hooker's corps, near Keedysville, and on the ridge of the first line of hills overlooking the Antietam, and between the turnpike and Fry's house on the right of the road, were placed Capts. Taft's, Langner's, Von Kleizer's, and Lieut. Weaver's batteries of 20-pounder Parrott guns; on

THE BURNSIDE BRIDGE OVER THE ANTIETAM.

the crest of the hill in the rear and right of bridge No. 3, Capt. Weed's 3-inch and Lieut. Benjamin's 20-pounder batteries. Gen. Franklin's corps and Gen. Couch's division held a position in Pleasant Valley in front of Brownsville, with a strong force of the enemy in their front. Gen. Morell's division of Porter's corps was *en route* from Boonsborough, and Gen. Humphreys's division of new troops *en route* from Frederick, Md. About daylight on the 16th the enemy opened a heavy fire of artillery on our guns in position, which was promptly returned; their lire was silenced for the time, but was frequently renewed during the day.

It was afternoon before I could move the troops to their positions for attack, being compelled to spend the morning in reconnoitring the new position taken up by the enemy, examining the ground, finding fords, clearing the approaches, and hurrying up the ammunition and supply-trains, which had been delayed by the rapid march of the troops over the few practicable approaches from Frederick. These had been crowded by the masses of infantry, cavalry, and artillery pressing on with the hope of overtaking the enemy before he could form to resist an attack. Many of the troops were out of rations on the previous day, and a good deal of their ammunition had been expended in the severe action of the 14th.

My plan for the impending general engagement was to attack the enemy's left with the corps of Hooker and Mansfield, supported by Sumner's and, if necessary, by Franklin's; and as soon as matters looked favorably there, to move the corps of Burnside against the enemy's extreme right, upon the ridge running to the south and rear of Sharpsburg, and, having carried their position, to press along the crest towards our right; and whenever either of these flank movements should be successful, to advance our centre with all the forces then disposable.

About two P.M. Gen. Hooker, with his corps, consisting of Gens. Ricketts's, Meade's, and Doubleday's divisions, was ordered to cross the Antietam at a ford, and at bridge No. 1, a short distance above, to attack and, if possible, turn the enemy's left. Gen. Sumner was ordered to cross the corps of Gen. Mansfield (the 12th) during the night, and hold his own (the 2d) corps ready to cross early the next morning. On reaching the vicinity of the enemy's left a sharp contest commenced with the Pennsylvania reserves, the advance of Gen. Hooker's corps, near the house of D. Miller. The enemy was driven from the strip of woods where he was first met. The firing lasted until after dark, when Gen. Hooker's corps rested on their arms on ground won from the enemy.

When I returned to the right, and found that Hooker's preparations were not yet complete, I went to hurry them in person. It was perhaps half-past three to four o'clock before Hooker could commence crossing and get fairly in motion up the opposite slopes. I accompanied the movement, at the head of the column, until the top of the ridge was fairly gained, indicated the new direction to be taken, and then returned to headquarters-not to the camp, but to a house further in advance (Fry's house), where I passed the night.

During the night Gen. Mansfield's corps, consisting of Gens. Williams's and Greene's divisions, crossed the Antietam at the 'same ford and bridge that Gen. Hooker's troops had passed, and bivouacked on the farm of J. Poffenberger, about a mile in rear of Gen. Hooker's position.

At daylight on the 17th the action was commenced by the skirmishers of the Pennsylvania reserves. The whole of Gen. Hooker's corps was soon engaged, and drove the enemy from the open field in front of the first line of woods into a second line of woods beyond, which runs to the eastward of and nearly parallel to the Sharpsburg and Hagerstown turnpike. This contest was obstinate, and as the troops advanced the opposition became more determined and the number of the enemy greater. Gen. Hooker then ordered up the corps of Gen. Mansfield, which moved promptly toward the scene of action.

The first division, Gen. Williams's, was deployed to the right on approaching the enemy; Gen. Crawford's brigade on the right, its right resting on the Hagerstown turnpike; on his left Gen. Gordon's brigade. The second division, Gen. Greene's, joining the left of Gordon's, extended as far as the burnt buildings to the north and east of the white church on the turnpike. During the deployment that gallant veteran, Gen. Mansfield, fell mortally wounded while examining the ground in front of his troops. Gen. Hartsuff, of Hooker's corps, was severely wounded while bravely pressing forward his troops, and was taken from the field.

The command of the 12th corps fell upon Gen. Williams. Five regiments of the first division of this corps were new troops. One brigade of the second division was sent to support Gen. Doubleday.

The 124th Penn. Volunteers were pushed across the turnpike into the woods beyond J. Miller's house, with orders to hold the position as long as possible.

The line of battle of this corps was formed, and it became engaged about seven A.M., the attack being opened by Knapp's

(Penn.), Cothran's (N. Y.), and Hampton's (Pittsburgh) batteries. To meet this attack the enemy had pushed a strong column of troops into the open fields in front of the turnpike, while he occupied the woods on the west of the turnpike in strong force. The woods (as was found by subsequent observation) were traversed by outcropping ledges of rock. Several hundred yards to the right and rear was a hill which commanded the debouch of the woods, and in the fields between was a long line of stone fences, continued by breastworks of rails, which covered the enemy's infantry from our musketry. The same woods formed a screen behind which his movements were concealed, and his batteries on the hill and the rifle-works covered from the fire of our artillery in front.

For about two hours the battle raged with varied success, the enemy endeavoring to drive our troops into the second line of wood, and ours in turn to get possession of the line in front.

Our troops ultimately succeeded in forcing the enemy back into the woods near the turnpike, Gen. Greene with his two brigades crossing into the woods to the left of the Dunker church. During this conflict Gen. Crawford, commanding 1st division after Gen. Williams took command of the corps, was wounded and left the field.

Gen. Greene being much exposed and applying for reinforcements, the 13th N. J., 27th Ind., and the 3d Md. were sent to his support with a section of Knapp's battery.

At about nine o'clock A.M. Gen. Sedgwick's division of Gen. Sumner's corps arrived. Crossing the ford previously mentioned, this division marched in three columns to the support of the attack on the enemy's left. On nearing the scene of action the columns were halted, faced to the front, and established by Gen. Sumner in three parallel lines by brigade, facing toward the south and west; Gen. Gorman's brigade in front, Gen. Dana's second, and Gen. Howard's third, with a distance between the lines of some seventy paces. The division was then put in motion and moved upon the field of battle, under fire from the enemy's concealed batteries on the hill beyond the roads. Passing diagonally to the front across the open space, and to the front of the first division of Gen. Williams's corps, this latter division withdrew.

Entering the woods on the west of the turnpike, and driving

the enemy before them, the first line was met by a heavy fire of musketry and shell from the enemy's breastworks and the batteries on the hill commanding the exit from the woods. Meantime a heavy column of the enemy had succeeded in crowding back the troops of Gen. Greene's division, and appeared in rear of the left of Sedgwick's division. By command of Gen. Sumner, Gen. Howard faced the third line to the rear preparatory to a change of front to meet the column advancing on the left; but this line, now suffering from a destructive fire both in front and on its left which it was unable to return, gave way towards the right and rear in considerable confusion, and was soon followed by the first and second lines.

Gen. Gorman's brigade, and one regiment of Gen. Dana's, soon rallied and checked the advance of the enemy on the right. The second and third lines now formed on the left of Gen. Gorman's brigade and poured a destructive fire upon the enemy.

During Gen. Sumner's attack he ordered Gen. Williams to support him. Brig.-Gen. Gordon, with a portion of his brigade, moved forward, but when he reached the woods the left of Gen. Sedgwick's division had given way; and finding himself, as the smoke cleared up, opposed to the enemy in force with his small command, he withdrew to the rear of the batteries at the second line of woods. As Gen. Gordon's troops unmasked our batteries on the left they opened with canister; the batteries of Capt. Cothran, 1st N. Y., and "I," 1st Artillery, commanded by Lieut. Woodruff, doing good service Unable to withstand this deadly fire in front and the musketry-fire from the right, the enemy again sought shelter in the woods and rocks beyond the turnpike.

During this assault Gens. Sedgwick and Dana were seriously wounded and taken from the field. Gen. Sedgwick, though twice wounded and faint from loss of blood, retained command of his division for more than an hour after his first wound, animating his command by his presence.

About the time of Gen. Sedgwick's advance Gen. Hooker, while urging on his command, was severely wounded in the foot and taken from the field, and Gen. Meade was placed in command of his corps. Gen. Howard assumed command after Gen. Sedgwick retired.

The repulse of the enemy offered opportunity to rearrange

the lines and reorganize the commands on the right, now more or less in confusion. The batteries of the Pennsylvania reserve, on high ground near J. Poffenberger's house, opened fire and checked several attempts of the enemy to establish batteries in front of our right, to turn that flank and enfilade the lines.

While the conflict was so obstinately raging on the right Gen. French was pushing his division against the enemy still further to the left. This division crossed the Antietam at the same ford as Gen. Sedgwick, and immediately in his rear. Passing over the stream in three columns, the division marched about a mile from the ford, then, facing to the left, moved in three lines towards the enemy: Gen. Max Weber's brigade in front, Col. Dwight Morris's brigade of raw troops-undrilled, and moving for the first time under fire-in the second, and Gen. Kimball's brigade in the third. The division was first assailed by a fire of artillery, but steadily advanced, driving in the enemy's skirmishers, and encountered the infantry in some force at the group of houses on Roulette's farm. Gen. Weber's brigade gallantly advanced with an unwavering front and drove the enemy from their position about the houses.

While Gen. Weber was hotly engaged with the first line of the enemy, Gen. French received orders from Gen. Sumner, his corps commander, to push on with renewed vigor to make a diversion in favor of the attack on the right. Leaving the new troops, who had been thrown into some confusion from their march through cornfields, over fences, etc., to form as a reserve, he ordered the brigade of Gen. Kimball to the front, passing to the left of Gen. Weber. The enemy was pressed back to near the crest of the hill, where he was encountered in greater strength posted in a sunken road forming a natural rifle-pit running in a northwesterly direction. In a cornfield in rear of this road were also strong bodies of the enemy. As the line reached the crest of the hill a galling fire was opened on it from the sunken road and cornfield. Here a terrific fire of musketry burst from both lines, and the battle raged along the whole line with great slaughter.

The enemy attempted to turn the left of the line, but were met by the 7th Va. and 132d Penn. Volunteers and repulsed. Foiled in this, the enemy made a determined assault on the front, but were met by a charge from our lines which drove them back with severe loss, leaving in our hands some 300 prisoners and several stands of colors. The enemy, having been repulsed by the terrible execution of the batteries and the musketry-fire on the extreme right, now attempted to assist the attack on Gen. French's division by assailing him on his right and endeavoring to turn this flank; but this attack was met and checked by the 14th Ind. and 8th O. Volunteers, and by canister from Capt. Tompkins's battery, 1st R. I. Artillery. Having been under an almost continuous fire for nearly four hours, and the ammunition nearly expended, this division now took position immediately below the crest of the heights on which they had so gallantly fought, the enemy making no attempt to regain their lost ground.

On the left of Gen. French, Gen. Richardson's division was hotly engaged. Having crossed the Antietam about 9.30 A.M. at the ford crossed by the other divisions of Sumner's corps, it moved on a line nearly parallel to the Antietam, and formed in a ravine behind the high grounds overlooking Roulette's house; the 2d (Irish) brigade, commanded by Gen. Meagher, on the right; the 3d brigade, commanded by Gen. Caldwell, on his left, and the brigade commanded by Col. Brooks, 53d Penn. Volunteers, in support. As the division moved forward to take its position on the field, the enemy directed a fire of artillery against it, but, owing to the irregularities of the ground, did but little damage.

Meagher's brigade, advancing steadily, soon became engaged with the enemy posted to the left and in front of Roulette's house. It continued to advance under a heavy fire nearly to the crest of the hill overlooking Piper's house, the enemy being posted in a continuation of the sunken road and cornfield before referred to. Here the brave Irish brigade opened upon the enemy a terrific musketry-fire.

All of Gen. Sumner's corps was now engaged - Gen. Sedgwick on the right, Gen. French in the centre, and Gen. Richardson on the left. The Irish brigade sustained its well-earned reputation. After suffering terribly in officers and men, and strewing the ground with their enemies as they drove them back, their ammunition nearly expended, and their commander, Gen. Meagher, disabled by the fall of his horse shot under him, this brigade was ordered to give place to Gen. Caldwell's brigade, which advanced to a short distance in its rear. The lines were passed by the Irish brigade breaking by company to the rear, and Gen. Caldwell's by company to the front, as steadily as on drill. Col. Brooks's brigade now became the second line.

The ground over which Gens. Richardson's and French's divisions were fighting was very irregular, intersected by numerous ravines, hills covered with growing corn, enclosed by stone walls, behind which the enemy could advance unobserved upon any exposed point of our lines. Taking advantage of this, the enemy attempted to gain the right of Richardson's position in a cornfield near Roulette's house, where the division had become separated from that of Gen. French's. A change of front by the 52d N. Y. and 2d Del. Volunteers, of Col. Brooks's brigade, under Col. Frank, and the attack made by the 53d Penn. Volunteers, sent further to the right by Col. Brooks to close this gap in the line, and the movement of the 132d Penn. and 7th Va. Volunteers, of Gen. French's division, before referred to, drove the enemy from the cornfield and restored the line.

The brigade of Gen. Caldwell, with determined gallantry, pushed the enemy back opposite the left and centre of this division, but, sheltered in the sunken road, they still held our forces on the right of Caldwell in check. Col. Barlow, commanding the 61st and 64th N. Y. regiments, of Caldwell's brigade, seeing a favorable opportunity, advanced the regiments on the left, taking the line in the sunken road in flank, and compelled them to surrender, capturing over 300 prisoners and three stands of colors.

The whole of the brigade, with the 57th and 66th N. Y. regiments, of Col. Brooks's brigade, who had moved these regiments into the first line, now advanced with gallantry, driving the enemy before them in confusion into the cornfield beyond the sunken road. The left of the division was now well advanced, when the enemy, concealed by an intervening ridge, endeavored to turn its left and rear.

Col. Cross, 5th N. H., by a change of front to the left and rear, brought his regiment facing the advancing line. Here a spirited contest arose to gain a commanding height, the two opposing forces moving parallel to each other, giving and receiving fire. The 5th, gaining the advantage, faced to the right and delivered its volley. The enemy staggered, but rallied and advanced desperately at a charge. Being reinforced by the

81st Penn., these regiments met the advance by a counter-charge. The enemy fled, leaving many killed, wounded, and prisoners, and the colors of the 4th N. C., in our hands.

Another column of the enemy, advancing under shelter of a stone wall and cornfield, pressed down on the right of the division; but Col. Barlow again advanced the 61st and 64th N. Y. against these troops, and, with the attack of Kimball's brigade on the right, drove them from this position.

Our troops on the left of this part of the line having driven the enemy far back, they, with reinforced numbers, made a determined attack directly in front. To meet this Col. Barlow brought his two regiments to their position in line, and drove the enemy through the cornfield into the orchard beyond, under a heavy fire of musketry, and a fire of canister from two pieces of artillery in the orchard, and a battery further to the right throwing shell and case-shot. This advance gave us possession of Piper's house, the strong point contended for by the enemy at this part of the line, it being a defensible building several hundred yards in advance of the sunken road. The musketry-fire at this point of the line now ceased. Holding Piper's house, Gen. Richardson withdrew the line a little way to the crest of a hill-a more advantageous position. Up to this time the division was without artillery, and in the new position suffered severely from artillery-fire which could not be replied to. A section of Robertson's horse-battery, commanded by Lieut. Vincent, 2d Artillery, now arrived on the ground and did excellent service. Subsequently a battery of brass guns, commanded by Capt. Graham, 1st Artillery, arrived, and was posted on the crest of the hill, and soon silenced the two guns in the orchard. A heavy fire soon ensued between the battery further to the right and our own. Capt. Graham's battery was bravely and skilfully served, but, unable to reach the enemy, who had rifled guns of greater range than our smooth-bores, retired by order of Gen. Richardson, to save it from useless sacrifice of men and horses. The brave general was himself mortally wounded while personally directing its fire.

Gen. Hancock was placed in command of the division after the fall of Gen. Richardson. Gen. Meagher's brigade, now commanded by Col. Burke, of the 63d N. Y., having refilled their cartridge-boxes, was again ordered forward, and took position in the centre of the line. The division now occupied one line in close proximity to the enemy, who had taken up a position in the rear of Piper's house. Col. Dwight Morris, with the 14th Conn. and a detachment of the 108th N. Y., of Gen. French's division, was sent by Gen. French to the support of Gen. Richardson's division. This command was now placed in an interval in the line between Gen. Caldwell's and the Irish brigades.

The requirements of the extended line of battle had so engaged the artillery that the application of Gen. Hancock for artillery for the division could not be complied with immediately by the chief of artillery or the corps commanders in his vicinity. Knowing the tried courage of the troops, Gen. Hancock felt confident that he could hold his position, although suffering from the enemy's artillery, but was too weak to attack, as the great length of the line he was obliged to hold prevented him from forming more than one line of battle, and, from his advanced position, this line was already partly enfiladed by the batteries of the enemy on the right, which were protected from our batteries opposite them by the woods at the Dunker church.

Seeing a body of the enemy advancing on some of our troops to the left of his position, Gen. Hancock obtained Hexamer's battery from Gen. Franklin's corps, which assisted materially in frustrating this attack. It also assisted the attack of the 7th Me., of Franklin's corps, which, without other aid, made an attack against the enemy's line, and drove in skirmishers who were annoying our artillery and troops on the right. Lieut. Woodruff, with battery I, 2d Artillery, relieved Capt. Hexamer, whose ammunition was expended. The enemy at one time seemed to be about making an attack in force upon this part of the line, and advanced a long column of infantry towards this division; but on nearing the position, Gen. Pleasonton opening on them with sixteen guns, they halted, gave a desultory fire, and retreated, closing the operations on this portion of the field. I return to the incidents occurring still further to the right.

Between twelve and one P.M. Gen. Franklin's corps arrived on the field of battle, having left their camp near Crampton's Pass at six A.M., leaving Gen. Couch with orders to move with his division to occupy Maryland Heights. Gen. Smith's division led the column, followed by Gen. Slocum's.

It was first intended to keep this corps in reserve on the east side of the Antietam, to operate on either flank or on the centre, as circumstances might require; but on nearing Keedysville the strong opposition on the right, developed by the attacks of Hooker and Sumner, rendered it necessary at once to send this corps to the assistance of the right wing.

On nearing the field, hearing that one of our batteries-A, 4th U. S. Artillery, commanded by Lieut. Thomas, who occupied the same position as Lieut. Woodruff's battery in the morning-was hotly engaged without supports, Gen. Smith sent two regiments to its relief from Gen. Hancock's brigade.   On inspecting

McCLELLAN AT ANTIETAM.

the ground Gen. Smith ordered the other regiments of Hancock's brigade, with Frank's and Cowen's batteries, 1st N. Y. Artillery, to the threatened position. Lieut. Thomas and Capt. Cothran, commanding batteries, bravely held their positions against the advancing enemy, handling their batteries with skill.

Finding the enemy still advancing, the 3d brigade of Smith's division, commanded by Col. Irvin, 49th Penn. volunteers, was ordered up, and passed through Lieut. Thomas's battery, charged upon the enemy, and drove back the advance until abreast of the

Dunker church. As the right of the brigade came opposite the woods it received a destructive fire, which checked the advance and threw the brigade somewhat into confusion. It formed again behind a rise of ground in the open space in advance of the batteries.

Gen. French having reported to Gen. Franklin that his ammunition was nearly expended, that officer ordered Gen. Brooks, with his brigade, to reinforce him. Gen. Brooks formed his brigade on the right of Gen. French, where they remained during the remainder of the day and night, frequently under the fire of the enemy's artillery.

It was soon after the brigade of Col. Irvin had fallen back behind the rise of ground that the 7th Me., by order of Col. Irvin, made the gallant attack already referred to.

The advance of Gen. Franklin's corps was opportune. The attack of the enemy on this position, but for the timely arrival of his corps, must have been disastrous, had it succeeded in piercing the line between Gens. Sedgwick's and French's divisions.

Gen. Franklin ordered two brigades of Gen. Slocum's division, Gen. Newton's and Col. Torbert's, to form in column to assault the woods that had been so hotly contested before by Gens. Sumner and Hooker; Gen. Bartlett's brigade was ordered to form as a reserve. At this time Gen. Sumner, having command on the right, directed further offensive operations to be postponed, as the repulse of this, the only remaining corps available for attack, would peril the safety of the whole army.

Gen. Porter's corps, consisting of Gen. Sykes's division of regulars and volunteers, and Gen. Morell's division of volunteers, occupied a position on the east side of Antietam creek, upon the main turnpike leading to Sharpsburg, and directly opposite the centre of the enemy's line. This corps filled the interval between the right wing and Gen. Burnside's command, and guarded the main approach from the enemy's position to our trains of supplies.

It was necessary to watch this part of our line with the utmost vigilance, lest the enemy should take advantage of the first exhibition of weakness here to push upon us a vigorous assault for the purpose of piercing our centre and turning our rear, as well as to capture or destroy our supply-trains. Once having penetrated this line, the enemy's passage to our rear could have met with but feeble resistance, as there were no reserves to reinforce or close up the gap.

Towards the middle of the afternoon, proceeding to the right, I found that Sumner's, Hooker's, and Mansfield's corps had met with serious losses. Several general officers had been carried from the field severely wounded, and the aspect of affairs was anything but promising. At the risk of greatly exposing our centre, I ordered two brigades from Porter's corps, the only available troops, to reinforce the right. Six battalions of Sykes's regulars had been thrown across the Antietam bridge on the main road, to attack and drive back the enemy's sharpshooters, who were annoying Pleasonton's horse-batteries in advance of the bridge. Warren's brigade, of Porter's corps, was detached to hold a position on Burnside's right and rear; so that Porter was left at one time with only a portion of Sykes's division and one small brigade of Morell's division (but little over 3,000 men) to hold his important position.

Gen. Sumner expressed the most decided opinion against another attempt during that day to assault the enemy's position in front, as portions of our troops were so much scattered and demoralized. In view of these circumstances, after making changes in the position of some of the troops, I directed the different commanders to hold their positions, and, being satisfied that this could be done without the assistance of the two brigades from the centre, I countermanded the order, which was in course of execution.

Gen. Slocum's division replaced a portion of Gen. Sumner's troops, and positions were selected for batteries in front of the woods. The enemy opened several heavy fires of artillery on the position of our troops after this, but our batteries soon silenced them.

On the morning of the 17th Gen. Pleasonton, with his cavalry division and the horse-batteries, under Capts. Robertson, Tidball, and Lieut. Haines, of the 2d Artillery, and Capt. Gibson, 3d Artillery, was ordered to advance on the turnpike towards Sharpsburg, across bridge No. 2, and support the left of Gen. Sumner's line. The bridge being covered by a fire of artillery and sharpshooters, cavalry skirmishers mere thrown out, and

Capt. Tidball's battery advanced by piece and drove off the sharpshooters with canister sufficiently to establish the batteries above mentioned, which opened on the enemy with effect. The firing was kept up for about two hours, when, the enemy's fire slackening, the batteries were relieved by Randall's and Van Reed's batteries, U. S. Artillery. About three o'clock Tidball, Robertson, and Haines returned to their positions on the west of Antietam, Capt. Gibson having been placed in position on the east side to guard the approaches to the bridge. These batteries did good service, concentrating their fire on the column of the enemy about to attack Gen. Hancock's position, and compelling it to find shelter behind the hills in rear.

Gen. Sykes's division had been in position since the 15th, exposed to the enemy's artillery and sharpshooters. Gen. Morell had come up on the 16th, and relieved Gen. Richardson on the right of Gen. Sykes. Continually under the vigilant watch of the enemy, this corps guarded a vital point.

The position of the batteries under Gen. Pleasonton being one of great exposure, the battalion of the 2d and 10th U. S. Infantry, under Capt. Pollard, 2d Infantry, was sent to his support. Subsequently four battalions of regular infantry, under Capt. Dryer, 4th Infantry, were sent across to assist in driving off the sharpshooters of the enemy.

The battalion of the 2d and 10th Infantry, advancing far beyond the batteries, compelled the cannoneers of a battery of the enemy to abandon their guns. Few in numbers, and unsupported, they were unable to bring them off. The heavy loss of this small body of men attests their gallantry.

The troops of Gen Burnside held the left of the line opposite bridge No. 3. The attack on the right was to have been supported by an attack on the left. Preparatory to this attack, on the evening of the 16th, Gen. Burnside's corps was moved forward and to the left, and took up a position nearer the bridge.

I visited Gen. Burnside's position on the 16th, and, after pointing out to him the proper dispositions to be made of his troops during the day and night, informed him that he would probably be required to attack the enemy's right on the following morning, and directed him to make careful reconnoissances.

Gen. Burnside's corps, consisting of the divisions of Gens.

Cox, Wilcox, Rodman, and Sturgis, was posted as follows: Col. Crook's brigade, Cox's division, on the right, Gen. Sturgis's division immediately in rear; on the left was Gen. Rodman's division, with Gen. Scammon's brigade, Cox's division, in support.

Gen. Wilcox's division was held in reserve. The corps bivouacked in position on the night of the 16th.

Early on the morning of the 17th I ordered Gen. Burnside to form his troops and hold them in readiness to assault the bridge in his front, and to await further orders.

At eight o'clock an order was sent to him by Lieut. Wilson, topographical engineers, to carry the bridge, then to gain possession of the heights beyond, and to advance along their crest upon Sharpsburg and its rear.

After some time had elapsed, not hearing from him, I despatched an aide to ascertain what had been done. The aide returned with the information that but little progress had been made. I then sent him back with an order to Gen. Burnside to assault the bridge at once and carry it at all hazards. The aide returned to me a second time with the report that the bridge was still in the possession of the enemy. Whereupon I directed Col. Sackett, inspector-general, to deliver to Gen. Burnside my positive order to push forward his troops without a moment's delay, and, if necessary, to carry the bridge at the point of the bayonet ; and I ordered Col. Sackett to remain with Gen. Burnside and see that the order was executed promptly.

After these three hours' delay the bridge was carried at one o'clock by a brilliant charge of the 51st N. Y. and 51st Penn. Volunteers. Other troops were then thrown over and the opposite bank occupied, the enemy retreating to the heights beyond.

A halt was then made by Gen. Burnside's advance until three P.M.; upon hearing which I directed one of my aides, Col. Key, to inform Gen. Burnside that I desired him to push forward his troops with the utmost vigor and carry the enemy's position on the heights; that the movement was vital to our success; that this was a time when we must not stop for loss of life, if a great object could thereby be accomplished; that if, in his judgment, his attack would fail, to inform me so at once, that his troops might be withdrawn and used elsewhere on the field. He replied that he would soon advance, and would

45

go up the, hill as far as a battery of the enemy on the left would permit. Upon this report I again immediately sent Col. Key to Gen. Burnside with orders to advance at once, if possible to flank the battery, or storm it and carry the heights; repeating that if he considered the movement impracticable, to inform me, so that his troops might be recalled. The advance was then gallantly resumed, the enemy driven from the guns, the heights handsomely carried, and a portion of the troops even reached the outskirts of Sharpsburg. By this time it was nearly dark, and strong reinforcements just then reaching the enemy from Harper's Ferry attacked Gen. Burnside's troops on their left flank, and forced them to retire to a lower line of hills nearer the bridge.

If this important movement had been consummated two hours earlier, a position would have been secured upon the heights from which our batteries might have enfiladed the greater part of the enemy's line, and turned their right and rear. Our victory might thus have been much more decisive.

The ground held by Burnside beyond the bridge was so strong that he ought to have repulsed the attack and held his own. He never crossed the bridge in person!

The following is the substance of Gen. Burnside's operations, as given in his report:

Col. Crook's brigade was ordered to storm the bridge. This bridge, No. 3, is a stone structure of three arches, with stone parapets. The banks of the stream on the opposite side are precipitous, and command the eastern approaches to the bridge. On the hill-side immediately by the bridge was a stone fence running parallel to the stream. The turns of the roadway as it wound up the hill were covered by rifle-pits and breastworks of rails, etc. These works and the woods that covered the slopes were filled with the enemy's riflemen, and batteries were in position to enfilade the bridge and its approaches.

Gen. Rodman was ordered to cross the ford below the bridge. From Col. Crook's position it was found impossible to carry the bridge.

Gen. Sturgis was ordered to make a detail from his division for that purpose. He sent forward the 2d Md. and 6th N. H. These regiments made several successive attacks in the most gallant style, but were driven back.

The artillery of the left were ordered to concentrate their fire on the woods above the bridge. Col. Crook brought a section of Capt. Simmons's battery to a position to command the bridge. The 51st N. Y. and 51st Penn. were then ordered to assault the bridge. Taking advantage of a small spur of the hills which ran parallel to the river, they moved towards the bridge. From the crest of this spur they rushed with bayonets fixed and cleared the bridge. The division followed the storming party; also the brigade of Col. Crook as support. The enemy withdrew to still higher ground some five or six hundred yards beyond, and opened a fire of artillery on the troops in the new positions on the crest of the hill above the bridge.

Gen. Rodman's division succeeded in crossing the ford after a sharp tire of musketry and artillery, and joined on the left of Sturgis; Scammon's brigade crossing as support. Gen. Wilcox's division was ordered across to take position on Gen. Sturgis's right.

These dispositions being completed about three o'clock, the command moved forward, except Sturgis's division left in reserve. Clark's and Darell's batteries accompanied Rodman's division, Cooke's battery with Wilcox's division, and a section of Simmons's battery with Col. Crook's brigade. A section of Simmons's battery, and Muhlenberg's and McMullan's batteries, were in position. The order for the advance was obeyed by the troops with alacrity. Gen. Wilcox's division, with Crook in support, moved up on both sides of the turnpike leading from the bridge to Sharpsburg; Gen. Rodman's division, supported by Scammon's brigade, on the left of Gen. Wilcox. The enemy retreated before the advance of the troops. The 9th N. Y., of Gen. Rodman's division, captured one of the enemy's batteries and held it for some time. As the command was driving the enemy to the main heights on the left of the town, the light division of Gen. A. P. Hill arrived upon the field of battle from Harper's Ferry, and with a heavy artillery-fire made a strong attack on the extreme left. To meet this attack the left division diverged from the line of march intended, and opened a gap between it and the right. To fill up this it was necessary to order the troops from the second line. During these movements Gen. Rodman was mortally wounded. Col. Harland's brigade, of Gen. Rodman's

division, was driven back.   Col. Scammon's brigade, by a change
of front to rear on his right flank, saved the left from being
driven completely in.   The fresh troops of the enemy pouring in,
and the accumulation of artillery against this command, destroyed all hope of its being able to accomplish anything more.

It was now nearly dark.   Gen. Sturgis was ordered forward
to support the left.   Notwithstanding the hard work in the
early part of the day, his division moved forward with spirit.
With its assistance the enemy mere checked and held at bay.

The command was ordered to fall back by Gen. Cox, who
commanded on the field the troops engaged in this affair beyond
the Antietam.

Night closed the long and desperately contested battle of
the 17th.   Nearly two hundred thousand men and five hundred pieces of artillery were for fourteen hours engaged in this
memorable battle.   We had attacked the enemy in a position
selected by the experienced engineer then in person directing
their operations.   We had driven them from their line on one
flank, and secured a footing within it on the other.   The Army
of the Potomac, notwithstanding the moral effect incident to
previous reverses, had achieved a victory over an adversary invested with the prestige of recent success.   Our soldiers slept
that night conquerors on a field won by their valor and covered
with the dead and wounded of the enemy.

Thirteen guns, 39 colors, upwards of 15,000 stands of small
arms, and more than 6,000 prisoners mere the trophies which
attest the success of our arms in the battles of South Mountain, Crampton's Gap, and Antietam.   Not a single gun or color
was lost by our army during these battles.

When I was on the right on the afternoon of the 17th I
found the troops a good deal shaken-that is, some of them who
had been in the early part of the action.   Even Sedgwick's division commenced giving way under a few shots from a battery
that suddenly commenced firing from an unexpected position.
I had to ride in and rally them myself.   Sedgwick had been
carried off very severely wounded.   The death of Mansfield,
the mounding of Hooker, Richardson, and Sedgwick, were irreparable losses in that part of the field.   It was this afternoon,
when I was on the right, that on the field of battle I gave Hancock a division - that of Richardson, who was mortally wounded.

Early next morning (the 18th) Burnside sent to ask me for a fresh division to enable him to hold his own. I sent word that I could send none until I came myself to see the state of affairs, and in a few minutes rode over there and carefully examined the position. Burnside told me that his men were so demoralized and so badly beaten the day before that were they attacked they would give may. I told him I could see no evidences of that, but that I would lend him Morell's division for a short time, though I would probably need it again elsewhere in a few hours. I instructed him to place one brigade on some heights that ran across the valley on our left, in order to cover the left flank, the rest on the heights in rear of the bridge, to cover the retreat of his men, should that prove necessary. The division was accordingly sent to him, and towards evening I learned that he had thrown it across the river and withdrawn his own men, his excuse to me being that he could not trust his men on the other side! The evening before he was at my headquarters, and told some of my aides that his men were badly beaten.

Long afterwards I learned from Col. Grif. Stedman (11th Conn. regiment) that on the night of the 17th he was with his then colonel (Kingsbury), who was mortally wounded and lying in a house on our side of the bridge, close to it. Burnside came by and gave orders for the wounded to be removed still further to the rear, stating that the corps were entirely defeated and demoralized, and that the house in question would soon be occupied by the enemy. As Kingsbury was in no condition to be removed, Stedman determined to remain with him and share his fate. It is needless to say that the house was not occupied by the enemy, and that Burnside was in no condition to know the real state of his command, as he had not been with it. But I have mentioned enough to show what his real opinions and state of mind were on the evening of the 17th and the morning of the 18th. Yet in face of all this he subsequently testified before the Committee on the Conduct of the War that he had on the morning of the 18th asked me for the reinforcement of a division to enable him to renew the attack, stating at the same time that his men were in superb condition, ready for any work, and that I had committed a great error in not renewing the battle early on the morning of the 18th. The real facts, so far as Burnside was concerned, were as I have given them above. But although his men were not, perhaps, in magnificent condition, they were by no means so demoralized as he represented them to be. I cannot, from my long acquaintance with Burnside, believe that he would deliberately lie, but I think that his weak mind was turned; that he was confused in action; and that subsequently he really did not know what had occurred, and was talked by his staff into any belief they chose.

I have only adverted to the very pernicious effects of Burnside's inexcusable delay in attacking the bridge and the heights in rear. What is certain is that if Porter or Hancock had been in his place the town of Sharpsburg would have been ours, Hill would have been thrown back into the Potomac, and the battle of Antietam would have been very decisive in its results.

[In a monograph prepared by Gen. William B. Franklin, "IN MEMORY OF GENERAL McCLELLAN," that distinguished soldier thus speaks of the Maryland campaign and its results, and specially of the result of the battle of Antietam:

"Without orders placing him in command other than the verbal request of the President, and without orders of any kind from any one, he started on the Maryland campaign to find the enemy, who had been so foolish as to invade a State which had remained true to the Union. The victories of Turner's and Crampton's gaps of South Mountain, and of Antietam, were the results, the last battle followed by the hurried retreat of Gen. Lee beyond the Potomac. History will some day tell why the Confederate army was not driven into the Potomac instead of across it. It will show that its escape was not due to want of generalship of the commanding general, nor to the absence of necessary orders to subordinates."

At the time of his death Gen. McClellan was about to write a condensed account of the battle of Antietam for the *Century* magazine. He had reviewed the events preceding South Mountain when his pen was arrested. From among the papers found lying on his writing-table, where he had left them four hours before his death, the editor regards the letters of Gen. Sackett, which here follow, as important to be published for the purposes of that history which has not heretofore been written.]

LETTERS FROM GEN. SACKETT.

"FEB. 20, 1876.

"MY DEAR GENERAL: In reply to your note I will state that, at about nine o'clock on the morning of the battle of Antietam, you told me to mount my horse and to proceed as speedily as possible with orders directing Gen. Burnside to move his troops across the bridge or stream in his front at once, and then to push them forward vigorously, without a moment's delay, to secure the heights beyond.

"You moreover directed me to remain with Gen. Burnside until I saw his troops well under way up the heights in the direction of Sharpsburg, and then to return and report to you.

"I started at once, as fast as my horse could carry me. I found Gen. Burnside on an elevated point (near the position of Lieut. Benjamin's 20-pounder battery) commanding an extensive view of the battle-field. I gave him your orders, which seemed to annoy him somewhat, as he said to me: 'McClellan appears to think I am not trying my best to carry this bridge; you are the third or fourth one who has been to me this morning with similar orders.' I told him I knew you were exceedingly anxious, and regarded his getting across the stream and moving on Sharpsburg with rapidity and vigor at once as of vital importance to a complete success.

"Gen. Burnside ordered assaults to be made on the bridge, which were for a long time unsuccessful. I had been at his headquarters for fully three hours when Col. Key arrived from your headquarters with positive orders to push across the bridge and to move rapidly up the heights; to carry the bridge at the point of the bayonet, if necessary, and not stop for loss of life, as sacrifices must be made in favor of success.

"As soon as Col. Key had gone I suggested to Gen. Burnside, were he to go down near the bridge, his presence among the troops could have the effect to encourage and stimulate the men to renewed efforts. He said he would, and immediately mounted his horse and rode in the direction of the bridge, but soon returned saying the bridge had been carried and the troops were crossing over as rapidly as possible. He likewise mentioned at this time that Col. Henry Kingsbury had been mortally wounded in the assault on the bridge.

"Gen. Burnside at once issued instructions for the move in the direction of Sharpsburg, but for some unaccountable reason things moved slowly and there was a long delay in getting the troops in motion.

"Col. Key again returned with instructions to Gen. Burnside to push forward his troops rapidly and with vigor, to secure the heights, as every moment gained was of the utmost importance to our success.

"I remained with Gen. Burnside until his troops were well, and seemingly successfully, under way up the heights - they having gallantly driven the enemy from the field for fully one-half the distance in the direction of Sharpsburg.

"Seeing this, and everything apparently going well, I returned to headquarters, where I found Gen. Fitz-John Porter, you being away temporarily on a visit to the right of the battle-field. It was at this time past four o'clock in the afternoon.

"It was not long after this that the check and repulse of Gen. Burnside's advance was witnessed.

"Often since that time I have thought what a serious misfortune was the death of the noble and energetic Reno. Had not that chivalric soldier fallen at South Mountain, Antietam certainly would have been in its results a very different affair. It would have been one of the most, if not the most, complete and important battle of the war.

"I am, general, very truly yours,

" D. B. SACKETT,
"Inspector-Gen., U. S. A.

"To Gen. GEO. B. McCLELLAN."

"NEW YORK CITY, March 9, 1876.

"MY DEAR GENERAL: I will state, in respect to a conversation had in my presence between Gen. Burnside and yourself that late in the evening of the day of the battle of Antietam I was with you in your tent when Gen. Burnside entered. The position occupied, and the condition of his command, became at once the topic of conversation with you two.

"As I understood the matter, Gen. Burnside desired to withdraw his troops to the left bank of the stream, giving as a reason for the move the dispirited condition of his men; stating further that if he remained in his present position and an attack was made by the enemy, he very much feared the result.

"You replied: 'General, your troops must remain where they are and must hold their ground.' Gen. Burnside then said: 'If I am to hold this position at all hazards I must be largely reinforced' - and, if not much mistaken, he mentioned the number of men necessary for the purpose at 5,000.

"You then replied (with emphasis): 'General, I expect you to hold your own, and with the force now under your command.'

"At this point other general officers arrived, and I left the tent and heard nothing more of the conversation.

"Afterward, in looking over Gen. Burnside's testimony before the Committee on the Conduct of the War, I was a good deal surprised to read:

" ' I went to Gen. McClellan's tent, and in course of conversation I expressed the same opinion (that the attack might be renewed the next morning at five o'clock), and told him that if

I could have 5,000 fresh troops to pass in advance of my line I would be willing to commence the attack on the next morning.'

"This statement brought back to my mind vividly that evening's conversation after Antietam. The conversation between Gen. Burnside and yourself, as I heard it, and Gen. Burnside's testimony before the committee, differ widely.

"I may be mistaken, but it has always appeared to me that the conversation to which I was a witness, and the statement made before the War Committee, must have referred to one and the same matter - the fighting condition of Gen. Burnside's command on the night after the battle of Antietam.

"I am, general, very truly yours,

"D. B. SACKETT,
"Inspector-Gen. U. S. A.

"To Gen. GEO. B. McCLELLAN."

CHAPTER XXXVII.

PRIVATE LETTERS.

[*Sept.* 15 to *Oct.* 1, 1862.]

Telegram - *Headquarters, Army of the Potomac, Sept.* 15. - We have carried the heights near here after a hard engagement, and gained a glorious victory. All your particular friends well.

Sept. 15, Monday, 9.30 - A.M., *Bolivar.* - . . . Just sent you a telegram informing you that we yesterday gained a glorious and complete victory; every moment adds to its importance. I am pushing everything after them with the greatest rapidity, and expect to gain great results. I thank God most humbly for His great mercy. How glad I am for my country that it is delivered from immediate peril! I am about starting with the pursuit and must close this. . . . If I can believe one-tenth of what is reported, God has seldom given an army a greater victory than this. . . .

Telegram - Near *Sharpsburg, Sept.* 16, 1862, 7 A.M. - Have reached thus far, and have no doubt delivered Pennsylvania and Maryland. Army in excellent spirits.

Sept. 18, 8 A.M., *camp near Sharpsburg* - . . . We fought yesterday a terrible battle against the entire rebel army. The battle continued fourteen hours and was terrific; the fighting on both sides was superb. The general result was in our favor; that is to say, we gained a great deal of ground and held it. It was a success, but whether a decided victory depends upon what occurs to-day. I hope that God has given us a great success. It is all in His hands, and there I am content to leave it. The spectacle yesterday was the grandest I could conceive of; nothing could be more sublime. Those in whose judgment I rely tell me that I fought the battle splendidly and that it was a masterpiece of art. I am well-nigh tired out by anxiety and
612

want of sleep. God has been good in sparing the lives of all my staff. Gens. Hooker, Sedgwick, Dana, Richardson, and Hartsuff, and several other general officers, wounded. Mansfield is dead, I fear, but am not certain. I just learn that he is not mortally wounded.

Sept. 20, 8 A.M., *camp near Sharpsburg.* - . . . Yesterday the enemy completed his evacuation of Maryland, completely beaten. We got many prisoners, muskets, colors, cannon, etc. His loss in killed and wounded was very great; so was ours, unfortunately. Gen. Mansfield was killed (or rather died of his wounds). Gens. Sedgwick, Richardson, Dana, Brooks, Hooker, Weber, Rodman, and two others were wounded on Wednesday. Poor Henry Kingsbury died of his wounds the day after the battle. The battle lasted fourteen hours, and was, without doubt, the most severe ever fought on this continent; and few more desperate were ever fought anywhere.

9 A.M. - . . . Am glad to say that I am much better to-day; for, to tell you the truth, I have been under the weather since the battle. The want of rest, and anxiety, brought on my old disease. The battle of Wednesday *was* a terrible one. I presume the loss will prove not less than 10,000 on each side. Our victory was complete, and the disorganized rebel army has rapidly returned to Virginia, its dreams of "invading Pennsylvania" dissipated for ever. I feel some little pride in having, with a beaten and demoralized army, defeated Lee so utterly and saved the North so completely. Well, one of these days history will, I trust, do me justice in deciding that it was not my fault that the campaign of the Peninsula was not successful. . . . Since I left Washington, Stanton has again asserted that *I*, not Pope, lost the battle of Manassas No. 2 ! . . . I am tired of fighting against such disadvantages, and feel that it is now time for the country to come to my help and remove these difficulties from my path. If my countrymen will not open their eyes and assist themselves they must pardon me if I decline longer to pursue the thankless avocation of serving them.

Sept. 20, 9 P.M., *camp near Sharpsburg.* - . . . I feel that I have done all that can be asked in twice saving the country. If I continue in its service I have at least the right to demand a guarantee that I shall not be interfered with. I know I cannot have that assurance so long as Stanton continues in the position of Secretary of War and Halleck as general-in-chief. . . . I can retire from the service for sufficient reasons without leaving any stain upon my reputation. I feel now that this last short campaign is a sufficient legacy for our child, so far as honor is concerned. . . . You should see my soldiers *now!* You never saw anything like their enthusiasm. It surpasses anything you ever imagined. . . . My tent is filled quite to overflowing with trophies in the way of captured secesh battle-flags. We have more than have been taken in all battles put together, and all sorts of inscriptions on them. . . .

Sept. 21, *Sunday,* A.M.- . . . Do you know that I have not heard one word from Halleck, the President, nor the Secretary of War about the last great battle! All, except fault-finding, that I have had since leaving Washington was one from the President about the Sunday battle, in which he says, "God bless you and all with you!" That is all I have; but plenty from Halleck couched in almost insulting language and prophesying disaster! I telegraphed him last night that I regretted the uniformly fault-finding tone of his despatches, and that he had not as yet found leisure to notice the recent achievements of my army. . . .

Sept. 22, 9 A.M. - . . . I rode out on the battle-field yesterday. The burial of the dead is by this time completed; and a terrible work it has been, for the slain counted by thousands on each side. . . . I look upon this campaign as substantially ended, and my present intention is to seize Harper's Ferry and hold it with a strong force; then go to work and reorganize the army ready for another campaign. . . . I shall not go to Washington, if I can help it, but will try to reorganize the army somewhere near Harper's Ferry or Frederick. . . . It may be that, now that the government is pretty well over their scare, they will begin again with their persecutions and throw me overboard again. I don't care if they do. I have the satisfaction of knowing that God has, in His mercy, a second time made me the instrument for saving the nation, and am content with the honor that has fallen to my lot. I have seen enough of public life. No motive of ambition can now retain me in the service. The only thing that *can* keep me there will be the conviction that my country needs my services and that circumstances make it necessary for me to render them. I am confident that the poison still rankles in the veins of my enemies at Washington, and that so long as they live it will remain there. . . . I have received no papers containing the news of the last battle, and do not know the effect it has produced on the Northern mind. I trust it has been a good one, and that I am re-established in the confidence of the best people of the nation. . . . Everything quiet to-day; not a shot fired as yet. I am moving troops down to Harper's Ferry, and hope to occupy it to-morrow. Then I will have the Potomac clear. . . .

Sept. 23, Tuesday, 8 A.M., *Sharpsburg camp.* - . . . The weather is splendid, though I should like a little rain to raise the Potomac slightly. We are all well. I am entirely well now, and rather better for my little attack of illness. . . .

Sept. 25, 7.30 A.M. - . . . We are so near the mountains that it is quite cold at night. . . . I think the health of our men is improving much: they look a great deal better than they did on the Peninsula; eyes look brighter and faces better. . . . My plans are not easily given, for I really do not know whether I am to do as I choose or not. I shall keep on doing what seems best until brought up with a round turn. My own judgment is to watch the line of the Potomac until the water rises, then to concentrate everything near Harper's Ferry, reorganize the army as promptly as possible, and then if secesh remains near Winchester to attack him. If he retires, to follow him up and attack him near Richmond. . . . It is very doubtful whether I shall remain in the service after the rebels have left this vicinity. The President's late proclamation, the continuation of Stanton and Halleck in office, render it almost impossible for me to retain my commission and self-respect at the same time. . . . It is a mercy of God that none of my staff have been hit, considering how much they have been exposed to danger. They have had plenty of horses killed, sabres hit, clothes cut, etc., but have thus far escaped unhurt. . . . Am going on a visit to Harper's Ferry this morning. . . .

Sept. 26, 10.30 P.M., *Sharpsburg camp.* - . . . Pretty well tired out by a long ride to Harper's Ferry to-day. I rode down in my ambulance, but when there took a long and fatiguing ride on horseback over the Maryland Heights to determine upon the question of its defence. I did not have time to go over the Virginia side, but propose doing that to-morrow. Our camp will be thrown a little down in that direction to-morrow, so I shall not have quite so far to travel in returning. . . . It is so cool this evening that I have a fire in front of my tent and am sitting in my overcoat. . . .

Sept. 29, *Sharpsburg,* A.M. - . . . I think secesh has gone to Winchester. The last I heard last night was to that effect. If he has gone there I will be able to arrange my troops more with a view to comfort, and, if it will only rain a little so as to raise the river, will feel quite justified in asking for a short leave. . . . We are having very fine weather. . . . Not yet even have I a word from any one in Washington about the battle of the Antietam, and nothing in regard to South Mountain, except from the President in the following: "Your despatch received. God bless you and all with you! Can't you beat them some more before they get off?" I don't look for any thanks.

P.M. - I have been hard at work all day upon a preliminary report of the recent battles, and find that, in order to arrive at anything like the truth, I must to-morrow take all my aides to the ground and talk with them there. I would really prefer fighting three battles to writing the report of one. You can hardly imagine the difficulties of such a task. You are necessarily combating the *amour propre* of every officer concerned when you say one word in commendation of anybody else. I ought to treat Burnside very severely, and probably will; yet I hate to do it. He is very slow; is not fit to command more than a regiment. If I treat him as he deserves he will be my mortal enemy hereafter. If I do not praise him as he thinks he deserves, and as I know he does not, he will be at least a very lukewarm friend. I mention this merely as an instance that you will comprehend.

Oct. 1, 7.30 A.M. - . . . A cloudy day. If it does not rain I think I will go to Williamsport and Hagerstown to-day, to see that part of the country; for there is no telling but that I might have to fight a battle there one of these days, and it is very convenient to know the ground. In this last battle the rebels possessed an immense advantage in knowing every part of the ground, while I knew only what I could see from a distance. . . . I rode all over the battle-field again yesterday, so as to be sure that I understood it all before writing my report. I was but the more impressed with the great difficulties of the undertaking and the magnitude of the success. Did I tell you that our losses at South Mountain and Antietam amounted to within one or two hundred of 15,000; that we took some 6,000 prisoners, 39 colors, 14 guns, 14,500 small arms, etc., etc.? Pretty fair trophies after a battle so stubbornly contested. . . . Yesterday I received at last a telegram from Halleck about the battle of Antietam. . . . I don't know where we are drifting, but do not like the looks of things; time will show. . . . I do not yet know what are the military plans of the gigantic intellects at the head of the government. . . .

CHAPTER XXXVIII.

After the battle - The position reviewed - Condition of the army - Reorganization and supply - Visit of the President - He approves McClellan's course - Details of supplies needed and not received - Shoes, clothing, blankets, tents, horses - Dates of receipt of supplies - Plans of advance into Virginia.

THE night brought with it grave responsibilities. Whether to renew the attack on the 18th, or to defer it, even with the risk of the enemy's retirement, was the question before me.

After a night of anxious deliberation and a full and careful survey of the situation and condition of our army, the strength and position of the enemy, I concluded that the success of an attack on the 18th was not certain. I am aware of the fact that, under ordinary circumstances, a general is expected to risk a battle if he has a reasonable prospect of success; but at this critical juncture I should have had a narrow view of the condition of the country had I been willing to hazard another battle with less than an absolute assurance of success. At that moment - Virginia lost, Washington menaced, Maryland invaded - the national cause could afford no risks of defeat. One battle lost, and almost all would have been lost. Lee's army might then have marched as it pleased on Washington, Baltimore, Philadelphia, or New York. It could have levied its supplies from a fertile and undevastated country; extorted tribute from wealthy and populous cities; and nowhere east of the Alleghanies was there another organized force able to arrest its march.

The following are among the considerations which led me to doubt the certainty of success in attacking before the 19th:

The troops were greatly overcome by the fatigue and exhaustion attendant upon the long-continued and severely contested battle of the 17th, together with the long day-and-night marches to which they had been subjected during the previous three days.

The supply-trains were in the rear, and many of the troops had suffered from hunger. They required rest and refreshment.

618

One division of Sumner's and all of Hooker's corps on the right had, after fighting most valiantly for several hours, been overpowered by numbers, driven back in great disorder, and much scattered, so that they were for the time somewhat demoralized.

In Hooker's corps, according to the return made by Gen. Meade commanding, there were but 6,729 men present on the 18th ; whereas on the morning of the 22d there were 13,093 men present for duty in the same corps, showing that previous to and during the battle 6,364 men were separated from their command.

Gen. Meade, in an official communication upon this subject, dated Sept. 18, 1862, says:

"I enclose a field return of the corps, made this afternoon, which I desire you will lay before the commanding general. I am satisfied the great reduction in the corps since the recent engagements is not due solely to the casualties of battle, and that a considerable number of men are still in the rear, some having dropped out on the march, and many dispersing and leaving yesterday during the fight. I think the efficiency of the corps, so far as it goes, good. To resist an attack in our present strong position I think they may be depended on, and I hope they will perform duty in case we make an attack, though I do not think their *morale* is as good for an offensive as a defensive movement."

One division of Sumner's corps had also been overpowered, and was a good deal scattered and demoralized. It was not deemed by its corps commander in proper condition to attack the enemy vigorously the next day.

Some of the new troops on the left, although many of them fought well during the battle and are entitled to great credit, were, at the close of the action, driven back and their *morale* impaired.

On the morning of the 18th Gen. Burnside, as before stated, requested me to send him another division to assist in holding his position on the other side of the Antietam, and to enable him to withdraw his corps if he should be attacked by a superior force.

A large number of our heaviest and most efficient batteries had consumed all their ammunition on the 16th and 17th and it was impossible to supply them until late on the following day.

46

Supplies of provisions and forage had to be brought up and issued, and infantry ammunition distributed.

Finally, reinforcements to the number of 14,000 men - to say nothing of troops expected from Pennsylvania-had not arrived, but were expected during the day.

The 18th was, therefore, spent in collecting the dispersed, giving rest to the fatigued, removing the wounded, burying the dead, and the necessary preparations for a renewal of the battle.

Of the reinforcements, Couch's division, marching with commendable rapidity, came up into position at a late hour in the morning. Humphreys' division of new troops, in their anxiety to participate in the battle which was raging, when they received the order to march from Frederick at about half-past three P.M. on the 17th, pressed forward during the entire night, and the mass of the division reached the army during the following morning. Having marched more than 23 miles after half-past four o'clock on the preceding afternoon, they were, of course, greatly exhausted, and needed rest and refreshment. Large reinforcements expected from Pennsylvania never arrived. During the 18th orders were given for a renewal of the attack at daylight on the 19th.

On the night of the 18th the enemy, after passing troops in the latter part of the day from the Virginia shore to their position behind Sharpsburg, as seen by our officers, suddenly formed the design of abandoning their position and retreating across the river. As their line was but a short distance from the river, the evacuation presented but little difficulty, and was effected before daylight.

About 2,700 of the enemy's dead were, under the direction of Maj. Davis, assistant inspector-general, counted and buried upon the battle-field of Antietam. A portion of their dead had been previously buried by them.

When our cavalry advance reached the river on the morning of the 19th it was discovered that nearly all the enemy's forces had crossed into Virginia during the night, their rear escaping under cover of eight batteries placed in strong positions upon the elevated bluffs on the opposite bank. Gen. Porter, commanding the 5th corps, ordered a detachment from Griffin's and Barnes's brigades, under Gen. Griffin, to cross the river at dark and carry the enemy's batteries. This was gallantly done under the fire of the enemy; several guns, caissons, etc., were taken, and their supports driven back half a mile.

The information obtained during the progress of this affair indicated that the mass of the enemy had retreated on the Charlestown and Martinsburg roads towards Winchester. To verify this, and to ascertain how far the enemy had retired, Gen. Porter was authorized to detach from his corps, on the morning of the 20th, a reconnoitring party in greater force. This detachment crossed the river and advanced about a mile, when it was attacked by a large body of the enemy lying in ambush in the woods, and driven back across the river with considerable loss. This reconnoissance showed that the enemy was still in force on the Virginia bank of the Potomac: prepared to resist our further advance.

It was reported to me on the 19th that Gen. Stuart had made his appearance at Williamsport with some 4,000 cavalry and six pieces of artillery, and that 10,000 infantry were marching on the same point from the direction of Winchester. I ordered Gen. Couch to march at once with his division and a part of Pleasonton's cavalry, with Franklin's corps within supporting distance, for the purpose of endeavoring to capture this force. Gen. Couch made a prompt and rapid march to Williamsport, and attacked the enemy vigorously, but they made their escape across the river.

I despatched the following telegraphic report to the general-in-chief :

HEADQUARTERS, ARMY OF THE POTOMAC,
SHARPSBURG, Sept. 19, 1862.

I have the honor to report that Maryland is entirely freed from the presence of the enemy, who has been driven across the Potomac. No fears need now be entertained for the safety of Pennsylvania. I shall at once occupy Harper's Ferry.

G. B. McCLELLAN,
Maj.-Gen. Commanding.

Maj.-Gen. H. W. HALLECK,
Commanding U. S. Army.

On the following day, Sept. 20, I received this telegram from Gen. Halleck:

"We are still left entirely in the dark in regard to your own movements and those of the enemy. This should not be so. You should keep me advised of both, so far as you know them."

To which I answered as follows:

Sept. 20. - Your telegram of to-day is received. I telegraphed you yesterday all I knew, and had nothing more to inform you of until this evening. Williams's corps (Banks's) occupied Maryland Heights at one P.M. to-day. The rest of the army is near here, except Couch's division, which is at this moment engaged with the enemy in front of Williamsport; the enemy is retiring, *via* Charlestown and Martinsburg, on Winchester. He last night reoccupied Williamsport by a small force, but will be out of it by morning. I think he has a force of infantry near Shepherdstown.

I regret that you find it necessary to couch every despatch I have the honor to receive from you in a spirit of fault-finding, and that you have not yet found leisure to say one word in commendation of the recent achievements of this army, or even to allude to them.

I have abstained from giving the number of guns, colors, small arms, prisoners, etc., captured, until I could do so with some accuracy. I hope by to-morrow evening to be able to give at least an approximate statement.

On the same day I telegraphed as follows to Gen. Halleck:

Sept. 20. - As the rebel army, now on the Virginia side of the Potomac, must in a great measure be dependent for supplies of ammunition and provisions upon Richmond, I would respectfully suggest that Gen. Banks be directed to send out a cavalry force to cut their supply communication opposite Washington. This would seriously embarrass their operations, and will aid this army materially.

Maryland Heights were occupied by Gen. Williams's corps on this day, and on the 22d Gen. Sumner took possession of Harper's Ferry.

It will be remembered that at the time I was assigned to the command of the forces for the defence of the national capital, on the 2d day of Sept., 1862, the greater part of all the available troops were suffering under the disheartening influences of the serious defeat they had encountered during the brief and unfortunate campaign of Gen. Pope. Their numbers were greatly reduced by casualties, their confidence was much shaken, and they had lost something of that *esprit de corps* which is indispensable to the efficiency of an army. Moreover, they had left behind, lost, or worn out the greater part of their clothing and camp equipage, which required renewal before they could be in proper condition to take the field again.

The intelligence that the enemy was crossing the Potomac into Maryland was received in Washington on the 4th of Sept., and the Army of the Potomac was again put in motion, under my direction, on the following day, so that but a very brief interval of time was allowed to reorganize or procure supplies.

The sanguinary battles of South Mountain and Antietam, fought by this army a few days afterwards, with the reconnoissances immediately following, resulted in a loss to us of ten general officers, many regimental and company officers, and a large number of enlisted men, amounting in the aggregate to (15,220) fifteen thousand two hundred and twenty. Two army corps had been badly cut up, scattered, and somewhat demoralized in the action of the 17th.

In Gen. Sumner's corps alone, 41 commissioned officers and 819 enlisted men had been killed; 4 general officers, 89 other commissioned officers, and 3,708 enlisted men had been wounded, besides 548 missing; making the aggregate loss of this splendid veteran corps, in this one battle, 5,209.

In Gen. Hooker's corps the casualties of the same engagement amounted to 2,619.

The entire army had been greatly exhausted by unavoidable overwork, fatiguing marches, hunger, and want of sleep and rest, previous to the last battle.

When the enemy recrossed the Potomac into Virginia the means of transportation at my disposal were inadequate to furnish a single day's supply of subsistence in advance.

Many of the troops were new levies, some of whom had fought like veterans, but the *morale* of others had been a good deal impaired in those severely contested actions, and they required time to recover, as well as to acquire the necessary drill and discipline.

Under these circumstances I did not feel authorized to cross the river with the main army, over a very deep and difficult ford, in pursuit of the retreating enemy, known to be in strong force on the south bank, and thereby place that stream, which was liable at any time to rise above a fording stage, between my army and its base of supply.

I telegraphed on the 22d to the general-in-chief as follows:

As soon as the exigencies of the service will admit of it this army should be reorganized. It is absolutely necessary, to secure its efficiency, that the old skeleton regiments should be filled up at once and officers appointed to supply the numerous existing vacancies. There are instances where captains are commanding regiments, and companies are without a single commissioned officer.

On the 23d the following was telegraphed to the general-in-chief:

From several different sources I learn that Gen. R. E. Lee is still opposite to my position, at Leestown, between Shepherdstown and Martinsburg, and that Gen. Jackson is on the Opequan creek, about three miles from its mouth, both with. large force. There are also indications of heavy reinforcements moving towards them from Winchester and Charlestown. I have, therefore, ordered Gen. Franklin to take position with his corps at the cross-roads about one mile northwest of Bakersville, on the Bakersville and Williamsport road, and Gen. Couch to establish his division near Downsville, leaving sufficient force at Williamsport to watch and guard the ford at that place. The fact of the enemy remaining so long in our front, and the indications of an advance of reinforcements, seem to indicate that he will give us another battle with all his available force.

As I mentioned to you before, our army has been very much reduced by casualties in the recent battles, and in my judgment all the reinforcements of old troops that can possibly be dispensed with around Washington and other places should be instantly pushed forward by rail to this army. A defeat at this juncture would be ruinous to our cause. I cannot think it possible that the enemy will bring any forces to bear upon Washington till after the question is decided here; but if he should, troops can soon be sent back from this army by rail to reinforce the garrison there.

The evidence I have that reinforcements are coming to the rebel army consists in the fact that long columns of dust extending from Winchester to Charlestown, and from Charlestown in this direction, and also troops moving this way, were seen last evening. This is corroborated by citizens. Gen. Sumner, with his corps and Williams's (Banks's), occupies Harper's Ferry and the surrounding heights. I think he will be able to hold his position till reinforcements arrive.

On the 27th I made the following report:

> HEADQUARTERS, ARMY OF THE POTOMAC,
> Sept. 27, 1862, 10 A.M.

All the information in my possession goes to prove that the main body of the enemy is concentrated not far from Martinsburg, with some troops at Charlestown; not many in Winchester. Their movements of late have been an extension towards our right and beyond it. They are receiving reinforcements in Winchester, mainly, I think, of conscripts - perhaps entirely so.

This army is not now in condition to undertake another campaign nor to bring on another battle, unless great advantages are offered by some mistake of the enemy, or pressing military exigencies render it necessary. We are greatly deficient in officers. Many of the old regiments are reduced to mere skeletons. The new regiments need instruction. Not a day should be lost in filling the old regiments - our main dependence - and in supplying vacancies among the officers by promotion.

My present purpose is to hold the army about as it is now, rendering Harper's Ferry secure and watching the river closely, intending to attack the enemy should he attempt to cross to this side.

Our possession of Harper's Ferry gives us the great advantage of a secure debouch, but we cannot avail ourselves of it until the railroad bridge is finished, because we cannot otherwise supply a greater number of troops than we now have on the Virginia side at that point. When the river rises so that the enemy cannot cross in force, I purpose concentrating the army somewhere near Harper's Ferry, and then acting according to circumstances - viz., moving on Winchester, if from the position and attitude of the enemy we are likely to gain a great advantage by doing so, or else devoting a reasonable time to the organization of the army and instruction of the new troops, preparatory to an advance on whatever line may be determined. In any event I regard it as absolutely necessary to send new regiments at once to the old corps, for purposes of instruction, and that the old regiments be filled at once. I have no fears as to an attack on Washington by the line of Manassas. Holding Harper's Ferry, as I do, they will not run the risk of an attack on their flank and rear while they have the garrison of Washington in their front.

I rather apprehend a renewal of the attempt in Maryland, should the river remain low for a great length of time, and should they receive considerable addition to their force. I would be glad to have Peck's division as soon as possible. I am surprised that Sigel's men should have been sent to Western

Virginia without my knowledge. The last I heard from you on the subject was that they were at my disposition. In the last battles the enemy was undoubtedly greatly superior to us in number, and it was only by very hard fighting that we gained the advantage we did. As it was, the result was at one period very doubtful, and we had all we could do to win the day. If the enemy receives considerable reinforcements and we none, it is possible that I may have too much on my hands in the next battle. My own view of the proper policy to be pursued is to retain in Washington merely the force necessary to garrison it, and to send everything else available to reinforce this army. The railways give us the means of promptly reinforcing Washington, should it become necessary. If I am reinforced as I ask, and am allowed to take my own course, I will hold myself responsible for the safety of Washington. Several persons recently from Richmond say that there are no troops there except conscripts, and they few in number. I hope to give you details as to late battles by this evening. I am about starting again for Harper's Ferry.

G. B. McCLELLAN, Maj.-Gen. Commanding.

Maj.-Gen. HALLECK,
    Gen -in- Chief, Washington.

The work of reorganizing, drilling, and supplying the army I began at the earliest moment. The different corps were stationed along the river in the best positions to cover and guard the fords. The great extent of the river-front from near Washington to Cumberland (some one hundred and fifty miles), together with the line of the Baltimore and Ohio Railroad, was to be carefully watched and guarded, to prevent, if possible, the enemy's raids. Reconnoissances upon the Virginia side of the river, for the purpose of learning the enemy's positions and movements, were made frequently, so that our cavalry, which from the time me left Washington had performed the most laborious service, and had from the commencement been deficient in numbers, was found totally inadequate to the requirements of the army.

This overwork had broken down the greater part of the horses; disease had appeared among them, and but a very small portion of our original cavalry force was fit for service.

To such an extent had this arm become reduced that when Gen. Stuart made his raid into Pennsylvania on the 11th of October with 2,000 men, I could only mount 800 men to follow him.

Harper's Ferry was occupied on the 22d, and, in order to prevent a catastrophe similar to the one which had happened to Col. Miles, I immediately ordered Maryland, Bolivar, and Loudon Heights to be strongly fortified. This was done as far as the time and means at our disposal permitted.

The main army of the enemy during this time remained in the vicinity of Martinsburg and Bunker Hill, and occupied itself in drafting and coercing every able-bodied citizen into the ranks, forcibly taking their property where it was not voluntarily offered, burning bridges, and destroying railroads.

On the first day of October his Excellency the President honored the Army of the Potomac with a visit, and remained several days, during which he went through the different encampments, reviewed the troops, and went over the battle-fields of South Mountain and Antietam. I had the opportunity during this visit to describe to him the operations of the army since the time it left Washington, and gave him my reasons for not following the enemy after he crossed the Potomac.

He was accompanied by Gen. McClernand, John W. Garrett, the Secretary of State of Illinois, and others whom I have forgotten. During the visit me had many and long consultations alone. I urged him to follow a conservative course, and supposed from the tenor of his conversation that he would do so. He more than once assured me that he was fully satisfied with my whole course from the beginning; that the only fault he could possibly find was that I was perhaps too prone to be sure that everything was ready before acting, but that my actions were all right when I started. I said to him that I thought a few experiments with those who acted before they were ready would probably convince him that in the end I consumed less time than they did. He told me that he regarded me as the only general in the service capable of organizing and commanding a large army, and that he would stand by me. We parted on the field of South Mountain, whither I had accompanied him. He said there that he did not see how we ever gained that field, and that he was sure that, if I had defended it, Lee could never have carried it.

We spent some time on the battle-field and conversed fully on the state of affairs. He told me that he was entirely satisfied with me and with all that I had done; that he would stand by

me against "all comers"; that he wished me to continue my
preparations for a new campaign, not to stir an inch until fully
ready, and when ready to do what I thought best.   He repeated
that he was entirely satisfied with me; that I should be let alone;
that he would stand by me. I have no doubt that he meant
exactly what he said.   He parted from me with the utmost cordiality. We never met again on this earth.

He had hardly reached Washington before Cox's division
was taken from me and the order of Oct. 6 reached me! A
singular commentary on the uncertainty of human affairs!

On the 5th of Oct. the division of Gen. Cox (about 5,000
men) was ordered from my command to Western Virginia.

On the 7th of Oct. I received the following telegram from
Gen. Halleck:

"*Oct.* 6. - I am instructed to telegraph you as follows: The
President directs that you cross the Potomac and give battle to
the enemy or drive him south. Your army must move now
while the roads are good. If you cross the river between the
enemy and Washington, and cover the latter by your operation,
you can be reinforced with 30,000 men. If you move up the
valley of the Shenandoah not more than 12,000 or 15,000 can
be sent to you. The President advises the interior line between
Washington and the enemy, but does not order it.   He is very
desirous that your army move as soon as possible. You will
immediately report what line you adopt and when you intend
to cross the river; also to what point the reinforcements are to
be sent.   It is necessary that the plan of your operations be positively determined on before orders are given for building bridges
and repairing railroads.   I am directed to add that the Secretary
of War and the general-in-chief fully concur with the President
in these instructions."

On the 10th of Oct. Stuart crossed the river at McCoy's Ferry
with 2,000 cavalry and a battery of horse-artillery, on his raid
into Maryland and Pennsylvania, making it necessary to use all
our cavalry against him. This exhausting service completely
broke down nearly all of our cavalry horses, and rendered a
remount absolutely indispensable before we could advance on
the enemy.

At the time I received the order of Oct. 6 to cross the river
and attack the enemy the army was wholly deficient in cavalry,

and a large part of our troops were in want of shoes, blankets, and other indispensable articles of clothing, notwithstanding all the efforts that had been made since the battle of Antietam, and even prior to that date, to refit the army with clothing as well as horses. I at once consulted with Col. Ingalls, the chief-quartermaster, who believed that the necessary articles could be supplied in about three days. Orders were immediately issued to the different commanders who had not already sent in their requisitions to do so at once, and all the necessary steps were forthwith taken by me to insure a prompt delivery of the supplies. The requisitions were forwarded to the proper department at Washington, and I expected that the articles would reach our depots during the three days specified; but day after day elapsed, and only a small portion of the clothing arrived. Corps commanders, upon receiving notice from the quartermasters that they might expect to receive their supplies at certain dates, sent the trains for them, which, after waiting, were compelled to return empty. Several instances occurred where these trains went back and forth from the camps to the depots as often as four or five different times, without receiving their supplies, and I was informed by one corps commander that his wagon-train had travelled over one hundred and fifty miles, to and from the depots, before he succeeded in obtaining his clothing.

The corps of Gen. Franklin did not get its clothing until after it had crossed the Potomac and was moving into Virginia. Gen. Reynolds's corps was delayed a day at Berlin to complete its supplies, and Gen. Porter only completed his on reaching the vicinity of Harper's Ferry.

I made every exertion in my power, and my quartermasters did the same, to have these supplies hurried forward rapidly; and I was repeatedly told that they had filled the requisitions at Washington, and that the supplies had been forwarded. But they did not come to us, and of course were inaccessible to the army. I did not fail to make frequent representation of this condition of things to the general-in chief, and it appears that he referred the matter to the quartermaster-general, who constantly replied that the supplies had been promptly ordered. Notwithstanding this, they did not reach our depots.

The following extracts are from telegrams upon this subject:

To Gen. Halleck, Oct. 11. - We have been making every effort to get supplies of clothing for this army, and Col. Ingalls has received advices that it has been forwarded by railroad; but, owing to bad management on the roads, or from some other cause, it comes in very slowly, and it will take a much longer time than was anticipated to get articles that are absolutely indispensable to the army, unless the railroad managers forward supplies more rapidly.

To Gen. Halleck, Oct. 11. - I am compelled again to call your attention to the great deficiency of shoes, and other indispensable articles of clothing, that still exists in some of the corps in this army. Upon the assurances of the chief-quartermaster, who based his calculation upon information received from Washington that clothing would be forwarded at certain times, corps commanders sent their wagons to Hagerstown and Harper's Ferry for it. It did not arrive as promised, and has not yet arrived. Unless some measures are taken to insure the prompt forwarding of these supplies, there will necessarily be a corresponding delay in getting the army ready to move, as the men cannot march without shoes. Everything has been done that can be done at these headquarters to accomplish the desired result.

To Gen. Halleck, Oct. 15. - I am using every possible exertion to get this army ready to move. It was only yesterday that a part of our shoes and clothing arrived at Hagerstown. It is being issued to the troops as rapidly as possible.

To Col. Ingalls, Oct. 15. - Gen. Franklin reports that there is by no means as much clothing as was called for at Hagerstown. I think, therefore, you had better have additional supplies! especially of shoes, forwarded to Harper's Ferry as soon as possible.

To Col. Ingalls, Oct. 16. - Gen. J. F. Reynolds just telegraphs as follows: "My quartermaster reports that there are no shoes, tents, blankets, or knapsacks at Hagerstown. He was able to procure only a complete supply of overcoats and pants, with a few socks, drawers, and coats. This leaves many of the men yet without a shoe. My requisitions call for 5,255 pairs of shoes."

Please push the shoes and stockings up to Harper's Ferry as fast as possible.

From Gen. Sumner, Oct. 7. - "I have given orders upon

orders about the clothing, but my officers can get nothing from Washington, and some staff officers there had the impudence to say that I had no right to sign requisitions."

From Col. Ingalls, Oct. 9. - "You did right in sending clothing to Harper's Ferry. You will not be able to send too much or too quickly. We want blankets, shoes, canteens, etc., very much."

From Col. Ingalls to Quartermaster in Philadelphia, Oct. 10. - "Shipments to Hagerstown must be made direct through, to avoid the contemptible delays at Harrisburg. If Col. Crosman was ordered to send clothing, I hope he has sent it, for the suffering and impatience are excessive."

From Col. Ingalls, Oct. 13. - "Has the clothing arrived yet? If not, do you know where it is? What clothing was taken by the rebels at Chambersburg? Did they capture any property that was *en route* to you? Have we not got clothing at Harrisburg? Send an agent over the road to obtain information and hurry up the supplies. Reply at once."

From Gen. Halleck, Oct. 13. - "Your telegram in regard to supplies has been referred to the quartermaster-general, and he replies that everything asked for had been sent or ordered. The movement of your reinforcements by railroads has probably delayed the transportation of some portion of them. It is difficult to supply the waste of horses."

From F. Lowry, Capt. and Quartermaster, Oct. 15. - "I have just returned from Hagerstown, where I have been for the clothing for the corps. There was nothing there but overcoats, trousers, and a few uniform coats and socks. There were not any shoes, blankets, shirts, or shelter-tents. Will you please tell me where and when the balance can be had? Shall I send to Harper's Ferry for them to-morrow? The corps surgeon has just made a requisition for forty-five hospital-tents. There are none at Hagerstown. Will you please to inform me if I can get them at Harper's Ferry?"

From Assist.-Quartermaster G. W. Weeks, Oct. 15. - "I want" at least ten thousand (10,000) suits of clothing in addition to what I have received. It should be here now."

From A. Bliss, Capt. and Assist.-Quartermaster, Oct. 22. - "We have bootees, 12,000; greatcoats, 4,000; drawers and shirts are gone; blankets and stockings nearly so; 15,000 each of these four articles are wanted."

From Col. Ingalls, Oct. 24. - "*Please* send to Capt. Bliss, at Harper's Ferry, 10,000 blankets, 12,000 caps, 5,000 overcoats, 10,000 pairs bootees, 2,000 pairs artillery and cavalry boots, 15,000 pairs stockings, 15,000 drawers, and 15,000 pants. The clothing arrives slowly. Can it not be hurried along faster? May I ask you to obtain authority for this shipment?"

From Capt. Weeks, Oct. 30. - "*Clothing* has arrived this morning. None taken by rebels. Shall I supply Franklin, and retain portions for Porter and Reynolds until called for?"

The following statement, taken from a report of the chief-quartermaster with the army, will show what progress was made in supplying the army with clothing from the 1st of Sept. to the date of crossing the Potomac on the 31st of Oct., and that a greater part of the clothing did not reach our depots until after the 14th of Oct.:

Statement of clothing and equipage received at the different depots of the Army of the Potomac from Sept. 1, 1862, to Oct. 31, 1862.

Received at the depots.	Drawers.	Forage-caps.	Stockings.	Sack-coats.	Cavalry-jackets.	Canteens.	Flannel shirts.	Haversacks.	Trousers (mounted).	Boots.	Shelter-tents.
From Sept. 1 to Oct. 6	10,700	4,000	6,200	4,190	3,000	6,000	6,200	6,000	4,200	4,200	11,100
From Oct. 6 to Oct. 15	17,000	11,000	22,025	......	500	10,221	18,325	12,989	1,000	6,000	3,000
From Oct.15 to Oct. 25	40,000	19,500	65,200	......	1,250	9,000	18,876	5,000	2,500	3,600	9,000
From Oct 25 to Oct. 31	30,000	......	30,000	......	1,500	3,008	2,200	9,900	5,000	20,040	......
Total........	97,700	34,500	123,425	4,190	6,250	28,229	45,601	33,889	12,700	33,840	23,100

Statement of clothing and equipage received, etc. - Continued.

Received at the depots.	Camp-kettles.	Mess-pans.	Overcoats (foot).	Artillery-jackets.	Blankets.	Overcoats (mounted).	Felt hats.	Infantry-coats.	Trousers (foot).	Bootees.	Knit shirts.
From Sept.1 to Oct. 6	799	2,030	3,500	1,200	20	1,200	2,200	2,000	2,000	2,000	.....
From Oct. 6 to Oct. 15	1,302	2,100	12,000	500	.....	875	7,000	12,060	9,500	7,000	2,655
From Oct.15 to Oct. 25	1,894	4,500	14,770	1,750	6,500	3,500	.....	22,500	39,620	52,900	2,424
From Oct.25 to Oct. 31	.....	.....	.....	1,000	4,384	2,015	.....	7,500	25,000	.....	11,595
Total......	3,995	8,630	30,270	4,450	10,904	7,590	9,200	44,060	76,120	61,900	16,674

Col. Ingalls, chief-quartermaster, in his report upon this subject says:

"There was great delay in receiving our clothing. The orders were promptly given by me and approved by Gen. Meigs, but the roads were slow to transport, particularly the Cumberland Valley Road.

"For instance, clothing ordered to Hagerstown on the 7th Oct. for the corps of Franklin, Porter, and Reynolds did not arrive there until about the 18th, and by that time, of course, there were increased wants and changes in position of troops. The clothing of Sumner arrived in great quantities near the last of Oct., almost too late for issue, as the army was crossing into Virginia. We finally left 50,000 suits at Harper's Ferry, *partly on the cars just arrived,* and partly in store."

The causes of the reduction of our cavalry force have already been recited. The difficulty in getting new supplies from the usual sources led me to apply for and obtain authority for the cavalry and artillery officers to purchase their own horses. The following are the telegrams and letters on this subject:

To Gen. Halleck, Oct. 12. - "It is absolutely necessary that some energetic means be taken to supply the cavalry of this army with remount horses. The present rate of supply is (1,050) ten hundred and fifty per week for the entire army here and in front of Washington. From this number the artillery draw for their batteries."

To Gen. Halleck, Oct. 14. - "With my small cavalry force it is impossible for me to watch the line of the Potomac properly, or even make the Reconnoissances that are necessary for our movements. This makes it necessary for me to weaken my line very much by extending the infantry to guard the innumerable fords. This will continue until the river rises, and it will be next to impossible to prevent the rebel cavalry raids. My cavalry force, as I urged this morning, should be largely and immediately increased, under any hypothesis, whether to guard the river or advance on the enemy, or both."

The following was received Oct. 25, 1862, from Washington, 4.50 P.M.:

"To Maj.-Gen. McClellan:

"I have just received your despatch about sore-tongued and fatigued horses. Will you pardon me for asking what the horses of your army have done since the battle of Antietam that fatigues anything?

" A. LINCOLN."

HEADQUARTERS, ARMY OF THE POTOMAC,
Oct. 25, 6 P.M., 1862.

His Excellency the President:

In reply to your telegram of this date I have the honor to state that from the time this army left Washington on the 7th of Sept. my cavalry has been constantly employed in making Reconnoissances, scouting, and picketing. Since the battle of Antietam six regiments have made one trip of two hundred miles, marching fifty-five miles in one day while endeavoring to reach Stuart's cavalry. Gen. Pleasonton in his official report states that he, with the remainder of our available cavalry, while on Stuart's track marched seventy-eight miles in twenty-four hours. Besides these two remarkable expeditions, our cavalry has been engaged in picketing and scouting one hundred and fifty miles of river-front ever since the battle of Antietam, and has made repeated Reconnoissances since that time, engaging the enemy on every occasion. Indeed, it has performed harder service since the battle than before. I beg you will also consider that this same cavalry was brought from the Peninsula, where it encountered most laborious service, and was at the commencement of this campaign in low condition, and from that time to the present it has had no time to recruit.

If any instance can be found where overworked cavalry has performed more labor than mine since the battle of Antietam, I am not conscious of it.

GEO. B. MCCLELLAN,
Maj.-Gen.

The following was received Oct. 24 from Cherry Run, 12 M.:

" *To Col. A. V. Colburn:*

"I have great difficulty in obtaining spies and guides without payment. Would it not be well to have sent to my acting division quartermaster, First Lieut. John S. Schutz, five hundred dollars for that purpose? Col. Williams reports, eleven (11) A.M. to-day:

"'I have in camp 267 horses belonging to officers and men. Of these 128 are positively and absolutely unable to leave the camp from the following causes-viz., sore tongue, grease and consequent lameness, and sore backs. For example, the 5th U. S. Cavalry has now in camp 70 horses. Of these 53 are worthless from the above causes. Out of 139 horses, the remainder, I do not believe 50 can trot eight miles. The other portion of my command, now absent on picket duty, has horses which are about in the same condition, as no selection, unless absolutely necessary, has been made. The number of sore-back horses exceedingly small; the diseases are principally grease, sore tongue. The horses which are still sound are absolutely broken down from fatigue and want of flesh. I will also remark that the men of my command are much in want of clothing.

" 'Col. WILLIAMS.'

"The cavalry should therefore be changed, I think, and their number increased to 1,000, with one battery of horse-artillery. I would respectfully desire to have Col. Williams in command.

"JOHN NEWTON,
"*Brig.-Gen. Commanding.*"

Col. Colburn telegraphed from Washington, Oct. 25:

"To GEN. MCCLELLAN: I went this morning to see Gen. Halleck, and spoke to him about the bridges, etc., and also about rebuilding the road to Winchester and prolonging it to Strasburg; also about the forces to be left at Harper's Ferry, and what was to be done in the Shenandoah provided the enemy fell back. The only answer I could get was that they had nothing to do with the present campaign, and that you ought to be able to decide in the premises. There was no use of trying to explain matters to him, because he would not listen to anything. When I spoke to him about the cavalry horses he said that that was the quartermaster's business and he had nothing to do with it. I will try again, but think it no use."

The following is an extract from the official report of Col. Ingalls:
47

"Immediately after the battle of Antietam efforts were made to supply deficiencies in clothing and horses. Large requisitions were prepared and sent in. The artillery and cavalry required large numbers to cover losses sustained in battle, on the march, and by diseases. Both of these arms were deficient when they left Washington. A most violent and destructive disease made its appearance at this time, which put nearly 4,000 animals out of service. Horses reported perfectly well one day would be dead-lame the next, and it was difficult to foresee where it would end or what number would cover the loss. They were attacked in the hoof and tongue. No one seemed able to account for the appearance of this disease. Animals kept at rest would recover in time, but *could not be worked.* I made application to send West and purchase horses at once, but it was refused, on the ground that the outstanding contracts provided for enough; but *they were not delivered sufficiently fast,* nor in sufficient numbers, until late in October and early in November. I was authorized to buy 2,500 late in October, but the delivery was not completed until in November, after we had reached Warrenton."

In a letter from Gen. Meigs, written on the 14th of Oct. and addressed to the general-in-chief, it is stated: "There have been issued, therefore, to the Army of the Potomac, since the battles in front of Washington, to replace losses, (9,254) nine thousand two hundred and fifty-four horses."

What number of horses were sent to Gen. Pope before his return to Washington I have no means of determining; but the following statement, made upon my order, by the chief-quartermaster with the army, and who had means for gaining accurate information, forces upon my mind the conclusion that the quartermaster-general was in error :

"HEADQUARTERS, ARMY OF THE POTOMAC,
"CHIEF-QUARTERMASTER'S OFFICE, Oct. 31, 1862.

"Horses purchased Sept. 6, 1862, by Col. Ingalls, chief-quartermaster, and issued to the forces under the immediate command of Maj.-Gen. George B. Mc-Clellan.. . . . . , ... 1,200
"Issued and turned over to the above force by Capt. J. J. Dana, assistant-quartermaster (in Washington). 2,261
"Issued to forces at and near Washington which have since joined the command.. 352

"Total purchased by Col. Ingalls, and issued and turned

over by Capt. Dana to the forces in this immediate
command. 3,813
"Issued by Capt. J. J. Dana, assistant-quartermaster, to
the forces in the vicinity of Washington. 3,363

"Grand total purchased by Col. R. Ingalls, chief-quar-
termaster, and issued and turned over by Capt. J. J.
Dana, assistant-quartermaster, to the entire Army of
the Potomac and the forces around Washington. . . 7,176
"About 3,000 horses have been turned over to the quarter-
master's department by officers as unfit for service; nearly 1,500
should now be turned over also, being worn out and diseased.
"Respectfully   submitted.
"FRED. MYERS,
"*Lieut.-Col. and Quartermaster.*"

This official statement, made up from the reports of the
quartermasters who received and distributed the horses, exhibits the true state of the case, and gives the total number of
horses received by the Army of the Potomac and the troops
around Washington, during a period of eight weeks, as (7,176)
seven thousand one hundred and seventy-six, or (2,078) two
thousand and seventy-eight less than the number stated by the
quartermaster-general.

Supposing that (1,500) fifteen hundred were issued to the
army under Gen. Pope previous to its return to Washington, as
Gen. Meigs states, there would still remain (578) five hundred
and seventy-eight horses which he does not account for.

The letter of the general-in-chief to the Secretary of War
on the 28th of Oct., and the letter of Gen. Meigs to the general-in-chief on the 14th of Oct., convey the impression that, upon
my repeated applications for cavalry and artillery horses for the
Army of the Potomac, I had received a much greater number
than was really the case.

It will be seen from Col. Myers's report that of all the horses
alluded to by Gen. Meigs, only (3,813) three thousand eight hundred and thirteen came to the army with which I was ordered
to follow and attack the enemy. Of course the remainder did
not in the slightest degree contribute to the efficiency of the
cavalry or artillery of the army with which I was to cross the
river. Neither did they in the least facilitate any preparations
for carrying out the order to advance upon the enemy, as the
general-in-chief's letter might seem to imply.

During the same period that we were receiving the horses alluded to about (3,000) three thousand of our old stock were turned into the quartermaster's department, and 1,500 more reported as in such condition that they ought to be turned in as unfit for service; thus leaving the active army some 700 short of the number required to make good existing deficiencies, to say nothing of providing remounts for men whose horses had died or been killed during the campaign and those previously dismounted. Notwithstanding all the efforts made to obtain a remount, there were, after deducting the force engaged in picketing the river, but about a thousand serviceable cavalry horses on the 21st day of Oct.

In a letter dated Oct. 14, 1862, the general-in-chief says: "It is also reported to me that the number of animals with your army in the field is about 31,000. It is believed that your present proportion of cavalry and of animals is much larger than that of any other of our armies."

What number of animals our other armies had I am not prepared to say, but military men in European armies have been of the opinion that an army to be efficient, while carrying on active operations in the field, should have a cavalry force equal in numbers to from one-sixth to one-fourth of the infantry force. My cavalry did not amount to one-twentieth part of the army, and hence the necessity of giving every one of my cavalry soldiers a serviceable horse.

Cavalry may be said to constitute the antennœ of an army. It scouts all the roads in front, on the flanks, and in the rear of the advancing columns, and constantly feels the enemy. The amount of labor falling on this arm during the Maryland campaign was excessive.

To persons not familiar with the movements of troops, and the amount of transportation required for a large army marching away from water or railroad communications, the number of animals mentioned by the general-in-chief may have appeared unnecessarily large; but to a military man who takes the trouble to enter into an accurate and detailed computation of the number of pounds of subsistence and forage required for such an army as that of the Potomac, it will be seen that the 31,000 animals were considerably less than was absolutely necessary to an advance.

As we were required to move through a country which could not be depended upon for any of our supplies, it became necessary to transport everything in wagons and to be prepared for all emergencies. I did not consider it safe to leave the river without subsistence and forage for ten days. The official returns of that date show the aggregate strength of the army for duty to have been about 110,000 men of all arms. This did not include teamsters, citizen employees, officers' servants, etc., amounting to some 12,000, which gave a total of 122,000 men.

The subsistence alone of this army for ten days required for its transportation 1,830 wagons at 2,000 pounds to the wagon, and 10,980 animals.

Our cavalry horses at that time amounted to 5,046, and our artillery horses to 6,836.

To transport full forage for these 22,862 animals for ten days required 17,832 additional animals; and this forage would only supply the entire number (40,694) of animals with a small fraction over half-allowance for the time specified.

It will be observed that this estimate does not embrace the animals necessary to transport quartermasters' supplies, baggage, camp equipage, ambulances, reserve ammunition, forage for officers' horses, etc., which would greatly augment the necessary transportation.

It may very truly be said that we did make the march with the means at our disposal; but it will be remembered that we met with no serious opposition from the enemy, neither did we encounter delays from any other cause. The roads were in excellent condition, and the troops marched with the most commendable order and celerity.

If we had met with a determined resistance from the enemy, and our progress had been very much retarded thereby, we would have consumed our supplies before they could have been renewed. A proper estimate of my responsibilities as the commander of that army did not justify me in basing my preparations for the expedition upon the supposition that I was to have an uninterrupted march. On the contrary, it was my duty to be prepared for all emergencies; and not the least important of my responsibilities was the duty of making ample provision for supplying my men and animals with rations and forage.

Knowing the solicitude of the President for an early movement, and sharing with him fully his anxiety for prompt action, on the 21st of October I telegraphed to the general-in-chief as follows:

Oct. 21. - Since the receipt of the President's order to move on the enemy I have been making every exertion to get this army supplied with clothing absolutely necessary for marching.

This, I am happy to say, is now nearly accomplished. I have also, during the same time, repeatedly urged upon you the importance of supplying cavalry and artillery horses to replace those broken down by hard service, and steps have been taken to insure a prompt delivery.

Our cavalry, even when well supplied with horses, is much inferior in number to that of the enemy, but in efficiency has proved itself superior. So forcibly has this been impressed upon our old regiments by repeated successes that the men are fully persuaded that they are equal to twice their number of rebel cavalry.

Exclusive of the cavalry force now engaged in picketing the river, I have not at present over about one thousand (1,000) horses for service. Officers have been sent in various directions to purchase horses, and I expect them soon. Without more cavalry horses our communications, from the moment we march, would be at the mercy of the large cavalry force of the enemy, and it would not be possible for us to cover our flanks properly, or to obtain the necessary information of the position and movements of the enemy in such a way as to insure success. My experience has shown the necessity of a large and efficient cavalry force.

Under the foregoing circumstances I beg leave to ask whether the President desires me to march on the enemy at once or to await the reception of the new horses, every possible step having been taken to insure their prompt arrival.

On the same day Gen. Halleck replied as follows:

"*Oct.* 21. - Your telegram of twelve M. has been submitted to the President. He directs me to say that he has no change to make in his order of the 6th instant.

"If you have not been, and are not now, in condition to obey it, you will be able to show such want of ability. The President does not expect impossibilities, but he is very anxious that all this good weather should not be wasted in inactivity. Telegraph when you will move and on what lines you propose to march."

From the tenor of this despatch I conceived that it was left for my judgment to decide whether or not it was possible to move with safety to the army at that time; and this responsibility I exercised with the more confidence in view of the strong assurances of his trust in me, as commander of that army, with which the President had seen fit to honor me during his last visit.

The cavalry requirements, without which an advance would have been in the highest degree injudicious and unsafe, were still wanting.

The country before us was an enemy's country, where the inhabitants furnished to the enemy every possible assistance; providing food for men and forage for animals, giving all information concerning our movements, and rendering every aid in their power to the enemy's cause.

It was manifest that we should find it, as we subsequently did, a hostile district, where we could derive no aid from the inhabitants that would justify dispensing with the active co-operation of an efficient cavalry force. Accordingly I fixed upon the 1st of November as the earliest date at which the forward movement could well be commenced.

The general-in-chief, in a letter to the Secretary of War on the 28th of Oct., says: "In my opinion there has been no such want of supplies in the army under Gen. McClellan as to prevent his compliance with the orders to advance against the enemy."

Notwithstanding this opinion, expressed by such high authority, I am compelled to say again that the delay in the reception of necessary supplies up to that date had left the army in a condition totally unfit to advance against the enemy; that an advance under the existing circumstances would, in my judgment, have been attended with the highest degree of peril, with great suffering and sickness among the men, and with imminent danger of being cut off from our supplies by the superior cavalry force of the enemy, and with no reasonable prospect of gaining any advantage over him.

I dismiss this subject with the remark that I have found it impossible to resist the force of my own convictions that the commander of an army who, from the time of its organization, has for eighteen months been in constant communication with its officers and men, the greater part of the time engaged in active service in the field, and who has exercised this command in many battles, must certainly be considered competent to determine whether his army is in proper condition to advance on the enemy or not; and he must necessarily possess greater facilities for forming a correct judgment in regard to the wants of his men and the condition of his supplies than the general-in-chief in his office at Washington City.

The movement from Washington into Maryland, which culminated in the battles of South Mountain and Antietam, was not a part of an offensive campaign, with the object of the invasion of the enemy's territory and an attack upon his capital, but was defensive in its purposes, although offensive in its character, and would be technically called a "defensive-offensive campaign." It was undertaken at a time when our army had experienced severe defeats, and its object was to preserve the national capital and Baltimore, to protect Pennsylvania from invasion, and to drive the enemy out of Maryland. These purposes were fully and finally accomplished by the battle of Antietam, which brought the Army of the Potomac into what might be termed an accidental position on the upper Potomac.

Having gained the immediate object of the campaign, the first thing to be done was to insure Maryland from a return of the enemy; the second, to prepare our own army-exhausted by a series of severe battles, destitute to a great extent of supplies, and very deficient in artillery and cavalry horses-for a definite offensive movement, and to determine upon the line of operations for a further advance. At the time of the battle of Antietam the Potomac was very low, and presented a comparatively weak line of defence unless watched by large masses of troops. The reoccupation of Harper's Ferry and the disposition of troops above that point rendered the line of the Potomac secure against everything except cavalry raids. No time was lost in placing the army in proper condition for an advance, and the circumstances which caused the delay after the battle of Antietam have been fully enumerated.

I never regarded Harper's Ferry or its vicinity as a proper base of operations for a movement upon Richmond. I still considered the line of the Peninsula as the true approach, but for obvious reasons did not make any proposal to return to it.

On the 6th of Oct., as stated above, I was ordered by the

President, through his general-in-chief, to cross the Potomac and give battle to the enemy or drive him south. Two lines were presented for my choice:

1st. Up the Valley of the Shenandoah, in which case I was to have 12,000 to 15,000 additional troops.

2d. To cross between the enemy and Washington-that is, east of the Blue Ridge - in which event I was to be reinforced with 30,000 men.

At first I determined to adopt the line of the Shenandoah, for these reasons: The Harper's Ferry and Winchester Railroad, and the various turnpikes converging upon Winchester, afforded superior facilities for supplies. Our cavalry being weak, this line of communication could be more easily protected. There was no advantage in interposing at that time the Blue Ridge and the Shenandoah between the enemy and myself.

At the period in question the Potomac was still very low, and I apprehended that if I crossed the river below Harper's Ferry the enemy would promptly check the movement by re-crossing into Maryland, at the same time covering his rear by occupying in strong force the passes leading through the Blue Ridge from the southeast into the Shenandoah Valley.

I anticipated, as the result of the first course, that Lee would fight me near Winchester, if he could do so under favorable circumstances; or else that he would abandon the lower Shenandoah, and leave the Army of the Potomac free to act upon some other line of operations.

If he abandoned the Shenandoah he would naturally fall back upon his railway communications. I have since been confirmed in the belief that if I had crossed the Potomac below Harper's Ferry in the early part of October, Gen. Lee would have re-crossed into Maryland.

As above explained, the army was not in condition to move until late in October and in the meantime circumstances had changed.

The period had arrived when a sudden and great rise of the Potomac might be looked for at any moment; the season of bad roads and difficult movements was approaching, which would naturally deter the enemy from exposing himself very far from his base, and his movements all appeared to indicate a falling back from the river towards his supplies. Under these circum-

48

stances I felt at liberty to disregard the possibility of the enemy's, recrossing the Potomac, and determined to select the line east of the Blue Ridge, feeling convinced that it would secure me the largest accession of force and the most cordial support of the President, whose views from the beginning were in favor of that line.

The subject of the defence of the line of the upper Potomac after the advance of the main army had long occupied my attention. I desired to place Harper's Ferry and its dependencies in a strong state of defence, and frequently addressed the general-in-chief upon the subject of the erection of field-works and permanent bridges there, asking for the funds necessary to accomplish the purpose. Although I did my best to explain, as clearly as I was able, that I did not wish to erect permanent works of masonry, and that neither the works nor the permanent bridges had any reference to the advance of the army, but solely to the permanent occupation of Harper's Ferry, I could never make the general-in-chief understand my wishes, but was refused the funds necessary to erect the field-works, on the ground that there was no appropriation for the erection of permanent fortifications; and was not allowed to build the permanent bridge, on the ground that the main army could not be delayed in its movements until its completion.

Of course I never thought of delaying the advance of the army for that purpose, and so stated repeatedly.

CHAPTER XXXIX.

Crossing the Potomac - The march of a great army - Overtaking the enemy - Another battle imminent - Removed from the command- Burnside brings the order - Farewells to the army.

ON the 25th of Oct. the pontoon-bridge at Berlin was constructed, there being already one across the Potomac and another across the Shenandoah at Harper's Ferry.

On the 26th two divisions of the 9th corps and Pleasonton's brigade of cavalry crossed at Berlin and occupied Lovettsville.

The 1st, 6th, and 9th corps, the cavalry, and reserve artillery crossed at Berlin between the 26th of Oct. and the 2d of Nov.

The 2d and 5th corps crossed at Harper's Ferry between the 29th of Oct. and 1st of Nov.

Heavy rains delayed the movement considerably in the beginning, and the 1st, 5th, and 6th corps were obliged to halt at least one day at the crossings to complete, as far as possible, the necessary supplies that could not be procured at an earlier period.

The plan of campaign I adopted during the advance was to move the army well in hand parallel to the Blue Ridge, taking Warrenton as the point of direction for the main army; seizing each pass on the Blue Ridge by detachments as we approached it, and guarding them, after we had passed, as long as they would enable the enemy to trouble our communications with the Potomac. It was expected that we would unite with the 11th corps and Sickles's division near Thoroughfare Gap. We depended upon Harper's Ferry and Berlin for supplies until the Manassas Gap Railway was reached; when that occurred the passes in our rear were to be abandoned and the army massed ready for action or movement in any direction.

It was my intention, if, upon reaching Ashby's or any other pass, I found that the enemy were in force between it and the

Potomac, in the Valley of the Shenandoah, to move into the valley and endeavor to gain their rear.

I hardly hoped to accomplish this, but did expect that by striking in between Culpeper Court-House and Little Washington I could either separate their army and beat them in detail, or else force them to concentrate as far back as Gordonsville, and thus place the Army of the Potomac in position either to adopt the Fredericksburg line of advance upon Richmond or to be removed to the Peninsula if, as I apprehended, it were found impossible to supply it by the Orange and Alexandria Railroad beyond Culpeper.

On the 27th of Oct. the remaining divisions of the 9th corps crossed at Berlin, and Pleasonton's cavalry advanced to Purcellville. The concentration of the 6th corps, delayed somewhat by intelligence as to the movements of the enemy near Hedgesville, etc., was commenced on this day, and the 1st corps was already in motion for Berlin.

On the 28th the 1st corps and the general headquarters reached Berlin.

On the 29th the reserve artillery crossed and encamped near Lovettsville. Stoneman's division, temporarily attached to the 9th corps, occupied Leesburg; Averill's cavalry brigade moved towards Berlin from Hagerstown; two divisions of the 9th corps moved to Wheatland, and one to Waterford. The 2d corps commenced the passage of the Shenandoah at Harper's Ferry, and moved into the valley east of Loudon Heights.

On the 30th the 1st corps crossed at Berlin and encamped near Lovettsville, and the 2d corps completed the passage of the Shenandoah. The 5th corps commenced its march from Sharpsburg to Harper's Ferry.

On the 31st the 2d corps moved to the vicinity of Hillsborough; the 6th corps reached Boonsborough; the 5th corps reached Harper's Ferry, one division crossing the Shenandoah.

On the 1st of Nov. the 1st corps moved to Purcellville and Hamilton; the 2d corps to Wood Grove; the 5th corps to Hillsborough; the 6th corps reached Berlin, one division crossing. Pleasonton's cavalry occupied Philomont, having a sharp skirmish there and at Bloomfield.

On Nov. 2 the 2d corps occupied Snicker's Gap; the 5th corps, Snickersville; the 6th corps crossed the Potomac and

encamped near Wheatland; the 9th corps advanced to Bloomfield, Union, and Philomont. Pleasonton drove the enemy out
of Union. Averill was ordered to join Pleasonton. The enemy
offered no serious resistance to the occupation of Snicker's Gap,
but advanced to gain possession of it with a column of some
5,000 to 6,000 infantry, who were driven back by a few rounds
from our rifled guns.

On the 3d the 1st corps moved to Philomont, Union, Bloomfield, etc.; the 2d corps to the vicinity of Upperville; the 5th
corps remained at Snicker's Gap; the 6th corps moved to Purcellville; the 9th corps moved towards Upperville. Pleasonton
drove the enemy out of Upperville after a severe fight.

On the 4th the 2d corps took possession of Ashby's Gap; the
6th corps reached Union; the 9th corps, Upperville; the cavalry
occupied Piedmont. On the 5th the 1st corps moved to Rectortown and White Plains; one division of the 2d corps to the
intersection of the Paris and Piedmont with the Upperville and
Barber's road; the 6th corps to the Aldie pike, east of Upperville; the 9th corps beyond the Manassas Railroad, between
Piedmont and Salem, with a brigade at Manassas Gap. The
cavalry under Averill had a skirmish at Manassas Gap, and the
brigade of Pleasonton gained a handsome victory over superior
numbers at Barber's cross-roads. Bayard's cavalry had some
sharp skirmishing in front of Salem.

On the 6th the 1st corps advanced to Warrenton, the 2d corps
to Rectortown; the 5th corps commenced its movement from
Snicker's Gap to White Plains; the 9th corps to Waterloo and
vicinity on the Rappahannock; the 11th corps was at New Baltimore, Thoroughfare and Hopewell's Gaps; Sickles's division
guarding the Orange and Alexandria Railroad from Manassas
Junction towards Warrenton Junction; the cavalry near Flint
Hill; Bayard to cut off what there might be in Warrenton, and
to proceed to the Rappahannock Station.

Nov. 7, Gen. Pleasonton was ordered to move towards Little Washington and Sperryville, and thence towards Culpeper
Court-House.

Nov. 8, the 2d corps moved half-way to Warrenton; the
5th corps to New Baltimore.

Nov. 9, the 2d and 5th corps reached Warrenton; the 6th
corps New Baltimore.

Late on the night of the 7th I received an order relieving me from the command of the Army of the Potomac, and directing me to turn it over to Gen. Burnside, which I at once did.

I had already given the orders for the movements of the 8th and 9th; these orders were carried into effect without change.

The position in which I left the army, as the result of the orders I had given, was as follows:

The 1st, 2d, and 5th corps, reserve artillery, and general headquarters at Warrenton; the 9th corps on the line of the Rappahannock, in the vicinity of Waterloo; the 6th corps at New Baltimore; the 11th corps at New Baltimore, Gainesville, and Thoroughfare Gap; Sickles's division, of the 3d corps, on the Orange and Alexandria Railroad, from Manassas Junction to Warrenton Junction; Pleasonton across the Rappahannock at Amissville, Jefferson, etc., with his pickets at Hazel river, facing Longstreet, six miles from Culpeper Court-House; Bayard near Rappahannock Station.

The army was thus massed near Warrenton, ready to act in any required direction, perfectly in hand, and in admirable condition and spirits. I doubt whether, during the whole period that I had the honor to command the Army of the Potomac, it was in such excellent condition to fight a great battle. When I gave up the command to Gen. Burnside the best information in our possession indicated that Longstreet was immediately in our front near Culpeper; Jackson, with one, perhaps both, of the Hills, near Chester and Thornton's Gaps, with the mass of their force west. of the Blue Ridge.

The reports from Gen. Pleasonton on the advance indicated the possibility of separating the two wings of the enemy's forces, and either beating Longstreet separately or forcing him to fall back at least upon Gordonsville to effect his junction with the rest of the army.

The following is from the report of Gen. Pleasonton:

"At this time, and from the 7th instant, my advance pickets were at Hazel river, within six miles of Culpeper, besides having my flank pickets towards Chester and Thornton's Gaps extended to Gaines's cross-roads and Newby's cross-roads, with numerous patrols in the direction of Woodville, Little Washington, and Sperryville.

GEN. McCLELLAN'S FAREWELL TO THE ARMY.

"The information gained from these parties, and also from deserters, prisoners, contrabands, as well as citizens, established the fact of Longstreet, with his command, being at Culpeper, while Jackson, with D. H. Hill, with their respective commands, were in the Shenandoah Valley, on the western side of the Blue Ridge, covering Chester and Thornton's Gaps, and expecting us to attempt to pass through and attack them. As late as the 17th of November a contraband just from Strasburg came into my camp and reported that D. H. Hill's corps was two miles beyond that place, on the railroad to Mount Jackson. Hill was tearing up the road and destroying the bridges under the impression that we intended to follow into that valley, and was *en route* for Staunton. Jackson's corps was between Strasburg and Winchester. Ewell and A. P. Hill were with Jackson. Provisions were scarce, and the rebels were obliged to keep moving to obtain them."

On the 10th of Nov. General Pleasonton was attacked by Longstreet, with one division of infantry and Stuart's cavalry, but repulsed the attack.

This indicates the relative position of our army and that of the enemy at the time I was relieved from the command.

Had I remained in command I should have made the attempt to divide the enemy, as before suggested; and could he have been brought to a battle within reach of my supplies, I cannot doubt that the result would have been a brilliant victory for our army.

[The following discretionary authority to Gen. Halleck, in the handwriting of Mr. Lincoln, was found among the papers of Gen. Halleck after his death, and transmitted by his widow to the War Department. It is not probable that Gen. McClellan ever heard of it :]

"EXECUTIVE MANSION, WASHINGTON,

"'By direction of the President, it is ordered that Maj.-Gen. McClellan be relieved from the command of the Army of the Potomac, and that Maj.-Gen. Burnside take the command of that army. Also, that Maj.-Gen. Hunter take command of the corps in said army which is now commanded by Gen. Burnside.

"'That Maj.-Gen. Fitz-John Porter be relieved from the command of the corps he now commands in said army, and that Maj.-Gen. Hooker take command of said corps.'

"The general-in-chief is authorized, in discretion, to issue an order substantially as the above, forthwith or so soon as he may deem proper.

"Nov. 5, 1862."

"A. LINCOLN.

When we broke up the camps on the upper Potomac and moved in advance, the army was in fine order for another battle; the troops in the best of spirits, full of confidence in me, and I was then, I believe, capable of handling an army in the field as I had never been before. I felt that I could fight a great battle. The march was admirably conducted, and is worthy of study. In the course of the 7th of Nov. I heard incidentally that a special train had brought out from Washington Gen. Buckingham, who had left the railway very near our camp, and, without coming to see me, had proceeded through a driving snow-storm several miles to Burnside's camp. I at once suspected that he brought the order relieving me from command, but kept my own counsel. Late at night I was sitting alone in my tent, writing to my wife. All the staff were asleep. Suddenly some one knocked upon the tent-pole, and, upon my invitation to enter, there appeared Burnside and Buckingham, both looking very solemn. I received them kindly and commenced conversation upon general subjects in the most unconcerned manner possible. After a few moments Buckingham said to Burnside: "Well, general, I think we had better tell Gen. McClellan the object of our visit." I very pleasantly said that I should be glad to learn it. Whereupon Buckingham handed me the two orders of which he was the bearer:

"HEADQUARTERS OF THE ARMY,
"WASHINGTON, NOV. 5, 1862.
"Maj.-Gen. McClellan, Commanding etc.:
"GENERAL: On receipt of the order of the President, sent herewith, you will immediately turn over your command to Maj.-Gen. Burnside, and repair to Trenton, N. J., reporting on your arrival at that place, by telegraph, for further orders.
"Very respectfully, your obedient servant,
"H. W. HALLECK,
"Gen.-in-Chief."

49

General Orders, No. 182.

"War Department,
"Adjutant-General's Office,
"Washington, Nov. 5, 1862.

"By direction of the President of the United States, it is ordered that Maj.-Gen. McClellan be relieved from the command of the Army of the Potomac, and that Maj.-Gen. Burnside take the command of that army.

"By order of the Secretary of War.

"E. D. Townsend,
" *Assist. Adj.- Gen.* "

I saw that both-especially Buckingham - were watching me most intently while I opened and read the orders. I read the papers with a smile, immediately turned to Burnside, and said: "Well, Burnside, I turn the command over to you."

They soon retired, Burnside having begged me to remain for a few days with the army, and I having consented to do so, though I wished to leave the next morning.

Before we broke up from the Maryland side of the Potomac I had said to Burnside that, as he was second in rank in the army, I wished him to be as near me as possible on the march, and that he must keep himself informed of the condition of affairs. I took especial pains during the march to have him constantly informed of what I was doing, the positions of the various corps, etc., and he ought to have been able to take the reins in his hands without a day's delay.

The order depriving me of the command created an immense deal of deep feeling in the army - so much so that many were in favor of my refusing to obey the order, and of marching upon Washington to take possession of the government. My chief purpose in remaining with the army as long as I did after being relieved was to calm this feeling, in which I succeeded.

I will not attempt to describe my own feelings nor the scenes attending my farewell to the army. They are beyond my powers of description. What words, in truth, could convey to the mind such a scene - thousands of brave men, who under my very eye had changed from raw recruits to veterans of many fields, shedding tears like children in their ranks, as they bade good-by to the general who had just led them to victory after the defeats they had seen under another leader? Could they have foreseen the future their feelings would not have been less intense!

[The following was McClellan's farewell to the army:]

HEADQUARTERS, ARMY OF THE POTOMAC,
CAMP NEAR RECTORTOWN, VA., Nov. 7, 1862.

Officers and Soldiers of the Army of the Potomac:
An order of the President devolves upon Maj.-Gen. Burnside the command of this army. In parting from you I cannot express the love and gratitude I bear to you. As an army you have grown up under my care. In you I have never found doubt or coldness. The battles you have fought under my command will proudly live in our nation's history. The glory you have achieved, our mutual perils and fatigues, the graves of our comrades fallen in battle and by disease, the broken forms of those whom mounds and sickness have disabled-the strongest associations which can exist among men-unite us still by an indissoluble tie. We shall ever be comrades in supporting the Constitution of our country and the nationality of its people.

GEO. B. MCCLELLAN,
Maj.-Gen. U. S. Army.

CHAPTER XL.

Private Letters.

[*Oct.* 1 to *Nov.* 10, 1862.]

Oct. 1, *Sharpsburg,* 7.30 P.M. - . . . Received this morning a mysterious despatch from which I inferred that the President was on his way hither. Went to Harper's Ferry and found him with half a dozen Western officers. He remains at Harper's Ferry to-night. . . .

Oct. 2, A.M. - . . . I found the President at Gen. Sumner's headquarters at Harper's Ferry; none of the cabinet were with him, merely some Western officers, such as McClernand and others. His ostensible purpose is to see the troops and the battle-field; I incline to think that the real purpose of his visit is to push me into a premature advance into Virginia. I may be mistaken, but think not. The real truth is that my army is not fit to advance. The old regiments are reduced to mere skeletons, and are completely tired out. They need rest and filling up. The new regiments are not fit for the field. The remains of Pope's army are pretty well broken up and ought not to be made to fight for some little time yet. Cavalry and artillery horses are broken down. So it goes. These people don't know what an army requires, and therefore act stupidly. . . .

Oct. 3. - . . . I was riding with the President all yesterday afternoon, and expect to do the same to-day. He seems in quite a good-humor; is accompanied only by Western people.

Oct. 4. - . . . The President is still here and goes to Frederick this morning. I will probably accompany him as far as the battle-field of South Mountain, so that my day will be pretty well used up.

654

Oct. 5. - . . . The President left us about eleven yesterday morning. I went with him as far as over the battle-field of South Mountain, and on my way thither was quite surprised to meet Mr. Aspinwall *en route* to my camp. . . . The President was very kind personally; told me he was convinced I was the best general in the country, etc., etc. He was very affable, and I really think he does feel very kindly towards me personally. I showed him the battle-fields, and am sure he departed with a more vivid idea of the great difficulty of the task we had accomplished. Mr. Aspinwall is decidedly of the opinion that it is my duty to submit to the President's proclamation and quietly continue doing my duty as a soldier. I presume he is right, and am at least sure that he is honest in his opinion. I shall surely give his views full consideration. He is of the opinion that the nation cannot stand the burdens of the war much longer, and that a speedy solution is necessary. In this he is no doubt correct, and I hope sincerely that another successful battle may conclude my part of the work.

Oct. —, 1862, *Pleasant Valley* - I received to-day a very handsome series of resolutions from the councils of Philadelphia, thanking me for the last campaign. The councils pitch into the government for not thanking me, most beautifully. The phrase about my having "organized victory" is a cut at Stanton, who last winter issued an order scouting the idea of "organizing victory," and rested on the sword of Gideon and Donnybrook Fair. I believe I will try to acknowledge them now, so I can send you the resolutions to-morrow. Pray keep them for May, with the thanks of Congress, etc. I have also some resolutions of the councils of Baltimore, which I have not yet replied to, and which I will send you in a day or two.

Oct. 25. - . . . I hope my bridge at Berlin is finished, and if so I can cross some troops to-day, and shall be all ready to march the moment the cavalry is ready, which will be shortly. I don't think Lee will fight us nearer than Richmond. I expect no fight in this vicinity. . . . My report is at last finished, and will, I presume, be copied to-day. . . . I see that there is much impatience throughout the country for a move. I am just as anxious as any one, but am crippled by want of horses. . . . I sent Bishop McIlvaine over to Harper's Ferry in my ambulance. He is accompanied by the Rev. Mr. Clements.

Oct. 26. - . . . I move a respectable number of troops across the Potomac to-day, the beginning of the general movement, which will, however, require several days to accomplish, for the cavalry is still terribly off. Yesterday a telegram received from the President asking what my "cavalry had done since the battle of Antietam to fatigue anything." It was one of those little flings that I can't get used to when they are not merited.

Pleasant Valley, Oct. -. - Since about three this morning it has been blowing a perfect gale; several tents blown over, etc. The bishop preached a very good extempore sermon on faith; a very impressive one it was, too. Service was in the little brick church that you remember just beyond the camp in the direction of Brownsville. They are working very hard to tie my tent fast with ropes; hope they will succeed. I strongly suspect our chances for breakfast are decidedly slim. Your father and I have been waiting for a very long time, and affairs don't seem to make progress. I confess that I am becoming hungry and cross-very hungry and *rather* cross. . . . You had better send me two uniform frock-coats. I begin to present a terribly poverty-stricken appearance. Ah! Andrew says that breakfast will soon be ready-that "the wittles is very slow cooking this here windy morning." I hope his estimate of time will not be out of the way much.

Pleasant Valley, Oct. 27. - I commenced the crossing yesterday. I returned a few moments ago from a trip to the —s to say good-by to the bishop and to present your album. The visit was so characteristic that I can't omit telling you of it. I found the family at dinner in the kitchen. They wanted me to take some dinner in the dining-room, but I insisted upon sitting down with them in the kitchen, which delighted them beyond measure. The old lady went nearly frantic-" to think of Gen. McClellan sitting down to dinner in the kitchen just like any common man," etc., etc. I got a little more than I bargained for in the shape of "the guard" coming in before I got through; but I kept on. The guard was rather more put out than I was, as he was a regular; but he could not get out of the scrape without a scene, so *he* went through with it. The album created a terrific scene of delight. More "O mys" were expended on it than I have heard for a couple of years or so. The old lady went almost out of her senses. I put the photographs in it for them, and wrote her name, with your regards, on one of the blank leaves. All sorts of inquiries were made about you, the baby, and mamma, and when I left Mrs. - wished me to kiss the baby for her and "give gold love" to you. The old lady said that "she'd been a mind to send to me for some beef," so I told Bates just now to get a good large piece and take it up to them. They would not take any pay from the bishop, because Col. Hammond had sent more money to pay his bill than they thought right, so they squared accounts and cleared their consciences by refusing any pay from the bishop. Some artist of an illustrated paper had been there taking a sketch of the house, and left them a very good copy, which delighted them much. I gave them that copy of the President and myself which you sent them, so that I think they are now a very happy family. All of them sent very kind messages to you, which you can consider delivered.

Oct. - , Berlin. - We are now near Berlin, and have a much better camp than the last one. My tent is at the bottom of a wooded ravine, and is perfectly sheltered from the wind. I am as comfortable as can be in a tent, and have a grass carpet instead of the dust and dirt which made the floor of my last tent.

Oct. 30, Berlin. - . . . I have just been put in an excellent humor (?) by seeing that, instead of sending the drafted men to fill the old regiments (as had been promised me), they are forming them into new regiments. Also that, in face of the great want of cavalry with this army, they are sending the new cavalry regiments from Pennsylvania to Louisville instead of hither! Blind and foolish they have ever been in Washington, and so, I fear, they will continue to the end.

Berlin, Oct. - - - . . . It will not do for me to visit Washington now. The tone of the telegrams I receive from the authorities is such as to show that they will take advantage of anything possible to do me all the harm they can, and if I went down I should at once be accused of purposely delaying the movement. Moreover, the condition of things is such that I ought not to leave just now. The army is in the midst of the preliminary movements for the main march, and I must be at hand in this critical moment of the operation. . . . If you could know the mean character of the despatches I receive you would boil over with anger. When it is possible to misunderstand, and when it is not possible; whenever there is a chance of a wretched innuendo, then it comes. But the good of the country requires me to submit to all this.

Berlin, Oct. 31. - . . . I don't expect to move headquarters from here for a couple of days; but in the meanwhile the troops are constantly crossing and the army getting into position for the advance.

Oct. 31. - If you can get to a comparatively permanent place you had better write to Dr. V- to send the sash and sabre by express to you, for I should hate to lose the ugly, rusty old thing - that is, if you would value it any; and perhaps our little child might value it after you and I are dead and gone. Miss - - and two Misses - - were at camp to-day. Of course there was a general row among the youngsters, and I came in for my share of the trouble in the shape of a visitation for an hour or so. . . . I had a long visit from Mr. Bancroft, the historian, to-day.

Oct. 31 *(after midnight).* - . . . From the despatches just received I think I will move headquarters over the river to-morrow. The advance is getting a little too far away from me, and I wish to have everything well under my own hands, as I am responsible.

Nov 2, *Berlin.*- . . . We are about starting to Wheatland, some eight or nine miles on the other side of the river. . . . Pleasonton had considerable skirmishing yesterday with Stuart's cavalry. They exceed ours vastly in numbers. There may be some infantry skirmishing to-day, but nothing serious.

Nov. 4. - . . . Slept under a tree last night, sharing what I had in the may of a bed with Gen. Reynolds. . . . There is some prospect of a fight to-day, but cannot tell exactly until I catch the extreme advance a couple of miles further on.

Nov. 4, 11.30 P.M., *near Middleburg.* - . . . We are in the full tide of success, so far as it is or can be successful to advance without a battle. . . . To-morrow night I hope to strike the railroad and telegraph again; no telegraph within twenty-five miles of this. . . .

Nov. 5, 9 P.M., *camp near Rectortown.* - . . . After a considerable amount of marching and skirmishing we have worked our way thus far down into rebeldom. We have had delightful weather for marching and a beautiful country to travel through. . . . We left Berlin on Sunday morning, the headquarters stopping at Wheatland; but I heard firing and rode to the front, going all the way to Snicker's Gap (to the top of the mountain) and spending the night at Snickersville. Next morning I rode to meet the train, but heard some more firing, and rode again towards the front, and spent the night near Bloomfield, camp being some miles back. At Snickersville I got a bed in a house to sleep in; at Bloomfield I slept under a tree in the moods; so that last night I was very glad, after another long ride, to get to my tent again. . . . Pleasonton has been doing very well again; has had some skirmishing pretty much every day; to-day he came across Jeb Stuart and thrashed him badly. Jeb outnumbered him two to one, but was well whipped; there were some very pretty charges made. . . .

Nov. 6, 1 P.M., camp near *Rectortown.* - . . . The army still advances, but the machine is so huge and complicated that it is slow in its motions.

Nov. 7, 2 P.M. — . . . Sumner returned last night. Howard returned this morning. I go to Warrenton to-morrow. Reynolds is there now, Burnside at Waterloo, Bayard in front. Pleasonton and Averill are trying to catch Jeb Stuart again near Flint Hills. Couch is here, and moves to-morrow towards Warrenton. Porter and Franklin are at White Plains. Porter moves to-morrow to New Baltimore, thence next day to Warrenton. Franklin moves day after to-morrow to New Baltimore. Sigel will remain at Thoroughfare Gap and the vicinity. The Manassas Gap road is in such bad order that we cannot depend upon it thus far up for supplies. Gainesville will be the depot until the Orange and Alexandria Railroad is open to Warrenton. We will have great difficulty in getting supplies by the Orange and Alexandria Railroad; its capacity has been overrated. Lee is at Gordonsville. G. W. Smith was yesterday driven out of Warrenton. . . .

11.30 P.M. - Another interruption - this time more important, It was in the shape of Burnside, accompanied by Gen. Buckingham, the secretary's adjutant-general. They brought with them the order relieving me from the command of the Army of the Potomac, and assigning Burnside to the command. No cause is given. I am ordered to turn over the command immediately and repair to Trenton, N. J., and on my arrival there to report by telegraph for further orders. . . . Of course I was much surprised; but as I read the order in the presence of Gen. Buckingham I am sure that not the slightest expression of feeling was visible on my face, which he watched closely. . . . They have made a great mistake. Alas for my poor country! I know in my inmost heart she never had a truer servant. I have informally turned over the command to Burnside, but shall go to-morrow to Warrenton with him, and perhaps remain a day or two there in order to give him all the information in my power. . . . Do not be at all worried - I am not. I have done the best I could for my country; to the last I have done my duty as I understand it. That I must have made many mistakes I cannot deny. I do not see any great blunders; but no one can judge of himself. Our consolation must be that we have tried to do what was right; if we have failed it was not our fault.

8 A.M. - . . . I am about starting for Warrenton. . . .

Warrenton, Sunday, A.M. . - . . . I expect to start to-morrow morning, and may get to Washington in time to take the afternoon train. . . . I shall not stop in Washington longer than for the next train, and will not go to see anybody. I shall go on just as quietly as I can and make as little fuss as possible . . . The officers and men feel terribly about the change. . . . I learn to-day that the men are very sullen and have lost their good spirits entirely. It made me feel very badly yesterday when I rode among them and saw how bright and cheerful they looked and how glad they were to see me. Poor fellows! they did not know the change that had occurred. . , .

Warrenton, Nov. 10, 2 P.M. - . . . I am very well and taking leave of the men. I did not know before how much they loved me nor how dear they were to me. Gray-haired men came to me with tears streaming down their cheeks. I never before had to exercise so much self-control. The scenes of to-day repay me for all that I have endured.

THE END.

INDEX.

Abbott, Lieut. H. C., 124.
Abercrombie, Gen. J. J., in Virginia, 240, 241 ; Fair Oaks, 379.
Abert, Capt. W. S., 123.
Acquia creek, Va., 106, 493-496, 500, 506, 508, 509, 529-531.
Administration, unfitness, 175, 176.
Alexander, Col. B. S., 119, 124.
Alexandria, Va., 80, 89, 96, 239, 509-527, 536.
Allen's Field, Va. – see Savage's Station.
Anderson, Gen. J. R., 347, 351, 371, 374.
Anderson, Gen. Richard, at Williams burg, 324, 325; South Mountain, 561, 573.
Anderson. Lieut.-Col. Robert, 580.
Annandale, Va., 515-519.
Antietam, Md., battle of, 584-613.
Arlington Heights, Va., 67, 68, 73, 80.
Army, Confederate, discipline, 72 ; entrenchments, 75 ; advantages, 253 ; at Yorktown, 257, 260, 267, 272, 285-291, 311, 312, 319; Williamsburg, 324-326, 333; West Point, 337 ; Hanover C. H., 369-372; Fair Oaks, 378-384 ; in Union rear, 390-393 ; Gaines's Mill, 416-418 ; Savage's Station, 426-428 ; Charles City road, 431, 432: Glendale, 430-433 ; Malvern Hill, 436, 437 ; Crampton's Gap, 562, 563; South Mountain, 572-579 ; Antietam, 584-606.
Army, Union, discipline, demoralized, 40; 68, 71, 87, 200.
Army of Potomac, under McClellan. composition, 67 ; reorganized, 69. 70, 198; deficient in officers, 73, 97 force, 75-79, 85. 163; divisions, 61, 114 ; mutinies, 86, 99 ; results of reviews, 98. Organization: staff, 83. 112, 114, 120-135 ; brigades, 112, 114 ; divisions, 114; artillery, 114-118; cavalry, 118, 119 : engineers. 119, 124, 125 ; adj.-gen.'s dept., 122; personal staff, 123; insp.-gen.'s dept.

124; medical dept., 126; commissary dept , 130 ; ordnance dept., 131 ; dept. of justice, 134; signal corps, 134 ; telegraph dept., 135. Medical record of, at Washington, 126 ; lack of stores, 128; provisioning, 130 ; artillery plenty, infantry arms needed, 131, 132. In Peninsula : artillery, 116; cavalry, 119; engineer officers, 124 ; troops withdrawn, 155, 163, 165, 261 ; advance, 222, 228; route, 227 ; transportation, 235, 237. 251, cost 238; maps, 253, 264; Yorktown, 272-288; lack of food, 301, 302, 340 ; Williamsburg, 319-333 ; in pursuit, 338 ; new corps, organization, 342 ; Mechanicsville, 363 ; Hanover C. H., 368-376; Fair Oaks, 377-384, 398 ; Gaines's Mill, 410-421, 442; Savage's Station, 426-428 ; White Oak Swamp, 428, 430 ; Charles City road, 431, 432 ; Glendale, 430, 433; Malvern Hill, 433-437, 484 ; Harrison's Landing, 444-468, 481-507 ; to Acquia creek, 464, 469-471, 493. 494-505. With Pope, 508-547 ; Fairfax C. H., 518, 519, 526. Maryland campaign : exhausted, 551 ; Crampton's Gap, 558-565; South Mountain, 572-583 ; Antietam, 584-613 ; material needed, 629-640, Ingalls's, Meigs's, and Myers's reports 633, 636, 637.
Army of Virginia, 552.
Army corps, formation, 222, 342.
Army organization : infantry, 108 ; artillery, 108 ; cavalry, 109 ; engineers, 110: staff, 110-112.
Aspinwall, W. H., 451, 655.
Astor. Jr., Col. J. J., 123. 251.
Averill, Gen. W. W., at Washington, 222. In Peninsula, 239 ; Yorktown, 260 ; Williamsburg, 339 ; Malvern. 438; White Oak Swamp, 494. In Maryland campaign, 647, 659.
Ayres, Capt., 301, 430.

234, 239 ; complains of McClellan, 243 ; commander-in-chief, 450, 452; treatment of McClellan, 467, 504; asks McClellan's co-operation, cordial feelings, 473 ; agrees with McClellan, 474, condemns his operations 475 ; charges delay, 500, 501, responsibility 539 ; refuses to thank army, 506, 507 ; in Pope's campaign, 508-547; ignorant of Pope's position, 503, 529 ; charges neglect 510 ; asks McClellan's assistance, 525, 541 ; unable to go to front, 534; order to McClellan, 538, 546; responsible for Pope's defeat, 538 ; helpless, 539; false testimony, 539, 542 ; contemptuous action, 550 : anxious, misquotes despatch of 11th Sept., '62, 555, 556; extract from testimony, 556 ; fault-finding, 614, 622 ; shirks responsibility, 635 ; on supplies to army, 641 ; refuses funds, 644 ; order of removal, 651.

Haller, Maj. G. O., 134.

Hamilton, Gen. C. S., in Peninsula, 239, 246, 256 ; Yorktown, 260, 261, 263.

Hampton, Capt , 592,

Hancock, Gen. W. S., 81, 140; at Yorktown, 285, 300 ; Williamsburg, 325, 326, 330, 331 ; in pursuit, 352 ; Savage's Station, 428 ; Antietam, 597-599, 602, 606.

Hanover Court-House, Va., battle of, 363-376.

Hardie, Lieut -Col. J. A., 122.

Harland, Col., 578. 605.

Harper's Ferry, Va., 94, 192 ; (Md. campaign) 550, 555, 556, 558-565, 570-573, 614, 622, 625, 627, 643, 644-646.

Harris, Hon. I., Keyes's letter to, 267.

Harrison, Capt, 371.

Harrison's Landing, Va., 430, 437, 440-468, 481-507.

Hartsuff, Gen. G. L., 581, 591, 613.

Hatch, Gen. J. P., 579-581.

Haupt, Col., 509, 517.

Hazard, Capt., 427. 428, 430.

Heintzelman, Gen. S. P., 80, 61, 96, 138, 306. In Peninsula, 250-252 ; Yorktown, 260, 261, 289, 298, 299, 304; Williamsburg, 320, 322, 325, 330, 332, 333 ; in pursuit, 348 ; Fair Oaks, 377-384; Old Tavern, 392; Gaines's Mill, 419, 420 ; Savage's Station, 427; Glendale, 430, 432 ; Malvern, 433, 436; Berkley, 444;

brevetted, 475. In Pope's campaign, 509, 510, 529, 532, 536.

Hexamer, Capt., 598.

Hill, Gen. A. P., at Williamsburg, 353 ; Seven Days, 401, 402, 431, 432 ; Antietam, 605 ; Shenandoah, 648, 650.

Hill, Gen. D. H , at Yorktown, 319, 324; Williamsburg, 334, 353 ; Fair Oaks, 378 ; South Mountain, 561, 562, 573 ; Shenandoah, 645, 650.

Hitchcock. Gen E. A., 137.

Hockaday's Springs, Va., 339, 340.

Hodges, Capt. H. C., 238.

Hoffmann, Lieut.-Col , 581.

Hooker, Gen. J., 50, 81, 96, 161. In Peninsula, 257 ; Yorktown, 278, 298, 299 ; Williamsburg, 301, 302, 304, 320-326, 332, 333 ; in pursuit, 311, 352 ; Fair Oaks, 379, 382, 333 ; Glendale, 430, 432 ; Malvern, 434, 436, 462, 492. 493 In Maryland campaign : South Mountain, 561, 574, 575, 577, 579, 532 ; Antietam, 584, 588, 590, 591, 593, 599-601, 606, 613, 619, 623.

Howard, Gen. O. O., 81 ; at Fair Oaks, 382, 383 ; Antietam. 592, 593.

Howard's bridge, Va., 254, 256, 259, 307.

Howe, Capt., 60.

Hudson, Lieut-Col. E., 123, 381.

Huger, Gen. B., 378.

Humphreys, Gen. A. A., 125, 589,620

Hunt, Gen. H. J., 80, 114, 116, 117; in Peninsula, 264, 302, 356.

Hunter, Gen. D., 80, 137, 225, 243.

Huttonsville, Va., 61, 62, 64.

Ingalls, Lieut.-Col. R., 128, 129, 140, 238, 251, 501 ; report, 633, 636.

Irvin, Col., 563, 599, 600.

Irwin, Capt. R, B , 122.

Jackson, Gen. Stonewall. In Peninsula, 230, 390-393 : Gaines's Mill, 415 ; Glendale, 443 ; Pope's campaign, 454, 466; South Mountain, 561, 562, 573 ; after Antietam, 624, 648. 640.

James river, Va., 203, 227, 235, 268, 269, 289, 343, 346. 411, 482, 485, 486, 497.

Jameson, Gen. C. D., 81, 379-381.

Johnston, Gen. J., in Virginia, 54, 85, 222, force 76. In Peninsula, 267 ; Yorktown, 319, 333 ; Williamsburg, 334, 337, 353 ; Fair Oaks. 399, 400, 402.

50

Bringing the Past into the Future

More Great Books Brought Back by DSI

Lincoln

ies 1 includes a total of nine volumes: *The Life of Abraham*
* Ida Tarbell, a four-volume set; *Debates of Lincoln and*
Six Months at the White House with Lincoln by F. B.
; and *Herndon's Lincoln: The True Story of a Great Life*,
nes unabridged, written by Lincoln's law partner of more
ty years.
ISBN 1-58218-084-9

of Abraham Lincoln

Tarbell. Illustrations and maps. 4 vols. Originally
by the Lincoln Historical Society in 1900.
he incredible facts of the life of Abraham Lincoln, a man
ged the fabric of America forever. Read in his own words
n equality and ending slavery. This work details Lincoln's
including the origins of the Lincoln family, his entry into
ry during the Black Hawk War, his important law cases,
political career, the Civil War, his personal life with Mary
devastating loss of one of their children, and his constant
th depression.
ISBN 1-58218-017-2
ISBN 1-58218-002-4

of Lincoln and Douglas

prepared by the reporters of each party at the times of their
Originally published by Follett & Foster in 1860.
he most consequential artifact of American election
ng and its political arguments. Political debates between
aham Lincoln and Hon. Stephen A. Douglas, in the
campaign of 1858 in Illinois. Included are the preceding
of each at Chicago, Springfield, etc., as well as the two
ches of Lincoln in Ohio in 1859, published at the times
livery.
ISBN 1-58218-009-1
ISBN 1-58218-000-8

Custer

ies 2 includes both *A Life of Major Gen'l George A. Custer*
ck Whittaker and *Tenting on the Plains* by Custer's wife,
Also included are the National Archives' transcripts
g the Court Martial of Custer (1867) and the Court of
Reno (1879) for his actions at Little Big Horn.
ISBN 1-58218-081-4

Major Gen'l George A. Custer

ck Whittaker. *Originally published in 1876*
marked advantages of education or wealth to command
on, Custer yet passed through a career so brilliant that his
household words, his "Last Stand" against Sioux and
warriors at Little Big Horn an enduring legend in
history. Truth and sincerity, honor and bravery, tenderness
athy, unassuming piety and temperance were the
g of Major Gen'l Custer, the man.
ISBN 1-58218-042-3
ISBN 1-58218-040-7

Tenting on the Plains

By Elizabeth Custer. Includes illustrations by Frederic Remington.
Originally published in 1889.

Elizabeth Custer was just a young girl when she fell in love with
one of the most controversial Indian fighters of the late 1800s, and
barely a woman when she defied her father to marry him. She went
on to earn literary fame as well as financial independence with her
entertaining tales of frontier life as the wife of General George
Custer. Her stories of life on the Plains are as colorful today as
when they first appeared over a century ago.
CD-ROM ISBN 1-58218-052-0
Softcover ISBN 1-58218-050-4

Series 3: Generals

Special Series 3 includes *Personal Memoirs of U. S. Grant, Memoirs*
of General W. T. Sherman, Personal Memoirs of P. H. Sheridan, and
McClellan's Own Story.
CD-ROM ISBN 1-58218-082-2

Personal Memoirs of U. S. Grant

Illustrations, Maps, and Facsimiles of Handwriting. 2 vols. Originally
published in 1885.

Published by Mark Twain under the Charles L. Webster Company
imprint, this memoir is widely admired as one of the finest military
autobiographies ever written. Grant recounts the failings and
triumphs of his leadership in strong, clear prose including his
boyhood in Ohio, his graduation from West Point, his marriage to
Julia Dent, his brilliant military campaigns, and his presidency.
CD-ROM ISBN 1-58218-029-6
Softcover ISBN 1-58218-005-9

Memoirs of General W. T. Sherman

With a map showing the marches of U.S. forces under his command.
2 vols. Originally published in 1890.

General William Tecumseh Sherman, a great man both in his gifts
and his achievements, was altogether a solider in the habits of mind.
A natural student of the topography of the countryside, this
characteristic of true military genius served Sherman well in
planning his devastating march from Atlanta, across Georgia to the
sea, the most striking achievement of the Civil War. The memoirs
of this courageous, patient, and self-sacrificing "Old Warrior" are
certain of a permanent place in literature.
CD-ROM ISBN 1-58218-025-3
Softcover ISBN 1-58218-004-0

Personal Memoirs of P. H. Sheridan

Illustrated. Twenty-six maps, prepared specially for this book by the
War Department. 2 vols. Originally published in 1888.

General Phil Sheridan revolutionized the handling of mounted men
in this country and abroad as commander of America's army. A hell-
for-leather cavalryman, Sheridan was as deliberate and careful as he
was brave. His memoirs vividly depict the brilliant campaigns he
masterminded, including his victory at Appomattox where his men
blocked Lee's retreat to force his surrender, ending the Civil War.
CD-ROM ISBN 1-58218-033-4
Softcover ISBN 1-58218-006-7

McClellan's Own Story

Illustrations from sketches drawn on the field of battle by A. R. Waud, the great war artist. Originally published in 1886.

After Bull Run, Lincoln appointed 34-year-old Gen. George B. McClellan as commander of the newly created Army of the Potomac. An able administrator and drillmaster, McClellan proceeded to reorganize the army for what he expected to be an overwhelming demonstration of Northern military superiority. "Our George," as his soldiers lovingly called him, was one of the ablest commanders which the United States has ever produced.

CD-ROM ISBN 1-58218-037-7
Softcover ISBN 1-58218-007-5

History of Massachusetts in the Civil War

By William Schouler, Late Adjutant-General of the Commonwealth. Originally published in 1868.

Massachusetts played a prominent part in the Civil War, from the beginning to the end; not only in furnishing soldiers for the army, sailors for the navy, and financial aid to the government, but in advancing ideas, which though scoffed at in the early months of the war, were afterwards accepted by the nation, before the war could be brought to a successful end.

CD-ROM ISBN 1-58218-013-X
Softcover ISBN 1-58218-001-6

Series 4: Indians

Special Series 4 includes George Catlin's *North American Indians* and *Indian Tribes of North America*. Also included are Indian Treaties from the National Archives.

CD-ROM ISBN 1-58218-083-0

North American Indians

By George Catlin. Illustrations and maps. 2 vols. Originally published in 1903.

Explore the territories of the North American Indian with the historical text, illustrations, and maps of George Catlin. Catlin gave up the practice of law to pursue his self-taught art, travelling throughout the American West from 1832 to 1840, painting portraits and writing on his encounters with various Indian tribes. Scholars and researchers alike will delight in the descriptions and portraits that portray this moment in history with such vivid detail.

CD-ROM ISBN 1-58218-021-0

Civil War Prison Stories

Daring and Suffering: A History of the Great Rai Adventure

By Lieut. William Pittenger, One of Andrews' Raiders. Originally published in 1863.

This courageous raid into Georgia ranks high amo striking and novel incidents of the Civil War. Pitteng his comrades embarked on a secret raid deep into Conf territory to cut the rail link between Mariett Chattanooga, only to run out of fuel after a lor dangerous chase. Those that survived the mission w first soldiers at rank of private to be awarded the Congr Medal of Honor.

CD-ROM ISBN 1-58218-077-6
Softcover ISBN 1-58218-075-X

Beyond the Lines: A Yankee Loose in Dixie

By Capt. J. J. Geer. Originally published in 1864.

Geer narrates the suffering endured as a prisoner Southern Confederacy. After being captured at the b Shiloh, Geer was tried on the most frivolous charg subsequently chained with slaves' chains and cast into r prisons and common jails. He managed to escape, over malarious marshes and bloodhounds only to be recap

CD-ROM ISBN 1-58218-085-7
Softcover ISBN 1-58218-088-1

Prison Life in Dixie

By Sergeant Oats. Originally published in 1880.

The author describes his harrowing capture and imprisc by the Rebels at Sumter Prison a.k.a. "Andersonville Pen". Renowned as one of the worst prisons of the Civ the Andersonville pen spread over only 11 acres, with foot wall surrounding over 33,000 Union soldiers. T endeavors to furnish such descriptions and incidents th the reader a true picture of Rebel prisons and the mea methods of either surviving or dying in them.

CD-ROM ISBN 1-58218-101-2
Softcover ISBN 1-58218-100-4

Forthcoming Titles

Herndon's Lincoln: The True Story of a Great Life
By William H. Herndon, Lincoln's friend and law partner

Six Months at the White House with Lincoln
By F. B. Carpenter

Reminiscences of Winfield Scott Hancock
By his wife, A. R. Hancock

The Battle of Gettysburg
By Comte de Paris

Sheridan's Troopers on the Border
By De B. Randolph Keim

Genesis of the Civil War
By Samuel Wylie Crawford

Following the Guidon
By Elizabeth Custer

The Indian Tribes of North America
By McKenney and Hall

The History of Philip's War
By Thomas Church

Book of the Indians of North America
By Samuel G. Drake

Digital Scanning, Inc. • 344 Gannett Road, Scituate, MA 02066 • www.digitalscanning.com • toll-free 1-888-34!